NOVELS
for Students

Advisors

Jayne M. Burton is a teacher of English, a member of the Delta Kappa Gamma International Society for Key Women Educators, and currently a master's degree candidate in the Interdisciplinary Study of Curriculum and Instruction and English at Angelo State University.

Mary Beth Maggio teaches seventh grade language arts in Schaumburg, Illinois.

Tom Shilts is the youth librarian at the Okemos branch of Capital Area District Library in Okemos, Michigan. He holds an MSLS degree from Clarion University of Pennsylvania and an MA in U.S. History from the University of North Dakota.

Amy Spade Silverman hastaught at independent schools in California, Texas, Michigan, and New York. She holds a bachelor of arts degree from the University of Michigan and a master of fine arts degree from the University of Houston. She is a member of the National Council of Teachers of English and Teachers and Writers. She is an exam reader for Advanced Placement Literature and Composition. She is also a poet, published in *North American Review*, *Nimrod*, and *Michigan Quarterly Review*, among others.

Mary Turner holds a BS in Secondary Education from East Texas State University and a Master of Education from Western Kentucky University. She teaches English 7 and AP English 12 literature and composition at SBEC in Southaven, Mississippi.

Brian Woerner teaches English at Troy High School in Troy, Ohio. He is also a Program Associate of the Ohio Writing Project at Miami University.

NOVELS
for Students

**Presenting Analysis, Context, and Criticism
on Commonly Studied Novels**

VOLUME 44

Sara Constantakis, Project Editor

Foreword by Anne Devereaux Jordan

GALE
CENGAGE Learning·

Detroit • New York • San Francisco • New Haven, Conn • Waterville, Maine • London

Novels for Students, Volume 44

Project Editor: Sara Constantakis

Rights Acquisition and Management: Sheila Spencer

Composition: Evi Abou-El-Seoud

Manufacturing: Rhonda Dover

Imaging: John Watkins

Product Design: Pamela A. E. Galbreath, Jennifer Wahi

Digital Content Production: Allie Semperger

Product Manager: Meggin Condino

For product information and technology assistance, contact us at
Gale Customer Support, 1-800-877-4253.
For permission to use material from this text or product,
submit all requests online at **www.cengage.com/permissions.**
Further permissions questions can be emailed to
permissionrequest@cengage.com

While every effort has been made to ensure the reliability of the information presented in this publication, Gale, a part of Cengage Learning, does not guarantee the accuracy of the data contained herein. Gale accepts no payment for listing; and inclusion in the publication of any organization, agency, institution, publication, service, or individual does not imply endorsement of the editors or publisher. Errors brought to the attention of the publisher and verified to the satisfaction of the publisher will be corrected in future editions.

Gale
27500 Drake Rd.
Farmington Hills, MI, 48331-3535

ISBN-13: 978-1-4144-9487-6
ISBN-10: 1-4144-9487-4

ISSN 1094-3552

This title is also available as an e-book.
ISBN-13: 978-1-4144-9273-5
ISBN-10: 1-4144-9273-1
Contact your Gale, a part of Cengage Learning sales representative for ordering information.

Printed in Mexico
1 2 3 4 5 6 7 17 16 15 14 13

Table of Contents

The Informed Dialogue: Interacting with Literature

When we pick up a book, we usually do so with the anticipation of pleasure. We hope that by entering the time and place of the novel and sharing the thoughts and actions of the characters, we will find enjoyment. Unfortunately, this is often not the case; we are disappointed. But we should ask, has the author failed us, or have we failed the author?

We establish a dialogue with the author, the book, and with ourselves when we read. Consciously and unconsciously, we ask questions: "Why did the author write this book?" "Why did the author choose that time, place, or character?" "How did the author achieve that effect?" "Why did the character act that way?" "Would I act in the same way?" The answers we receive depend upon how much information about literature in general and about that book specifically we ourselves bring to our reading.

Young children have limited life and literary experiences. Being young, children frequently do not know how to go about exploring a book, nor sometimes, even know the questions to ask of a book. The books they read help them answer questions, the author often coming right out and *telling* young readers the things they are learning or are expected to learn. The perennial classic, *The Little Engine That Could, tells* its readers that, among other things, it is good to help others and brings happiness:

> "Hurray, hurray," cried the funny little clown and all the dolls and toys. "The good little boys and girls in the city will be happy because you helped us, kind, Little Blue Engine."

In picture books, messages are often blatant and simple, the dialogue between the author and reader one-sided. Young children are concerned with the end result of a book—the enjoyment gained, the lesson learned—rather than with how that result was obtained. As we grow older and read further, however, we question more. We come to expect that the world within the book will closely mirror the concerns of our world, and that the author will *show* these through the events, descriptions, and conversations within the story, rather than *telling* of them. We are now expected to do the interpreting, carry on our share of the dialogue with the book and author, and glean not only the author's message, but comprehend how that message and the overall affect of the book were achieved. Sometimes, however, we need help to do these things. *Novels for Students* provides that help.

A novel is made up of many parts interacting to create a coherent whole. In reading a novel, the more obvious features can be easily spotted— theme, characters, plot—but we may overlook the more subtle elements that greatly influence how the novel is perceived by the reader: viewpoint, mood and tone, symbolism, or the use of humor. By focusing on both the obvious and more subtle literary elements within a novel, *Novels for Students* aids readers in both analyzing for message and in determining how and why that message is communicated. In the discussion on Harper Lee's *To Kill a Mockingbird* (Vol. 2), for example, the mockingbird as a symbol of innocence is dealt with, among other things, as is the importance of Lee's use of humor which "enlivens a serious plot, adds depth to the characterization, and creates a sense of familiarity and universality." The reader comes to understand the internal elements of each novel discussed—as well as the external influences that help shape it.

"The desire to write greatly," Harold Bloom of Yale University says, "is the desire to be elsewhere, in a time and place of one's own, in an originality that must compound with inheritance, with an anxiety of influence." A writer seeks to create a unique world within a story, but although it is unique, it is not disconnected from our own world. It speaks to us *because* of what the writer brings to the writing from our world: how he or she was raised and educated; his or her likes and dislikes; the events occurring in the real world at the time of the writing, and while the author was growing up. When we know what an author has brought to his or her work, we gain a greater insight into both the "originality" (the world of the book), and the things that "compound" it. This insight enables us to question that created world and find answers more readily. By informing ourselves, we are able to establish a more effective dialogue with both book and author.

Novels for Students, in addition to providing a plot summary and descriptive list of characters—to remind readers of what they have read—also explores the external influences that shaped each book. Each entry includes a discussion of the author's background, and the historical context in which the novel was written. It is vital to know, for instance, that when Ray Bradbury was writing *Fahrenheit 451* (Vol. 1), the threat of Nazi domination had recently ended in Europe, and the McCarthy hearings were taking place in Washington, D.C. This information goes far in answering the question, "Why did he write a story of oppressive government control and book burning?" Similarly, it is important to know that Harper Lee, author of *To Kill a Mockingbird,* was born and raised in

Monroeville, Alabama, and that her father was a lawyer. Readers can now see why she chose the south as a setting for her novel—it is the place with which she was most familiar—and start to comprehend her characters and their actions.

Novels for Students helps readers find the answers they seek when they establish a dialogue with a particular novel. It also aids in the posing of questions by providing the opinions and interpretations of various critics and reviewers, broadening that dialogue. Some reviewers of *To Kill A Mockingbird,* for example, "faulted the novel's climax as melodramatic." This statement leads readers to ask, "Is it, indeed, melodramatic?" "If not, why did some reviewers see it as such?" "If it is, why did Lee choose to make it melodramatic?" "Is melodrama ever justified?" By being spurred to ask these questions, readers not only learn more about the book and its writer, but about the nature of writing itself.

The literature included for discussion in *Novels for Students* has been chosen because it has something vital to say to us. *Of Mice and Men, Catch-22, The Joy Luck Club, My Antonia, A Separate Peace* and the other novels here speak of life and modern sensibility. In addition to their individual, specific messages of prejudice, power, love or hate, living and dying, however, they and all great literature also share a common intent. They force us to *think*—about life, literature, and about others, not just about ourselves. They pry us from the narrow confines of our minds and thrust us outward to confront the world of books and the larger, real world we all share. *Novels for Students* helps us in this confrontation by providing the means of enriching our conversation with literature and the world, by creating an *informed* dialogue, one that brings true pleasure to the personal act of reading.

Sources

Harold Bloom, *The Western Canon, The Books and School of the Ages,* Riverhead Books, 1994.

Watty Piper, *The Little Engine That Could,* Platt & Munk, 1930.

Anne Devereaux Jordan
Senior Editor, TALL (Teaching and Learning Literature)

Introduction

Purpose of the Book

The purpose of *Novels for Students* (*NfS*) is to provide readers with a guide to understanding, enjoying, and studying novels by giving them easy access to information about the work. Part of Gale's "For Students" Literature line, *NfS* is specifically designed to meet the curricular needs of high school and undergraduate college students and their teachers, as well as the interests of general readers and researchers considering specific novels. While each volume contains entries on "classic" novels frequently studied in classrooms, there are also entries containing hard-to-find information on contemporary novels, including works by multicultural, international, and women novelists. Entries profiling film versions of novels not only diversify the study of novels but support alternate learning styles, media literacy, and film studies curricula as well.

The information covered in each entry includes an introduction to the novel and the novel's author; a plot summary, to help readers unravel and understand the events in a novel; descriptions of important characters, including explanation of a given character's role in the novel as well as discussion about that character's relationship to other characters in the novel; analysis of important themes in the novel; and an explanation of important literary techniques and movements as they are demonstrated in the novel.

In addition to this material, which helps the readers analyze the novel itself, students are also provided with important information on the literary and historical background informing each work. This includes a historical context essay, a box comparing the time or place the novel was written to modern Western culture, a critical essay, and excerpts from critical essays on the novel. A unique feature of *NfS* is a specially commissioned critical essay on each novel, targeted toward the student reader.

The "literature to film" entries on novels vary slightly in form, providing background on film technique and comparison to the original, literary version of the work. These entries open with an introduction to the film, which leads directly into the plot summary. The summary highlights plot changes from the novel, key cinematic moments, and/or examples of key film techniques. As in standard entries, there are character profiles (noting omissions or additions, and identifying the actors), analysis of themes and how they are illustrated in the film, and an explanation of the cinematic style and structure of the film. A cultural context section notes any time period or setting differences from that of the original work, as well as cultural differences between the time in which the original work was written and the time in which the film adaptation was made. A film entry concludes with a critical overview and critical essays on the film.

To further help today's student in studying and enjoying each novel or film, information on media adaptations is provided (if available), as well as suggestions for works of fiction, nonfiction, or film on similar themes and topics. Classroom aids include ideas for research papers and lists of critical and reference sources that provide additional material on the novel. Film entries also highlight signature film techniques demonstrated, and suggest media literacy activities and prompts to use during or after viewing a film.

Selection Criteria

The titles for each volume of *NfS* are selected by surveying numerous sources on notable literary works and analyzing course curricula for various schools, school districts, and states. Some of the sources surveyed include: high school and undergraduate literature anthologies and textbooks; lists of award-winners, and recommended titles, including the Young Adult Library Services Association (YALSA) list of best books for young adults. Films are selected both for the literary importance of the original work and the merits of the adaptation (including official awards and widespread public recognition).

Input solicited from our expert advisory board—consisting of educators and librarians—guides us to maintain a mix of "classic" and contemporary literary works, a mix of challenging and engaging works (including genre titles that are commonly studied) appropriate for different age levels, and a mix of international, multicultural and women authors. These advisors also consult on each volume's entry list, advising on which titles are most studied, most appropriate, and meet the broadest interests across secondary (grades 7–12) curricula and undergraduate literature studies.

How Each Entry Is Organized

Each entry, or chapter, in *NfS* focuses on one novel. Each entry heading lists the full name of the novel, the author's name, and the date of the novel's publication. The following elements are contained in each entry:

Introduction: a brief overview of the novel which provides information about its first appearance, its literary standing, any controversies surrounding the work, and major conflicts or themes within the work. Film entries identify the original novel and provide understanding of the film's reception and reputation, along with that of the director.

Author Biography: in novel entries, this section includes basic facts about the author's life, and focuses on events and times in the author's life that inspired the novel in question.

Plot Summary: a factual description of the major events in the novel. Lengthy summaries are broken down with subheads. Plot summaries of films are used to uncover plot differences from the original novel, and to note the use of certain film angles or other techniques.

Characters: an alphabetical listing of major characters in the novel. Each character name is followed by a brief to an extensive description of the character's role in the novel, as well as discussion of the character's actions, relationships, and possible motivation. In film entries, omissions or changes to the cast of characters of the film adaptation are mentioned here, and the actors' names—and any awards they may have received—are also included.

Characters are listed alphabetically by last name. If a character is unnamed—for instance, the narrator in *Invisible Man*—the character is listed as "The Narrator" and alphabetized as "Narrator." If a character's first name is the only one given, the name will appear alphabetically by that name.

Variant names are also included for each character. Thus, the full name "Jean Louise Finch" would head the listing for the narrator of *To Kill a Mockingbird*, but listed in a separate cross-reference would be the nickname "Scout Finch."

Themes: a thorough overview of how the major topics, themes, and issues are addressed within the novel. Each theme discussed appears in a separate subhead. While the key themes often remain the same or similar when a novel is adapted into a film, film entries demonstrate how the themes are conveyed cinematically, along with any changes in the portrayal of the themes.

Style: this section addresses important style elements of the novel, such as setting, point of view, and narration; important literary devices used, such as imagery, foreshadowing, symbolism; and, if applicable, genres to which the work might have belonged, such as Gothicism or Romanticism. Literary terms are explained within the entry but can also be found in the Glossary. Film entries cover how the director conveyed the meaning, message, and mood of the work using film in comparison to the author's use of language, literary device, etc., in the original work.

Historical Context: in novel entries, this section outlines the social, political, and cultural climate in which the author lived and the novel was created. This section may include descriptions of related historical events, pertinent aspects of daily life in the culture, and the artistic and literary sensibilities of the time in which the work was written. If the novel is a historical work, information regarding the time in which the novel is set is also included. Each section is broken down with helpful subheads. Film entries contain a similar Cultural Context section because the film adaptation might explore an entirely different time period or culture than the original work, and may also be influenced by the traditions and views of a time period much different than that of the original author.

Critical Overview: this section provides background on the critical reputation of the novel or film, including bannings or any other public controversies surrounding the work. For older works, this section includes a history of how the novel or film was first received and how perceptions of it may have changed over the years; for more recent novels, direct quotes from early reviews may also be included.

Criticism: an essay commissioned by *NfS* which specifically deals with the novel or film and is written specifically for the student audience, as well as excerpts from previously published criticism on the work (if available).

Sources: an alphabetical list of critical material used in compiling the entry, with full bibliographical information.

Further Reading: an alphabetical list of other critical sources which may prove useful for the student. It includes full bibliographical information and a brief annotation.

Suggested Search Terms: a list of search terms and phrases to jumpstart students' further information seeking. Terms include not just titles and author names but also terms and topics related to the historical and literary context of the works.

In addition, each novel entry contains the following highlighted sections, set apart from the main text as sidebars:

Media Adaptations: if available, a list of audiobooks and important film and television adaptations of the novel, including source information. The list also includes stage adaptations, musical adaptations, etc.

Topics for Further Study: a list of potential study questions or research topics dealing with the novel. This section includes questions related to other disciplines the student may be studying, such as American history, world history, science, math, government, business, geography, economics, psychology, etc.

Compare and Contrast: an "at-a-glance" comparison of the cultural and historical differences between the author's time and culture and late twentieth century or early twenty-first century Western culture. This box includes pertinent parallels between the major scientific, political, and cultural movements of the time or place the novel was written, the time or place the novel was set (if a historical work), and modern Western culture. Works written after the mid-1970s may not have this box.

What Do I Read Next?: a list of works that might give a reader points of entry into a classic work (e.g., YA or multicultural titles) and/or complement the featured novel or serve as a contrast to it. This includes works by the same author and others, works from various genres, YA works, and works from various cultures and eras.

The film entries provide sidebars more targeted to the study of film, including:

Film Technique: a listing and explanation of four to six key techniques used in the film, including shot styles, use of transitions, lighting, sound or music, etc.

Read, Watch, Write: media literacy prompts and/or suggestions for viewing log prompts.

What Do I See Next?: a list of films based on the same or similar works or of films similar in directing style, technique, etc.

Other Features

NfS includes "The Informed Dialogue: Interacting with Literature," a foreword by Anne Devereaux Jordan, Senior Editor for *Teaching and Learning Literature* (*TALL*), and a founder of the Children's Literature Association. This essay provides an enlightening look at how readers interact with literature and how *Novels for Students* can help teachers show students how to enrich their own reading experiences.

A Cumulative Author/Title Index lists the authors and titles covered in each volume of the *NfS* series.

A Cumulative Nationality/Ethnicity Index breaks down the authors and titles covered in each volume of the *NfS* series by nationality and ethnicity.

A Subject/Theme Index, specific to each volume, provides easy reference for users who may be studying a particular subject or theme rather than a single work. Significant subjects, from events to broad themes, are included.

Each entry may include illustrations, including photo of the author, stills from film adaptations, maps, and/or photos of key historical events, if available.

Citing Novels for Students

When writing papers, students who quote directly from any volume of *NfS* may use the following general forms. These examples are based on MLA style; teachers may request that students adhere to a different style, so the following examples may be adapted as needed.

When citing text from *NfS* that is not attributed to a particular author (i.e., the Themes, Style, Historical Context sections, etc.), the following format should be used in the bibliography section:

> "*The Monkey Wrench Gang.*" *Novels for Students.* Ed. Sara Constantakis. Vol. 43. Detroit: Gale, Cengage Learning, 2013. 157–193. Print.

When quoting the specially commissioned essay from *NfS* (usually the first piece under the "Criticism" subhead), the following format should be used:

> Holmes, Michael Allen. Critical Essay on "*The Monkey Wrench Gang.*" *Novels for Students.* Ed. Sara Constantakis. Vol. 43. Detroit: Gale, Cengage Learning, 2013. 173–78. Print.

When quoting a journal or newspaper essay that is reprinted in a volume of *NfS,* the following form may be used:

> Bryant, Paul T. "Edward Abbey and Environmental Quixoticism." *Western American Literature* 24.1 (1989): 37–43. Rpt. in *Novels for Students.* Vol. 43. Ed. Sara Constantakis. Detroit: Gale, Cengage Learning, 2013. 189–92. Print.

When quoting material reprinted from a book that appears in a volume of *NfS,* the following form may be used:

> Norwick, Steve. "Nietzschean Themes in the Works of Edward Abbey." *Coyote in the Maze: Tracking Edward Abbey in a World of Words.* Ed. Peter Quigley. Salt Lake City; University of Utah Press, 1998. 184–205. Rpt. in *Novels for Students.* Vol. 43. Ed. Sara Constantakis. Detroit: Gale, Cengage Learning, 2013. 183–85. Print.

We Welcome Your Suggestions

The editorial staff of *Novels for Students* welcomes your comments and ideas. Readers who wish to suggest novels to appear in future volumes, or who have other suggestions, are cordially invited to contact the editor. You may contact the editor via e-mail at: **ForStudentsEditors@cengage.com.** Or write to the editor at:

Editor, *Novels for Students*

Gale

27500 Drake Road

Farmington Hills, MI 48331-3535

Literary Chronology

1835: Samuel Butler is born on December 4 in Bingham, Nottinghamshire, England.

1843: Henry James is born on April 15 in New York, New York.

1876–1877: Henry James's *The American* is published.

1896: Giuseppe Tomasi di Lampedusa is born on December 23 in Palermo, Sicily.

1902: Samuel Butler dies of unspecified causes on June 18 in London, England.

1903: Samuel Butler's *The Way of All Flesh* is published.

1905: Dalton Trumbo is born on December 9 in Montrose, Colorado.

1916: Henry James dies of complications from a stroke on February 28 in London, England.

1923: Walter Michael Miller Jr. is born on August 12 in Martinsburg, West Virginia.

1931: Edgar Lawrence (E. L.) Doctorow is born on January 6 in New York City, New York.

1932: Miloš Forman is born on February 18 in Čáslav, Czechoslovakia (present-day Czech Republic).

1935: Ken Kesey is born on September 17 in La Junta, Colorado.

1937: Anita Desai is born on June 24 in Mussorie, India.

1939: Toni Cade Bambara is born on March 25 in Harlem, New York.

1939: Dalton Trumbo's *Johnny Got His Gun* is published.

1942: Isabel Allende is born on August 2 in Lima, Peru.

1944: Alice Walker is born on February 9 in Eatonton, Georgia.

1944: Amy Tan is born on February 19 in Oakland, California.

1953: Dalton Trumbo earns the Academy Award for Best Story for *Roman Holiday*.

1954: Louise Erdrich is born on June 7 in Little Falls, Minnesota.

1956: Dalton Trumbo earns the Academy Award for Best Story for *The Brave One*.

1957: Giuseppe Tomasi di Lampedusa dies of lung cancer on July 23 in Rome, Italy.

1958: Giuseppe Tomasi di Lampedusa's *The Leopard* is published.

1959: Walter M. Miller Jr.'s *A Canticle for Leibowitz* is published.

1962: Ken Kesey's *One Flew over the Cuckoo's Nest* is published.

1970: Alice Walker's *The Third Life of Grange Copeland* is published.

1975: Markus Zusak is born on June 23 in Sydney, Australia.

1975: E. L. Doctorow's *Ragtime* is published.

1975: The film *One Flew over the Cuckoo's Nest* is released.

1975: Miloš Forman is awarded the Academy Award for Best Director for *One Flew over the Cuckoo's Nest*.

1975: Jack Nicholson is awarded the Academy Award for Best Actor in a Leading Role for *One Flew over the Cuckoo's Nest*.

1975: Louise Fletcher is awarded the Academy Award for Best Actress in a Leading Role for *One Flew over the Cuckoo's Nest*.

1975: Michael Douglas and Saul Zaentz are awarded the Academy Award for Best Picture for *One Flew over the Cuckoo's Nest*.

1975: Bo Goldman and Lawrence Hauben are awarded the Academy Award for Best Writing (Screenplay Adapted from Other Material) for *One Flew over the Cuckoo's Nest*.

1976: Dalton Trumbo dies of lung cancer on September 10 in Los Angeles, California.

1980: Toni Cade Bambara's *The Salt Eaters* is published.

1980: Anita Desai's *Clear Light of Day* is published.

1981: Miloš Forman's film version of *Ragtime* is released.

1982: Miloš Forman's film version of *Ragtime* is nominated for eight Academy Awards.

1983: Alice Walker is awarded the Pulitzer Prize for Fiction for *The Color Purple*.

1995: Amy Tan's *The Hundred Secret Senses* is published.

1995: Toni Cade Bambara dies of colon cancer on December 9 in Philadelphia, Pennsylvania.

1996: Walter M. Miller Jr. dies of suicide on January 6 in Daytona Beach, Florida.

1998: Louise Erdrich's *The Antelope Wife* is published.

2001: Ken Kesey dies of a liver tumor on November 10 in Eugene, Oregon.

2005: Markus Zusak's *The Book Thief* is published.

2005: Isabel Allende's *Zorro* is published.

Acknowledgements

The editors wish to thank the copyright holders of the excerpted criticism included in this volume and the permissions managers of many book and magazine publishing companies for assisting us in securing reproduction rights. We are also grateful to the staffs of the Detroit Public Library, the Library of Congress, the University of Detroit Mercy Library, Wayne State University Purdy/Kresge Library Complex, and the University of Michigan Libraries for making their resources available to us. Following is a list of the copyright holders who have granted us permission to reproduce material in this volume of PfS. Every effort has been made to trace copyright, but if omissions have been made, please let us know.

COPYRIGHTED EXCERPTS IN NfS, VOLUME 44, WERE REPRODUCED FROM THE FOLLOWING SOURCES:

Robert James Butler, "Alice Walker's Vision of the South in 'The Third Life of Grange Copeland'," *African American Review*, vol. 27, no. 2, Summer 1993, pp. 192–204. Copyright © 1993 by Robert James Butler. All rights reserved. Reproduced by permission.—Barbara Mujica, "Zorro and the Zahir," *Américas* (English edition), vol. 57, no. 6, Nov.-Dec. 2005, p. 62. Copyright © 2005 by *Américas*. All rights reserved. Reproduced by permission.—Bill Ott, "Review of 'The Antelope Wife'," *Booklist*, vol. 94, no. 13, March 1, 1998, p. 1044. Copyright © 1998 by Booklist Publications. All rights reserved. Reproduced by permission.—Brad Hooper, "Review of 'Zorro'," *Booklist*, vol. 101, no 12, February 15, 2005, p. 1035. Copyright © 2005 by American Library Association. All rights reserved. Reproduced by permission.—Katherine Rushton, "Death Warmed Up," *The Bookseller*, vol. 18, no. 2, November 17, 2006. Copyright © 2006 by The Bookseller Media Group. All rights reserved. Reproduced by permission.—Shouri Daniels, "Anita Desai's 'Clear Light of Day'," *Chicago Review*, vol. 33, no. 1 , Summer 1981, pp. 107–112. Copyright © 1981 by *The Chicago Review*. All rights reserved. Reproduced by permission.—Roger Ebert, "Review of 'Ragtime'," *Chicago Sun Times*, January 1, 1981. Copyright © 1981 by *Chicago Sun Times*. All rights reserved. Reproduced by permission.—Roger Ebert, "Review of 'One Flew Over the Cuckoo's Nest'," *Chicago Sun Times*, February 2, 2003. Copyright © 2003 by *Chicago Sun Times*. All rights reserved. Reproduced by permission.—Jay Parini, "The Afterlife of Henry James," *Chronicle of Higher Education*, vol. 57, no. 27, March 6, 2011. Copyright © 2011 by Jay Parini. All rights reserved. Reproduced by permission.—Arun P. Mukherjee, "Other Worlds, Other Texts: Teaching Anita Desai's 'Clear Light of Day' to Canadian Students," *College Literature*, vol. 22, no. 1, February 1995, p. 192. Copyright © 1995 by *College Literature*. All rights reserved. Reproduced by permission.—Katherine Mullen, "The 'L' Word in Henry James' Fiction,"

Way of All Flesh': Overview," ***Reference Guide to English Literature***, 1991. © 1991 Cengage Learning.—Peter Faulkner, "Samuel Butler: Overview," ***Reference Guide to English Literature***, 1991. Copyright © 1991 Gale, a part of Cengage Learning, Inc. Reproduced by permission. www.cengage.com/permissions.—Alberto Manguel, "Tenderness, Wisdom and Irony," ***Spectator***, vol. 315, no. 9515, January 8 2011, p. 35. Copyright © 2011 by The Spectator (1828) Ltd. All rights reserved. Reproduced by permission.—Beverly Guy-Sheftall and Toni Cade Bambara, "Commitment: Toni Cade Bambara Speaks," in ***Sturdy Black Bridges***, Roseann P. Bell, Bettye J. Parker, Beverly Guy-Sheftall, eds. Anchor Press/Doubleday, 1978, pp. 230–249. Copyright © 1978 by Beverly Guy-Sheftall. All rights reserved. Reproduced by permission.—Linda Ross, 'Dalton Trumbo: Overview," ***Twentieth-Century Young Adult Writers***, 1E. © 1994 Gale, a part of Cengage Learning, Inc. Reproduced by permission. www.cengage.com/permissions.—Paul Skenazy, "Doing Time," ***Threepenny Review***, no. 10, Summer 1982, pp.21–23. Copyright © 1982 by Paul N. Skenazy. All rights reserved. Reproduced by permission.—"A Bitter Legacy," ***Times Literary Supplement***, vol. 71, May 22, 1903, p. 158.—D. Murphy, "Review of 'One Flew Over the Cuckoo's Nest'," ***Variety***, November 18, 1975. Copyright © 1975 by *Variety*. All rights reserved. Reproduced by permission.—"Review of 'Ragtime'," ***Variety***, December 31, 1980. Copyright © 1980 by *Variety*. All rights reserved. Reproduced by permission.—Bruce Allen, "Mysteries and Miracles," ***The World and I*** Online (WorldandIJournal.com), vol. 16, no. 9, September 2001, p. 223. Copyright © 2001 by *The World and I* Online. All rights reserved. Reproduced by permission.

Contributors

Susan Andersen: Andersen has a PhD in English. Entry on *Clear Light of Day*. Original essay on *Clear Light of Day*.

Bryan Aubrey: Aubrey holds a PhD in English. Entry on *The Third Life of Grange Copeland*. Original essay on *The Third Life of Grange Copeland*.

Rita M. Brown: Brown is an English professor. Entry on *The Leopard*. Original essay on *The Leopard*.

Catherine Dominic: Dominic is a novelist and a freelance writer and editor. Entry on *The American*. Original essay on *The American*.

Kristen Sarlin Greenberg: Greenberg is a freelance writer and editor with a background in literature and philosophy. Entries on *The Hundred Secret Senses* and *Zorro*. Original essays on *The Hundred Secret Senses* and *Zorro*.

Michael Allen Holmes: Holmes is a writer with existential interests. Entry on *Johnny Got His Gun*. Original essay on *Johnny Got His Gun*.

David Kelly: Kelly is an instructor in literature and creative writing. Entry on *Ragtime*. Original essay on *Ragtime*.

Amy Lynn Miller: Miller is a graduate of the University of Cincinnati and currently resides in New Orleans, Louisiana. Entry on *One Flew over the Cuckoo's Nest*. Original essay on *One Flew over the Cuckoo's Nest*.

Michael J. O'Neal: O'Neal holds a PhD in English. Entry on *The Way of All Flesh*. Original essay on *The Way of All Flesh*.

April Paris: Paris is a freelance writer with an extensive background writing literary and educational materials. Entry on *The Antelope Wife*. Original essay on *The Antelope Wife*.

Rachel Porter: Porter is a freelance writer who holds a bachelor of arts in English literature. Entry on *The Salt Eaters*. Original essay on *The Salt Eaters*.

Bradley A. Skeen: Skeen is a classicist. Entry on *A Canticle for Leibowitz*. Original essay on *A Canticle for Leibowitz*.

Greg Wilson: Wilson has written essays and articles examining a wide range of topics related to popular culture, from contemporary best-selling fiction to World War II memoirs. Entry on *The Book Thief*. Original essay on *The Book Thief*.

The American

HENRY JAMES

1876–1877

The American is one of the early novels of prolific novelist, short-story writer, and literary critic Henry James. An American-born author who was educated abroad and who later became a British citizen, James often used his fiction to explore the cultural differences between American and European society. The action of *The American* takes place almost exclusively in Europe. In the novel, James contrasts American ideas of wealth, success, and class with those of the French.

James's protagonist is the wealthy American businessman Christopher Newman, who is traveling in Europe. In Paris, Newman becomes acquainted with an aristocratic French widow whom he hopes to marry. Throughout the course of the novel, Newman's attempts to win over the countess Claire de Cintré and her scornful family, the Bellegardes, are incorporated with James's observations on French society and French perceptions regarding Americans. Although Claire initially accepts Newman's proposal, she and her family ultimately reject him. Newman subsequently learns that Claire's mother and brother are implicated in the death of her father. After Claire enters a convent, having succumbed to her mother's wish that she renounce Newman, Newman considers using his knowledge of the family secret to seek revenge. He decides, however, to not pursue this course of action, and his destruction of the evidence of the murder comprises the novel's conclusion.

Henry James *(© Reginald Haines / Hulton Archive / Getty Images)*

The American was initially published in serial form, in 1876 and 1877, in the *Atlantic Monthly*. It was first published in novel from in 1877. James later revised the novel when it was published by Charles Scribner's Sons in 1907. This final version of the novel is available in a modern edition published in 1999 by Oxford University Press.

AUTHOR BIOGRAPHY

James was born on April 15, 1843, in New York City. He was the second child of parents Henry James Sr. and Mary Walsh James. The family traveled to Paris and London during the first year of James's life and then returned to New York. James grew up in Albany and New York City. From 1855 through 1858, James attended various schools in Geneva, Switzerland; London, England; and Boulogne-sur-Mer, France. He also received private tutoring.

In 1858, his family, which by now included James and four siblings, settled in Newport, Rhode Island. James continued to travel between the United States and Europe, studying in Geneva and in Bonn, Germany, before he returned to Newport in 1860. While serving as a volunteer fireman, James injured his back and was consequently unable to serve in the Union Army during the Civil War (1861–1865). After studying at Harvard briefly, James once again traveled to Europe and wrote unsigned fiction and reviews.

James published his first novel, *Watch and Ward*, in 1870. For the next several years, James continued to write and travel abroad. He settled in Paris and later in London. Between 1876 and 1877, his novel *The American* was published in serial form in the *Atlantic Monthly*. James wrote prolifically during this time, publishing a number of novels over the course of a decade, including one of his best-known works, *The Portrait of a Lady*, in 1881. Spending much of the 1880s and 1890s in Europe, James wrote numerous novels and plays, including the highly regarded novel *The Turn of the Screw*, published in 1898. After living in England for many years, James became a British subject in 1915. In December of that year, James suffered a stroke, which led to further health problems. He died not long after, on February 28, 1916, in London.

PLOT SUMMARY

Chapters I–V

The American opens with the protagonist, Christopher Newman, relaxing in the Louvre after perusing the museum's offerings. He approaches a young Parisian woman who has set up an easel to paint copies of the artwork. She introduces herself as Mademoiselle Noémie Nioche, and she is soon joined by her father, Monsieur Nioche. Newman offers to buy her painting. Noémie also convinces her father to offer Newman French lessons. Newman then encounters an old friend, Tom Tristram, who has taken up residence in Paris. The two catch up as they stroll through Paris. In this conversation, Newman's status as a successful American businessman who is vacationing in Europe is introduced.

The following day, Newman is invited to Tristram's home, where he meets Tom's wife, Lizzie Tristram. Newman and his friends discuss his business success and the differences in the way Europeans and Americans view wealth.

MEDIA ADAPTATIONS

- The PBS production of Henry James's *The American* originally aired in 1998 and was released on DVD in 2009 by BBC Productions. The film stars Matthew Modine as Christopher Newman. It is available in a boxed set, *The Henry James Collection: The American, The Portrait of a Lady, The Wings of the Dove, The Golden Bowl, The Spoils of Poynton.*

Mrs. Tristram also asks Newman about his marriage prospects and agrees to introduce him to one of her friends, a widow from an aristocratic family. Not long after, Newman meets the widow, Madame Claire de Cintré, when she is visiting Lizzie Tristram. Intrigued, Newman attempts to visit Claire at her home but is told she is not present. He is surprised to learn that one of her brothers is a count and the other a marquis.

Meanwhile, Newman begins his French lessons with Monsieur Nioche. Nioche and Newman converse about Nioche's daughter and their family's dire financial circumstances. Hoping to help Nioche provide a dowry for his daughter so that she may attract a husband, Newman commissions Noémie to paint several more pictures for him. When Noémie meets with Newman, she reveals that she is not talented enough to do as he asks and that she is frustrated with her father and the arrangements he has made on her behalf. Knowing that Claire will be away from Paris for the summer, Newman, at Mrs. Tristram's urging, decides to tour Europe. In Holland, Newman meets a young American minister, Benjamin Babcock. They decide to travel together. In Venice, they part ways.

Chapters VI–X

Once Newman has returned from his travels, he meets with Mrs. Tristram to discuss again the prospect of seeing Claire. Mrs. Tristram explains

to Newman that Claire is in many ways at the mercy of her older brother, Urbain de Bellegarde, and her mother, Madame de Bellegarde. Mrs. Tristram goes on to tell Newman that Claire's brother and mother forced her into a marriage she did not want many years ago. Furthermore, Mrs. Tristram believes that Claire's mother and brother seek to marry her off again, because Claire's elderly, wealthy husband has been deceased for several years. After Mrs. Tristram suggests that Newman should save Claire by trying to marry her himself, Newman once again visits the Bellegarde home.

He converses with Claire, Claire's younger brother, Valentin, and the younger Madame de Bellegarde, who is the wife of Claire and Valentin's older brother, Urbain. The young Madame de Bellegarde asks Newman about his commercial endeavors in America. Not long after this visit, Valentin calls on Newman. As the gentlemen discuss Claire, among other topics, a friendship is fostered. Newman has become increasingly fascinated with Claire and asks Valentin to speak well of him to his sister. Newman further reveals that he would like to marry Claire, and although Valentin alludes to obstacles Newman will face, he agrees to do his best to advance Newman's suit.

The next day, Newman once again visits Claire and declares his desire to wed her. Claire seems at once intrigued and upset, yet she encourages Newman to see her again provided he wait six months before he once again mentions marriage. Soon after, the elder Madame de Bellegarde—Claire's mother—invites Newman to speak with her. Newman also meets Claire's older brother Urbain at this time. Madame de Bellegarde seems disapproving of Newman, until he discusses his wealth. Newman is tacitly given permission to continue to call on Claire.

Chapters XI–XV

Monsieur Nioche visits Newman. Nioche expresses his frustration with his daughter, who visits the Louvre but does not work on Newman's paintings. Newman decides to find Noémie at the museum and question her. Instead, he finds Valentin, who has been waiting in the museum to meet a relative who has not shown up. Newman describes Noémie to Valentin and explains his association with her to his friend. Valentin is curious about Noémie and expresses a desire to meet her. After Newman finds Noémie, she tells Newman she has not worked on his paintings at all. She departs with her father. Valentin then reveals that he is attracted to Noémie. Newman attempts to discourage Valentin from pursuing her.

Several days after Newman has been introduced to the Bellegarde family, he is invited to dinner. After dinner, when the gentlemen have retired to the smoking room with their cigars, Valentin informs Newman that he has formally been accepted as a candidate for Claire's hand in marriage. Valentin and Urbain allude to the fact that Newman faces obstacles he cannot understand and that cannot be openly discussed. The underlying suggestion is that the social class difference between Newman and the Bellegardes will be problematic.

Over the course of the next six weeks, Newman pays Claire numerous visits. During one such visit, Newman has the opportunity to speak with Mrs. Bread, an Englishwoman who is servant to the elder Madame de Bellegarde. Mrs. Bread urges Newman to remain steadfast in his pursuit of Claire; she seems to fear for Claire's well-being. When Newman questions Claire about her family's support of him, she insists that they have not spoken ill of him. Madame de Bellegarde introduces Newman to a distant relative of the family, Lord Deepmere. Not long after, Newman again visits Claire and reminds her of his promise to not speak of marriage to her for a period of several months. Since that time has now expired, Newman expresses his love for Claire and his desire to marry her. She responds favorably.

The next day, he returns to the Bellegarde home. Mrs. Bread approaches him, seeming fearful, and hints that the marriage will be opposed. Madame Bellegarde and Urbain have learned that Claire has accepted Newman. They give their permission to allow the wedding to take place but clearly remain disapproving of Newman. When Newman announces to the Bellegardes that he wishes to throw a party to celebrate the engagement, Madame de Bellegarde insists that she will organize her own event first.

Meanwhile, Valentin has been seeing Noémie Nioche. Newman has grown concerned that Monsieur Nioche has stopped visiting him and arranges a visit. As they converse, Nioche reveals his fears about his daughter: that he is losing control of her entirely. She appears at the café where the men are talking and treats her father rudely. Later, when Valentin and Newman discuss Valentin's relationship with Noémie, Newman once again cautions his friend to steer clear of her.

Chapters XVI–XX

Newman enjoys daily visits with Claire, and the two grow increasingly close. At the party the Bellegardes throw, Newman exhibits his pride and excitement at the prospect of his marriage to Claire. He is introduced to and reacquainted with the Bellegarde's social circle. Lord Deepmere is present, and Newman observes him having private conversations with Madame de Bellegarde and with Claire.

Shortly after this occasion, Newman attends an opera. There, he spies Noémie Nioche, Valentin, and another man. As the evening progresses, Newman has the opportunity to once again try and warn Valentin to avoid Noémie. However, Noémie fans the flames of an altercation between Valentin and the other man, later identified as Stanislas Kapp of Strasbourg. The men agree to a duel as a means of settling their disagreement. Newman disapproves.

When he next visits Claire, Mrs. Bread informs Newman that Claire is about to leave Paris. Newman intercepts Claire, and she informs him that she cannot marry him, although she will not tell him why. Newman accuses Madame de Bellegarde and Urbain of abusing or coercing Claire into making this decision and of interfering in the matter of their engagement. The only explanation Newman is given is that the Bellegardes object to Newman as a businessman; he is not of their social standing. Newman is hurt and confused and can only assume Claire's mother and brother have bullied her into obedience to their demand that the engagement be called off. Claire departs for a small town in the French countryside.

When Newman tells Mrs. Tristram of his troubles, she suspects that Claire is to be married off to Lord Deepmere. Before Newman is able to follow Claire, he receives a telegram from Valentin telling him that Valentin is extremely ill. In fact, as Newman soon discovers, Valentin has received a life-threatening injury in the duel with Kapp. Newman remains with Valentin as Valentin's condition worsens. When Newman reveals what has transpired with Claire, Valentin informs him of a secret he has closely held for many years. He suggests that his mother and his brother Urbain were involved in his father's death and claims that they were motivated by their desire to silence the Marquis de Bellegarde, because he opposed his daughter Claire's marriage to the elderly Comte de Cintré. Valentin hopes Newman will be able to use this information to his advantage, to blackmail Madame de Bellegarde into letting Claire marry Newman. Valentin dies shortly after this conversation.

Newman travels to Geneva and writes to Claire, telling her that he will visit her soon. Once he arrives, Newman again pours out his heart to Claire, hoping to find a way to convince her to marry him. Claire then reveals her intention to become a nun and live in seclusion for the remainder of her life. Newman is shocked and heartbroken. They share one kiss before Claire departs.

Chapters XXI–XVI

Devastated by Claire's decision, Newman begins to plot his revenge against the Bellegardes. He enlists the aid of Mrs. Bread, who, according to Valentin, knew everything about the death of the Marquis de Bellegarde. Mrs. Bread eventually describes the role Urbain and Madame de Bellegarde played in the death of the Marquis. Mrs. Bread also reveals that she possesses a document signed by the dying Marquis de Bellegarde that identifies his wife as his murderer, and she hands this letter over to Newman.

Once back in Paris, Newman visits Mrs. Tristram and enlists her aid in helping him get into the chapel where he hopes he will be able to talk to Claire, who has already resigned herself to the nunnery. At the chapel, he finds that Urbain and Madame de Bellegarde have also come, hoping to see Claire. Claire, however, is not present. With the help of Urbain's wife, Newman arranges an encounter with Claire's brother and mother. Newman alludes to the information he possesses and threatens to make it public. Urbain and Madame de Bellegarde appear unconcerned. Newman threatens to tell one of the family's most influential friends, the duchess, Madame d'Outreville, what he knows of Henri-Urbain de Bellegarde's death. After arranging a meeting with the Duchess, Newman finds he cannot go through with his plan. Mrs. Tristram advises him to travel once again, to leave Paris until his grief has ebbed.

In London, Newman once again encounters Monsieur Nioche and his daughter. Noémie is now romantically involved with Lord Deepmere.

Newman returns briefly to the United States but eventually finds himself in Paris once again. He visits the gates of the convent where Claire is now locked away and finally finds he can move on. As he spends time with Lizzie and Tom-Tristram, Newman reveals to them that he possesses a document that proves that Madame de Bellegarde murdered her husband. He then burns the letter.

CHARACTERS

Benjamin Babcock

Benjamin Babcock is an American Unitarian minister whom Newman meets in Holland. The two subsequently travel through Europe together but part ways after spending time in Venice. The conservative and contemplative Babcock is critical of Newman's expansive and hurried approach to travel and pleasure.

Madame Emmeline de Bellegarde, the Marquise de Bellegarde

Madame de Bellegarde is the mother of three grown children: Urbain, Claire, and Valentin. When Newman first encounters her, he finds her to be cold and dismissive, as well as disapproving of his desire to court Claire. Although Madame de Bellegarde never gives Newman her blessing where Claire is concerned, she does not initially obstruct Newman's courtship of Claire. Cruelly, she allows the relationship to evolve and assents to the marriage, only to later demand that Claire reject Newman. Madame de Bellegarde makes it clear that Newman has been rejected because he is a businessman who has worked for his wealth; he has not been born into an aristocratic family

As Valentin suggests and Mrs. Bread finally confirms, Madame de Bellegarde had a hand in killing her husband many years before Newman's arrival in Paris. She was motivated by her desire for Claire to marry the wealthy Comte de Cintré, despite her husband's objection to the match. Mrs. Bread, who was with Henri-Urbain de Bellegarde just before his death, possesses a letter from Henri-Urbain in which he states that his wife has killed him. Mrs. Bread's observations indicate that Madame de Bellegarde withheld the treatment that was keeping Henri-Urbain alive. Madame de Bellegarde seems unconcerned that Newman will be able to prove anything or will have the power to diminish her social standing in any way.

Monsieur Henri-Urbain de Bellegarde, the Marquis de Bellegarde

Monsieur de Bellegarde is the dead husband of the elder Madame de Bellegarde and the father of Valentin, Claire, and Urbain. He was murdered by his wife because he opposed the marriage of his daughter to the Comte de Cintré.

Madame de Bellegarde, the Marquise de Bellegarde

The younger Madame de Bellegarde is the wife of Urbain de Bellegarde. She is often referred to as the young Marquise, to differentiate her from her mother-in-law, who holds the same title. The younger Madame de Bellegarde is depicted as youthful and animated, a woman who enjoys her wealth and title but who is not necessarily enamored of her husband.

Urbain de Bellegarde, the Marquis de Bellegarde

Urbain de Bellegarde is the oldest son of Madame de Bellegarde. He is steadfast in his devotion to his mother throughout the novel, and Valentin and Mrs. Bread both indicate that Urbain knew of and supported his mother's plan to kill his father. Newman finds Urbain unlikable, not only because of Urbain's blind obedience to his mother but also in the way he, like Madame de Bellegarde, looks down upon him as a social inferior.

Valentin de Bellegarde, the Comte de Bellegarde

Valentin de Bellegarde is the younger son of Madame de Bellegarde. After a few conversations with Newman, Valentin not only becomes an increasingly close friend to Newman but also grows supportive of Newman's desire to marry Claire. He promises to be an advocate on Newman's behalf. As Newman courts Claire, he additionally spends time with Valentin socially.

Unlike his cold older brother and his reserved sister, Valentin seem the most open and carefree of the Bellegarde siblings, yet he expresses to Newman that he is growing bored with the limited range of options open to him. Newman attempts to convince Valentin to come with him to America after he has wed Claire. Newman promises to set Valentin up as a businessman and is eager to be a part of Valentin's

prosperity and independence from his family. Valentin considers this proposal but becomes entangled with Noémie Nioche.

After arguing with another of Noémie's admirers, Stanislas Kapp, Valentin is fatally injured in a duel with Kapp. Until his last breath, Valentin asserts that his choice to duel was an honorable one. Before he dies, he tells Newman that his mother was involved in his father's death and that Mrs. Bread knows the details of the affair.

Mrs. Catherine Bread

Mrs. Bread is a servant of the Bellegarde family. She traveled with Madame de Bellegarde from England, before she was wed to the Marquis de Bellegarde. She helped raise the family's children and is particularly close to Claire and Valentin. Mrs. Bread appears timid and fearful to Newman when he first meets her. After Claire calls off her engagement to Newman at her mother's command and following Valentin's death, Mrs. Bread reveals the secret she has held for many years regarding Madame de Bellegarde's role in her husband's death. For her loyalty to him, Newman offers Mrs. Bread a position in his own household.

Madame Claire de Cintré, the Comtesse de Cintré

Claire is the only daughter of Madame de Bellegarde. She is characterized as mild and obedient to her mother and her elder brother, Urbain. Despite her trepidation at marrying an elderly stranger, Claire weds the Comte de Cintré when she is a very young woman. After her husband's death just a few years later, she promises her mother to always obey her, if she will only allow her a period of ten years to remain unwed. Madame de Bellegarde complies.

Claire is described to Newman by the Tristrams as refined, beautiful, and haughty. Despite her reservations about marriage, Claire is curious about Newman and appears to look forward to his visits and to thrive under his attention. She accepts his proposal to marry but later obediently acquiesces to her mother's request to break off the engagement to Newman. Claire expresses her fear of her mother, and Newman wonders what Madame de Bellegarde could do to Claire that would frighten her so.

Although Newman pleads with Claire and her family to allow the marriage, Claire remains steadfast in her obedience to her mother's wishes, but rather than agree to marry Lord Deepmere, Claire resigns herself to a life of solitude as a nun. Newman is crushed by this decision, and after her retreat to the convent, Claire disappears from the story except as a memory and an obsession for Newman.

Monsieur le Comte de Cintré

Monsieur le Comte de Cintré is the man to whom Claire was married. Elderly and extremely wealthy, he was an ideal match for Claire, from Claire's mother's point of view. Claire's father opposed the marriage, and because he took this stance, his wife murdered him by withholding the medical treatment he needed to survive. After the Comte's death, Claire tells her mother that she will do anything she asks in the future, as long as she does not have to remarry for ten years.

Lord Deepmere

Lord Deepmere is a distant cousin of the Bellegardes on their mother's side of the family. Madame de Bellegarde wishes to have Claire wed him rather than Newman. Lord Deepmere appears briefly in the story, at the party the Bellegardes throw for Newman and Claire. Later, when Newman escapes to London after being rejected by Claire and her family, he learns that Lord Deepmere has become involved with Noémie Nioche.

Monsieur de Grosjoyaux

Monsieur de Grosjoyaux is a friend of Valentin's. He is with Valentin during the duel and afterward, as Valentin dies.

Monsieur Stanislas Kapp

Stanislas Kapp is first introduced as a rival to Valentin for Noémie Nioche's attention. The three are seated together at an opera Newman is also attending. Kapp and Valentin argue, although Valentin is vague when describing this altercation to Newman. Valentin tells Newman that he and Kapp have exchanged cards, meaning that they have agreed to duel. They leave the country to do so. Although Valentin opts to only inflict a minor injury on Kapp during the duel, Kapp uses the second shot he is allotted to shoot Valentin in the chest. Valentin dies from his injury not long after, while Kapp departs Switzerland hastily.

Monsieur Ledoux

Like Monsieur de Grosjoyaux, Monsieur Ledoux is Valentin's friend. He is at Valentin's side during and after the duel.

Christopher Newman

Christopher Newman is the protagonist of *The American* and is in fact "the American" to whom the title refers. In many ways, he is regarded as the culmination of James's own observations garnered through his travels through Europe. Newman's name has been regarded by critics as significant. He is a "new man" in the sense of being an American reimagining himself, re-creating himself, in Europe. He is also a new man in that he is a product of a newly industrialized, post-Civil War America. He is an American who has made his fortune through industry and investment and is part of the "nouveau riche," or newly wealthy, class of Americans that made their money through their own efforts rather than inheriting it from wealthy generations past.

At times, James pokes fun at the perceptions surrounding Newman—those he has of himself as a wealthy American entitled by virtue of this fact to everything Europe has to offer and those his acquaintances have of him, as when Mrs. Tristram tells Newman he is "the great Western Barbarian, stepping forth in his innocence and might, gazing a while at this poor corrupt old world and then swooping down on it." Despite such characterizations, Newman demonstrates a work ethic of which he is deservedly proud and a compassion for Claire as a woman forced by her family into situations she finds repugnant.

Initially, Newman seeks to acquire a wife who will enhance the world's perception of his success. Before Mrs. Tristram even mentions Claire to Newman, he states that if he were married, "if people notice my wife and admire her I shall count it as part of my success." Despite this attitude, Newman grows increasingly sympathetic to Claire as Mrs. Tristram describes her situation to Newman. Once Newman meets Claire, his ideas begin to evolve. Although he still sees it as a great accomplishment to marry her and although he regards her in some ways as a prize to brag about, he grows increasingly affectionate toward her. By the end of the novel he has expressed his love for her and suffers anguish at the loss of a future with her.

Throughout the novel, Newman is differentiated from his European counterparts as a man with a unique set of values and beliefs. He seems to feel at home wherever he is, even though the Bellegardes express their disdain for all he represents as a businessman who has earned his wealth. The Bellegardes' rejection of him forces him to question who he is. He asks them, "What's the matter with me?," as though it is the first time he has ever had to wonder this. His anguish leads him to pursue a course of revenge, which he ultimately gives up. Newman relinquishes his need for power, opting instead for a quiet retreat from Paris.

Monsieur Nioche

Monsieur Nioche is the father of the spirited Noémie Nioche. Nioche is surprised by Newman's interest in Noémie's paintings and initially reluctant to tutor Newman in French as his daughter urges. Although Newman gradually comes to regard Nioche as a friend, Nioche is aware that he and Newman are not on equal footing in terms of social class. However, he continues to teach Newman and reveals that he hopes to wed Noémie to a respectable man. Newman extends an offer to Noémie through her father to buy several paintings. He hopes, through a business arrangement such as this, to provide Nioche with the dowry he needs to secure a marriage for his daughter. Nioche, however, finds that his daughter will not comply. He loses authority over her, as she begins to openly pursue wealthy men outside of their social circle, men such as Valentin de Bellegarde, Stanislas Kapp, and, later, Lord Deepmere. Eventually Nioche sparks little more than pity in Newman.

Noémie Nioche

Noémie Nioche is the beautiful daughter of Monsieur Nioche. Newman first finds her in the Louvre, where she is painting copies of famous works of art. Newman offers to buy the paintings, indulging his own sense of himself as a worldly art collector, despite the fact that Noémie's art is not very good, at least according to Noémie. Through Noémie, Newman strikes up a friendship with Monsieur Nioche and begins to learn French under Nioche's tutelage.

Newman's judgment of Noémie becomes increasingly harsh, as he observes the way she seeks to elevate her own social status by attracting the interest of wealthy and noble men. Newman warns Valentin to stay away from Noémie, whom Newman now knows to be calculating and manipulative. Noémie encourages the disagreement between Valentin and Stanislas Kapp that leads to the duel and ultimately to Valentin's death. Newman is not surprised to see how little remorse Noémie later expresses about Valentin.

Madame d'Outreville

The duchess, Madame d'Outreville, is a wealthy and powerful friend of the Bellegarde family. Newman meets her on several occasions and is interested to see the deference with which the Bellegardes treat her. He capitalizes on this observation, when, after having been rejected by the Bellegardes, he seeks an audience with the Duchess. Newman intends to reveal Madame de Bellegarde's secret to the Duchess, in hopes of damaging the Bellegardes in any way he can. Newman does not follow through on his plan for revenge, however, and leaves the perplexed duchess's home without revealing the secret.

Lizzie Tristram

Lizzie Tristram is Tom Tristram's wife. She is well acquainted with Parisian society, and when Newman expresses his interest in finding a wife, Mrs. Tristram immediately thinks of her friend, the widow Claire de Cintré, with whom she attended a private school at a convent. Throughout the novel, Mrs. Tristram offers advice to Newman, and in fact the two establish a closer relationship as friends and confidantes than the relationship that exists between Newman and Tom Tristram. Mrs. Tristram encourages Newman's pursuit of Claire but seems unsurprised that Newman meets interference from Claire's family. She is there to console Newman when the Bellegardes reject him, and she expresses her pity that Claire was not able to escape her family and spend the rest of her life with Newman.

Tom Tristram

Tristram is an old friend of Newman's. He once fought alongside Newman in the Civil War but has since settled in Paris and married a fellow expatriate, Lizzie. Newman is irritated by Tristram's often-disdainful attitude toward America, but he nevertheless enjoys being welcomed by the Tristrams into their home and social circle.

THEMES

American Identity

James treats the subject of American identity in the late 1860s through the character of Christopher Newman. In some ways, James satirizes American identity by describing Newman in overly idealistic terms. Newman is described as "the superlative American; to which affirmation of character he was partly helped by the general easy magnificence of his manhood." He goes on to comment on the impressiveness of Newman's "health and strength." Newman, in the opening scene of the novel, is observed to be confident, virile, and at ease in the distinctly Parisian environment that is the Louvre. James maintains a lightly comic thread through a good portion of the novel, and by describing Newman in this manner, he gently pokes fun at the way Americans abroad regard themselves or believe they are regarded by the Europeans among whom they are traveling.

Despite this arguably satiric depiction of Newman as the ultimate expression of American strength and vitality, Newman reveals himself to be something more. As a successful American businessman, Newman is deeply proud of the hard work that has enabled him to rise to the prosperous status he now enjoys. He describes to the Bellegardes and the Tristrams the way his efforts allowed his rise from poverty to prosperity. Uncomfortable with the current idleness—vacationing in Europe—that he has permitted himself, Newman leaves Paris to continue his travels at Mrs. Tristram's prompting. Later, as he becomes more intimately acquainted with the Bellegardes, Newman displays astonishment at the fact that Valentin simply does *nothing* with his time. Business endeavors are regarded as beneath someone of Valentin's status. Further, Newman's pride in what he has accomplished, his lauding of his American work ethic, is shocking to the Bellegardes, who seem to expect humility or shame from someone with Newman's commercial background.

However, Newman is at ease in his own skin and in any environment, a trait that could be regarded alternately as well-earned American pride or a characteristically American overdeveloped sense of entitlement. Valentin de Bellegarde observes to Newman, "It's a sort of air you have of being imperturbably, being irremoveably [sic] and indestructibly (that's the thing!) at home in the world." That James cultivates sympathy for Newman suggests that his portrait of the American identity is only partially satirical. At the same time, Newman does not seek to assimilate into European society but rather seeks to pluck Claire from it. Although he negatively views the culture in which Claire was raised, he does so from a sense of fairness and independence rather than from a sense of superiority. Claire's culture does not allow her the freedom to chose her spouse; she is subject to her mother's authority and to the demands of her class.

Social Class

Closely tied to the theme of American identity is that of social class. In *The American*, James links the notion of social class standing with the idea of wealth but contrasts American and European views on wealth and class. The Bellegardes convey their distaste for Newman and his commercial nature. At the same time, they appear to, at least initially, indulge Newman's interest in Claire based on his financial holdings. James demonstrates that wealth that one has gained through hard work and an enterprising nature is regarded as a source of pride for Newman. It allows Newman the freedom to do as he pleases.

In France, however, where Newman seeks to wed Claire, his very American wealth and the class status that Newman believes go with it in fact get him nowhere with the Bellegardes, who are a family with an ancient noble lineage and inherited wealth. Newman's status as a self-made businessman is frowned upon by Madame de Bellegarde and her son Urbain, who both prefer to not discuss how Newman has earned his wealth. Valentin de Bellegarde and Claire, despite their affection for Newman, refer to the fact that Newman is simply incapable of understanding the finer points about French upper-class society.

Newman's objection to the duel between Valentin and Stanislas Kapp is pointed to as one example of Newman's ignorance about matters of class. Valentin regards the duel as a noble way in which gentlemen settle their disputes, but Newman sees it as foolish and dangerous. The fact that Valentin is needlessly slain in this duel underscores, for Newman, the validity of his objections, but Valentin, before his death, simply points out that Kapp failed to act as a true gentlemen.

When Newman's pursuit of Claire is rejected by the Bellegardes, despite the fact that Newman was allowed to see Claire and that their

TOPICS FOR FURTHER STUDY

- *The American* is set in the Gilded Age. Research this time period in American history and create a presentation in which you explore the factors that led to the era being characterized in this fashion. Who were notable individuals during this time? What political leaders and businessmen shaped American economic policy and business ethics of the era? What writers contributed to defining the qualities that characterized these years? What key events occurred during this era? Prepare a written research paper on this topic, being sure to cite all of your sources.

- In *The American*, James depicts the experience of an expatriate American traveling through Europe. In the 2011 young-adult novel *Inside Out and Back Again*, Vietnamese-native Thanhha Lai relates the story of a young Vietnamese girl who flees Vietnam during the Vietnam War and settles in America. Lai draws on her own experiences and writes her novel in verse. With a small group, read Lai's novel. Compare the protagonist's experience as a foreigner in America with Newman's experience as an American in a foreign country. Despite their obvious differences, do Newman and Kim Hà share any similar experiences? Consider as well the challenges Hà faces in her new school. How is Hà perceived by her classmates? Discuss these issues in an online blog or forum your group creates to share ideas about Lai's and James's novels.

- As a work of realistic fiction, *The American* attempts to accurately and objectively depict American and European cultural identities and differences and surveys Parisian society in the late 1860s. The work focuses on the relationships among the characters, and the plot is driven by conflicts between these characters rather than on melodramatic events (in melodrama, plot and action are more important than characterization). Write a realistic short story in which you depict a small group of characters and the realistic tensions these characters experience. Your short story should include dialogue and should avoid the use of melodrama. Share your story with the class by reading it aloud, by sharing a recording of yourself reading it, or by making it available online for your class to review.

- In *The American*, James demonstrates a sustained interest in the role of women in society and portrays the limited range of choices available to women. Elsewhere, he directly explores American feminism. Using print and online sources, research the history of American feminism during the nineteenth century. Examine the issues that feminists focused on and the political issues they embraced. Who were the prominent feminist activists during this time period, and what did they fight for? What successes did the movement achieve? Create a time line—either as poster or as an electronic time line using PowerPoint or online tools and/or sites—and share your presentation with the class.

---

engagement was announced and celebrated, Madame de Bellegarde tells him, "It's not your personal character that we object to, it's your professional—it's your antecedents. We really can't reconcile ourselves to a commercial person." Newman is perplexed and refuses to accept their reasoning. He asks the family, "What's the matter with me? . . . What if I *am* a commercial person? I'll be any sort of person you want. I never talked to you about business—where on earth does it come in?" Newman is doomed from the beginning, as the Bellegardes return to their original objections to Newman. Despite his wealth, he has no "antecedents." He has no

James's works frequently incorporated an "international" theme and the setting of nineteenth-century Europe. (© Morphart Creation / Shutterstock.com)

ancestors of noble birth to precede him, no acceptable family history. Newman has believed throughout the novel that his wealth bought him access to whatever social circles he desired to infiltrate, yet as the Bellegardes point out, in their world, riches cannot buy social class.

STYLE

Realism

Literary realism refers to the depiction of people and places in a fashion that corresponds to real world experiences. American literary realism developed as a movement in the latter half of the nineteenth century. In *The American*, James draws upon his own experiences as an American living abroad and traveling extensively through Europe. His novel is informed by the attention to detail with which he describes Paris and its surrounding countryside, as well as by an understanding of cross-cultural perceptions concerning Americans and Europeans.

James infuses his realism with overtones of comedy and satire, as he humorously depicts Newman at times in an overly idealistic fashion. In this manner, James also gently mocks the sentimental romance novels in fashion during this time period. James's realism has been regarded as a reaction against this type of fiction, in which characters and locations are idealized, and melodramatic turns of events characterize the plot. Although the satire of sentimentalism is a component of *The American*, James infuses the novel with serious commentary on American and European perceptions of wealth and social class and the American cultural identity. Valentin perishes because of his devotion to an antiquated notion of the noble class and its obligations, while Claire is at the mercy of a cruel and narrow-minded mother as a result of her adherence to norms associated with her social class. James realistically portrays the conflicts these characters face and additionally captures Newman's indignant and anguished response to the dire consequences of Valentin's and Claire's decisions.

Sentimental Romanticism

Some critics have argued that the final third of *The American* hinges on plot developments that lean toward the type of melodrama typical in the sentimental romantic novel from which James had attempted to distance himself, like other realist writers at the time. In *The Cambridge Introduction to American Literary Realism*, Phillip J. Barrish describes the way James, as a literary critic, harshly assessed a novel by Rebecca Harding Davis, which James asserted was dripping with trivial sentimentalism. Although romantic plots remain within the purview of realist novels, the sentimentalization of characters and events through the use of melodrama was something James increasingly steered clear of throughout his career. However, Valentin's death, Claire's rejection of Newman, the discovery of Madame de Bellegarde's role in her husband's death, and Claire's escape to the nunnery all create a melodramatic tone in the final third of *The American*.

Kendall Johnson, in *Henry James and the Visual*, describes the "generic classification" (that is, the classifying of the work into a specific genre) as a "quandry." Johnson asks, "Is it a romance, a realistic novel, or as James labels it in his 1907 preface, 'an arch-romance'?" In Eric Haralson and Kendall Johnson's *Critical Companion to Henry James: A Literary Reference to His Life and Work*, the authors point out that the 1907 preface was written long after *The American*'s initial 1877 publication and that James had earned "the license to redefine the terms of romance and realism." Although James had distanced himself from sentimentality, he continued to justify the validity of romance in realism. Johnson and Haralson comment that "the line between the genres of romance and realism is blurry" and that "the confusion between the 'romantic' and 'realistic' is James's opportunity to outline the method of his writing craft."

HISTORICAL CONTEXT

The Gilded Age and the Rise of the American Nouveau Riche

The term "Gilded Age" refers to a period in American history from the late 1860s through the 1890s. This was a time of rapid industrialization and urbanization in America, and these forces reshaped American society, allowing for the middle classes and the upper classes to thrive. Many Americans moved West, finding their fortunes in mining, ranching, and farming. At the same time, industrial developments brought formerly rural workers to urban factories.

It was Twain's novel *The Gilded Age: A Tale of Today*, published in 1873, that inspired the dubbing of this time period in American history as the "Gilded Age." The novel, which Twain published in collaboration with Charles Dudley Warner, satirized the materialism of this time period and explored the greed and excess of the age. The economic expansion that occurred during this prosperous time gave rise to a new class of upwardly mobile Americans who became known as the "nouveau riche." This term, which means "newly rich," refers to formerly middle-class entrepreneurs, investors, manufacturers, industrialists, and businessmen who accumulated enough wealth to put them on par, economically, with the wealthiest Americans. These upper-class Americans, whose wealth was typically inherited rather than earned, were often referred to as "old money."

The expanding class of nouveau riche were typically frowned upon by upper-class Americans. These wealthy Americans often regarded the nouveau riche as having middle-class manners and comportment despite the wealth that they had earned. James's protagonist in *The American* is regarded as nouveau riche, as is the eponymous character Silas Lapham in William Dean Howells's *The Rise of Silas Lapham*, published in 1885. Describing the place of the nouveau riche in the Gilded Age, Pat Reeve states, in *Class in America: An Encyclopedia*, "To be sure, this was an age of political venality, unrivaled capital accumulation, and conspicuous consumption on the part of the nouveau riche." Reeve goes on to note that the time period, so near to the close of the Civil War, was also characterized by increasingly vigorous activism in the area of civil rights. Activists seeking to rebuild a damaged democracy led movements to protect the rights of women, the urban working class, farmers, and African Americans.

American Literary Realism in the Late Nineteenth Century

James was writing during a time of transition in American literature. During the mid-1800s,

COMPARE & CONTRAST

- **1870s:** Many Americans travel and live abroad during the prosperous Gilded Age. They travel for various reasons. Some, including many writers, seek a European education, while others vacation or live permanently abroad. Paris, France, is a popular destination for traveling and expatriate Americans. In 1870, approximately five thousand Americans are living in Paris.

  Today: Many Americans live abroad in the twenty-first century. Estimated U.S. State Department figures indicate that nearly 6.32 million Americans live abroad in 2012 and that approximately 1.6 million of them are settled in Europe.

- **1870s:** American literature is increasingly focused on the realistic portrayals of American and European society and culture. Henry James's *The American* (1876–1877), Mark Twain's *The Adventures of Tom Sawyer* (1876), and William Dean Howells's *A Foregone Conclusion* (1875) are examples of prominent realist novels of the time.

  Today: Twenty-first century American novelists continue to use realism to explore American society and the contemporary American family and to discuss culture and

identity, among other themes. Works such as David Eggers's *A Heartbreaking Work of Staggering Genius* (2001), Philip Roth's *Everyman* (2006), Jeffrey Eugenides's *Middlesex* (2007), Jennifer Eagen's *A Visit from the Good Squad* (2010), and Jonathan Franzen's *Freedom: A Novel* (2010) exemplify this trend.

- **1870s:** The economy during the 1870s is experiencing a period of expansion, and many Americans enjoy enough prosperity to rise from middle-class to upper-class status. Their new wealth, acquired through their efforts in business, industry, and investment, establishes them as the nouveau riche class of what becomes known as the Gilded Age.

  Today: After a US recession, which was further impacted negatively by a global financial crisis in 2008, the US economy shows signs of a moderate but definite recovery in 2012. Gross domestic product, a measure of the value of goods and services produced by a country, grew in the third quarter of 2012. Further, the unemployment rate is 7.7 percent in November of 2012. This represents the lowest level of unemployment since December of 2008.

American fiction was dominated by romantic portrayals of people, places, and events. This type of writing was marked by an idealization of characters and settings. Some writers incorporated melodramatic plot turns in their fictions and sentimentalized the relationships between their characters and the society in which they lived. Gradually, a number of writers began moving toward more realistic depictions of characters and settings. Writers such as Sarah Orne Jewett, Mark Twain, and Kate Chopin focused on capturing accurately the significance of place and attempted to convey local dialects and

scenery with accuracy. Such writers became referred to as local colorists, or regionalists.

Joel Schrock discusses this development in *The Gilded Age*, stating, "This regional literature had a realist focus but at times exhibited a streak of nostalgia and romanticism." Concurrent with this development was an increasing emphasis on the realistic depiction of people, places, and society. Writers such as Henry James and William Dean Howells, for example, sought to write with objective attention to detail as they explored the social realities of their rapidly changing time. Additionally,

One of the first scenes in The American *takes place in the Louvre.* (© BMCL | Shutterstock.com)

Mark Twain was noted not only as a local colorist or regionalist but also as a realist. As Schrock notes, "In many ways, realism was the literary attempt to understand and control the forces of change assailing Gilded Age America in a truthful way that was not exaggerated, romantic, or sensationalized."

CRITICAL OVERVIEW

Contemporary critical reception of *The American* was mixed. Some critics regarded it favorably, particularly when compared with James's earlier work. An unsigned review in the *New York Tribune* written in 1877 comments that in depicting his characters, James remains "untouched by any sympathy with them." Although this objectivity is regarded in a positive light, the reviewer later faults James for portraying Claire and Newman in such a cold manner that it is difficult for the reader to sustain an interest in their fate.

A critic for *Literary World* writes in 1877 that James's novel accurately represents American and European character yet asserts, "the story is exceedingly simple and devoid of incident." The critic further comments on the tragic elements of the novel's conclusion and maintains that because of the reader's lack of interest in the story and characters, "No gentle reader will shed a tear or heave a sigh over the most tragic of its pages." That James chose to end the work in an almost unresolved and clearly unhappy manner also garnered criticism. James's friend and contemporary, fellow realist author William Dean Howells, complained to James about the lack of a more "cheerful" ending, according to Collin Meissner in *Henry James and the Language of Experience.*

Modern critics have focused heavily on matters of genre. Marita Nadal observes in *Etudes Britanniques Contemporaines,* the novel's "structure and indefinite mode (melodrama/comedy/romance) have been regarded as the flaws that spoil the work." Nadal goes on to examine the way the work anticipates postmodernist literary techniques of the blurring of genres and the use of irony to undercut the story's romantic or comedic elements. Chiyo Yoshii, in *Papers on Language and Literature,* comments on what appears to be an incongruity between the realist and the romantic sections of the novel. However, Yoshii maintains that the work is integrated through James's focus on and critique of social class. Yoshii states, "James repeatedly foregrounds the social world lying behind but suppressed by Newman's romantic fantasies."

CRITICISM

Catherine Dominic

Dominic is a novelist and a freelance writer and editor. In the following essay, she explores James's depiction of women and their resistance to marriage in The American, *arguing that James demonstrates a sensitivity to the struggles women face during this time period and an awareness of the strength women exhibit in subverting the expectations their society and their families place upon them.*

In *The American*, James depicts a number of distinctly different female characters, all of whom attempt, with varying levels of success, to assert power in a world dominated by patriarchal views regarding the roles of women in society. Elsewhere in his work, particularly in the later novel *The Bostonians*, published in 1886, James explicitly treats women's issues. *The Bostonians* explores the American feminist movement in Boston during the late 1870s. Although critics remain divided on whether or not this novel reveals James to be a feminist, his concern with women and their power in the world is evident.

In *The American*, James portrays French society as one in which women are at the mercy of their families. Their fates are arranged for them and are rooted wholly within the institution of marriage. However, James's female characters struggle against these bonds and find ways to respond to their families' expectations that are vehement and sometimes violent. Through such characters as the expatriate Lizzie Tristram, the beautiful and defiant Noémie Nioche, the mild widow Claire de Cintré, and the elderly and cruel Madame de Bellegarde, James narrates a range of responses to the marital expectations that rule the lives of women during the late 1860s.

James is often described as objective to the point of coldness in the way he depicts his characters—he is a true observer—yet by

JAMES IS OFTEN DESCRIBED AS OBJECTIVE TO THE POINT OF COLDNESS IN THE WAY HE DEPICTS HIS CHARACTERS—HE IS A TRUE OBSERVER—YET BY EXAMINING THE WORDS AND ACTIONS OF THESE KEY FEMALE CHARACTERS, THE READER GAINS A DEEPER UNDERSTANDING OF WOMEN'S STRUGGLES IN THIS ERA."

examining the words and actions of these key female characters, the reader gains a deeper understanding of women's struggles in this era. Further, the lengths to which some of the women go to assert power in situations in which their patriarchal society expects them to be impotent suggest that James possessed an awareness of women's issues that perhaps tinged his otherwise objective portrayals with hints of sympathy.

Lizzie Tristram, the wife of Christopher Newman's old acquaintance Tom Tristram, is described as being indifferent to her husband. She had in fact been in love with someone else, who had slighted her, and "she had been perfectly at liberty not to marry" Tom Tristram. Yet, marry him she did. Now, she openly disagrees with Tom on any and all matters and is free with her advice to Newman and the attention she lavishes on him. For his part, Newman is aware of the discord between Tom and Lizzie: "he was sure one or other of them must be very unhappy. Yet he knew it was not Tristram."

This unhappiness manifests itself in Lizzie's forward nature with Newman. She eagerly spends time with him, and Newman, who enjoys the attention, often prefers to lounge with Lizzie on her balcony than accompany Tom to a club for drinks and cards. Lizzie also offers to help Newman find the wife he seeks. Later, after Lizzie has suggested that Newman should set out to wed Claire de Cintré, Lizzie tells Newman about Claire's previous marriage and how she might be forced to wed against her will again. Newman is astounded that women in France can be "thumb-screwed" into marrying objectionable

WHAT DO I READ NEXT?

- *The Portrait of a Lady* is counted among James's finest works. First published in serial form in 1880–1881, the novel is concerned with protagonist Isabel Archer, an independent American woman traveling in Europe.

- In *The Bostonians*, originally published in 1885–1886, James focuses on Boston society and the feminist movement and explores the struggle of Basil Ransom and Olive Chancellor, a feminist activist, for the affections of Verena Tarrant, Olive's feminist protégé.

- William Dean Howells's *The Rise of Silas Lapham*, published in 1885, is a realist novel featuring the nouveau riche Lapham, who made and lost his fortune in Boston during the Gilded Age.

- Mark Twain and Charles Dudley Warner's 1873 novel *The Gilded Age: A Tale of Today* is the satirical story that gave the Gilded Age its name. The novel exposes the corruption and greed of politicians, bankers, and speculators.

- African American author Jesmyn Ward examines life in a coastal Mississippi town in *Salvage the Bones: A Novel*, published in 2011. The work is a young-adult novel that uses the realist style to expose rural poverty and comment on contemporary rural society.

- *Henry James: The Young Master* by Sheldon M. Novick traces James's life from his birth through the early portion of his career. The highly acclaimed critical biography, published in 1996, assesses the influence of James's personal experiences on his writing.

- *Olivia and Jai*, a 1991 novel by an author who is a native of India, narrates the story of a young American woman who comes to stay with British relatives in India. The story is set in the mid-nineteenth century and is concerned with Olivia's romantic relationship with a man of Indian descent. As in James's *The American*, cultural differences impede the romance.

men. Lizzie replies, "Helpless women, all over the world, have a hard time of it. . . . There's plenty of the thumb-screw for them everywhere." The image is forceful, in that it implies the torture women endure in marriages they have not sought. Newman naively characterizes this situation as unique to France, but Lizzie reveals a deeper understanding of the issue and does not dismiss his use of the thumb-screw image. Rather, she asserts that the coercion women experience to marry men they do not wish to marry is a universal phenomenon.

This statement further underscores the unhappiness Newman astutely observed in Lizzie earlier. Near the novel's conclusion, when a heartbroken Newman comes to tell Lizzie that he has been rejected by Claire, Lizzie reveals to some degree an attraction that was hinted at with the earlier attention she had shown Newman. Lizzie tells Newman how compelling his unspoken eloquence is and adds:

> To resist you a woman must have a very fixed idea or a very bad conscience. I wish I had done you a wrong—that you might come to me and make me so feel it; and feel *you*, dear man, just you.

She then urges Newman to appeal once again to Claire. Unhappy in her own marriage and attracted to Newman, Lizzie nevertheless urges Newman to try to change Claire's mind. She sees Newman's worth and, knowing she cannot have him for herself, attempts to use her own powers to ensure that her friend Claire can have the happy marriage that she lacks.

Whereas Lizzie, in an unhappy marriage, attempts to secure a happy one for her widowed friend, Noémie Nioche seeks to avoid marriage altogether. Monsieur Nioche, Noémie's father, would like nothing more than to marry his spirited daughter off to a respectable suitor. He laments that he has lost much of his wealth and cannot provide his daughter with the dowry expected to attract a suitable mate. Additionally, he worries that his daughter's beauty and independent nature will bring trouble. When Noémie and Newman discuss her father's plans for her, Noémie grows angry. She does not wish to consider "grocers and butchers" as potential suitors. Having been described by her father as a "free spirit," Noémie envies Newman's own freedom, equating it with pure happiness. She tells Newman that she would rather throw herself into the Seine than to toil at needlecrafts as a way to earn a living and that she would prefer to not marry at all if she cannot do better than butchers and grocers.

Noémie goes on to pursue her own course as the novel continues, attracting the attention of Valentin de Bellegarde and Stanislas Kapp, among other men. She moves on to Lord Deepmere after Valentin is killed in a duel by Kapp, a duel resulting from an altercation that she encouraged and inflamed. Near the conclusion of the novel, Newman tells Noémie's father, "She has done a devilish mischief; it doesn't matter what. She's a public nuisance; she ought to be stopped." Despite Noémie's manipulations and her coldheartedness in the wake of Valentin's death, she nevertheless successfully avoids the fate of an unhappy marriage, through the only means she feels are at her disposal, that is, her charm and beauty and her ability to manage her meek father.

Claire de Cintré, unlike Lizzie and Noémie, has already experienced one unhappy marriage and escaped from it. Lizzie describes her friend's past by explaining, "She was married at eighteen, by her parents, in the French fashion, to a man with advantages of fortune, but objectionable, detestable, on other grounds, and many years too old." After Monsieur de Cintré's death only a few years after his marriage to Claire, Claire begged her mother to allow her to remain unwed for ten years. Madame de Bellegarde allowed this concession. Claire, at the age of twenty-eight, is now in danger of being married off again. Lizzie Tristram advises Newman, "Pounce down, seize her in your talons and carry her off. Marry her yourself."

When Newman asks Valentin his thoughts on his desire to marry Claire, Valentin asks, "Why should she put her head back into the noose?" He suggests his sister might be ambitious enough to hold out for a prince or an ambassador but admits to not knowing what might motivate her. Valentin does, however, admit that he approves of Newman's intentions. However, Claire only has the illusion of choice. After Madame de Bellegarde and Urbain allow Newman to pursue Claire, she hesitatingly grows interested in him and his attention, while Madame de Bellegarde seems to have allowed the courtship only because of her interest in Newman's vast wealth, a topic he candidly discusses with her when she asks.

When the Bellegardes further allow the engagement of Newman and Claire to be announced, Newman thinks he has won. He characterizes this period as the "happiest [he] had ever known" and is convinced of Claire's affections because of the contentment she displays and the "charming and tender things" she says to him. Madame de Bellegarde, however, reins in the lovers' illusions when she insists that Claire reject Newman. The Bellegardes decide that Newman's wealth cannot make up for his lack of noble ancestry. Madame de Bellegarde further attempts to have Claire marry Lord Deepmere instead.

Although Claire acquiesces to her mother's demand where Newman is concerned, she decides that rather than marry Deepmere or anyone else her mother would chose for her should she refuse Deepmere, she will escape for the rest of her life into the convent where she will live sequestered from society. Claire objects to the notion of defying her mother, and she feels compelled by her ancestry to make the choices she does. She tells Newman, "I've things to reckon with that you don't know. I mean I've feelings. I must do as they force me—I must, I must." She believes there is a "curse" upon her family that she sought to "escape" through marriage to Newman. She claims to now realize that wish was a "selfish" one. She goes on to insist, "I'm not made for boldness and defiance. I was made to be happy in a quiet natural way." Finally, she states, "I was made to do gladly and gratefully what is expected of me." Yet, in removing herself from society altogether, in committing herself to the convent, Claire *is* defying her mother and rejecting "what is expected" of her. She refuses to defy her mother in order to marry Newman, but Claire is resolute in her decision to enter the convent, thereby defying her mother by refusing to marry *anyone*. Claire escapes marriage—unhappy or otherwise—completely.

In the character of Claire's mother, Madame de Bellegarde, James offers one more portrait of escape from marriage. When Madame de Bellegarde intuits her husband's resistance to Claire's pending marriage to the Comte de Cintré, she finds she can no longer live under the constraints that her marriage to Henri-Urbain de Bellegarde has put upon her and her ambitions. After Monsieur de Bellegarde falls ill, Madame de Bellegarde tends to him in solitude. She pours out the medicine that

James's works often feature a wealthy American traveling in Europe. (© *Aleksei Makarov | Shutterstock.com*)

has been keeping her husband's illness at bay and watches him die. Madame de Bellegarde effectively takes matters into her own hands, becoming the mistress of her own fate by permanently eliminating the husband who opposed her.

Throughout *The American*, James observes the way marriage is forced upon women. Through his characters, he demonstrates the way marriage can suffocate and how it inspires fear and bitterness. Through Lizzie Tristram, James depicts the acute emotional suffering and longing endured by a woman in a loveless marriage. Lizzie's only recourse is to attempt to prevent the same fate from being forced upon her friend Claire. Seeing in Newman a strong and confident man who expresses his horror at what Claire has already endured, Lizzie hopes to help foster a match between Claire and Newman. She is nearly successful.

Noémie and Claire explore different means of escaping an unwanted marriage. Noémie escapes the fate of marriage through outright defiance of her father and through her own ambitious pursuit of prominent men, while Claire literally and figuratively escapes by withdrawing herself from society entirely and entering a convent. Claire's mother demonstrates a more violent but equally final means of escaping a marriage she finds confining: Madame de Bellegarde murders the man who stands in her way.

James has been accused of being objective to a fault in his portrayal of his characters and their struggles. However, in depicting several women who are all motivated by a desire to control their own destinies and by a need to flee situations—marriages—they view as undesirable, he demonstrates an awareness, if not a sympathetic understanding, of the challenges women face in his society.

Source: Catherine Dominic, Critical Essay on *The American*, in *Novels for Students*, Gale, Cengage Learning, 2014.

Jay Parini

In the following excerpt, Parini discusses James's popularity in current times, which comes in part from his "international" theme, first established in The American.

. . . James's understanding of the material world and its connection to power makes him extraordinarily relevant in an era when vast killings are made on Wall Street and on the Internet, turning our times into a kind of new Gilded Age. James would have had much to say about the shenanigans of investment bankers and real-estate moguls. He would have fashioned mythic tales of greed and social climbing, putting a finger on the moral bankruptcy everywhere in evidence. That's what he was good at.

Part of the attraction of James also lies in his famous "international" theme: the story of a confrontation between Old World and New World values. An early novel, *The American* (1877), established the paradigm for this kind of fiction, which often involves a rich young American going to Europe and facing its refinements and harsh realities.

In James's time, only wealthy Americans could travel to European capitals and visit the monuments of high culture. Now it's quite ordinary for middle-class travelers—many of them college students on their Wanderjahr—to visit London, Florence, and Paris. The corridors of the National Gallery, the Uffizi, and the Louvre teem with innocents abroad, guidebooks in hand. The novels and stories of Henry James come alive every day in these palaces of high culture. Is it any wonder they remain popular?

Of course, their popularity is relative. I doubt that readers en masse will ever flock to the *The Golden Bowl*, or even to *The Portrait of a Lady* or *Daisy Miller*, the most accessible James novels. His works remain highly challenging, with their endless loops of consciousness reflected in interwoven syntactical layers, in dazzling but complex formulations. But the taste of some readers for such fiction will not go away. There is something disheartening about the tele-graphic prose of many best-selling writers—James Patterson comes to mind, with his inch-long sentences and thumbnail paragraphs, his sheer disdain for complication of any kind. That is the common style of our time, often reflected in popular films and television shows. . . .

Source: Jay Parini, "The Afterlife of Henry James," in *Chronicle of Higher Education*, Vol. 57, No. 27, March 6, 2011.

Katherine Mullen

In the following essay, Mullen claims that Henry James's "interest in the lives and perspectives of women even included a thinly disguised lesbian theme in his 1877 novel The American.*"*

Denied a voice of their own by social and legal prohibition through most of Western history, women have often had to allow men to speak for them. The scarcity of women writers, much less lesbian writers, means that the lives of women have either been ignored or interpreted by male writers attempting to fathom their point of view. Still, in some cases it is better to have men speak for women than for women to have no voice at all. One example is Henry James, whose interest in the lives and perspectives of women even included a thinly disguised lesbian theme in his 1877 novel *The American*.

Now Henry James was a gay man, albeit a rather closeted one, and in this respect he is not alone in showing an uncanny insight into the subjectivities of women (Oscar Wilde and Tennessee Williams come immediately to mind). Perhaps because they've suffered many of the same kinds of oppression, gay men and women often show a special understanding of one another. In earlier periods, especially the late 19th century, when women had very little voice, gay men would integrate the plight of lesbians into their writing through subtle asides and implied story lines. Henry James—whose sister may have been a lesbian—was a master of such coded gay stories. Many of his novels and short stories have been studied by GLBT scholars for their gay subtext, including strong lesbian undertones in his novel *The Bostonians*, which has been thoroughly dissected.

While this theme is most pronounced in *The Bostonians*, it is certainly present in other James novels. The relationship between Lizzie Tristram and Claire de Cintre is an integral component of *The American*. Mrs. Tristram is largely absent from the story, but her connection to Christopher Newman and Claire de Cintre has her intertwined in the central plot. Though never explicitly stated, [there] is clearly a love connection between Mrs. Tristram and Claire de Cintre. Indeed, this relationship is the driving force behind the narrative. Lizzie and Claire attended school at a convent, where they formed a very close and intimate friendship. Such bonds between two women were not uncommon in 19th-century American life, and they appeared in the literature of the time, often transforming traditional love triangles. In *The American*, James inverts the notion of erotic love triangles described by the late Eve Kosofsky Sedgwick. Instead of the usual formation of two men and

**IN *THE AMERICAN*, HOWEVER, IT IS NEWMAN
WHO IS USED AS A COMMODITY."**

one woman, James places a man in the pivotal position between two women.

The exact nature of the "romantic friendship" between two women in 19th-century America has been much debated (how physical was it?), but it was clearly an uncommonly intimate and loving relationship in many cases. Lillian Faderman has argued that "being 'in love' meant experiencing intense feelings of affection and devotion, which were more likely to have found occasional expression in generalized sensual rather than specifically genital contact." This was due in large part to the strict gender roles that governed society and the restrictions on intimacy between the sexes, so that husbands and wives were often emotionally isolated from each other. James was no stranger to the idea of intimate relations between women: George Eliot (nee Mary Ann Evans), one of his muses, is said to have had a female "admirer." A relationship between Claire and Mrs. Tristram would have been fairly normal.

James uses a commonly occurring phenomenon for establishing the connection between Lizzie Tristram and Claire. Intimate bonds between two women were commonly formed while they were away at school. Carroll Smith-Rosenberg traces several such relationships: "Sarah Butler Wister first met Jeannie Field Musgrove while vacationing with her family.... During two subsequent years spent together in boarding school, they formed a deep and intimate friendship." Another pair, "Molly and Helena met in 1868 while both attended the Cooper Institute School of Design for Women in New York City." This pattern was also employed in literature. In Henry Wadsworth Longfellow's *Kavanagh* (1849), Cecilia and Alice Archer, the two "lovers," are described as "bosom-friend[s] at school." In Oliver Wendell Holmes' *A Moral Antipathy* (1886), Euthymia and Lurida are also schoolmates. This pattern appeared in both life and literature, and James employs it in *The American*. Claire and Lizzie met at the convent,

where they attended school together. Mrs. Tristram views this meeting as the redeeming facet of having had to attend the convent school. In her own words: "I took a tremendous fancy to her, and she returned my passion as far as she could."

The closeness between Claire and Mrs. Tristram finds no parallel in either woman's connection to any other character, including their husbands. Claire very much keeps to herself. The only time we encounter her outside of her home or the convent is when she's first introduced at Mrs. Tristram's house. Claire also makes another exception for Mrs. Tristram. When Christopher Newman proposes marriage to Claire, he's the one who has to take the initiative to hold her hand, and she does not let this intimacy last long. When she first appears at Mrs. Tristram's, however, it is Claire who takes hold of Lizzie's hand, and she makes no attempt to keep the contact brief.

The exclusion of men is further underscored by the lack of intimacy exhibited between husbands and wives. Mr. and Mrs. Tristram certainly don't enjoy marital bliss: "Newman hated to see a husband and wife on these terms, and he was sure one or other of them must be very unhappy." Claire is also unlucky in marriage. She does not, in fact, want to marry in the first place. As Claire's younger brother Valentin explains to Christopher, it was only a month before the wedding that Claire first encountered her intended, and everything had already been arranged: "She turned white when she looked at him, and white she remained till her wedding-day. The evening before the ceremony she swooned away, and she spent the whole night in sobs." Indeed, after her first marriage Claire promises never to marry again, in effect swearing off men for life. She doesn't even want Newman. When she's searching for a reason why she might accept him, he says, "Your only reason is that you love me," and Claire's response, described by the narrator, is not exactly a ringing endorsement: "for want of a better reason Madame de Cintre reconciled herself to this one." Newman basically accepts his own proposal.

According to Sedgwick, "the power relationships between men and women appear to be dependent on the power relationships between men and men, [which] suggests that large-scale social structures are congruent with the male-male-female erotic triangles." In *The American*, Mrs. Tristram is the one with the power; the relationship between Claire and Christopher is ultimately her doing. Mrs. Tristram is the first to introduce the idea that Newman ought to marry: "Mrs. Tristram suddenly observed to Christopher Newman that it was high time he should take a wife." She then builds up Madame de Cintre in Newman's mind by extolling her in the way a lover might praise a beloved. She refers to her as "the loveliest woman in the world. . . . Among all women I have known she stands alone; she is of a different clay." Through her description she sows the seed of Newman's admiration. She is also responsible for persuading Claire to indulge Newman's attempts at courting.

In the scene when Newman first meets Claire, Mrs. Tristram clearly communicates a desire for Claire to consider Christopher as a suitor. She and Claire are holding hands in farewell when "Mrs. Tristram seemed to have formed a sudden and somewhat venturesome resolution, and she smiled more intensely. . . . 'I want Mr. Newman to know you,' she said, dropping her head on one side and looking at Madame de Cintre's bonnet ribbons." When Claire expresses how this would please her, she's looking at Mrs. Tristram, not at Newman. She's indulging Mrs. Tristram's desire; she is not attracted to the American. Newman's success is dependent on Mrs. Tristram's influence over Claire as a result of their intimacy. The triangulation of power that Sedgwick highlights is inverted in this situation: Newman's power over Claire is dependent on the power relationship between the two women.

Traditionally, women were seen as a commodity to be exchanged, as Sedgwick points out: "The total relationship of exchange which constitutes marriage is not established between a man and a woman, but between two groups of men, and the woman figures only as one of the objects in the exchange, not as one of the partners." In *The American*, however, it is Newman who is used as a commodity. Being rich, he can offer Claire a continued life of comfort, including escape from her overly controlling family. In addition, as Newman is a friend of Mrs. Tristram's, it is also possible that she would get to see Claire more often, considering that Newman gives Claire the choice of living anywhere she wishes. Of course, this might not happen.

As Newman is an American, it is possible that the two might decide to leave France. Mrs. Tristram undoubtedly recognizes this danger, for when Newman tells her about his first proposal to Claire, she exhibits some signs of jealousy: "she had counted too much on her own disinterestedness." However, she continues to support the union, because it would still serve as retribution. Claire had to give Mrs. Tristram up after the convent because the latter was not a part of her social circle. Mrs. Tristram sees this as an offense, and she refers to Claire's circle as "terrible people." Newman is a means of exacting her revenge. She knows that Claire's mother Madame Bellegarde will not approve of Newman, and his marrying Claire would be an affront to the Bellegardes in the eyes of the Marquise.

Mrs. Tristram establishes a relationship between Claire and Newman for a purpose. There is a possibility that the marriage will bring her and Claire closer together, but, failing this, their union will serve as vengeance. Using Newman in this fashion is a power play; here the woman wields the power, not the man. This is a clear inversion of Sedgwick's triangle theory: "in any male-dominated society, there is a special relationship between male homosocial desire and the structures for maintaining and transmitting patriarchal power." Newman holds no power over Claire except that which he has by virtue of Mrs. Tristram; thus patriarchal power is not at issue. According to Sedgwick, "[Male] homosexuality is the law that regulates the sociocultural order"; however, the female-female bond governs Newman's interaction with Claire.

Mrs. Tristram constantly apologizes to Newman, claiming that his relationship with Claire was her doing; this says it quite well. She is the instigator of Newman's courtship of Claire, and she's able to do this because of an intimate bond that she shares with Claire. As these relationships were quite common in 19th century life and literature, it makes sense that Henry James would use such a connection in his novel. In employing such a structure of intimacy, he inverts the more frequent triangle involving a woman between two men, and instead places a man at the center. Neither Claire nor Mrs. Tristram wants a man; they are far closer to each other than to their respective husbands or suitors. Their inability to be together was the sad fate of homosexual relationships at the time; such relationships could not be overtly recognized. Therefore, Christopher's courtship of Claire is the talk of the novel, but Mrs. Tristram's connection to her is the engine.

Source: Katherine Mullen, "The 'L' Word in Henry James' Fiction," in *Gay & Lesbian Review Worldwide*, Vol. 16, No. 4, July–August 2009, pp. 30–32.

William F. Buckley Jr.

In the following review, Buckley laments that The American *"may be the single most boring book ever published."*

The sickbed serves to distract attention, but it is unsafe to assume as a corollary that such distraction is enjoyable or even productive. It may have lessened, for a few days, preoccupation with street warfare in Baghdad, but beware the seductions of innocent diversion.

Many years ago, just graduated from college, just married, I purchased a shelf-load of newly printed "classics"—to be read sometime, somewhere, or left to grandchildren to read. Such books rest, of course, in the uppermost reach of one's library, but I tipped one out en route to the hospital last month and found myself reading *The American* by Henry James.

It is 488 pages long, and it may be the single most boring book ever published. It is at least the single most venerated bad book ever published.

Now Henry James (1843–1916) is captivating when describing people and situations. I once wrote about his travel books that "you can close your eyes and open either volume at any page and find yourself reading prose so resplendent it will sweep you off your feet. Yet after a while, after a long while, you will recognize that you do, really, have to come down to earth because there are so many other things to do. And besides, if you stay with him for too long, in that engrossing, scented, colored, brilliant, absorbing world, you feel strung out, feel something like hanging moss."

On the matter of writing, and how to get it done, Richard Powers in the *New York Times* recently wrote an exalted essay in praise of dictation, made economically feasible in the modern world by speech-recognition devices. "I write these words from bed," Powers tells us, "under the covers with my knees up, my head propped and my three-pound tablet PC—just a shade heavier than a hardcover—resting in my lap, almost forgettable. I speak untethered, without a headset, into the slate's microphone array. The words appear as fast as I can speak."

One reads on, even if internally apprehensive at the prospect of a multiple increase in reading matter, and numb after completing *The American*. "Not that efficiency has always been dictation's prime selling point," Powers writes. "In dictating his own last few baggy monsters, Henry James perfected such fluid elocution that, according to Edith Wharton, he couldn't even ask directions without releasing a torrent of 'explanatory ramifications.'"

Henry James! In his travel books James demonstrates his extraordinary powers of discrimination. Geneva suffers from "the want of humor in the local atmosphere, and the absence, as well, of that aesthetic character which is begotten of a generous view of life." OK. But what about the Swiss in general? They have, James found, "an insensibility to comeliness or purity of form—a partiality to the clumsy, coarse, and prosaic, which one might almost interpret as a calculated offset to their great treasure of natural beauty, or at least as an instinctive protest of the national genius for frugality."

One or two mechanical points should be made here. One of them is that James's *The American*, lionized in American literary history, was written in 1877—which was before he took to dictating his work. A second mechanical point is that transcribers didn't have the skill, in the 19th century, to record as fast as people could speak. Another, non-mechanical point: It is the responsibility of men and women who seek an audience for their writing beyond the family to instruct or entertain, or to die trying. The ratio is not definitively established, between skills disposed of and weight of literary production.

The grand meaning of this lesson being that eminent people can write eminently awful books and get away with it, and that medical science falls short of shielding us from bad books.

Source: William F. Buckley Jr., "Bed Reading," in *National Review*, Vol. 59, No. 2, February 12, 2007, p. 54.

George Perkins

In the following essay, Perkins offers an overview of James's work and illustrates the ways in which The American *developed his main literary themes.*

Few who accord the novels and short stories of Henry James the attention they deserve come away from the experience unmoved by the subject matter and unenlightened by the artistry, yet it is probably true that James would be little read today if it were not for the continuing enthusiasm of individuals who discover him first as a reading assignment in a college or university course. More than almost any other great novelist, James is a writer whose best works require a sympathetic power of attention that the casual reader is not disposed to give. For most people James is an acquired taste. Unless they approach him in the right spirit they never acquire the taste at all. Yet he is certainly one of the great writers in English, one of those artists of another era who nevertheless seems perennially modern.

His dedication to literature for fifty years from the Civil War until his death in 1916 produced a body of work of monumental scope. He never married, never carried on anything resembling a conventional courtship. His friendships were virtually all rooted in shared literary or artistic enthusiasms. He travelled—often, it seems, merely to reinvigorate himself for a new assault upon his artistic problems. With less talent and similar dedication he might have produced novels and tales that consisted mainly of the same stories retold, the same techniques exploited again and again in order to recapture prior successes. Something of this tendency resides in his work as it does in the work of all masters, but there is also an extraordinary continual development that reaches its peak in three late masterpieces: *The Wings of the Dove*, *The Ambassadors*, and *The Golden Bowl*. The late work of some poets can best be read largely in the light of the education gained by studying their earlier efforts: James is one of a relatively few novelists whose work cries out to be approached in a similar manner.

"It's a complex fate being an American," James once wrote, "and one of the responsibilities it entails is fighting against a superstitious valuation of Europe." Herein is expressed the essence of the "international theme" that runs through much of his work. In a time when more than a few novelists were making capital out of the social complications that arise when individuals from one side of the Atlantic confront the natives of the other side upon their home ground, James made this subject peculiarly his own by returning to it in work after work. So doing, he lifted it outside the confines of drawing room comedy and placed it squarely at the crossroads of the two great traditions of the 19th-century novel in English. Among the best of James's international novels and tales are *The American*, *The Europeans*, *Daisy Miller*,

> AN IMPORTANT PART OF HIS WORK IS ALSO THE THEME OF AWARENESS THAT COMES TOO LATE. HIS PEOPLE ARE CONCERNED ABOVE ALL WITH THE QUESTION OF HOW TO LIVE, BUT MOST OF THEM HAVE NOT ANY CLEAR IDEA OF HOW TO BEGIN."

The Portrait of a Lady, *The Wings of the Dove*, *The Ambassadors*, and *The Golden Bowl*. In these works the central concerns of previous novelists in English come together in a confrontation almost mythic in its implications. Simply expressed, the central concern of English novelists from Austen through Scott, Dickens, and Eliot was the accommodation of individual aspirations within the sheltering embrace of the social framework; both their social view and their art were shaped by a realistic vision of compromise. Just as simply expressed, the central concern of American novelists from James Fenimore Cooper through Nathaniel Hawthorne, Herman Melville, and Mark Twain, was with those individual aspirations that are incapable of accommodation within any social framework except the as-yet-unrealized American dream of perfect freedom, equality, and justice; their social view and their art were shaped by a vision that looked toward a world considerably more ideal than the world they lived in. James brought these visions together in an amalgamation inherently tragic. His best works express in metaphor how much the condition of modern man hangs continually in the balance between the European dream of social accommodation and the American dream of perfect freedom.

Closely related to the international theme is James's continual emphasis upon partial perspectives. Human knowledge, he insists, and consequently human action, is sharply limited by inescapable conditions of time and place. From Christopher Newman to Lambert Strether his Americans achieve their destiny because the perspectives forced upon them by birth and education allow them no choices except the ones they inevitably make. From Madame de Cintre to Madame de Vionnet his Europeans are similarly limited. This at least is the theory: the novel is realistic, as James most often intended it should be, when the fates of the characters follow inevitably from the conditions that surround them; it is romantic, as James sometimes allowed, when the fates evolve from conditions imposed by the author that are quite distinct from the facts of observable reality. The realistic effect that he intended for most of his novels derives from the success with which he developed techniques for objectifying the partial perspectives from which humans direct their lives.

An important part of his work is also the theme of awareness that comes too late. His people are concerned above all with the question of how to live, but most of them have not any clear idea of how to begin. Sometimes they are wealthy, like Christopher Newman in *The American*, Millie Theale in *The Wings of the Dove*, and Maggie Verver in *The Golden Bowl*. Sometimes they become wealthy, like Isabel Archer in *The Portrait of a Lady*. Sometimes they live in expectation of wealth, like Kate Croy in *The Wings of the Dove*. In most instances they have at least, like Lambert Strether in *The Ambassadors*, enough to enable them to live comfortably, though it is often true of the less attractive figures that they suppose themselves in need of more than they possess. In any event they are mostly free of the more mundane cares of life and have nearly total leisure in which to pursue happiness through courtship, marriage, liaisons, social activity, travel, the search for culture: whatever, in short, seems most attractive to them. To live most fully, James makes clear in a number of places, is to be most fully aware of one's possibilities so that one may make the best of them. Since, however, the most interesting possibilities come from human relationships which are inherently a tissue of subtle complexities, to be most fully aware is to possess a depth of sympathetic insight that comes to few people until it is too late to take advantage of it. Total freedom for James's characters involves the freedom to make social commitments different from those that all too often they make, wrongly, in bondage to some mistaken understanding, or do not make at all because, sadly, they fail to perceive the opportunity that lies before them.

A great critic, James is also a great technical experimenter. The best of his criticism is preserved in individual essays such as "The Art of Fiction" and in his *Notebooks* and the prefaces that he wrote for the New York edition of his works. All are read most profitably in conjunction with the example of his fiction. His technical experiments are most readily approached through those many fictions in which he enforces the theme of partial perspectives by contriving severely limited perspectives from which to narrate. Some of the easier works in which this theme and this method are important are the early *Daisy Miller* and the late "The Beast in the Jungle." Because Daisy is never seen except from the partial view that Winterbourne enjoys, the reader remains in danger of sharing Winterbourne's misunderstanding of her character. Because May Bartram, in "The Beast in the Jungle," is never seen except in a view accessible to Marcher, the same potential exists. Fundamentally simple in these works, both theme and technique become more complex in "The Aspern Papers," *The Turn of the Screw*, and *The Sacred Fount*. In all three the careful reader is aware that there may be some aspect of the truth that remains dark to the central vision of the narrator; in *The Turn of the Screw* there are good reasons to suppose both that the ghosts do and do not exist; in *The Sacred Fount* the puzzle that begins the novel becomes not less but more of a puzzle as it ends. In *The Portrait of a Lady*, *The Wings of the Dove*, *The Ambassadors*, and *The Golden Bowl*, the theme of partial perspectives (which involves often the theme of too late awareness) merges with the international theme to provide the substance of James's most lasting achievement.

Many of James's fictions conclude upon a sense of loss. In his deepest vision human life is fundamentally tragic because of the eternal tension between the individual's sense of his vast human opportunities and his frequently inadequate awareness of his personal limitations. Like Isabel Archer or Lambert Strether, 20th-century readers, too, are possessed by dreams of boundless freedom. Like both, they make in the end the choices that they can make—which are often not all the choices that they would make if they lived in a world in which a just and equal perfect freedom came less insistently into conflict with the requirements of social accommodation.

Source: George Perkins, "Henry James: Overview," in *Reference Guide to American Literature*, 3rd ed., edited by Jim Kamp, St. James Press, 1994.

SOURCES

Barrish, Phillip J., "American Literary Realism," in *The Cambridge Introduction to American Literary Realism*, Cambridge University Press, 2011, pp. 1–73.

Haralson, Eric, and Kendall Johnson, "*The American*," in *Critical Companion to Henry James: A Literary Reference to His Life and Work*, Facts on File, 2009, pp. 34–48.

James, Henry, *The American*, Oxford University Press, 1999.

Johnson, Kendall, "Rules of Engagement: The Arch-Romance of Visual Culture in *The American*," in *Henry James and the Visual*, Cambridge University Press, 2007, pp. 85–122.

Meissner, Collin, "The Experience of Divestiture: Toward and Understanding of the Self in *The American*," in *Henry James and the Language of Experience*, Cambridge University Press, 1999, pp. 36–79.

Nadal, Marita, "Tradition and Modernity in Henry James's *The American*," in *Etudes Britanniques Contemporaines*, No. 8, 1995, pp. 51–66.

Reeve, Pat, "Gilded Age," in *Class in America: An Encyclopedia*, Vol. 1, edited by Robert E. Weir, Greenwood Press, 2007, pp. 308–11.

Review of *The American*, in *Literary World* (Boston), July 1877, reprinted in *Henry James*, edited by Kevin J. Hayes, Cambridge University Press, 1996, pp. 37–38.

Review of *The American*, in *New York Tribune*, May 8, 1877, reprinted in *Henry James*, edited by Kevin J. Hayes, Cambridge University Press, 1996, pp. 21–22.

Schlup, Leonard C., "Gilded Age," in *Historical Dictionary of the Gilded Age*, edited by Leonard C. Schlup and James G. Ryan, M.E. Sharpe, 2003, pp. 186–87.

Shrock, Joel, "Literature," in *The Gilded Age*, Greenwood, 2004, pp. 151–82.

"6.32 Million Americans (Excluding Military) Live in 160-Plus Countries," The Association of Americans Resident Overseas website, http://www.aaro.org/about-aaro/6m-americans-abroad (accessed December 20, 2012).

Smith, Mark M., "The Past as a Foreign Country: Reconstruction, Inside and Out," in *Reconstructions: New Perspectives on the Postbellum United States*, edited by Thomas J. Brown, Oxford University Press, 2006, pp. 117–40.

Weller, Christian E., "Economic Snapshot for December 2012," Center for American Progress website, December 17, 2012, http://www.americanprogress.org/issues/economy/report/2012/12/17/48232/economic-snapshot-for-december-2012/ (accessed December 20, 2012).

White, Craig, "Henry James," in *Dictionary of Literary Biography*, Vol. 189, *American Travel Writers, 1850–1915*, Gale Research, 1998, pp. 199–221.

Yoshii, Chiyo, "*The American* and the Romance of Modernity," in *Papers on Language and Literature*, Vol. 33, No. 2, Spring 1997, pp. 142–68.

FURTHER READING

Anesko, Michael, *Letters, Fictions, Lives: Henry James and William Dean Howells*, Oxford University Press, 1997.
Anesko's work explores the relationship between these two realist authors and demonstrates the ways in which they influenced and criticized each other's work. Anesko's assessments are supported by the letters reproduced in each chapter.

Nagel, James, and Tom Quirk, eds., *The Portable American Realism Reader*, Penguin, 1997.
The editors offer a sampling of the short fiction of prominent realist writers. They include the works of prominent authors, such as Mark Twain, Sarah Orne Jewett, and Henry James, as well as the works of lesser-known writers.

Wayne, Tiffany K., *Women's Roles in Nineteenth-Century America*, Greenwood Publishing, 2007.
Wayne analyzes the role of women in nineteenth-century American society, focusing on the expectations regarding marriage and motherhood, education, and employment, among other topics.

West, Elliot, and Paula Petrik, eds., *Small Worlds: Children and Adolescents in America, 1850–1950*, University Press of Kansas, 1992.
West and Petrik present a series of essays in which the daily lives of young people in the second half of the nineteenth century and the first half of the twentieth century are portrayed. The personal experiences and contributions to society of young people are discussed, as are the hardships children endured.

SUGGESTED SEARCH TERMS

Henry James AND The American

Henry James AND expatriates

Henry James AND feminism

Henry James AND social class

Henry James AND realism

Henry James AND melodrama

Henry James AND social satire

Henry James AND the Gilded Age

Henry James AND William Dean Howells

Henry James AND romanticism

The Antelope Wife

LOUISE ERDRICH

1998

The Antelope Wife, by Louise Erdrich, is a lyric and historical novel that weaves elements of magic realism throughout the narrative. First published in 1998, the story is typical of Erdrich's work because it is circular rather than linear, meaning that the events do not occur in sequence. Narrated by multiple characters, *The Antelope Wife* explores the themes of love, revenge, family, identity, and destiny.

Erdrich follows the stories of three different families whose fates are forever united in the 1800s when a US cavalry officer kills an Ojibwa woman. Although the story takes place in a Native American setting, readers from all backgrounds will appreciate Erdrich's skill as a storyteller and the book's universal lessons. The novel does contain language, sexual scenes, and violence that some readers may find offensive.

AUTHOR BIOGRAPHY

Karen Louise Erdrich was born in Little Falls, Minnesota, on June 7, 1954. Her mother was French Ojibwa (also styled Chippewa or Ojibwe) and her father a German American. The oldest of seven children, Erdrich grew up in Wahpeton, North Dakota, where her parents worked at the Bureau of Indian Affairs boarding school. Erdrich is a member of the Turtle Mountain Band of Chippewa, and her cultural heritage

Louise Erdrich (© Ulf Andersen / Getty Images Entertainment / Getty Images)

shaped her literary career. She showed an interest in writing from an early age, which her father encouraged. He paid her a nickel for every story she wrote, which she confirmed in an interview in the *Paris Review*. She stated, "My father is my biggest literary influence."

In 1972, Erdrich attended the first coed class at Dartmouth College, in New Hampshire. There, she became friends with Michael Dorris, the chair of the Native American Studies Program. As an undergraduate, Erdrich showed a talent for writing poetry. She earned the American Academy of Poets Prize her junior year, and she went on to teach writing and poetry after she graduated. In 1979, she completed her master's degree in creative writing from Johns Hopkins University. Erdrich returned to Dartmouth as a writer in residence, and she married Dorris in 1981. This was also the year that her first book of poetry, *Imagination*, was published.

In 1984, Erdrich's first novel, *Love Medicine*, was published. The novel's release coincided with

the publication of her second book of poetry, *Jacklight*. *Love Medicine* was praised by critics and helped establish Erdrich's career as a novelist, earning her the National Book Critics Circle Award. Her next three novels, *The Beet Queen* (1986), *Tracks* (1988), and *The Bingo Palace* (1994), continue the stories of the characters in *Love Medicine*. Erdrich also wrote nonfiction based on her experience as a mother called *The Blue Jay's Dance*.

Erdrich and Dorris collaborated on *The Crown of Columbus*, published in 1991. The couple separated in 1995, and Dorris committed suicide in 1997. Erdrich continued her literary career with *The Antelope Wife* in 1998. Erdrich owns the Birchbark Books store in Minneapolis, and she continues to write fiction and poetry. She was awarded the National Book Award for *Roundhouse* in 2012.

PLOT SUMMARY

The Antelope Wife has multiple narrators. The story is not told in sequence and shifts between characters and times.

Part One: Bayzhig

Erdrich introduces the myth of twin sisters who bead the fate of the world. One works with light beads and the other with dark. Each sister is trying to disrupt the balance of power.

1: FATHER'S MILK

Scranton Roy: This chapter is told in the third person. It begins when Scranton Teodorus Roy, a US cavalry private, takes part in a raid against the peaceful Ojibwa tribe, who are mistaken for the Sioux. Violence is new to Roy, the son of Quakers. He kills an old woman with a bayonet. She says the word *Daashkikaa* as she dies, and Roy sees an image of his mother before observing a baby being carried away by a dog on a cradle board with blue beads.

Roy follows the dog and eventually manages to reach the infant. The little girl is too young to eat and attempts to nurse on Roy. After a few days of persistence, she is successful.

Ms. Peace McKnight: Peace is a Scottish schoolteacher in the Great Plains. She becomes the teacher and friend of Roy's six-year-old daughter, Matilda. Matilda insists that Peace should move

MEDIA ADAPTATIONS

- Released by Harper Audio 1998, *The Antelope Wife* audiobook is an abridged version of Erdrich's novel. The book may be downloaded from Audible.com and the running time is six hours and twenty-six minutes.
- Harper Audio released an unabridged audio version of *The Antelope Wife* in 1998. This is available on cassette.

---

into their house when it is too cold for the young teacher to stay in the school.

Scranton Roy: Roy has named the infant he found Matilda, after his mother. He considers marrying Peace because she is already like a mother to Matilda.

Matilda Roy: Matilda is conflicted about her father. She loves him, but she tests his love by holding her breath to discover if he will save her.

Kiss: Matilda sees Peace and Scranton kiss. She is shocked and relieved.

Ozhawashkwamashkodeykway / Blue Prairie Woman: Matilda's mother mourns the loss of her child. She is given a puppy to nurse, which becomes her constant companion. Her husband, Shawano, returns, and she becomes pregnant. Still, she remains haunted by her first child. The elders order her renamed, and the namer chooses the place that Blue Prairie Woman must go to rescue her child.

Other Side of the Earth: Other Side of the Earth is Blue Prairie Woman's second name because she must travel west. With her new name, she lives in both the present and past. She remains in her village long enough to give birth to her twin daughters.

A Dog Named Sorrow: The puppy Blue Prairie Woman nursed is grown and follows her when she searches for her lost child. Blue Prairie Woman leaves her twins, Mary and Josephette, who is called Zosie in Ojibwa, with their grandmother when she searches for her daughter.

Matilda Roy: Peace is sick with a fever when Matilda's mother shows up. The girl leaves a note before departing with her mother.

Scranton Roy: Scranton's marriage with Peace is tense. She is pregnant when she contracts a fever. When she goes into labor, a blizzard makes it impossible for him to get the midwife. Her labor lasts three days, and the baby is not breathing when he is born. Scranton saves his child, but Peace dies. Scranton feeds their son.

Blue Prairie Woman: Blue Prairie Woman is dying with the fever that killed Peace. She gives Matilda the spirit name Other Side of the Earth to protect her. She kills and cooks the dog so that her daughter will not starve. As she is dying, she sings and summons the antelope. Matilda follows them and joins the herd.

2: THE ANTELOPE WIFE
Klaus Shawano: Narrating in the first person, Klaus explains how he found his great love at a powwow in Elmo. There to trade, he sees a group of beautiful women, a mother with her daughters. He decides that he must have the mother and asks the medicine man from the plains, Jimmy Badger, how to hunt antelope. Jimmy tells him antelope will come when they are curious. He warns Klaus against pursuing the antelope women.

Klaus flicks a piece of calico to catch their attention the next morning. They come to his stall, where he feeds them and offers the daughters a place to sleep. He lures the mother into his van and drives away with her. He ties her to him with the calico he used to catch her attention.

Once in the city, she is lost and no longer tries to escape. She never speaks, and he calls her Sweetheart Calico. Their relationship swings in extremes from devotion to hate. Klaus is miserable and calls Jimmy Badger. Jimmy advises him to release the woman, but Klaus cannot let her go.

3: SEAWEED MARSHMALLOWS
Rozina Whiteheart Beads: Rozina, also called Rozin, explains her family's relationship with Sweetheart Calico. Rozin is a Roy, and her family is descended from Blue Prairie Woman's twin

daughters. She is a twin, but her sister is dead. Rozin is married to Richard Whiteheart Beads, and she has twin daughters named Cally and Deanna.

After seeing Sweetheart Calico outside of a bakery, she goes inside and meets Frank Shawano. She falls in love with him and feels conflicted when she thinks about her daughters.

4: WHY I AM NO LONGER FRIENDS WITH WHITEHEART BEADS
Klaus Shawano: Klaus explains that he and Richard were partners in a disposal company. At a company party, Richard offers him two tickets to Hawaii. The tickets are in Richard's name, but he gives Klaus his identification. Klaus decides to take Sweetheart Calico with him.

Klaus becomes suspicious when two men from the plane follow them to the hotel. He discovers that they are with the IRS. They think Klaus is Richard and arrest him.

5: SWEETHEART CALICO
This brief chapter is told in the third person. Sweetheart Calico is lost is the city. She is tied to Klaus and cannot find her way home.

6: THE GIRL AND THE DEER HUSBAND
Cally: Cally tells this part of the story. She remembers seeing Frank and Rozin when at the park with her father. Richard tells her that it is not her mother. Cally agrees that she does not know the happy woman.

II: Cally considers how happy Frank and Rozin were together.

III: At home, Rozin is herself again. Cally's grandmothers, Mary and Zosie, watch Cally and Deanna dance. They tell the girls that they are descended from deer.

IV: The grandmothers begin the story of their ancestor, So Hungry. The people fear she is a *windigo*, a creature from Native American mythology believed to eat human flesh, and she leaves for the woods. One day, she is cooking a stew and a deer comes to her. Rather than eat the deer, she shares her food. For the first time she is full. She loves him and becomes part of the deer's family.

V: The grandmothers refuse to tell more of the story.

VI: Cally recalls Frank coming to their house with cookies.

VII: The grandmothers return to their story. So Hungry's brothers kill her deer and bring her home. She is renamed Blue Prairie Woman and marries a Shawano. A deer warns her about the raid before Scranton Roy kills her grandmother.

VIII: Rozin lies to Richard about Frank. Richard soon discerns the truth and confronts her about the affair.

IX: Cally remembers Rozin crying herself to sleep in her arms.

7: YELLOW PICKUP TRUCK
This chapter is told in the third person. Rozin tells Richard that Frank has cancer, and she is taking the children to live with Frank.

Cally and Deanna have enjoyable days at school while Richard processes the news. He confronts Rozin after school is out, and Deanna walks in on their argument. Richard drinks until he passes out, and Deanna promises to fix her parents' marriage.

That night, Richard decides to kill himself from carbon monoxide poisoning by running his truck in the garage. Deanna hides herself in the truck because she thinks her father is leaving. Richard locks himself out of the garage while the truck is running.

Part Two: Neej
The sisters bead cruelly. The dark or light beads dominate depending on which sister falls asleep first.

8: ALMOST SOUP
Windigo Dog: This chapter is told from a dog's point of view. He is a descendant of Sorrow, but as a white puppy on a reservation, he is at risk of being made into soup. One day, a grandmother intends to cook him. To save himself, he gets the attention of a visiting granddaughter. She demands the puppy and names him Almost Soup. His new owner is Cally.

9: THE LAZY STITCH
Almost Soup: Almost Soup continues his story. Rozin and Cally are staying with Mary and Zosie after Deanna's death. Rozin does not know which of them is her biological mother. Cally is playing outside one day when she loses her *indis*,

which is her umbilical cord. She becomes sick, and a storm makes reaching help difficult.

Almost Soup hides in the car when they are finally able to take her to the hospital. He sneaks into the hospital and returns Cally's life to her, which he had taken into himself to protect during her illness.

10: NIBI

Klaus and Richard are alcoholics living on the street and asking for money.

Part Three: Niswey

This introduction explains how the Shawano ancestor Sounding Feather dyed her quills. Her actions and feelings from the previous day always affected their color.

11: GAKAHEBEKONG

Cally: Cally tells her own story. After losing her *indis*, she feels the need to wander. At the age of eighteen, her mother sends her to Frank in Minneapolis, or Gakahebekong. She agrees to work in the bakery and hopes to find her grandmothers and ask them about her spirit name, Ozhawashk-wamashkodeykway. Rozin still loves Frank but refuses to speak to him because she believes their love killed Deanna.

Sweetheart Calico lives with Frank, while his brother, Klaus, is on the street. Cally calls her Auntie Klaus, and the silent woman frightens her. Frank's sister Cecille, who owns a kung fu studio, also lives with Frank. Cally notices that Frank has lost his sense of humor, and Cecille tries to restore it. Meanwhile, Frank attempts to reconstruct a recipe called *blitzkuchen*.

Cally attempts to contact her grandmothers, but they lead busy lives and are never available. One day, Zosie comes into the bakery, but Cally finds herself unable to ask about her name. Zosie warns her that Richard is not well. Cally says that she does not want to see him as he and Klaus walk through the door. He thinks Cally is Deanna's ghost and leaves. Klaus is reunited with Sweetheart Calico.

12: WINDIGO DOG

This chapter is told in the third person. Klaus is visited by a *windigo* dog he believes Sweetheart Calico sent. The dog mocks the name Klaus.

13: THE BLITZKUCHEN

Klaus Shawano: Klaus explains the origin of his name. After World War II, an elder advises his father to take a German slave brother to avenge the death of a cousin. His father and some other men kidnap a young man from a nearby camp. In an attempt to save his life, the prisoner, Klaus, signs that he will cook for the men in the clan. Klaus makes *blitzkuchen*, and it is so delicious that he is made part of the clan. He is Klaus Shawano's namesake.

14: THE GRAVITRON

Cally continues her story. Two years later, Rozin moves in with Mary and Zosie. Rozin works at a supermarket and is studying to become a lawyer. She finally agrees to go out with Frank and Cally. At the state fair, Rozin is not able to hide her love for Frank after a mishap on a ride.

15: TEARS

Klaus Shawano: Klaus is living in a recovery lodge with Richard. Klaus gets the priest when Richard is inconsolable. Richard has created a fantasy about the death of his children. Klaus is finally so frustrated that he confronts Richard with the truth. Richard accuses Klaus of kidnapping Sweetheart Calico, and the priest has to separate them.

16: KAMIKAZE WEDDING

This chapter is told in the third person. Frank's and Rozin's families prepare for the wedding. Cecille is annoyed that no one is paying attention to her telling a story. She answers the phone and tells everyone that Richard is threatening to come, but no one believes her. Richard arrives at the wedding and attempts to jump off a cliff. The reverend and Sweetheart Calico save him.

Richard gives a note to Rozin at the reception, claiming that he poisoned the cake. He admits that it is a lie when she leaves with him. Klaus hits him on the head. They cut the cake when Rozin returns, and everyone realizes that Frank has finally perfected the *blitzkuchen* recipe.

After another plot to ruin the wedding fails, Richard shoots himself outside Rozin and Frank's hotel room.

Part Four: Neewin

One twin sells everything for beads that her hungry children eat. She chases them with a knife.

17: FOOD OF THE DEAD

Rozin hears Deanna's voice as she mourns Richard. While she mourns and fasts, she believes a *windigo* visits her. Rozin makes peace with her loss and the bond between life and death.

18: NORTHWEST TRADER BLUE

Cally: The family has Christmas dinner at Frank and Rozin's home. Cally is overcome with the word *Daashkikaa* when her grandmothers arrive.

Windigo Story I: Augustus Roy marries Zosie but promises to take care of Mary, and she moves in with the couple.

A break returns to the Christmas dinner.

Windigo Story II: Mary and Augustus are having an affair. Zosie soon discovers the truth.

A break returns to the present. Cecille asks the twins what they did to Augustus Roy when he disappeared.

Windigo Story III: Zosie manipulates her family. Mary confesses, and the sisters make it impossible for Augustus to tell them apart. Frustrated, Augustus bites Zosie's earlobe to mark her.

A break returns to the present. The sisters do not answer Cecille's question.

After dinner, Cally asks Zosie the meaning of *Daashkikaa*. Zosie says it is an old name that means "cracked apart." Zosie believes Cally is the new namer and agrees to explain the origin of her spirit name.

Zosie says she once longed for beads called Northwest Trader Blue that she saw as a girl. She also reveals that she is Rozin's mother.

Other Side of the Earth: When Zosie is pregnant, she gambles her life and the lives of her children with a woman for the coveted beads. She wins and gambles for the woman's spirit names, which she gives to Cally and Deanna: Deanna is Other Side of the Earth, and Cally is Blue Prairie Woman. Cally asks where the beads are, and Zosie tells her that their new owner is Sweetheart Calico. Sweetheart Calico offers Cally the beads and speaks for the first time, saying, "Let me go."

Cally spends the night wandering the city with Sweetheart Calico, who talks incessantly. In the morning, Cally wakes up outside, and she realizes that her wandering days are over.

19: SWEETHEART CALICO

Sweetheart Calico feels a sense of freedom. She wonders how Klaus took it from her.

20: WINDIGO DOG

Windigo Dog comes to Klaus again. Klaus realizes he will only stop drinking if he releases Sweetheart Calico.

21: SWEETHEART CALICO

Klaus uses the original calico to tie himself to Sweetheart Calico. They walk until they reach the countryside, where he releases her.

22: THE SURPRISE PARTY

Frank and Rozin surprise each other for their anniversary. She plans an intimate evening, and he plans a party. On the night of their anniversary, he calls her downstairs, where the family is secretly waiting. She walks down the stairs without any clothes. Rozin begins laughing, and Frank laughs for the first time in years.

23: SCRANTON ROY

The spirit of the Ojibwa woman Scranton killed haunts him. He tells her that he will find her people and begins a journey with his grandson, Augustus Roy. When they arrive at the village, Augustus trades his whiteheart beads and other items to Midass to marry her great-granddaughter, Zosie. The beads are used in a blanket for a pregnant woman who names her child after them.

CHARACTERS

Almost Soup

Almost Soup is a descendant of Sorrow. He is a white dog, which puts him at risk of being made into soup. Cally saves him from this fate when he is a puppy and names him Almost Soup. Later, he saves Cally by taking her life into him and keeping it from death.

Jimmy Badger

Jimmy Badger is a medicine man who warns Klaus Shawano to stay away from the antelope women. After Klaus take Sweetheart Calico, her daughters create bad luck for Jimmy's people.

Blue Prairie Woman

Originally named So Hungry, the villagers, who believe she is a *windigo*, shun her, and she lives with the deer in her youth. She is renamed Blue Prairie Woman when her brothers bring her back to the village. She marries Shawano and is the mother of Matilda Roy as well as the original Mary and Zosie, the namesakes of the Mary and Zosie present in the story.

Blue Prairie Woman is warned about the cavalry attack by the deer and ties her daughter's cradle board to a dog to protect her. She is devastated when Scranton kills her grandmother, and she is inconsolable when her baby cannot be found. She nurses the dog Sorrow and is renamed Other Side of the Earth, which is where she must travel to find her lost child.

Blue Prairie Woman finds her daughter but catches Peace's illness and dies on the way home. Before she dies, she cooks Sorrow and gives Matilda the spirit name Other Side of the Earth. She also calls the antelope to her daughter, who joins the herd.

Josephette

See Zosie Roy

Klaus

Klaus is a German soldier who was kidnapped by the Shawano clan. He bakes a *blitzkuchen* to save his life and is adopted into the clan.

Auntie Klaus

See Sweetheart Calico

Mary

Mary is Zosie's twin sister. She is Blue Prairie Woman's granddaughter, and she and Zosie share their names with the first twins. Mary loves Augustus Roy and has an affair with her sister's husband. After she confesses her betrayal to Zosie, Mary helps her sister punish Augustus by disguising her identity from Augustus. She raises Rozin with Zosie as a co-mother. In fact, Rozin is not sure which of the twins is her mother.

Peace McKnight

A Scottish schoolteacher on the Great Plains, Peace is Matilda's teacher and friend. She marries Scranton Roy and dies in childbirth after a long illness. Her son and grandson both are named Augustus Roy.

Midass

Midass is the mother of Blue Prairie Woman and raises the first Mary and Zosie. She is also the great-grandmother of the second Mary and Zosie. Augustus Roy trades whiteheart beads to Midass in order to marry Zosie.

Other Side of the Earth

See Blue Prairie Woman, Matilda Roy, and Deanna Whiteheart Beads

Augustus Roy

Augustus Roy is Scranton Roy's grandson. He trades his whiteheart beads and other possessions to marry Zosie, the granddaughter of Blue Prairie Woman. Augustus loves Zosie, but he also loves her twin sister, Mary, who lives with the couple. He and Mary have an affair, which Zosie discovers. The sisters punish him by making it impossible for him to tell them apart from each other. Augustus attempts to tell them apart by biting Zosie's ear. He eventually disappears from his grandfather's cabin and is never seen again.

Matilda Roy

Matilda Roy is the daughter of Blue Prairie Woman and Shawano. Her mother ties her cradle board to a dog to save her from the cavalry raid. But Scranton Roy finds her, names her Matilda, and raises her as his daughter. When Blue Prairie Woman seeks out and finds her, Matilda leaves with her mother, who becomes sick on the way back to the village. Her mother gives her the name Other Side of the Earth and calls the antelope to protect her. Matilda joins the antelope herd and becomes the ancestor of Sweetheart Calico.

Scranton Teodorus Roy

Scranton Roy is a son of Quakers who enlisted in the US cavalry after suffering a broken heart. He takes part in a raid against a peaceful Ojibwa village and kills an old woman with a bayonet. As she dies, she curses him with the name *Daashkikaa*, which means "cracked apart," and he sees a vision of his own mother in her place. Scranton leaves the battle and chases a dog with a baby. The infant is too young to eat solid food and nurses on Scranton until she successfully feeds. He names the girl Matilda, after his mother. He raises her as his daughter until her mother comes for her. Scranton marries Peace McKnight, but she dies in childbirth. He raises his son, Augustus, on his own, and he later raises his grandson.

The woman he murdered haunts him when he is old. In an effort to appease her spirit, Scranton takes his grandson, also named Augustus, to the woman's village to make amends. There, Augustus sees Zosie and trades everything to marry her.

Zosie Roy
Named for Blue Prairie Woman's daughter, Zosie is the Ojibwa name for Josephette. Mary is her twin sister and lifelong companion. Zosie marries Augustus Roy and takes revenge on him when she discovers his affair with Mary. She and Mary make it impossible for him to tell them apart, and they torment him until he disappears.

Zosie is Rozin's biological mother, but she never reveals this to her daughter. She indirectly tells this information to Cally when she explains the origins of her granddaughter's spirit name and its connection to Northwest Trader Blue beads that she gambled her life and the lives of her children to obtain.

Shawano
Blue Prairie Woman's husband is from the Shawano clan. He is a younger Shawano and the father of Matilda and the first twins, Mary and Zosie.

Cecille Shawano
Cecille is Frank Shawano's younger sister. She owns a kung fu studio and lives with Frank. Cecille is prone to exaggerate, and she makes it her mission to restore Frank's sense of humor.

She tries to be the center of attention, but it often backfires. On Frank's wedding day, she answers the phone when Richard calls, but no one will believe her. At Christmas, she insists on discussing Richard's suicide and confronts Mary and Zosie about what they did to Augustus.

Frank Shawano
Frank is a baker in Minneapolis. He falls in love with Rozin while she is married to Richard Whiteheart Beads. When Frank develops cancer, Rozin plans to move in with him. Unfortunately, Deanna's death prevents this from happening. Rozin leaves the city and refuses to speak to Frank because she believes that their love killed Deanna.

Frank survives the cancer, but he loses his sense of humor. He takes in Cally at her mother's request, and he takes care of Sweetheart Calico

for Klaus. He is obsessed with perfecting the original *blitzkuchen* (which finally occurs on his wedding day).

Rozin returns to Minneapolis and agrees to go out with him, and they are soon preparing for a wedding. Richard attempts to sabotage their wedding and then shoots himself at the door of their hotel room. Frank refuses to leave Rozin when she orders him to go away while she mourns Richard. At the end of the story, Frank finally laughs again when he and Rozin plan conflicting surprises for each other.

Klaus Shawano
Klaus is a trader who kidnaps Sweetheart Calico from a powwow. He is miserable with her, but he cannot let her go. Klaus becomes an alcoholic and loses everything. He lives on the street with his former business partner, Richard Whiteheart Beads. Frank, Klaus's brother, takes care of Sweetheart Calico while Klaus is homeless. Klaus finally realizes that he can only stop drinking if he releases Sweetheart Calico.

So Hungry
See Blue Prairie Woman

Sorrow
Sorrow is the name of the dog nursed by Blue Prairie Woman. The dog is her constant companion. The dog is sacrificed to feed Matilda when Blue Prairie Woman realizes that she is dying.

Sounding Feather
Sounding Feather is the great-grandmother of the first Shawano.

Sweetheart Calico
Sweetheart Calico's true name is never revealed. She is Matilda Roy's descendant and lives with the antelope on the plains. Klaus kidnaps her from a powwow, and she is bound to him by a piece of calico. She cannot find her way home once he takes her to Minneapolis. Sweetheart Calico never speaks until she asks Cally to let her go. She is completely free when Klaus releases her.

Cally Whiteheart Beads
Cally is the daughter of Richard and Rozin Whiteheart Beads. She is Deanna's twin sister and the owner of Almost Soup. She loses her *indis* or umbilical cord as a child, which she believes makes her prone to wander. That same

night she becomes sick, and the illness progresses dangerously. Almost Soup saves her life by taking it into himself.

At the age of eighteen, Cally moves to Minneapolis to live with and work for Frank Shawano. She also wants to ask her grandmothers about the meaning of her spirit name. Cecille Shawano, Frank's sister, and Sweetheart Calico also live with Frank. Sweetheart Calico makes Cally nervous.

Two years later, Rozin moves to the city, and Cally is torn as she watches her mother's love for Frank develop. On Rozin's wedding day, Cally is concerned that her father will come uninvited, and her anxiety is justified when he kills himself.

The following Christmas, Cally hears the word *Daashkikaa* in her head. She asks Zosie what it means. Her grandmother tells her that it means "cracked apart," and she believes Cally is the new namer. Zosie explains that Cally's spirit name means Blue Prairie Woman and Deanna's spirit name was Other Side of the Earth. Zosie needed these names to possess the Northwest Trader Blue beads that she gambled her life to attain.

Cally learns that Sweetheart Calico, whom she calls Auntie Klaus, is now the owner of the beads. Auntie Klaus shows her the beads and asks Cally to let her go. Cally spends the night wandering the city with Sweetheart Calico, and when she wakes up the next morning, her own desire to wander is gone.

Deanna Whiteheart Beads
Deanna is the daughter of Richard and Rozin Whiteheart Beads. She is Cally's twin sister, and she accidentally dies of carbon monoxide poisoning when she is eleven. Her spirit name is Other Side of the Earth.

Richard Whiteheart Beads
Richard is a descendant of the child who was given the blanket made with the whiteheart beads that Augustus traded to marry Zosie. Richard runs a waste disposal company with Klaus, and he plots so that his partner is taking his place when the IRS comes to arrest him.

He is married to Rozin, and he is Cally and Deanna's father. His marriage to Rozin falls apart, but he initially ignores the signs that she is having an affair. He is surprised when Rozin announces that she is going to leave him to be with Frank, who is being treated for cancer.

Angry, Richard decides to kill himself out of spite, but his attempt at carbon monoxide poisoning is unsuccessful. Unfortunately, his daughter, Deanna, hides in the car without his knowledge and dies. Richard never recovers from her death and sinks deeper into depression and alcoholism. Rozin divorces him, and he lives on the street with Klaus.

Richard is determined to ruin Rozin's wedding day and win her back. He arrives at the ceremony uninvited and attempts to jump off a cliff. After he is rescued, he lies and tells Rozin that he poisoned the cake. Finally, he shoots himself in front of the newlyweds' hotel room.

Rozina "Rozin" Whiteheart Beads
Formally named Rozina, Rozin is the daughter of Zosie and Augustus Roy, although she is never told if Mary or Zosie is her biological mother. She is a twin in a long line of twins, but her sister is dead. She has twin daughters named Deanna and Cally. Rozin falls in love with Frank Shawano while she is married to Richard Whiteheart Beads and has an affair.

Rozin decides to leave Richard when Frank develops cancer. As a result, Richard attempts suicide and accidentally kills Deanna. Rozin blames her daughter's death on her love for Frank. She leaves Minneapolis for the reservation, and she does not speak to Frank for years. When Cally is twenty, Rozin moves back to Minneapolis, where she begins dating Frank and studying to become a lawyer. They get married, but Richard attempts to sabotage the wedding and then shoots himself in front of their hotel room. Rozin grieves Richard's death but comes to terms with the connection between life and death. By the end of the story, Rozin is a lawyer and happily married to Frank.

Windigo Dog
Windigo Dog is a spirit that visits Klaus Shawano. He humiliates Klaus, and Klaus believes that Sweetheart Calico sent the spirit.

THEMES

Family
The theme of family dominates *The Antelope Wife*. Many of the characters are related to Blue Prairie Woman, an individual whose desire to reunite her family has profound consequences

TOPICS FOR FURTHER STUDY

- Read Sherman Alexie's novel *Reservation Blues* (1995). An example of magic realism, the novel tells of how blues legend Robert Johnson gives Spokane Reservation residents Thomas, Victor, and Junior the guitar he traded his soul to obtain. Write a short story in which one character from *The Antelope Wife* interacts with the characters from *Reservation Blues*.

- Read *Black Eagle Child: The Facepaint Narratives* (1992), by Ray A. Young Bear. Young Bear is a contemporary Native American novelist who explores some of the same concepts that Erdrich does. Write an essay comparing this novel with *The Antelope Wife*. What are the similarities and differences in the themes and style? Present your paper in front of the class.

- Research the art of Ojibwa beading, and create a video or multimedia presentation of the art form. Be sure to include pictures of the different patterns and designs. Choose any image from *The Antelope Wife* and create your own beaded artwork to show with the presentation.

- Read *Caramelo* (2002), a young-adult novel by Sandra Cisneros. Like *The Antelope Wife*, this examines a family's story over generations, set in Mexico and the United States. Young Lala Reyes attempts to discover the history of her family and find her own identity. Using PowerPoint, create a design of a social network page for both Lala and Cally Whiteheart Beads. What do they have in common? How do their families influence their personal identities? Create a transcript of an online interaction between the two characters.

- Research Ojibwa myths and legends. Be sure to include *windigos* in your research. Create a web page that provides an overview of the different Ojibwa myths, legends, and spirits. Include links that expand information on the topics.

for both her daughter and herself. She risks everything to find Matilda, and she loses her life in the attempt. Her legacy of strength and love, however, lives on in her descendants.

Blue Prairie Woman unites all of the characters in the book in some way. This family unity is seen in Cally's heritage. As she says, "I am a Roy, a Whiteheart Beads, a Shawano by the way of the Roy and Shawano proximity." In many ways, the characters are defined by their family heritage. They also, however, define family for themselves.

The definition of family, for example, is explored in the relationship between Scranton and Matilda. As his adopted daughter, Matilda loves her father, but she is always troubled by "an anxious sorrow." When Matilda leaves with her mother, the narrator states, "she has tasted his disconcerting hatred for her kind and also protection." Matilda senses Scranton's love and hatred alike. The existence of his hatred enables Matilda to reunite with her self-sacrificing mother. After her mother's death, Matilda joins the antelope and becomes part of their family.

Revenge

Revenge is a theme that appears throughout *The Antelope Wife*. For example, Sweetheart Calico's daughters take revenge on Jimmy Badger's people when their mother is kidnapped by Klaus. They do so by bringing bad luck. Jimmy says, "Our luck is changing. Our houses caved in with the winter's snow and our work is going for grabs."

The theme of revenge is also echoed in the actions of Richard Whiteheart Beads. Richard first attempts suicide when Rozin says she is leaving him. In his desire for revenge, Richard, "is comforted by the thought that once he is gone and later, when Frank dies, she will be lonely." Richard acts on his need for revenge again when he attempts to ruin Rozin's wedding to Frank. When this is unsuccessful, he takes his final revenge by shooting himself outside of their hotel room.

Like Richard, Zosie takes revenge on her spouse for his betrayal. She carefully manipulates Mary and Augustus. Mary becomes Zosie's ally against Augustus because she blames him for breaking her bond with her twin. The two women dress and style their hair alike, making it impossible for him to discern between them. This

The Antelope Wife *looks at the relationships forged between generations.* *(© Thomas Barrat | Shutterstock.com)*

confusion tortures Augustus, who wants to hide his affair from Zosie.

No one who takes revenge in *The Antelope Wife* considers how it will harm others. Sweetheart Calico's daughters punish Jimmy's people, not Klaus. Richard is willing to leave his children fatherless in his first suicide attempt, and he accidentally kills Deanna. Zosie's actions leave her daughters without a father, and unhappy marriage becomes part of a vicious family cycle.

Destiny

Erdrich questions how much control people have over their own lives, beginning with the myth of the twins beading the world. The characters face the events in their lives questioning their destiny. Cally, for example, says, "Family stories repeat themselves in patterns and waves generation to generation, across bloods and time." The history of the family does seem to repeat itself between generations. There are sets of twins, unhappy marriages, and complicated loves. These patterns are visible in the lives of Mary, Zosie, and Rozin. The family history seems to indicate that life is predetermined and beyond the control of those who live it.

The end of the book, however, suggests that destiny can be altered. When referring to Richard Whiteheart Beads, the narrator makes a surprising revelation: "He would have died in his sleep on his eighty-fifth birthday, sober, of a massive stroke, had his self-directed pistol shot

glanced a centimeter higher." Richard's actions alter his destiny. The narrator brings up the question of destiny again in the closing paragraph. She asks, "Who are you and who am I, the beader or the bit of colored glass sewn onto the fabric of this earth?" The readers must answer this question for themselves.

STYLE

Historical Novel

According to William Harmon's *A Handbook to Literature*, a historical novel is "a novel that reconstructs a past age." Traditionally, it "calls for an age when two cultures are in conflict." *The Antelope Wife* begins with a conflict between the US cavalry and an Ojibwa village in the 1800s. The conflict specifically engulfs Scranton Roy and Blue Prairie Woman when he kills her grandmother and then takes her baby. The conflict between these two families continues over the years through their descendants.

Erdrich does not tell a linear story. Rather, the events shift back and forth between the 1800s and the present. Each generation, in some way, repeats the actions of their predecessors. They create a pattern that is rooted in the original conflict between Scranton Roy and Blue Prairie Woman.

COMPARE
&
CONTRAST

- **1800s:** Many Native Americans hand over their lands in a series of treaties, some legitimate, some not. As a result, they are limited to reservations, which are typically allotted portions of land that American citizens do not want.

  Today: Many Native Americans still live on reservations, but the Relocation Program of the 1950s to the 1980s began a migration to cities. Roughly one-third of Native Americans now live in cities, according to the American Indians' Cultural Network website.

- **1800s:** Native Americans are not offered the rights of citizenship. Citizenship is only possible if an individual is one-half Native American or less. Even members of ally tribes are denied citizenship status.

  Today: The 1924 Indian Citizenship Act granted Native Americans citizenship. Reservations today still have their own sovereignty, but their citizens are also citizens of the United States.

- **1800s:** There is little respect for Native American culture and traditions. US agencies and institutions attempt to assimilate Native Americans into Anglo-American culture in efforts to make them "civilized." For example, schools force the children to speak English.

  Today: There is growing interest in Native American history and culture. The works of Native American artists, musicians, and authors are respected internationally.

Lyric Novel

As a poet, Erdrich is a master of the lyric and creates lyric novels. Harmon quotes Ralph Freedman's definition of the lyric novel as one that "transforms 'the materials of fiction (such as characters, plots, or scenes) into patterns of imagery.'" The lyric style appears throughout *The Antelope Wife*. For example, Zosie's manipulation of Mary and Augustus is described in lyric terms: "The two never saw the stitch work that kept them sewed to her side. They never saw the fabric upon which their passion was marked out in chalk."

Magic Realism

The Antelope Wife is an example of magic realism. Erdrich weaves elements of myth and magic throughout the novel. Harmon defines *magic realism* as occurring when "the frame or surface of the work may be conventionally realistic, but contrasting elements—such as the supernatural, myth, dream, fantasy—invade the realism and change the whole basis of the art." In Erdrich's novel, Sweetheart Calico is part of an antelope herd, and a *windigo* dog visits Klaus.

Additionally, Almost Soup guards Cally's life from death, and Cally hears spirit names. All of these events are examples of magic realism.

HISTORICAL CONTEXT

Ojibwa Treaties

The Ojibwa, also spelled Ojibway and Ojibwe, are also referred to as the Chippewa people. One of the larger and more influential tribes in the United States and Canada, the Ojibwa people were hunters and gatherers. They had a totem clan system that began in the woodlands of the North, including Michigan, Wisconsin, Minnesota, and Ontario. The Ojibwa had a predominantly peaceful relationship with the United States, fighting mainly with the Sioux. The tribe signed numerous treaties with the United States in the 1800s.

These treaties typically involved seceding land to the United States, which was not always in the best interest of the Ojibwa. In his article for *Minnesota History*, Edmund J. Danziger Jr. notes

The Antelope Wife *concludes in modern-day Minneapolis.* (© Henryk Sadura | Shutterstock.com)

that this led to a migration north. After a treaty in 1842, for example, the Ojibwa people were allowed to stay on the land near Lake Superior that they signed away because of the "white farmers' lack of interest." In 1850, President Zachary Taylor ordered them to be removed, but the order was halted after his death. Additionally, the Ojibwa refused to move, and some American citizens supported them.

The US commander of Indian affairs, according to Danziger, believed that the Ojibwa would need to "be allowed to remain on small reservations." In 1854, a new treaty was signed, promising two decades of paid annuities to the Ojibwa. In many ways, the reservations this treaty established were preferable because the Ojibwa were allowed to keep some of their native land and were given annuities.

Over time, however, the annuities ended, and the people of this hunter-gatherer society were not effective farmers. Additionally, the treaty made the timberland available for logging. The woodland was destroyed, and the people suffered in poverty by the beginning of the twentieth century.

Plains Ojibwa

The Plains Ojibwa, or Bungi, were descendants of Woodland Ojibwa who migrated to the plains. This migration was a response to the expansion of the fur trade in the late 1700s. Over time, Ojibwa culture and traditions were adapted to suit their new environment. For example, they moved from hunting deer to antelope and buffalo. They required hard-soled shoes instead of soft moccasins, and they developed the Sun Dance to bring rain. According to James Howard's article in *Plains Anthropologist*, regarding the Plains Ojibwa,

> although it is true that they are descended from Woodland Ojibwa and Ottawa groups, a century and a half of separate political and cultural existence entitle them to designation as a distinct tribe in their own right.

The differences are clearly seen in the characters in *The Antelope Wife*. Martha McCullough in the *Encyclopedia of the Great Plains* notes that the "similarities between the Plains and Woodland Ojibwas continued in the areas of social organization and belief systems."

CRITICAL OVERVIEW

Erdrich's first novel, *Love Medicine*, was a critical success, earning her the respect of her literary peers. For example, Toni Morrison, as quoted by the *Voices from the Gaps* database, says, "the beauty of *Love Medicine* saves us from being devastated by its power." The book earned her the National Book Critics Circle Award and the Los Angeles Times Book Award. Her second novel, *TheBeet Queen*, received equal praise from Michiko Kakutani, who compares Erdrich to Faulkner in her *New York Times* review.

Subsequent criticism for Erdrich's books has been positive, in part due to her use of poetic language and multiple plot lines. However, critics have commented that the sinister aspects of her stories are extreme. As Kakutani says, "At times, Ms. Erdrich dwells a bit too insistently on the darker aspects." Critics are also divided on how well she represents Native Americans. For example, Howard Meredith, in his *World Literature Today* review of *The Antelope Wife*, questions her use of Ojibwa/Chippewa dialects.

The *Antelope Wife* was published in 1998, and the story did not have the same reception as *Love Medicine*. Meredith states that it "lacks the verve of Erdrich's previous novels. Frustration hangs over the book." Other critics, such as Betsy Kline of Pittsburgh's *Post-Gazette*, disagree with his negative criticism. Kline believes that "the reader can only marvel at Erdrich's artistry and revel in her characters' unquenchable spirit."

Despite some negative criticism, Erdrich has continued to receive praise for her work. Her 2009 novel *The Plague of Doves* was nominated for the Pulitzer Prize for Fiction, and *The Roundhouse* won the National Book Award for Fiction in 2012.

WHAT DO I READ NEXT?

- Published in 1989, *Holding Our World Together: Ojibwe Women and the Survival of Community*, by Brenda J. Child, examines the essential social roles of Native American women. Child's history goes back to the time of European colonization and through life on the reservations.
- *The Master Butchers Singing Club*, published by Erdrich in 2003, is a novel about German migration to the United States. She examines her father's heritage in this book.
- *Ojibwa Myths and Legends*, by Bernard Coleman, Ellen Frogner, and Estelle Eich, was first published in 1961. This nonfiction text provides valuable insight into the myths and legends of the Ojibwa and how they influenced culture and society.
- *Ojibwein Minnesota*, by Anton Steven Treuer, is a nonfiction book published in 2010. This expansive history is helpful for anyone who desires a greater understanding of the culture and history of the Ojibwa in the state.
- Published in 1997, *The God of Small Things*, by Arundhati Roy, is set in India. Like in *The Antelope Wife*, magical elements abound in this fictional story of family and identity.
- Amy Harmon's young-adult novel *Running Barefoot* was published in 2012. This fictional story follows the relationship between Samuel Yazzie, a Navajo teenager, and Josie Jensen. The love story includes themes of family and identity.

CRITICISM

April Paris

Paris is a freelance writer with an extensive background writing literary and educational materials. In the following essay, she argues that beadwork and food are the images and metaphors used to draw people together in The Antelope Wife.

Louise Erdrich uses the metaphors of beading and food to show the connections between her characters in *The Antelope Wife*. Beading draws them together, and food helps unite them. Beading is the dominant metaphor in the book. As Diana Postlethwaite explains in her *New York Times* review of the novel, "The intricate craft of Native American beadwork is the central metaphor upon which Erdrich strings her multiple, intertwined narratives." The book begins with the myth of twin sisters beading light and dark into the fabric of the world. Each one is attempting to outperform the other, and this competition throws off the balance between light and dark. The beading patterns of these twins cause the narrator to question how much of life is chosen and how much is fated.

Jonathan Little explains this concept of beading and fate in an essay for *Contemporary Literature*: "On one level, the battle between the twins can be read metaphorically as different fates (fortune and misfortune) warring against each other, both being equally present in the rich tapestry of life." Regardless of whether they experience fortune or misfortune, the characters are all part of a larger beaded pattern. This pattern draws the characters together and unites them.

The metaphor of beading extends beyond the realm of the mythical twins. The beading of mortal women is equally important. It is through beading that Rozin expresses her sorrow to Mary and Zosie after the death of Deanna. She bares her soul as she discusses her pain and grief while she beads with them. Beading creates a communal bond that facilitates open discussions of emotional and spiritual matters. The act of beading with her mothers spiritually unites her with them. Besides filling an emotional need, beading provides Rozin with the ability to assert some sort of control over her life and her feelings.

The dog Almost Soup understands the significance of women beading as he watches Rozin with her mothers. He reports, "They are sewing us all into a pattern, into life beneath their hands. . . . We are the tiny pieces of the huge design that they are making—the soul of the world." He explains that the word for beads means "little spirit seed." Each bead placed in the pattern is spirit. Thus, Rozin imbues part of herself into the patterns that she beads. For example, Almost Soup notes that her stitches are "agonizing" and that she uses "harrowing orange" while Cally is ill. The pattern takes on Rozin's feelings and her spirit. Her life is reflected in what she creates.

The influence that beading has on human lives can also be seen in the relationship between Rozin's mothers and her father. Beading helps define the lives of Mary and Zosie. Mary lives with Zosie and her husband, Augustus, and they are all happy for a time. The two sisters sit

> BEADWORK UNITES THE CHARACTERS INTO A SINGLE PATTERN, AND HUNGER AND FOOD BRING THE CHARACTERS TOGETHER IN UNITY. THROUGHOUT THE NOVEL, THESE METAPHORS NOT ONLY PROVIDE INSIGHT INTO THE INDIVIDUAL CHARACTERS BUT ALSO SHOW HOW THEY ARE ALL CONNECTED WITH EACH OTHER."

together and bead different patterns each night, working in unison. Mary, however, eventually betrays her sister and has an affair with Augustus. Zosie discerns the truth while beading with Mary, but she keeps the knowledge to herself. At this moment, she becomes the beader, and Augustus and Mary are her beads. In an act of revenge, Zosie manipulates all of their destinies and seals their fates. Consumed by guilt, Mary confesses her indiscretion, unaware that her sister already knows the truth. With this confession, Zosie "saw exactly the course of her pattern." She creates a pattern of deception that involves Mary's cooperation.

In seeking revenge on Augustus, Mary and Zosie reflect the mythical twin sisters who bead the world. Mary and Zosie, however, disrupt the balance when they both choose to work with darkness and deception. United in purpose, they make it impossible for Augustus to tell them apart, which becomes a source of constant strain and torment. The relationship between Augustus and the sisters begins to deteriorate. Desperate, he resorts to violent measures to find peace of mind. He bites Zosie's ear in an attempt to permanently mark her. The dark pattern continues until Augustus disappears.

While it is true that Zosie acts as the beader in her marriage, it could be argued that she was only following the path that was established when Scranton Roy committed murder. Augustus is the grandson of the man who murdered the ancestor of Mary and Zosie. As Little points out, the sisters have the right to hate him: "Through their revenge they mend or at least counter the Daashkikaa of his grandfather's blood sins in the glitteringly cruel pattern of what has gone before." The conflict between the Roy family and the family of Blue Prairie Woman is part of a larger pattern that is simply repeated in the lives of Mary and Zosie. In this way, the two generations and families are drawn together and united in the same pattern.

Postlethwaite points out, "Beadwork is not the only metaphor that unifies 'The Antelope Wife.' There is also abundant food." Judyth Hills, quoted in a Shirley Brozzo essay for *Studies in American Indian Literatures*, explains, "This is the food that unites us, that tells the story of who we have been, and whom we have met and what we may together become." Food is both personal and cultural, and it provides valuable insight into the different characters of *The Antelope Wife*. The different images and metaphors show how hunger and desire motivate the actions of the characters. It also shows that people sometimes confuse their appetites.

Food and hunger have a long history in Cally's family. Blue Prairie Woman was once named Apijigo Bakaday, which means So Hungry. As a girl, the people in her village begin to fear that she is a *windigo* because of her endless appetite. She faces rejection by her own people and chooses to separate herself from them. The girl goes into the forest alone, but her hunger is endless until a deer comes to her camp. Rather than killing the deer, she shares her stew with him. She realizes that she loves the deer and the deer loves her, and for the first time, she no longer feels hunger. She becomes part of the deer's family, and her hunger for love is finally satisfied.

Food and hunger are tied to emotion, but it is easy to mistake the connection, like Frank Shawano does. Food defines Frank Shawano's life. As a baker, he is surrounded by it; food makes up his life experiences. For example, he gives Rozin fresh bread when they first meet. After he and Rozin begin their affair, Frank brings over cookies for Cally and Deanna. Although Frank is immersed in food, he does not fully understand it.

Brozzo argues, "Frank has become assimilated into the dominant [white] culture." This assimilation alters his perception of food. She points out that his recipes are not traditional Ojibwa recipes. They are made with sugar and refined flour. His creations contribute to diabetes in people, like Mary, who were unaccustomed to eating sweet food. Although Frank does show signs of assimilation, the recipe that he attempts to perfect is, arguably, a family one. Frank is obsessed with remaking the *blitzkuchen* he ate as a child.

The *blitzkuchen* is a cake that was created by a young German named Klaus, whom Frank's father and other men kidnapped after World War II. The act was perpetrated in order to avenge a cousin who died in the war. Although he cannot communicate with his captors, the prisoner understands that he is in danger. The young man offers to cook for the men, which he hopes will save his life. He works in fear, but he is successful. The recipe effectively connects the men who "had for a long unbending moment the same heartbeat, same blood in their veins, the same taste in their mouths." The *blitzkuchen* not only saves Klaus's life, but it also unites him with his captors. Klaus is made part of the Shawano clan because of the *blitzkuchen*. This makes the recipe part of the Shawano family's heritage.

Frank spends his life attempting to recreate Klaus's recipe, but he is unsuccessful. When Zosie tastes one attempt, she pronounces that the cake needs something. But he "does not talk about the old ways or the traditions he is using for the recreation of the blitzkuchen," as Brozzo points out. He forgets the link between emotion and creation, a lesson that his ancestor, Sounding Feather, learned when her emotions affected the colors of the quills she dyed.

The recipe is finally perfected when Frank cuts the wedding cake. As Brozzo notes, "He stumbles on the secret ingredient that made that cake taste so special . . . fear." After Richard Whiteheart Beads's suicide attempt and his threat of poisoning the cake, every one of the guests is tense with emotion. This emotion recreates the original recipe. The cake does more than unite the wedding guests. It also unites the generations: "The ones who had gone on before, the dead, even they came back for a little taste."

The characters in *The Antelope Wife* are all connected in ways that they do not always understand. Erdrich uses metaphor and symbolism to show these connections. Beadwork unites the characters into a single pattern, and hunger and food bring the characters together in unity. Throughout the novel, these metaphors not only provide insight into the individual characters but also show how they are all connected with each other.

Source: April Paris, Critical Essay on *The Antelope Wife*, in *Novels for Students*, Gale, Cengage Learning, 2014.

Erdrich's works often examine the forces affecting the lives of Native Americans. (© Everett Collection / Shutterstock.com)

Bruce Allen

In the following excerpt, Allen provides a brief biography of Erdrich and calls the novel "a rich book, which effectively juxtaposes colorful ancestral tales."

BEGINNINGS

. . . Born in 1954 in Little Falls, Montana, Louise Erdrich grew up near the Turtle Mountain Reservation in North Dakota. Both her Chippewa mother and her German-American father were teachers at a boarding school run by the Bureau of Indian Affairs. The eldest of seven children, she was a writer from early childhood, encouraged by her parents and stimulated by the presence of Native American culture and history, all around her, and specifically embodied by her Chippewa grandfather, a Turtle Mountain tribal chairman.

Erdrich entered Dartmouth College in 1972—another in a varied round of activities that also included employment as a waitress, poetry teacher, lifeguard, and construction gang "flagger." At Dartmouth, she met writer Michael Dorris (himself part Modoc Indian), head of the college's Native American Studies program and a single adoptive father. Louise graduated in 1976; several years later they met again at a poetry reading (according to Dorris' account in *The Broken Cord*) and began a romantic relationship. They began collaborating on fictional projects as well; a joint story of theirs, "The World's Greatest Fisherman," won a $5,000 Nelson Algren prize. They married in 1981, after Louise completed graduate work at Johns Hopkins University.

The marriage seemed perfect, and each began publishing critically acclaimed and highly popular books: Louise's widely reviewed and respected early fiction (particularly *Love Medicine* and *The Beet Queen*), and Michael's robust first novel *A Yellow Raft in Blue Water* (1987) and award-winning memoir of raising an adoptive son born with fetal alcohol syndrome, *The Broken Cord* (1989). Three daughters were born to the couple, joining their three adopted sons.

But the marriage failed, and by 1996, the couple had separated and planned to divorce. Under a cloud of allegations that he had sexually abused his adopted children, Dorris took his own life in 1997. Understandably, Erdrich has told interviewers little about the last years of her marriage or her bereavement.

Erdrich has gradually become an even more visible figure in recent years, serving on the executive board of the PEN Writers Union, submitting to numerous interviews, producing further installments in her many-paneled Native American saga, and, not coincidentally, acquiring local fame as proprietor of a busy Minneapolis shop named Birch Bark Books, Herbs, and Native Arts. She is the new mother (at age forty-six) of a fourth daughter.

Still, the world knows her best as the author of the phenomenally successful *Love Medicine* (1984), which won the National Book Critics Circle Prize for Fiction. A loosely episodic "novel," it introduced members of the Lazarre, Lamartine, Morrissey, Kashpaw, and other families who reappear throughout her subsequent books. She has published seven adult novels, several children's books (including *Grand-mother's Pigeon* and *The Birchbark House*), two volumes of poetry (*Jacklight* and *Baptism of Desire*), and a luminous memoir of pregnancy and motherhood, *The Blue Jay's Dance: A Birth Year* (1995).

A NEW SAGA

. . . With *The Antelope Wife* (1988), Erdrich enters new territory. Set mostly in and near Minneapolis, it introduces an entirely new set of characters in an ambitious multigenerational tale whose separate stories are explicitly compared to beads stitched together by a patient craftsman, which form a design that isn't discernible until the work is completed. (One wonders whether Erdrich is offering this as a metaphor for her own tightly knit, seemingly formally amorphous work in progress.)

It begins stunningly, following a U.S. cavalry raid on an Ojibwe village, when white soldier Scranton Roy sights a dog escaping from the carnage with a baby tied to its back. Roy rescues

and raises the child (a girl, whom he names Matilda): an act of both love and assimilation that is destined to be cruelly thwarted, as the novel's subsequent incidents dramatize the painful incompatibility of white and Ojibwe cultures.

It's a rich book, which effectively juxtaposes colorful ancestral tales, told by both human and canine narrators (such as that of Blue Prairie Woman, who becomes the wife of a stag), with a grim account of the downward path trod by Richard Whiteheart Beads, an Ojibwe activist and spokesman who cannot survive in the world outside the reservation. Marital troubles, alcoholism, and Richard's grief-stricken guilt over the accidental death of his beloved daughter (who succumbed to carbon monoxide poisoning in a truck left running in a closed garage, where Richard had planned to kill himself) exact their toll in a troubling novel, which, one cannot help guessing, may be a partial fictionalization of the short, unhappy life of Michael Dorris. . . .

Source: Bruce Allen, "Mysteries and Miracles," in *World and I*, Vol. 16, No. 9, September 2001, p. 223.

Barbara Hoffert

In the following review, Hoffert expresses conflicting emotions about The Antelope Wife*, calling it at once terrific and a bit disappointing.*

As the U.S. Cavalry sweeps down on the Ojibwa village, a baby girl is carried away on the back of a dog. Private Scranton Roy follows, rescues her, and—literally—nurses her back to health. But though he raises her as his own, when her mother finally comes to retrieve her, the little girl knows—and follows, spending time with a herd of antelope after her mother dies before finally returning to her village. Now the Antelope Wife, she has mysterious powers, and she links together several generations of her white and Native families in a constant dance of passion and sorrow that replicates the relationship between the two races generally. With elliptical storytelling, almost mythic women, and startlingly lyrical assays (as brilliant as the beadwork that serves here as motif), this is vintage Erdrich. It's absolutely terrific and also a bit disappointing; the language and the easy superiority of the women can seem a bit suffocating, and one feels that Erdrich has done this all before.

Source: Barbara Hoffert, "Review of *The Antelope Wife*," in *Library Journal*, Vol. 123, No. 5, March 15, 1998, p. 92.

Bill Ott

In the following review, Ott praises Erdrich's "image-rich prose."

In reviewing *Tales of Burning Love* (1996), we observed that "the power of narrative and the salvation of love have always been Erdrich's quintessential themes." Those themes remain crucial to her latest novel, but here they only sporadically shine through a cloudy sky: "History is grief and no passion is complete without its jealous backdrop." In her characteristically swirling narrative style, Erdrich tells the story of two intertwined Ojibwa families, the Roys and the Shawanos, and the fiery love that scars their souls and inhibits their freedom. We hear many voices in these overlapping and interconnected stories, jumping in time and place from a cavalryman who bayonets an Indian woman and then saves an infant girl to a reservation dog who avoids the soup pot and becomes a canine Greek chorus, but the axis around which the entire cast rotates is an event, not a person: when a smooth-talking trader abducts (or maybe just entices) a beguilingly beautiful woman from a powwow and takes her with him to Minneapolis, a tremor is felt on the mythic seismograph, echoing the past and foreshadowing the future. Some readers may have difficulty with the narrative jumps and the rich overlay of magic realism, but for those willing to slowly immerse themselves in this nonlinear world as one soaks in a hot bath, the rewards are many. Erdrich's image-rich prose seduces the reader just as her trader lures his Antelope Wife and as the other lovers across generations forge their connections ("His low, vibrant voice sank down the front of Mary's dress"), And while it is those passionate connections that again provide salvation for Erdrich's storm-tossed characters, we feel equally the power of connections to constrain, to keep *Antelope Wife* from stretching the horizon.

Source: Bill Ott, "Review of *The Antelope Wife*," in *Booklist*, Vol. 94, No. 13, March 1, 1998, p. 1044.

Publishers Weekly

In the following review, a contributor to Publishers Weekly *calls* The Antelope Wife *"a beautifully articulated tale of intertwined relationships among succeeding generations."*

"Family stories repeat themselves in patterns and waves, generation to generation, across blood and time." Erdrich (*Love Medicine*, etc.) embroiders this theme in a sensuous novel that brings her back to the material she knows best, the emotionally dislocated lives of Native Americans who try to adhere to the tribal ways while yielding to the lure of the general culture. In a beautifully articulated tale of intertwined relationships among succeeding generations, she tells the story of the Roy and the Shawano families and their "colliding histories and destinies." The narrative begins like a fever dream with a U.S. cavalry attack on an Ojibwa village, the death of an old woman who utters a fateful word, the inadvertent kidnapping of a baby and a mother's heartbreaking quest. The descendants of the white soldier who takes the baby and of the bereaved Ojibwa mother are connected by a potent mix of tragedy, farce and mystical revelation. As time passes, there is another kidnapping, the death of a child and a suicide. Fates are determined by a necklace of blue beads, a length of sweetheart calico and a recipe for blitzkuchen. Though the saga is animated by obsessional love, mysterious disappearances, mythic legends and personal frailties, Erdrich also works in a comic vein. There's a dog who tells dirty jokes and a naked wife whose anniversary surprise has an audience. Throughout, Erdrich emphasizes the paradoxes of everyday life: braided grandmas who follow traditional ways and speak the old language also wear eyeliner and sneakers. In each generation, men and women are bewitched by love, lust and longing; they are slaves to drink, to carefully guarded secrets or to the mesmerizing power of hope. Though the plot sometimes bogs down from an overload of emotional complications, the novel ultimately celebrates the courage of following one's ordained path in the universe and meeting the challenges of fate. It is an assured example of Erdrich's storytelling skills.

Source: "Review of *The Antelope Wife*," in *Publishers Weekly*, Vol. 245, No. 6, February 9, 1998, p. 72.

Charles de Lint

In the following review, de Lint discusses how The Antelope Wife *involves multiple stories each with its own issues, though there is a thread of themes leading the reader from beginning to end.*

Where to begin?

Erdrich's latest novel is such a rich tapestry of a book, cutting across family generations and various times in history, that any attempt to explain its plot in simple terms runs the risk of making it all seem far too complex and bewildering for easy reader access. This is truly one of those cases where, if the author could have made her point in a few pithy sentences, there'd have been no reason to write a whole book. But there is no one single point. Like the best novels, *The Antelope Wife* sweeps us up into many stories, each with its own issues to explore.

There is, however, a thread that leads from beginning to end, beaded with all these stories and the characters inhabiting them. Part of that thread is the background setting of Minneapolis and the nearby reservations from which native people have been continually drawn to what was once an important trading center and hunting ground, and is now a concrete metropolis. And many of the beads are various members of the extended Roy and Shawano families, whose destinies seem forever entangled with each other, as well as with beings not quite human.

Perhaps the story starts when the trader Klaus Shawano kidnaps the antelope woman at a powwow, bringing her back to Minneapolis as his wife. However, like the selchies of Scottish folklore, such a mystical woman cannot thrive without her freedom, without the wild plains from which she was stolen. Bad luck will fall upon the community where she is being held, Shawano is told. And bad luck will also fall on the community from which she has been taken. But Shawano doesn't care; the antelope woman has become more important to him than communities or family.

Or perhaps it starts earlier, when the cavalry soldier Scranton Roy follows a dog out of an Ojibway village, a dog bearing a small child on its back, a child Roy nourishes at his breast with the impossibility of father's milk, a child who will go on to live in the wilds and run with antelope.

But wherever it starts, most of it takes place in the city, with this community of Roys and Shawanos, delineating their sorrows and joys, and how their relationships bang up against each other in both humorous and tragic circumstances. And shot through the narrative are wonderful bits of tall tale—native style—as well as myth and folklore, such as the ribald stories and bad jokes told by the dog Almost Soup, the myths of the Windigo people, and a baker's obsession to recreate a perfect cake, tasted once, decades ago. There are the series of twins

that run in the Roy family, said to be descended from Blue Prairie Woman, to whom more bad luck comes the further they stray from their true names. There's the tragic wedding, and the hilarious first year anniversary party.

You can see the trouble I'm having here. *The Antelope Wife* provides a rich panorama of character, culture, and ideas in its relatively few pages. It moves effortlessly between urban Indians and old ways, lending a mythic quality to dialogues between, say, a pair of drunk, broken braves, living on the street, or to Cally Roy's—she's the youngest of the Roy twins—confusing quest to find out which of the elusive grandmothers, Zosie or Mary, gave birth to her own mother.

But it all comes together in the end, a stew of humor, despair, and magical moments that takes the false romance and over-wrought sentiment out of the Native condition, but leaves in their place the far richer wealth of a cast of characters that the reader will not soon forget, never mind their cultural background. Which isn't to say that the Native material doesn't lend weight to this magical story, but rather, that Erdrich has given the characters to us as people first, and then gone back to show us how they've become who they are.

Highly recommended.

Source: Charles de Lint, "Review of *The Antelope Wife*," in *Magazine of Fantasy and Science Fiction*, Vol. 95, No. 3, September 1998, p. 48.

Brad Stone

In the following interview, Stone and Erdrich discuss how readers will notice familiar themes of Erdich's works in The Antelope Wife, *including "ill-fated love, unalterable ancestral patterns and the political forces molding the lives of Native Americans." They go on to examine the echoes of Erdrich's own family tragedy, which occurred after Erdrich completed the writing of the novel.*

Just looking at her as she sits in a deli in Minneapolis, you'd never suspect this woman is one of the most celebrated writers of her generation—or that she's been through hell in the past year. Louise Erdrich is dressed in jeans and a turtleneck; her red winter coat is draped over the back of her chair. She smiles, laughs easily. But then she begins talking about all the letters of support she got after the much-publicized suicide last April of her estranged husband, the writer Michael Dorris. "I had never requested kindness before," she says, dabbing at her eyes with a paper napkin. "And all of a sudden it was keeping me and my children alive."

Erdrich, 43, has come for an interview with *Newsweek*, to talk about her seventh and latest novel, *The Antelope Wife*. But there's no way to avoid [the] subject—especially since *The Antelope Wife*, which Erdrich says she'd finished before Dorris's death, involves a husband who's left by his wife and descends into alcoholism, obsession and, finally, suicide. "It was written by a writer who was afraid of what was about to happen and didn't know how to stop it," she says, almost in a whisper. "It was written out of dread." Erdrich's readers will recognize the shifting narrative perspectives, the lyrical prose, the surrealist humor and the familiar themes: ill-fated love, unalterable ancestral patterns and the political forces molding the lives of Native Americans. But they'll also recognize echoes of her own family's tragedy.

Erdrich began *The Antelope Wife* three years ago; she had just finished it when Dorris washed down pills with a bottle of vodka and tied a plastic bag over his head in a New Hampshire motel room. They had been separated for more than a year and were barely speaking. Their marriage, Erdrich now says, had suffered since the terrible trauma of the 1991 death of their older adopted son, Abel, who was hit by a car. "That was a huge blow," she says. "These things tend to isolate people and make them go deeper and change. I know very few people who could have stayed together after that." Only after Dorris's suicide was it reported that he, the author of the moving family memoir *The Broken Cord*, had been under investigation for sexually abusing two of their three biological daughters. "I don't think it's fair to talk about this since he can't defend himself," says Erdrich. "I don't think I ever want to address it."

Erdrich's editors at HarperCollins worried about how the press would handle the eerily prescient plot of *The Antelope Wife*, and briefly floated the idea of making the husband's suicide less central; in the end, no significant changes were made. Rozin, the wife in the book, repeatedly tries to leave the marriage—not unlike the wife in Dorris's 1997 novel, *Cloud Chamber*. After her husband's suicide, Rozin overcomes feelings of guilt and marries her lover. Erdrich's real life wasn't so tidy. With her husband dead,

his estate contested in court by their adopted daughter, Madeline, and conflicting accounts of the family's life appearing in the media, Erdrich felt fiercely protective of her kids and racked with guilt. "You are not supposed to take responsibility for another person's decision," she says. "But it's impossible not to." And transmuting her premonitions into art didn't prove entirely therapeutic. "It was as though I was trying to prepare myself for what might happen. But it didn't come near to being helpful to me. It shows a poverty of my imagination."

These days, Erdrich says she's "recommitting to hanging in," and she's fallen back into the sustaining patterns of life. Her parents help, they live less than three hours away. Erdrich wakes every morning at 6:30 to get her daughters off to school. She's reached out to Madeline and her other adopted son, Sava, settling their disputes with her husband's estate. Madeline, in fact, drops by the deli during the interview, and they hug their hellos. "Write this down," Erdrich says. "Maddie is a brave person and I love her." Erdrich is also taking piano lessons and Chippewa-language classes and is working on a children's book and—of course—a new novel. She and the children do normal things, like going to see *Titanic*. Did it make her cry? Well, not exactly. But Erdrich says the scene where the crew tries to avoid hitting the iceberg haunted her. "I thought about it for a long time. I thought the two of us had been doing that for years. Michael had his hands on the wheel, we were both trying to steer. Only in opposite directions. And we ended up hitting it dead on."

Source: Brad Stone, "Scenes from a Marriage: Louise Erdrich's New Novel—and Her Life," in *Newsweek*, Vol. 131, No. 12, March 23, 1998, p. 69.

SOURCES

"American Indians Today," American Indians' Cultural Network website, http://www.american-indians.net/today.htm (accessed December 1, 2012).

Brozzo, Shirley, "Food for Thought: A Postcolonial Study of Food Imagery in Louise Erdrich's *Antelope Wife*," in *Studies in American Indian Literatures*, Series 2, Vol. 17, No. 1, Spring 2005, pp. 1–15.

Callahan, Kevin L., "An Introduction to Ojibway Culture and History," University of Minnesota website, 1998, http://www.tc.umn.edu/~call0031/ojibwa.html (accessed December 1, 2012).

Danziger, Edmund J., Jr., "They Would Not Be Moved: The Chippewa Treaty of 1854," in *Minnesota History*, Vol. 43, No. 5, Spring 1973, pp. 175–85.

Erdrich, Louise, *The Antelope Wife*, HarperFlamingo, 1998.

Halliday, Lisa, "Louise Erdrich, the Art of Fiction No. 208," in *Paris Review*, http://www.theparisreview.org/interviews/6055/the-art-of-fiction-no-208-louise-erdrich (accessed December 1, 2012).

Harmon, William, "Historical Novel," "Lyrical Novel," and "Magic Realism," in *A Handbook to Literature*, 9th ed., Prentice Hall, 2003, pp. 246, 293, 297.

Howard, James H., "The Identity and Demography of the Plains-Ojibwa," in *Plains Anthropologist*, Vol. 6, No. 13, August 1961, pp. 171–78.

Kakutani, Michiko, "Book of the Times," in *New York Times*, August 20, 1986, http://www.nytimes.com/1986/08/20/books/books-of-the-times-293786.html?ref=louiseerdrich (accessed December 1, 2012).

Kline, Betsy, Review of *The Antelope Wife*, in *Post-Gazette* (Pittsburgh, PA), May 3, 1998, http://old.post-gazette.com/books/reviews/19980503review28.asp (accessed December 1, 2012).

Little, Jonathan, "Beading the Multicultural World: Louise Erdrich's 'The Antelope Wife' and the Sacred Metaphysic," in *Contemporary Literature*, Vol. 41, No. 3, Fall 2000, pp. 495–524.

McCollough, Martha L., "Ojibwas," in *Encyclopedia of the Great Plains*, edited by David J. Wishart, University of Nebraska–Lincoln website, 2011, http://plainshumanities.unl.edu/encyclopedia/doc/egp.na.076 (accessed December 1, 2012).

McNally, Amy Leigh, and Piyali Nath Dalal, "Louise Erdrich," *Voices from the Gaps*, University of Minnesota website, May 27, 1999, http://voices.cla.umn.edu/artistpages/erdrichLouise.php (accessed December 1, 2012).

Meredith, Howard, Review of *The Antelope Wife*, in *World Literature Today*, Vol. 74, No. 1, Winter 2000, pp. 214–15.

Postlethwaite, Diana, "A Web of Beadwork," in *New York Times*, April 12, 1998, http://www.nytimes.com/books/98/04/12/reviews/980412.412post.html (accessed December 1, 2012).

FURTHER READING

Blackbird, Andrew J., *History of the Ottawa and Chippewa Indians of Michigan: A Grammar of Their Language, and Personal and Family History of the Author*, BiblioLife, 2010.

This volume is republished from Blackbird's 1887 history. An interpreter for the US government, Blackbird explores his own culture as well as the prejudice that he faced.

Erdrich, Louise, *Original Fire: Selected and New Poems*, HarperCollins, 2003.

Erdrich combines new poems with selections from *Jacklight* and *Baptism of Desire* in this collection. The volume displays her poetic skill and growth.

Johnston, Basil, *Ojibway Heritage*, Columbia University Press, 1976.

Johnston provides information about myths of the Ojibway culture. He also explains prayers, songs, rituals, and ceremonies in a way that anyone outside the tribe can understand.

Stookey, Lorena L., *Louise Erdrich: A Critical Companion*, Greenwood Press, 1999.

Stookey examines Erdrich's life and how it shaped her writing. She also offers critical insight into Erdrich's work.

Tanner, Helen Hornbeck, *The Ojibwa*, Chelsea House, 1992.

Created for a young-adult audience as part of the Indians of North America series, this nonfiction book is a useful history. Tanner explores the tribe's origins and transformations through the twentieth century.

Treuer, Anton, ed., *Living Our Language: Ojibwe Tales and Oral Histories*, Minnesota Historical Society Press, 2001.

Treuer interviewed ten elders to create this collection. His translation of the tales allows readers to glimpse the oral tradition of the Ojibwe.

SUGGESTED SEARCH TERMS

Louise Erdrich

Louise Erdrich AND biography

Louise Erdrich AND The Antelope Wife

Ojibwe OR Ojibway OR Ojibwa OR Chippewa

Ojibwe AND history

Native American AND literature

Louise Erdrich AND criticism

Ojibwe AND culture

Ojibwe AND reservations

Louise Erdrich AND Ojibwe

The Book Thief

MARKUS ZUSAK

2005

Markus Zusak's novel *The Book Thief* features a unique narrator telling the tale of Liesel Meminger, a young German girl who finds her life during World War II increasingly tied to books—many of which, as the title suggests, are stolen. Seemingly abandoned by her parents and witness to younger brother's death by illness, Liesel is sent to live with a foster family in a small town outside Munich. There, she begins a relationship with books that challenges and sustains her during the darkest moments of war—and, ultimately, even saves her life.

Zusak was already a successful children's book author before *The Book Thief*, with four previously published novels. One of these, *I Am the Messenger* (originally published in Australia as *The Messenger*, 2002), was even chosen as Book of the Year by the Children's Book Council of Australia. However, *The Book Thief* was a special work for the author: The youngest child of German and Austrian parents who later settled in Australia, Zusak grew up hearing tales of wartime Germany. He wanted to show readers that not all Germans were hateful and brutal. As Zusak states in an interview featured in the reader's guide of the paperback edition of the novel, "I wanted them to see people who were unwilling to fly the Nazi flag, and boys and girls who thought the Hitler Youth was boring and ridiculous."

Published first in Australia in 2005, *The Book Thief* became one of the most popular

Markus Zusak (© David Levenson | Getty Images Entertainment | Getty Images)

works of young-adult fiction of 2006 internationally, topping the *New York Times* children's best-seller list and enjoying significant readership among adults as well. The book was Zusak's second named a Michael L. Printz Honor Book; more importantly, it has sparked the imaginations of readers around the world with its resonant message about the power of words. As Zusak himself puts it,

> I thought of Hitler destroying people with words, and now I had a girl who was stealing them back. . . . She writes her own story—and it's a beautiful story—through the ugliness of the world that surrounds her.

AUTHOR BIOGRAPHY

Markus Zusak was born on June 23, 1975, and raised in Sydney, Australia. He is the youngest child of a German mother and an Austrian father. Growing up, he heard many tales about life and the times in Germany during World War II. Some of these events, such as the Allied bombing of Munich and the marching of Jews through towns to nearby concentration camps, would serve as key elements in *The Book Thief*.

Zusak's first novel was *The Underdog*, published in Australia in 1999. The book concerns a teenager named Cameron Wolfe and his struggles to become a man in his working-class Australian neighborhood. Two more novels followed, *Fighting Ruben Wolfe* and *When Dogs Cry* (published in the United States as *Getting the Girl*), also about Cameron and the Wolfe clan. *When Dogs Cry* was selected as an Honor Book by the Children's Book Council of Australia. Zusak's follow-up, *The Messenger* (2002; US release as *I Am the Messenger* in 2005), earned Zusak further acclaim. The novel was named a Michael L. Printz Honor Book, a young-adult commendation given by the American Library Association, and was nominated for the *Los Angeles Times* Book Prize.

Zusak's most successful work to date is *The Book Thief*, which has topped the best-seller lists in several countries and became the author's second Michael L. Printz Honor Book. The novel won the 2006 National Jewish Book Award for Children's and Young Adults' Literature. As of 2012, Zusak was living with his wife and children in his native Sydney, where he occasionally works as an English teacher and continues to write.

PLOT SUMMARY

Prologue: A Mountain Range of Rubble

The Book Thief begins with an introduction by its narrator, Death. He offers a brief explanation for his involvement in the story about to begin. As Death, he explains, he occupies himself by taking note of the color of the sky at the moment he takes the soul of a dying person. This is also, he points out, a way to keep from noticing the living—the survivors "who are left behind, crumbling among the jigsaw puzzle of realization, despair, and surprise." Sometimes, however, a survivor catches his eye during the course of his work; one of these is a girl he calls "the book thief," whom he has seen three times while taking the souls of others.

The first time he saw the girl he was outside a train in the snow, under a blinding white sky.

MEDIA ADAPTATIONS

- An unabridged audio recording of *The Book Thief* was released by Listening Library in 2006. The book is read by Allan Corduner and is available on compact disc or as an audio download through Audible.com.

- An e-book version of *The Book Thief* was released by Knopf Books for Young Readers in the Kindle format in 2007, available online at Amazon.com.

The girl's young brother had suddenly died as the two journeyed by train with their mother. The second time was years later, when the girl appeared at the site of a crashed plane under a black sky; the pilot was not yet dead when she arrived. The third time was under a glowing red sky, among the ruins of a devastated city. The girl, standing dazed in the bombed-out remains of her former neighborhood, dropped the book she was holding. Death watched as workers piled the book onto a stack of garbage to be hauled away, and on an impulse he acted: "I climbed aboard and took it in my hand, not realizing that I would keep it and view it several thousand times over the years." The story that follows is the tale of the book thief and her experiences between Death's first and third encounter with her.

Part One: The Grave Digger's Handbook

In January 1939, the book thief—whose name is Liesel Meminger—is only nine years old. She and her brother are being taken by their mother to Munich, where they are to be taken in by foster parents with the hope of receiving a better life. Their father is absent, and though Liesel does not understand why, she draws a connection between him and the word "Communist," which she hears in hushed adult conversations. Riding on the train toward Munich, Liesel wakes from a nap and notices that her brother Werner has died.

Liesel and her mother bury Werner at the next town. While at the cemetery, Liesel—who has trouble understanding the loss of her brother—stumbles upon a small black book that has been dropped in the snow. She takes it.

Outside Munich, in the small town of Molching, Liesel is left with a woman who drives her to her new home. Her foster parents are Rosa and Hans Hubermann, a middle-aged couple who live on Himmel Street in an impoverished section of town. Their own two children are grown and living away from home. Hans is a soft-spoken man whose eyes are "made of kindness, and silver," while Rosa is a plump, abrasive woman who refers to most people as filthy pigs—in German, *Saukerl* (for males) or *Saumensch* (for females). Hans is a painter by trade, though he also loves playing the accordion and rolling his own cigarettes. Rosa washes laundry for some of the wealthier Molching families—including Mayor Hermann and his wife—as a way of bringing in some much-needed money.

Liesel is enrolled in both school and the BDM, a Hitler Youth group for young girls. Though she has already taken a book—which she keeps under her mattress—Liesel cannot read or write when she begins school. She is also haunted nightly by nightmares about her brother's death. Both problems are dealt with by Hans, who sits with Liesel each night when she wakes in terror; eventually they begin late-night readings of the book she took from the cemetery, which she discovers is called *The Grave Digger's Handbook*. Hans begins teaching her to write on the only paper in the house: the backsides of sandpaper sheets he uses when painting. When the sandpaper runs out, they begin painting words on the walls of the basement.

Liesel makes a few friends at school, most notably Rudy Steiner, a boy known throughout the neighborhood for blackening himself with charcoal and impersonating Jesse Owens three years prior. She also has one notable enemy, however, at least for a time: Ludwig Schmeikl, a boy who takes pleasure in ridiculing Liesel's still-faltering skills at reading. Liesl is already upset and humiliated. Ludwig's words break her confidence, and she beats him up during recess.

Part Two: The Shoulder Shrug

By the close of 1939, Liesel has finished reading *The Grave Digger's Handbook* with Hans and has adjusted well to her new life in Molching. For Christmas, she receives two books from her foster father; she discovers that he traded away much of his treasured tobacco ration in order to buy them.

The following month, Liesel and her classmates are tasked with writing a letter. She chooses to write to her biological mother and sends it through the foster-care agency, hoping that somehow the letter will find her mother and bring a response. She watches the mail each day for three months, even after foster-care agents admit to not knowing the mother's location. Liesel even mails off additional letters by taking portions of Rosa's ever-dwindling laundry earnings in order to buy stamps. She is discovered, and starts to receive a beating; when Rosa finds out the reason for the thievery, however, she apologizes. Liesel comes to the realization that "she would never see her mother again."

In April 1940, the entire town of Molching prepares to celebrate Hitler's birthday with a bonfire. The adult Hubermann children, Hans Junior and Trudy, also return home for the event. Hans Junior, a zealous member of the Nazi Party, butts heads with his more moderate father, who has yet to be accepted as a member of the party but does not seem to mind. Trudy works as a housemaid in Munich, and Liesel finds her quiet but pleasant. During an argument, Hans Junior calls his father a coward and storms out of the house. Death hints at his future fate: "Yes, the boy was gone, and I wish I could tell you that everything worked out for the younger Hans Hubermann, but it didn't."

Liesel leaves the house to attend the bonfire as part of her Hitler Youth group. She is stunned when she discovers that the fuel for the bonfire is a mountain of books. She is further taken aback when the Nazi speaker rattles off a list of enemies to Germany—including "communists," a word somehow connected to her father. She struggles to escape through the crowd and finds an unlikely ally among the press of people: Ludwig Schmeikl, the boy she had beaten up for teasing her. His ankle has been injured during the chaos, and she helps him to safety. The two apologize for their past behaviors to each other.

Later, Liesel meets her foster father by the smoking remains of the bonfire. She asks him if her mother was a Communist, and if Hitler took her away. He answers honestly: "I think he might have, yes." When she tells him that she hates

Hitler, he slaps her and warns her never to say such a thing in public again. It is an uncharacteristic act for the normally gentle man, which drives home the importance of the message. While her foster father speaks with an acquaintance, Liesel watches as workers dampen the embers and shovel away the burned remains of the bonfire. Near the bottom of the heap, she sees three books that have escaped the flames. When no one is looking, she reaches in and pulls out the closest of the books. She shoves it into her jacket, though it is still hot and smoking. Only afterward does she realize that someone has seen her thievery—the mayor's wife, Ilsa Hermann.

Part Three: Mein Kampf

On the way home from the bonfire, Hans discovers Liesel's secret theft. Rather than becoming upset, it seems to spark an idea in him. He later walks to the local Nazi Party office and trades some money and cigarettes for a used copy of Hitler's autobiography, *Mein Kampf*.

Soon after, Liesel visits the mayor's house to drop off laundry for her mother. She is relieved when the mayor's wife makes no mention of the book-stealing incident. The next time she visits, Ilsa Hermann beckons Liesel inside. The woman shows the girl a wondrous sight: an entire room with each wall filled to the ceiling with books. Thereafter, every time she stops at the mayor's house for laundry delivery or pickup, she spends time reading books in the library while Ilsa looks on. Liesel discovers that the Hermanns had once had a son, but he died during World War I. Ilsa Hermann is certain that he froze to death, and in a sort of punishment to herself, she always leaves the window to the library open—even in the dead of winter.

Hans sends the used copy of *Mein Kampf* to a Jew in hiding named Max Vandenburg, along with a key taped inside the cover. Hans knows that any other shipment might be suspect, but a copy of *Mein Kampf* is likely to pass unnoticed by an official searching through parcels; it would also divert suspicion from a Jew if he were to be seen reading the book in public. Max leaves his hiding place in Stuttgart and, using fake identification, boards a train headed toward Molching. He walks the last portion of the journey and arrives at the Hubermann household at night. He uses the key from the book to let himself in.

Part Four: The Standover Man

Hans Hubermann's connection to Max Vandenburg is revealed: Hans Hubermann fought during World War I with Max's father, Erik. Indeed, Erik was the one who taught Hans how to play the accordion. One day, just before their company entered combat, the sergeant asked for a volunteer with good penmanship. Knowing that the volunteer would avoid combat and have the best chance at surviving the day, Erik recommended his friend Hans for the job. In doing so, he saved Hans's life and lost his own. Hans was later given the only possession of Erik's that was too big to send home to his family: his accordion. After the war, Hans visited Erik's widow in Stuttgart; to his surprise, he discovered that Erik had a son. Hans left the woman his name and address in Molching and told her to contact him if she ever needed a favor, such as painting her apartment—his only skill.

The root of Hans's uneasy relationship with the Nazi Party is also revealed: as a painter, he became infamous for helping Jews whose homes and businesses had been painted over with slurs and insults. Also, although he had applied to be a member of the party in 1937, he made a clumsy and aborted attempt to withdraw his application after seeing some vandals throwing bricks through the window of a Jewish businessman's shop. Thereafter, he was regarded with suspicion.

Hans also reveals how Max came to their home. Hans was visited in June 1939 by a man named Walter Kugler from Stuttgart. Walter was a longtime friend—and frequent fist-fighting opponent—of Max Vandenburg. Walter had been hiding Max for two years but was fearful that he would be discovered. Walter found Hans thanks to the scrap of paper he had left with Max's mother twenty years before; seeing it as a way to repay his long-dead friend, Hans agreed to help Max.

Once in the Hubermann house, Max sleeps for three days straight. When Max wakes, Liesel's is the first face he sees. Hans explains the situation to Liesel, making clear that the presence of Max must never be revealed to anyone. For everyone's safety, Hans fashions a small, secret living space under the basement stairs for Max; when winter arrives, however, Max is allowed upstairs at night to sleep near the fire. In February, when she turns twelve, Liesel receives a book titled *The Mud Men*. Max, unable to give her anything, comes up with an idea: he removes some of the pages from the copy of *Mein Kampf* that Hans sent him, paints over the words, and writes his own story—featuring himself, Liesel, and crude illustrations—called "The Standover Man." She treasures it.

Part Five: The Whistler

Throughout the spring of 1941, Liesel continues her visits to Ilsa Hermann's library every time she stops by for laundry pickup. She becomes hooked on a book called *The Whistler*, about a murderer who whistled as he fled the scenes of his crimes. She also strengthens her bond with Max; she brings him discarded newspapers so he can do the crosswords, and she tells him what the weather is like since he cannot venture outdoors himself. The whole family also helps Max paint over the remaining pages of *Mein Kampf* so he can continue his writings and sketches.

In June, as the war intensifies in places far from Molching, Ilsa Hermann hands Liesel a letter terminating her foster mother's employment—and with it, the last trace of Rosa Hubermann's meager income. Ilsa also insists that Liesel take *The Whistler* as a gift. She does, but later returns to give back the book and unload a torrent of anger and insults at the wealthy woman.

Meanwhile, Rudy Steiner endures frequent abuse at the hands of his Hitler Youth leader, Franz Deutscher. One day, after being humiliated by Deutscher, Rudy asks Liesel to go steal something with him to improve his mood. Liesel takes him to the mayor's house, knowing that Ilsa Hermann leaves the window open in the library. Instead of stealing food like Rudy wants, she sneaks in and steals *The Whistler*. Rudy stops attending Hitler Youth in order to avoid Deutscher; eventually, thanks to his brother Kurt, Rudy is reassigned to a different Hitler Youth group.

Part Six: The Dream Carrier

Shortly after Christmas 1942—an event highlighted by Liesel, her foster parents, and Max building a snowman in the basement using buckets of snow from outside their house—Max's health begins to decline. In February, he collapses and falls unconscious. The Hubermanns place him upstairs in Liesel's bed to recover. Liesel gathers discarded items from the outside world and leaves them next to him as gifts, somehow believing they might help him get better and wake up. She also reads to him each day, and even makes a trip with Rudy to the mayor's house to steal another book for Max to listen to; the book is called *The Dream Carrier*.

Max remains unconscious for over a month, and the Hubermanns begin to fear that he will die—leaving them not only with grief, but also with the additional danger of having a dead Jew in their house. Finally, one day while Liesel is at school, Rosa visits on the pretense of yelling at the girl for stealing her hair brush; the real message, however—whispered under her breath—is that Max is finally awake. By April, he has fully recovered and reclaimed his living space in the basement.

In June, however, members of the Nazi Party make the rounds throughout the neighborhood, inspecting basements to determine which are the deepest—and therefore most suitable to serve as bomb shelters in the event of an Allied attack. Liesel notices the inspectors and acts quickly to warn her family. They contemplate moving Max out of the basement, but Hans decides it would be best to leave him hidden there behind the drop sheets and paint cans that cover his living space. The Nazi inspector spends three long minutes in the basement, to then inform Hans that it is too shallow to serve as a bomb shelter. Max has gone undiscovered, and they all narrowly escape an awful fate.

Part Seven: The Complete Duden Dictionary and Thesaurus

As the citizens of Molching prepare for possible attack, Hans Hubermann enjoys a resurgence in his painting business, blackening windows to make internal lights invisible to nighttime bombers. Liesel often goes with her father to help him paint and loves hearing him tell stories of his life.

Throughout the summer, Rudy practices his running in preparation for a competition at a Hitler Youth carnival. Rudy wins three of the four race events, relishing his victories over Franz Deutscher. In his final event, however, he is disqualified for jumping the starting gun. Rudy later confesses that he did it on purpose, though he does not explain himself.

Liesel steals another book from the library of the mayor's house, titled *A Song in the Dark*. Soon after, Rudy shows Liesel something unusual: at the mayor's house, the window to the library is closed, but a book rests against it on the inside. Liesel lifts the window and takes it. The book is *The Complete Duden Dictionary and Thesaurus*, and inside is a letter for Liesel from Ilsa Hermann. Ilsa informs Liesel that she knows the girl has been entering the library and stealing books, but she does not mind. She writes, "My only hope is that one day you will knock on the front door and enter the library in the more civilized manner."

One September night, the Hubermann household wakes to the sirens warning of a coming air raid. They hurry to the nearest approved shelter, the basement of a family named the Fiedlers. Other occupants include Rudy and his family and Frau Holtzapfel—a spiteful neighbor engaged in a long-standing feud with Rosa Hubermann. This first warning, they later discover, was a false alarm. It is soon followed, however, by another real warning. Crowded in a basement filled with fearful civilians, Liesel opens *The Whistler* and begins reading in an attempt to calm everyone down. Soon enough, they are all engrossed in the tale; when the siren sounds to indicate safety, they all remain in place to allow Liesel to finish reading the first chapter. They return home to find that Molching has narrowly escaped the bombs.

In the days that follow, Frau Holtzapfel appears at the Hubermanns' front door. She tells Liesel that she enjoyed the first chapter of *The Whistler* and would like the girl to come to her house regularly and read her the rest of the book. In exchange, Frau Holtzapfel agrees to stop spitting on the Hubermanns' front door—a nasty tradition spawned from her feud with Rosa—and also agrees to give the Hubermanns her ration of coffee.

Soon after, a group of Nazi soldiers decides to march their cargo of Jews through the streets of Molching on their way to the concentration camp at Dachau. As the residents watch, one of the Jews falls behind and repeatedly drops to his knees, only to be forced back to his feet by the soldiers. As he passes, Hans Hubermann walks out into the assembly of Jews and gives the man a piece of bread. Both the Jew and Hans receive lashes from a whip; Hans's paint cart is overturned, and he is called a Jew lover.

Only afterward does Hans realize that his actions have placed his family and Max in jeopardy. Fearing that Nazi officials will come to search their house, Max packs his things and departs under cover of night. He tells Liesel that he has left her something but that she will not receive it until the time is right.

Part Eight: The Word Shaker

Despite Hans Hubermann's fears, Nazi officials come not for him but for Rudy Steiner. His excellent academic and athletic abilities have attracted their attention, and they would like the boy to attend a special school. His fearful father, however, refuses to let him go.

In November, Hans Hubermann is surprised to finally receive a letter approving his application to be a member of the Nazi Party. It is followed soon after by a draft notice enlisting him to serve in the German army. Liesel soon discovers that Rudy's father, Alex, will suffer the same fate. One night, after Hans has left for the war, Liesel wakes to find Rosa—usually so loud and often outwardly callous—sitting on her bed, silently holding her husband's accordion.

Instead of being sent to Russia as he fears, Hans remains in Germany as part of a unit of soldiers known among themselves as "Dead Body Collectors," tasked with cleaning up the devastation caused by Allied air raids. Alex serves in Vienna, using his skills as a tailor to repair clothing destined for soldiers fighting in Russia.

In December 1942, another parade of Jews is marched through Molching. Rudy decides to leave bread in the street for the hungry Jews to take—inspired by Hans Hubermann's infamous act of generosity—and Liesel helps him. They are chased off by Nazi soldiers, but only after some of the Jews find and eat the offerings. Liesel is both disappointed and gladdened that Max is not among the captured Jews. For Christmas, Rosa gives Liesel a final gift from Max, which she had been holding onto at his request. It is another book created by him, titled *The Word Shaker*. It is a dreamlike tale of a girl, the power of words, and the young man who inspires her to use them.

Part Nine: The Last Human Stranger

Liesel returns to the mayor's house and takes another book, *The Last Human Stranger*, along with a plate of cookies that has been left for her. She is surprised when Ilsa Hermann opens the door and finds her there; they have a brief but pleasant conversation. Later, Liesel meets Frau Holtzapfel's son Michael, who lost a hand fighting in Stalingrad; her other son, Robert, died there. Michael informs Rosa that Hans Junior is fighting there as well, but his fate is unknown.

Hans, while preparing to ride out with his unit for clean-up duty, is forced to switch seats with an intimidating soldier named Reinhold Zucker. The truck they ride in blows a tire and loses control, flipping several times. Hans suffers a broken leg, but Zucker—having taken Hans's usual seat—is killed. Because of his injury, Hans is sent back home.

Part Ten: The Book Thief

In July 1943, a few months after Hans has returned home, Michael Holtzapfel hangs himself, guilt-ridden over the loss of his brother. In August, Liesel—who makes a habit of searching the occasional parades of captured Jews—finds Max Vandenburg. She runs to Max and embraces him, undeterred by the cracking whips of the Nazi overseers. The soldiers separate them, and Rudy holds Liesel back as Max is taken away. She later reveals the secret of Max's hiding to Rudy.

Liesel sneaks once more into Ilsa Hermann's library for another book, but she becomes angry over the unfairness of the world and instead tears a book apart. She leaves a letter of apology and promises never to return. Three days later, Ilsa Hermann visits her at home. She brings a special book as a gift: a book of empty pages. She tells the girl, "I thought if you're not going to read any more of my books, you might like to write one instead." Liesel takes her advice, and working in the basement that once housed a hidden Jew, she begins writing a memoir of her life from the time her young brother died. She calls it *The Book Thief*. She finishes the book in October with the following line: "I have hated the words and I have loved them, and I hope I have made them right."

Five nights later, while Liesel is in the basement rereading her book, the bombs finally fall on Molching without warning, as the city sleeps. Everyone on her street is killed—Hans and Rosa Hubermann, Frau Holtzapfel, Rudy Steiner and his siblings—except Liesel, who happened to be in the safest place possible. She is buried beneath the rubble, but when workers find her, she is unhurt. Dazed and unable to comprehend the devastation, she drops her book and cries out for her papa, Hans.

Epilogue: The Last Color

Death does not encounter Liesel Meminger for many years after that. In fact, he states, "I should tell you that the book thief died only yesterday."

When Death finally visits Liesel as an old woman in Sydney, Australia, he is able to glimpse additional details of her life after the bombing through fragments of her memories. After her street was destroyed, Liesel was taken in by Ilsa Hermann and her husband, the mayor. Erik Steiner returned from the war to find that his family had been killed; eventually he reopened his clothing shop, and Liesel often worked there with him. In October 1945, after the end of the war, Liesel was reunited with Max Vandenburg, who was fortunate enough to survive the concentration camps.

Conversing with Death, Liesel is surprised that he has kept and read her book so many times. She wants to know if it is possible for Death to understand a story so centered on life and living. Death simply responds, "I am haunted by humans."

CHARACTERS

Arthur Berg

Arthur Berg is the leader of a group of youngsters who steal various things in and around Molching. Rudy and Liesel briefly join his gang of thieves, stealing items such as potatoes and onions. He is a generous leader, sharing his various takes with Liesel and Rudy. Arthur later moves to Cologne, where his younger sister is killed—presumably by Allied bombing.

Herbert Bollinger

Herbert Bollinger is an old acquaintance of Hans Hubermann's. When Hans notices in the mid-1930s that the number of customers for his painting business are dwindling, Bollinger points out that he should be a member of the Nazi Party if he wants to keep working.

Viktor Chemmel

Viktor Chemmel is the young man who takes over as leader of the gang of young thieves previously led by Arthur Berg. After Viktor offers Liesel and Rudy almost nothing for their efforts on a thievery run, Rudy insults him, and Viktor beats him up. Later, Viktor throws one of Liesel's books into the river.

Death

Death is the narrator of *The Book Thief* and participates in the story by taking the lives of many of the characters at various times. He first notices Liesel when he takes the life of her young brother, Werner. Later, after he collects the many victims of the bombing on Himmel Street, he finds Liesel's memoir on a pile of trash and takes it. From it he learns Liesel's story, which he shares with the reader.

Franz Deutscher

Franz Deutscher is Rudy Steiner and Tommy Müller's sadistic Hitler Youth leader. When Tommy fails to hear his commands during marching, both Tommy and Rudy—who stands up for his friend—become his favorite targets of punishment. After Rudy moves to a different Hitler Youth group, he takes pleasure in winning several events at an athletic competition as Deutscher looks on.

Frau Diller

Frau Diller is the owner of the corner shop on Himmel Street. An avid supporter of the Nazi Party, she demands that everyone offer a salutary "*heil* Hitler" when they enter her store.

The Fiedlers

The Fiedlers are the family with the deepest basement on Himmel Street, which is thus chosen as the meeting location for Himmel Street residents in the event of an air raid. It is in their basement that Liesel calms both the children and adults by reading excerpts from *The Whistler*. Like the others on Himmel Street, they die during a surprise bombing by Allied planes.

Rolf Fischer

Rolf Fischer is a leading member of the Nazi Party in Molching. In 1937, he sees Hans Hubermann painting over the door of Joel Kleinmann, a Jewish store owner, after it had been marked by a Star of David and the words "Jewish filth." This is part of the reason why Hans Hubermann is not accepted as a member of the Nazi Party until many years later.

Frau Heinrich

Frau Heinrich is the foster-care agent who transports Liesel on her final journey to her new home with the Hubermanns. When Liesel arrives, she is at first unwilling to get out of Frau Heinrich's car. Later, when Hans Hubermann contacts her regarding the whereabouts of Liesel's biological mother, she states that she does not know where the woman is.

Heinz Hermann

Heinz Hermann is the mayor of Molching and husband of Ilsa Hermann. In June 1941, he mentions in an interview for the local paper that the citizens of Molching should prepare for harder times to come. A week later, he and his wife fire Rosa Hubermann as their launderer. After the bombing of Himmel Street, Heinz and Ilsa take Liesel in and raise her as their own.

Ilsa Hermann

Ilsa Hermann is the wife of the mayor of Molching, Heinz Hermann. Liesel's foster mother, Rosa, washes their laundry, and the Hermanns are her last remaining customers until they, too, must stop using her services as the war rages on. On the day of the bonfire, she sees Liesel steal a book from the charred remains; she later invites Liesel to use her library, which Liesel does on a regular basis, forging a bond between the two. After Himmel Street is destroyed, Ilsa and Heinz Hermann take Liesel in as their own.

Frau Holtzapfel

Frau Holtzapfel is the next-door neighbor of the Hubermanns. She and Rosa Hubermann are longtime enemies for an unknown reason, and Frau Holtzapfel faithfully spits on the Hubermann's front door every time she passes. After being huddled together in a basement during an air raid, Frau Holtzapfel makes a deal with Rosa: she will stop spitting on her door if Liesel will visit her regularly and read to her from one of her books.

Michael Holtzapfel

Michael Holtzapfel is one of Frau Holtzapfel's two sons. He loses his hand fighting in Stalingrad, while his brother dies there. After he returns home to live with Frau Holtzapfel, he cannot overcome the guilt of surviving when his brother did not. He eventually commits suicide by hanging himself.

Hans Hubermann

Hans Hubermann is Liesel's foster father, her reading teacher, and eventually the most significant person in her life. He is a tall, quiet man with a gentle nature whose sympathy for Jews results in his being eyed with suspicion by local members of the Nazi Party, as well as by his son, Hans Junior. He agrees to secretly harbor a Jew named Max Vandenburg in his basement, an arrangement that places him and his family in

great danger. Although he escapes death twice as a soldier, he is killed during the Allied bombing of Himmel Street.

Hans Hubermann Junior

Hans Hubermann Junior is the adult son of Hans and Rosa Hubermann. A faithful member of the Nazi Party, he has arguments with his father over the older man's apparent lack of support for Nazism. After one argument, on the day of Hitler's birthday celebration, Hans Junior leaves his parents' house and never returns. He later dies in combat in Russia.

Rosa Hubermann

Rosa Hubermann is Liesel's foster mother and lives on Himmel Street in the small town of Molching with her husband, Hans. She is a brash, strict woman who frequently refers to those around her as filthy pigs. Later, Liesel realizes that Rosa's harsh exterior masks a deep love for the people in her life. Like most of the residents of Himmel Street, she is killed by Allied bombs during an air strike.

Trudy Hubermann

Trudy is the adult daughter of Hans and Rosa Hubermann. She works as a housemaid for a family in Munich and occasionally returns to Molching on holidays to visit her parents. She is quiet but kind, like her father.

Joel Kleinmann

Joel Kleinmann is the Jewish owner of a shoe store in Molching. When his shop is vandalized in 1937, Hans Hubermann paints over a slur that has been written on his door.

Walter Kugler

Walter Kugler is a childhood friend of Max Vandenburg's. The two often fist-fought each other as part of a friendly rivalry. When Max faces persecution and possible imprisonment as a Jew, Kugler—who is not a Jew and therefore safe from the reach of Nazis—hides Max for nearly two years. When Kugler finds out he is being relocated to Poland, he meets with Hans Hubermann to see if Hans will help Max hide.

Liesel Meminger

Liesel Meminger, the main character in *The Book Thief*, is a girl who is left in the care of a foster family at a young age. Her brother dies on the way to the foster home, and at the cemetery where he is buried, Liesel sees a book resting in the snow. She takes it, and thus begins her career as a book thief. Ilsa Hermann catches her stealing a book and invites her to borrow more books from her massive library. Liesel becomes an avid reader, and Ilsa Hermann eventually encourages her to write her own book. She does, working in the basement of her foster family's home, where she once spent time with Max Vandenburg, a Jew in hiding. One night, while Liesel is reading over her finished book in the basement, Allied forces bomb Himmel Street, killing everyone except for Liesel. She is then taken in and raised by Ilsa Hermann and her husband, the mayor. The book she has written, lost in the rubble of Himmel Street, is found by Death and kept as an example of how humans are as capable of wonderful things as they are of horrible things.

Paula Meminger

Liesel's biological mother, Paula Meminger, leaves Liesel with a foster family in Munich and, though Liesel later tries to contact her, disappears. Liesel later figures out that it is likely she was taken away by Hitler for being a Communist.

Werner Meminger

Werner Meminger, Liesel's younger brother, dies after having a coughing fit on the train journey to Munich with his mother and sister. Liesel and her mother bury the boy at a local cemetery before continuing their journey; this cemetery is where Liesel steals her first book, *The Grave Digger's Handbook*.

Tommy Müller

Tommy Müller is a boy who lives on Himmel Street and goes to school with Liesel and Rudy. Plagued by chronic ear infections and scarred by several related operations, Tommy is partially deaf and prone to facial twitches. Rudy Steiner stands up for Tommy during Nazi Youth activities after he fails to hear commands, and both boys are frequently punished together. Like the others on Himmel Street, he is killed during the Allied bombing.

Pfiffikus

Pfiffikus is a foul-mouthed old man who lives on Himmel Street. No one seems to know his real name, but he is called Pfiffikus because he constantly whistles a tune as he walks. He is one of the Himmel Street residents who later shares the Fiedlers' basement during air raids.

Boris Schipper

Sergeant Boris Schipper is Hans Hubermann's commanding officer when he is called to serve as a clean-up soldier during World War II. After Hans is injured when their transport truck rolls over, Schipper—who likes Hans due to his generosity when he wins at cards—recommends that Hans be allowed to return home and work in an office in Munich.

Ludwig Schmeikl

Ludwig Schmeikl is a boy in Liesel's class who teases her for being unable to read during her first months in Molching. One day during recess, after he relentlessly insults her, Liesel snaps and gives him a serious beating. The two later make amends during the bonfire at Hitler's birthday celebration.

Stephan Schneider

Stephan Schneider is the officer in charge of Hans Hubermann and Erik Vandenburg's unit during their service in World War I. One day, he offers one soldier a chance to perform a non-combat-related task. Knowing that the other men will face the possibility of death, Erik recommends Hans for the job.

Alex Steiner

Alex Steiner is Rudy Steiner's father. He works as a tailor and owns his own clothing store in Molching. When Nazi officials want to take Rudy to a special officer's school due to his athletic and academic prowess, Alex refuses to let him go. Because of this, he is sent off to help with the war effort. Though he survives, his entire family is killed by the bombing of Himmel Street.

Kurt Steiner

Kurt Steiner is Rudy Steiner's older brother. When Rudy begins to have trouble with Frans Deutscher, Kurt manages to get Rudy transferred to a different Hitler Youth division.

Rudy Steiner

Rudy Steiner is Liesel's best friend, frequent companion, and occasional partner in thievery. He often looks out for Liesel and frequently attempts—unsuccessfully—to get her to kiss him. Rudy is terrorized by his Hitler Youth leader, Franz Deutscher; after switching Hitler Youth groups, however, he excels at both athletics and academics. Nazi officials notice this and ask his parents to allow him to attend a special Nazi officer's school they are creating. Rudy's parents refuse to let him go. He dies with his mother and siblings when the bombs are dropped on Himmel Street.

Erik Vandenburg

Erik Vandenburg is Hans Hubermann's closest friend. The two served together during World War I. Vandenburg, a Jew, teaches Hans how to play the accordion and is responsible for Hans surviving when Vandenburg and everyone else in their unit are killed in combat: he saves Hans by recommending him for a noncombat project. Hans keeps Vandenburg's accordion and promises his wife that he will do whatever he can to repay the debt he owes to Vandenburg for saving his life.

Max Vandenburg

Max Vandenburg, the son of Erik Vandenburg, is a Jew who is taken in by Hans Hubermann. He lives for a time in the Hubermanns' basement and becomes close friends with Liesel. He makes Liesel two books of stories and sketches. Eventually, he leaves the Hubermanns' basement because he fears capture. Later, he is indeed captured, and Liesel sees him being marched through town on the way to a concentration camp. Max survives, and after the war he reunites with Liesel.

Reinhold Zucker

Reinhold Zucker is a fellow soldier in Hans's unit during World War II. When playing cards, he is a gloating winner and a sore loser. After Hans takes all of his cigarettes (used in place of money), Zucker gets angry and holds a grudge against him. Later, Zucker forces Hans to change seats with him on the transport truck as they head out to duty. The truck rolls over, and Zucker is the only one on board who is killed.

THEMES

Storytelling

Perhaps the most important theme found in *The Book Thief* is the power of stories. Most of the major events in the story revolve around this theme. Even Hitler's rise to power, it is suggested, is largely the result of the popularity of his autobiography, *Mein Kampf*. Later, the power of this book is used against the Nazi cause: Hans hides the key he sends to Max inside a copy of it, knowing that no one would suspect the sender (or receiver) of such a book to be engaging in suspicious activities. The book serves a final purpose when Max tears out its pages and paints over them to create his own stories.

For Liesel, her first book helps her hold on to the memory of her dead brother and absent mother. It is also the gateway for Liesel to forge a loving relationship with Hans, who teaches her how to read using the book. Stories later bind Liesel to Max, who creates his own homemade books as gifts to her since he has nothing else to offer. Ilsa Hermann is tied to Liesel by books as well: she spies the girl stealing one from the burning remains of the bonfire, and later invites her into her massive library. Their relationship is almost ended by written words—the letter Ilsa gives her for Rosa Hubermann, terminating her employment—and is also saved by them when Ilsa writes Liesel a letter of apology and gives her a dictionary.

Finally, stories save Liesel's life. Because she is in the basement, rereading her work on her own memoir, she is the only survivor on Himmel Street when the Allied bombs are dropped. It is this book that leads Death to remember and share Liesel's story with the reader.

The novel, however, also depicts certain limitations to the power of stories and the written word. For Hans, letters are insufficient to convey his thoughts and emotions while he is away as a soldier. Also, books are dependent upon one thing for their power: a reader. The books lining the walls of Ilsa Hermann's library serve no function—and indeed, the room itself appears cold and lifeless—until Liesel begins reading there. Liesel's own story is never read by another living soul and is tossed onto a pile of trash after the bombing. It is very nearly lost before Death spots it and saves it.

Dualism

Dualism is the presence of different—often opposing—forces or traits in a single thing or person. Duality is used throughout *The Book Thief* to emphasize both the wonderful and terrible possibilities of humankind.

This natural dualism is shown in nearly every character, including the most virtuous. Liesel herself is, as the title suggests, a thief;

TOPICS FOR FURTHER STUDY

- One of the most important and tragic events in *The Book Thief* is the nighttime air bombing of Himmel Street by Allied forces. Indeed, World War II was the first war to feature large-scale bombings of nonmilitary targets, also known as "strategic bombing." Research the topic of strategic bombing during World War II. Who engaged in it, for what reasons, and how were the targets chosen? What did this accomplish, and what were the consequences? In your opinion, was the practice justified by what it accomplished? Do you think the bombing of civilian targets is justified in other situations? Why or why not? In an oral report accompanied by a presentation with multimedia or visual support (such as graphs showing civilian casualty figures), summarize your findings and take a position on the issue of strategic bombing.

- A popular childhood chant states, "Sticks and stones may break my bones, but names will never hurt me." Victims of insults are often told that the offense is "just words." Under most circumstances in the United States, the accepted definition of assault is that it begins not when someone shouts abuse at another person, but when physical contact is made. The main message of *The Book Thief*, however, is rather opposite: that words are among the most powerful tools known to humankind. Do you think words hold the same power as physical action? Why or why not? Provide examples—from your personal experience or from historical research—to support your point in a reflective essay.

- The Hitler Youth organization was meant to indoctrinate young Germans in the ideas and beliefs of the Nazi Party. Enrolling in the Hitler Youth was made mandatory in 1939, though enforcement was often lax; many young people, as shown in *The Book Thief*, thought the organization was beneficial only as an athletic or social organization, and ignored or dismissed its ideological underpinnings. After the end of World War II, however, many members of the Hitler Youth were persecuted for their implied support of the Nazis. Watch the movie *Swing Kids* (1993), about young adults coming of age in Nazi Germany, paying close attention to the significance of characters' participation in Hitler Youth groups. Do you think it is fair to condemn young people who participated in the Hitler Youth as supporters of Nazism? What about adults who were drafted to fight for Nazi Germany? In your opinion, at what point is the statement "I was just doing what I was forced to do" not an acceptable reason for unethical action? Giving consideration to these questions and others, write an essay comparing the depictions of the Hitler Youth in *The Book Thief* and *Swing Kids*.

- Books, stories, and words play significant roles in the upkeep of morale and even in the survival of characters in *The Book Thief*. Read *Balzac and the Little Chinese Seamstress* (2000), a novel by Dai Sijie that is suitable for young adults, and consider the role played by literature in the lives of his protagonists during China's Cultural Revolution. Write an essay comparing and contrasting the influence of stories on the characters in Zusak's and Sijie's novels.

---

taken out of the context of her life, many of her actions would be considered immoral or worthy of punishment. She steals books, food, and even money from her foster mother, and she destroys one of Ilsa Hermann's books. Hans Hubermann, described as having eyes "made of kindness," strikes Liesel hard across the face when she makes a disparaging statement about Hitler in public. He later threatens her with awful consequences if she ever reveals the secret of Max Vandenburg. He does these things for her protection, and he does them reluctantly; however, this illustrates the potential within even the most virtuous people to hurt those they love.

Rosa Hubermann is a clearer example of duality. She is brash, insulting, and speaks venomously of nearly everyone with whom she comes into contact—especially her husband, Hans. When Hans is conscripted to serve in the war, however, her true feelings about him are revealed: Liesel discovers her sitting on the edge of her bed, cradling his accordion—an instrument she previously seemed to despise—and silently praying for his safe return. Similarly, though she constantly refers to Liesel as "*Saumensch*," Liesel eventually realizes that boundless love exists just beneath the superficial insult.

Duality is perhaps most dramatically shown in Death's observations of humans. Seeing people's lives end day after day, often at the hands of other people, Death notes that he is "constantly overestimating and underestimating the human race." In his final conversation with Liesel, he states about humans, "I wanted to ask her how the same thing could be so ugly and so glorious, and its words and stories so damning and brilliant."

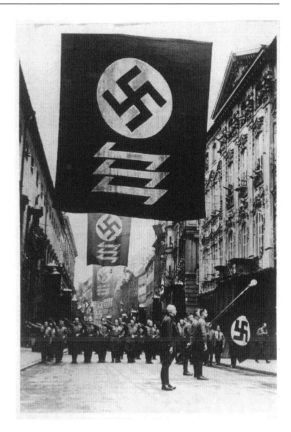

The Book Thief is set in Nazi Germany. (© Mary Evans Picture Library / Alamy)

Fate

Through cause and effect as well as chance, characters in *The Book Thief* are sometimes depicted as deserving of their fates owing to their past actions. But on the whole, as told from Death's perspective, the book suggests that the universal fate of all human beings, an end to life, is simply unavoidable. As the narrator, Death takes great pains to delineate the interconnected nature of the actions and reactions of the characters. Although many events might be described as lucky or unlucky occurrences, their causes are nearly always revealed. Hans Hubermann, for example, manages to avoid death twice during military service—once during World War I, and again during World War II. The first time, he is saved because his friend Erik Vandenburg recommends him for a noncombat assignment; the indebtedness he feels to Erik, who dies that day, eventually results in him taking in Erik's son Max, a Jew in hiding, twenty years later. This in turn causes dramatic changes in the lives of Liesel and Rosa

as well. At the same time, Hans's friendship with Max results in an enduring sympathy for persecuted Jews, which ultimately leads to Max having to leave the Hubermann's basement for fear of discovery by Nazis suspicious of Hans. It also leads Hans back to military duty, pressed into service as a sort of punishment for his sympathizing with Jews.

Similarly, Hans escapes death a second time because he beats his fellow soldiers at cards—a game largely of chance. Even though he is gracious and offers some of his winnings back to the other players, his win angers another soldier, who later forces Hans to change seats with him on their transport truck. During that trip, the truck rolls over, and the other soldier—sitting where Hans would have sat—is the only casualty. In addition, Hans's generosity when winning at cards persuades his sergeant to recommend that he be able to return home to his family. This lucky turn of events results in Hans being present on Himmel Street when the

Allied bombs are dropped, resulting in his death. However kindhearted all the people of Himmel Street may be, only Liesel is lucky enough to escape the fate of an untimely death in the bombing.

STYLE

Memoir

The Book Thief is written in the form of a memoir. A memoir is a personal record of events in the writer's own life. Hitler's *Mein Kampf*, mentioned often in the novel, is a memoir, as is the book that Liesel writes about her own experiences. In addition, *The Book Thief* itself often serves as a memoir for its narrator, Death; in addition to Death's own experiences with Liesel and the people in her life, there are also sections throughout the book labeled "Death's Diary" that relate brief glimpses of the narrator's other grim work during World War II.

Foreshadowing and Flash-Forwards

Foreshadowing, or the suggestion of what will happen later in the story, is used extensively in *The Book Thief*. The narrator frequently hints of what is to come later, as when he states in the prologue, "I saw the book thief three times." The author also uses flash-forwards, or glimpses at events that take place beyond the story's current time frame. For example, after revealing how many times he saw the book thief, the narrator goes on to provide detailed descriptions of each occasion—though two of those events will not take place until near the end of the book. Another example of foreshadowing occurs when Liesel convinces herself that Ilsa Hermann did not see her take a book from the bonfire. The narrator quickly offers, "The mayor's wife had seen her, all right. She was just waiting for the right moment." Similarly, when Viktor Chemmel threatens to make Rudy pay for spitting at him, the narrator informs the reader, "It took him approximately five months to turn his statement into a true one." The act of vengeance occurs twenty-five pages later.

The foreshadowing in *The Book Thief* often explicitly reveals the fates of the characters. The narrator tells the reader in no uncertain terms what will happen, as when he states about Reinhold Zucker shortly after introducing him, "He would die with his mouth open." The narrator also makes clear that Rudy Steiner will die, though the circumstances of his death are kept vague until the event occurs.

Stories within Stories

The Book Thief contains many stories within the main tale being told by the narrator. These include brief asides by the narrator that touch upon events not directly related to Liesel's story. In addition, the books Liesel reads are mostly fictional works, and the basic plot of each is described for the reader, often along with snippets of text from the book.

The clearest examples of stories within the story, however, are the ones Max creates for Liesel. They are even presented in a different format than the rest of the book, in what is meant to represent Max's own handwritten and hand-drawn work.

HISTORICAL CONTEXT

The Rise of the Nazi Party and Hitler Youth

The Nazi Party, or the National Socialist German Workers' Party, rose to power in the wake of the economic turmoil Germany suffered after being defeated in World War I. Founded in 1918, the party focused on a platform of national unity and pride, coupled with the darker goals of driving Jews out of the country and expanding Germany's borders at the expense of neighboring countries. Adolf Hitler became a party member and quickly rose to the highest ranks due to his ambition and oratory skills. He attempted to seize control of the German government in 1923 but was unsuccessful and instead spent a little over one year in jail. During this time, he wrote *Mein Kampf* (My Struggle), a book that offered a positive and persuasive view of his actions and political beliefs.

As economic conditions worsened in the years that followed—in part due to the Great Depression, which had a drastic effect on the global economy—Hitler's promises of a prosperous Germany won over a large percentage of the population. By the early 1930s, the Nazi Party had won substantial power in the Reichstag, or German parliament, not by force but by election. Hitler, however—despite his popularity—was not elected. Instead, as the governing bodies of Germany fell into chaos, the president

Death is the narrator of The Book Thief, *and Zusak presents a very different characterization of Death than the standard Grim Reaper stereotype.* (© Mayovskyy Andrew | Shutterstock.com)

appointed Hitler chancellor of Germany. He quickly seized control of government and military offices, silencing his critics and any other social elements he considered undesirable.

The Hitler Youth was created in 1922, composed primarily of the children of Nazi Party members. Like the Nazi Party itself, the organization grew slowly but steadily until 1930, when membership expanded dramatically; between 1930 and 1934, Hitler Youth membership skyrocketed from 26,000 to over 3.5 million. As Michael H. Kater points out in *Hitler Youth*, "Many if not most of the youth cohort for the period of the 1920s and very early 1930s felt cheated out of what chances they had thought were theirs and increasingly looked to radical alternatives." The group was briefly banned in 1932 but was quickly reinstated in recognition of Hitler's influence and popularity.

The organization was meant to serve as premilitary training, and older members of the Hitler Youth almost inevitably went on to become Nazi soldiers fighting on the front lines or officers in charge of expanding Hitler Youth membership. Equivalent organizations for females and for younger children were also formed; these more closely resembled activity clubs than military groups, though they also provided the Nazi Party with an opportunity to indoctrinate youngsters with their beliefs. Although Hitler Youth began with voluntary membership, it was later required for all eligible German children.

As the German war effort faltered in the early 1940s, the Nazi Party began to call up younger and younger members of the Hitler Youth to active duty in the national militia. Members as young as fourteen were called upon to serve in antiaircraft units and were killed in the increased bombings within Germany's borders. With the defeat of Germany in 1945 by Allied forces, the Hitler Youth and its related organizations were quickly disbanded. Many German children who had been forced into compulsory Hitler Youth programs were often stigmatized later in life due to their involvement with organizations so closely associated with Nazism.

The Allied Bombing of German Cities

As Allied forces waged war against Germany and the other Axis powers during World War II, British (and later American) air forces began bombing raids on German-occupied areas of Europe that were not considered combat locations. The justification for these bombings was twofold: to begin with, the targets for these bombings were often strategic pieces of German industry or infrastructure, meaning that their destruction would weaken Germany's ability to continue supporting its troops with weaponry and other essentials; also, it was believed that destruction of some nonmilitary targets would serve to weaken the morale of German citizens and erode support for Hitler and the Nazi Party.

Between the British Royal Air Force and the United States Air Force, over 1.5 million tons of bombs were dropped on Germany between 1939 and 1945. Munich, the large city near which Liesel and her foster family live in *The Book Thief*, was subjected to over seventy separate bombing attacks by air. One of the worst bombings, however, was reserved for the city of Dresden in February 1945. The city was obliterated in two days of nonstop attacks, as the bombs set off fires that raged uncontrolled in their wake. Conservative estimates of civilian casualties in Dresden—deaths of those not involved in combat in any way—exceed 20,000, and some believe that as many as 40,000 German citizens were killed.

In all, historians estimate that approximately 600,000 German civilians were killed by Allied bombings during the war—dwarfing the estimated loss of around 14,000 British citizens due to German air attacks. One in every nine German civilian casualties was a child. Because of these startling statistics, the practice of bombing in city areas has been a source of great controversy ever since.

CRITICAL OVERVIEW

When *The Book Thief* was published in 2005 as a book for children and young adults, it met with initial skepticism regarding its length (over five hundred pages) and its subject matter (a child living in Nazi Germany surrounded by death, as narrated by Death). However, reviews for the novel were overwhelmingly positive, which helped to propel the book to the status of best seller.

Most of the praise for the work centered on the resonant power of the story, though the author's skill with language was also complimented in many reviews. Francisca Goldsmith, in a review for *School Library Journal*, calls the book "an extraordinary narrative." Goldsmith observes that the author "not only creates a mesmerizing and original story but also writes with poetic syntax." Claire E. Gross, reviewing the novel for the *Horn Book* magazine, refers to it as a "deeply affecting tale." She remarks, "Exquisitely written and memorably populated, Zusak's poignant tribute to words, survival, and their curiously inevitable entwinement is a tour de force to be not just read but inhabited."

Michael Cart, in a brief recommendation from *Booklist*, expresses pleasant surprise over the novel's achievements: "Who would have thought that Death could be such an engaging—even sympathetic—narrator? And has there ever been a better celebration of the lifesaving and affirming power of books and the reading of them?" In a review for *School Libarary Journal*, Barbara Wysocki compliments the "richly evocative imagery and compelling characters" of the novel, while April Brannon, writing for the *Journal of Adolescent and Adult Literacy*, points out the "surreal and often stunning" imagery created by the author.

Some reviews of the book included brief cautions about the subject matter and its appropriateness for young readers. Brannon notes that the book "is set in the bleakest of circumstances but is a surprisingly hopeful story about the atrocities that occurred during the Nazi years in Germany." She suggests that the book "would work best with high school audiences." Goldsmith seems to agree, stating that the novel "deserves the attention of sophisticated teen and adult readers."

Lev Grossman, in a review for *Time*, recommends the book for "more ambitious younger readers." He specifically notes that the opening pages of the book are "rather challenging." Grossman further notes, "Zusak doesn't sugarcoat anything, but he makes his ostensibly gloomy subject bearable the same way Kurt Vonnegut did in *Slaughterhouse-Five*: with grim, darkly consoling humor." A reviewer in *Publishers Weekly* calls Zusak's novel "a challenging book in both length and subject, and best suited to sophisticated older readers." The reviewer also notes that despite the often dark subject matter, the author's "playfulness with language leavens the horror and makes the theme even more resonant." The reviewer does point out, however, that the narrator "has a bad habit of forecasting" upcoming events. Hazel Rochman, in her largely positive review for *Booklist*, concedes that the novel has "too much commentary at the outset, and too much switching from past to present time."

The Book Thief earned the top spot on the *New York Times* children's best-seller list and remained on the list for over five months. It has also been a number-one seller in Ireland, Taiwan, and Brazil. The book was named a Michael L. Printz Honor Book in 2007, and it earned the Kathleen Mitchell Award and the Teen Book Award from the Association of Jewish Libraries. Hailed as a phenomenal title for adults and younger readers alike, *The Book Thief* has continued to enjoy widespread popularity into the 2010s.

CRITICISM

Greg Wilson

Wilson has written essays and articles examining a wide range of topics related to popular culture, from contemporary best-selling fiction to World War II memoirs. In the following essay, he argues that the author's use of Death as the narrator of The Book Thief *conflicts with the most basic theme of the novel.*

Markus Zusak's young-adult novel *The Book Thief* has received wide acclaim for its unique portrayal of the life of a young girl growing up in Nazi Germany. Upon its publication, critics lauded its characters and story; Hazel Rochman of *Booklist* compliments the book's "astonishing characters," while Francisca Goldsmith of *School Library Journal* calls the work "an extraordinary narrative." Many other critics also celebrated the book's unique narrator—Death—and his playful presentation of the tale. Indeed, Zusak's story and characters are memorable, and even haunting. In addition, he employs numerous techniques to convey the otherworldly nature of the narrator. However, these techniques amount to a narratorial intrusion in the story that weakens its most basic—and most important—message.

Death is obviously not just any old character, and it stands to reason that his "voice" as

> ANOTHER CHARACTERISTIC OF THE NOVEL, AGAIN SENSIBLY ATTRIBUTED TO THE NARRATOR'S INHUMAN NATURE, IS THE CONSTANT USE OF FORESHADOWING. SOMETIMES THE FORESHADOWING PRECEDES THE EVENTS THEMSELVES BY MERELY A PARAGRAPH."

conveyed in the novel should have something of the ineffable about it. Zusak accomplishes this in several ways, one of which is his use of synesthetic and otherwise "impossible" descriptions.

Synesthesia is a condition in which a victim suffers from an uncontrolled commingling or interconnection of the senses. For example, a person with synesthesia may be able to "see" colors when certain sounds are heard. Neurologist Richard E. Cytowic, in his book *Synesthesia: A Union of the Senses*, sums up the condition:

> Is synesthesia a real perception of a sense datum or just a projection? Is there actually the rare individual who can *really* hear colors and taste shapes? Yes, there is, and his existence does not rely on our wanting to believe the impossible.

Zusak uses synesthetic descriptions—combining seemingly contradictory sensory information—throughout *The Book Thief*. Synesthesia is suggested by the narrator's connection of certain colors to the deaths of different people, but it also appears more explicitly, as when the narrator refers to his appreciation for death-colors in the following way: "A billion or so flavors, none of them quite the same, and a sky to slowly suck on." Later, when Liesel discovers the fate of her biological parents, there is another example: "Even Papa's music was the color of darkness." When Liesel enters Ilsa Hermann's library after Christmas, the narrator states, "The room tasted like sugar and dough, and thousands of pages."

Similarly, the narrator also associates sensory information with the abstract, making for descriptions that are impossible but evocative. This is seen in the chapter heading "The Smell of Friendship." Another example can be found in Liesel's farewell with Max Vandenburg: "She

WHAT DO I READ NEXT?

- *I Am the Messenger* is a 2002 novel by Zusak. Unlike *The Book Thief*, it is a contemporary tale; it concerns a young man named Ed Kennedy who becomes an accidental hero when he stops a bank robbery. Soon after, he begins receiving messages prompting him to perform other acts of justice and beneficence. The novel was chosen as the Book of the Year by the Children's Book Council of Australia, where it was originally published as *The Messenger*.

- Anne Frank's memoir *The Diary of a Young Girl* (1947) is one of the best-known personal accounts of a Jew who lived in hiding during World War II. Anne's account was actually written during the ordeal, as her family and a few others lived in a hidden portion of a building in Amsterdam, Netherlands, during the Nazi occupation. Though Anne herself died in the Bergen-Belsen concentration camp in 1945—days before Allies arrived to save the remaining prisoners—her tale has endured as a testament to the spirit of survival shown by victims of Nazi Germany.

- *In My Hands: Memories of a Holocaust Rescuer* (1999), by Irene Gut Opdyke with Jennifer Armstrong, is an autobiographical account of a Polish woman who risked her life to help save Jews in her Nazi-occupied homeland. Forced to work as a waitress for German officers, she used her position to gain information about German plans and shared it with the local Jews, with whom she sympathized for the hellish treatment they experienced. Later, after becoming a maid for a German major, she used the officer's own villa as a secret hideout for a dozen Jews.

- In *Number the Stars* (1989), by Lois Lowry, which is suitable for younger teens, ten-year-old protagonist Annemarie Johansen and her friend Ellen Rosen cope with the inconveniences and dangers of the Nazi occupation of Denmark, as Ellen must go into hiding.

- *Slaughterhouse-Five* (1969), by Kurt Vonnegut, is a dark, funny look at a man named Billy Pilgrim who has become "unstuck" in time thanks to a race of aliens. Throughout the book, Pilgrim experiences snippets of events from throughout his life, one of the most significant being as a prisoner of war who lives through the firebombing of Dresden during World War II.

- A different facet of World War II is presented in J. G. Ballard's *Empire of the Sun* (1984), based on the true story of the author's boyhood internment in a Japanese-controlled camp outside of Shanghai, China. The book was adapted to film by director Steven Spielberg in 1987.

could smell his breath of goodbye." It also appears in Reinhold Zucker's far more pedestrian "smell of victory." Speaking of Frau Diller, the narrator notes, "Her voice was like suicide, landing with a clunk at Liesel's feet." Speaking of the uneasiness one experiences while harboring a Jew: "The fear is shiny." Describing Hans Hubermann's eyes: "They were made of kindness, and silver."

If one assumes that the author's extensive use of such unusual description is meant to reflect the voice of his narrator, then perhaps this would help to suggest the narrator's unique, otherworldly state of being. The problem is, descriptions such as these are deliberately showy; they stop the reader's eyes as they scan, either forcing the reader to try and visualize something one cannot or asking the reader to acknowledge that they are, indeed, clever turns of phrase. They interrupt the story in order to showcase the narrator's voice (or the author's).

Another characteristic of the novel, again sensibly attributed to the narrator's inhuman nature, is the constant use of foreshadowing.

Sometimes the foreshadowing precedes the events themselves by merely a paragraph. Some examples are simply confusing, as when the narrator mentions—just after Liesel arrives in Munich at the beginning of her tale—a half-dozen events that will not occur for hundreds of pages. Nearly every major event in the novel is foretold in some way; for example, scarcely halfway through the novel, we are told about Rudy Steiner, "He did not deserve to die the way he did," even though he does not die for another two years. Many foreshadowed moments are detailed enough to qualify as flash-forwards, such as Death's descriptions of his encounters with Liesel in the prologue.

This technique would seem to suggest a narrator who either has trouble with human conceptions of time, or has so memorized the tale of Liesel that he cannot help but flit from piece to piece, excitedly forecasting upcoming events the way a theatergoer who has already seen a movie gently nudges the audience member next to him and whispers, "Ooh, here comes a great part." In either case, the device itself seems to make sense for the choice of narrator. However, this also tends to rob the story of much of its surprise and impact.

Another technique of the narrator's—again giving the author the benefit of the doubt and assuming he meant it to reflect his narrator's voice, and not his own—is the repeated use of callouts within the body of the story. They occur on almost every page as centered and headlined blocks of bolded text. They are clearly meant as asides to the story at hand, with titles like "A SMALL QUESTION AND ITS ANSWER" or "SOME FACTS ABOUT RUDY STEINER." However, most of these attention-seeking blurbs would have fit quite naturally in the regular flow of text, without the showy headlines. And some others are such deliberate attempts at artful turns of phrase that they just do not fit at all, such as the callout titled "A PAINTED IMAGE" that refers to Liesel seeing her foster mother sadly wearing her foster father's accordion after he is called away to war. It reads in full: "Rosa with accordion. Moonlight on Dark. 5′1″ x Instrument x Silence." Obviously there is no painted image, and this is just a pretentious way of framing the scene as if it were a piece of art identified by a placard on the gallery wall. One can choose to view this as an author's attempt to experiment with description, or as the narrator's attempt to do the same. Either

way, it fails; worse yet, it stomps on an otherwise touching moment when Liesel realizes the true depths of her foster parents' relationship.

The narrator also seems able to describe in vivid detail scenes at which he was not present. He clearly indicates in the beginning that he has only seen the book thief three times (though this is not quite true, since he also sees her when she dies as an old woman). Yet the remainder of the book includes extensive descriptions of events that even Liesel was not present for, such as the flashbacks of Hans Hubermann and Max Vandenburg. In addition, many of the narrator's descriptions seem to presume knowledge inside the heads of characters other than Liesel. Even if we allow that Death is telling us a story based on Liesel's memoir—which is by and large the only source of information he would have access to—we would also have to concede that these descriptions are then based upon Liesel's recollections and interpretations. It would seem, then, that the story we are being told consists entirely of at least secondhand and largely thirdhand information (Death interpreting Liesel's words interpreting another character's behavior or words).

This begs the question: what purpose does the narrator serve? Why not do away with the device of the narrator altogether? Why do we, the readers, not get to enjoy Liesel's words ourselves? We see very brief snippets, and we are offered a rather lame excuse about the book having deteriorated from so many read-throughs by the narrator that it has fallen apart.

The reason this becomes problematic has to do with the main theme of the novel. The obvious message of *The Book Thief* is simple: words—especially books—are powerful. They can sway a nation, as with Hitler's *Mein Kampf*; they can serve as a link to past experiences, as *The Grave Digger's Handbook* does for Liesel; they can capture the imagination so thoroughly that a group of terrified Germans huddled in a basement briefly forget about the threat of bombs dropping upon them; they can literally save a person's life, as they do for both Max Vandenburg and Liesel.

It is disappointing that this underlying conceit of the novel—that words wield such amazing power, especially in book form—is undermined by the fact that we as readers are kept at a distance from Liesel's own words—her own powerful book. What better way to illustrate the power of books than to give us access to Liesel's own?

Instead we are given an intermediary—and a showy, contrived one at that—who gives us a secondhand version of her tale.

Why did Zusak choose to tell the story in a way that undermines its most basic theme? In an interview taken from the reader's guide of the paperback edition of the book, Zusak states, "I thought, 'Here's a book set during war. Everyone says war and death are best friends.' Death is ever-present during war, so here was the perfect choice to narrate *The Book Thief.*" The only problem with this line of thinking is that the book is not *about* war—it is about the power of books. Based upon the amount of attention the novel earned due to its high-concept narrator, one has to wonder if the idea just so tickled Zusak with its cleverness and audacity—the same way it later tickled many potential readers, who knew almost nothing else about it but were compelled to pick it up—that he found a way to make sure he fit his story into that framework, regardless of how much shoving it took to get it in.

This trick up Zusak's sleeve in *The Book Thief* is a device no less gimmicky than the one Alice Sebold employed in *The Lovely Bones,* coincidentally—or perhaps not—another young-adult novel that achieved great success among adult readers. With Sebold's novel, the gimmick—that the narrator was murdered before the tale begins—masked a comparatively meatless and mawkish story, making it at first appear far better than it actually is. For Zusak's tale, the gimmick of Death as narrator results in a far more serious crime: he takes his own wonderful, resonant story and lessens its impact in exchange for the alluring, self-indulgent rush of high-concept buzzworthiness. It is entirely possible that this made *The Book Thief* more popular; however, it most certainly did not make the book better.

Source: Greg Wilson, Critical Essay on *The Book Thief,* in *Novels for Students,* Gale, Cengage Learning, 2014.

Shannon Maughan

In the following review, Maughan examines the surprisingly steady increase in sales of The Book Thief *since its publication.*

The Book Thief, a novel by Australian author Markus Zusak set in Germany during WWII, was published by Knopf Books for Young Readers to much critical acclaim in March 2006. By early 2007 it had appeared on many Best Books lists and won a Printz Honor.

But what has been truly unusual about *The Book Thief* is that its sales—to adults as well as young readers—have risen steadily since publication. The book is a regular fixture on bestseller lists more than four years later, and it has sold more than 1.5 million copies across print, audio, and e-book formats in North America.

It's a success story that not even Zusak imagined. "I honestly thought it would be my least successful book," he recently told the *Palm Beach Post.* "I thought, 'A book set in Nazi Germany, narrated by Death, and it's 580 pages long. Who wants to read that?' It shows that I know nothing about publishing and what readers want to read."

The folks at Random House have been surprised by the book's trajectory, too, though they were always certain that *The Book Thief* was something special. "We had published Markus's remarkable *I Am the Messenger* the year before, and it did well," said Chip Gibson, president and publisher of Random House Children's Books. "So we were delighted to have another book from this extraordinary Australian writer."

A 10,000–15,000 first printing was initially planned, but that quickly changed, Gibson recalled. "I was on a flight with our sales director, Joan DeMayo, who loved to load up with manuscripts before a trip and then shed pages along the way. She brought *The Book Thief*—and the manuscript was quite fat; carrying it around was a commitment! By the time we landed, Joan could not stop reading. She said, 'We have something amazing,' and insisted that I take it immediately. I had the same reaction. The whole company fell headlong in love with the book and all our expectations were recalibrated."

In Zusak's native Australia *The Book Thief* was marketed as an adult book. Erin Clarke, senior editor at Knopf BFYR, had acquired both *I Am the Messenger* and *The Book Thief* as YA titles, and Gibson believed there was no reason to change that. The strategy was to get readers to read it, regardless of age. Gibson felt strongly that *The Book Thief* was a title that begged to be talked about; one promotional effort included offering free books to book clubs. "It's a book about books, and about the power and resonance of the written word," he said. "It's the kind of book you inhabit, and then you want to tell people where you've been living."

The book club push helped get the ball rolling, but booksellers were in the mix early as well.

"I still have the reader's copy," said Ann Seaton, manager of Hicklebee's in San Jose, Calif. Hicklebee's voted the title its Book of the Year for 2006. "It's a huge favorite, still," said Seaton. "I don't know of anything else that covers all aspects of war from all different angles."

At University Book Store in Seattle, *The Book Thief* nabbed that store's 2007 UBIE Award for the favorite novel of the year, according to children's book buyer Lauren Mayer: "We're pretty upfront about the subject matter, letting people know that there are difficult issues, but the book is so beautifully written and so moving that it deserves to be read."

For Becky Anderson, owner of Anderson Bookshops in Naperville, Ill., "*The Book Thief* has been that perfect read-one that crosses over both ways from adult to young adult and back. New readers to this phenomenal title are coming in all the time."

The Book Thief continues to reach new audiences via such platforms as Community Read programs and the Jewish Community Center festival circuit. This past spring, *The Book Thief* was chosen as the One Book, One Community title for Read Together Palm Beach County. Darlene Kostrub, executive director of the county's Literacy Coalition, said the selection of *The Book Thief*, though it exceeded the group's usual 400-page limit, proved a rousing success. "What really gave Markus a huge fan club here in Palm Beach was his appearance via Skype in May," she said. "We had 500–600 people at the event and Markus was so charming and self-effacing."

And so it goes. Gibson at Random House said that *The Book Thief* has transcended any normal velocity curves. "Sales are pretty steady. We might see a surge for graduation or back to school or Christmas. It ebbs and flows, but never ebbs too far." And Gibson is pleased to go with that flow as long as possible. "There's nothing better or more fun than to start with excitement in-house about a manuscript that's not out of nowhere—but almost—and share it and sell it."

Zusak's next book, a coming-of-age novel called *Bridge of Clay*, is scheduled for 2011, also from Knopf. And in *The Book Thief*'s wake, Gibson noted, "A lot of people are eager to read that."

Source: Shannon Maughan, "It's a Wonderful (Sales) Life: The Staying Power of 'The Book Thief,'" in *Publishers Weekly*, Vol. 257, No. 34, August 30, 2010, p. 16.

Judith Ridge

In the following review, Ridge claims that The Book Thief *delivers a striking message about how differences can and should be accommodated.*

Half a dozen years ago, Markus Zusak, a first-generation Australian of German and Austrian extraction, was being hailed as an important new voice. Grounded in his working-class Sydney roots, Zusak's three early novels—*The Underdog, Fighting Ruben Wolfe* and *Getting the Girl*—were acclaimed for their fresh take on suburban masculinity. The Australian papers were filled with anxious reports about declining reading habits among young males, and Zusak's intelligent but street-smart books for young adults were ardently welcomed.

Now, at the age of 30, Zusak has a new book that may be just as welcome, coming on the heels of last fall's race riots in Sydney's southern suburbs between white locals and Middle Eastern immigrants. *The Book Thief* is set in Germany during WWII, and concerns a German family on the outskirts of Munich that hides a young Jewish man. At a time when Australia is struggling with its own tolerance issues, *The Book Thief* delivers a message about how differences can and should be accommodated. Interestingly, in Australia, Zusak's new book is being aimed this time not at teenagers, but at adults.

Zusak has already won a number of prestigious literary awards, including a Printz Honor for *I Am the Messenger* (Knopf, 2005), which also won the Children's Book Council Book of the Year award for older readers in Australia, as well as several state literary awards. The appeal of his early books, at least in Australia, was in part due to his honest appraisal of working-class life. Zusak grew up in the suburban area known as The Shire, where the recent rioting was centered, and he has just moved back there after living elsewhere in Sydney for a few years. "I figure they need more people with names like Zusak down there," he observed with a wry grin as we walked to find a quiet coffee shop on a busy shopping strip.

As young post-WWII immigrants, Zusak's parents arrived in Australia knowing little English, and they weren't really book people, says Zusak—except in the sense that they encouraged their four children to read ("I've got every Dr Seuss book there is," Zusak says). His parent are, however, storytellers, and *The Book Thief* found its initial inspiration in two stories Zusak remembers being told as a child. The first was of a tale his mother told of Munich being bombed. "Everything was red, like the sky was on fire. That was a memory that I could see really clearly as a child, a very visual image," he says. The second story was of a teenage boy who took pity on an emaciated Jew being forced through the streets, and offered him some bread. Both were whipped by a soldier who witnessed this act of compassion.

Zusak originally planned *The Book Thief* to be a 100-page novella based on these two memories, but, "Once I started writing—it took three years to write—one thing turned into another. Once the ideas came they wouldn't stop."

PW called *The Book Thief* "an achievement—challenging in both length and subject." Indeed it is, clocking in at 560 pages and featuring as its narrator "Death." Death tells the tale of a girl, Liesel, orphaned when her Communist father is taken away to a concentration camp. Liesel goes to live with Hans and Rosa Hubermann in a small town outside Munich. Hans teaches Liesel to read, and thereafter she steals and reads every book she can get her hands on. The Hubermanns also take in Max, a young Jewish man, and the relationship between Liesel and Max forms the emotional and thematic core of the novel.

In writing about Nazi Germany, Zusak was aware that he was entering well-traveled terrain. Hence his decision to give the narration not to a living person but to Death itself. "I wrote the sentence, 'I have seen the colour of time on three occasions,'" he explains. "I wrote this about three deaths, and Death himself was the narrator." So he went with it.

The language of the book is striking. "I wanted Death to talk in a way that humans don't speak," Zusak says. "One thing I stood by [in the editing process] was when Death says things like 'the trees who stood' or 'the sky who was this color.' He refers to the sky and the trees and the clouds as though they're colleagues."

Zusak, who grew up speaking German—a rough, working-class argot, as in the book—is at pains to clarify that while the novel involves German characters sympathetic to and supportive of Jews, it isn't a pro-German tract, nor an apologia. "I'm not trying to get people to re-examine their views on Nazi Germany," the author says. "All I'm trying to do, like every writer does, is to tell a story that hasn't been told in this way before. It's the hope to examine one small story in the big story that we already know.

The Book Thief was published last September in Australia to wide acclaim, and was positioned by Pan Macmillan as Zusak's adult debut. Random House here has chosen to publish it as a YA, a situation that Zusak is comfortable with. "For a teenage audience, it's clearly for sophisticated readers. You just hope it gets into the right person's hands, whatever their age," he says.

Like most any writer, Zusak hopes that readers will "love the characters." But he also hopes that readers will appreciate his attempt at writing a different kind of book, where death is not a hidden theme but a dominant voice. "Whether it worked or not, you just want people to see the attempt," Zusak says. "You want them to see you've tried, and that you did try to give them something fresh."

Source: Judith Ridge, "Death Gets Its Say: Markus Zusak's New Novel Features an Unusual Narrator in Nazi Germany," in *Publishers Weekly*, Vol. 253, No. 8, February 20, 2006, p. 61.

Katherine Rushton

In the following article, Zusak discusses with Rushton the "crossover" appeal of The Book Thief.

As the author of *The Book Thief*, a harrowing crossover novel set in Nazi Germany, Markus Zusak cuts a surprising figure. He is a bright-eyed, straightforward Aussie guy, casual in his demeanour and endearingly uncomfortable on the subject of his book.

"At home, no one would ever get up and say: 'This is a great achievement.' You just don't do that," he says in his Antipodean lilt. "I see all that is wrong with [the book] now. It's a bit like a photo of yourself where everyone else seems to think you look really good, but you think: 'What, are you just lying?'"

But the book's success as an adult novel in Australia and as a children's title in the US proves it has merit. Random House plans to give it the same treatment as Mark Haddon's *The Curious Incident of the Dog in the Night-time*, and launch it in the UK in January with simultaneous adult and children's editions under Doubleday and Bodley Head.

The Book Thief is an altogether more harrowing tale than Haddon's, woven from the experiences of Zusak's German mother and Austrian father before they emigrated to Sydney after the war. It was originally conceived as a 100-page novella—and, Zusak jokes, likely to be his "least-read book"—but three years of redrafts crafted a 580-page, tear-jerking doorstopper.

"It came about just from the stories I'd heard my whole life," he says. "Stories of cities on fire, and teenage boys giving pieces of bread to starving Jewish people on their way to concentration camps. In almost the same way you learn to speak English or the language you grow up with, that world was in my head. It was given to me on a plate."

Zusak penned three young adult novels before *The Book Thief* and now writes full time, but he used to juggle part-time jobs as a cleaner, tutor and supply teacher. Being in the classroom was an experience he enjoyed, but—crippled by his own gentle manner—he questions his ability. "I don't know if teachers get the stick here that they get at home, but I think you need to have a certain killer instinct to do the job well," he says. "I was pretty bad." Writing was a better fit, and as "essentially quite a lazy person," it is also the occupation that makes him feel "most awake and happy."

Liesel in Love

The book thief after whom his new novel is named is Liesel, a 10-year-old girl who moves to live with foster parents in Molching, near Munich, and develops a habit of filching books from her neighbours and Nazi bonfires. The story focuses on her life in decidedly unheavenly Himmel Street, where she forms close friendships with the exuberant boy next door, Rudy; her accordion-playing foster father, who teaches her to read; and later a Jewish refugee who hides in their basement.

"In a lot of ways, the book is a love story between Liesel and everything around her," says Zusak. "Liesel and the books; Liesel and her foster father; even her foster mother, who can't even bring herself to say that she loves her."

If the formula feels familiar from countless other Holocaust-evacuation tales, Zusak has given it a twist by appointing Death as narrator—an omniscient, witty and reluctant transporter of dead souls, he is bound to work hand in glove with war but pricked by the sadness of his task. "Death is on hand to see all of our disasters, all of our miseries. He is haunted by everything he sees humans do, and he is telling this story to prove to himself that humans are actually worth it."

But if Death feels pangs when he kills the characters he has come to love, Zusak can sympathise: "I was a bit of a mess by the end, there's no other way of saying it. I was sitting there bawling my eyes out as I was making these things happen."

Youth Club

He cried most for Liesel's boy next door, Rudy, who was closely modelled on Zusak's father, and his hilarious recollections of Hitler Youth. "Dad said it was just this rabble," he laughs, recounting failed marching exercises, a far cry from the propaganda reels showing smart columns of boys and girls marching in perfect time. "Some of those experiences my dad went through—like running laps for not getting the Fuhrer's birthday right—those are the stories that I'm interested in: those little pockets where not too many hands have gone in to pull them out."

Zusak is unable to say whether he wrote the book for an adult or a young-adult audience, swearing allegiance "to the truth of the story more than any demographic." But while it certainly presents an emotional challenge for teenage readers, Zusak is convinced that many will appreciate his approach.

"There are some teenage and adult readers who don't need to be patronised," he explains. "We need books for teenagers that say: 'Here is a book for you. It is written in your voice. It is about your concerns in this world we live in today.' But we also need books that say: 'This is for you, but you've got to step up here.' If that's what *The Book Thief* is, I'm all the more happy for that."

Source: Katherine Rushton, "Death Warmed Up," in *Bookseller*, Vol. 18, No. 2, November 17, 2006, p. 1.

SOURCES

Blasingame, James, Cynthia Kiefer, David M. Pegram, Kyle Gillis, Bryan Gillis, April Brannon, and Megan Hoover, "Books for Adolescents," in *Journal of Adolescent & Adult Literacy*, Vol. 49, No. 8, May 2006, pp. 718–27.

Cart, Michael, "'Tis the Season," in *Booklist*, Vol. 103, Nos. 9–10, January 1, 2007, p. 74.

Davis, Richard G., *Bombing the European Axis Powers: A Historical Digest of the Combined Bomber Offensive, 1939–1945*, Air University Press, 2006.

Goldsmith, Francisca, Review of *The Book Thief*, in *School Library Journal*, Vol. 52, No. 3, March 2006, p. 234.

Gross, Claire E., Review of *The Book Thief*, in *Horn Book*, Vol. 82, No. 2, March–April 2006, pp. 199–200.

Grossman, Lev, "5 Great New Books: Dragons! Lip Gloss! Death! There's Life in Teen Books after Harry Potter," in *Time*, Vol. 167, No. 11, March 13, 2006, p. 63.

Harding, Luke, "Germany's Forgotten Victims," in *Guardian* (London, England), October 22, 2003, http://www.guardian.co.uk/world/2003/oct/22/worlddispatch.germany (accessed March 19, 2008).

Kater, Michael H., *Hitler Youth*, Harvard University Press, 2004, p. 6.

Lamers, Richard, "Destroyed Youth: Growing Up in Nazi Germany," Goethe-Institut website, November 2007, http://www.goethe.de/ges/pok/dun/en2744598.htm (accessed March 18, 2008).

Maughan, Shannon, "It's a Wonderful (Sales) Life: The Staying Power of 'The Book Thief,'" in *Publishers Weekly*, Vol. 257, No. 34, August 30, 2010, p. 16.

Rempel, Gerhard, *Hitler's Children: The Hitler Youth and the SS*, University of North Carolina Press, 1989.

Review of *The Book Thief*, in *Publishers Weekly*, Vol. 253, No. 5, January 30, 2006, pp. 70–71.

Rochman, Hazel, Review of *The Book Thief*, in *Booklist*, Vol. 102, Nos. 9–10, January 1, 2006, p. 88.

Wysocki, Barbara, Review of *The Book Thief*, in *School Library Journal*, Vol. 53, No. 3, March 2007, p. 79.

Zusak, Markus, *The Book Thief*, Knopf, 2007.

FURTHER READING

Gottfried, Ted, *Children of the Slaughter: Young People of the Holocaust*, Twenty-First Century Books, 2001.
    This compact volume discusses both the young Jewish victims of the Holocaust and the German young people manipulated through the Hitler Youth. With text presented in capsule format, the book is especially readable for young adults.

Hitler, Adolf, *Mein Kampf*, translated by Ralph Manheim, Educa Books, 2006.
    This book, part autobiography and part political diatribe, reveals the thoughts, motivations, and goals of one of the world's most destructive leaders. Written before his rise to prominence and after his first failed attempt to take over the government, *Mein Kampf* contains the same fervent nationalism, brutality, and racial hatred that later marked the era of Nazi rule. It provides important insight for those interested in understanding the tragic roots of World War II and the Holocaust.

Wall, Donald D., *Nazi Germany and World War II*, 2nd ed., Thomson/Wadsworth, 2003.
    Historian Donald D. Wall provides a comprehensive overview of Germany before and during World War II. The book covers the conditions that brought about the rise of Hitler and the Nazi Party, the German perspective on Hitler, and how such a massive atrocity as the Holocaust could have happened at all.

Wiesel, Elie, *Night*, Hill & Wang, 2006.
    This haunting memoir chronicles the author's experiences as a young man in concentration camps at Dachau and Buchenwald. Wiesel received a Nobel Peace Prize in 1986, primarily for the impact of this work, which was first published in Yiddish in the mid-1950s and was translated into English in 1960.

SUGGESTED SEARCH TERMS

Markus Zusak AND The Book Thief

The Book Thief AND Holocaust

Holocaust AND young adult literature

Holocaust AND children's literature

The Book Thief AND death

Nazi Party AND Hitler Youth

Nazi Party AND literature

Markus Zusak AND interview

A Canticle for Leibowitz

WALTER M. MILLER JR.

1959

Published in 1959 at the height of the Cold War, Walter M. Miller Jr.'s *A Canticle for Leibowitz* is acknowledged as perhaps the greatest novel to deal with the potential disaster of a nuclear war. At the time of its publication, a war between the Soviet Union and the United States seemed almost inevitable and would have resulted in something between the destruction of technological civilization and the extermination of all life on earth. Miller takes as his starting point the commonplace that a nuclear war would, at a minimum, plunge humanity into a new dark ages. He develops this theme literally, telling his story as the history of a Catholic monastery in the American Southwest founded by Isaac Leibowitz, one of the few engineers left, and dedicated to preserving the few scraps of technical information that survived the war that the monks refer to as the Flame Deluge. In Miller's vision, history repeats itself exactly with a new Renaissance, fueled in part by the work of the monastery of St. Leibowitz, and a new Cold War, and finally another and more devastating nuclear war. The Order of Leibowitz finally renews its role of scientific preservation by helping to transport human civilization to an interstellar colony. Miller also deals presciently with the problems of abortion and euthanasia that have come to the fore of American culture in the twenty-first century, a debate that touched Miller personally as he struggled with suicidal depression from what today would be called

A Canticle for Leibowitz begins 600 years after nuclear war destroyed civilization. *(© Sebastian Kaulitzki / Shutterstock.com)*

post-traumatic stress disorder following his service as a bomber crewman in World War II. In this way Miller, like any great writer, transcends the limits of genre. Contrary to expectation, *A Canticle for Leibowitz* (like Stanley Kubrick's film *Dr. Strangelove, or How I Learned to Stop Worrying and Love the Bomb*, perhaps the greatest artistic treatment of nuclear war in any medium) is not a tragedy but a comedy. Perhaps there is no other way to approach the insanity of its subject matter, which is ultimately the suicide of the entire human race.

AUTHOR BIOGRAPHY

Walter M. Miller Jr. was born in New Smyrna Beach, Florida, on January 23, 1923. His father was a railroad employee. During World War II, Miller served as a radioman and tail-gunner in the Mediterranean theater and flew fifty-three combat missions on B-25 bombers. He was especially affected by a mission in 1944 to bomb Monte Casino, the site of the oldest active monastery in Western Europe but also a key mountaintop position for the German Gustav Line. Attacking the historic landmark was controversial, and even the Nazis agreed to a truce to allow time to evacuate its art treasures and manuscripts. After the war, Miller studied engineering at the University of Texas, but he did not complete a degree before taking work with a series of rail lines. He seems to have worked at this career throughout his adult life. In 1945 he married Anne Louise Becker, with whom he had four children. He converted to Catholicism in 1947.

Recuperating from a car accident, Miller began to write and publish short stories, eventually specializing in the science fiction genre, and also produced scripts for the *Captain Video* television show. In 1950, he had an affair with the science fiction author Judith Merril (who had published *Shadow on the Hearth* in 1950, probably the first novel based on the aftermath of a nuclear war), though he later reconciled with his wife. In 1955, Miller won the Hugo Award (the most prestigious literary award in the science fiction genre) for his short novel *The Darfsteller*, which concerns the replacement in mass culture of human artistic creativity by computer-generated entertainment. Between 1955 and 1957, Miller published three more short novels in *The Magazine of Fantasy and Science Fiction*, which he reworked into his major work, *A Canticle for Leibowitz*, in 1959. While he was revising the first section, which takes place in the bombed-out ruins of an American city, he realized that he was working through his mental anguish over his role in the bombing of Monte Casino. *A Canticle for Leibowitz* also won the Hugo Award in 1960. It also became a best seller, crossing over to mainstream readers, and it has remained in print since its initial publication.

Miller quickly became disenchanted with his celebrity and retreated from the science fiction and literary worlds, publishing nothing else during his lifetime (though he did edit *Beyond Armageddon*, an anthology of post–nuclear war stories, in 1985). He spent much of his later years writing *Saint Leibowitz and the Wild Horse Woman*. But following years of depression, Miller killed himself on January 9, 1996, shortly after the death of his wife, leaving the work unfinished. This novel takes place in the same continuity as *A Canticle for Leibowitz*, about a century after the "Fiat Lux" section. His literary estate arranged for it to be completed by the science fiction author Terry Bisson.

PLOT SUMMARY

Fiat Homo

This section takes place during the twenty-sixth century. *Fiat homo* is Latin for "Let there be a man."

The novel begins with Brother Francis Gerard of Utah lurking about a field of ruins. The rather strong impersonal narrative voice that tells the story slowly reveals two facts through dropping hints to the reader rather than telling them outright. Francis is a teenage boy undergoing a Lenten vigil of fasting and renunciation

MEDIA ADAPTATIONS

- Clark Fuller adapted *A Canticle for Leibowitz* in 1967 as a brief play intended for community and other amateur theater groups.

- In 1981, *A Canticle for Leibowitz* was adapted as a fifteen-part radio drama by John Reed for a production broadcast on National Public Radio. A recording is available at the Internet Archive: http://archive.org/details/ACanticleForLiebowitz.

- In 1993, the BBC produced a radio drama by Donald Campbell based on the "Fiat Homo" and "Fiat Lux" sections of *A Canticle for Leibowitz*.

in the ruins prior to gaining admittance to a monastery founded by and dedicated to the blessed (*beatus*) Leibowitz. The monastery is located somewhere in the Four Corners area of the United States (the area where the borders of present-day Colorado, New Mexico, Arizona, and Utah meet); the ruins are a few miles away from it. The other fact is that the story takes place six hundred years in the future, long after a devastating nuclear war, known as the Flame Deluge, was fought in the early 1960s (the near future when the book was published). One immediate reaction to the war had been a rejection on the part of the survivors of the technological civilization that had made it possible; this rejection inspired the lynching of surviving scientists and intellectuals and the burning of any remaining books (the Great Simplification). Leibowitz had managed to survive both the war and the murder of scientists and technicians, and he made it his mission to gather together what books he could and hide them in a Catholic monastery he founded.

Francis is soon visited by someone he thinks of as a pilgrim. Although Francis does not know what a Jew is, it is obvious that the pilgrim is Jewish from the characteristic prayer he says over his meal and the fact that he speaks and writes Hebrew. Francis mistakes him at first for one of the class of people called the Pope's Children. These are individuals born with notable physical deformities because of their ancestors' exposure to nuclear fallout. In line with Catholic teaching about the sanctity of life, the Papacy (based in New Rome—a city founded probably in southern Missouri after the war, since Rome itself had been completely destroyed in the war) forbids them to be killed. Nevertheless, they are at this time generally driven out of human communities as they become old enough to fend for themselves, and they often live as bandits and cannibals. These people and the fallout itself are thought of as literal monsters: "Brother Francis visualized a Fallout as half-Salamander, because, according to tradition, the thing was born in the Flame Deluge, and as half-incubus who despoiled virgins in their sleep," giving rise to mutations and physical deformities.

Francis assures the pilgrim that he will be given food and water. To thank him for the generosity, the pilgrim finds a rock that is the perfect shape to fit into the shelter that Francis is building to protect himself from the wolves that prowl the ruins at night. Beneath the rock, Francis discovers a buried doorway marked "Fallout Survival Shelter; Maximum Occupancy: 15." Francis is terrified, thinking that the door leads to the lair of a group of fallout demons. But his curiosity eventually overcomes his fear, and Francis goes into the room. There he discovers a toolbox with some letters, a planner, and a blueprint, which had been written by Leibowitz himself.

Francis soon reveals all this to his confessor, Father Cheroki, who thinks the boy must have been driven mad by heatstroke. He sends him back to the monastery. When something of Francis's story has been confirmed by examination of the contents of the toolbox, he is summoned to an interview with the abbot, Father Arkos. Talking to organize his thoughts more than to explain things to the lowly novice, Arkos reveals that the discovery Francis has made might well be of sufficient significance to persuade the Papal authorities in New Rome to finally canonize Leibowitz. But he knows that other proposed canonizations have failed because they have become associated with fantastic miracle stories that the Church officials investigating the case have dismissed as superstitious. Already, wild rumors are circulating through the monastery that the pilgrim was a visitation by Leibowitz himself. Arkos therefore

demands that Francis deny that the pilgrim was Leibowitz and that there was anything miraculous or supernatural about his discovery of the fallout shelter. Francis, although he believes nothing of the kind and has played no part in exaggerating the story, does not feel he can, since he has no definite knowledge of whether the pilgrim was Leibowitz or not. The Abbot whips him, but he still refuses to make the denial that Arkos demands. As a result, Francis is not admitted to the order. Instead, he is required to spend another year as a novice, and he is sent back into the desert during Lent the following year. At the end of that time, Francis's interview with Arkos is repeated, with same result, and again and again for seven years, until he is finally made a monk. Francis begins to work as a copyist of what the monks call the memorabilia, the books that Leibowitz managed to save as well as others that the monks of the monastery had managed to salvage in the intervening centuries.

Eventually the claim of Leibowitz to sainthood is investigated and accepted. In the mean time, Francis had made a copy of the blueprint he discovered, and he is sent to take it and the original to New Rome to present to the Pope during the ceremony of canonization. On the journey, Francis is waylaid by bandits—Pope's Children—who steal the copy, thinking it is the precious original. Neither the Pope nor Francis is able to understand anything of what the blueprint means (the reader, however, realizes it is a circuit diagram), demonstrating that Leibowitz's legacy of trying to preserve technological civilization has little meaning at this time. The pope gives Francis gold to buy back his copy from the bandits, but when he attempts to do so, he is simply killed by other bandits, after again encountering the pilgrim who found the fallout shelter. The pilgrim buries Francis's body.

Fiat Lux

This section begins in the year 3174, about another six hundred years later than the first section. *Fiat lux* means "Let there be light"; it is a quotation from the Vulgate version (Latin translation of the Bible) of Genesis 1:3.

The section begins with Monsignor Apollo, the Papal nuncio, or ambassador, at the court of Hannegan, mayor (in effect, king) of Texarkana. Hannegan is engaged in diplomatic and military preparations to unite the south-central portion of the former United States, or the civilized world as it is known to the characters. At the same time Hannegan's cousin, Thon Taddeo, a leading scholar, is alerted to the memorabilia preserved at the Leibowitz Abbey by a letter from Brother Kornhoer, who is beginning to make practical advances based on the old writings, including an electrical generator.

When Apollo proves unable to have the documents brought to Texarkana, Taddeo goes to the abbey. On the way Taddeo meets with Madbear, a chieftain of the plains nomads with whom Hannegan is in alliance. Meanwhile Benjamin, the Jewish hermit who claims to be the same pilgrim who showed brother Francis the fallout shelter six hundred years ago, tells the new abbot, Paulo, with whom he is old friends, that Taddeo will use the memorabilia to start a new Renaissance. An unnamed poet is also living at the monastery, finding the events that unfold before him as a source of cynical humor.

Taddeo is amazed by the secrets revealed by the memorabilia, but his guardsmen are plainly plotting to seize the abbey for Texarkana. Taddeo has no concern for how the scientific discoveries might be used, even in the face of the destruction of civilization by technologically advanced weapons. Once Hannegan launches his war, he executes Apollo as a spy; the Church reacts by excommunicating Hannegan. In response, Hannegan creates a secular state separated from the Church's authority. In a postscript to the section, the poet is killed in a skirmish with refugees fleeing Hannegan's forces across the plains.

Fiat Voluntas Tua

This section takes place in the year 3781, another six hundred years in the future. *Fiat voluntas tua* ("Let your will be done") is a quotation from the Vulgate translation of the Bible, Matthew 26:42, where it signifies Jesus's acceptance of the crucifixion.

Civilization has advanced to the point where technology is somewhat more advanced that it had been in 1960. For example, Miller describes computers with voice transcription software and self-driving cars. Nuclear power has been rediscovered, but since it is known that civilization had once been destroyed in a nuclear war, the main rival powers in North America and Eurasia have had a long-standing agreement never to use nuclear weapons. Space colonization and interstellar travel have been developed. Nevertheless,

the rival powers proceed with the secret development of nuclear bombs. As a political and military crisis looms, the Leibowitz order, now under Abbot Zerchi, prepares to move its memorabilia as well as the totality of scientific knowledge to a human colony in the star system of Alpha Centauri.

As this plan goes into action, the narrative of the novel moves to a smaller story about human society. Mrs. Graels is a poor woman who sells produce to the abbey. Because of genetic damage resulting from fallout released during the previous war, she has a second head, that is, a partially formed conjoined twin. Although the head, which she calls Rachel, has human features, it lacks any sign of life. Mrs. Graels is anxious to have Rachel baptized, which is contrary to church practice in such cases.

There is a limited nuclear exchange between the powers (resulting in the destruction of Texarkana), followed by a ten-day truce. Official announcements about what is happening and why are quoted, but the characters neither understand nor trust them, leaving the reader even more in the dark about why the war is happening. The Church rushes forward with its plans for its interstellar transfer of human knowledge and the Church hierarchy. Refugees from Texarkana flee to the Leibowitz Abbey. Many are dying protracted deaths from radiation poisoning. The Green Star (analogous to our Red Cross) doctors treat them following government policy by offering euthanasia, which Abbot Zerchi opposes, following Church teaching. He intervenes in the case of one young woman. She and her baby both suffered fatal exposure to radiation, which will mean a few days of lingering agony and then death. She wants to have the baby and herself euthanized, and Zerchi tries to persuade her not to but is unsuccessful.

Eventually the war comes with a general nuclear exchange, and with the more sophisticated weapons used, all life on earth outside of the deep oceans is exterminated. Abbot Zerchi and Mrs. Gales are trapped together in the rubble of the Abbey during the brief interval between the first shock wave from a bomb and the final firestorm of destruction. Mrs. Gales is already dead, but Rachel suddenly wakes up, and Zerchi begins to baptize her. But she refuses and instead gives the priest the last rites. The Church's interstellar mission succeeds in getting away before the attack.

CHARACTERS

Monsignor Apollo

Apollo is the Papal nuncio at the court of Texarkana at the time of the "Fiat Lux" section of
the novel. He provides exposition to the reader
to describe the political situation and other
background.

Abbot Arkos

Arkos is the abbot of the Leibowitz Abbey during "Fiat Homo." He is mainly concerned with
the canonization of his order's founder, which he
thinks may be imminent, depending on the political climate. In particular, he thinks the relics
found by Francis will ensure the canonization,
if they are handled in the right way, and is willing
to bring terrible psychological pressure to bear
on the novice to help bring this about.

Father Cheroki

Father Cheroki is an old and rather irascible
monk in charge of the discipline of the novices,
including acting as their confessor.

Benjamin Eleazar bar Joshua

See Pilgrim.

Brother Francis Gerard of Utah

Francis is the main character of the "Fiat
Homo" section. He was raised as a slave in
Utah and entered the Leibowitz Abbey after
running away. During his novitiate, he finds
important relics of the Blessed Leibowitz in an
old fallout shelter near the abbey. His discovery
is met with disbelief by his superiors, and with
wildly exaggerated tales of the supernatural by
other young monks and novices. His personality
is rather retiring, and he endures years of chas-
tisement from Abbot Arkos rather than flatly
state that the pilgrim who led him to the fallout
shelter was not a supernatural apparition of Leibowitz, simply because he cannot know something like that for certain. He tends to faint when
put under pressure. When he eventually becomes
a copyist of the memorabilia he shows great
devotion to his work, even though he is completely unable to understand the documents he is
working on. He is not really dedicated to the
mission of Leibowitz, to preserve whatever is
left of the records of technological civilization
(a concept he cannot grasp), but simply realizes
that he has no way to make a life outside the
monastery.

Mrs. Graels

Mrs. Graels is a woman whose ancestors' genetic
code had been damaged by nuclear fallout from
the first nuclear war. She has a second head,
Rachel, which the Church refuses to baptize.
During the second war, when Mrs. Graels dies,
Rachel comes to life and acts a priest, in the short
time before she is vaporized, along with the
whole abbey. The pilgrim does not survive this
war, but Rachel's instinctive action as a priest
suggests that Rachel is the second coming of
Christ that the pilgrim had been waiting for.

Brother Kornhoer

Kornhoer is a monk at the time of "Fiat Lux."
He is the first person since the Great Simplification to understand the scientific literature preserved at the abbey, and he constructs an arc
light and an electrical generator run from a
treadmill. He is interested in the practical applications of technology, in contrast to the theoret-
ical approach of Thon Taddeo.

Isaac Edward Leibowitz

Leibowitz does not appear directly as a character, but he is frequently referred to by other
characters, and a number of his letters and journal entries are quoted. His character underlies
the whole action of the novel. Before the war,
Leibowitz had been an engineer or technician
working in the design or manufacture of nuclear
weapons. The monks of the Leibowitz Abbey do
not know much about him, and the reader has to
infer a great deal from the traditions that the
monks preserve but do not understand, and
from the documents that they hold and that are
quoted in the text. He was on a trip at the time of
the war and would otherwise have been killed in
the attack, living near a prime target. His wife
seems to have died in the fallout shelter that
Francis later discovers near what must have
been Leibowitz's house.

Leibowitz also managed to survive the murder of scientists and engineers of the Great Simplification. Thereafter he took on the task of
saving what books he could in the hopes that
they would one day prove useful in rebuilding
civilization. Although he was Jewish, he founded
a Catholic monastery to hide them, guessing that
the generation that survived the war would tolerate only religious books, not technical material. In later ages the monks remembered their
original task to preserve the books, which they
called the memorabilia (perhaps a term coined

by Leibowitz to hide their true nature from out-siders), but are just as keen to have the founder of their order recognized as a saint by the Church. At the beginning of the novel Leibowitz is already recognized as a *beatus* (Latin for "blessed"), which is a step on the way to becom-ing canonized as a saint. This final step is accom-plished in the first section of the novel. Leibowitz is undoubtedly the "man" referred to by the section title, *Fiat Homo* ("Let there be a man").

Canticle is the English version of the Latin translation of the Greek term *psalm* ("song"). In particular it refers to the various songs dedicated to saints and prophets song by monks according to the calendar of their daily service. The monks of the Leibowitz Abbey undoubtedly sang a can-ticle for their founder, although its words are never quoted in the novel. The title *A Canticle for Leibowitz* refers to the whole refounding of civilization being a hymn of praise for Leibowitz, the only man who tried to save it when it failed. Miller probably meant it also as a lament for his own part in helping to destroy the past of civili-zation by bombing the Monte Casino monastery.

Madbear

Madbear is a mighty chieftain of the plains nomads. Although they occupy the same regions as the former Plains Indians, their culture is based more nearly on the steppe nomads of inner Asia, such as the Huns or Mongols, in that they keep herds of cattle rather than follow-ing wild herds.

Abbot Paulo

Paulo is abbot of the Leibowitz Abbey during "Fiat Lux." He is dying of stomach cancer when Taddeo comes to the abbey. He realizes that a secular Renaissance is about to start which will complete the task of the abbey in preserving the memorabilia, but he wonders what that accom-plishment will mean for the future of the order.

Thon Taddeo Pfardentrott

Taddeo is a high-ranking nobleman in the state of Texarkana. Originally intended for the priest-hood, he was educated at a Benedictine monas-tery, but he was called to succeed his father as head of a territory when his half-brother died. He is embittered against both the Church and the secular world. But he is a remarkable genius, and as a professor in the college at Texarkana, he is making new breakthroughs in natural his-tory as the level of civilization is rising. According

to Apollo the Papal nuncio, Taddeo "has a mind like a loaded musket, and it can go off in any direction." He is interested in the prewar science and technical writings kept at the Leibowitz Abbey, which are largely unknown to the outside world. *Thon* is the respectful title *Don* after hav-ing undergone linguistic change over the centuries.

Pilgrim

The pilgrim is the only character to appear in more than one section of the novel. He is a hermit who lives in the mountains above the Leibowitz Abbey. In "Fiat Homo" he wanders down to the vicinity of the abbey and acciden-tally directs Brother Francis to find the fallout shelter containing the relics of Leibowitz. He is physically unimpressive, even ridiculous: "The pilgrim was a spindly old fellow with a staff, a basket hat, a brushy beard, and a waterskin slung over one shoulder." In "Fiat Lux," he is an old friend of Abbot Paulo and is known to the monks by the typically Jewish name Benjamin Eleazar bar Joshua. He claims at that time to be more than 3,200 years old, though the monks dismiss this as madness or lying.

Although Miller offers no explanation of how this pilgrim could live through the 1,800-year span of the novel, it may be explained through the European folklore of the Wandering Jew. In the Gospel of Matthew, Jesus addresses a crowd, saying, "Verily I say unto you, There be some standing here, which shall not taste of death, till they see the Son of Man coming in his kingdom" (Matthew 16:28, King James Version). This contributes to the theme of the urgency of the coming of the Kingdom (interpreted as the second coming of Christ in the Middle Ages) throughout the Gospels. This incident gave rise to a medieval legend that in fact one of the Jews in the crowd must still be alive and will live until the end of the world. The Wandering Jew was further identified with various characters from the Gos-pels, especially those who mocked Christ, but Miller identifies him with Lazarus. Miller uses this legend to link together the three disconnected parts of his story. Since the monks occasionally mistake him for Leibowitz, this builds up Miller's idea of the cyclical nature of history. Although the pilgrim claims to have been about sixty or seventy years old at the time of the crucifixion (traditionally dated to 33 AD), Leibowitz becomes a new Wandering Jew for the new Middle Ages of the novel, making an implied comparison between the catastrophe of the cruci-fixion (described in cosmic terms in Matthew) and the disaster of the Flame Deluge.

The Poet

The poet, unnamed, is a semipermanent guest of the Leibowitz Abbey in "Fiat Lux." He is the only character to believe that the hermit Benja-min is the same pilgrim whom Brother Francis met six centuries before. He provides an ironic comment on events he witnesses.

The Pope

When Francis sees the Pope (never named) who canonizes Leibowitz, he is overawed by the cere-monial grandeur of the Papal court and images him to be a stern, larger-than-life figure. But when Francis briefly meets him in private, he realizes that the Pope is an ordinary man, as ignorant and powerless as the rest of mankind in the wake of the destruction of civilization.

Rachel

See Mrs. Graels.

Abbot Jethrah Zerchi

Zerchi is the abbot of the Leibowitz Abbey dur-ing "Fiat Voluntas Tua." Though he excels in his administrative tasks, he is well adapted neither to the monastery's work with the memorabilia nor to the spiritual task of the order:

> Like other abbots before him, the Dom Jethrah Zerchi was by nature not an especially contem-plative man. . . . His nature impelled him toward action even in thought; his mind refused to sit still and contemplate. There was a quality of restlessness about him which had driven him to the leadership of the flock.

He selflessly devotes himself to administer-ing the Leibowitz interstellar mission, whose success he knows will also mean his own death, and then to trying to uphold Church teachings about the sanctity of life in the face of an indif-ferent government.

THEMES

Roman Catholicism

A Canticle for Leibowitz takes place for the most part at the Leibowitz Abbey, and most of the characters are monks. Miller is careful to accu-rately depict monastic life, with its tendency for gossip and petty squabbles for insignificant power within the monastery (which monastic bureaucrat will control which rooms of the abbey, and so on). This interest probably derives from Miller's guilt in his role in the destruction of the Monte Casino monastery during World War II. The Catholic Church that Miller presents is essentially identical to the medieval Church, down to the use of Latin as an official and liturgical language (since his Church exists only in North America, and since he shows some interest in the evolution of regional dialects of English into new languages, he might have cast modern English in this role). As the Church of the medieval period was headquartered at Rome, Miller's North American church is based in New Rome (possibly in southern Mis-souri). This Church is a political agent as much as a religious institution, negotiating for power between the various secular states of the region, attempting to guarantee its own independence. The Church is the one connection to the prewar world, before the Flame Deluge; it is not re-created by the cyclical advance of history. Miller shows a remarkably detailed knowledge of Cath-olic theology, but he also implies that this theol-ogy was not preserved through the Great Simplification any more completely than scien-tific knowledge. For instance, Zerchi the abbot speaks of "A vegetable soul? And the animal soul? Then the rational human soul, and that's all they list in the way of incarnate vivifying principles, angels being disembodied."

Nuclear Warfare

The first description of a nuclear bomb and nuclear war occurs in H. G. Wells's novel *The World Set Free* (1914). He realized, perhaps before the scientists themselves did, that advan-ces in understanding of the structure of matter indicated that such terrible weapons were possi-ble. Indeed, Leo Szilárd, one of the leading phys-icists to work on the Manhattan project, which actually constructed the first nuclear bomb, was directly inspired by Wells's story. Wells immedi-ately realized that such an unprecedentedly destructive weapon would change the nature of warfare and many other institutions, and risked destroying civilization:

> The atomic bomb had dwarfed the interna-tional issues to complete insignificance. . . . We speculated upon the possibility of stopping the use of those frightful explosives before the world was utterly destroyed. For to us it seemed quite plain that these bombs and the

TOPICS FOR FURTHER STUDY

- *Barefoot Gen* is a Japanese manga series that began publication in 1973 and has had several English publications, beginning in 1978 (it was adapted into an anime in 1982, which was released in an English version in 1999). Its author, Keiji Nakazawa, was a survivor of the nuclear attack on Hiroshima in 1945. The main character, Gen, is a ten-year-old boy who is orphaned by the nuclear attack. The comic book deals with unprecedented realism with the immediate effects of the nuclear bombing. In the future history of *A Canticle of Leibowitz*, every American city was destroyed by a nuclear bomb in the same way as Hiroshima. Draw and write your own comic book depicting the aftermath of a nuclear attack on your community.

- Since 1960, a great deal of research has been done to determine the actual effects of a nuclear war, and especially since the end of the Cold War, many government documents from both sides have been declassified detailing the actual strategies that would have been used in the event of a nuclear war. Much of this material is posted on the Internet, either at government websites or at the websites of anti-nuclear organizations. Familiarize yourself with this material and make a PowerPoint presentation to help you present your findings to your class. By what mechanisms do the bombs cause destruction (heat, blast, radioactivity)? Would the damage caused by a general war in the early 1960s have been even more severe than Miller imagined?

- The day-to-day business of the monks of the Leibowitz Abbey is making handwritten manuscript copies of the books that they preserve in their memorabilia, just as monks did in medieval monasteries. Select a page of text from a printed book (perhaps one of the ancient books quoted in *A Canticle for Leibowitz*) and make a copy of it using medieval techniques. Information about how to do this is available on the web (use search terms such as *paleography*, *quill pens*, and *vellum*). At a minimum, use a broad-tipped pen on a sheet of unlined vellum (these materials can be found at an art supply store). Lay out the sheet using a ruler and pencil. For a more ambitious version of the project, use a metal pen hand-dipped into an inkwell, or even make your own goose-quill pen. Make sure you practice forming letters with the pen before starting your final copy; it will feel quite different from writing with a ball-point pen.

- All of the records of the nuclear war available to the future described in *A Canticle for Leibowitz* were written in highly figurative language, imitating the Bible or church texts. Write a description of a real-world catastrophic event, such as the landfall of Hurricane Sandy or the 9/11 terrorist attacks, in the same kind of highly colored language.

---

still greater power of destruction of which they were the precursors might quite easily shatter every relationship and institution of mankind.

Wells imagined that the only possible response to nuclear weapons would be to end national rivalries by creating a single world government, though he realized that the threat of terrorist attacks with a nuclear bomb would remain.

Later science fiction writers frequently turned to nuclear war as a theme of their writings. *A Canticle for Leibowitz* is recognized as one of the greatest literary achievements along these lines, with its working out of the results of a nuclear war over centuries. The novel begins six hundred years after such a war, which is described only through the quotation of older texts, written in the fictional future history of the

A Canticle for Leibowitz was inspired by Miller's experience in the Allied bombing of the monastery at Monte Cassino during WWII. (© Anthony Ricci | Shutterstock.com)

novel. Since these are ascribed to the Catholic Church, Miller carefully echoes the forms of ancient and medieval Jewish and Christian writings. One of the most famous passages of the novel is a liturgy based on the Litany of Deliverance, conceiving of nuclear fallout as demonic beings:

> From the place of ground zero,
>
> *O Lord, deliver us.*
>
> From the rain of the cobalt,
>
> *O Lord, deliver us.*
>
> From the rain of the strontium,
>
> *O Lord, deliver us.*
>
> From the rain of the cesium,
>
> *O Lord, deliver us.*

The Church's history of the war, written in imitation of the Book of Job, presents the cause of the Flame Deluge as a wager between God and Satan. Satan tests the leading prince of earth by reducing his power, but unlike Job the prince aggressively lashes out, as do his fellow rulers:

> The princes of Earth had hardened their hearts against the law of the Lord, and of their pride there was no end. And each of them thought within himself that it was better for all to be destroyed than for the will of other princes to prevail over his.

It also describes a nuclear attack in mythological terms:

> Over each city a sun appeared and was brighter than the sun of heaven, and immediately that city withered and melted as wax under the torch, and the people thereof did stop in the streets and their skins smoked.

STYLE

Science Fiction

Nineteenth-century authors such as H. G. Wells and Jules Verne, whose novels were called "scientific romances" at the time, are today seen as progenitors of science fiction. Verne was the more traditional author, celebrating the wonders that were being created by the rapid advance of science and technology. Wells often took a more cautionary tone, suggesting that science might also bring new troubles. The genre became firmly established in the 1920s in pulp magazines (named after the cheap quality of paper they were printed on) marketed to teenage boys. The first generation of science fiction stories were generally of the Verne type, promising a new world filled with the wonders of space travel and exciting adventure. By the 1950s, however, the increasing destructive power of weapons refined by science, above all the atomic bomb, as well as the dawning consciousness of problems such as overpopulation and ecological harm, made it clear that scientific advancement was not purely good. This new pessimistic mood about the future began to be reflected even in the science fictions pulps, as authors such as Philip K. Dick and Ray Bradbury produced a more cautionary type of story in the tradition of Wells. It was in this vein that Miller began writing science fiction in the 1950s, although he did not, like so many of that period's writers, come from the science fiction fan community and had not grown up in the genre. His stories, such as *The Darfsteller*, reflected the fear that technological advancement might be destructive of the human spirit. The ultimate extension of this trend was nuclear war. Although nuclear war as a theme was an extrapolation of the future effects of technology, there was nothing fantastic about it. This theme made it possible for the first time for science fiction writers to break out of their genre market to the mainstream, notably in Bradbury's *Martian Chronicles* and Miller's *A Canticle for Leibowitz*. Because of its obvious relevance, mainstream authors, such as Nevil Shute in *On the Beach* and William Golding in *Lord of the Flies*, took up nuclear war as subject matter. As people realized that a nuclear war was possible and would result in the end of civilization and very probably their own death, speculative writing about the future suddenly took on a new meaning. The shock that the American public received from the Soviet launch of the first satellite, Sputnik (which was proof that the Soviet Union could attack the United States successfully), acted as a similar spur. In the 1960s, technological change would continue to accelerate, especially in its power to transform daily life. Nevertheless, science fiction remains largely a genre confined to a narrow—though wider than it once was—fan base, and novels by mainstream writers on typical science fiction

themes, such as Doris Lessing's Canopus in Argos series or Margaret Atwood's *Oryx and Crake*, do not penetrate the fan community.

Typography

Typography refers to the use of fonts and the arrangement of text on a printed page. Its potential as a form of artistic expression is generally neglected (although some artistic publications in the 1920s and 1930s made good use of it). It is almost startling to see any typographical variation in a mass-produced novel; such works are generally printed uniformly in the same font and layout. Miller makes some use of the possibilities of typography, however, during the interviews between Abbot Arkos and Brother Francis in the "Fiat Homo" section. The difference of status and emotion between the two characters is shown by typographical variation throughout the conversations. As Arkos builds into a towering rage, his words are printed with greater and greater emphasis until they are in all capital letters to convey shouting. This is not so unusual, but the increasing meekness and submissiveness of Francis's response is shown by a reduction in the font size of his words. Even this minor typographical variation is very rare in mainstream publishing.

HISTORICAL CONTEXT

The Cold War

After World War II, the victorious Allies of the Soviet Union and the United States became known as superpowers, as opposed to the mere great powers spoken of earlier in the century, because of their unprecedented military capabilities. In particular, the United States from 1945, and the Soviet Union from 1949, possessed nuclear weapons, whose destructive power went far beyond any military use and, it was recognized, could have exterminated all life on earth. Each superpower was politically and ideologically hostile to the other, to a degree that might ordinarily have been expected to spark a third world war between them, but the facts that each side had arsenals consisting of thousands of nuclear weapons and that an open war would almost certainly result in the annihilation of the civilian populations of both countries and of Europe (at least) made each side refrain from open hostilities. The political maneuvering of

COMPARE & CONTRAST

- **1950s:** The United States lives in constant fear of a nuclear attack.

  Today: With the end of the Cold War, it is considered unlikely that the United States could come under a general nuclear attack, although the threat of terrorists setting off one or a few bombs remains a remote possibility.

- **1950s:** The improvement of science education is a top national priority, as scientific advancement is seen as the only hope of defending America in the Cold War in the face of events such as the first Soviet nuclear bomb test in 1949 and the Soviet launch of the Sputnik satellite in 1957.

  Today: With the ease of Cold War anxieties, science education is under attack by well-funded fundamentalist religious organizations that believe science is incompatible with their religious traditions.

- **1950s:** Fallout shelters, underground bunkers of the kind used during World War II to protect against conventional bombing, are commonly built and encouraged by the government as a defense against nuclear attack (especially in schools and other public buildings), although technical experts of the time recognize they would be useless in the vicinity of a nuclear explosion, as Miller demonstrates in *A Canticle for Leibowitz*.

  Today: Particularly after the end of the Cold War in 1989, most fallout shelters have been decommissioned, although they are still built by extremists as a political statement.

---

both sides, as well as wars fought by proxies (as in Korea, Vietnam, and Afghanistan), was referred to as a Cold War. Nevertheless, it was widely expected at the time that some crisis or other would inevitably escalate to open warfare between the superpowers and a full-scale nuclear attack and counterattack. This was symbolized by the editorial staff of the *Bulletin of the Atomic Scientists* through a Doomsday Clock, showing how close they believed the world was to such a war. A condition of secure peace would have shown twelve hours to midnight, but throughout the Cold War they set the clock at between two and seventeen minutes to midnight, the closest call coming in 1953 when Douglas MacArthur, the American commander in Korea, openly called for a nuclear attack on China. Another close call came in 1962 during the Cuban Missile Crisis, when the United States considered invading Soviet-aligned Cuba, where Soviet troops were already stationed with orders to destroy any American invasion force with tactical nuclear weapons.

A Canticle for Leibowitz is set during the aftermath of a nuclear war fought between the superpowers at some point in the early 1960s. Many novels of the period, including Shute's *On the Beach*, Bradbury's *The Martian Chronicles*, and Golding's *Lord of the Flies*, deal with the extinction of human life or civilization through a nuclear war. In *A Canticle for Leibowitz*, Miller succeeds in offering a simultaneously pessimistic and optimistic view of humanity and its prospects. During the next two thousand years of history after the war, civilization is rebuilt, following a course through periods analogous to the Middle ages, the Renaissance, and the Scientific Revolution, only to inevitably result in a new Cold War between powers based in North America and Eurasia. Warned by the knowledge of the earlier nuclear war, the new superpowers show more restraint in avoiding war, but this merely allows them time to perfect even more devastating weapons until another war is fought in the year 3781, this time exterminating all life on earth outside the deep oceans. But the same

Set in a Catholic monastery, A Canticle for Leibowitz *takes place after a nuclear war.* *(© kavram /*
Shutterstock.com)

time gained allows for the advance of space flight
and the establishment of human colonies outside
of our solar system, ensuring the survival of the
human race and civilization.

CRITICAL OVERVIEW

Miller's *A Canticle for Leibowitz* crossed over
from a specialized audience to a mainstream readership, but it has not drawn much attention from
mainstream critics (compared with, for examples,
Gore Vidal's historical novels from the same
period). When scholars approach Miller's novel,
it is usually in the context of other nuclear war
literature. Paul Brians, in his 1987 *Nuclear Holocausts: Atomic War in Fiction, 1895–1984*, points
out that the original structure of the book as three
individual novellas makes the final text uneven in
literary quality, citing the "Fiat Lux" section as
the weakest. Nevertheless, Brians is impressed not
merely with Miller's skill as a futurist, but as a
writer, judging that the "story is so rich in detail

and so sympathetic in characterization that one
cannot help but feel for the poor monks even
while one is laughing at them." Brians was perhaps the first to offer the opinion that the real
strength of *A Canticle for Leibowitz* lies in Miller's
engagement with the Catholic Church, not in the
distant future, but around social issues that have
become increasingly important in the decades
since it was written: "In a world of grotesque
mutations and radiation disease the Church's
stands on abortion, euthanasia, and suicide—
although they are thoughtfully considered and
not merely caricatured—are presented as ultimately inhumane." While Brians sees that Miller,
himself a Catholic convert as an adult, escapes the
trap of anti-clerical hysteria that is common in
post–nuclear war literature (he is thinking of Fritz
Leiber's 1950 novel *Gather, Darkness!*), he
accuses Miller of descending to cliché by giving
a "version of the traditional science fiction
panacea for the world's problems, the exploration
of space." But perhaps it is the only solution
that a writer can offer to the insoluble problem
of nuclear war. Brians also provides a useful

bibliography and, uniquely, a survey of the nuclear war theme in Miller's earlier short stories. Martha A. Bartter, in her 1988 *The Way to Ground Zero: The Atomic Bomb in American Science Fiction*, stresses the cyclical nature of the novel: "Miller's *Canticle for Leibowitz* operates out of existential shame. There is no hope for humanity. All human efforts, no matter how well intentioned, will inevitably lead to the next war." Albert E. Stone, in his 1994 *Literary Aftershocks: American Writers, Readers, and the Bomb*, views *A Canticle for Leibowitz* as a development of Bradbury's *Martian Chronicles*: "Miller's romance extends Bradburyian time greatly in both directions: backward a thousand years into an imaginary dark ages, several thousand years forward into a science fiction world of spaceships and interplanetary escape." David N. Samuelson, writing in *Science Fiction Studies* in 1976, emphasizes Miller's engagement with American society, giving a depth to his work beyond run of the mill science fiction. Miller treated his themes "with respect to their social implications particularly for the United States, but perhaps more importantly, with regard to their effect on individual behavior, including that side of behavior which can only be termed religious."

CRITICISM

Bradley A. Skeen

Skeen is a classicist. In the following essay, he examines Miller's view of history in A Canticle for Leibowitz.

Historical novels are set within the framework of past events as known to historians. A writer might, for example, set a series of novels in ancient Rome. It could concern members of the same family in three different periods, for example, at the time of the Second Punic War (third century BCE), the time of the Emperor Augustus (turn of the era), and finally the time of Constantine (fourth century CE). In each case the writer could consult the historical record to discover the circumstances the characters would encounter: the social arrangements, the type of government, the religions, the cultural interests of each period, and so on. But in a science fiction story that takes place in the future, no such resource is available. The science fiction author has to create not only a story but the whole world that the story will take place in. This

> MILLER IS ASKING THE READER TO CONSIDER THE REALITY THAT WOULD RESULT FROM A WAR THAT SEEMED INEVITABLE IN HIS OWN TIME."

world-building, indeed, is one of the main points of genre science fiction, to show how society will be transformed in the future by new technological developments, such as nuclear power and space travel. That kind of imaginative structure is sufficient for a single story, but when episodes stretch over centuries or millennia of the future, the author must construct a whole future history, showing the changes that take place over time, which will be at least as great as those that took place in the past. Once the author has established how the world might be one thousand years in the future, he or she must imagine again the ways in which it will have changed even more two thousand years in the future.

In most science fiction novels, even series of novels, a future history framework is not necessary, as in E. E. Smith's *Lensmen* series, which all take place over a relatively short interval. The first future history in science fiction was established by Robert A. Heinlein in stories he began writing in the 1930s. He did not do so purposefully, but soon found that by reusing favorite themes and characters, he had set up a coherent narrative of the future, and after 1941 he outlined the future chronology (published in the 1941 issue of the science fiction pulp magazine *Astounding*) and thereafter intentionally placed many of his stories in his fictitious future. Heinlein's editor, John W. Campbell, coined the term *future history* to describe this setting. The series begins with the exploitation of the solar system through a space program run by private enterprise, and eventually sees the development of worldwide communication (analogous to the Internet) lead to a one-world dictatorial government based on Christian fundamentalism, which lasts several centuries before it is overthrown and government embraces Heinlein's libertarian ideals. The series ends about the year 5000 CE with the development of time travel and the ability to travel between parallel universes. After Heinlein, the technique of creating a future

WHAT DO I READ NEXT?

- Miller's *Saint Leibowitz and the Wild Horse Woman* (1997) is a sequel to *A Canticle of Leibowitz*. Unfinished at the time of Miller's suicide, it was prepared for publication by Terry Bisson. It takes place about seventy-five years after "Fiat Lux," and its plot concerns the struggle for power between the Church and the empire of Texarkana. It is a meditation on the moral character of suicide.

- James N. Yamazaki was a Japanese American physician who worked on the genetic study made of children affected by the fall from the atomic bombings of Japan and later atomic tests in the South Pacific. *Children of the Atomic Bomb: An American Physician's Memoir of Nagasaki, Hiroshima, and the Marshall Islands* (1996) is a presentation of his research and experience, aimed at a general readership.

- Rose Secrest's *Glorificemus: A Study of the Fiction of Walter A. Miller, Jr.* (2002) offers a summary of Miller scholarship and an overview of his work, together with a literary analysis of *A Canticle for Leibowitz* from a fannish rather than a scholarly perspective.

- Fritz Leiber's *Gather, Darkness!* (serialized in *Astounding* in 1943 and published in book form in 1950) is a science fiction novel set some thousands of years after a nuclear war. In this future, the earth is ruled by a tyrannical Catholic Church, which monopolizes science under the guise of magic that only its priests can control.

- *Black Rain* (1965; English translation, 1966), by Masuji Ibuse, tells the story of a young adult who was left orphaned by the nuclear attack on Hiroshima. Her aunt and uncle must take care of her, and in the middle-class Japan of that era, that means arranging an advantageous marriage for her. But this proves difficult because potential suitors fear that she was affected by the nuclear fallout, or "black rain," from the attack.

- *Walter M. Miller, Jr.: A Bio-Bibliography* (1992) by Robert L. Battenfeld and William Roberson is the foundational scholarly work on Miller. It gives an encyclopedic review of Miller's works and Miller criticism, and it offers new biographical and interpretative essays.

---

history became common in science fiction, and another relevant science fiction future history was created by Ray Bradbury in the 1940s. His *Martian Chronicles* is not really a novel but rather a series of short stories connected only by taking place in the same future history time line, which envisions the colonization of Mars and the survival of the human race there after a nuclear war on earth.

The idea of creating a future history has points of contact with the ancient idea of being able to predict or see into the future through methods of divination (the use of ritual to discover things that are humanly impossible to know, including the course of future events)

such as astrology. But it is different also insofar as a future history is acknowledged as fictional. The writer does not predict that what is claimed in the story will happen but merely records what rational speculation suggests may happen, or what the writer hopes will happen, or simply something that would be interesting to write about. The 1930s was not the first era to think about the future in this systematic way. The ancient religious genre of the apocalypse is a kind of future history. The Book of Daniel in the Hebrew Bible from the second century CE is an early apocalypse that illustrates the genre's new approach to history and historical progression compared with earlier prophetic writings.

In Daniel, the author describes in some detail the crisis that the Jewish nation was going through during the Maccabean revolt against the Seleucid Empire, reaches his own time of writing, and then just as assuredly begins to narrate events in his own future. The author argues that under human control, history has become unmanageable and is producing one disaster after another (represented by the state's insults to the writer's religious views), but in the future, God will take control of history and restore it to the proper course. This too is a wish, as any writing about the unknowns of the future has to be, and one that has become a central idea in Western culture. Whatever the current crisis perceived by an apocalypse's author, it will be resolved in a utopian future. This outline—perhaps one might say this *message*— was picked up by nineteenth-century positivism with its vision of a future where all problems are solved by science and technology, and made it into science fiction and its future histories. While a science fiction future history must begin with a crisis in order to create the dramatic structure of fiction, such crises are as a rule resolved in a utopia created by science. The initial impulse of the science fiction genre that began in the 1920s was that progress in the form of science and technology would inevitably make civilization and human lives perfect, inheriting the Victorian myth of progress and its precursor the Judeo-Christian doctrine of redemptive salvation.

An exception to the science fiction future history of infinite progress is the future history that encompasses nuclear war. In Bradbury's *Martian Chronicles*, the human race manages to survive, but the outcome is anything but ideal. The tone of the message is nevertheless prophetic: if things go on as they are, the world will end in disaster. Miller thinks beyond this moment of catastrophe to the history that will come afterward. His pattern for the future is based closely on the Middle Ages and Renaissance of Western Europe in some detail. For instance, he paints a detailed linguistic background for his future history. Under the circumstances, writing ceases (outside the Church, which reverts to Latin), so English is freed of the fixative power of writing: "The vulgar dialects of the people had neither alphabet nor orthography." Separated into geographic regions that did not contact each other for centuries, English gives rise to several new languages, just as Latin once gave rise to Spanish, French, Romanian, and other Romance languages. This is revealed when Abbot Zerchi talks about the difficulties of translation between the various new languages: "Do you speak Alleghenian? . . . Neither do I, and Cardinal Hoffstraff doesn't speak SouthWest."

As civilization progresses, it inevitably moves toward nuclear war, repeating the cycle of the previous age. The idea that civilization proceeds in repeating cycles is ancient. The Stoic philosophers of ancient Greece believed that the elements that make up the universe were formed from an initial fire, that history proceeds in a fixed course, and that the universe will eventually resolve back into fire; the process will repeat exactly and infinitely, so that there will be another Trojan war, another Roman Empire, and so on. This is contrary to the ancient Christian belief that history proceeds from the creation through the fall to a climax in the crucifixion and return of Christ and the end of history.

Miller frames the cyclical nature of his story with a coda to each of the three sections of the novel. In the first two, vultures eat the body of one of the characters, and the narrative stresses their role in the natural cycle of life. At the end of "Fiat Homo," "the buzzards laid their eggs in season and lovingly fed their young. Earth had nourished them bountifully for centuries." This is repeated at the end of "Fiat Lux": "As always the wild black scavengers of the skies laid their eggs in season and lovingly fed their young." In the end of "Fiat Voluntas Tua," the vultures are killed on the wing by the nuclear blast, and the only surviving scavengers are sharks: "The shark swam out to his deepest waters and brooded in the cold clean currents. He was very hungry that season."

Although the characters in *A Canticle for Leibowitz* speculate about the influence of divine providence on the evident repetition of history, what Miller proposes is perfectly natural in his own eyes. In 1960, all evidence suggested that nations cannot resolve their differences by any means short of war and that they do not limit the destructive power of the weapons they use in war. The natural extrapolation of these tendencies suggested that technological civilization would inevitably result in nuclear war. Miller's point, in showing this through a second cycle with the same result, is to warn that such a war seemed inevitable if nothing was done to prevent

An examination of the struggle between the Church and the state plays a large role in A Canticle for Leibowitz. *(© Margaret M Stewart / Shutterstock.com)*

it in the future that still stretched ahead in 1960. So he is in fact not writing about a fictional future, but about his own age. Miller is asking the reader to consider the reality that would result from a war that seemed inevitable in his own time.

Source: Bradley A. Skeen, Critical Essay on *A Canticle for Leibowitz*, in *Novels for Students*, Gale, Cengage Learning, 2014.

Denise Dumars

In the following excerpt, Dumars describes the plot of A Canticle for Leibowitz *and recommends it for book clubs.*

. . . Walter M. Miller's 1959 classic *A Canticle for Leibowitz* foresees a postapocalyptic future in which Catholic monks try to learn and then preserve the secrets of Earth's lost technology. The Albertian order venerates St. Leibowitz, an engineer from our time who left a grocery list as a relic. Brother Francis seeks to understand the mysterious Leibowitz (including

the list and a blueprint) in order to bring hope to a world that has descended into a new dark age. There is a lot of black humor in this novel, and its revelation of the Second Coming is like no other. Miller's cautionary tale has stood the test of time and transcends its genre. It's also highly recommended for book discussion groups. . . .

Source: Denise Dumars, "Out of This World: SF for Novices," in *Library Journal*, Vol. 126, No. 13, August 2001, p. 196.

Brian Aldiss

In the following review, Aldiss addresses the status of A Canticle for Leibowitz *as a classic science-fiction book, despite his dislike of the tedium of religious life in the text.*

The term "Classic" applied to a book generally means that the book is out of copyright, with all profits accruing from its sale collected by publisher and bookseller. Only an innocent will believe the term has some connection with the readability of a book. Thus, *Lorna Doone* is totally impenetrable and a Classic and, incidentally, a World's Classic.

The science fiction industry, in its endearingly doomed bid to be taken seriously, is keen on the label. Any book possessing something of that same stodgy quality as *Lorna Doone* merits the term, although "science fiction classic" is in its way an oxymoron. A journalistic element in SF militates against the enduring qualities of the true classic (Homer being a name that leaps to mind here). It is precisely for this journalistic quality that SF is valued, where it is valued at all. A warm water ocean on Jupiter's moon Europa? Let's go! Let's speculate on that one!

Just occasionally, a story or novel emerges concerning something so confounding, so likely to remain unlikely, so imaginative and so imaginatively written, that it does achieve a desired longevity. Mary Shelley's *Frankenstein*, some novels of Jules Verne, and almost anything H. G. Wells wrote before the Great War, fall into this category.

The new paperback edition of Walter Miller's *A Canticle for Leibowitz* is described on its cover as "The Classic Novel of a New Dark Age and New Renaissance." Phew! Renaissance, eh? The picture of the man on an ass also commands respect. There are those who dislike their SF respectable, but this novel is aimed at (and has acquired) a wider audience.

I thought of *Lorna Doone* while re-reading it. Well, I thought of a lot of things while re-reading it, as we trudge through another page of meandering in the desert, such as other SF novels which deal with religion and are immeasurably more entertaining, notably James Blish's *Case of Conscience* or Kurt Vonnegut's satirical *Cat's Cradle*.

Canticle plods along in an American nowhere, six centuries after nuclear devastation. There's the journalistic bit. The novel was first published in parts in an SF magazine, from 1955 to 1957—a period when those who had power over the globe were preparing to blow it to bits.

In this ignorant and violent future time, the Catholic Church endeavours to hold together what is left of civilisation, just as it does today in Ireland. The monks spend much of their time copying and embroidering blueprints found in the ruins of former periods. Brother Francis finds a note written by one I. E. Leibowitz, a technician who worked on a missile site and is now due for canonisation by the authorities in New Rome.

Brother Francis also spends many years copying and adorning a blueprint with Leibowitzian associations. A sense of futility overpowers the know-all humour of the activity. As the Doanes scour Dartmoor, so the monks scour the desert.

It's a clearly written novel in which the best passages contain moral and religious arguments. What to do for those suffering radioactive burns, doomed not to survive? The arguments for and against euthanasia between Abbot Zerchi and Doctor Cars are powerful. They come towards the end of the book, when more years have passed. The Church has lost power. A new scientific age dawns. Again the nuclear bombs are falling. History is repeating itself with an accuracy only fiction can achieve. The monks and sisters, gathering up children, climb into a spaceship and head for other worlds.

Despite the brilliant arguments, the tedium of religious life was too much for me. It was so when the stories first appeared, and again when the book was first published in 1960, and is so now.

That's three times I have read *Canticle*, so it must be a classic, at least in SF terms. But the SF industry has another trick up its sleeve, a trick much persevered in by Isaac Asimov and Arthur C. Clarke, to name no lesser mortals.

If a novel receives acclaim—a Foundation novel, say, or a 2001—then run the idea into the ground with a sequel, or sequels. Terry Bisson has taken up and completed a Miller sequel to *Canticle*. It begins with an impenetrable precis. Again the Catholic Church is involved in a struggle with the earthly powers. Son of Lama Doone? This reviewer faltered. Not again, he cried. Not a fourth time . . . Please . . .

Source: Brian Aldiss, Review of *A Canticle for Leibowitz*, in *New Statesman*, Vol. 126, No. 4353, September 26, 1997, p. 65.

SOURCES

Bartter, Martha A., *The Way to Ground Zero: The Atomic Bomb in American Science Fiction*, Greenwood, 1988, pp. 127, 146–47, 230–31.

Bradbury, Ray, *The Martian Chronicles*, Doubleday, 1958, pp. 205–11.

Brians, Paul, *Nuclear Holocausts: Atomic War in Fiction, 1895–1984*, Kent State University Press, 1987, pp. 80–82, 260–62.

Miller, Walter M., *A Canticle for Leibowitz*, J. B. Lippincott, 1960.

Samuelson, David N., "The Lost Canticles of Walter M. Miller, Jr.," in *Science Fiction Studies*, Vol. 3, No. 1, 1976, pp. 3–26.

Stone, Albert E., *Literary Aftershocks: American Writers, Readers, and the Bomb*, Twayne, 1994, p. 55.

Wells, H. G., *The World Set Free: A Story of Mankind*, E. P. Dutton, 1914, p. 146.

FURTHER READING

Kearny, Cresson, *Nuclear War Survival Skills*, Oak Ridge National Laboratory, 1979.

> This work was a pioneering guide on its subject matter, including material on specialized first aid and low-technology devices for the construction of fallout shelters and survival in a post-nuclear war world (although many of its assumptions may be optimistic). It was originally intended to be disseminated freely and is widely available on the Internet, for example in a PDF file available at: http://www.homeland civildefense.org/nwss/nwss.pdf.

Miller, Walter M., *The Best of Walter M. Miller, Jr.*, Pocket Books, 1980.

> This volume collects Miller's short stories and novellas from the period before *A Canticle for*

Leibowitz and is invaluable since they are otherwise not generally available. Unusually for science fiction of the 1950s, these stories deal with the possible limitations on the human spirit that technology might produce and frequently have strong female characters.

Miller, Walter M., and Martin H. Greenberg, eds., *Beyond Armageddon*, Bison Books, 1985.

> *A Canticle for Leibowitz* was the first novel to deal at length with the aftermath of nuclear war. This anthology collects short stories on the same subject written over the next twenty-five years, of which the most notable is Harlan Ellison's "A Boy and His Dog." Miller writes an introduction to the volume and comments and notes on each story.

Roberson, William H., *Walter M. Miller, Jr.: A Reference Guide to His Fiction and Life*, McFarland, 2011.

> In this volume, Roberson updates his previous work on Miller to cover the author's suicide as well as the publication of *Saint Leibowitz and the*

Wild Horse Woman. It is encyclopedic in nature, including entries on large topics such Miller's biography and *A Canticle for Leibowitz*, as well as minutia such as translations of every Latin phrase in Miller's work.

SUGGESTED SEARCH TERMS

Walter M. Miller Jr.

A Canticle for Leibowitz

science fiction

nuclear war

post-apocalyptic

Cold War

monasticism

Hiroshima

Clear Light of Day

ANITA DESAI

1980

Anita Desai is one of the best-known postcolonial writers of India and one of the founders of the Indian literary renaissance referred to as Indian English Literature, or Indo-Anglian literature, written in English by natives of India. Indo-Anglian fiction actually predates Indian Independence, which started in 1947, but women novelists like Desai came to the fore during the decades afterwards as women's roles were changing and the country was modernizing. Her early novels like *Cry, the Peacock* (1963) helped illuminate the psychological struggles of women to become individuals. Desai gradually broadened her focus to include the inner portraits of whole families who have grown up in India's modern cities, detailing their difficult adjustments to postcolonial life. Her fiction has been hailed as a turning point in Indian literature for delving into psychological territory. Some of her themes include alienation, the search for identity, the fragmentation of tradition in city life, and self-understanding. Her novel *In Custody* (1984) was made into a Merchant Ivory film, and her 1983 children's book *The Village by the Sea* became a TV series. Desai has been shortlisted for the coveted Booker prize in fiction three times.

Clear Light of Day (1980) is the last of her early novels exploring the inner reality of the characters, without much reference to external action. Historical issues like Indian independence and Partition are only felt in the background of

Anita Desai (© Jeremy Sutton-Hibbert / Alamy)

the thoughts of the Das children, who come of age along with the country. The four siblings are shown to have different memories of growing up in Old Delhi. Their impressions are compared during a family reunion in middle age as they try to patch up old wounds.

AUTHOR BIOGRAPHY

Anita Mazumdar was born in Mussoorie, near Delhi, India, on June 24, 1937, to a German mother, Toni Nime, and a Bengali businessman father, D. N. Mazumdar. Although she grew up speaking German with her family of three other siblings, she spoke Urdu, Hindi, Bengali, and English as well. At school she studied and wrote creatively in English from the age of seven and published in children's magazines. She attended Queen Mary's Higher Secondary School in Delhi and Miranda House at Delhi University, where she graduated with a bachelor's degree in English

literature in 1957. In 1958, she married Ashvin Desai, a businessman. They had four children, including Kiran Desai, who is also a novelist.

In later life, Desai separated from her husband and traveled, teaching in England at Girton and Smith College and in America at Mount Holyoke College, Baruch College, and Massachusetts Institute of Technology. She is a fellow of the Royal Society of Literature, of the American Academy of Arts and Letters, and of Girton College and writes for the *New York Review of Books*. Since 1993, she has taught creative writing at Massachusetts Institute of Technology in Cambridge, Massachusetts, where she is now professor emeritus.

Desai wrote and published short stories early in her career. Her first novel, *Cry, the Peacock* (1963), set the trend for a new kind of Indian fiction in English with its psychological probing of characters. Her books *Voices of the City* (1965), *Where Shall We Go This Summer* (1975), *Fire on the Mountain* (1977), *Games at Twilight and Other Stories* (1978), and *Clear Light of Day* (1980) follow this trend. In her later books, *In Custody* (1984), *Bomgartner's Bombay* (1987), *Journey to Ithaca* (1995), *Fasting, Feasting* (1999), *Diamond Dust and Other Stories* (2000), *The Zig-Zag Way* (2004), and *The Artist of Disappearance* (2011), Desai developed her style to include social issues as well as psychological, in a variety of postcolonial settings. Desai has been shortlisted for the Booker Prize in fiction three times, including for *Clear Light of Day*, and won the Guardian Children's Fiction Prize for *The Village by the Sea* (1983). Her daughter, Kiran, to whom Desai has been a mentor, won the Booker in 2006 for *Inheritance of Loss*.

PLOT SUMMARY

Clear Light of Day is written in four parts. It is like a long short story where a character discovers something important near the end. The author shows what time has done to four characters, the children of the Das family, a middle-class Hindu family in Old Delhi, India. Part I covers the present in the late 1970s; part II flashes back to the summer of 1947 when India was gaining its independence; part III is the Das childhood of the late 1930s; and part IV is the present again when the main character, Bim, has her moment of life-changing insight. There is

MEDIA ADAPTATIONS

- A 1993 Ivory Merchant film production of *In Custody*, Anita Desai's 1984 novel, tells the story of Deven, a professor of Hindi in love with Urdu poetry. He is thrilled to get an interview with the great Urdu poet Nur. This tale elaborates on the theme of Raja's passion for Urdu poetry in *Clear Light of Day*, illustrating conflict between modernity and tradition. It is directed by Ismail Merchant, with a screenplay by Anita Desai and Shahrukh Husain, and stars Om Puri, Sashi Kapoor, and Shabana Azmi.

little external action, although there are many fascinating details and poetic descriptions of Indian landscapes and characters. Most of the story consists of the memories and mental impressions of the siblings: Bim, Raja, Tara, and Baba. The third-person narration freely switches from one point of view to another.

Part I

Part I centers on Tara's memories as she comes home to visit her elder sister, Bim, who has never married. Dialogue provides the contrasting views of the sisters. Tara, married to Bakul, a diplomat, is a world traveler, but she comes to visit her family home where her elder spinster sister, Bim, who is a college lecturer in history, and her younger brother, Baba, who is mentally handicapped, still live. Their other brother, Raja, lives in Hyderabad with his family. Tara tries to persuade Bim to come to a family wedding in Hyderabad with Baba. Raja's eldest daughter is getting married.

Tara tries to patch up the breach between Bim and Raja, who were close when growing up but are now estranged. Tara wants to understand the influence of their childhood, the old house, and especially what happened to Bim and Raja. Tara wonders why Bim is so angry. Bim was left with all the family responsibility when

Raja and Tara escaped as teenagers to find their own lives. Tara feels guilt for this. Tara and Bakul have two teenaged daughters and a glamorous life, but Bim has to support and look after Baba and also had to nurse their Aunt Mira as she died and care for Raja when he was ill. Tara is still intimidated, however, by Bim's intellectual superiority and sarcasm, which she uses as a weapon to subdue her younger sister. Tara's childhood fears overwhelm her as she examines the now dilapidated house she grew up in. Bim has a limited income and is not able to keep up appearances.

The story opens as Tara gets up in the morning and goes out to the verandah to find Bim walking in the unkempt garden. Bim has a habitual tone of condescension towards Tara, so they cannot be close. Tara sees that nothing has changed, except everything is going to ruin in the extreme heat of summer. Bim says Old Delhi never changes; it just decays. She teases Tara about living in the wide world while she lives a dull life at home. Tara is hurt by Bim's distancing tactics. She wants to feel a nostalgic connection with the past. Just then, they hear the loud music of an old phonograph, coming from Baba's room. He plays the same records over and over every day—American music from the 1940s, such as the song "Smoke Gets in Your Eyes." Tara does not know how Bim can stand it.

Baba comes out for tea on the verandah, where Bakul sits waiting for his wife to serve him. Bim says she must get ready for her students, who are coming for a tutorial. Bim asks Baba if he will go the office today and sign papers for the manager, Mr. Sharma—the conversation is a kind of ritual with them, for it is obvious Baba cannot go anywhere. He goes back to his room and plays records. Tara and Bakul argue about their plans for the day. Bakul sends for a car, so he can visit in the city, but Tara refuses to go with him. She wants to stay and visit with Bim and Baba.

Tara goes to Baba's room, thinking she can get him to go out and do something. He appears to her as an unchanged angel. Though once shy, Tara has been trained by Bakul to be an outgoing and forceful person. Baba is not used to her commands. Distressed, he runs out of the house where he is hit by a bicycle. He sees a driver whipping his horse, and Baba feels like he himself is being whipped. He runs home in terror. Bim is giving a tutorial to college girls.

She treats them as her children and buys them ice cream, giving a cone to Baba to soothe him.

Tara contrasts the dirty old house with her neat flat in Washington. She remembers how their parents neglected them by playing bridge at their club. She had a fear as a child that their father was killing their mother, but she now understands that he was injecting her with insulin because she was diabetic. Now Tara still feels fear and hopelessness in the house, although Bim seems not to notice. Bim reminds Tara of Raja's fascination with their landlord, Hyder Ali, riding his white horse by the river. Raja was the family poet and wrote poems in Urdu, trying to impress Hyder Ali's Muslim friends.

Bim shows Tara the letter Raja wrote her that caused the break between them. After he married Hyder Ali's daughter and inherited his wealth, Raja told Bim he would never raise her rent on the family house, thinking he was being generous. She took this as a supreme insult, for he was acting like her landlord, not her brother. He was apparently abandoning her and Baba to take care of themselves. Tara is shocked by this falling out, for Bim and Raja were inseparable growing up, until he grew ashamed of his family and started spending more time at the Hyder Ali home. They lived in a grand house and were part of a cultured circle of Muslim poets and artists. Raja married the daughter, Benazir, and moved with her family to Hyderabad, thus ending the relationship with his sister, Bim, who cannot forgive him.

Tara, Bim, and Bakul visit the neighbors, the Misra family. The middle-aged Misra sisters keep a day school to support their father and lazy brothers, who do not work. One brother, Mulk, thinks he is a singer and throws expensive parties, while the sisters go hungry.

Bim confesses to Tara she used to see Aunt Mira's ghost near the house after she died. She mentions the terrible summer of 1947 when the fires of Partition riots burned in the city. Tara is glad they can never be young again.

Part II

This chapter is a flashback to the Das children in adolescence, mostly from Bim's point of view, during the summer so many things happened to change their lives. It was the summer of 1947 when India was preparing for independence from Britain, and the Partition riots, Hindus versus Muslims, could be seen from the rooftop of the Das home. Bim watches and then rushes to the bedside of her brother, Raja, too sick with tuberculosis to go see for himself. He is anxious because his friend, the landlord, Hyder Ali, has left his house without saying good-bye. Bim reminds him that the Hyder Alis are Muslim and had to escape the violence. Bim admires her brother for his liberal attitude towards Muslims, for his college friends try to get him to join a Hindu terrorist group. Raja has endangered himself by expressing Muslim sympathy. He has always wanted to be a heroic rebel, like Lord Byron, whose poetry Bim reads aloud to quiet him down.

Raja had studied Urdu poetry, which he found superior to anything in Hindi, but his father would not allow him to pursue Islamic studies because of the political climate, with the Muslims asking Britain to partition India into two states: India and Pakistan. Everyone knows there will be bloodshed.

Their mother has recently died. When Raja attended Hindu College and studied English literature, Bim became his companion, reading and keeping up with his interests. Now as the city burns, Bim nurses Raja and reads to him. She takes on more and more responsibility as Tara escapes to the neighbors, the Misras. When Bim herself goes to college, Tara comes home with her suitor, Bakul, whom she met at the Misras. The marriage has to be arranged by Bim, for their father dies suddenly in a car accident. He leaves the family insurance business to Raja, but as soon as Raja is well, he escapes to Hyderabad to be with the Hyder Alis. The country explodes into violence. Bim is left with the family house, business, Baba, and a dying Aunt Mira.

Dr. Biswas, the doctor attending first Raja and then the alcoholic Aunt Mira, begins courting Bim. She is reluctant to accept his attentions. He is a timid but cultured man who studied in Germany and plays Mozart on the violin. He takes Bim to meet his mother, and she gets a taste of what having a domineering mother-in-law would be like. On their way home, they hear of Mahatma Gandhi's assassination. Bim drops Dr. Biswas and finishes college, deciding to stay at home with Aunt Mira and Baba, who have no one else. Dr. Biswas thinks Bim is one of the self-sacrificing women devoted to family, but Bim is angry at being misunderstood. She wants her independence.

Part III

Part III goes back in time even further to the childhood of the Das children, in the late 1930s, principally from Tara's fearful point of view. Tara remembers as a child seeing her diabetic mother pregnant with Baba. She was sickly and distracted herself by playing cards and leaving the children to the servants. The new baby was slow and difficult, so the mother sent for her cousin, Mira-*masi*, widowed at fifteen and passed around among relatives like damaged goods. She looks like a scarecrow, but she gives the children the nurturing they need, playing with them and telling them stories. The small and especially insecure Tara is devoted to Mira-*masi*. In a childhood game, Raja says he will be a hero when he grows up, Bim says she will be a heroine, but Tara blurts out she wants to be a mother. The older children laugh at her, and she runs to Aunt Mira for comfort.

The children learn their mother has diabetes and only stays alive through injections. Their world with Mira-*masi* is removed from their parents. Even Mira-*masi* cannot reverse the seeming curse of illness, death, and depression over the house. She convinces the parents to buy a cow to provide fresh milk for the children, but the cow wanders to the backyard and falls in the dark well there and drowns. Her calf dies also. Ever after the children are terrified by the well and haunted by the event.

As Raja grows up, he rejects Mira-*masi* and the feminine circle, seeking local boys to play with or going to the Hyder Ali house for books and music. Raja is a romantic; Hyder Ali riding a white horse is his ideal. Bim tries to keep up with her brother in studies and games. She adopts a more masculine attitude towards Tara, playing tricks on her, like cutting her hair off, telling her it will curl better. The children begin to feel suffocated in the house, full of dullness and decay. They escape in books, especially the English classics. The children are joyful, however, when they play on the banks of the Jumna River together.

In school Bim is a leader and eventually becomes head girl. Tara is afraid of challenge and clings to home. She feels she is a coward, remembering the time on the picnic at the Lodi Gardens when Bim was attacked by a swarm of bees, and Tara ran away. She believes she has always let Bim down. A failure at home and school, Tara escaped to the Misras for company.

They took her to parties and through them, she met her husband, Bakul. She married at eighteen and left Bim with Baba and Mira-*masi*.

Part IV

The narrative returns to the present (the late 1970s) and appears as an argument between the two sisters and their points of view. They each have a different memory of the past. As a dust storm rages outside, Bim sits at the dining table correcting papers, and Tara writes a letter to her daughters. Tara tries to persuade Bim to come to the family wedding. Bim says she is bored with rich, fat, and selfish people like Raja. Tara argues that Bim does not even know Raja now. She argues that people can change.

Tara thinks of Bim's anger in comparison with the dust storm, creating havoc. She realizes, however, that she does not see Bim objectively because she sees the past from her own point of view. She observes that children never know what is really going on. Bim corrects her, saying children notice everything. Tara feels pulled down when Bim disagrees with her, yet she suddenly bursts out in a guilty apology for deserting Bim when she was stung by bees. Bim says the incident was unimportant, but Tara is disappointed that Bim will not give her the forgiveness she feels she needs. Bim continues to think of herself as the family martyr.

Near the end of the visit, the ice between the sisters thaws a little, and they have their first real conversation where they admit their fears from the past to each other. They laugh at how their fates seemed reversed—Bim, who wanted to be a heroine, stayed home, and Tara, who was timid, embraced the world. Tara is still dissatisfied, wishing to solve the mystery of Bim's character.

Bim carries her unresolved anger about the past to Baba. She roughly asks Baba if he would like to go live with Raja now. Baba's hurt shows on his face, and Bim's anger disappears. She feels that Baba's silence and innocence complete her as a person and give her the answers she needs. She realizes she has always loved her whole family because they are a part of her. The clear light of day is revealed: how she must forgive and perfect her love for them. She stays up all night cleaning out her desk and throws away Raja's insulting letter.

In the morning, Bim's nieces arrive, and she happily embraces them. Bim sends them all off to the wedding, telling Tara she wants to see

Raja at last and asking him to come see her. The sisters have reached a greater understanding. Bim goes to a musical soiree with Baba at the Misras after they leave. Mulk sings in a young man's voice, but his old teacher sings like an old man at the end of his journey. Suddenly Bim remembers the lines in T. S. Eliot's *The Four Quartets* about time being both a destroyer and preserver. She understands in a flash that despite apparent differences, all of her family members have influenced each other's journeys deep down where they are unified by their past.

CHARACTERS

Hyder Ali Sahib

Hyder Ali is the Das family's landlord. His own family lives in a nearby grand house in Old Delhi near the river, where he rides his white horse every evening. "Sahib" is a polite form of address meaning "mister" or "master," used because he is an owner or landlord: a gentleman. The young Raja is drawn to Hyder Ali's wealthy house of fine Muslim learning and culture, including a library of great literature. Raja learns to read and recite Urdu poetry there in a circle of intellectuals. He is attracted also by the warmth of the family and by the daughter, Benazir. Hyder Ali has to flee during the Partition riots. He goes to Hyderabad, where he continues being a wealthy landowner. He leaves his business to Raja, who becomes his son-in-law.

Bakul

Bakul is Tara's husband. He is in the diplomatic service. He is exacting and domineering but not unkind to his wife. He chooses her over Bim because she is softer and more attractive and pliable. He trains her to be outgoing and to get over her inferiority complex from childhood. Stationed in Washington in the present, he comes back to India for the wedding of Raja's eldest daughter. Bakul respects Bim for her intelligence and thinks his wife is a bit empty-headed, emotional, and talkative.

Benazir

Benazir is the daughter of the Muslim landlord, Hyder Ali. She is an only child and pampered, treated as a child even as a young woman. Bim notes with disgust her shallow tastes and childish ways when she sees Benazir's bedroom in Hyder Ali's house after the family has moved away. Baba takes Benazir's phonograph and pop records from the 1940s. Later, Bim describes her as fat and overfeeding her pampered children.

Dr. Biswas

Dr. Biswas is the thin and timid Bengali doctor who cares for Raja and Aunt Mira. Bim is rather abrupt with him, but he pursues her, takes her to a concert, and finally takes her to tea with his mother, after which she promptly backs out of the relationship. He believes it is because she is devoted to nursing her family, but actually she likes her independence.

Baba Das

Baba Das is the youngest Das child, mute and mentally handicapped because Mrs. Das was a diabetic and had him late in life. He has a sweet and innocent character, described as angelic by his siblings. He likes routine and plays the same records over and over. He is too sensitive to cope with going out in public by himself. He is taken care of by Bim.

Bimla Das

Bimla Das (Bim) is the main character, the eldest and most complex of the family. While young, she is an enthusiastic leader and companion of her brother, Raja, keeping up with him in sports and reading. Bim is intelligent and competitive. She wins school prizes and becomes head girl. She learns the poetry and poets Raja is interested in.

When Raja wants to be a hero, Bim wants to be a heroine like Joan of Arc or Florence Nightingale. Bim identifies intensely with Raja until he rejects her for the male world. She even tries on his clothes, wishing she had a man's power. However, she is very motherly, tending to her younger siblings when the parents desert the children and spend time at their club. Bim cares for Baba all his life and nurses Raja through tuberculosis for an entire year. She is the one left to nurse the dying and alcoholic Mira-*masi*. She is shown to be affectionate with her pets, rescues the Hyder Ali's dog, and helps a servant who was left behind.

After Raja leaves, Bim is courted by Dr. Biswas, but finding marriage to be a trap, she goes to college and becomes a history teacher at a girls' college. Bim is somewhat bitter, abrupt, and sarcastic in her manner. She finds the neighbors, the Misras, too dull for her. As an adult she is somewhat reclusive and messy in her habits, focusing on her work. She is left in genteel poverty after her brother leaves for Hyderabad. He does not contribute to her or Baba's support. Although Tara visits Bim, Raja and Bim never speak as adults. Bim feels he is uncaring and arrogant, seeing her as a poor relation, but she is willing to make up after having an epiphany of love during Tara's visit.

Raja Das

Raja Das is the darling of his sisters, admired for all he does. He is extremely romantic, making his sisters read the English romantic poets like Byron. He also takes the Muslim neighbor and landlord, Hyder Ali Sahib, as his mentor, borrowing his books of Urdu poetry, even trying to write Urdu poetry himself. His admiration for the aristocratic Hyder Ali knows no bounds, especially when he rides by on his white horse. Raja falls in love with the whole family, and when they leave during Partition, he follows them to Hyderabad and marries Benazir. They have five children, and he inherits the family fortune as a businessman. Bim criticizes him for selling out his romantic dreams for a fat life of luxury. When Raja's eldest daughter is to marry, it brings out the family wound in the open, and healing of the breach can begin.

Tara Das

Tara Das is the youngest next to Baba. She was largely neglected as a young child, unable to keep up with her older siblings. She is described as a normal child rather than extraordinary like Bim and Raja. She clings to Aunt Mira as a mother substitute. Fearful of everything, she hates the Das house but does not like school any better. Tara is full of guilt for crimes she imagines she committed as a child. She feels that she has never lived up to her responsibility and that she abandoned Bim and Baba. She keeps seeking Bim's forgiveness.

Growing up, Tara spends her time with the mediocre but more normal neighbors, the Misras, who introduce her to her husband, Bakul. Tara's only ambition is to be a mother; she marries at eighteen and leaves home as soon as she can. Bakul trains her to be a competent diplomat's wife, and she travels the world with him. They have two teenaged daughters and have kept in touch with Raja and his family. On the way to Raja's oldest daughter's wedding, Bakul and Tara visit Bim. Tara keeps prodding Bim

about old family memories, triggering Bim's revelation of what her life has meant.

Mira-masi (Aunt Mira)

Mira-*masi* is a distant cousin of Mrs. Das who comes to take care of the children, especially the developmentally delayed child, Baba. *Masi* means "maternal aunt" or "one who is like a mother." Indians frequently call any female relative or friend of the family "auntie." Mira-*masi* was married at twelve, widowed at fifteen, and forced into a life of servitude with in-laws. Widows had no standing in Hindu society and were in some ways considered to have died with their husbands, so they could not remarry. They wore white, the color of death, and had no finery. Mira is said to be too ugly for the brothers-in-law to abuse sexually. She is passed around as an undesirable object. When she arrives at the Das home, she is anxious to please the children so they will want her to stay, for she has nowhere else to go. The younger children are especially grateful for her attention, but the older ones soon outgrow her company, wanting books instead. When the children grow up, Mira becomes an alcoholic out of desperation and dies, with Bim nursing her.

Jaya and Sarla Misra

Jaya and Sarla Misra are sisters in the family next door. Bim considers them too mediocre for her interest, but Tara becomes good friends with them, and they treat her as one of the family. They marry as young ladies, but their husbands, who are rough, send them back to their family where they are forced to open a day school for girls and teach a dance class at night to support their father and brothers. They are thin and often go hungry to give food to the men in the family.

Mulk Misra

Mulk Misra is one of the Misra brothers who all married as young men, but then, as with their sisters, their spouses left them. They sit at home doing nothing while their sisters support them. Mulk has ambitions to be an artist and spends a lot of money on singing lessons and soirees where he can perform.

Mr. Sharma

Mr. Sharma is the manager of the family insurance business. Mr. Das let him run the business and hardly did anything himself. After Mr. Das died, Bim had to keep up the business by signing papers. Mr. Sharma does all the work, but he also takes most of the profits. Bim does not like to deal with him, because she does not know the business or what he is up to.

THEMES

Family Relationships

In *Clear Light of Day*, the decaying family home in Old Delhi, the mother's diabetes, the absence of the parents, the close bond of the siblings, the mentally handicapped younger brother, and Aunt Mira as a mother substitute all play an important part in shaping the lives of the Das children. Bim reminds Tara that children notice everything, and the smallest incident takes on major significance. Desai's contribution to this familiar theme of family is to apply psychological insight to Indian families, for every culture has its own customs and issues.

Family is very important in Indian culture, and the family members generally exert a very great influence on the decisions and personalities of the other members. In fact, Indian culture has always favored family and tradition over individuality. Desai shows the difficulty Indian families experience in the modern world with the pull of Eastern tradition on the one hand and the Western drive to be an individual on the other.

Traditionally, a person of Indian culture did not have to make many choices, for social roles were laid out clearly by sex, class, and religion; careers were pursued according to the family trade. *Clear Light of Day* shows the postmodern struggle of the Indian middle classes, as women strive to be individuals, not just someone's wife, and as a man decides to marry a woman from another religion. Although the Das family is modern and secular in focus, with the parents playing bridge at their club and the children going to college, there are echoes of the Hindu tradition of child marriage with Aunt Mira's history, and there is also the volatile conflict of religious beliefs causing Partition riots.

The novel's emphasis is on Bim's choices and what it cost her to refuse marriage and have a career as a single woman. Raja also runs up against his father when he wants to major in Islamic studies. Clearly, if the parents had not died, Raja would have had a difficult time moving to Hyderabad and becoming part of a Muslim family, and Bim would have been pressured into marriage. Bim has done her best to avoid being like Mira-*masi*, stuck with taking care of others in the family, by keeping some independence. Tara's life too has been shaped by the family. Her guilt and insecurity all stem from early childhood; she has taken a more traditional role as wife and mother. Bim and Raja had to push against the family and social grain to realize their own dreams. The family reunion when the siblings are middle-aged allows them to take a look at their relationships and how they were formed by the past but also to realize they are not cut in stone.

Time

Desai says that time is the fourth dimension of *Clear Light of Day*. She is interested in how time functions in a family and especially in memories. In the Das family, past, present, and future are not distinct but continue to interact with each other as the characters try to recollect and gauge the importance of what they have been through together. The past was clearly perceived by Tara, Bim, and Raja to be disappointing, for they have all gone separate ways, yet they each have a distinct remembrance of their childhoods.

Raja did not want to be tied down to a family that was falling into physical and emotional ruin. He identified with the Hyder Alis, rich and intellectually vibrant. His choice to leave with the Muslims during Partition effectively partitioned the Das family as well, with Bim and Raja totally estranged during their adult lives. Tara confesses to Bim how the past made her fearful and why she also had to escape in marriage. Bim is surprised by Tara's completely negative evaluation of their childhood. Bim has anger about Raja's desertion in the past and struggles in the present with the family business. She vows to change the future for her female students by teaching them self-sufficiency.

Bim feels stuck because she sees time in a straight and unforgiving line. By going back and looking at the past, yet speaking of it in the present, Tara begins to remind Bim that there can be change for the future, for change is also a function of time. Tara sees that Bim has created a new feeling in the house, for instance. She coaxes Bim to get reacquainted with Raja. Bim's epiphany in a moment of intuition both espouses and transcends time, because she realizes that family relationships go back in time and

TOPICS FOR FURTHER STUDY

- *Cracking India* (1991; originally *Ice Candy Man*, 1988) by Bapsi Sidhwa tells the story of Indian Partition from the point of view of an eight-year-old Pakistani girl. *Waiting for the Rain* (1996) by Sheila Gordon discusses the problem of apartheid in South Africa where two childhood friends, black and white, grow up on opposite sides of apartheid and must fight each other. Read these two young-adult novels about countries that tried to segregate the people who lived there based on religion or race. The class should organize a discussion by blog around these novels and other similar examples to discuss whether nations are successful in efforts to classify and contain certain groups and whether it is ever moral or justified to segregate certain groups in a population.

- Watch the film *Water* by Deepa Mehta (2005) and then write a short paper on the treatment of widows in India, before and after Independence, using both electronic and book sources. Why were child widows like Mira-masi treated so harshly? Give examples from film and book to illustrate your points.

- Raja in *Clear Light of Day* is greatly attracted to a culture other than his own. Find examples of people being attracted to another culture and doing something creative because of it (artists, writers, politicians, or scientists). Create a website celebrating cultural diversity and creativity, posting such examples.

- Do a group presentation using PowerPoint or slides on the Hindu and Muslim religions. What are their beliefs and how do they differ? Why have they had a violent history of conflict in India?

- Find relevant websites showing how Mahatma Gandhi was able to unify the diversity of Indian cultures around the issue of independence. Use Delicious.com as your social bookmarking service to share results. Then share visually on a large screen sample websites and your conclusions to the class.

- The Das children were well read in the poetry of many languages. Read Western and Indian lyric poets (William Wordsworth, Pablo Neruda, Emily Dickinson, Rabindranath Tagore, and Muhammad Iqbal, for instance) and make a PowerPoint presentation on Poetry East and West. How does poetry cross over cultural lines and have a universal appeal?

---

continue to spread out in time. Time is a destroyer, but it is also a healer. Bim is willing to consider a different future with her family by looking at the past.

Postcolonialism

Since India gained its independence in 1947, its writers have used the novel and short story as an artistic vehicle to express the contemporary condition of their country. There are many native languages in India, but English, the language of the former oppressor, Great Britain, has the advantage of being a common second language for India's millions. Through fiction written in English, writers from diverse backgrounds and languages have been able to share their vision and memories of India.

Salman Rushdie in 1981, with the publication of *Midnight's Children*, announced a new and serious art form for India, the secular postcolonial novel. The name of his novel refers to the children born after Indian Independence into a different world than traditional India, and it has stuck as a name for a whole generation and way of life. He used a hybrid language—English generously peppered with Indian terms—to convey a

Desai explores the theme of the forgotten, abandoned, and left behind. (© SeanPavonePhoto | Shutterstock.com)

new vision of the country. The Indian postmodern novel is also represented in such works as Rohinton Mistry's *A Fine Balance* (1995) and Anita Desai's *Fasting, Feasting* (1999).

Desai's fiction often focuses indirectly on politics or social conditions, but it is postcolonial in that it probes the confusion of values and the displacement and loneliness of characters that are both traditional and modern at the same time, the legacy of having been colonized by England for two and a half centuries. Anita Desai's poetic prose recalls the writing of her favorite writers: Hawthorne, Melville, Faulkner, Virginia Woolf, and D. H. Lawrence. She also identifies with other postcolonial writers, such as Gabriel García Márquez, Milan Kundera, and Gunter Grass.

STYLE

Indo-Anglian Literature

Indian authors today write in English or one of their own official languages such as Hindi, Urdu, or Bengali. Indo-Anglian literature or Indian literature in English describes the poetry and prose by writers from India who write in the English language. English is a suitable language for describing the postcolonial concerns of authors who are largely modern and secular and were brought up with English culture. It is also associated with the writings of the Indian diaspora, those authors like Salman Rushdie, who were born in India but live in another country. Anita Desai is one of these authors who wrote her early work in India but lives now in the United States. Writing in English allows for a worldwide audience.

Indo-Anglian literature is only one and a half centuries old. R. K. Narayan is an early writer in English who influenced Desai with his humorous local color stories about Indian life in his fictitious small town of Malgudi. Mulk Raj Anand wrote harsher stories about divisions of caste, class, and religion. Anita Desai is often referred to as the Indian Virginia Woolf, bringing in a new concern for the inner psychological dimension of the modern Indian city dweller, such as housewives or children or artists. Other Indo-Anglian authors include Salman Rushdie,

Vikram Chandra, Kiran Desai, Arundhati Roy, Jhumpa Lahiri, Amit Chaudhuri, Amitav Ghosh, and Vikas Swarup.

Indian Women's Fiction in English

Indian women began writing fiction in English starting in the late-nineteenth century, but it was not until after Independence in 1947 that there was a spread of literacy, English education, and greater freedom of movement for women in India. The status of women in India changed rapidly with modernization, and women's fiction gained maturity as it took up the new social awareness accompanying the political emancipation of India. Mainly from middle or upper classes, women novelists wrote of nationhood, everyday trials, poverty, clash of customs, modernity, and women in the family.

Anita Desai is among the first generation of women writers after World War II who achieved enduring greatness, along with Kamala Markandaya (*Nectar in a Sieve*, 1954), Santha Rama Rau (*Remember the House*, 1956), Attia Husain (*Sunlight on a Broken Column*, 1961), Ruth Prawer Jhabvala (*Heat and Dust*, 1975), and Nayantara Sahgal (*Rich Like Us*, 1985). Anita Desai's great contribution was her stream-of-consciousness exploration of the individuality of women. In her novels, the political and social backgrounds are peripheral, while the individual woman's thoughts and emotions form a plot of self-discovery, usually ending in some moment of truth for the character. Desai was influenced by Western writers such as Jane Austen, the Brontës, Emily Dickinson, and Virginia Woolf.

Point of View

Desai exploits the ability of the novel to illuminate multiple points of view. The Das children shared the past, but each got something different from it. Only when they begin to share or compare points of view are healing and understanding able to take place. Individuality is thus a paradox like time, both fragmenting and enriching. Tara points out this paradox when she tells Jaya Misra that even though she and Bim differ, they have everything in common.

Because of the various points of view, there are several versions of the same events. The fine figure of Hyder Ali riding by on his white horse thrills Raja's heroic imagination, but the same image terrifies the simple awareness of Baba, who is almost trampled by the horse. For him, ever after

horses are frightening animals. Tara is fixated by guilt over the childhood picnic to Lodi Gardens where Bim was stung by a swarm of bees, and she ran away. However, the incident is shrugged off by Bim as unimportant. Tara realizes she has only seen Bim through her own childish perspective. She is shocked to hear Bim's version of their brother, Raja, who is nothing like the brother she knows. She urges Bim to revise her viewpoint.

Point of view turns out to be everything in this story. Bim acknowledges her own fragmented vision when she admits that if she could join her jaded self to the innocent Baba, together they would be a whole person. She vows that in future she has a lot of work to do mending the misperceptions of her family.

Stream-of-Consciousness Narration

The stream-of-consciousness style of narration looks at the thought and creative process from the inside of a character's mind, using symbols, lyric description, interior monologues, memory, and association. James Joyce's *Ulysses* (1922), Virginia Woolf's *Mrs. Dalloway* (1925), and William Faulkner's *The Sound and the Fury* (1928) are classics in this style. The plots are often not chronological but fragmented, going forward and backward in time. Desai has added a depth to the psychological realism in Indian fiction in the way she applies symbolism, stream of consciousness, and point of view to Indian concerns such as the tension between tradition and modernity in India, the lack of freedom for women, and family dynamics. Tara's thoughts, for instance, are not logical but range freely between past and present, triggered by associations or conversations. First, the inside of Tara's mind is followed and then the inside of Bim's; sometimes the narrative follows the hallucinations of Mira-*masi* or Baba's restricted understanding. The narration is unified not through plot but through symbols, such as the old well in the yard, a symbol of death, or the snail in the garden that indicates the slowness of life in the family house. Instead of an action climax, there is a personal revelation or epiphany.

HISTORICAL CONTEXT

Colonial India

The British East India Company was given permission by a Mughal emperor in 1617 to trade in India. In protecting its trading interests,

COMPARE
&
CONTRAST

- **1947:** Although a college education is possible for a woman, most women marry and stay at home. Child marriages like Mira-*masi*'s are not uncommon.

  Late 1970s: Prime Minister Indira Gandhi as the head of state typifies the new middle-class women of India: educated, married, and able to have a career. Desai gives voice to women who feel stifled by old traditions but feel challenged by the forces of modernity.

  Today: Indian middle-class women in cities tend to live in nuclear rather than extended families where they can pursue both family and career. They juggle the demands of tradition with the demands of modern society.

- **1947:** India gains its independence from Britain but is partitioned into Pakistan and India, causing great upheaval and suffering with millions of people displaced. The young country focuses on becoming stable.

  Late 1970s: Although India under Indira Gandhi enters the modern world as a competing player, Gandhi's State of Emergency in the late 1970s makes her a virtual dictator and creates great national uneasiness.

  Today: India is a modern secular state, the most populous democracy in the world. It is a leader in telecommunications, the film industry, world trade, cuisine, textiles, art, and music, and it plays an important part in the world balance of power.

- **1947:** A few Indian authors who write in English, like R. K. Narayan, are known in the West. Narayan's fictional town of Malgudi (*Swami and Friends*, 1935; *The English Teacher*, 1945) is loved by both Indian and English readers but hardly known in the United States.

  Late 1970s: Modern Indian artists, such as filmmaker Satyajit Ray and novelists Kamala Markandaya and Anita Desai, are known and respected in India and Europe. Americans are just beginning to hear of Desai with the publication of *Fire on the Mountain* in 1977.

  Today: Anita Desai is taken seriously by the literary world and has been nominated three times for the Booker prize. Indian fiction in English has gained worldwide prestige, with several Indians winning the British Booker prize, such as Salman Rushdie for *Midnight's Children* (1981), Arundhati Roy for *The God of Small Things* (1996), and Kiran Desai for *The Inheritance of Loss* (2006).

Britain used more and more military force, until it took over large areas of India and its administration, with the cooperation of local rulers. In 1857, after the rebellious Indian Mutiny, the English Crown took over the whole country, adding India to its empire. The British ruled in India with many Indians as part of their administrative staff. The upper classes of India lost their traditional power, and in order to gain advancement in the new system, Indians had to have an English education and training to get positions in the British Raj. In the novel, the Das children are born while India is still a colony, and they attend schools with British or British-trained teachers.

India's Independence

From the 1920s, leaders such as Mohandas Gandhi sought to rouse the Indians from their colonial bondage. Gandhi taught the people to boycott English products and to make their own cloth and salt. He used the principle of nonviolence to protest the presence of the British and gained a following of millions. He was initially able to unify all the religious

Raja is fascinated with Muslim culture and eventually integrates himself into it. (© *Kirsz Marcin* / *Shutterstock.com*)

factions of India, particularly the Hindus and Muslims, who were rivals.

Partition

In *Clear Light of Day*, Raja reads and quotes from the Islamic poet Iqbal. Sir Allama Muhammad Iqbal (1877–1938) wrote Urdu poetry, was a philosopher, and inspired Pakistani nationalism. Separatists protested for a Muslim country, resulting in the bloody and tragic Partition of India into two countries at the time of Indian Independence in 1947. Perhaps a million were killed, and millions more were forced to flee their homes because of their religion, with Muslims relocating to Pakistan and Hindus to India. The fact that Raja, a Hindu, took part in Hyder Ali's Muslim intellectual gatherings and married a Muslim had huge political implications during the time of Partition.

Old Delhi was the scene of clashes between Muslims and Hindus, because the plain where Delhi is located in northeastern India is the land where Krishna and the Pandavas fought the battle of Kurukshetra described in the Hindu epic the *Mahabharata*. Bim refers to the Yamuna or Jumna river where they played as children as the holy river where Krishna played his flute. Old Delhi, however, was also an important place later for the Mughal dynasty with its famous Islamic landmarks and bazaars. It became Old Delhi in 1931 when the British built New Delhi to be the capital of India.

Postcolonial India

Although India today is a secular and modern democracy, it is one of the postcolonial nations that has endured periods of confusion and mixed values, trying to sort out its new identity. *Clear Light of Day* opens in the time of the virtual dictator, Indira Gandhi (late 1970s), who took over the government on the pretext of a State of Emergency, a source of embarrassment to the Misras when they ask Bakul what others think of their supposedly democratic country. The tradition of extended families has also broken down, with the Das children moving far away, living in nuclear families, and marrying whom they please. Most of Desai's fiction takes place in large cities like Bombay or Delhi where Western lifestyles are the norm for the middle class.

CRITICAL OVERVIEW

From her first publication in 1963, Anita Desai was recognized as an important writer in India. Ramesh Srivastava, in his introduction to *Perspectives on Anita Desai*, summarizes the reception of *Cry the Peacock* (1963) in India: it was described as "a trend-setting novel" and "a significant achievement." Still two decades later in 1984, an American critic, Evelyn Damashek Varady, in "The West Views Anita Desai: American and British Criticism of *Games at Twilight and Other Stories*," asserts, "As a novelist, Anita Desai's reputation is secure in India. In America, however, she remains virtually unknown." Desai's worldwide fame steadily increased once she published *Fire on the Mountain* in London in 1977, winning enthusiastic reviews from the British press and many awards.

Clear Light of Day (1980) is reviewed in the *Times Literary Supplement* by Gabrielle Annan as a "carefully constructed, beautifully written, sensitive, funny, atmosphere work." The novel was shortlisted for the prestigious Booker Prize in fiction, thus forever securing Desai's status as a global author. By the late 1980s and in the 1990s, when Desai was well known and teaching in British and American universities, many monographs and collections of essays begin to appear on her work. In Jasbir Jain's *Stairs to the Attic: The Novels of Anita Desai*, for instance, Jain clearly delineates the inner journey that Desai's characters attempt to make from a fragmented self to wholeness, in their task of modern self-fashioning. S. Indira, in *Anita Desai as An Artist*, praises her experimentation with the novel form, noting that *Clear Light of Day* is Desai's last novel that focuses solely on the inner life of the character as she begins in her later novels to include outer events and their effect on individuals.

In "Introduction: The Fiction of Anita Desai" in *The Fiction of Anita Desai*, Suman Bala and D. K. Pabby point out that Desai's treatment of time in *Clear Light of Day* puts her in the company of European existential philosophers. They sum up Desai's major achievements as a fiction writer over the last forty years,

citing her blend of Western psychological analysis and Indian sensibility to focus on the status of women and the family in postcolonial India. Anita Desai is internationally known in the twenty-first century as one of the great fiction writers of India.

CRITICISM

Susan Andersen
Andersen holds a PhD in literature. In the following essay, she examines heroism as an act of consciousness by the main character Bim in Anita Desai's Clear Light of Day.

In Anita Desai's *Clear Light of Day*, Bimla Das comes of age during the time of Partition in India. The splitting of the Das family in 1947 mirrors the splitting of the nation into India and Pakistan. The Das children grow up and go their own ways, leaving a troubled wake behind. Bim is angry because she has taken on the woman's role of family martyr, staying at home to care for weaker family members and to keep the family home in Old Delhi. Her siblings have more exciting lives: Tara as a diplomat's wife in Washington and Raja as a wealthy businessman in Hyderabad. Bim journeys to her realization that she too has had a good life at home, even with the family burdens. Loss is transformed to acceptance and satisfaction through an act of consciousness. Bim's childhood dream of being a heroine plays out in a dimension she could not have foreseen.

The novel is set in postcolonial India as it attempts to accommodate both modernity and tradition. Bim exhibits the paradox in her personality. She is a new woman because she makes her own decision to stay single and have a career as a teacher, but at the same time, she seems stuck in the past, living in the decaying family home with a bitter feeling of being lonely and abandoned. She feels she has somehow taken Mira-*masi*'s place as the family drudge.

Although Desai is concerned with feminism and other postcolonial issues, she does not tackle them head on but rather filters the issues through the inner lives of the characters. Desai is famous for her ability to show women dealing with their marginality in Indian society. In *Clear Light of Day*, Aunt Mira (Mira-*masi*) is the main study of a traditionally subjugated Hindu woman, forced to marry at twelve, widowed at fifteen while still

WHAT DO I READ NEXT?

- *The House on Mango Street* (1984) is a young-adult novel by Mexican American writer Sandra Cisneros. It tells the story of Esperanza Cordero, a Latina girl growing up with her siblings in Chicago. Esperanza wants to escape poverty for a better life but vows to come back to help those she leaves behind. As with *Clear Light of Day*, the narration is subjective and poetic.

- *Women in Modern India* by Geraldine Forbes (2007) follows the history of Indian women from colonial times to the twentieth century after Independence. She shows how education gave women a public voice.

- Anita Desai's young-adult novel *The Village by the Sea: An Indian Family Story* (1983) tells the story of a lower-class Indian family falling on hard times. Thirteen-year-old Lila and her twelve-year-old brother Hari try to keep the family together. Hari goes to Bombay to earn his fortune and returns with plans for the future.

- *Hullabaloo in the Guava Orchard* (1998) is a novel by Kiran Desai, Anita Desai's daughter, offering a humorous look at the contradictions of growing up in a postcolonial culture. In a small town in India, a young man wants to run away from modern confusion, deciding to live in a tree with monkeys. He is mistaken for a holy man and consulted by the people.

- Novelist Ruth Prawer Jhabvala, like Anita Desai's mother, is a German Jew who married an Indian. *Heat and Dust* (1975) depicts the European fascination with India, as an English woman travels to India to discover the unconventional life of her step-grandmother Olivia during the British Raj in the 1920s.

- Kamala Markandaya, one of the pioneering modern women novelists of India, became famous with *Nectar in a Sieve* (1955) about suffering farmers in rural India, a story often compared to Pearl Buck's *The Good Earth* (1931), about farmers in China.

- Salman Rushdie's *Midnight's Children* (1981) with its magic realism is an important example of postcolonial literature about India. The novel's protagonist, Saleem Sinai, is born at midnight on August 15, 1947, the moment of Indian Independence, and is thus endowed with telepathic powers as are all others born at that time. This novel won the Booker prize for fiction.

- Virginia Woolf's *To The Lighthouse* (1927) is a stream-of-consciousness novel concerning the differing memories of the Ramsay family holidays as they try to visit a lighthouse in the Hebrides. One of Anita Desai's influences, Woolf excels in inner portraits of sensitive and alienated characters, written in rich poetic language.

---

a virgin, and then a household slave for the rest of her life, passed around as a servant. She has no dignity in the adult world, but as long as the Das children are small and dependent, they thrive from her warmth and attention: "She was the tree that grew in the centre of their lives and in whose shade they lived." Desai's novels show mothering as a two-edged sword. After Aunt Mira gives everything to the children, they grow up and do not need her. She is thrown away like an old rag and dies an alcoholic with hallucinations of being burned and drowned and suffocated by the very children she raised. She feels she will die, as the family "bride-like cow" died, when it fell into the black well in the yard and drowned.

Bim, even as a modern woman, is still trapped in her position. In Hindu society, an unmarried woman has no status. Dr. Biswas can only interpret her refusal of marriage as

> **BIM'S CHILDHOOD DREAM OF BEING A HEROINE PLAYS OUT IN A DIMENSION SHE COULD NOT HAVE FORESEEN."**

self-sacrifice in the traditional woman's way of taking care of others. He does not imagine she is trying to be independent. Now, however, she must take on both traditionally male and female roles in the household. She takes the father's role in marrying off her sister, taking care of the family business, and then supporting her mentally challenged brother with her salary. She plays the role of mother too: nurturing to her family, to her students, to the servants, and to her pet animals. Like Mira-*masi*, Bim is the tree in the center of the family, holding them all together, in the past and the present. She complains the family has deserted her, yet she is exhausted by Tara's visit in the paradox of "Loving them and not loving them. Accepting them and not accepting them."

The Das house is a major symbol in the novel. Like Poe's House of Usher, its decay symbolizes the depression of consciousness experienced by those who enter it. It also has a tarn or well, like the Usher mansion, that swallows up living things in death, such as the family cow. The children are terrified to get near it or look into it. Tara feels overcome when she first arrives by "the spirit of the house" with its "hopeless atmosphere of childhood." Tara traces this to "The secret, hopeless suffering of their mother . . . at the root of this subdued greyness, this silent desperation that pervaded the house." The house is female. Tara tells Bim the house always seemed cursed with "illness passing from one generation to the other so that anyone who lived in it was bound to become ill." That is why Tara escaped.

Desai had read *Wuthering Heights* at the age of nine, and in many ways the Das children growing up in their own world apart from their parents suggests the Brontë children in the parsonage where their mother died, and they all became ill and died young too. As Charlotte Brontë tried to compete with her Byronic brother, Branwell, so does Bim compete with her romantic and poetic brother, Raja, who,

during the Partition riots, longs to rush out like Lord Byron fighting for Greek liberty. When Raja becomes disinterested in Bim, she goes to his room and puts on his clothes, to see what it is like to be male. She imagines she would have more power if she could wear pants and smoke cigarettes.

Bidulata Choudhury, in *Women and Society in the Novels of Anita Desai*, quotes Desai on her interest in characters that turn against the common current and make a stand. Tara is the sister who went with the flow, while Bim did not. Bim is not one of Desai's tragic women, however. Bakul remarks of Bim's life, "She *made* what she wanted." Jaya Misra tells Tara that Bim has her own mind and "can take care of herself." These are great achievements for an Indian woman of her generation. Yet Bim is also upset that she was not prepared to participate in the world; her father expected Raja to run the office, and Bim has no idea how to direct business affairs. She tries to teach her students, college girls in jeans, "to be different from what we were at their age," for she still feels herself to be "badly handicapped."

Elizabeth Jackson in *Feminism and Contemporary Indian Women's Writing* points out that traditional Indian society is hierarchical in sex, caste, age, wealth, education, and kinship and that even with modernity, "individualism tends to be curtailed by existing societal and family situations." Raja has grown up expecting women and servants to wait on him, just as Bakul still waits for his wife to pour his tea. Bim sees what is waiting for her if she marries Dr. Biswas: she would be subservient to both his needs and the commands of his manipulative mother, because the extended family, although an eroding institution in modern India, still exists.

In "Feminist Critical Theory and the Novels of Anita Desai," Gajendra Kumar sees Desai's work as a manifesto against Indian patriarchy and female confinement. Purnima Mehta, in "Dehumanization of the Male in Anita Desai's Fiction," accuses Desai of presenting men unfairly through the lens of the female point of view and not portraying the normal give and take between men and women. Actually, Raja, as with many of Desai's male characters, is not portrayed as cruel, but instead he seems completely unaware of female individuality or needs. That is what hurts Bim; Raja does not see her as a person but as a dependent, like Mira-*masi*. She finds more solace in the company of her mentally handicapped brother, Baba, for he has no social ideas about her. He lives in a world of direct experience, and she appreciates his nonjudgmental innocence.

India, caught in its postcolonial double-value system of Eastern and Western ideas, is one reason why many intellectual women, like Anita Desai herself, are part of India's diaspora to Western countries. Western modernity, however, is no guarantee of happiness, as Desai has clearly pointed out in her book *Fasting, Feasting* and as Bim discovers. There is no one telling her what to do, but she pays a price in existential loneliness.

Indians are traditionally family-oriented. Desai's fiction, portraying highly individual female characters, with a full and private inner life, has been an important revelation in Indian English literature. She shows girls, wives, and old women having their own thoughts, feelings, reactions, and versions of events. Jackson points out, however, that Indian feminism has different concerns than Western feminism. While Indian feminism attacks the abuses of patriarchy, it sometimes sees Western feminism as too focused on individual rights and destructive of Indian cultural values. Community is very important to Indians, as is the role of the nurturing mother. The lack of a mother, such as in the Das household, is felt as a deep spiritual wound. In India, God has a mother's face as well as a father's. Mothers are sacred trees that give shade, sacred cows that give milk. Desai shows Bim heroically achieving a balance between her individuality and her motherly care for the needs of others. She stays home, but she is not really an abused martyr like Aunt Mira, and she has to make an inner journey in consciousness to see this.

In an interview with Ramesh Srivastava, Desai calls time the fourth dimension of the novel, a field in which the mind can travel forward and backward in its search for meaning: "I wanted Time to be an element, like light, or darkness, that is pervasive . . . a part of their everyday consciousness." Time, which has been such a problem for the Das family, separating them in hurts and misunderstandings, is also a ground of healing as it brings Bim to her realization. The novel at the end quotes T. S. Eliot on time as both destroyer and preserver. As Desai explains to Srivastava, with *Clear Life of Day* she wished to show that "nothing is lost, nothing comes to an end."

Desai is sometimes called the Indian Virginia Woolf for her sensitive stream-of-consciousness depiction of the inner life of women. *Clear Light of Day* in some ways recalls Virginia Woolf's "Moments of Being: Slater's Pins Have No Points," when Fanny understands the life of her piano teacher Julia through a transcendent moment of being where the other's wholeness is revealed to her. Similarly, Bim finds her own moment of being where she and all her family members are validated for her: "There could be no love more deep and full and wide than this one, she knew. . . . They were really all parts of her." Moments of being are actually not the property of Western literature, because American and European authors, such as T. S. Eliot, whom Desai quotes, borrowed freely from Eastern spiritual classics to express such ideas. While some critics refer to Bim's moment of enlightenment, Ushe Bande in *The Novels of Anita Desai: A Study of Character and Conflict* prefers to see Bim's moment of being as self-actualization of the kind described by the holistic psychologist Abraham Maslow. No matter the wording, Desai is known for wedding her stream-of-consciousness technique to her theme of women's growth of awareness, as Jackson points out.

Desai may have been inspired by Woolf, but she creates an Indian masterpiece with unforgettable scenes that have different meanings to an Indian sensibility than to a Western one. The ploys of Aunt Mira trying to win the children over with homemade gifts from her tin trunk is as poignant a scene as the one in Satyajit Ray's film *Pather Panchali* (1955) showing the unwanted old aunt getting food only through the kindness of the children.

Bim's moment of being is not completely solitary, because it is triggered by family members. It is Tara's constant probing into the past and into Bim's anger that leads to the discovery. Bim also is moved to her insight by the mute Baba who only responds to love and kindness. Bim said as a child she wanted to be a heroine. In her middle age, it is a heroic act to drop her stiff resentment and make a new direction for herself and her family that will heal the past. This new direction is not a ready-made one given by society but forged in the depths of her own self.

Source: Susan Andersen, Critical Essay on *Clear Light of Day*, in *Novels for Students*, Gale, Cengage Learning, 2014.

Clear Light of Day *incorporates Indian culture into the text.* *(© AJP | Shutterstock.com)*

Arun P. Mukherjee

In the following excerpt, Mukherjee explores the dependence of Clear Light of Day *on symbols of Indian culture and the cultural familiarity the reader must possess to understand the text.*

. . . I would now like to focus on one particular fictional text, Anita Desai's *Clear Light of Day*, and elaborate on my pedagogical strategies as well as my students' responses. I have chosen this text since it is widely taught and has also received considerable critical attention. However, few of the research articles in journals and books—focusing on aspects such as intertextuality of the text with British literature and American pop music, "universal" themes such as quest, search for identity, loss of innocence, and, more recently, post-colonial "resistance" to the colonizer's impositions—provide much help to my students in coming to grips with the cultural premises that are embedded in the text and account for its "Indianness."

> AGAINST THE CONFLICTLESS HIGH CULTURE'S PROMOTION BY BAKUL, WHO IS APPROPRIATELY A HIGH-RANKING CIVIL SERVANT, THE NOVEL UNCOVERS THE ANGUISHED HISTORY OF FRATRICIDE, OF PARTITION, OF RELIGIOUS BIGOTRY, OF TREATMENT AND REPRESENTATION OF WOMEN, AND FINALLY, OF THE DESTRUCTION OF ISLAMIC INDIAN CULTURE."

It is these cultural premises that I am interested in exploring and explaining to my students so that they may become aware of the dependence of the literary text on the totality of the symbolic resources of the culture the text emanates from. Often, it is the questions or the interpretations of my students that alert me to the culture-specific aspect of these symbolic codes as I had passed over them in my own reading, unaware of my own special knowledge as a "cultural insider" in my encounter with the text. For instance, if the text were being taught in India to Indian students, the teacher would not have to inform the students that the white sari of Mira Masi signifies her widowhood. However, the Canadian students need to be informed of this symbolism. Such realizations on our part make me and my students aware how culture-specific literary texts are and how important it is to know the social text if we really want to understand the literary text.

. . . The text, however, inverts these narratives of joyous adulterous love by pointing out their patriarchal underpinnings. While these narratives idealize the explicit sexuality of the Krishna-Radha legend as the allegorical rendering of the pining of a devotee for the incarnate God, Desai's use of the legends brings out their total irrelevance to the lived experience of Indian women. She suggests that dancing and teaching these stylized dances celebrating the love of Radha and Krishna is no exhilarating experience for Jaya and Sarla, the Misra sisters:

> Walking up the Misras' driveway, they [Bim and Tara] could hear instead the sounds of

the music and dance lessons that the Misra sisters gave in the evenings after their little nursery school had closed for the day, for it seemed that they never ceased to toil and the pursuit of a living was unending. . . . Bim stood apart, feeling a half-malicious desire to go into the house and watch the two grey-haired, spectacled, middle-aged women—once married but both rejected by their husbands soon after their marriage—giving themselves up to demonstrations of ecstatic song and dance, the songs always Radha's in praise of Krishna, the dance always of Radha pining for Krishna. She hadn't the heart after all. . . . After a while, the teachers, too, emerged on the veranda. They too drooped and perspired and were grey with fatigue. There was nothing remotely amusing about them.

The emphasis on "always" in "the songs always Radha's in praise of Krishna, the dance always of Radha pining for Krishna," brings out the selectiveness and repetitiveness of the thematizations utilized by the classical schools of Indian dancing, which are all heavily focused on the theme of Radha's and Krishna's lovemaking, carried out "always" in terms of Krishna's flirtations and ultimate abandonment of Radha. Desai's questioning of this art form pokes holes in the vocabulary of high seriousness that Indian dance critics employ. Her vocabulary seems to parody the mystical-formalistic mode of dance critics like Ananda Coomaraswamy, Sunil Kothari, and Kapila Vatsyayan whose studies of Indian classical dance have been published in expensive, lavishly illustrated books: "The poor Misra girls, so grey and bony and needle-faced, still prancing through their Radha-Krishna dances and impersonating lovelorn maidens in order to earn their living. . . . Bim shook her head."

As the term "always" had emphasized the frozen-in-time quality of the form, the term "prancing" mocks those who speak of it only in terms like "fluidity," "ecstasy," and "gracefulness." It asks us whether watching and enacting the same theme over and over again does not risk boredom. And it asks us to question the disjunction between the "lovelorn maidens" and the aging Misra sisters who must "impersonate" them in order to make their living. The novel, by giving voice to the plight of these aging and abandoned sisters, sets itself up in antithesis to the art form they must practise despite the fact that it obliterates their own sad realities. Unlike the novel, the dance has no room for women other than "lovelorn maidens."

One can only understand the boldness of this attack if one knows about the discursive idealizations of this dance form in the official cultural discourses of India that occurred under the nationalist project of manufacturing a new cultural identity. Beginning in the 40s, nationalist cultural critics sanitized the history of India's classical dance forms by renaming the dance as well as writing out of its history the prostitutes and temple dancers (Devdasis) who made their living by performing these dances for the entertainment of their rich clients. In fact, temple dancing by Devdasis was outlawed by the passage of a Bill in the Madras legislative assembly in 1947 in the name of morality and national honor. The dance was then "revived" under the aegis of "nationalization of Indian art and life and its almost 'religious' idealization . . . was in no small measure itself an effect of westernisation" (Srinivasan 196).

Supported by huge subsidies from the government and business patrons, India's classical dances were given a new cultural script. Nowadays, India's classical dancers present the eternal love play of Krishna and Radha in opulent concert halls, both at home and abroad. Indian dance critics comment on the "spirituality" of these dances in expensively produced and subsidized hard-cover volumes. Their exalted language hides the inability of the exponents of the dance form to connect and expand their art to encompass the lives of flesh and blood women. Desai's narrative, by bringing out the repetitiveness and frozen-in-time aspect of these dance forms creates a dissonance in the discursive consensus around India's high culture, which speaks of such things as "the attainment of the Infinite," and "absolute bliss in the Brahman" (Vatsyayan 5) etc., but not about the plane of day-to-day life and its iniquities.

This idealized view of classical Indian art is further critiqued in the novel in an exchange between Bakul and Bim that occurs only a few paragraphs after the passages quoted earlier:

> Elegantly holding his cigarette in its holder at arm's length, Bakul told them in his ripest, roundest tones, "What I feel is my duty, my vocation, when I am abroad, is to be my country's ambassador. . . . I refuse to talk about famine or drought or caste wars or—or political disputes. . . . I choose to show them and inform them only of the best, the finest."
>
> "The Taj/Mahal?" asked Bim.

"Yes, exactly," said Bakul promptly. "The Taj Mahal—the Bhagvad Gita—Indian philosophy—music—art—the great, immortal values of ancient India."

I tell my students that Bakul's view presents the officially sanctioned view of Indian culture—the culture Indian government exhibits at great cost at Indian fairs held in New York and Moscow. It is a view of culture frozen in the past and unable to encompass "famine or drought or caste wars." And it is highly selective. In Susie Tharu's words, this nationalist construction has produced "an almost unbearably tasteful past and an exquisite tradition." In it, "Women are no longer people, but goddess spirits. And as such, not alive or growing, but sculpted by the requirement of the emerging power" (262–63).

Desai's ironic uncovering of this "exquisite tradition" is, for me, the achievement of her text. Against the conflictless high culture's promotion by Bakul, who is appropriately a high-ranking civil servant, the novel uncovers the anguished history of fratricide, of partition, of religious bigotry, of treatment and representation of women, and finally, of the destruction of Islamic Indian culture. Raja's inability to go to Jamia Milia to pursue a degree in Islamic studies and the inability of his sisters to read his verses written in Urdu thematize the deliberate erasure of Islamic culture and Urdu literature in modern India. The Hindu bias in post-independence Indian historiography and Indian literary history are themes that are now being written about in oppositional terms by Muslim writers like Rahi Masoom Raza and Manzoor Ehtesham. Anita Desai's contribution to this oppositional discourse is indeed a gesture of tremendous integrity.

However, this oppositional aspect of the novel will remain inaccessible to my students unless I acquaint them with the politics of language and culture in modern India. Part of my work is done by Attia Hosain's powerful novel *Sunlight on a Broken Column*, which I teach before teaching *Clear Light of Day*. It describes vividly to them the partition of the country on the basis of religion and prepares them for the events and politics narrated in *Clear Light of Day*. Some stories still need to be told by me, however. I tell them about my father's education in English, Persian, and Urdu whereas my mother was educated, like Bim and Tara, in English, Hindi, and Punjabi. I tell them that this was so because of the combined impact of gender and religion. And, finally, I tell them of my own lack of education in Urdu and of the gap it leaves in my knowledge of my past. I tell them of major Indian writers like Prem Chand who wrote in both Hindi and Urdu, and how their Urdu writings have been forgotten.

The text's radical questioning of this forgetting and its intertextualizing of such famous Urdu poets as Zauq, Ghalib, Daag, Hali, and Iqbal can only be appreciated if we know the politics of language in contemporary India. For Canadian students, these aspects of the text, once explained, become illuminative of their own country's struggles around language and culture.

. . . I will end with one more passage from the novel that appears quite transparent on the surface but is really a deconstructive intertextualization with one of the grand themes of Bengali literature and culture. Dr. Biswas, the Bengali doctor who has been trying to court Bim, unsuccessfully, thinks that her reluctance to marry him is caused by her responsibility for looking after Mira-masi, Raja, and Baba:

> "Now I understand why you do not wish to marry. You have dedicated your life to others—to your sick brother and your aged aunt and your little brother who will be dependent on you all his life. You have sacrificed your own life for them."

Desai's heroine, Bim, is shocked "at being so misunderstood, so totally misread." Desai's use of the term "misread" once again reminds us of the power of social texts. For Dr. Biswas's "misreading" of Bim is informed by scores of Bengali novels and films. The rejection of marriage and love on the part of a young woman for the sake of providing for her family is a perennial theme in Bengali literature and has also been rendered on screen by such talented filmmakers as Ritvik Ghatak in his classic film *Meghe Dhaka Tara*.

On the surface, Bim's predicament appears quite similar to these sacrificing heroines of Indian fiction and Indian cinema who abjure marriage because of family responsibilities, and it is because of the cultural ubiquity of this theme that Dr. Biswas so confidently "misreads" Bim. By making Bim "reject" Dr. Biswas because she considers him a wimp and not because she is burdened by dependent family members, Desai parodies the sacrificial, sentimental heroine popularized by the stalwarts of Bengali fiction and cinema. By creating a heroine who wants autonomy rather than domestic bliss, and having her turn down the Bengali doctor, Desai creates a new script for Indian women at the same time that she mocks the earlier ones. There is perhaps no other heroine in Indian literature(s) who utters words such as Bim's with such emotional force:

> She was looking down, across the lighted, bustling garden to her own house, dark and smouldering with a few dim lights behind the trees, and raised her hands to her hair, lifting it up and letting it fall with a luxuriant, abundant motion. "I shall work—I shall do things," she went on, "I shall earn my own living—and look after Mira-masi and Baba and—and be independent. There'll be so many things to do—when we are grown up—when all this is over—" and she swept an arm out over the garden party, dismissing it. "When we are grown up at last—then—then—" but she couldn't finish for emotion, and her eyes shone in the dusk.

While the emotional charge of these words is not hard for my students to understand, surrounded and influenced as they are by feminist theories and feminist activism, they appreciate the text's radical stance even better when they learn about its oppositional intertextuality with the Bengali and Hindi texts about the sacrificing spinster who remains unappreciated by her ungrateful family members and ends up in a sanatorium. By creating a spinster heroine who refuses to be "read" in the framework of these discourses and by refusing to render her, as they do, as the object of pity and guilt, Desai's text engages in a discursive battle with the texts about sentimentalized femininity that continue to be churned out in great numbers in India. The terms of its battle are specific, not universal, just as the constructions of gender and femininity are culture-specific.

My classroom, then, is a place to explore the kind of meanings that a text generates in its place of production. Such an exploration presupposes that human beings, both the author and her/his characters, are social and historical beings, and their subjectivity is formed by their response to their concrete historical situation. To the extent that I focus on the text's relationship with the other discourses and material realities of a society, I steer my students away from the notions of universality as they operate in literary criticism, both in terms of technique and themes. I see my goal as a teacher to be to wean my students away from the ethnocentric universality that unproblematically applies the thought and behavior patterns of a critic's own culture to the rest of humanity, refusing to acknowledge and/or value

difference. If I succeed in making my students aware of the universalizing tendencies of Western literary theory, consider my teaching to have attained its desired goal. . . .

Source: Arun P. Mukherjee, "Other Worlds, Other Texts: Teaching Anita Desai's *Clear Light of Day* to Canadian Students," in *College Literature*, Vol. 22, No. 1, February 1995, p. 192.

Richard Cronin

In the following essay, Cronin examines Desai's treatment of India and Indian life and culture in Clear Light of Day.

Like *Midnight's Children*, *Clear Light of Day* is at once a family chronicle and a history of modern India. But there is a crucial difference. In *Clear Light of Day* history is glimpsed only out of the corner of the eye. In the partition riots Delhi is ablaze, but the fires are on the horizon. The novel takes place in Old Delhi's Civil Lines, 'where the gardens and bungalows are quiet and sheltered behind their hedges,' and the residents only imagine that they 'hear the sound of shots and of cries and screams.' It is here that the family live, the four children—Raja, his two sisters, Bim and Tara, and Baba, the youngest son, the retarded baby of the family. Raja and Tara leave, Raja to marry the daughter of a rich Muslim businessman, and Tara to marry a diplomat and enter on the displaced life of the embassy, shifting from country to country, returning to India from time to time in a forlorn attempt to 'keep in touch.' Bim teaches history at the local college. Her life oscillates between history and memory, between the comfortingly distant history of the Moghul empire that she teaches at college, and the memories that she broods over at home: sad memories for the most part, of her aunt's lapse into alcoholism, and of the rupture that took place between herself and her brother, embittering the love that she still feels for him.

It is a noisy house. Badshah, the dog on which Bim lavishes her affection, irritates the neighbours with his non-stop barking, and Baba plays over and over again at full volume his small collection of 1940s records. The noise grates on the nerves of visitors, sometimes on Bim's nerves too, but the noise works only to drown out the noises of the outside world. However paradoxically, it works to preserve a silence, the silence in which Bim has chosen to live out her days.

Time stopped for her in 1947. Then her sister married, and her beloved brother left home. She lives with her memories, two memories in particular—the one associated with her aunt, the other with her brother. The aunt—really a poor relation taken in by Bim's mother so that she need not be distracted by her children from her bridge—recommended buying a cow. The cow broke its tether, stumbled into the garden well, and was drowned. That image—the white cow, green slime and black water—haunted Bim's aunt as she lay dying. The white cow is balanced by a white horse. 'Can you remember,' Bim asks Tara 'playing on the sand late in the evening and the white horse riding by, Hyder Ali Sahib up on it, high above us, and his peon running in front of him, shouting, and the dog behind him, barking.' It is the image that first inspired Raja with a vision of the grace of Islam, the glamour of India's Moghul past, and the beauty of Urdu. It gave him the ambition to become when he grew up a poet or a hero, a second Iqbal, or someone who might single-handed heal the wounds of his country's partition by the practice of a reckless magnanimity. Bim's emotional life is suspended between a white dream and a white nightmare, between love and bitterness.

Raja married Hyder Ali's daughter, became his heir, and wrote Bim a letter assuring her that he would not increase the rent she pays for the family house. Bim has never recovered from the shock of her brother, her hero, diminishing to a landlord. She keeps the letter by her, until, at the end of the novel, she destroys it, as a sign that she has recovered from her sterile obsession with the past. It is the progression figured in the novel's third white memory, a memory associated with Tara. Tara was running after her mother as her mother strolled through the rose garden. She spied something gleaming from under a heap of fallen rose petals, a pearl, or a silver ring. But what Tara finds when she bends to look is a 'small blanched snail.' 'Her face wrinkling with disgust her mother turned and paced on without a word, leaving Tara on her knees to contemplate the quality of disillusion.' The incident is recalled again later in the novel, but, as it is repeated, it is transformed. Tara stayed for a while on her knees 'crushed with disappointment, then lifted the snail onto a leaf and immediately delight gushed up as at a newly mined well at seeing the small creature unfold, tentatively protrude its antennae, and begin to slide forward on a stream of slime.' The loss of

childish illusions need not after all be sad: it may mark the beginning of the adult's capacity to find joy in looking at the world undeceived. At the end of the novel Bim forgives her brother, forgives him for being not what she dreamed he might be, a pearl, a silver ring, a hero, but for being what he is.

In the novel's last scene Bim has left her house, left her garden. She has not been released into a full possession of the great and wonderful land of India—Anita Desai's novels do not work like that—she has only gone next door, to listen to her neighbour singing. She still lives in her house as if in a shell, and she can only progress as snails do, slowly. But she is no longer self-enclosed: her horns have emerged and are alert to the world around her. After the neighbour, his teacher sings in his old man's voice: 'All the storms and rages and pains of his life were in that voice, impinging on every song he chose to sing, giving the verses of love and romance a harsh edge that was mocking and disturbing.' It is a voice that redeems by its beauty the ravages of time, the pain, and the disillusionment that it embodies: 'Vah! Vah! someone called out in rapture—it might have been the old man listening above on the veranda—and the singer lifted a shaking hand in acknowledgement.' So the novel ends, not with Baba playing over and over again his collection of 1940s records with their depressingly ironic titles—'Don't fence me in'—but with an old man making beauty not by ignoring the passage of time, but by accepting it.

Bim's was a family overtaken by history, unprepared for life in an independent India. Her parents spent their lives playing bridge at the club, intently conning their hands, unaware of the movement of history that was bringing their way of life to an end. Their children were educated in English, in Christian schools, educated into a culture that in 1947 packed its bags and left, condemning them to live their lives as a futile exercise in nostalgia, dreaming like Bing Crosby on Baba's record of a white Christmas. Bim is offered no magic release. Even when she listens to the old man's song, what it brings to her mind is a line from *Four Quartets*. She and Raja will be friends again: the partition in the family will be healed. But the incident has no national implications, for *Clear Light of Day* determinedly refuses allegory. All that Bim is offered is a moment; a Hindu singing a song by Iqbal, Pakistan's national poet, and herself responding with a verse of T.S. Eliot's—a privileged moment in which her own, and India's, fragmented cultural heritage becomes one, and Bim feels at peace with herself and at peace with her land. . . .

Source: Richard Cronin, "The Quiet and the Loud: Anita Desai's India," in *Imagining India*, Macmillan Press, 1989, pp. 45–58.

Shouri Daniels

In the following review, Daniels discusses the themes, characterization, and narrative structures in Clear Light of Day.

Clear Light of Day is an English novel (as distinct from American, Russian or French), and it surpasses all other novels in English set in India in characterization, poetic use of landscape and integrity of vision. As might have been expected, the publisher's description finds in the novel "echoes we haven't heard since E. M. Forster's *A Passage to India*." This is somewhat misleading. Anita Desai's novel brings to mind not the Forster of *A Passage* but the Forster of *Howard's End*. In broad conception, the similarities between the two novels are obvious: the atmosphere of both novels is built around a house, both might have been titled *Two Sisters* (in Desai's novel, the sisters—Bim and Tara—share an inner sensibility that sets them apart from others, as is the case with the Schlegel sisters in Forster's novel); both belong to the tradition of the comedy of manners; both use the domestic to suggest the larger social fabric; both rely on symbols that are drawn from the inner as well as the outer world, while managing to convey the nineteenth-century view of man as something continuous with nature.

In *Clear Light of Day* Tara returns to her childhood home on Bela Road, Civil Lines, Old Delhi, to visit her sister Bim and their retarded brother Baba. (Civil Lines is a leafy residential area where one can find families with old money.) The time is summer. The days are dry and dusty; the reunion throws up images of past years. We move through the present to the past and back again through the separate perspectives of the sisters. A fourth member of the family, the older brother, Raja, lives in Hyderabad. Bim and Raja once perceived themselves to have affinities and heroic aspirations in common, but they are now estranged.

> ANITA DESAI'S SUCCESS HERE PROVES THAT THE COMEDY OF MANNERS IS PARTICULARLY SUITED TO REPRESENTING INDIAN LIFE WHERE THE HEROIC AND THE ANTI-HEROIC INVARIABLY HAVE A DOMESTIC FRAME."

The narrative of the story concerns the forthcoming wedding of Raja's daughter, an event Tara means to attend with her diplomat husband and daughters, but Bim cannot bring herself to go. Her sense of injury and hurt isolates her. Today in every Indian family there is a Bim, a daughter who stays home to take care of members of the family who have nowhere to go and no means of support. Such women seldom discover the luxury of self-definition and do not see themselves in a heroic light. The society demands it of them, and they are taken for granted. (The fatted calves are reserved for the prodigals.) Tara is aware that she deserted Bim. Though morally sensitive, Tara resists the circle of oppression, and the resulting ambiguity and tension between the two sisters has a compelling reality. The final movement of the novel is toward harmony, as in many English novels. When Tara and her family pile into a car with their American suitcases, even though Bim's face seems made of "dried clay that had cracked," there is a recognition of affinities between Tara and Bim, and a suggestion of a possible meeting with the absentee head of the household, Raja.

Bim is the strongest character in the novel. She perceives Old Delhi as a city that does not change, but merely decays. Old Delhi, she says, quoting one of her students, "is a cemetery, every house a tomb. Nothing but sleeping graves." Just as Old Delhi has more life in its burial grounds than is suspected by Bim, Bim has more vitality than is suspected on the surfaces of the narration. Tara perceives her sister as "part of the pattern." For Tara, the pattern had grown old, and

> Bim, too, gray-haired, mud-faced, was only a brown fleck in the faded pattern. If you struck her, dust would fly out. If you sniffed, she'd make you sneeze. An heirloom, that was all— not valuable, not beautiful, but precious on account of age. Precious to whom?

The question is an ironic one. Bim had stayed on to nurse the sick, cremate the dead, and watch the retarded. Abandoned to this task, she endured—earned a degree, found work, held herself and her world together. She had perceived herself as the center of that world, but there was no one left in it other than the near-mute brother who could do nothing at all except listen all day to "Lili Marlene" and "Don't Fence Me In" on an old gramophone.

To escape the waiting, the wanting, the sense of oppression and absence that hung over their house, Tara married a diplomat. The parents were obsessed with their games of bridge after the Roshanara Club; they came home to sleep or dress. The mothering the children received came from a hand-me-down aunt, Mira, a widow who had served another household of relatives from her twelfth year, as unpaid servant—for that is the lot of widows. Mira had been paying off her guilt of widowhood. Finding her unattractive and useless, her in-laws wished to place her with another family. A new home was now to "find some use for her: cracked pot, torn rag, picked bone." Tara needed her most, and folded herself in Mira's white sari, yet it was Bim who nursed her when Mira finally drank herself to madness and death. At the end of the novel, the parallel between Bim and Mira is brought up defensively by Tara.

The poetic way the novel gains depth might be best seen in the symbol of the cow and the well. Mira persuades the parents to buy a cow for the children's supply of milk, soon after she joins their household. Within a week the cow drowns in the well and

> the well then contained death as it once had contained merely water, frogs and harmless floating things. The horror of that death by drowning lived in the area behind the cavanda hedge like a mad relation, a family scandal or hereditary illness waiting to re-emerge.

It does re-emerge. In her final delirium, Aunt Mira is obsessed with the well,

> the hidden, scummy pool in which the bride-cow they had, had drowned, and to which she (Aunt Mira) seemed drawn. Bim held her wrists all night, wondering why of all things in this house and garden it was the well she wanted, to drown in that green scum that had never shown a ripple in its blackened crust since the cow's death.

The use of the word "bride-cow" extends the image of the cow to Aunt Mira:

There was something bride-like about her white face, her placid eyes and somewhat sullen expression. The children fondled her pink, opaque ears that let in the light and glowed shell-pink in the sun.

Mira, scarcely a bride-child, had been interred after the death of her husband (who was sent abroad for an education). The green scum would then be the appropriate spot for one who had lived and been exploited for most of her life. The image does not end there, it goes on to envelop Bim, whose life takes on the complexion of her aunt's life:

> . . . for Bim dreamt night after night of her bloated white body floating on the surface of the well. Even when drinking her morning tea, she had only to look into the tea-cup to see her aunt's drowned face in it, her fine-spun hair spread out like Ophelia's, floating in the tea.

Bim takes on the guilt, though least guilty. Bim endures; Tara escapes. Bim has a power, therefore, that Tara's moral nature dreaded:

> That rough, strong, sure grasp—dragging her down, down into a well of oppression, of lethargy, of ennui. She felt the waters of her childhood closing over her head—black and scummy as in the well at the back.

The two sisters pick up the image of the well, each in her own way; they have a moral dimension that is lacking in the male characters in the novel. Neither the parents, nor the absent brother, nor the wastrel sons of the Misra family next door, have any qualms. The Misra men live off the earnings of their widowed sisters. The novelist wisely refrains from any authorial remarks on the sociology of a situation that is becoming all too common in Indian cities.

Old man Misra sits on his patriarchal divan—he eats, sleeps and lives on the veranda—casting his patriarchal eye on his sons, and remarks to Bim:

> Look at them—fat, lazy slobs, drinking whisky. Drinking whisky all day that their sisters have to pay for—did you hear of such a thing?

He nonchalantly goes on to admit that he was not any different at their age, but boasts:

> When my sister's husband died, I brought her to live with us. She has lived here for years, she and her children. Perhaps she is still here, I don't know. I haven't seen her.

The irony underscores the callousness and the piety. The reader guesses there is an Aunt Mira in the Misra home.

Desai does not preach; she presents a narrative in which there is not one man who has a moral consciousness. And Desai's style is not tilted. She gives the absent brother full scope in the remembrance of things past. He had fallen in love with the image of a man (their Nawab-like Muslim neighbor and landlord, Hyder Ali) on a white horse on the white banks of the River Jumna, a peon ahead of him, a dog behind him, riding each evening. Entranced, Raja took to Urdu poetry, Islamic culture, pro-Muslim politics (during the holocaust years of Partition) and finally followed Hyder Ali to Hyderabad, where he married the Muslim's daughter, inherited his wealth and lived out the life of his dream man. Raja is now Bim's landlord. He writes her a letter in which he decides not to raise the rent!

Traditional Indian families were bastions of male privilege, and with the privilege went certain duties. Family identity, caste names, communal affiliations and familial functions defined a person. In *Clear Light of Day*, the family name (Des) is revealed just once after the parents' deaths. Desai's voice is quiet and ironic, but she has a sure understanding of how to project a fractured tradition. The persecution of widows, the burning of brides, the economic exploitation of women in Indian family life—these would be too horrible in a novel of sensibility, where a little goes a long way.

Desai has a gift for evoking a physiognomy with a phrase (for example, Aunt Mira's "bird-boned wrist" at her death, or her "bride-like face" on arrival) and she can bring alive an entire way of life in a few lines, as in the case of the surly driver who continues to sit outside the garage door, after the family car has been sold, sometimes smoking, "staring over the caps of his knees," till finally they permit him to be the gardener's helper.

It seems a shame to cavil at so splendid an offering, but cavil I must. Anita Desai seems to be intoxicated with similitude. When these work, they are brilliant and refreshing and add to the immediacy of the writing (". . . his mouth shut in astonishment so that he looked like a fish that had snapped up a hook by accident") but sometimes they do not work: ". . . his voice rising to a shrill peak and then breaking on Baba's head like eggs, or slivers of glass," or "Just one injection and the old woman lay still, slipping neatly as a little tube into heavy sleep." There are too many passages, as well, each about a page long, where the stream-of-consciousness technique is used, and each time it throws the narrative out of focus without adding anything to it.

Although the sisters are negative about the house and the old city, the reader's reaction could with justification be different, if only because the world within the novel pulsates with life in an unexpected way. It has memorable moments with mynahs, koels, kites, pigeons, egrets, budgerigars, hornbills, horses, crickets, frogs, snails, caterpillars, cats (a cat stalks a butterfly), and dogs and river birds. Never have so many flowers, creepers, bushes, trees raised their heads in fiction: the bougainvillea, the spider lilies, the asparagus ferns, the cannas, the jasmine, the chamelis, the hibiscus, the roses (smelling of tea-leaves), the begonias, the oleanders, the jacaranda, the papaya, the guava, the lemon trees, the fig trees, the silver oaks, the mulberry, the eucalyptus, the castor oil plant . . . Never since the nineteenth century has a city raised such "jocund" company.

One enjoys Desai's sudden clairvoyance: "The navel of the world it (the well) was, secret and hidden in thick folds of grass, from which they all emerged and to which they must return, crawling on their hands and knees." And anyone who has written fiction will notice the success of the concluding insight: "'Nothing's over,' she agreed. 'Ever,' she accepted." Desai takes a cliché ending from the popular English tradition and makes it work—the character who utters the concluding insight ("Nothing's over") has earned the right to say it, and the "English" design of the novel is fulfilled by suggesting continuity and connections, while, at the same time, a deeply Indian attitude is reflected in such a closure.

This novel was not written for "Export Only," as too many Indian novels in English tend to be. Anita Desai's success here proves that the comedy of manners is particularly suited to representing Indian life where the heroic and the anti-heroic invariably have a domestic frame.

Source: Shouri Daniels, "Anita Desai's *Clear Light of Day*," in *Chicago Review*, Vol. 33, No. 1, Summer 1981, pp. 107–12.

SOURCES

Annan, Gabrielle, "Dreams in Old Delhi," in *Times Literary Supplement*, September 5, 1980, p. 948.

Bala, Suman, and D. K. Pabby, "Introduction: The Fiction of Anita Desai," in *The Fiction of Anita Desai*, edited by Suman Bala and D. K. Pabby, Khosla Publishing House, 2002, pp. 1–23.

Bande, Usha, *The Novels of Anita Desai: A Study in Character and Conflict*, Prestige Books, 1988, p. 141.

Choudhury, Bidulata, *Women and Society in the Novels of Anita Desai*, Creative Books, 1995, p. 49.

Desai, Anita, *Clear Light of Day*, Harper & Row, 1980.

Indira, S., *Anita Desai as an Artist: A Study in Image and Symbol*, Creative Books, 1994, p. 196.

Jackson, Elizabeth, *Feminism and Contemporary Indian Women's Writing*, Palgrave, 2010, pp. 1–11, 115.

Jain, Jasbir, *Stairs to the Attic: The Novels of Anita Desai*, Printwell Publishers, 1987, p. 112.

Jena, Seema, "The Place of Anita Desai among Indian Woman Fiction Writers in English," in *Voice and Vision of Anita Desai*, Ashish Publishing House, 1989, pp. 1–15.

Kumar, Gajendra, "Feminist Critical Theory and the Novels of Anita Desai," in *Indian Women Writers*, edited by Jaydipsinh K. Dodiya and K. V. Surendran, Sarup & Sons, 1999, pp. 21–23.

Mehta, Purnima, "Dehumanization of the Male in Anita Desai's Fiction," in *Indian Women Writers*, edited by Jaydipsinh K. Dodiya and K. V. Surendran, Sarup & Sons, 1999, pp. 36–37.

Naikar, Basavraj, "The Paradox of Time in *Clear Light of Day*," in *The Fiction of Anita Desai*, edited by Suman Bala and D. K. Pabby, Khosla Publishing House, 2002, pp. 225–40.

Srivastava, Ramesh, "Anita Desai at Work," in *Perspectives on Anita Desai*, edited by Ramesh Srivastava, Vimal Prakashan Publishers, 1984, pp. 224–25.

———, Introduction to *Perspectives on Anita Desai*, edited by Ramesh Srivastava, Vimal Prakashan Publishers, 1984, pp. xiii, xvi.

Varady, Evelyn Damashek, "The West Views Anita Desai: American and British Criticisms of *Games at Twilight and Other Stories*," in *Perspectives on Anita Desai*, edited by Ramesh Srivastava, Vimal Prakashan Publishers, 1984, p. 194.

Brewer, Wanda E., "T.S. Eliot's *Four Quartets* and the Four-Fold Pattern of Anita Desai's *Clear Light of Day*," in *Literary History, Narrative, and Culture*, edited by Wimal Dissanayake and Steven Bradbury, University of Hawaii Press, 1989, pp. 132–39.

> Brewer discusses the influence of T. S. Eliot on Desai and the themes of his poetry in her novel.

Iqbal, Muhammad Allama, *Tulip in the Desert: A Selection of the Poetry of Muhammad Allama Iqbal*, translated by Mustansir Mir, McGill-Queen's University Press, 2000.

> Iqbal (1887–1938) is one of the great Urdu and Persian poets and philosophers, influential in inspiring the creation of Pakistan. The introduction explains his place in Islamic thought.

Khan, Yasmin, *The Great Partition: The Making of India and Pakistan*, Yale University Press, 2008.

> Yasmin Khan is a British historian who shows the terrible human cost of the political decision to split India into two hostile countries.

Riemenschneider, Dieter, "History and the Individual in Anita Desai's *Clear Light of Day* and Salman Rushdie's *Midnight's Children*," in *The New Indian Novel in English: A Study of the 1980s*, edited by Viney Kirpal, Allied Publishers, 1990, pp. 187–99.

> Both novels concern the days of Independence and Partition and were written during Indira Gandhi's State of Emergency. Both Desai and Rushdie avoid historical realism and treat history from subjective and imaginative narrative viewpoints.

Rushdie, Salman, and Elizabeth West, eds., *Mirrorwork: 50 Years of Indian Writing, 1947–1997*, Henry Holt, 1997.

> This important anthology presents an overview and excerpts of the significant writers of the Indian renaissance in English, including both Anita Desai and her daughter, Kiran Desai. Rushdie's introduction is a defense of Indian writers using English, the colonial language, instead of Indian languages.

FURTHER READING

Afzal-Khan, Fawzia, *Cultural Imperialism and the Indo-English Novel: Genre and Ideology in R. K. Narayan, Anita Desai, Kamala Markandaya, and Salman Rushdie*, Pennsylvania State University Press, 1993.

> Afzal-Khan uses the postcolonial theories of Frantz Fanon, Fredric Jameson, Edward Said, and others to understand how the novelists named in the title attempted to break away from colonial constraints through the way they use the genre of the novel. She discusses the tension between myth and realism in Desai's work.

SUGGESTED SEARCH TERMS

Anita Desai

Clear Light of Day

Indian English literature OR Indo-Anglian literature

stream-of-consciousness novel

Indian Partition

postcolonial novel

history of India

Old Delhi

women Indian novelists

The Hundred Secret Senses

AMY TAN

1995

In an interview with the Academy of Achievement, Amy Tan tells that, when she was growing up, "There was a lot of storytelling going on in our house: family stories, gossip, what happened to the people left behind in China." These stories were clearly significant to Tan because she includes autobiographical elements in many of her books, including *The Hundred Secret Senses* (1995). Just as Olivia in the novel learns that her father left behind a daughter when he came to America to find a better life, Tan herself learned that she had half-sisters in China. As an adult, Tan traveled to China with her mother after she recovered from a serious illness, much as Olivia and Kwan return to China: both Tan's and Olivia's journeys brought better understanding of cultural heritage, the importance of family, and self. Drawing from her personal experience allows Tan to breathe life into her characters, filling them with emotion.

The Hundred Secret Senses includes sexual situations, some descriptions of war-time violence, and casual references to recreational drug use. It is therefore more appropriate for older students.

AUTHOR BIOGRAPHY

Tan was born on February 19, 1952, in Oakland, California. Her mother, a nurse, and her father,

Amy Tan *(© Frank Capri / Archive Photos / Getty Images)*

an electrical engineer and Baptist minister, immigrated separately from China. "My parents had very high expectations," Tan said in an interview with the Academy of Achievement. "They expected me to get straight A's from the time I was in kindergarten." They also hoped that she might become a surgeon or a concert pianist, but Tan knew she wanted to be a writer from the time she was eight years old, when she won an essay contest in a local newspaper.

When Tan was fourteen, both her brother and her father died of brain tumors, and Tan and her mother moved to Switzerland. There Tan attended an expensive private school and developed a rebellious streak. This teenage rebellion was the beginning of a difficult relationship between mother and daughter.

Tan finished high school in 1969, and the family moved back to the United States. Her mother pressured her into enrolling at a Baptist college. Tan went on a blind date with Louis DeMattei, the man who would become

her husband, and dropped out of school to follow him to San Jose. Tan graduated from San Jose State University with honors, majoring in English and linguistics. She continued at San Jose State, earning a master's degree in linguistics. She then enrolled as a doctoral student at Berkeley but did not complete her degree. After leaving school, Tan used her background in linguistics, working as a consultant helping to develop programs for disabled children. She also worked as a freelance business writer.

The idea for Tan's first book, *The Joy Luck Club*, began as a short story called "The Rules of the Game." A literary agent saw the story in *Seventeen* magazine and encouraged Tan to continue writing. Tan expanded the idea into a novel that was published in 1989. It became a best seller, was nominated for the National Book Award, and was adapted into a successful film. Other fiction followed: *The Kitchen God's Wife* (1991), *The Hundred Secret Senses* (1995), *The Bonesetter's Daughter* (2001), and *Saving Fish from Drowning* (2005). She has also published various essays and short stories.

Tan published *The Opposite of Fate: A Book of Musings*, her first full-length nonfiction work, in 2003. The book describes how Tan struggled with Lyme disease for years before she was correctly diagnosed, which greatly hindered her writing until she finally received proper treatment. As of 2013, Tan lives in San Francisco and New York with her husband.

PLOT SUMMARY

The scenes in the novel are not in chronological order. The narrative describes Kwan's previous life in China in 1864, as well as modern times, jumping back and forth between various periods throughout Olivia's life.

Part I

CHAPTER 1: THE GIRL WITH YIN EYES

Olivia, the primary narrator, describes how her family learned about her half-sister, Kwan, her father's daughter from his marriage in China. His first wife died, and he left Kwan with her aunt in a small village and went to Hong Kong to find work. When the communists took over China in 1949, their father could not get back to Kwan and left for America.

MEDIA ADAPTATIONS

- Tan herself reads *The Hundred Secret Senses* in the Audible Audio Edition, which was released in 1999. This audiobook is abridged, and the length is approximately six hours.

- In 2008, Playaway released *The Hundred Secret Senses* as a library edition on a pre-loaded digital audio player. This version is unabridged, but it may be difficult to acquire.

- An unabridged version of *The Hundred Secret Senses* is available on audio cassette from Books on Tape. It is read by Frances Cassidy and was released in 1996.

Olivia's mother, Louise, keeps her promise to her dying husband to bring Kwan to America, but she is nothing like they expected: she is not a "Chinese Cinderella," shy and half-starved but still somehow glamorous. Instead she is "like a strange old lady, short and chubby." Because Olivia's mother is still in a "honeymoon phase" with Bob, her new husband, Olivia is often left in Kwan's care. Instead of appreciating her, Olivia resents her.

Kwan tells Olivia a "forbidden secret": that she has "yin eyes" and can see people who have died. Olivia, frightened, tells her mother, and when Bob finds out, he puts Kwan into a mental institution. Kwan, however, does not blame Olivia for not keeping her secret.

Olivia loves Kwan because they are sisters, but she often gets annoyed at her. Olivia reveals that she and her husband are divorcing, and Kwan will not accept it. She tells Olivia that she talked with one of her "yin people," Lao Lu, who said that if Olivia, Kwan, and Simon go to China together, everything will work out.

CHAPTER 2: FISHER OF MEN

Kwan relates some of her past life in 1864, when she was a young girl named Nunumu. An American military leader called General Cape convinces most of the people living in a small mountain village to join the leader called the "Heavenly King" and rebel against the Man-chus, but the general then betrays them. Nunumu saves an American woman, Miss Banner, and her servant Lao Lu after they fall into a river. Nunumu stays to work in the house where Miss Banner lives with a group of American missionaries.

CHAPTER 3: THE DOG AND THE BOA

Olivia and Simon argue as they negotiate their separation. Kwan tells the story of Miss Banner's life. Nunumu helps Miss Banner learn to speak Chinese and tries to teach her to see the world as a Chinese person does. Olivia remembers how, influenced by Kwan, she also began to see ghosts. At first she only pretended, but then she started to truly believe she saw ghosts.

CHAPTER 4: THE GHOST MERCHANT'S HOUSE

Olivia's mother comes over to cheer her up after her break-up with Simon but instead makes her feel resentful. She remembers a Christmas when her mother and Bob went on a trip, leaving Kwan to care for the younger children.

Kwan tells Olivia that she saw Lao Lu in church and continues the story of life in 1864. Miss Banner explains that her sweetheart has deserted her. She translates the sermon every Sunday even though she is not a true believer because if she does not, Pastor Amen will not let her continue living in the house. Nunumu discovers that Miss Banner's sweetheart is the trai-tor General Cape.

CHAPTER 5: LAUNDRY DAY

Olivia reminisces about meeting Simon in college. She quickly falls in love with him, but he is oblivious because he is devoted to his late girlfriend, Elza. Olivia brings her laundry to Kwan's house and has dinner with her. Kwan tells more about her past life: one day when Nunumu is hanging the laundry in the garden, she finds General Cape and his assistant, Yiban Johnson. Miss Banner is very glad to be reunited with General Cape, and she is angry with Nunumu for saying that he will betray her.

Part II

CHAPTER 6: FIREFLIES

Olivia and Simon kiss for the first time. Simon feels guilty and explains that Elza was killed six months before in a skiing accident.

Elza feared she might be pregnant, and they had a big argument just before she died.

CHAPTER 7: THE HUNDRED SECRET SENSES

Olivia competes with Elza's memory—trying to do things she would have liked. She hopes that this will make things work with Simon. Simon and Olivia go to Kwan's house for dinner, and Kwan talks to Elza in the yin world. Kwan gives lots of details, and it seems to convince Simon that she is truly speaking to Elza's spirit. Kwan tells Simon that Elza wants him to forget her. Olivia thinks she herself sees Elza and that she desperately wants Simon to remember her and be loyal, but Olivia keep this a secret.

CHAPTER 8: THE CATCHER OF GHOSTS

Simon and Olivia get married. Their decision to marry is completely unromantic—they do it for tax reasons. The wedding does not go well. They learn that they cannot have children. When they buy an apartment and move in, lots of strange noises convince Olivia that it is haunted. Kwan tries to trap whatever is making the sounds but concludes that it is "not ghost."

CHAPTER 9: KWAN'S FIFTIETH

Olivia becomes increasingly frustrated with her marriage. She feels the shadow of Elza all the time and worries that she and Simon are not connecting. Simon comes up with a plan for a trip to China. He will write an article about village cuisine, and Olivia will take pictures. They send a proposal to travel and food magazines.

Olivia finds a computer file: Simon is writing a book about a character named Eliza, clearly based on Elza. They argue and Simon moves out. Olivia watches a video of Kwan's fiftieth birthday party. She contrasts herself on the video, looking like a "zombie," with Kwan, who is very happy and full of life.

Part III

CHAPTER 10: KWAN'S KITCHEN

Olivia has dinner with Kwan, who passes on Lao Lu's message that Olivia must stay with Simon. Kwan continues the tale of her life in 1864. Miss Banner takes General Cape back even though he abandoned her before. Miss Banner will not speak to Nunumu because she knows that Nunumu disapproves of the relationship. Yiban Johnson tells Nunumu about his life as a half-Chinese, half-American man.

CHAPTER 11: NAME CHANGE

Olivia learns that her downstairs neighbor is the one causing the eerie sounds in her apartment. The proposal for the article is accepted, and Kwan wants all three of them to go, but Olivia says no. Kwan tells Olivia that Yee is not their father's real name. He changed his name because he found papers for a man named Jack Yee that would get him into America. Kwan says they must go to China to find his real name.

CHAPTER 12: THE BEST TIME TO EAT DUCK EGGS

Simon tells Olivia he thinks she should go to China without him. This kindness makes Olivia ask him to go along after all. Kwan is "tipsy with happiness."

Kwan explains how in her past life she made "thousand-year duck eggs," which are fresh eggs preserved in a mixture of lime and salt. Miss Banner and General Cape disappear. Everyone assumes they have run off together, but the next day Nunumu finds Miss Banner in the garden. General Cape left her behind. Miss Banner asks Nunumu to kill her because she is sad and ashamed. Instead, Nunumu ties Miss Banner to a tree so that everyone thinks Miss Banner tried to stop the general. Yiban finds her bag, which makes it obvious she intended to leave as well, but he makes it clear that he will keep this a secret.

Miss Banner and Yiban become friends and start flirting. Nunumu is jealous. Nunumu starts a flirtation with the peddler who trades her jars for her duck eggs. Pastor Amen, Doctor Too Late, and Yiban go to see if the boat is coming from Canton, bringing them money to buy food and supplies. They get caught up in Chinese clans fighting among themselves and fighting against British rule. Pastor Amen becomes unbalanced. They run out of food and are forced to eat bugs and mice. Nunumu breaks into her treasured store of preserved duck eggs so that they do not starve.

CHAPTER 13: YOUNG GIRL'S WISH

Olivia wakes up on the first morning in China. She is worried about getting food poisoning or parasites and wants to eat in the hotel, but Kwan convinces her to go out and get breakfast from the vendors outside. Kwan talks to the man who sells them their breakfast, who says that Changmian, Kwan's hometown, is cursed. They go to a bird market and rescue an owl. Kwan plans to release it from the mountains once they are home and make a wish, according to a local tradition.

CHAPTER 14: HELLO GOOD-BYE

They find a driver, Rocky, to take them to Changmian. During the drive, they see a serious bus accident, but Rocky says there is nothing they can do to help and refuses to stop. Olivia and Simon find Changmian charming because it is not modernized.

Kwan is greeted by old friends. She thinks she sees her aunt, Big Ma, who raised her until she left for America, but the neighbors explain that she went by bus to greet them and will be back later. There is a welcome party, and an official comes to tell them that Big Ma was killed in the accident they saw that morning from their taxi. Kwan lets the owl go.

CHAPTER 15: THE SEVENTH DAY

Kwan mourns Big Ma. She explains that the "secret sense" that helps her see into the yin world is the "language of love."

Back in 1864, Zeng tells Nunumu that the Heavenly King is dead, and that the Manchus are taking revenge against his followers. Zeng asks Nunumu to run away with him, but she is concerned for Miss Banner and the others. Zeng agrees to take them as well. When Nunumu tells the missionaries about the danger, only Miss Banner, Yiban, and Lao Lu agree to go. While they are waiting for Zeng, General Cape comes with soldiers, who kill Lao Lu. Miss Banner sends Nunumu to find Yiban and keep him safe, knowing that General Cape will kill everyone if she tries to leave. Nunumu sees Zeng as a ghost. He tells her where to hide and says he will wait for her forever. Yiban and Nunumu hide in a mountain cave.

CHAPTER 16: BIG MA'S PORTRAIT

Kwan, Olivia, and Simon take Big Ma's body back to Changmian. Kwan chats with Big Ma and learns that she wants Olivia to take her picture. They go to Big Ma's house and meet Du Lili, an old family friend. In the small house, Simon and Olivia must share a bed with Kwan. Olivia asks Du Lili if she believes in Kwan's yin people, but Du Lili will not answer.

Kwan and Olivia go to the community hall to take Big Ma's picture while a crowd of villagers watches. Du Lili asks Olivia to take her photograph and is shocked that she looks so old. Kwan tells Olivia that Du Lili had an adopted daughter who died. Du Lili was "crazy with sorrow" and came to believe that she was her own daughter.

CHAPTER 17: THE YEAR OF NO FLOOD

Kwan explains that when she and Du Lili's daughter, who was called Buncake, were five years old, Buncake drowned. A flood came and washed Kwan and Buncake down a flooded ditch. When Kwan woke up, Big Ma and Du Yun (Du Lili's original name) thought she was a ghost. She seemed to be in Buncake's body instead of her own. Kwan explains that she went to the yin world but returned because Olivia's spirit came to say she would be born soon and made her promise to wait.

CHAPTER 18: SIX-ROLL SPRING CHICKEN

Olivia does not know what to think about Kwan's story. Olivia cannot speak the local dialect and therefore cannot ask anyone for the truth. Olivia and Simon watch Kwan and Du Lili preparing a meal. Du Lili kills a chicken and uses its blood in the stew, and they are served "pickle-mouse wine." At first, Simon and Olivia are shocked, but they open themselves to the new experience and end up laughing.

After dinner they are looking at the mountains, and Kwan tells them about a village of caves inside the mountains. Simon wants to explore, thinking there might be prehistoric dwellings there. He hopes to write a story that he will sell to a big publication like *National Geographic*. When they go to bed that night, Olivia is crowded between Kwan and Simon in Big Ma's bed.

CHAPTER 19: THE ARCHWAY

When Olivia wakes, Kwan is gone, and she and Simon are snuggled up together. She tries to resist, but the intimacy of being close and Simon's teasing win her over. Kwan later sees Olivia smiling and knows that she and Simon are starting to reconcile.

Simon and Olivia explore the caves in the mountains. It begins to rain heavily, and they take shelter in one of the caves. They argue. Olivia claims that their marriage fell apart because of Elza, but Simon believes Olivia made Elza "the scapegoat for all [her] insecurities." Olivia runs back to Big Ma's house, leaving Simon in the cave.

CHAPTER 20: THE VALLEY OF STATUES

When Simon still has not returned by afternoon, Olivia and Kwan go to look for him. Olivia lets her fear overcome her and loses her way. Kwan finds her; she is bearing a wooden box. The two women decide to wait together for Simon to appear, lighting a small camp stove to keep warm. Kwan opens the chest, explaining to Olivia that it is the music box belonging to Miss Banner. Olivia is not sure whether that is true, but she knows Kwan well and believes "it isn't in her nature to lie." Olivia admits to herself that she might have been Miss Banner in her previous life.

CHAPTER 21: WHEN HEAVEN BURNED

Kwan finishes the story of what happened in 1864. Nunumu leads Yiban to a safe cave and then returns to the village for Miss Banner. Everything is in chaos at the missionaries' house. Pastor Amen went mad (or was possessed by Lao Lu) and killed General Cape, accidentally hitting Miss Banner and breaking her leg. Fearing what the Manchus would do to them, Miss Mouse, Doctor Too Late, and Pastor Amen and his wife all committed suicide. Nunumu helps Miss Banner flee from the village. They cannot find Yiban, and they are killed.

CHAPTER 22: WHEN LIGHT BALANCES WITH DARK

Kwan explains that many of the people from Changmian hid in the caves that night in 1864. Some people went home and let it be believed that they were ghosts, which is why some now call the village cursed. Kwan tells Olivia that she first saw Lao Lu and Yiban as yin people when she was six years old. She claims that Simon is Yiban reincarnated and that he is waiting for Olivia the way Yiban waited for Miss Banner. Kwan goes to find Simon, and Olivia waits at their makeshift campsite. Simon appears, but Kwan does not return.

Part IV

CHAPTER 23: FUNERAL

Various search teams look for Kwan in the caves, but no one is able to find her. After Big Ma's funeral, Olivia digs in the garden and finds the crumbling duck eggs that Nunumu buried so long before.

CHAPTER 24: ENDLESS SONGS

Olivia describes what happened to everyone in the two years since Kwan's death. Kwan's husband, George, remarries. Olivia and Simon have a fourteen-month-old daughter. No one can explain why they are able to have a baby now when they tried before without success, but Olivia calls her daughter "a gift from Kwan" and says that she and her baby took Kwan's last name, Li. Simon and Olivia are still living separately, but they are "practicing being a family." The baby loves Miss Banner's box, and the final image of the book is Olivia dancing with her daughter to its music.

CHARACTERS

Pastor Amen

The pastor's surname is really "Hammon or Halliman, something like that," but Nunumu and the other servants began calling him "Pastor Amen" because they were supposed to shout "Amen" during his sermons when he cued them to do so by raising his eyebrows. Pastor Amen leads the missionaries, none of whom are able to accomplish much in terms of truly teaching any of the villagers about Christianity. When the turmoil between the Hakka people and the Manchus approaches their village, Pastor Amen becomes unbalanced. Whether because of his mental instability or because he was possessed by the vengeful spirit of Lao Lu, Pastor Amen kills General Cape and accidentally injures Miss Banner.

Mrs. Amen

Mrs. Amen is the pastor's wife.

Nelly Banner

Miss Banner is the American woman who becomes friends with Nunumu in 1864. Kwan believes that Olivia is Miss Banner reincarnated. Miss Banner has relationships with several different men before the start of the story, including General Cape, who abandons her twice. She seems to have a genuine connection to Yiban, and her most important relationship by far is her friendship with Nunumu. She alone among the missionary household makes an effort to get to know the Chinese servants as individuals. Miss Banner's music box becomes an important symbol in the book. It is the music box that makes Olivia begin to believe that Kwan's stories of 1864 might be true, and at the close of the book, the box's music gives Olivia hope for the future and a continued connection with Kwan.

Big Ma

Big Ma is Kwan's aunt, who raised her after her father left for Hong Kong to find work. She was not very kind to Kwan. Big Ma dies in an accident just as Kwan, Olivia, and Simon get to China.

Simon Bishop

Simon is Olivia's husband. When they first meet in college, he is still devoted to his last girlfriend, Elza, who died in a skiing accident. Throughout their entire relationship, Olivia feels she has to compete with Elza's memory. She resents it, though she is the one who encourages Simon to keep thinking about Elza by bringing her up and pursuing activities that she would have enjoyed.

Buncake

Buncake is Du Lili's adopted daughter. She is called "Lili" because that's all she says when she is first found, but soon everyone calls her by the nickname "Buncake" because of her chubby cheeks. She is killed in a flood that Kwan survives. After Buncake dies, Du Yun takes her name and becomes Du Lili.

General Cape

General Cape is an American military leader who becomes involved in Chinese politics, encouraging the villagers to join the Heavenly King in revolting against the Manchu leadership. He deserts the villagers, however, just as he deserted Miss Banner. He is responsible for Lao Lu's death and is killed in turn by Pastor Amen, who may have been possessed by Lao Lu's vengeful ghost.

Doctor Too Late

The doctor's real name, Swan, sounds like the Chinese for "too late," earning him this nickname.

Betty Dupree

Betty is Louise's cousin. Olivia and her brothers call her "Aunt Betty." She comes to the hospital when Jack is dying.

Jaime Jofré

Jaime is one of Louise's boyfriends after she divorces Bob Laguni. Louise is upset to discover that Jaime is married.

Yiban Johnson

Yiban's name comes from the Chinese *yiban ren*, which means "one-half man." He is called this because his father was American, an old friend of General Cape, and his mother was a young Chinese woman who killed herself when Yiban's father abandoned her. Yiban is General Cape's assistant and translator. When General Cape abandons Miss Banner for the second time, she becomes close friends with Yiban, and they plan to escape together. Kwan tells Olivia that Simon is Yiban reincarnated and that he is waiting for her just as Yiban waited for Miss Banner.

Bob Laguni

Bob is Louise's second husband and Olivia's stepfather. Olivia and her brothers call him "Daddy Bob." Bob does not seem to like having Kwan with the family. When Olivia admits that Kwan told her she can see ghosts, Bob sends her to a mental institution. Bob and Louise eventually divorce.

Louise Kenfield Yee Laguni

Louise is Olivia's mother. She is more interested in her "volunteerism," which includes everything from serving dinner to the homeless to being a foster mother to terriers, than in being a mother to her children. She often leaves Olivia in the care of her stepsister, Kwan. As a girl, Louise longed to be more exotic; as a result, all of the men she falls in love with as an adult are of different ethnicities.

Kevin Yee Laguni

Kevin is one of Olivia's brothers.

Tommy Yee Laguni

Tommy is one of Olivia's brothers.

George Lew

George is Kwan's husband. Kwan believes that he is Zeng reincarnated. George seems like a good husband to Kwan, and he is a "wretched mess" when he accepts that Kwan is not coming back.

Kwan Li

Kwan, as Nunumu, is the first-person narrator of the parts of the story that take place in 1864. She is Jack Yee's daughter from his first marriage in China. She is half-sister to Olivia, Kevin, and Tommy. Kwan confides in Olivia that she has "yin eyes." This means that she can see people in the yin world, which is a kind of afterworld where Kwan can speak to people who have died and people whom she knew in her past life.

Kwan is an exuberant and happy person; she does not seem to understand that she sometimes annoys Olivia, and she always forgives Olivia for being short-tempered or unkind. Kwan believes that in 1864, Olivia's spirit inhabited Miss Banner, and she herself was Nunumu, a girl from a mountain village who became Miss Banner's servant and then her friend. Kwan does not accept Olivia's separation from Simon. She is certain that they will reconcile, in part because Kwan believes them to be reincarnations of Miss Banner and Yiban, who promised to always wait for each other.

Olivia Yee Laguni Bishop Li

Olivia is the first-person narrator of the parts of the story that take place in modern times. She is Louise and Jack's daughter, Bob Laguni's stepdaughter, Simon's wife, and Kwan's half-sister. These relationships, in this order, explain her lengthy name. Kwan, with her imperfect English, pronounces Olivia's name "Libby-ah." Olivia has a troubled relationship with her half-sister. Kwan is very affectionate and tells Olivia her secrets, but as a child, Olivia says unkind things and resents Kwan for "taking my mother's place." Louise is more to blame for this: she is always volunteering for things like helping the homeless and stray dogs. While these are good causes, she pursues them instead of caring attentively for her children, and she often leaves Olivia in Kwan's care. Indeed, Olivia's relationship with her mother is also strained.

Olivia's marriage to Simon is breaking down throughout the novel. From the time they first met in college, Simon felt guilty and obsessed over his late girlfriend, Elza. Olivia allowed Elza's memory to rule over her own relationship with Simon. At first Olivia used what she knew about Elza as a way to get close to Simon, and then later she constantly worried that Simon was always comparing her to Elza and finding her lacking.

Lili

See Buncake

Du Lili

Du Lili is a friend of Kwan's aunt, Big Ma. Du Lili had an adopted daughter about the same age as Kwan. Du Lili's real name is Du Yun, but when her daughter drowned, Du Lili went "crazy with sorrow" and took her daughter's name as part of her own.

Lao Lu

Lao Lu, like Nunumu, is one of the Chinese servants in the missionaries' house. Rather bad-tempered and always cursing, Lao Lu speaks rudely to General Cape and his soldiers, and they kill him. From the yin world, Lao Lu speaks to Kwan often. He insists that traveling to China with Kwan will save Olivia and Simon's marriage.

Miss Mouse

Miss Mouse is the nickname given to one of the missionary women because her true surname, Lasher, sounds like the Chinese word for "mouse."

Nunumu

Nunumu is Kwan's identity in her past life. The events in 1864 that Kwan narrates are from Nunumu's point of view. When Nunumu was seven years old, she was injured when a "rock tumbled down the side of the mountain and smashed out her eye." From that point on, she was called Nunumu after a character in a legend who also lost her eye. Because the girl in the story was brave and strong, Nunumu is proud of her nickname. Nunumu meets Miss Banner and becomes her servant. As Nunumu teaches Miss Banner to speak Chinese and to learn the Chinese way of life, they become friends. Nunumu tries to help Miss Banner when General Cape abandons her and when the Manchus are approaching the village, but she is killed.

Rocky

Rocky is the driver who takes Olivia, Kwan, and Simon to Changmian. He wants to practice his English so that he can go to America and become a martial arts movie star.

Mr. Shirazi

Mr. Shirazi is one of the men that Louise dates after her divorce from Bob Laguni. She brings him to Kwan's fiftieth birthday party.

Elza Vandervort

Elza is Simon's late girlfriend. She was adopted and never knew her birth parents. Her name was Elsie, but she changed it to Elza when she decided that she was descended from Polish Jews. Just before she died, she and Simon had a huge argument, and he feels guilty when he starts getting involved with Olivia. Throughout their marriage, Olivia blames Simon for their problems, but she is the one who cannot forget about Elza.

Jack Yee

Jack Yee is Louise's husband and Olivia and Kwan's father. Louise and her children are shocked to learn that he had been married before as a young man in China. On his deathbed, he asks Louise to promise that she will find his daughter and bring her to the United States. Later Olivia is surprised to learn that Jack Yee is not his real name. He found papers bearing that name and pretended to be Jack Yee so that he could leave Hong Kong, come to America, and attend college.

Du Yun

See Du Lili

Zeng

Zeng is the peddler who gives Nunumu jars to make her preserved duck eggs while they flirt. When the Manchus are coming Zeng offers to help Nunumu flee, but he is killed before they can escape. Kwan believes George is Zeng reincarnated.

THEMES

Family

Throughout *The Hundred Secret Senses*, the characters, especially Olivia, explore what it means to be a family. As soon as Olivia learns about her stepsister Kwan, she is full of doubt and insecurity. She believes that Kwan will replace her in the family. She asks angrily, "Why did I get Kwan for a sister? Why did she get me?" Olivia thinks that "in so many ways, Kwan never fit into our family." As a child, Olivia resists letting Kwan into her heart, and even as an adult, Olivia says,

> I'm not saying I don't love Kwan. How can I not love my own sister? In many respects, she's been more like a mother to me than my real one. But I often feel bad that I don't want to be close to her.

In spite of this, Kwan remains dedicated to Olivia, who does not understand Kwan's continued devotion, asking "Why do I remain her treasured little sister?" When Olivia needs help, however, whether because of Simon's obsession with Elza or because she believes her new apartment is haunted, she turns to Kwan. As the novel progresses, Olivia tries to be more kind to Kwan.

The trip to China is part of Olivia's resolution to change: she finally agrees to go because it

TOPICS FOR FURTHER STUDY

- In *The Hundred Secret Senses*, Olivia and Simon go to explore the caves and rocks near Changmian. Using the Internet, research karst rock formations like those in Shilin National Scenic Area in China. Make a PowerPoint presentation with images of these unique formations. Explain to your class how and when they were formed, and relate at least one legend that people tell about the rocks.

- Read *The Afterlife* by Gary Soto, in which teenager Chuy is killed during a misunderstanding. His ghost travels through his California town, finding out what others truly think of him and learning lessons he ignored in life. Create a scene, either as a short story or as dialogue from a play, where Tan's character Kwan, with her "yin eyes," meets Chuy.

- After reading Bapsi Sidhwa's young-adult book *An American Brat*, write an essay about the novel's heroine, Feroza Ginwalla, a Pakistani teenager sent to live for a while in America with her uncle. Compare Feroza's immigrant experience with Kwan's.

- Research nineteenth-century Chinese history. Make a time line that displays the historical events of the Opium Wars and the Taiping Rebellion and indicate where events in the novel fit into that time line. Share your time line with your classmates.

seems very important to Kwan. However, Olivia discovers many things on the trip that make her question whether Kwan is truly her half-sister. The story about the flood, where Kwan is swept away and wakes up, as she claims, in Buncake's body makes Olivia suspicious; she wonders if the village sent another girl to America because the real Kwan had drowned.

By the end of the novel, Olivia accepts that Kwan is her sister. Even if they are not related by blood, they are bound together because they have spent so much of their lives together and because they care for each other. It does not really matter whether Olivia truly believes that she and Kwan are the reincarnated spirits of Miss Banner and Nunumu. By accepting what Kwan believes and by promising to wait outside the cave while Kwan goes to look for Simon, Olivia brings Kwan "peace." Kwan feels as though Olivia has finally accepted her completely as part of her family.

The theme of family is also echoed in other small details of the novel. For example, Du Lili adopts Buncake and becomes her mother. Du Lili cares for her daughter so much that she becomes unbalanced when the child drowns. Also, Nunumu and the other servants in the merchant's house become a kind of family, as do the missionaries in their own way—relying on one another and trying to help each other through the hard times after General Cape has stolen their money and they are starving. Nunumu and Miss Banner, especially, become close. This may be why they are reincarnated as sisters. Perhaps the most important part of the theme of family in the novel is that blood ties matter less than ties of affection. A family is made up of people who care for each other, even if they are not related.

Abandonment

There is a recurring pattern of abandonment in *The Hundred Secret Senses*. This theme first appears in the opening scene when Olivia's father dies. Louise tells the children, "Daddy's left us." Of course, Jack Yee did not die by choice, but for a young child who cannot truly understand death, it is easy to get confused and feel abandoned by a parent who has died. Soon afterward, it is revealed that Jack abandoned his older daughter, Kwan. He left with good intentions, trying to find work to improve his daughter's life, but he still left her, allowing her to be cared for by an unkind aunt. He abandoned her again when the communists took over China, making it impossible for him to return from Hong Kong. He left for America and never made any effort to find her. He never even told his second wife about Kwan until he was dying.

There are several romantic relationships in the novel that are ruined by abandonment: General Cape abandons Miss Banner more than once, and Yiban's mother is driven to suicide

Tan's novels explore the importance of past and heritage, particularly her characters' Chinese heritage. (© feiyuezhangjie | Shutterstock.com)

when his father leaves them. Some of the happier relationships are ruined, if not by abandonment then by other kinds of separation. Several times, characters such as Miss Banner and Yiban or Olivia and Kwan promise to wait for each other and then are never able to reunite.

Abandonment also characterizes Olivia's relationship with her mother. Louise is infected by "seasonal rashes of volunteerism," during which she throws her time and energy into various causes but ignores her young daughter. Olivia is cared for by Kwan but comes to resent her for "taking my mother's place." Because Olivia feels that her mother abandoned her as a child, they never have a solid relationship once Olivia is an adult. Olivia's lasting resentment also affects her relationship with Kwan, though she seems to move past that by the end of the book.

STYLE

First-Person Narrator

Throughout the novel, the story alternates between two first-person narrators. The sections that take place in modern times are narrated by Olivia, and Kwan describes her past life as Nunumu in the scenes of 1864. By using both characters, Tan is able to present their very different perspectives. Readers cannot always assume that first-person narrators are reliable because, in contrast to an impartial, omniscient narrator, their emotions and their experiences color what they say. By comparing the way Olivia and Kwan (through Nunumu) see the world, readers may catch hints of where each of them makes mistakes.

Nonlinear Narrative

Tan does not present the events in *The Hundred Secret Senses* in chronological order. Instead, the chapters jump back and forth between the life of Nunumu in a small Chinese village in 1864 and the modern life of Olivia. Also, within Olivia's life, the story reveals events that occur in her childhood, while she is in college, and when she is an adult with a crumbling marriage. By using this nonlinear narrative, Tan reveals the plot and the characterization gradually, so the reader learns only a bit of the story with each chapter and has to figure out how the pieces fit into the time line.

For example, are readers meant to believe that Kwan really can see "yin people"? Was she truly Nunumu in a former life? When Kwan's secret is first revealed, she is sent to a mental institution—everyone thinks she must be crazy to believe that she can talk to ghosts. As pieces of the puzzle are revealed, both the reader and the character Olivia learn a little at a time and can slowly start to accept that Kwan is telling the truth. It is easy for Olivia not to argue with Kwan when she claims that General Cape is reincarnated as a loyal pet dog—it would seem silly to protest about something so unimportant and humorous. Having accepted this makes it easier for Olivia to later consider the possibility that she herself might be the reincarnation of Miss Banner. Having the novel reveal important information as it is relevant, rather than in chronological order, allows Tan to guide her readers' thoughts about the events and characters in the story.

HISTORICAL CONTEXT

The Taiping Rebellion

The political events in *The Hundred Secret Senses* revolve around the Taiping Rebellion (1850–1864). When Nunumu is a child, she sees General Cape giving supplies and uniforms to the people of her village. The first forces gathered for the rebellion came from villages like these, in minority Hakka areas of rural China. The Taiping armies were rebelling against the Qing dynasty, which was led by the Manchus.

The term "Manchu" was first used in 1635 and included people of various ethnic backgrounds, including Jurchen, Mongolian, Han Chinese, and Korean, who lived in northeast China. The Manchus were considered barbarians by the Han people of the Ming dynasty, but in spite of being heavily outnumbered, the Manchus conquered the Ming empire and established the Qing dynasty in 1644. Over the next thirty years, they conquered all of China.

By the middle of the nineteenth century, China's economy was suffering, and the Manchu leaders were blamed. The influence of foreign powers, such as Britain, was also criticized. Although China never became a part of the British Empire as India did, the British did make efforts to bring the Qing regime back into power because it seemed they had already learned to do what the British wanted.

The Taiping Rebellion was led by Hong Xiuquan, who was a farmer's son. Many of China's poorer people, living in hard times under an oppressive government, were encouraged by the things Hong said. He criticized the ruling class and promised to make things fair, taking away the power of landlords and making all citizens equal. Hong's followers were called "God worshippers" because he used elements of Christianity to appeal to the people. He claimed to be the son of God, the younger brother of Jesus, and was therefore called the "Heavenly King." Thousands joined the cause as Hong led the rebel forces to the imperial city of Nanjing, taking control from the Qing in 1853 and ruling from there for the next eleven years.

The dynasty that Hong established was very different from what he had promised. There was indeed a treasury to ensure that the common people had food and clothing. However, the vast majority had only the basics necessary for survival, while Hong and the other leaders lived in palaces with servants and many luxuries. Hong managed to keep the people's support by continuing to promise benefits, such as land reform, while in fact he killed many of those who protested his regime.

Qing armies attacked Nanjing in July 1864. The so-called Heavenly King had died, and the

COMPARE & CONTRAST

- **1860s:** The vast majority of Chinese people live in small rural villages. Many suffer under difficult economic times as political struggles, such as the Taiping Rebellion, are complicated by European involvement.

  Today: Approximately 50 percent of China's people still work in agriculture, but urban populations are growing as more people move to cities to find work. China is a communist country, but in recent years changes have been made to move toward a more free-market system. China now has one of the fastest-growing economies in the world.

- **1860s:** Taoism, Buddhism, and Confucianism are all observed in China, but the formal practices of these religions are often mixed with worship of local gods and old traditions of honoring ancestors. The goal of Christian missionaries is religious conversion.

  Today: After the Boxer Rebellion in 1900, during which China rejected most foreign influences, missionaries shift their focus to social reform, working to improve the lives of Chinese citizens, especially women. In the

  middle of the twentieth century, the rise of communism suppresses all religion, but in the 1970s, these restrictions are relaxed. The number of Christians in China is now growing.

- **1860s:** Approximately fifty-four thousand people immigrate from China to the United States, mostly to seek greater economic opportunities. Ethnic discrimination and non-Chinese workers' fears about losing jobs lead to the passage of the Chinese Exclusion Act, which stops all immigration of Chinese laborers for ten years. This legislation, enacted in 1882, marks the first time in American history that Congress placed major restrictions on immigration.

  Today: Although the Chinese communist leadership restricts emigration and some consider those who wish to leave "traitors," many hope to move to Western countries. Between 2000 and 2010, almost six hundred thousand Chinese people come to live permanently in the United States.

Manchus reclaimed the city and their power. They were merciless to those who had rebelled against them. Thousands were killed. In the novel, Nunumu and her friends die in this violent vengeance.

CRITICAL OVERVIEW

Tan's first book, *The Joy Luck Club*, was a huge success. Laura Shapiro describes the reaction in *Newsweek*: "Critics and readers went wild." After such sudden popularity, Tan must have found writing a second book "nerve-racking," according to Shapiro, who calls *The Kitchen God's Wife* "beautifully written . . . but melodramatic."

However, Shapiro believes Tan saved her reputation with the novel *The Hundred Secret Senses*, which is "more finely nuanced than her previous two."

In a *Booklist* review, Joanne Wilkinson calls *The Hundred Secret Senses* "mesmerizing and awkward." Diane Fortuna, in a review of the book for *America*, writes that Tan "has an impeccable ear for both contemporary West Coast speech and Chinese-American dialect." In *Contemporary American Women Fiction Writers: An A-to-Z Guide*, Carman C. Curton especially praises "Tan's acknowledgment of the wisdom and knowledge of her older female characters, subtly represented through layers of nested stories."

However, Fortuna describes how Tan's focus on this particular issue can become a weakness at

In The Hundred Secret Senses, *the co-heroine Kwan is uprooted from her life in rural China to move to San Francisco.* (© stephane106 / Shutterstock.com)

times: "Her canvas . . . seems limited to the relationships between Chinese and Chinese-American mothers and daughters." In contrast, the male characters, Fortuna feels, are "unaccountably mysterious or downright villainous or just unrealized." Ruth Pavey, in her review in *New Statesman & Society*, agrees, explaining: "Like Kwan in the caves of Guilin, the last part of this story gets a little lost" before Tan returns to familiar territory: "hope for the future, embodied in the relationship between mother and daughter."

Critics have nothing but praise for the portrayal of the character Kwan. Wilkinson writes, "Kwan steals every scene she appears in." The *Publishers Weekly* review says that "in Kwan, Tan has created a character with a strong, indelible voice," whereas "needy, petulant, skeptical Libby [Olivia] is not as interesting." Perhaps it is *Publishers Weekly* that best sums up the overall reaction to the novel: "Some readers may feel that the ending is less than satisfactory, but no one will deny the pleasure of Tan's seductive

prose and the skill with which she unfolds the many-layered narrative."

CRITICISM

Kristen Sarlin Greenberg

Greenberg is a freelance writer and editor with a background in literature and philosophy. In the following essay, she examines the significance of names in The Hundred Secret Senses.

Shakespeare proclaims in *Romeo and Juliet*, "That which we call a rose, By any other name would smell as sweet." Indeed it is true that whatever name we call a thing cannot change what it is. However, words and names are powerful. They can represent more than just their literal meaning. In *The Hundred Secret Senses*, Amy Tan uses the implications of names as a kind of shorthand to provide information about her characters' identities.

The first indication of the significance of names appears on the very first page of text,

WHAT DO I READ NEXT?

- Gene Luen Yang's *American Born Chinese* (2006) tackles issues of identity with humor. This graphic novel blends traditional tales of the Monkey King with the story of a Chinese American teenager trying to fit in at school.

- *Autumn in the Heavenly Kingdom: China, the West, and the Epic Story of the Taiping Civil War* (2012) by Stephen R. Platt is a well-reviewed history of the Taiping Rebellion.

- Tan's first novel, *The Joy Luck Club* (1989), explores many of the same themes as *The Hundred Secret Senses*, such as cultural identity and the relationships between mothers and daughters.

- Mother-daughter issues, secrets, and stories that span generations are also prominent in *Divine Secrets of the Ya-Ya Sisterhood: A Novel* (1996), by Rebecca Wells.

- Darlene Deibler Rose relates her experience as a missionary caught in political upheaval in *Evidence Not Seen: A Woman's Miraculous Faith in the Jungles of World War II* (1988).

- Early in *The Hundred Secret Senses*, Olivia mentions her mother's interest in the film *The Good Earth*, which was an adaptation of Pearl S. Buck's 1931 book. The novel won the Pulitzer Prize in 1932, and Buck was awarded the Nobel Prize for Literature in 1938.

---

where Olivia establishes the characters of "my father, Jack Yee" and "our mother, Louise Kenfield." The formality of these introductions draws attention to the names. Louise calls herself "American mixed grill, a bit of everything white, fatty, and fried," meaning that her heritage is composed of several different nationalities, presumably mostly European. When she was young, she dreamed of being "thin, exotic, and noble like Luise Rainer," who played a Chinese woman in the movie *The Good Earth*.

This desire to be different increases Louise's interest in Jack Yee. She takes his name when they marry, enjoying the label because she believes that "marrying out of the Anglo race makes her a liberal."

Names are also important in Louise's choice for her second husband. She assumes that he is of Mexican descent because of his last name: Laguni. The foreign sound of his name attracts her. It turns out that he is Italian American, and Olivia's brother Kevin learns on a trip to Italy that Laguni is "an orphan's name . . . a made-up name that nuns gave to orphans. Laguni—like 'lagoon,' isolated from the rest of the world." The meaning of the name stresses the lack of connection that Olivia feels.

The novel is full of other names that are important in outlining identities for the characters. For example, Simon's former girlfriend was "Elsie" for most of her life. Then she became convinced that she was descended from Polish Jews who died in a concentration camp and began calling herself "Elza." Du Yun takes on part of her adopted daughter's name and becomes Du Lili after the child's death, reflecting her devotion and sorrow, as well as her confused belief that she has actually become her daughter. When the missionaries begin to interact with their Chinese servants, everyone receives a nickname except for Miss Banner, which highlights the fact that she is the only foreigner who makes the effort to get to know the Chinese people as individuals.

Yiban Johnson's name also echoes who he is. When Tan first introduces the character, General Cape calls him "*yiban ren*," which means "one-half man" in Chinese, and the surname comes from his American father. His name, half-Chinese and half-American, portrays his confusion about his identity and his place in the world. "I have been both Chinese and foreign, this makes me neither," he tells Nunumu. "Tell me, whom do I belong to? What country? What people? What family?"

Perhaps Tan's most important use of names in the novel is Olivia's decision to change her name when she separates from her husband, Simon. Olivia's surname changed from her birth name of Yee to Laguni when her stepfather adopted her. It changed again, to Bishop, upon her marriage to Simon. When she and Simon decide to divorce, she wants to change her name to reflect this major change in her life,

Amy Tan often explores the relationship forged between mother and daughter. *(© leungchopan | Shutterstock.com)*

but she cannot make up her mind about which name to use. Olivia explains, "As I think more about my name, I realize I've never had any sort of identity that suited me, not since I was five at least, when my mother changed our last name to Laguni." She considers going back to her original surname, but she thinks the name "sounds alien, as though I'd become totally Chinese, just like Kwan. That bothers me a little." Olivia cannot be proud of her relationship with Kwan or comfortably associate herself with her Chinese heritage at this point even though, as Olivia says to her brother, "It's hip to be ethnic."

It is no accident that this issue is discussed almost exactly halfway through the novel. Tan is drawing attention to a central theme of the story: the search for one's identity. Olivia struggles with this issue throughout, but it is during this scene that she begins to consciously understand her problem. She asks herself, "Isn't it time to feel connected to somebody's name?" By this she means that she wants to identify herself with a name that reflects who she truly is and what is important to her.

When Olivia mentions to Kwan that she is planning on changing her name back to Yee, Kwan has a rather dramatic reaction. Olivia describes Kwan "vigorously shaking her head. Her face is scrunched up. Is she choking?" Kwan seems to understand that in giving up the name Bishop, Olivia is also giving up on any hope of reconciling with Simon. Kwan also admits that Jack Yee was not their father's true name. He adopted it because he found papers bearing that name that would allow him to travel to America, get an education, and create a better life. Kwan tells Olivia how their father changed when he changed his name. Kwan's mother watched him

> turn himself into this man Yee by putting on his clothes, cutting his hair. . . . He had no warm feelings anymore for my mother. She said it was as though he had become this man Yee . . . a man who was arrogant and powerful—eager to be rid of his past, in a hurry to start his new fate.

In other words, he turns into a man capable of leaving his daughter behind and keeping her a secret for over a decade.

This revelation confuses Olivia even more. If she cannot claim her original surname, she does not know what to do. However, by the close of the book, Tan makes it clear that Olivia has started to shape her identity. She has taken steps toward reconciling with Simon or has at least come closer to understanding her part in the deterioration of their relationship. The trip to China, although Kwan was lost, cemented the relationship between her and Olivia, allowing Olivia to feel at peace with the part of Kwan that she saw in herself. She calls her daughter "a gift from Kwan" and explains: "She and I took Kwan's last name. . . . What's a family name if not a claim to being connected in the future to someone from the past?" In taking Kwan's name as her own, Olivia shows that she has accepted Kwan as her true sister, learned to value her Chinese heritage, and figured out who she wants to be.

Source: Kristen Sarlin Greenberg, Critical Essay on *The Hundred Secret Senses*, in *Novels for Students*, Gale, Cengage Learning, 2014.

Benzi Zhang

In the following review, Zhang examines the way "the world of yin and the world of yang are presented adjacently and ambiguously" in The Hundred Secret Senses.

> I have to write what I have to write about, including the question of life continuing beyond our ordinary senses.—Amy Tan

In Amy Tan's novel *The Hundred Secret Senses* (1995), the world of yin and the world of yang are presented adjacently and ambiguously. As Laura Shapiro observes, Tan's book is somewhat like a hologram: "turn it this way and find Chinese-Americans shopping and arguing in San Francisco; turn it that way and the Chinese of Changmian village in 1864 are fleeing into the hills to hide from the rampaging Manchus." Readers can easily find cross-references of the same personae and their reincarnations in both yin and yang existences. As we move deeper into the heart of the book, we find that the yin/yang hologram produces a rebounding circularity that indicates an endless narrative recursion in which the narrative levels are relative without a clear hierarchy. In Olivia's dreamy narratives, Kwan is a character who reads and interprets Olivia's life against numerous yin characters. At the same time, Olivia, as well as her previous incarnations, is also a character in Kwan's stories

> BY JUXTAPOSING THE YIN AND YANG WORLDS AND BY LAYERING BOTH RATIONAL AND IRRATIONAL ELEMENTS IN LIFE, THE NOVEL CREATES AN IMAGE OF A LARGER, ETERNAL WHOLE OF WHICH ONE'S INDIVIDUAL LIFE AND EXPERIENCE ARE ONLY A TINY PART."

about the world of yin. In other words, the two main characters "create" each other in their own narratives, interpreting each other's lives in relation to their previous existences. These narratives, at once overarching and kaleidoscopic, shift without warning from one level to another, and from one existence to another. Moreover, the stories of their overlapping lives and deaths, which span two continents and two centuries, are convoluted in a manner of recursion: all versions/visions seem to coexist in a Chinese box of stories within stories and dreams within dreams. "With my half-awake mind," says Olivia, "I would trace my way back to the previous dream, then the one before that, a dozen lives, and sometimes their deaths." If we are to read Olivia's dreams and Kwan's stories about the world of yin as a series of echoing narratives, the distinction between dream and reality and between yin and yang is not clear-cut. The irrational states of the world of yin are correlated to the real situations and events in the world of yang. The process of relating the life of yang to the world of yin has intricate implications. On the one hand, the puzzling hologram connects with broad cultural, aesthetic, and spiritual issues; on the other, it suggests that Tan's art cannot be understood entirely in terms of Western rationalism. In more than one respect, Tan's novel moves toward the subversion of our rational perception of life, elaborating on "the question of life continuing beyond our ordinary senses."

The meaning of the novel is articulated through the interplay and cooptation of its related narratives. Through a process of reverberation, readers slowly realize that the stories of Olivia and Kwan in twentieth-century San

Francisco are actually an incarnated rendition of their previous lives in nineteenth-century Changmian. Furthermore, moving through the complex work of Tan's hologram, we find in the relation of yin and yang that boundaries of time and space collapse. The links between San Francisco and Changmian provide the foundation for both plot and narrative developments. Through the relation of yin and yang worlds, Tan attempts to present a broader vision of the various dimensions of life, a vision that is revealed only through the most elaborate and even conjectural strategy. The novel requires readers to adjust their ordinary senses to be willing to intertwine the real and the unreal.

Kwan's unshakeable belief in the world of yin presents a big challenge for Olivia's sense of reality. At first, Olivia is annoyed by Kwan's constant communication with people from the world of yin: "For most of my childhood, I had to struggle not to see the world the way Kwan described it." Growing up in modern Western civilization, Olivia is influenced by a scientific view of life and the universe, which emphasizes the observable realities of the material world, while playing down or overlooking the spiritual aspects of life. The world of yin, so to speak, mediates Olivia's experience against her own rational mind. As Olivia says, "Kwan saw what she believed. I saw what I didn't want to believe." "Because I'm not Chinese like Kwan. To me, yin isn't yang, and yang isn't yin. I can't accept two contradictory stories as the whole truth." Western rationalism and materialism have left Olivia with a limited view of life, and she cannot grasp the spiritual values embodied in Kwan's Chinese way of thinking.

Kwan's stories introduce an alternative way of looking at things, highlighting the secret senses—"the senses that are related to primitive instincts, what humans had before their brains developed language and the higher functions." Moreover, the secret senses seem to enable Kwan to have a pair of "yin eyes" with which Kwan "sees those who have died and now dwell in the World of Yin." The secret senses, therefore, not only provide a channel of communication between the yin and yang worlds, but also suggest an extrasensory aspect of human beings beyond that which medical doctors and scientists can understand. In the beginning of the novel Olivia describes how a group of doctors in San Francisco diagnose Kwan's secret senses "as a

serious mental disorder. They gave her electroshock treatments, once, she said, then twice, she cried, then over and over again. Even today it hurts my teeth to think about that." The secret senses, which modern science fails to explain, seem to connect to a mysterious, illusive part of the human world. Although she cannot fully grasp Kwan's Chinese way of thinking, Olivia decides to subject herself to her secret senses and to suspend her disbelief in Kwan's "make-believe." "In fact," she says, "the idea of searching for make-believe eggs in China sounds charming." Olivia is indeed charmed, when she finds jars of eggs in the Ghost Merchant's Garden in Changmian, which Kwan claims to have buried a century earlier. As a result, Olivia is galvanized to see life in a way that she has never anticipated: that is, the way of yin-sight. Relying on her secret senses, Olivia starts to perceive what she had failed to notice before—that is, a paradox of "light within dark, dark within light." Her recognition of the indivisible duality of light and dark, yang and yin, and the rational and the irrational allows her to understand life more fully. The image of a yin-yang hologram, in a sense, epitomizes the relationship of two halves of a divided whole. In Changmian, Olivia eventually finds "the other half" of herself: "being here, I feel as if the membrane separating the two halves of my life has finally been shed."

The name "Changmian" in Chinese has two possible meanings, suggesting the village's uncanny peculiarity: "Chang mean 'sing,' mian mean 'silk,' something soft but go on forever like thread. Soft song, never ending. But some people pronounce 'Changmian' other way, rising tone change to falling. . . . This way chang mean 'long,' mian mean 'sleep.' Long Sleep." Here, Tan purposely makes an interesting "slip," since the opposite is true: the falling tone of chang means "sing" while the rising tone indicates "long" in Mandarin Chinese. This slip successfully creates a transposition of two incompatible meanings that insinuate the juxtaposition of yin and yang, pointing to a cycle of death and rebirth. Moreover, the slip suggests a tangling of chronology and synchronicity, in which Olivia undergoes an "out-of-herself" experience that brings her beyond the limits of her life and time to reach "the other side"—the yin side—of the phenomenal world. The notion of other-sidedness transcends the realms of the empirically verifiable and the rational, as it touches the nerve of our spirituality. This moves the novel away from Western rationalism to a holistic revisionism that does not negate perceptions of other modes of existence. In this sense, the novel as a whole represents Olivia's journey, as guided by Kwan's yin-sight, to the other side of existence to explore the deeper dimensions of her life. [Tan's] novel, therefore, moves beyond the conventional understanding of the human world. Through its unique yin/yang hologram, Tan portrays Olivia's quest for relocating her sense of identity beyond the boundary of her empirical senses. Olivia admits that her previous effort to understand life rationally is a failure: "It was like fitting all the pieces of a jigsaw puzzle only to find the completed result was a reproduction of corny art, great effort leading to trivial disappointment." Through relating yin and yang, Olivia eventually transcends the limits of her ordinary senses and the one-sided view of rationality that blocks her in-sight, or rather yin-sight.

The yin/yang hologram reverberates with the long tradition of the Chinese cultural sensibility. By juxtaposing the yin and yang worlds and by layering both rational and irrational elements in life, the novel creates an image of a larger, eternal whole of which one's individual life and experience are only a tiny part. Olivia's rationalism obstructs her from fully grasping the world of yin. Toward the end of the novel, Olivia discovers the music box that Kwan claims to have hidden in the cave in her previous lifetime. The presence of the music box brings into focus not only a wide range of epistemological questions, but also an ontological conundrum about the relation between yin and yang, and between the real and the unreal. Olivia seems to have reached the limit of her ordinary senses: "if I believe what [Kwan] says, does that mean I now believe she has yin eyes?" The yin/yang hologram not only contextualizes the emotional and intellectual powerlessness that troubles Olivia, but also provides a wide cultural landscape for Olivia to relocate the deep dimension of her identity. Olivia struggles with the question of yin in a broad cultural context, since among all other things yin signifies her cultural roots—the depths and breadth of her identity.

In Olivia's dreams and Kwan's narratives, yin people and events constantly recur in confused regression with people in the yang world. One of Olivia's disturbing dreams is about the moments just before she "dies" in her previous life: "I've smelled my own musky fear as the rope tightens around my neck. I've felt the heaviness of flying through weightless air. I've heard the sucking creak of my voice just before life snaps to an end." Tan's novel highlights the mysterious nature of human life and rebirth, suggesting that if we deny the possibility of the recycling of life, part of the meaning of life will be lost. Looking back at Olivia's dreams through the prism of Kwan's multilayered death-before-life stories, we can understand what it is that Olivia fails to recognize: the necessity to accept the world of yin, which implies her previous existence and her connection with her ancestry. Through the reimposition of the yin and yang worlds as two sides of a hologram, Tan shows the extra dimensions of life and afterlife that lie just on the far side of yang existence. Facilitated by her unique "yin-eyes," Kwan helps Olivia perceive the mutually illuminating connectedness of yin and yang. From Kwan, Olivia learns how to view herself and the world in a new way: "[Kwan] pushed her Chinese secrets into my brain and changed how I thought about the world." Relating yin and yang enables Olivia to achieve an awareness of her cultural tradition and to assert an identity connected with her cultural ancestry.

At the end of the novel, after finishing all her stories about the world of yin, Kwan tells Olivia: "Now you know all my secret. Give me peace." With that, Kwan vanishes into the enigmatic cave in Changmian. Kwan's mysterious disappearance provokes a magical effect that can be found in a traditional "Chinese tale where the imperial architect, turning from the wrath of his emperor, opens the door in the drawing of the palace he has made and disappears inside." When Kwan, like the Chinese architect, enters the cave of her own stories and disappears "yin-side," readers are left with the feeling that the world of yin is eventually translated into real life. Readers are not only told that the relation of yin and yang is mysterious, but also that the undecipherable mystery might not be too far from "the truth of this fiction." As Olivia says, "I now believe truth lies not in logic but in hope" that can survive "all sorts of contradictions, and certainly any skeptic's rationale of relying on proof through fact." To represent the elusive world of yin is to represent the unrepresentable, to visualize the invisible, and to think the unthinkable. Tan's novel, therefore, encourages readers to pass through the world of sensory experience and to search for meaning in the negotiations between yin and yang, and between the ordinary and the extraordinary.

"By providing multiple versions of and varying perspectives on events that are central to the novel," E. D. Huntley writes, "Tan explores the ways through which storytellers create meaning on many levels and from different points of view." The hologram presented in Tan's novel highlights the coexistence, interaction, and interdependence of two perspectives that express simultaneously the various contents of the worlds within a single work. Tan's novel is not a sum of unrelated fragments, but a work in which the implicit dialogue or interplay intervenes between different worlds. Tan's work unveils "the very roots of Chinese thinking and feeling" wherein "lies the principle of polarity, which is not to be confused with the ideas of opposition or conflict," as Alan Watts observes. "In the metaphors of other cultures, light is at war with darkness, life with death"; but "to the traditional way of Chinese thinking, this is as incomprehensible as an electric current without both positive and negative poles. . . . Thus the art of life is not seen as holding to yang and banishing yin, but as keeping the two in balance."

The Hundred Secret Senses recognizes the nature of yin/yang multiplicity and balance. The meaning of the world of yin, therefore, resides in its relation to the world of yang—through yin we find the meaning of yang and through yang we understand the significance of yin. "The key to the relationship between yang and yin," Watts notes, "is called hsiang sheng, mutual arising or inseparability." This idea communicates the unusual wisdom of Oriental thinking. "If someone puts a question to you and asks about the existing," Zen master Tripitaka tells us, "mention the non-existent in your answer. If you are asked about the nonexistent, mention the existing in your answer. . . . [Thus] the mutual dependence of the two extremes will bring to light the significance of the 'mean." The notion of "mutual dependence" helps us understand Tan's hologram which comprises the "existing" and the "non-existent," life and death, yang and yin. By juxtaposing the yin and yang worlds and by layering both rational and irrational elements of life, the novel seems to tell us that "the world is not a place but the vastness of the soul."

Source: Benzi Zhang, "Reading Amy Tan's Hologram: *The Hundred Secret Senses*," in *International Fiction Review*, Vol. 31, Nos. 1–2, January 2004, p. 13.

Ruth Pavey

In the following review, Pavey explores the tensions established between the coheroines in The Hundred Secret Senses.

Kwan, the co-heroine of the *Hundred Secret Senses*, has yin eyes, second sight. At least she thinks she has, which is why she talks of relating to ghosts as an everyday experience. There is nothing fey about Kwan. Having spent the first 18 years of her life in rural China, she takes uncomplainingly to being uprooted to join her dead father's new family in San Francisco. But how is her much younger half-sister to accommodate Kwan's hotline to the past? From the first sentence of this novel, Amy Tan sets up a tension between Kwan's Chinese-born certainties and the distancing ironies of Olivia's San Francisco inheritance.

To begin with, Olivia, or Libby-ah, has a firm grip on the narration, which begins when she is already well over 30 and married to Simon. There seems little chance of her, or the reader, getting caught by Kwan's fancies. It is not long, however, before Kwan muscles in. She takes us back to a former life, in 1864, when she was a servant to an English missionary, Miss Banner, at the time of the Taiping rebellion. For the reader this is initially fine, a good story into which we dip. But for Libby-ah herself, Kwan's stories have always represented a strain—a long childhood of traction away from her own reality, back to the culture her father left.

Not only does Olivia have Kwan's past, or pasts, to put into the balance of her brittle, first-generation American life. There is another ghost. Before meeting her, Simon was in love with a girl who died young. Elsie, adopted by Mormon parents, had been convinced she was really Elza, of Polish-Jewish descent. Her unquiet presence has always disturbed Olivia's marriage.

By halfway through the novel, when Kwan, Olivia and Simon set off for China, there are already more than enough spirits clamouring to be put to rest. At this point, the strain Libby-ah has always felt about Kwan's unusual gifts starts to affect the reader. Apprehensions of a detour to Auschwitz prove unfounded, but it becomes clear that we too are being asked to accept the possibility that Kwan was indeed the servant girl and Olivia was Miss Banner. Like Kwan in the caves of Guilin, the last part of this story gets a little lost before returning to a favourite theme of

Tan's: hope for the future, embodied in the relationship between mother and daughter.

As a device for meshing several different periods into one fiction, yin eyes may not be as convincing as the straight-forward use Tan made of memory in *The Kitchen God's Wife*. But this does not detract from the great appeal of her character, Kwan (who combines saintly good humour with wit, practicality and guile), or the enjoyable liveliness of her style.

In a thoughtful book about being an orphan, the American writer Eileen Simpson observes that most Americans are more or less orphans, immigrants missing their past. The persistent themes of Amy Tan's novels seem to bear that out. In this one alone there are at least six orphans, and hardly anyone leading a settled, secure life.

Source: Ruth Pavey, Review of *The Hundred Secret Senses*, in *New Statesman & Society*, Vol. 9, No. 390, February 16, 1996, p. 38.

Publishers Weekly

In the following review, a contributor to Publishers Weekly *discusses how Tan grounds her novels in "family and the workings of fate."*

Again grounding her novel in family and the workings of fate, Tan (*The Kitchen God's Wife*) spins the tale of two sisters, two cultures, and several acts of betrayal. Kwan, who came to San Francisco from China when she was 18, remains culturally disjointed, a good-natured, superstitious peasant with a fierce belief that she has "yin eyes" which enable her to see ghosts. Kwan's younger half-sister Olivia (or Libby-ah, as Kwan calls her) is supremely annoyed by Kwan's habit of conversing with spirits and treats her with disdain. Despite herself, however, Libby is fascinated by the stories Kwan tells of her past lives, during one of which, in the late 1800s, she claims to have befriended an American missionary who was in love with an evil general. Kwan relates this story in installments that alternate with Libby's narration, which stresses her impatience with Kwan's clinging presence. But Kwan's devotion never cools: "She turns all my betrayals into love that needs to be betrayed," Libby muses. When circumstances take Kwan, Libby and Libby's estranged husband, Simon, back to Kwan's native village in China on a magazine assignment, the stories Kwan tells—of magic, violence, love and fate—

begin to assume poignant—and dangerous—relevance. In Kwan, Tan has created a character with a strong, indelible voice, whose (often hilarious) pidgin English defines her whole personality. Needy, petulant, skeptical Libby is not as interesting; though she must act as Kwan's foil, demonstrating the dichotomy between imagination and reality, she is less credible and compelling, especially when she undergoes a near-spiritual conversion in the novel's denouement. Indeed, some readers may feel that the ending is less than satisfactory, but no one will deny the pleasure of Tan's seductive prose and the skill with which she unfolds the many-layered narrative.

Source: Review of *The Hundred Secret Senses*, in *Publishers Weekly*, Vol. 242, No. 37, September 11, 1995, p. 73.

SOURCES

"Amy Tan: Biographical Information," City of Duluth Public Library website, http://www.duluth.lib.mn.us/Programs/JoyLuckClub/Bio.html (accessed December 2, 2012).

"Amy Tan: Biography," Academy of Achievement website, http://www.achievement.org/autodoc/page/tan0bio-1 (accessed December 2, 2012).

"Amy Tan: A Uniquely Personal Storyteller," Academy of Achievement website, http://www.achievement.org/autodoc/page/tan0int-1 (accessed December 2, 2012).

"Biography: Amy Tan," *Book Reporter* website, http://www.bookreporter.com/authors/amy-tan (accessed December 2, 2012).

Curton, Carman C., "Amy Tan," in *Contemporary American Women Fiction Writers: An A-to-Z Guide*, edited by Laurie Champion and Rhonda Austin, Greenwood Press, 2002, p. 361.

Dutkiewicz, Rebekah, "Missionary Work in China: An Unexpected Shift towards Social Reform," in *Mount Holyoke Historical Atlas*, https://www.mtholyoke.edu/courses/rschwart/hatlas/mhc_widerworld/china/index.html (accessed December 12, 2012).

Fortuna, Diane, Review of *The Hundred Secret Senses*, in *America*, Vol. 174, No. 15, May 4, 1996, p. 27.

"Milestones: 1866–1898: Chinese Immigration and the Chinese Exclusion Acts," Office of the Historian, Bureau of Public Affairs, U.S. Department of State website, http://history.state.gov/milestones/1866-1898/Chinese Immigration (accessed December 13, 2012).

Newsinger, John, "The Taiping Peasant Revolt," in *Monthly Review: An Independent Socialist Magazine*, October 2000, Vol. 52, No. 5.

Pavey, Ruth, Review of *The Hundred Secret Senses*, in *New Statesman & Society*, Vol. 9, No. 390, February 16, 1996, p. 38.

"Persons Obtaining Legal Permanent Resident Status by Region and Selected Country of Last Residence: Fiscal Years 1820 to 2011," in *2011 Yearbook of Immigration Statistics*, U.S. Department of Homeland Security, Office of Immigration Statistics, 2012, pp. 6–10.

Review of *The Hundred Secret Senses*, in *Publishers Weekly*, Vol. 242, No. 37, September 11, 1995, p. 73.

Russell, Terence C., "Religion, Folk: China," in *Encyclopedia of Modern Asia*, edited by Karen Christensen and David Levinson, Scribner, Vol. 5, 2002, pp. 64–69.

Ryder, Amanda, "Barbarian Emperors," in *China Now*, Vol. 135, December 1990, p. 30.

Shapiro, Laura, Review of *The Hundred Secret Senses*, in *Newsweek*, Vol. 126, No. 19, November 6, 1995, p. 91.

Stanford, Eleanor, "China," in *Countries and Their Cultures*, edited by Carol R. Ember and Melvin Ember, Macmillan Reference, 2001, pp. 466–83.

Tan, Amy, *The Hundred Secret Senses*, G. P. Putnam's Sons, 1995.

Wagner, Wieland, "Fleeing the People's Paradise: Successful Chinese Emigrating to West in Droves," in *Spiegel Online International*, February 24, 2012, http://www.spiegel.de/international/world/fleeing-the-people-s-paradise-successful-chinese-emigrating-to-west-in-droves-a-817092.html (accessed December 13, 2012).

Waley-Cohen, Joanna, "Taiping Rebellion: 1851–1864," in *Reader's Companion to Military History*, edited by Robert Cowley and Geoffrey Parker, Houghton Mifflin, 1996, p. 461.

Weiss, Antonio, "China: The Future of Christianity?" in *Guardian*, August 28, 2010, http://www.guardian.co.uk/commentisfree/belief/2010/aug/28/china-future-christianity (accessed December 13, 2012).

Wilkinson, Joanne, Review of *The Hundred Secret Senses*, in *Booklist*, Vol. 92, No. 2, September 15, 1995, p. 116.

FURTHER READING

Keay, John, *China: A History*, Basic Books, 2009.
    Keay examines five thousand years of Chinese history, from the early dynasties to the rise of communism, in a surprisingly concise volume.

Pao, Basil, *China Revealed: An Extraordinary Journey of Rediscovery*, Abbeville Press, 2007.
    Pao's book contains the remarkable photos he took during a trip across China's varied landscape, from mountains to tea plantations to bustling cities.

Paterson, Katherine, *Rebels of the Heavenly Kingdom*, E. P. Dutton, 1983.
    This young-adult novel tells the story of Wang Lee, a teenage Chinese peasant who is kidnapped and forced to join a secret rebel organization during the Taiping Rebellion.

Tan, Amy, *The Bonesetter's Daughter*, Ballantine Books, 2003.
    Like *The Hundred Secret Senses*, *The Bonesetter's Daughter* explores the complicated relationship between a mother and a daughter. Written in the form of the mother's diary, the novel also describes historical events in China.

SUGGESTED SEARCH TERMS

Amy Tan AND The Hundred Secret Senses

Amy Tan AND China

Amy Tan AND interview

Amy Tan AND mother-daughter relationship

Taiping Rebellion

missionaries AND China

Manchu

Hakka Chinese

Johnny Got His Gun

DALTON TRUMBO

1939

Dalton Trumbo's *Johnny Got His Gun*, the story of a badly wounded World War I soldier, is one of the most enduring antiwar novels in American literature. Although Trumbo was a burgeoning literary figure at the time of the book's publication in 1939, he would become famous not as a novelist but as a Hollywood screenwriter. Trumbo's cinematic inclinations can be detected in certain stylistic aspects of *Johnny Got His Gun*, as with the montage scene featuring lines like "Johnny get your gun get your gun get your gun" from George M. Cohan's war anthem "Over There." However, the novel is far more challenging than the average film.

As the book opens, Joe Bonham is laid up in a hospital and badly wounded, after an incoming shell exploded when he dove to take cover in a trench. The question is, how wounded is he? As the chapters progress, the answer unravels through Joe's intermittent dreams and memories. The next question is, how will he respond?

The book greatly impressed critics upon its publication, the notable timing of which was not entirely a coincidence: as Nazi Germany roiled and war seemed imminent in the late 1930s, Trumbo sought to finish and publish his novel in time for its antiwar statement to be relevant; it came out within a week after Germany invaded Poland and started World War II. The book was subsequently serialized in the American Communist Party's newspaper, the *Daily Worker*.

Dalton Trumbo *(© Everett Collection Inc | Alamy)*

The novel won one of the early National Book Awards, then presented by the American Booksellers' Association, for Most Original Book of 1939.

Although most of *Johnny Got His Gun* takes place away from the battlefield, a number of grievous injuries to soldiers are described in graphic detail.

AUTHOR BIOGRAPHY

James Dalton Trumbo was born in Montrose, Colorado, on December 9, 1905, and raised in Grand Junction by his avid home-farmer father, Orus, and Christian Scientist mother, Maud. Some of the details of his early life would find their way into *Johnny Got His Gun*; to begin with, the book's Shale City is acknowledged to be a stand-in for Grand Junction, Trumbo had two younger sisters named Catherine and Elizabeth, and as a youth he enjoyed camping trips in the wilderness with his father.

In high school, Trumbo became the successful captain of the debate team and president of a couple of other clubs, all while being ambitiously devoted to his job as cub reporter for the *Grand Junction Sentinel*. The family moved to Los Angeles while Trumbo was finishing what proved to be his only year at the University of Colorado; not long after, Orus became seriously ill. Maud's religion led her to decline to seek medical treatment for her husband. Orus passed away painfully at home, but it turned out his pernicious anemia was at the time untreatable. After his father's death, Trumbo worked a night shift at the Davis Perfection Bakery for about eight years to help support his family.

Drawing on the verbal skills that made him a success on the high-school debate team, Trumbo sought a career as a novelist, writing some half dozen unpublished novels while working at the bakery. After publishing a story in *Vanity Fair*, he began to contribute film reviews and essays to the magazine, and he gained work at Warner Bros. as a story-department reader. In 1935, he published his first novel, *Eclipse*, and at Warner was promoted to B-unit screenwriter. He wrote a number of screenplays for Columbia and RKO through the late 1930s, but none gained as much recognition as his third novel, *Johnny Got His Gun* (1939). After a prolonged courtship, Trumbo married Cleo Fincher in 1938; they lived on a ranch in Ventura County and had three children.

Among Trumbo's earliest screenwriting successes were *A Man to Remember* (1938) and *Kitty Foyle* (1940), which earned him his first Academy Award nomination and permanently elevated him above the studios' B units. In 1941, Trumbo published his fourth novel, *The Remarkable Andrew*, in which the oddly pacifist ghost of Andrew Jackson (hero of the War of 1812's Battle of New Orleans) helps a man defend himself against unjust accusations of embezzlement; it was Trumbo's last novel.

Despite his novels' antiwar sentiments, Trumbo wrote several patriotic films supportive of American involvement in World War II, a war effort he came to consider honorable. Still, his ideological inclinations led him to join the Communist Party, and when the House Un-American Activities Committee set its sights on Hollywood in 1947, Trumbo declined to testify and was indicted for contempt of Congress. He served just under a year in jail in Kentucky and was blacklisted from Hollywood. He would contribute screenplays under pseudonyms for the next thirteen years, including *The Brave One* (1956), for which he won an Academy Award; the script that brought him off the blacklist was *Spartacus* (1960). The credited author or coauthor of over four dozen screenplays, Trumbo was considered by many the greatest screenwriter of his era. He died of lung cancer in Los Angeles on September 10, 1976.

PLOT SUMMARY

Book I: The Dead

CHAPTERS 1–3

Johnny Got His Gun opens with the protagonist, Joe, walking through the bakery where he works to an endlessly ringing telephone. The caller is his mother: evidently his father is dead, and Joe heads home. There, the family gathers around, and the deceased is taken away; but a phone is ringing again; Joe is actually badly hurt in a hospital and has been dreaming. He is bandaged all over and apparently deaf, after the bombing of a dugout during trench warfare. He dreams of or imagines life in Colorado, where his father courted his mother over the telephone, with Macia giving impromptu piano concerts for Bill, as well as listeners all up the open line.

At home in Shale City, Joe's mother would sing while cooking and canning in the kitchen. On Saturday nights they would get special hamburgers from an outdoor vendor. A stunt pilot came through town, awing everyone. Social occasions included birthdays, the county fair, and swimming. As teenagers Joe and his friends focused on girls. The war broke out, but Joe thought little of it until the family moved to Los Angeles. Around then, even Romania, a country that he had known before only from geography classes, entered the fray, and two Canadians were crucified by the Germans on the battlefield. Joe was drafted. Now, badly hurt, he regrets having gotten involved.

Joe keeps rising and sinking in and out of consciousness. The doctors pinch and work on his arm, and he soon realizes they must have cut it off. He panics at the loss of his ring from his girlfriend, Kareen. The night before he left to enlist, they consummated their love for the first time. At the train station, bands played, the

MEDIA ADAPTATIONS

- The first adaptation of *Johnny Got His Gun* was an hour-long radio play produced in 1940, with Joe Bonham voiced by Jimmy Cagney.

- Trumbo himself wrote a screenplay and directed his adaptation of *Johnny Got His Gun*, produced by Bruce Campbell at World Entertainments, Ltd. in 1971. With the young Timothy Bottoms starring as Joe Bonham, the cast also included Jason Robards, Diana Varsi, Marsha Hunt, and Donald Sutherland. The film was a hit at the 1971 Cannes Film Festival, where it won the Prix spécial du Jury and also won the International Critics Award.

- An audiobook version of *Johnny Got His Gun* was produced on CD in 2008 by Tantor Audio, read by William Dufris, with a running time of seven hours, thirty minutes.

mayor gave a speech, his family wept, and he and Kareen embraced. Joe realizes that both his arms are now gone.

CHAPTERS 4–6

Joe is back in the Uintah desert with Howie, working on a section gang with some Mexican men laying railroad tracks. The heat is oppressive, and Joe and Howie brought no lunch. But the Mexican workers share their lunches, and Joe and Howie tag along on a break-time run—which proves two miles long—to swim in a mucky ditch. Back working, their legs are covered in thistles, their hands bleed, and Joe passes out at day's end. He signed up to forget about his former girlfriend Diane, who went on a date with another man, Glen Hogan; Howie, in turn, intended to forget Onie, but she has written a conciliatory letter. They both jump on a train back to Shale City, where Joe walks past Diane's to see her kissing Bill Harper, his former best friend. Once at home again, Joe cries.

Joe has a sense of drowning, as if while floating down a river, head back; through the dreamscape he feels explosive pain, then relief. His legs have been cut off. He finds he also has no mouth to scream with—he breathes through tubes below his throat—and no nose, yet surprisingly he is not dead. Calmly, he realizes he also has no eyes; he figures he must be still dreaming, but he is not. He grows terrified.

Joe drifts back to the bakery in California, where he would walk some eleven miles during his night shift. One night, a Puerto Rican named Jose, who is sheltering at the Mission for the winter but in warmer weather sleeps in the park, joins the staff. He had been a chauffeur back east, but a young woman in the family for whom he worked fell in love with him; she is seeking him out, but he cannot love her. Jose gets a dream job at a movie studio but sadly concludes, with Pinky Carson's encouragement, that he must destroy a huge batch of pies in order to lose his bakery job; after being fired, he pays for the damage. Joe has been dreaming again.

CHAPTERS 7–10

Joe's stumps have healed. He has a horrifying sense of being helplessly back in the womb, although he cannot even kick. He imagines that the preening doctors have considered him a fun challenge. He thinks of the appalling fates met by other soldiers, left in hospitals functioning through tubes or being driven insane. Joe cannot even dislodge the mask covering his face or turn over. He remembers seeing a rat chewing at a Prussian corpse during the war and then feels a rat gnawing at the wound in his side; he finds himself running through the hospital for help. A nurse tends to Joe. The rat was a dream. He has to figure out how to deter nightmares. He used to be able to wake himself from nightmares, but now the sensory boundaries between waking and sleeping have been obliterated. Joe feels he can never be sure of whether he is dreaming and of what is real.

Joe would spend summers with his father in the mountain wilderness. When Joe is fifteen, Bill Harper becomes his first other fishing buddy. They borrow Joe's dad's prized rod—and lose it to a powerful fish. A hardworking homesteading farmer, Joe's dad cannot afford a new rod, but he goes easy on Joe. This would be their last trip together. In the hospital, Joe is lonely.

Joe wonders why he even went to war. Supposedly they were fighting for liberty, but evidently not their own, since they signed away their lives. Joe cannot imagine that ideals of freedom, decency, or honor offer adequate rationales for fighting either. From his vantage point, he cannot see that any ideals could be worth a man's life; he believes that all the other millions dead from the war would agree with him, though none can speak. They surely all died regretting the war.

Book II: The Living

CHAPTERS 11–13

In his mind, Joe reviews what little he can remember of academic learning. Considering his life since the explosion back in September 1918—near the end of World War I—he grows determined to track time. He tallies the seconds, minutes, and hours and the nurses' visits but always loses count before figuring anything out. He figures his bedding is changed once every twelve nurse visits, probably every two days; he realizes he might be able to sense the change in temperature in the room at sunrise. He triumphantly identifies dawn and can envision the living world.

Having counted 365 days, Joe calls this night New Year's Eve and remembers those eves in the past. He can differentiate between nurses by the vibrations of their footsteps and patterns of activity. On Sundays, he imagines walking outside Paris, and he imagines sleeping with Kareen. Missing her, he wonders where he is—presumably still on foreign land, an anonymous casualty. Considering Britons versus Frenchmen, he remembers a Scot who refused to fight Bavarians. He remembers an enemy who was shot and left hanging on barbed wires; he was buried eventually but blown back out of the ground, twice, and dubbed Lazarus. A young English soldier stumbled upon the decomposing body and went crazy, and Joe sympathizes.

In the third year of his "new time world," Joe gets a new room and is astonished to be changed two days in a row and given a freshening spritz; four or five visitors file in the room, leaving him petrified. When they pin something on his chest and kiss his temples, he realizes he has received a medal; he thrashes, trying to expose his cavernous face, but the visitors file out. He at last thinks to send out deliberate vibrations—to communicate through Morse code. He taps his head on the pillow, but the nurse only strokes his forehead to subdue him.

CHAPTERS 14–16

Joe loses track of the days as he constantly taps his head, but the nurses misunderstand. The brisk day nurse gives him a massage that turns intimate. He remembers girls of the past—Ruby and Laurette in Colorado, Bonnie in Los Angeles, and Lucky in Paris. On leave in France, Joe—or any American soldier—would live it up but imagine a German shell somewhere out there had his name on it.

As Joe nearly loses his sanity, tapping has replaced thinking. He feels like a prisoner or a slave, although he imagines both are luckier than him. A doctor visits—perhaps summoned by a nurse over the tapping. Joe taps his head more frantically, but the doctor only gives him an injection, and he drops off into a haze.

Joe drifts through airiness and psychedelic colors and the music of the spheres. Then he is overcome by fear and battered by immense globes and goes whirling through light—until a woman's voice grounds him, asking about her sixteen-year-old son who was too young to have been enlisted out of jail in Tucson. Joe sees him—the son is Christ—walking through the desert. At a train station, ill-fated men are all playing blackjack, and Christ joins them. When the train disembarks, Christ rides on top and serves as the train's whistle. Along the way, Joe jumps off and runs to Christ in the desert.

CHAPTERS 17–20

A new day nurse attends to Joe, seeming lighter, younger, and sweeter. She traces the words "merry christmas" on his chest, and he remembers his mother reading "'Twas the Night before Christmas" and the story of Jesus's birth, which is related at length, stressing how Mary fears for her heavenly child.

Joe now taps his head for the nurse, and she tries everything to appease him, but he only shakes his head no and taps anew. Finally she taps back on his forehead; she gets it; she leaves to fetch someone. Joe imagines a phalanx of impressed doctors, but only a single person returns with the nurse. His heavy finger taps in Morse code on Joe's forehead, "What do you want?"

At first dumbstruck to be communicated with, Joe at length pleads for freedom—to be let out into the world, at least to feel around him fresh air and the presence and life of ordinary people. He proposes that he could pay his own expenses by becoming a traveling exhibit, visiting farms, workplaces, schools, colleges, parliaments, churches, everywhere—a deterrence to all those who might otherwise get sucked into the horrors of war.

The heavy feet leave the room, then eventually return. Joe is told that what he asks is against regulations; he realizes that he is being willfully hidden away. Ignoring the man's further questions, Joe begs again for release, but he is only doped up with another injection. As he fades into his visions he goes on tapping, imagining himself as a new Christ figure, one who foretells a rebellion of the masses against the warring wills of the leaders of the armies and nations.

CHARACTERS

Lincoln Beechy

Lincoln Beechy is the pilot who amazes everyone in Shale City with his stunts. He eventually dies in an accident out in California.

Kareen Birkman

Joe's girlfriend, Kareen, is short and beautiful. The memory of her sustains Joe after his trauma, but the reader learns little about Kareen. She has brown hair and was nineteen when he shipped out.

Mike Birkman

Understood to be Kareen's father, Mike Birkman resembles a big dwarf after stooping through tunnels for twenty-eight years in a Wyoming coal mine. He grants Kareen permission to bring Joe to her bedroom the night before he leaves for army training. Mike seems to be a widower.

Bill Bonham

Joe's father worked at a store while providing food for his family through home farming. He was not financially successful, making his treasured fishing rod of particular significance, but he prized his relationship with his son more and largely overlooked the rod's loss. His lack of wealth perhaps contributes to his early death at age fifty-one.

Catherine Bonham

Catherine is the older of Joe's sisters. She is thirteen in his memories. He imagines her snuggling against their father on Christmas Eve.

Elizabeth Bonham
Joe's younger sister, Elizabeth, is still a small child in his memories.

Joe Bonham
After being injured in the wartime bombing of a dugout, Joe Bonham can only passively absorb the experience of losing all four of his limbs—which are likely amputated owing to gangrene—and discovering that he no longer has a face; he is blind, mute, and deaf and cannot taste or smell. Simply discovering these facts is surreal and horrifying. His former existence as Joe Bonham is annihilated; his mind remains, but never again will he be able to participate in ordinary life. In these appalling circumstances, the slightest psychological lapses or breakthroughs are magnified beyond reason; he cannot help but be carried away by his dreams, visions, and thoughts, and he drifts toward insanity. His attempts to communicate with his caretakers only prove frustrating, since they cannot, or will not, give him what he wants: to get out of that lonesome hospital. Condemned to his interior life, Joe comes to conceive of himself as a martyred symbol of "a new order of things," one in which war might be somehow forsaken.

Macia Bonham
Joe's mother is a background presence throughout his memories and dreams. She is fondly remembered for singing while preparing and canning foods in the family kitchen. When Bill Bonham was courting her, she played the piano for him over the telephone, at a time when people along the line could listen in on others' calls.

Pinky Carson
The sly Pinky manages to persuade Jose that his only choice with regard to his quandary about quitting is to destroy a large number of pies in order to get fired. Pinky helps by signalling when Jody is watching.

Diane
Diane is one of Joe's former girlfriends. She disappointed him by cheating on him. Joe gets the job laying railroad tracks in the desert to forget her.

Bonnie Flannigan
Saying she went to school with him in Shale City, Bonnie picks up Joe in Los Angeles near the bakery. She is thrice married and may be a prostitute. She is obsessed with the notion that she looks like the model Evelyn Nesbitt Thaw.

Mr. Hargraves
Mr. Hargraves, the school superintendent, is inspired by Lincoln Beechy to hail the airplane as an instrument of world peace.

Bill Harper
Bill Harper is Joe's former best friend. He lost Joe's dad's prized fishing rod by letting a fish jerk the rod out of his hand. Bill clued Joe in to Diane's date with Glen Hogan, getting punched in response and inspiring Joe to leave town. When Joe returns from the desert, however, he finds Bill kissing Diane in front of her house.

Glen Hogan
Evidently a stud, Glen is the cause of girl trouble for both Joe and Howie, since Diane two-times Joe by dating Glen, and Onie perhaps could not get over Glen.

Howie
Though Joe considered Howie somewhat inferior socially, he joined him to work in the desert to forget about girls. Joe resents Howie's joy in receiving a warm letter from Onie, and Howie seems to rub it in when they return to Shale City.

Jose
The Mission, where homeless people take shelter, would at times dispatch cheap labor to the bakery where Joe worked in Los Angeles, and Jose was one of those men. The bakery regulars disbelieve his impressive anecdotes at first, but a letter from the rich young woman who loves Jose eventually proves that he has been sincere. Jose declines to take advantage of the woman, and he experiences a crisis of honor when he must quit the job that the bakery manager so benevolently gave him to work at a movie studio. He caves in to the outlandish suggestion that he destroy a huge batch of pies to get fired.

Laurette
Before leaving Shale City, Joe has a prolonged flirtation with a sweet young woman who apparently lives at a brothel but whom Joe could never bring himself to crudely proposition.

Lazarus

A Hun, or German soldier, accidentally wanders toward the British/American trenches and is mercilessly shot and left to rot on the barbed wire. Eventually he is buried but then is blown out of the ground (twice), leading him to be nicknamed Lazarus, after the biblical figure reportedly raised from the dead by Jesus Christ. The Lazarus story also reflects Joe's circumstances, since he is cut off from the living world by his injuries but eventually rejoins it through tactile communication.

Limey

During the war, Joe commiserates with poor Limey, an eighteen-year-old English soldier who went crazy after falling on the decomposing body of Lazarus.

Lucky

Lucky is a prostitute Joe met in Paris. She has a young son and always manages to cheer up the Americans who visit her.

Onie

Perhaps because Glen abandoned her for Diane, Onie coaxes Howie to return to Shale City from the work in the desert, and Howie agrees.

Ruby

The younger, rotund Ruby was the first girl Joe slept with.

Rudy

Rudy works at the bakery. He drove Joe home when his father died.

Scotchman

A man from Scotland in a British regiment refused to fight Bavarians because he considered their Stuart-descended king the rightful king of England.

Jody Simmons

After hiring Jose and admiring his work ethic, Jody, the bakery manager, is surprised and forgiving when Jose drops a half dozen pies. When Jose ruins one hundred and eighty pies, however, Jody has no choice but to fire him.

Stumpy Telsa

Telsa is the madam at the house where Laurette lives and works.

Corporal Timlon

Timlon was put in charge of burying Lazarus and was blamed when the burial failed. While reading the service during the second burial, he was shot in the posterior and sent away from his mostly doomed regiment.

THEMES

Dreams

From the opening scene of *Johnny Got His Gun*, the reader is immersed in a world that often seems dreamlike and fantastic, with time frames extended or compressed and occurrences that push beyond realistic expectations (as with the endlessly ringing telephone ignored by everyone but Joe). The reason for this dreamy uncertainty soon becomes apparent: Joe is in a hospital in such poor condition that his dreams have all but overtaken reality. He cannot see, hear, or smell anything going on around him, and in fact he has great difficulty discerning his dreams from real life; he can find no means of objectively determining whether or not he is awake.

Often when dreams play a role in a work of literature, they serve to illuminate aspects of a character's subconscious or even suggest a course of action that should or will be taken. Here, the role of Joe's dreams is less contextual and more metaphysical in nature, primarily serving to convey to the reader the experience of being trapped in a consciousness where dreams and reality merge. In fact, the content of Joe's dreams or visions is almost always memory based, allowing the reader insight not into his present psychology but into his past life. The only realistically random dreamlike experience is that where he seems to feel a rat gnawing on a wound in his side. Of course, in the absence of new stimuli (other than vibrations and that festering wound), it stands to reason that Joe's dreaming mind would primarily plummet through the past.

Helplessness

In ushering the reader through Joe's experience of being literally unable to get a grip on reality, Trumbo aptly conveys the sense of helplessness Joe feels. In and of itself, the dreaming state is often a helpless one, because the average person has little if any control over what goes on in dreams. For Joe this sense is intensified by his

TOPICS FOR FURTHER STUDY

- Watch Trumbo's award-winning film version of *Johnny Got His Gun*, and write a paper in which you express your opinions about the success of the adaptation. Address the aspects of the novel that made the adaptation to film especially challenging; the reasons why material was left out or added for the film and how the story line is affected by those changes; scenes in which either the book or the film has stronger impact and why; points in the film where Trumbo's status as a novice director seems evident; how the film might have been improved (keeping in mind that Trumbo was restricted to a shoestring budget); and the overall quality of the film.

- Read Margaret I. Rostkowski's young-adult novel *After the Dancing Days* (1986), about a girl named Annie whose uncle died in World War I and whose father works at a hospital caring for veterans. At the hospital, Annie makes the acquaintance of a young, badly injured veteran named Andrew. Write a paper in which you compare and contrast the postwar lives of Andrew and Joe Bonham from *Johnny Got His Gun*, noting ways in which Andrew is actually fortunate compared to Joe, how their personalities and daily lives are affected by their new limitations, what their logical conclusions

about their fates are, and any other relevant topics.

- Make your own audiobook recording of chapter 10 of *Johnny Got His Gun*. You should consider beforehand the overarching tones you plan to read with (ranging from depressed to melancholy, bitter, furious, and so forth) and the approach you will take regarding the absence of commas—whether to introduce pauses where commas ought to go, or randomly, or to read with as much continuous flow as the text suggests. Post your recording online or play it for your class, and ask for feedback regarding how effectively you produced the chapter.

- Research the experiences of conscientious objectors during World War I, and write a research paper detailing the different reasons why people objected in the United States (as well as European countries if you choose), how the process was carried out, and what the consequences were. Beyond the broader survey, focus on a particular group, such as Mennonites, if you wish, and consult at least one topic-specific print source, such as Yuichi Moroi's *Ethics of Conviction and Civic Responsibility: Conscientious War Resisters in America during the World Wars* (2008).

---

physical inability to do anything even in waking life: in response to his misfortune, he cannot punch a wall, nor run away, nor even scream out his fear; he cannot gain solace from expressing himself with words or gestures or body language, nor from hearing the soothing voice of a nurse or a friend, nor even from simple eye contact. All he can do is passively use his sense of touch, yet in the absence of any loved ones, for the majority of the book he is touched not in expressive or sensual ways but only in practical ways, as the nurses bathe and change him as

necessary. Indeed, it is difficult to imagine a more helpless state than the one in which Joe finds himself, short of a coma or death.

It is Joe's helplessness—not the pain of his injuries, which is addressed in the early chapters but minimized thereafter—that accounts for much of the angst and pathos of the book, and it also drives the plot: essentially, Joe can do nothing; and so what can he do? Foremost, he realizes, he can think. He absorbs himself in the possibility of using what little he can determine about reality to deduce his daily routine and keep track of the passage of time. It is during this period of mental absorption, in the tenth chapter, that Joe presents the book's most cogently articulated argument against war. Joe eventually realizes that he is not entirely helpless—he can tap his head, and so he can speak through Morse code. Thus does he seek to communicate what his helplessness should signify to the world.

Death

Once Joe proves able to communicate with his caretakers, he makes quite clear that "he would speak from the dead. He would talk for the dead. He would tell all the secrets of the dead." Signalling the central importance of this theme, the dichotomy of life versus death is foregrounded at the highest level of the novel's internal structure, with book I titled "The Dead" and book II titled "The Living." It is as if in the first book, Joe joins the dead—he departs from ordinary reality, loses almost all use of his physical body, and even experiences something like having his life flash before his eyes, in the form of dreams or visions of his past. When he discovers the extent of his injuries, Joe is actually astonished that he is not dead, that a fluke of fate has left him alive. However, for all his disconnectedness, he may as well be a ghost banished to a purgatorial existence; he is "dead while alive."

It is in this frame of mind that Joe finds himself in a position to speak for the dead, as elaborated in the last chapter of book I. From his perspective, regardless of their principles or reasons for fighting, the war's dead can have nothing but regret for the fact that they have lost their lives, because death automatically negates the principles one was living for by negating one's life. Joe, meanwhile, is not dead. When in book II he realizes that he can both determine the time of day and communicate—or at least try to communicate—with others, he rejoins "the living," and when he is at last understood, he tries to do precisely what he envisioned himself doing: speaking for the dead, protesting the wars that inevitably lead to so much death.

Wars

While the novel is founded in the tragedy of World War I, it expands in breadth through Joe's consciousness to become a polemic against all wars. Known at the time of Trumbo's writing rather as the Great War, the conflict is curiously not once mentioned by name in the novel. The year is not even given until halfway through the

Johnny Got His Gun *was inspired by the true story of a WWI soldier who lost all his limbs in the war.* (© Mondadori / Getty Images)

book, such that the overall sense of dislocation may be enhanced for the modern reader (though there are clues, like the novelty of the telephone, that do signal the era).

Outside of this single reference to the year, the setting is simply wartime. The combatants happen to be French, British, and German, but the politics of the war are omitted almost entirely, with the purported rationale behind the war—"to make the world safe for democracy"—only vaguely alluded to here and there. The novel never makes clear which side was the aggressor, which side was in the right, or which side was winning. Forsaking such historical details, Trumbo forged a universal novel that is simply about, and decidedly against, war and its potential consequences for the individual.

In Joe's final tirade against war, he hammers home the point that the people who want the wars are never the people who fight the wars. The military commanders take orders from the politicians, and no politician is an active member of his or her nation's armed forces. Ultimately, Joe imagines, the people will become fully conscious of how their very lives are gambled away by those in charge, and when those in charge call for war and put guns in their hands, the people will have the wherewithal to point the guns right back at those in charge and thus bring about peace.

STYLE

Stream of Consciousness

Johnny Got His Gun is a novel that presents a stream of consciousness in the most literal sense: the book must be conceived not as Joe recording or narrating aloud his own story, since he can neither write nor speak, but rather as the stream of thoughts taken directly from his mind. These thoughts are taken beginning sometime well after Joe's bombardment in September 1918, immediately immersing the reader in the highly altered reality in which Joe finds himself. This immersion is effective in part because the reader is thus made to share in Joe's disorientation; Trumbo might have begun the novel with, say, the scene in which Joe is so gravely injured, but this would have given the reader the chance to get a firm footing in the ordinary reality of the war, and thus Joe's altered state would have been approached as an extension of that reality. Part of the point of the novel is that Joe is so drastically cut off from that reality that he himself no longer has any footing in it—not with regard to time or to place or to the people around him. Accordingly, the reader is likewise allowed no footing in that reality. Throughout the novel, then, the reader shares firsthand in Joe's desperate process of coping with his unfortunate state.

A stylistic aspect connected with the stream of consciousness is the total lack of commas. Without commas, the natural pauses that would ordinarily be signaled remain hidden; the reader is left to either introduce pauses on his or her own or simply read straight through each sentence without pausing, which lends a steadily rolling, insistent cadence to the prose. In effect, the lack of commas leaves the prose one step removed from the rhythm of ordinary speech—which keeps the reader conscious of the fact that Joe is neither speaking nor writing; it is as if the words are simply tumbling out of his head.

The stream-of-consciousness angle is maintained through Joe's waking reality and dreams alike, although some of the supposedly dreamed episodes read less like dreams and more like envisioned remembrances—but Trumbo does leave room for the reader to consider them as such. Perhaps only once in the novel is the stream of consciousness disrupted: in the scene of Joe's parents' courtship by telephone; the scene is introduced in a way that suggests the parents remembering the courtship together in conversation at home, as overheard by Joe, but it is not clear whether Joe can be understood as vicariously remembering or reconstructing or dreaming the vivid imagery of that courtship. Still, this does not compromise the effectiveness of the scene. From a literary perspective, all of Joe's dreams or envisioned remembrances can be more succinctly classified as flashbacks, and a novelist need not account for the precise metaphysical nature of a flashback.

Modernism

In a sense, *Johnny Got His Gun* is the epitome of the modernist novel, since modernism is often understood as literature's response to the moral anarchy of World War I, and Trumbo's novel is both a direct product of that moral anarchy and an attempt to cure it. Among the most highly recognized modernist writers are James Joyce, Virginia Woolf, and Franz Kafka, whose works tend to stretch the bounds of realism to produce a literary reality that inherently questions the nature of truth and subjectivity. Likewise, Trumbo filters his novel's occurrences through the highly modified perceptive standpoint of the sense-deprived Joe Bonham, undermining the legitimacy and relevance of ordinary reality in Joe's experience. In other words, in being cut off from public reality, Joe is able to offer a unique and telling perspective on that reality.

In his essay "The Literature of Replenishment," the novelist and literary theorist John Barth lists a number of qualities common to modernist literature that are represented in Trumbo's novel. Barth cites "the radical disruption of the linear flow of narrative," which is accomplished by Joe Bonham's dreams/flashbacks. Regarding modernism's "frustration of conventional expectations concerning unity and coherence of . . . character," the ambiguity of Joe's consciousness and the drastic alteration of his physical condition result in a wounded Joe who comes to little resemble, both internally and externally, the prewar Joe. Furthermore, Joe's difficulty in identifying the nurses, doctors, and others around him means that those characters remain incoherent and mostly inaccessible to the reader. Perhaps most prominent in Trumbo's novel is what Barth terms "the opposition of inward consciousness to rational, public, objective discourse," since Joe comes to define himself by his conscious opposition to politicians' public rationale behind the fighting of war.

Interestingly, one additional minor aspect of modernist literature is represented in *Johnny Got His Gun*: Barth refers to modernists' devotion to "the special, usually alienated role of the artist in his society," calling to mind Joe's assertion that his father's means of escaping the publicly sanctioned world of "success stories and the job at the store" was his garden, his "way of being an artist." Joe laments that his father "was a failure" because he "couldn't make any money"—a classic modernist lament about the misguided ethics of the commercialized bourgeois world.

HISTORICAL CONTEXT

World War I and the United States

The First World War began through the assassination of Archduke Franz Ferdinand, heir to the throne of the Austro-Hungarian Empire, by a hooligan teenager in Sarajevo, Bosnia, on June 28, 1914. The war is considered in retrospect an especially tragic one because shrewd diplomacy and strategy might have greatly reduced the number of casualties; in all, some nine million combatants and twelve million civilians died during the conflict.

Myriad political and military factors contributed to the onset of what would be known in its era as the Great War: France and Germany had lingered as enemies since France's defeat in the Franco-Prussian War in 1871; Germany and Austria-Hungary were neighbors and ironclad allies; Austria-Hungary and Russia were poised to compete over the conquest of Balkan nations; Russia was aligned with Serbia through the rhetoric of Pan-Slavism, drawing on shared ethnic heritage; and Serbian nationalists—like Gavrilo Princip, Franz Ferdinand's assassin—were hoping to bring the Slavic populations of Austria-Hungary back within Serbian borders. France and Russia were also allies, while Great Britain, too, supported France. Meanwhile, internal

politics in Britain, where the Irish were seeking home rule, and Germany, where socialists were becoming a political force, may have encouraged leaders to forestall internal upheaval by welcoming external crisis. After the archduke's assassination, Germany pushed Austria-Hungary to respond aggressively, and it did, attacking Serbia in late July.

In his volume *World War I*, Neil M. Heyman makes plain the prevailing scholarly opinion with regard to the culpability of all of the belligerent nations' political and military leaders, noting that "their diplomatic ineptness and their antagonisms" were what brought the war about. In circumstances where neighboring nations were implicit and constant threats, Heyman states, "no civilian leader could ignore a high-ranking general claiming that a delay in mobilization would put the country's future in peril." Thus, upon Austria-Hungary's waging war against Serbia, in the span of only a week, Russia mobilized its military along its entire western border; Germany declared war against Russia, then France, and then invaded neutral Belgium to get to northern France; and Great Britain declared war against Germany. Numerous battles were fought on land and at sea over the ensuing months, which stretched into years. Among other nations involved, the Ottoman Empire (Turkey) joined the Central powers (Germany and Austria-Hungary) in late 1914, while Italy joined the Entente or Allied powers in mid-1915.

On the battlefields, the carnage was horrific, with advances in weaponry—especially the machine gun—neither countered by equivalent advances in protective technology nor adequately tactically adjusted for by military commanders. Most military leaders continued to believe in the necessity of bold offensives, although the ubiquitous trenches, barbed wire, and heavy artillery marking defensive positions made many offensives essentially suicidal and pointless. The German offensive at Verdun, France, in early 1916 led to a ten-month battle that saw some 400,000 French and 340,000 Germans killed or missing, while neither side gained any ground. In the summer of 1916, the British waged what they hoped would be a decisive attack at the Somme, a river in northern France, only to see some 20,000 killed and 40,000 wounded in a single day; after several months there, the battle lines had barely shifted, while over a million soldiers were killed

COMPARE & CONTRAST

- **1918:** After five years, World War I ends on November 11, when Germany signs the armistice ending hostilities with France, Great Britain, and the United States. Russia had already left the war.

  1939: In September, emboldened by a temporary nonaggression pact with Soviet Russia, Germany invades Poland and initiates World War II, which would last some six years. Germany's foremost enemies would be, again, Great Britain, France, and the United States, as well as the Soviet Union.

  Today: As of 2012, soldiers from the United States, Great Britain, and France were continuing to contribute through the North Atlantic Treaty Organisation (NATO) to the war in Afghanistan, begun in 2001 after the 9/11 terrorist attacks in the United States in the interest of rooting out the Taliban. NATO hopes to withdraw from the region in the near future.

- **1918:** President Woodrow Wilson takes a lead role in the post–World War I peace negotiations, with his Fourteen Points for peace in the postwar world and his conception of a communal League of Nations—precursor to the United Nations—earning international respect.

  1939: President Franklin D. Roosevelt and the US Congress amend the Neutrality Act in November to allow for the provision of arms to Britain and France, but otherwise the United States retains hope for a compromise peace—which the Allies consider already impossible.

  Today: President Barack Obama earns the 2009 Nobel Peace Prize for signalling as the new American president the onset of a new era of open, peaceable international relations, including between the Western and Muslim worlds. As of 2012, Obama has ended one of the wars—in Iraq—that he inherited from his predecessor.

- **1918:** In the wake of the Bolshevik Revolution of 1917, which saw the forced abdication of the czar, Russia becomes communist, with soldiers and workers hopeful for the equalization of society.

  1939: Soviet Russia has sealed itself off, keeping secret the extent of Joseph Stalin's reign of terror, while Great Britain, for one, fears Soviet aggression almost as much as German. Nonetheless, the ideals of communism appeal to many Americans, including Dalton Trumbo, whose *Johnny Got His Gun* is serialized in the *Daily Worker* and who will join the American Communist Party in 1943.

  Today: Following the 1991 collapse of the Soviet Union and the end of the Cold War, communism is looked at askance in democratic countries but not so much feared. China, the one remaining large communist nation, has become an economic superpower without international aggression (though internal suppression and human rights violations remain international concerns).

---

altogether. Meanwhile, owing to restricted news coverage, the full extent of the slaughter went unwitnessed and sometimes entirely unrecognized by civilian leaders and the public at large in most of the warring nations, and persistent wartime propaganda fed into the cycle of recruitment, ill-advised aggression, and slaughter.

After prolonged political efforts to remain neutral, the United States was finally drawn into the war in 1917. The threat of US involvement had earlier persuaded Germany to agree to wage only limited submarine warfare, but that year Germany decided to use its U-boats (undersea boats) without restriction, a strategy that would

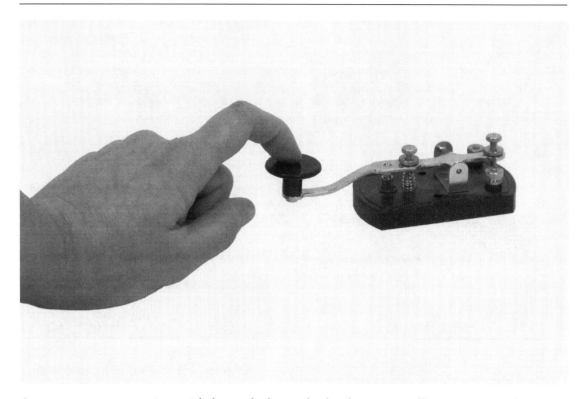

Joe attempts to communicate with doctors by hitting his head against a pillow in Morse Code. *(© Dani Simmonds | Shutterstock.com)*

cripple transatlantic trade and endanger American lives. President Woodrow Wilson, in Heyman's words, "abhorred war as wasteful," and he won reelection in 1916 with the slogan "He kept us out of war." However, the last straw was an intercepted telegram in which Germany promised to return southwestern US territory to Mexico in exchange for an alliance. Congress declared war against Germany in April 1917.

US Navy ships were immediately sent into battle, but American ground troops would not arrive in Europe until the following year. Meanwhile at home, the federal government's Committee of Public Information was in charge of stirring up support for the war effort. Some 75,000 public speakers dubbed the Four Minute Men were dispatched to American cities to address crowds, and propaganda films with titles like *The Prussian Cur* were dramatic (and racist) tools used to vilify the Germanic enemies. To augment the insufficient US armed forces—at the time the army and National Guard together boasted only some 300,000 men—Wilson authorized conscription. Some 3 million men were drafted, while another 1.5 million volunteered.

By 1918, the warring nations were on the verge of collapse. Following the Bolshevik Revolution of late 1917, Russia negotiated for peace in March 1918, eliminating the eastern front and thus intensifying the western front. American troops reached the front later that spring, waging combat in France at Château-Thierry and Belleau Wood. American contributions may have helped tip the balance on the battlefields, allowing for critical French and British advances, but the diplomacy of President Wilson was just as essential. His famous Fourteen Points outlining a plan for peace that did not punish the aggressors did much to persuade the German people that the war should end. In the fall of 1918, first Austria-Hungary, then Turkey, and finally Germany surrendered. In all, some 2 million American soldiers took part in the war, with some 115,000 losing their lives. Additionally, some 42,000 were discharged for psychological trauma termed "war neurosis," or shell shock. Even two decades later, nearly 10,000 veterans remained hospitalized or in treatment for psychological disturbance in the wake of the unparalleled modern, machine-enabled slaughter of World War I.

CRITICAL OVERVIEW

There was no shortage of praise for *Johnny Got His Gun* upon its release in 1939, with the *Washington Post*, *Boston Herald*, and *Chicago Daily News*, among other publications, offering glowing comments on Trumbo's singular achievement. Early reviewers almost universally categorized the book as terrifying, indicating the acuity of the book's psychological exploration of the tragically wounded Joe Bonham: Joe's terror becomes the reader's terror. In the *Dictionary of Literary Biography*, James Moore calls the novel "a tour de force." In a *Literature and Medicine* essay, Richard M. Zaner notes that the book is "known as a brilliant, anguished declaration against war" borne of the author's "amazing ingenuity."

Despite the novel's popular impact over the decades—it experienced a renaissance among the masses who opposed the Vietnam War—it has not received a great deal of critical attention. Tim Blackmore, in his 2000 essay "Lazarus Machine: Body Politics in Dalton Trumbo's *Johnny Got His Gun*," suggests that this may be in part due to "the novel's weakest moment," namely, the triumphant monologue that closes the book. Blackmore argues that the reader can only conceive of Joe, in his pitiable state, as doomed, so that ending the book on a high note rings false. The critic remarks that the author "is unable to face his own narrative's logic," by which he would have had "to push Joe Bonham into the abyss of the socius," that is, the modern social machine that propelled him into the war and his tragic fate. Still, while Blackmore laments "the failure of Trumbo's romantic conclusion," he finds the novel as a whole of great value. In particular, he asserts that stylistically the novel was ahead of its time, that with its fragmented portrait of a fragmented person it "sits at the edge of postmodernism, hailing it."

In his critical biography *Dalton Trumbo*, Bruce Cook calls the novel "one of the finest by an American in the thirties." Considering the book alongside the author's screenwriting achievements, Cook notes that he "uses film techniques to good advantage," such as with the cinematic flashbacks; though framed as dreams, the flashbacks function much like they would in a movie, offering straightforward dramatic presentations of circumstances from the past. Cook describes the flashbacks as "brilliantly realized . . . with the economy and vividness of film." He also finds the montage at the train station aptly cinematic, while in general "Joe's subjective experience of the passage of time . . . is like movie time, an emotional dimension, an empathetic reality." Cook, too, contends that despite the "impressive rhetoric" that closes the book, Trumbo's attempt "to elevate Joe from a figure of pathos to one of heroic dimensions . . . does not really work." Nonetheless, Cook affirms that the book merits high praise for constituting both an admirable antiwar statement and "a profoundly moving novel." As cited by Cook, in the words of *Saturday Review of Literature* critic Ben Ray, *Johnny Got His Gun* is "a book that can never be forgotten by anyone who ever reads it."

CRITICISM

Michael Allen Holmes

Holmes is a writer with existential interests. In the following essay, he considers the merits of the philosophical argument against war in Johnny Got His Gun.

The high praise bestowed on Dalton Trumbo's novel *Johnny Got His Gun* upon its publication in 1939 made clear the general consensus that the book offers a searing, haunting, even horrifying argument against war. In the twenty-first century the book is recognized as, in the words of Tim Blackmore in a *Mosaic* essay, "an anti-war classic," one whose message still resonates nearly a century after the war it treats took place. Indeed, modern readers are likely to approach the novel not as any mere story but specifically as an ideological statement against war—an approach encouraged by the modern jacket design, which features the small silhouette of an old-time soldier in motion near barbed wire, dwarfed by a cover-spanning hand with two fingers raised in a peace sign.

In its opposition to war, there is no questioning the novel's effectiveness. Trumbo masterfully plunges the reader directly into the experience of a man who has lost all his limbs and practically all his senses, an experience that would be otherwise unavailable to anyone but that very man. No one would want to end up in such a condition, and no one would argue that this man deserved to end up in such a condition; the reader's *emotional* response can only be that

WHAT DO I READ NEXT?

- Trumbo's first novel, *Eclipse* (1935), follows the experiences of a man who descends by misfortune from being one of the most successful and admired men in town to being divorced, disabled, and a financial failure.

- One well-regarded novel more closely examining the battlefield action of World War I is C. S. Forester's *The General* (1936), which focuses on a fictional general who takes command along the western front in the spring of 1915. The novel sheds light on the British attitudes that led to the horrific slaughters of the war.

- Nobel Prize–winner Ernest Hemingway gained early recognition with his novel *A Farewell to Arms* (1929), about the experiences of an American lieutenant in the Italian army's ambulance corps who develops a romance with an English nurse. The novel was inspired by Hemingway's own World War I experiences as an ambulance driver.

- Henri Barbusse, a French writer and soldier, helped spark the antiwar movement in literature with his 1916 novel *Le feu*, translated as *Under Fire*, which criticizes the political rhetoric and strategic risk-taking that compromised so many soldiers' lives.

- One of the most famous World War I novels was written by a German, Erich Maria Remarque: *Im Westen nichts Neues* (1929), or *All Quiet on the Western Front*. The book portrays the devastating reality of trench warfare from a German perspective.

- *Scarlet Fields: The Combat Memoir of a World War I Medal of Honor Hero*, by John Lewis Barkley, originally published in 1930 but retitled for a 2012 edition, offers a take on the experience of World War I by a sniper who proved essential in the heavy action seen by his platoon.

- Prior to World War I, the pacifist Norman Angell presented in *The Great Illusion* (1910) an argument against war on the basis of the broad foundation of economic interdependence among modern nations, which would make any war inevitably costly and futile.

- Michael Morpurgo's young-adult novel *Private Peaceful* (2004) follows two brothers, the younger being just fifteen years of age, as they fight in the Great War in the trenches in France.

- *Without Warning: Ellen's Story, 1914–1918* (2007) is a young-adult novel by Dennis Hamley about the experiences of a young English woman who enlists during World War I and serves as a nurse close to the front lines.

---

war is wrong. However, beyond the emotionally charged characterization and plot, Trumbo includes a fair amount of antiwar rhetoric, and it is worth considering how well that rhetoric itself withstands scrutiny.

Through the early chapters of the book, Joe Bonham is mostly just coming to grips with his condition, such that he makes only passing comments with regard to how the war has ruined his life. Still, even these comments are telling. At the end of chapter 2, he remarks, "This was no war for you. This thing wasn't any of your business.

What do you care about making the world safe for democracy?" A key strain throughout the book is Joe's indifference to societal principles, and the effect is notable. By chapter 2, the reader has already been fully plunged into Joe's consciousness, and although thus far only his deafness and the bandages covering his body have been revealed, there is the premonition, "you're hurt worse than you think." When one's physical health has been compromised, abstract principles can mean little; at that point in time, how could Joe care whether people an ocean away from

"WHAT FOLLOWS IS, RHETORICALLY SPEAKING, AN EPITOME OF RADICAL INDIVIDUALISM; QUITE LITERALLY, AS HE ALREADY NOTED, JOE IS THINKING ONLY FOR HIMSELF."

America are living under democracies or monarchies or any particular form of government?

Because the real-life importance behind "making the world safe for democracy"—a slogan employed by President Woodrow Wilson once America entered the war—is never explained in the novel and because the rationale remains abstract, the reader naturally sides with Joe on the matter. Trumbo allows this abstraction about the war to persist by having Joe be the sort of soldier who "never really knew what the fight was all about." As a single, relatively minor illustration of what "making the world safe for democracy" actually meant, one hundred and twenty-eight American lives were lost—out of over a thousand total deaths—in the sinking of a British ocean liner, the *Lusitania*, by a German submarine in May 1915. Even after this murder of civilians, the United States remained out of the war for nearly two years, after negotiating with Germany to ensure that such an attack would not happen again.

Over the next half dozen chapters, Joe is mostly absorbed in his dreams/memories and the shocking revelations of how much of himself he has lost. By chapter 10, he has settled down and come to realize that he "had plenty of time to think." A passage about how one comes to think while mired in such extreme inactivity and isolation as Joe's reveals much about the nature of the rhetoric to follow:

> You figured only for yourself without considering a single little thing outside yourself. It seemed that you thought clearer and that your answers made more sense. And even if they didn't make sense it didn't matter because you weren't ever going to be able to do anything about them anyhow.

By and large, a person thinks in order to resolve his or her problems. If one is having difficulty with schoolwork or a job, one may constantly churn over the nagging details of the task without even meaning to. If one is trying to improve at a sport or martial art or dance form, one may find oneself constantly reviewing the motions and thought sequences needed to perform the activity as well as possible. If one has been arguing with a significant other, one may find oneself arguing with the person in one's head as a means of resolving what to say and how to respond when the next quarrel arises. Joe, of course, has no one left to argue with, but this does not mean he has nothing to argue over. To the contrary, he is devastated by what has become of his life, and he undoubtedly has a psychological need to express his frustration with the war machine that has devoured him and to logically demonstrate how he has been wronged.

However, Joe can neither speak nor write to anyone, nor can he listen to or read a response. Before he thinks of the possibility of using Morse code, he believes that he now has no one to speak to but himself. Thus, what can he do but let his thoughts follow their natural course and give his understandable anger a focus and an outlet by delineating just how the state is to blame for his condition? He does not have any interest—at this point in time, at least—in justifying the war or conceiving of America's participation as reasonable, because his physical existence has been utterly suppressed, causing profound angst, and his angst needs a target (other than himself) in order to be released.

What follows is, rhetorically speaking, an epitome of radical individualism; quite literally, as he already noted, Joe is thinking only for himself. If his conceptions seemingly "made more sense," this may be less because they are ethically sound and more because they serve to give closure to the lingering questions and resentments in his mind—and truly, it only matters that these answers appease his own mind; no one else's mind matters.

Joe first objects to the fact that his life can be claimed by the government, in the form of the draft, without him having any choice in the matter: "You haven't even the right to say yes or no or I'll think it over." There is of course the counterargument that one agrees to live by the rules of one's country simply by living there, but this is not to say that one must find each and every rule in one's country just, even in a democracy. Regardless, Joe did have the choice to say no, by being a conscientious objector; his religion may not have obliged him to object, but he still could have objected that he did not wish to kill anyone, in which case he could have been assigned noncombat duty. If he still refused to serve, he might have been imprisoned, but either way, he presumably would have avoided his soldier's fate.

The next several pages of rhetoric deconstruct the words representing the concepts that American soldiers were supposedly fighting for. The first is *liberty*. Here, Joe first wonders whose liberty and how much of it was being fought for, neglecting to posit concrete answers to these concerns. He then descends into a moral equivalency where *liberty* generally could mean the liberty "of eating free ice cream cones" or of people "robbing anybody they pleased," two absurd formulations of the ordinarily high-minded concept *liberty* that together implicitly suggest that the term in and of itself is meaningless. He notes, "You tell a man he can't rob and you take away some of his liberty," which again devalues the bare notion of liberty by implying that no one has *total* liberty anyway.

As for whose liberty is being defended, the unstated answer might be the peoples of all the nations that a victorious Germany would harshly occupy. It is also worth recalling here that some twelve million civilians died during World War I, from causes ranging from direct attacks to starvation owing to disruptions of trade. Had the war been prolonged in the absence of American involvement, who knows how many more civilians as well as soldiers might have died? From this perspective, US soldiers were fighting for the liberty of innocent people simply to live. In Joe's mind, however—and thus in Trumbo's book—permitted to stand is the comment that "anybody who went out and got into the front line trenches to fight for liberty was a goddam fool and the guy who got him there was a liar." From here on, Joe continues to express that he simply does not believe he should be obligated to sacrifice his own life for anyone else's liberty.

Joe makes the additional point that as valiant a fight for liberty as the American Revolutionary War may have been, had the United States gained independence peacefully, as Canada proceeded to do, many lives would have been saved. This is an excellent rationale for not starting a war in the first place—but it was

the aggression between European countries that initiated World War I; for America in 1917, the question was not so much one of *fighting* a war but one of finally *ending* a war by getting involved.

Joe prepares the reader for the rhetoric to come by collectively devaluing the various concepts to be addressed: "If they weren't fighting for liberty they were fighting for independence or democracy or freedom or decency or honor or their native land or something else that didn't mean anything." Indeed, if such concepts are reeled off one after the other without any connotations, none of them means anything. Joe imagines that if the war is over by now "the world must be all safe for democracy. Was it? And what kind of democracy? And how much? And whose?" Of course, being exiled from historical time, Joe cannot answer any of these questions, and as such, the questions effectively hang in the air as meaningless.

It is worth considering how the European map would be redrawn following the defeat of the Central powers. With President Wilson advocating the formation of new states in accord not with imperial interests but with local nationalities, the Austro-Hungarian and German empires were broken down to help create the countries of Poland, Czechoslovakia, and Yugoslavia. Although this did not ensure everlasting peace in these countries, the intent was to minimize further animosity—and avert future wars and death—by collecting people of shared ethnicity within their own states. Viewed in this sense, the notion of *democracy* has clear significance and value.

Joe approaches *freedom* in much the way that he approached *liberty*. Were soldiers fighting for "freedom from work or disease or death? Freedom from your mother-in-law?" In the first question, it is obviously unreasonable to expect freedom from these things that are a part of every person's life; the second question, once more, devalues the bare notion of freedom through a frivolous connotation. Surely the soldiers were not fighting for these drily enumerated senses of freedom. Again, the most appropriate response might be that the soldiers were fighting for the freedom of innocent people simply to live.

As for *decency*, Joe points out that mere decency is irrelevant when a person is dead. In turn, *honor* is construed, through more moral relativism, as meaningless, because different nations have different conceptions of honor, such that there can be no one absolute definition. However, a certain philosophical conception of honor may adequately justify the occasional need to participate in war: Many people choose to live their lives in the most peaceful way possible, in such a way as to bring as much happiness to others as one is capable of—in other words, to increase the net happiness of the world as much as possible. To do so, to many people, feels like the most honorable thing one can do with one's life. Some do this by raising morally sound children who will do good in the world; some devote their lives to serving a nonprofit organization or charitable causes; some become religious figures who try to bring light and peace to others' souls; some do all of the above.

Certainly one can no longer increase the happiness of the world once one has died, but what if risking one's life potentially means saving, say, two lives? Some people would conceive that those two lives are worth more, in terms of total happiness in the world, than one's own life. If, in an extreme situation, one had the chance to push two people out of the way of a speeding car to save their lives while sacrificing one's own, would that action be taken? What if the two people were one's parents? Perhaps the parents would prefer that their child survive them. What if they were one's children? Perhaps a majority of parents would indeed directly sacrifice themselves for their children. What if they were total strangers? What if they were foreigners? Some people would not sacrifice their own lives for those of strangers, but some would. And such people could have easily conceived of their participation in the Great War in such a fashion: potentially, one soldier's sacrifice could mean that, say, two French children would be saved. It is of course impossible to literally equate any soldier's death with the preserved lives of any other particular individuals. Still, if one believes that risking one's life may help preserve the lives of others and allow for greater happiness in the world, then fighting a war is indeed an honorable thing to do. In such a formulation, there is certainly meaning in the word *honor*.

Joe's rhetoric continues in like fashion, and the counterargument continues in like fashion as well. Joe heralds and proclaims the right of the individual to live, to do what he chooses with his own life, to not have his death dictated by some abstract principle, but he never considers the plights of the individuals who indeed suffered because of the ongoing war, nor does he conceive of any moral obligation to help fellow humans in need, nor does he ever give substance to the principles he so readily criticizes. He claims that, being exiled from the world of the living, he can now speak for the dead, and he states that no dead soldier is glad that he is dead and that each would give anything, abandon any principle, to get his life back. However, such an argument must assume that the person lost his life for nothing; that nothing was gained through his death. Sadly, in the case of many soldiers in World War I especially, this was precisely the case: many died for nothing, marching directly into oncoming fire in accord with the dictates of an aggressive battle plan. Yet it goes without saying that no soldier in his right mind *wants* to die, nor does he need to be glad to be dead in order to validate the choice he made to enlist or to allow himself to be drafted and risk his life.

Joe concludes that "there's nothing worth dying for," but this does not also mean that there are no *people* worth dying for. Joe asserts that "there's nothing noble about dying," but this comes from someone who "never really knew what the fight was all about," from someone who did not morally justify his participation in the war in the first place. Viewing the war in retrospect from the prison cell of his hospital bed and his isolated mind, Joe no longer has any means of gaining such a moral justification. Throughout the novel, he considers war as a perfect abstraction—as fighting not for the sake of people but for the sake of various words, none of which has any concrete meaning because Joe himself has inadequate awareness of the circumstances behind the war. Therefore a reader may justifiably conclude that Joe's antiwar rationale, centered as it is on the idea of war in the absence of context, is not entirely valid.

Notably, even Trumbo himself later conceded that the pacifist rhetoric of *Johnny Got His Gun* is not without fault. In the introduction he penned for the novel in 1959, he begins by describing the atmosphere that fed into World War I as like a "summer festival" where military "fools" marched honorably away to what would prove "the last of the romantic wars"; in other words, the war was fit to inspire an antiwar novel such as his own. However, World War II would prove "an entirely different affair"—one that

Trumbo ultimately fully supported, even going so far as to advocate the establishment of an additional land front that would serve to relieve the war burden being borne by Russia.

When his book went out of print during World War II, Trumbo was fairly content. In fact, once Hitler's doom seemed imminent, Nazi-aligned interests hoped to have the book republished, thinking a push for peace could preserve what was left of the Third Reich, but as Trumbo explains in his 1959 introduction, he and his publisher agreed that "*Johnny* was exactly the sort of book that shouldn't be reprinted until the war was at an end." In other words, in presenting a one-sided rhetorical condemnation of war, the novel can unfortunately have a subversive influence even when an ongoing war is justified. Trumbo would write an addendum to his introduction in 1970, in the thick of the Vietnam War, when once again he believed that his book carried a crucial message that needed to be heard.

In the novel, Trumbo makes clear his antiwar inclinations, but it is worth keeping in mind that the author was a champion debater in high school, one who took delight in wielding rhetoric with aplomb. He was inspired to write the novel not only by his own antiwar sentiment but by an article he read about a visit by England's Prince of Wales to a Canadian veteran who had been precisely as severely debilitated as Joe Bonham finds himself: he had lost all four limbs, and the only sense that remained to him was touch. Naturally, then, in writing *Johnny Got His Gun*, Trumbo inhabited his protagonist—in the words of his wife Cleo, "in order to write *Johnny*, he had to *become* Johnny"—and elaborated precisely the sort of antiwar rhetoric one might expect to hear from a veteran who has suffered such a horrible fate. In sum, the impact of the novel is emotional above all. If the antiwar rhetoric falls short of offering a truly convincing argument against participation in war, the stunning power of the book's portrait of Joe Bonham remains.

Source: Michael Allen Holmes, Critical Essay on *Johnny Got His Gun*, in *Novels for Students*, Gale, Cengage Learning, 2014.

Tim Blackmore

In the following excerpt, Blackmore traces "an arc through modernity's idea of the body machine, and

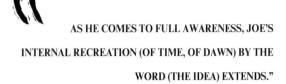

AS HE COMES TO FULL AWARENESS, JOE'S INTERNAL RECREATION (OF TIME, OF DAWN) BY THE WORD (THE IDEA) EXTENDS."

the way that machine acts in war, to the development of the postmodern body and war."

. . . In this essay, I trace an arc through modernity's idea of the body machine, and the way that machine acts in war, to the development of the postmodern body and war. I argue that Trumbo's text has been wrongly forgotten, that it sits at the edge of postmodernism, hailing it. If we read the narrative of the living corpse that Trumbo presents us, we can ignore complaints about sentiment and romance. We can use Trumbo's advice about myth and apply it to ourselves as we stare glumly (yet again) through the barrel of a cruise missile's video monitor, squinting at meaningless low-res images of what might be important military installations— or abandoned warehouses somewhere on a Hollywood back lot.

Johnny Got His Gun is the story of one body, a body in pain. The politics of that body appear to be personal, relatively unimportant. Elaine Scarry argues that "injury must at some point be understood individually because pain, like all forms of sentience, is experienced within, 'happens' within, the body of the individual" (65). But the inside story quickly becomes an outside one. As soon as the sufferer is able to twitch, and then to groan, the most basic pain narrative begins. In Joe Bonham's case, the narrative of the severed body so damaged that it cannot see, hear, smell, touch, taste must be told through thought; it is a fragmentary, almost postmodern, communication from a body pulverized by modernity's war. Postmodern communication, full of gaps, miss-takes, sudden arrests, can be frightening, disorienting enough so that Pope John Paul II, one of the apparent moral forces in the contemporary world, has been moved to attack postmodernism as "nihilism," which, he admits, "has been justified in a sense by the terrible experience of evil which has marked our age" (*Encyclicab*). The church's perpetual message of faith is contested by Trumbo's novel, which employs religious signs to examine a world of faithlessness, of erasure.

"Then take Lazarus," remembers Joe Bonham. "He showed up one gray morning when nothing was happening. All of a sudden out of the fog loomed this big fat Hun" (Trumbo). Lazarus, a dead German soldier, hangs for days rotting on the wire. No amount of shelling destroys the corpse. When the smell gets too horrific, Bonham's commander orders a detail, and out into "no man's land" the living go to bury Lazarus. True to his namesake, a shell hits the grave and resurrects the corpse, and the men once more confront their physical future in all its corruption. Booth notes that, "during the Great War, the most common soldier's nightmare was of being buried alive 'in a bunker by a heavy shell' [Leed 22]. This fear expresses how profoundly disturbing combatants found the lack of a clear boundary between life and death to be, for to be buried alive means literally to occupy the positions of life and death simultaneously—to become a conscious corpse" (Booth 61). Joe Bonham is that conscious corpse—awake, alive, and embedded in a flesh coffin: "It was as if all the people in the world the whole two billion of them had been against him pushing the lid of the coffin down on him tamping the dirt solid against the lid rearing great stones above the dirt to keep him in the earth. Yet he had risen" (Trumbo).

Joe struggles against the pressure of the *socius* that bears down on him, the forces that want him silenced, that want the propaganda machine to run unhindered by resistant voices. Trumbo assumes a powerful authorial position when he invokes the sign of Lazarus (until now, that has been Christ's signifying practice): "And when he thus had spoken, he cried with a loud voice, Lazarus, come forth" (John 11:43). Joe Bonham, Trumbo's Lazarus, emerges with a vengeance, aware of his predecessor's failings: "Never before in the world had the dead spoken never since Lazarus and Lazarus didn't say anything. Now he would tell them everything. He would speak from the dead. He would talk for the dead. He would tell all the secrets of the dead" (Trumbo). Trumbo speaks for the soldier buried alive and puts in Joe's tongueless mouth a message about modernity's war. Lazarus needs no voice because his existence is enough to cause a rupture in the Pharisees' story about orthodoxy (for us, faith in ethics, in the Hippocratic

oath). The result of the rupture is that the "chief priests consulted that they might put Lazarus also to death; Because that by reason of him many of the Jews went away, and believed on Jesus" (John 12:10–11). Trumbo's novel turns the reader away from the orthodoxy of patriotism and medical care, toward the logic of machines that use bodies for fuel and medicine for lubricant.

Inscribed in the Lazarus myth is a broken narrative and an uncertain future for those in power, for those who have held other beliefs; it is a resistant narrative about beating the odds, of hope for the forgotten, and a site of danger for the powerful. Lazarus is about the body's reclamation and the death of death. Michel Foucault argues that "death is the great analyst that shows the connexions by unfolding them, and bursts open the wonders of genesis in the rigour of decomposition: and the word decomposition must be allowed to stagger under the weight of its meaning" (144). But decomposition is only half the Lazarus story. Incorporation picks up where decomposition breaks down—a new corporatist power ousts birth and death. Joe knows how he looks: "He was nothing but a piece of meat like the chunks of cartilage old Prof Vogel used to have in biology. Chunks of cartilage that didn't have anything except life so they grew on chemicals," and he also knows there's more to the story: "He was one up on the cartilage. He had a mind and it was thinking" (Trumbo). Joe understands himself as a successful lab experiment. His leap from understanding a human as a doing creature to a thinking one gives him a taste of agency. Science may have created him, but, he hopes, it does not control every part of him. The soldier begins to understand science (including medicine) from a machinic perspective. While the mind thinks, the body machine confronts pressures, stresses, wheels, belts, gears—a panoply of industrial forces.

. . . The body is shipped to war like any unit off the line. The problems will be the same on the shop floor as on the war yard: how long can the human motor last before it burns out? The growing techno-structure puts trust in "the endless natural power available to human purpose while revealing an anxiety of limits—the fear that the body and psyche were circumscribed by fatigue and thus could not withstand the demands of modernity" (Rabinbach 12). At the centre of the machine experiment, and of progress, is the question of what power the human body really contains. Doubt about the BODY produces a rupture in the socius's expectant narrative where motion goes only forward. If the body is weak, progress will stall. Why, at this juncture, couldn't the machine borrow the Lazarus myth, reassure the body that it can always be replaced? Machines couple with machines, not spiritual flows. The medical army develops anti-fatigue vaccines rather than rely on old myths, magic: Lazarus is useful only for the resistant. While it seems as if the machine doesn't need the Lazarus myth, those who serve it still have large sections of faith intact. Industry borrows human mythology (as Von Harbou borrowed both the genesis [164–65] and underworld myths [21] for her visions of Met ropous) because humans are intimately connected to the machine. Humans serving the machine still need human stories.

Joe sees himself as the perfect war consumer: "I used to be a consumer. I've consumed a lot in my time. I've consumed more shrapnel and gunpowder than any living man" (Trumbo). Once he has been consumed, Joe understands. But his assessment that he "used to be a consumer" is wishful thinking. He continues to consume and be consumed—his illusions about agency have changed. He believes himself in charge of the consumption but admits that he consumes helplessly through the umbilicus plugged into his newly infantilized body. Virilio looks beyond the shattered body, beyond modernity's war, to the war that runs at full consumption without anxiety about exhaustion: "We notice that the doctrine of use—in other words knowledge at work in effectiveness, utilizations—has been completely squeezed out in favor of a doctrine of production: they make tools so that they exist for a war in its pure form, without worrying about what happens when you use them." Pure war annihilates the body. Until that point, the production is better than ever. If the product is ever consumed, even the "cut of meat" that is Joe Bonham won't exist to meditate on its errors. In modernity's war, the body persists; it is required in industrial quantity. Postmodern war causes the body to vanish. Robot missiles fly over [C.sup.3] I topographic zones, striking at military targets without killing people. NATO bombs Serbia to deny terrain, and when ground forces finally appear (called up as part of the final event) they find only mass graves left behind by the atrocity makers: the thousands of bombs that flew dropped perfectly and surgically (it is a war theatre, after all) on real estate. In Virilio's information suicide state, the body disappears before it is shipped to war: the state has already conscripted every body, and the subject agrees to conscription because there are payoffs.

Modernity exchanges labour for money, the body for an appropriately packaged set of signs of cultural value (standard of living, home, safety, freedom, democracy). The exchange has a finality to it. Once the deal has been struck, the inscription proceeds. If the body backs away from inscription, severe distress, rupture, danger threaten the system. Trumbo, one of the Hollywood Ten who defied the House Committee on Un-American Activities (HCUA) and refused to name names, was accused of the usual things an uncooperative witness could expect to be accused of. Famously, he answered the chief investigator: "Very many questions can be answered 'Yes' or 'No' only by a moron or a slave." For that, he went to prison and endured a ten-year blacklist. His resistant body, if it couldn't be inscribed, had to be put away out of view, as is Joe Bonham's. Modernity's war is no different, and it strikes the bargain for the body entire: "War may be understood as organizing itself not only according to our side vs. their side but also according to inside vs. outside, with each metaphorical formulation disrupting the other" (Booth 51–52). What happens to Joe Bonham's outside self (complete loss of physical agency) is followed by the sudden growth of his inside self ("He was one up on the cartilage. He had a mind and it was thinking"). Joe Bonham has already agreed to be racked up on the war line for consumption: Joe, and other citizens like him, have been socialized to agree with the machine. If the subject doesn't strenuously disagree, as Trumbo did, then the state expects obedience (stand and sing the anthem, salute the flag, see it our way, go to war). The deeper into the socius he sinks, the less chance Joe has of emerging.

Too late, Joe recognizes the economy he works in: "Give us a bill of sale drawn up plainly so we know in advance what we're getting killed for and give us also a first mortgage on something as security so we can be sure after we've won your war that we've got the same kind of freedom we bargained for" (Trumbo). Only after the fact can Joe see that he has exchanged his whole labouring self for inclusion in the socius.

When he frames the relationship, it is a financial transaction (a mortgage, a bill of sale); it is not the sign package he thought he had agreed to. But then, he didn't think, and the signifying engine that runs on advertising, war songs, propaganda posters, and nostrums about democracy drew up the documents, so the deal was never clear. The separation between self and not-self is chimerical, flickering: "If the inside story and the outside story seem interchangeable, this is precisely because it's the boundaries between inside and outside that are violently being renegotiated, transgressed, and reaffirmed" (Seltzer 162). Nothing shatters and reforms those boundaries more violently than war does. Possession of the body in a mill town or of a limbless chunk of flesh from a war zone is all part of the same logic: the latter is simply more extreme. Industry owns not only the workers' bodies but, arguably, also the whole town (as Michael Moore has demonstrated so graphically in the case of Flint, Michigan (*Roger and Mel*). When the civilian enters basic training, all so-called rights disappear: it is the first of many vanishing acts that the new soldier will experience. Joe is blind to the amount that has been given, taken, lost, absorbed.

Virilio reminds us that postmodernity's subjects are not any wiser than modernity's: "All of us are already civilian soldiers, without knowing it. And some of us know it. The great stroke of luck for the military class's terrorism is that no one recognizes it. People don't recognize the militarized part of their identity, of their consciousness (Virilio 26). But Trumbo recognizes it before the Calvaries of World War II, Korea, Vietnam, and the first and second Gulf wars. The inscribed soldier is evident: "Maybe times are bad and your salaries are low, [thinks Joe]. Don't worry boys because there is always a way to cure things like that. Have a war and then prices go up and wages go up and everybody makes a hell of a lot of money. There'll be one along pretty soon boys so don't get impatient. It'll come and then you'll have your chance" (Trumbo). For all the claims about the cyborg body I make in this essay, this engine of war, even of total war, operates with a naggingly similar logic. The body displays the inscription, the war machine's writing is clear on the skin's surface (and under it as well, where medicine engraves itself in the body, sculpting new organs).

Laughter must greet House minority leader Richard Gephardt's plaints about the timing of the presidential impeachment: "We strongly object to their matter coming up tomorrow or the next day or any day in which our young men and women in the military are in harm's way protecting the interests of the people of the United States" (Mitchell). But what is the definition of "harm's way"? Long before entering a war zone, the soldier is in "harm's way": the soldier's first beating is administered by the army, which bends the individual to suit the apparatus. Once at war, there is no safety zone, everything is free-lire, and the reasons for fire will be obscure, arbitrary, frightfully banal. Joe Bonham puts it succinctly: "How could you believe or disbelieve anything any more?" (Trumbo). The gap between 1999 and 1939 seems more like a slight fissure. The socius began moving to a body without organs long before Hobbes drew his picture of the Leviathan.

Prefiguring Deleuze and Guattari's idea of the body without organs is a creation by medical science: a set of organs without a body, confusion about inside and outside become chaos and terror. A human used to signifying himself as "free," not inscribed, is jolted by the body's revelation of loss: "He was so sure the idea of no mouth was a dream that he could investigate it calmly. He tried to work his jaws and he had no jaws." He explores what is in the gap: "The hole went too high to have any eyes in it. He was blind" (Trumbo). The presence of absence is mapped above and below: "Somewhere just below his hip joints they had cut both of his legs off. No legs" (Trumbo). In a book marked by its spill of words, multiple streams of consciousness and name-brand realism, here is a terrible lack of words that matches Joe's lack of body. Here is the scientific search; "investigate it calmly" and the result: "had no jaws," "blind, no legs." The words are chopped off—a sudden logo-amputation, linguistic, and physical aporia.

Modernity has an answer for bodily aporia. A discourse of power rushes in to the gaps: "'When the eye can no longer see, the ear cannot hear, or touch cannot feel, or even when the senses appear to deceive us, these instruments perform like a new sense with astonishing precision': what the writer's signs here trace is thus not the writer's 'own' desires or the writing self but the prosthetic language of the body and the mechanical and automatic inscription of the body's forces" (Seltzer 16). We've arrived at the body's piecemeal replacement by mechanical organs, where fatigue is a factor but not a fearful one. If a camera lens shatters, attach a new one. If an explosion lances an audio pickup, replace it. If the part simply becomes fatigued, what matter? The question is, how much, exactly, of the body do you really need to keep?

Such questions move us prematurely from the biosphere to the technosphere. Back in what is left of the body, panic burns a hole. The anxiety of attaching prostheses is connected to identity, to wholeness. Joe continues to think of himself by his cultural sign package: "When you have only a back and a stomach and half a head you probably look as much like a Frenchman or German or an Englishman as an American" (Trumbo). Joe's cautious surrender of America as his primary signifying system brings him the kind of freedom experienced by many expatriates: an ability to look back and see more clearly (even, perhaps especially, if you don't have eyes). Allyson Booth suggests: "Corpses collapse the distinction between ally and enemy and confuse the boundary between life and death." Joe, the living corpse, sees all boundaries transgressed; he is an adoptive child of the socius, no longer attached to a nation or creed. He is the zone of collapse. In him all binaries are liquefied, and growth perishes: "It was like a full grown man suddenly being stuffed back into his mother's body. He was lying in stillness. He was completely helpless" (Trumbo).

Joe's nurses preside over a creature who is no longer human, and yet has been born, who has no identity, and yet knows who he is. Joe's identity as produced by the state has been literally exploded. He is inside now, only thinking, and that thinking must create his new self. He is one of the first surviving children of the socius's war: "In a sense, the cyborg has no origin story in the Western sense—a 'final' irony since the cyborg is also the awful apocalyptic telos of the 'West's' escalating domination of abstract individuation, an ultimate self untied at last from all dependency, a man in space" (Haraway 150–51). The idea that humans control the war machine flickers past with modernity. Wars of conquest and revenge are replaced (at least in the West) by pure war, the socius's skin. Modernity created industrial war, the socius creates pure war. But unmodified humans can barely tolerate modernity's war—a new soldier must emerge, one that

has been amplified, improved, strengthened against fatigue: a cyborg soldier. The cyborg doesn't have Lazarus's history. Lazarus, the myth, suggests a richness of past, of combined narrative, that the cyborg cannot claim. The origin of modernity's Joe Bonham is Lazarus, but the postmodern continuation is a cyborg.

Joe thinks about his and others' new status as body-machines that have failed due to fatigue: "Oh hell there were a lot of funny things happened in this man's war. Anything could be true. [. . .] There were whole rooms filled with men who breathed through tubes. [. . .] Tubes were important" (Trumbo). The tubes signal the entrance of the socius under the skin, the forced creation of a creature that will continue like a machine. Worse than the panic, as Mark Seltzer would call it, of the prosthesis, is the final irrevocable agentic shift from human to socius. Joe cannot choose but to be fed: "He ate regular. He could feel them sliding stuff into his belly and he knew he was eating all right. Flavor didn't matter to him" (Trumbo). His assessment of the loss of agency is matched by a cold tone, the impersonal realization that "flavor didn't matter to him," that they can "slide stuff" into him the way you would slide a magazine into a machine. Lazarus appears to be dead finally, killed by the cyborg: "Modern medicine is also full of cyborgs, of couplings between organism and machine, each conceived as coded devices, in an intimacy and with a power that was not generated in the history of sexuality" (Haraway 150). What is the new myth for the human brain in the post-human body? What stories will we tell the children, if we can call them that?

Lost in his Underground, Dostoyevsky's enraged misanthrope scribbles:

> So perhaps I turn out to be more alive than you. Look harder! After all, we don't even know where "real life" is lived nowadays, or what it is, what name it goes by. Leave us to ourselves, without our books, and at once we get into a muddle and lose our way—we don't know whose side we are on or where to give our allegiance, what to love and what to hate. [. . .] We even find it difficult to be human beings, men with real flesh and blood of our own. [. . .] We are born dead [. . .] and we become more and more contented with our condition. We are acquiring a taste for it. Soon we shall invent a method of being born from an idea. (123)

Almost eighty years later, Trumbo has Joe Bonham ponder the same issue: "He had to start in like a baby and learn. He had to concentrate. He had to start in the beginning. He had to start with an idea" (Trumbo). The differences are manifest: where the Undergrounder exhorts us to look hard for a way out but concludes before the search begins that it has failed, Joe, the Cartesian, who has been chopped and charted, maps an answer that creates space, light, a self from grid coordinates. Joe uses the tools of modernity to reconstruct the self that modernity explodes. As he comes to full awareness, Joe's internal recreation (of time, of dawn) by the word (the idea) extends. He connects his internal recreation to external communication, transforming his body into a giant telegraph key. Joe uses his body to convert trench war to communication war, fulfilling the C'I evolution that is the basis for Virilio's pure war battlefield. For Joe Bonham, communication promises an end to his mute existence and the chance to be a vocal Lazarus.

. . . Perched on the edge of modernity, about to fall into the abyss of the information age, of the cyborg's magnetic impulses, Trumbo sees the beginning of the end. His picture of Joe Bonham's body has brought us a long way toward our cultural moment, toward a fall, as Seltzer would argue "from production to consumption (or from industry to luxury, or from use to exchange, etc.) that at times seems as crude as the claim that people grew things in the first half of the nineteenth century and ate them in the second half" (Seltzer 60). Trumbo knows that the human body is ripe for consumption, and sees the postmodern conclusion: erasure of the body, the self, the rise of the socius, the supremacy of the body without organs, the generation of a cyborg world. But it is too horrible, too brutal, too pure to follow through. And so he ends with Joe's helpless shrill warning to the war managers to beware.

Trumbo goes out into the world and in eleven years refuses to act like a moron or a slave" before the Committee, returning as a spectre to Hollywood, writing like Lazarus, [films] about finding light (*Spartacus, Bad Day at Black Rock, Lonely are the Brave, Papillon, Executive Action*), until finally Otto Preminger will roll back the stone of the blacklist and shine a light on him. . . .

Source: Tim Blackmore, "Lazarus Machine: Body Politics in Dalton Trumbo's *Johnny Got His Gun*," in *Mosaic* (Winnipeg), Vol. 33, No. 4, December 2000, p. 1.

Linda Ross

In the following essay, Ross suggests that much of the success of Johnny Got His Gun *was due to*

Trumbo's use of cinematic techniques and the reflective nature of the book.

World War I killed more than people, it killed an age of innocence. When the fighting began, singing mothers and wives who expected to see their men home by Christmas sent young men away with fanfare to the battlefields of the "war to end all wars." That Christmas did not come until four years later, and many of the men never returned. Armed primarily with a sense of national pride, the desire to serve God and country, and an archaic albeit glorious notion of war, the young soldiers were faced with a brutal reality. Modern war with its machine guns, chemicals, grenades, and mines ravaged the European countryside and the armies along with it. Not until Vietnam would the United States experience such trauma again.

In fact, the worst of the trauma was never revealed. This is the story Dalton Trumbo tells in his sole completed novel, *Johnny Got His Gun*. His compelling yet chilling account, though published in 1939, still wrenches the soul of the reader. Trumbo, best known for his screenplays and political activities, relates in his novel the story of Joe Bonham, a young veteran who was wounded during the war. Bonham was not simply wounded, however, he was marred beyond recognition as a human being. His face was completely disfigured and all four of his limbs were lost. He was, in essence, a stump. His mental functions, however, were completely intact—and trapped inside a body that allowed him no expression. The story is told completely from Bonham's perspective, thus the reader becomes engaged in the character's struggle to figure out what has happened to him, create order in a new universe of which he is the only inhabitant, and establish contact with the outside world.

Part of Trumbo's success with *Johnny Got His Gun* was his use of cinematic techniques to keep his audience involved. Most of the novel takes place in Joe Bonham's head, but Trumbo kept the reader engaged in the stream of consciousness flow through the extensive use of flashbacks and even, on one occasion, a montage. The sensual detail of Bonham's flashbacks is exquisite. Often the character remembers the sights, sounds, smells, and tastes of his childhood. Trumbo describes these memories with such clarity and finesse that the reader lives these scenes along with the character. Not only are these flashbacks individually well-crafted, each of them is essential to the progression of the plot. Each flashback reveals new bits of information about Joe's present condition and together, they provide fascinating suggestions about how the human mind uses memory.

Although the book is a cogent and passionate argument for pacificism, it retains a vital significance even in times of peace. Because of Bonham's severe injuries, one of the central issues with which he must grapple is what gives life meaning? What makes one human? Clearly, Bonham is still human and keeps the reader engaged as such. Yet he is one over whom debate would rage on the outside world. Is his life worth continuing? To what lengths should society go to sustain him?

Trumbo also invites an examination of society in this book. Interestingly, Bonham becomes more of a problem to society once he regains access to it. When he was non-responsive, the outside world could more or less ignore him. Once he could make his wishes known, however, they knew he still was an alert and aware human being. The thought of that—the obligations that implied—were beyond society's ability to handle. He held an unkind mirror to society. The people within the system wanted to appear magnanimous as is evidenced by their bestowing Bonham with medals and offering him such extensive care for the rest of his life. But once Bonham could make his desires known, the system was revealed to be cruel, callous, and self-serving.

Perhaps this reflective aspect of the book is its most significant contribution to young adults. The pacifist argument is certainly an important one—war is not a glorious undertaking and should not be portrayed as such. Yet war is not always at issue. The more constant issue within society is the meaning and value of life. Teaching young people to ponder these issues and form conscious convictions about them is, perhaps, the more urgent matter at hand. Trumbo provides a vehicle through which both sets of issues can be addressed.

Source: Linda Ross, "Dalton Trumbo: Overview," in *Twentieth-Century Young Adult Writers*, edited by Laura Standley Berger, St. James Press, 1994.

SOURCES

Baldwin, Hanson W., *The Crucial Years, 1939–1941: The World at War*, Harper & Row, 1976, pp. 51–55.

Barth, John, "The Literature of Replenishment: Postmodernist Fiction," in *The Friday Book: Essays and Other Non-fiction*, Johns Hopkins University Press, 1984, pp. 193–206.

Blackmore, Tim, "Lazarus Machine: Body Politics in Dalton Trumbo's *Johnny Got His Gun*," in *Mosaic*, Vol. 33, No. 4, December 2000, p. 1.

Cook, Bruce, *Dalton Trumbo*, Charles Scribner's Sons, 1977, pp. 12–13, 21, 34–40, 52–53, 124–31, 140–50.

De Groot, Gerard J., *The First World War*, Palgrave, 2001, pp. 1–22.

Douglas, Roy, *The Advent of War, 1939–40*, St. Martin's Press, 1978, pp. ix–xi, 1–2, 121.

Duffy, Michael, "Conscientious Objectors," FirstWorld War.com: A Multimedia History of World War One, August 22, 2009, http://www.firstworldwar.com/atoz/conscientiousobjectors.htm (accessed December 6, 2012).

Hanson, Peter, *Dalton Trumbo, Hollywood Rebel: A Critical Survey and Filmography*, McFarland, 2001, pp. 1, 7, 65, 79.

Heyman, Neil M., *World War I*, Greenwood Press, 1997, pp. xix–xxiii, 3–34, 63–80.

Howard, Michael, *The First World War*, Oxford University Press, 2002, pp. xxii–xv, 81–95, 146.

Keep, Christopher, Tim McLaughlin, and Robin Parmar, "Modernism and the Modern Novel," in *The Electronic Labyrinth*, 2000, http://www2.iath.virginia.edu/elab/hfl0255.html (accessed December 5, 2012).

Moore, James, "Dalton Trumbo," in *Dictionary of Literary Biography*, Vol. 26, *American Screenwriters*, edited Robert E. Morsberger, Stephen O. Lesser, and Randall Clark, Gale Research, 1984, pp. 324–31.

Review of *Johnny Got His Gun* (audiobook), read by William Dufris, in *Publishers Weekly*, Vol. 255, No. 21, May 26, 2008, pp. 60–61.

Ross, Linda, "Dalton Trumbo: Overview," in *Twentieth-Century Young Adult Writers*, edited by Laura Standley Berger, St. James Press, 1994.

Trumbo, Cleo, Foreword to *Night of the Aurochs*, by Dalton Trumbo, edited by Robert Kirsch, Viking Press, 1979, pp. ix–x.

Trumbo, Dalton, *Johnny Got His Gun*, Bantam Books, 2007.

———, Introduction to *Johnny Got His Gun*, L. Stuart, 1959.

Wilson, Scott, "President Obama Wins Nobel Peace Prize," in *Washington Post*, October 10, 2009, http://www.washingtonpost.com/wp-dyn/content/article/2009/10/09/AR2009100900914.html (accessed December 8, 2012).

Zaner, Richard M., "Sisyphus without Knees: Exploring Self-Other Relationships through Illness and Disability," in *Literature and Medicine*, Vol. 22, No. 2, Fall 2003, pp. 188–207.

FURTHER READING

Bauby, Jean-Dominique, *The Diving Bell and the Butterfly*, translated by Jeremy Leggatt, A.A. Knopf, 1997.

A Frenchman, Bauby suffered a debilitating stroke in 1995 that left him with the use of no more than his left eyelid, despite his mind remaining fully intact. With the help of therapists and software applications, he was able to compose this memoir—published just two days before he died of complications—of how the stroke altered his life and perspectives.

Capozzola, Christopher, *Uncle Sam Wants You: World War I and the Making of the Modern American Citizen*, Oxford University Press, 2008.

The 1917 transformation of American society into a war machine had profound consequences on American ideologies, the role of the federal government, and the national culture in general, all of which Capozzola explores in depth.

Early, Frances H., *A World without War: How U.S. Feminists and Pacifists Resisted World War I*, Syracuse University Press, 1997.

Early focuses on a pair of crusading women who sought to advocate pacifist interests during World War I and describes how activists criticized compromises to the democratic process and the poor treatment of conscientious objectors.

Scodari, Christine, "*Johnny Got His Gun*: Wartime Songs of Pacifism, Patriotism and Life Style in 20th-Century America," in *Popular Music and Society*, Vol. 18, No. 1, 1994, pp. 1–17.

In this essay, Scodari draws on Trumbo's title in exploring the impact that certain songs had on patriotic and pacifist sentiments during the nation's twentieth-century wars.

SUGGESTED SEARCH TERMS

Dalton Trumbo AND novel AND Johnny Got His Gun

Dalton Trumbo AND film AND Johnny Got His Gun

World War I AND casualties

World War I AND trench warfare

World War I AND veterans AND disabled OR hospital

World War I AND literature OR films

United States AND World War I

Johnny Got His Gun AND Vietnam War

Johnny Got His Gun AND Cindy Sheehan

Johnny Got His Gun AND communism

The Leopard

GIUSEPPE DI LAMPEDUSA

1959

The Leopard (1959), by Giuseppe Tomasi, the prince of Lampedusa, is perhaps the best-known modern Italian novel in the English-speaking world. Produced in a modern Italy that was trying to put the dismal history of Fascism behind it and had been split apart by economic changes after World War II that brought prosperity to the north but left the south in squalid poverty, *The Leopard* is a nostalgic meditation on the nation's past. The novel is closely based on Lampedusa's own family history and is set during the Risorgimento, the unification of Italy that took place around the same time as the American Civil War. Lampedusa's grandfather had been a great landholder in Sicily, but he died without a will, and his fortune was consumed by decades of legal wrangling among his heirs. Lampedusa, the inheritor of not much more than his title, grew up in the shadow of his ancestor's nobility and looked back on it as a lost paradise. In *The Leopard*, he conveys his heartbreaking longing for the world that had been swept away by modernity. For Lampedusa, the loss everyone feels when leaving childhood is magnified into the loss of an entire world.

AUTHOR BIOGRAPHY

Giuseppe Tomasi di Lampedusa was born on December 23, 1896, at his ancestral palace in Palermo, Sicily. Technically his surname was

Giuseppe Tomasi di Lampedusa with his wife and dogs *(© Mondadori | Getty Images)*

Tomasi, and he was the last person to hold the title of Prince of Lampedusa (a tiny island in the Mediterranean between Sicily and Tunisia). The Tomasi family had been members of the European nobility going back to the Middle Ages and had, particularly since the seventeenth century, controlled large estates on Sicily near Palermo. *The Leopard* is very much a reflection on Tomasi family history. Almost every character and event of the novel can be linked to a historical member of the Tomasi family and the details of their lives, but while the novel is in some sense a history, it is one that was transformed to become an artistic creation.

Prince Giulio, Lampedusa's grandfather and the model for Don Fabrizio in the novel, died without a will in 1885, and the subsequent division of his estate among his heirs, involving decades of legal battles, left the Tomasi family in a relatively diminished and impoverished position. Lampedusa fought in World War I and was captured by the Austrians, but he managed to escape from a prison camp in Hungary and return to Italy. Disgusted by the rise of the Fascist government in Italy, he devoted himself to the study of foreign literature and spent much of his life in London, where he met his wife, Alexandra Wolff von Stomersee, the daughter of the Latvian consul. They were married in 1932 but had to live much of their lives apart because of the tyrannical influence of Lampedusa's mother. During World War II, the Lampedusa palace in Palermo was destroyed by American bombing.

After the war, Lampedusa's wife became one of the leading psychoanalysts in Italy. She encouraged her husband to write memoirs exploring his childhood and early life. These eventually became the basis of *The Leopard*. The earliest version of these writings, *Places of*

My Infancy, has also been translated into English and was published in the collection *Two Stories and a Memory*. Lampedusa became attached to a circle of young intellectuals and writers in Rome, Italy, which included his cousin, the poet Luccio Piccolo, whom Lampedusa adopted. Lampedusa delivered lectures to this group on French and English literature; the text of these lectures has been published but not translated. *The Leopard* was rejected by several publishers during Lampedusa's lifetime because of its reactionary nature. Lampedusa died of lung cancer on July 23, 1957, in Rome. The manuscript of *The Leopard* circulated among Lampedusa's friends. It was finally published in 1959 and translated into English the following year.

PLOT SUMMARY

The Leopard is the translation of the Italian title *Il gattopardo*. However, the Italian word actually refers to a serval, a type of small spotted cat that was native to Sicily but that became extinct there in the middle of the nineteenth century. The serval, rather than the leopard, was the heraldic animal of the princes of Lampedusa, as it is of the princes of Salina in the novel.

Introduction to the Prince (May 1860)
The Leopard begins during the invasion of Sicily by Giuseppe Garibaldi and his thousand volunteers. This invasion sparks a civil war in the kingdom of the two Sicilies, leading to the unification of Italy into a single modern state under the ruling house of Piedmont from northern Italy.

The novel begins in the Salina palace in Palermo as the prince, Don Fabrizio, and his family are being led in saying the rosary by their chaplain, Father Pirrone. Afterward, the prince walks in his garden with his dog, Bendico. He recalls the dismembered body of a Neapolitan soldier that was recently found there, killed by Garibaldi's "Redshirt" soldiers, who are massing in the hills above the city. That night, the prince visits his mistress in the city. He takes Father Pirrone with him so that he can visit the Jesuit house in town, where he learns how alarmed the Church authorities are about the invasion and uprising. Don Fabrizio spends his days doing astronomical work (he is a prominent amateur astronomer) and in looking after

MEDIA ADAPTATIONS

- *The Leopard* was filmed by Luchino Visconti in 1963, staring the American actor Burt Lancaster as Don Fabrizio. The film won the Palme d'Or at the Cannes Film Festival. While European audiences saw a version in Italian with Lancaster's lines dubbed, the American release used Lancaster's voice and dubbed the other actors into English. The American version was also shorter by twenty-four minutes. The recent Criterion Collection DVD release contains both the full (subtitled) and edited versions.

the affairs of his estate, particularly in meetings with his accountant, Ciccio Ferrara, and his chief agent, Pietro Russo. These scenes give the prince scope to express his disgust with the rising middle class who are going to be propelled into power by the coming revolution, but also his helplessness in the face of the future. His beloved nephew, Tancredi, and Russo are both are secretly allied with the building revolution. Tancredi visits his uncle and explains to him that change is inevitable and that he must join the revolution in order to guide it in a way that will protect the family's way of life. In fact, Tancredi is going to openly join Garibaldi's army. The prince thinks about the contrasts between Tancredi and his own eldest son and heir, Paolo, whom he considers ineffectual and boorish, and his favorite son, Giovanni, who has run away to England to find freedom in making a life for himself without depending on his father's influence. The prince receives an anonymous letter advising his family to go to his country estate of Donnafugata, where they will be safe.

Donnafugata (August 1860)
Once in his country palace outside the small town of Donnafugata, the prince learns that Calogero Sedàra, the local mayor, had been quick to ally himself with the Redshirts and has amassed a large fortune, nearly equal to the

prince's own, through sharp business dealings, usually at the expense of aristocrats. Father Pirrone brings Don Fabrizio a message from his daughter Concetta: she is in love with Tancredi and believes that he is on the verge of proposing to her, and she wants to know how her father wishes her to answer. But the prince does not give a definite answer. Sedàra and other prominent commoners are invited to dinner at the palace that evening. Sedàra brings his daughter Angelica, who is remarkably beautiful and who sets her romantic sights on Tancredi. Father Pirrone retreats from her erotic allure and takes refuge in the Bible, but he reads the stories of Delilah, Judith, and Esther, all women who used their feminine wiles to bring about the downfall of men. Tancredi tells stories of his adventures in the recent war (now over in Sicily, but continuing on the mainland), including a raid on a convent. Concetta finds this outrageous and takes personal offense. The next day, Tancredi takes up the same line, when the family makes a visit to a convent of which the prince is the patron, and she reacts just as strongly. Thereafter, Tancredi begins courting Angelica.

The Troubles of Don Fabrizio (October 1860)

Fabrizio grows dissatisfied with his diminished role in the new world created by the revolution. Tancredi is back with Garibaldi's army at the siege of Gaeta, but he continues his courtship of Angelica through letters. She is a daily visitor at the palace. While Fabrizio is out hunting with his friend Ciccio Tumeo, the church organist, Fabrizio discusses the recent vote on whether Sicily should join the Kingdom of Piedmont and move toward Italian unification. The prince had voted yes, but Ciccio had voted against it, clinging to his traditional loyalties. Yet the election results from Donnafugata, certified by Sedàra, had supposedly been unanimously in favor. Both men are appalled that the election has been falsified, and they realize that it exposes the utopian promises of the new régime as false. Ciccio starts to speak against Sedàra, but the prince stops him, telling him the man is soon to become Tancredi's father-in-law and must be respected. This deeply shocks Ciccio, who had thought that Tancredi was only trying to seduce Angelica in order to humiliate her father, Sedàra.

In a meeting with Sedàra, Fabrizio arranges the marriage of Tancredi and Angelica. They realize that whatever their feelings, they need each other. The Salina family needs Sedàra's wealth for Tancredi, and Sedàra needs the Salina connection for prestige.

Love at Donnafugata (November 1860)

Tancredi, now commissioned in the royal army of Piedmont, visits Donnafugata and spends blissful days with Angelica, showing her the estate and introducing her to the family traditions. Although the novel reveals little of their married life together, the narrative voice remarks on the contrast between this time of happiness and their future, miserable married life. Don Fabrizio is visited by Aimone Chevalley di Monterzuolo, a representative of the Piedmontese crown, who is there to offer him the position of senator. But the prince refuses, realizing that he has no place in the new world that is being created around him. The next day the prince sees the emissary off at the train station, and they observe the poverty that oppresses the lives of the peasants in Donnafugata. They would both like to see it change; Monterzuolo believes that it will, while the prince believes that it cannot.

Father Pirrone Pays a Visit (February 1861)

This chapter is a digression from the plot of the novel and is nearly a stand-alone short story. Father Pirrone visits his home village. He finds that the land rented by the local peasants had been transferred from the nearby Benedictine monastery to a peasant moneylender, considerably worsening the peasants' economic rights and position. He comes to believe that the nobles like his patron Don Fabrizio are doing nothing to correct these evils because they live in a world apart and have no practical understanding of what is happening. He becomes involved in a marriage matter that is a mirror reflection of that between Angelica and Tancredi. His own niece has become pregnant out of wedlock, and he arranges a marriage with the father, which also ends an age-old feud between the two peasant families involved. However, this had all been carefully planned by the other family to seize the priest's brother's property as a dowry.

A Ball (November 1862)

Back in Palermo, the Salina family attends a ball that is the highlight of the social calendar of the city's nobility. It will be Angelica's presentation to noble society. At the ball, Fabrizio realizes that not only is his youth over but the very way of life he grew up in is gone. The other aristocrats at the ball seem to him like so many inbred pygmies, the motions of their dance like the circling of crows over a corpse. Seeing Angelica and Tancredi dance, he realizes that theirs is a union of greed and ambition, but he cannot help but love them. The ball lasts until dawn, and the prince walks home while his family goes ahead in their carriages. He observes a cartload of slaughtered bulls, a symbol of the death of the Italian nobility, and contrasts it with the unchanging beauty of the heavens, particularly the planet Venus, which, still visible, fills him with a sense of joy.

Death of a Prince (July 1888)

Twenty-six years after the last chapter, Don Fabrizio is dying. He and his family are returning to Sicily by train from a visit to a specialist physician in Naples. Tancredi is rising in the government, and the prince's heir, Paolo, has died in a riding accident, leaving the prince's grandson Fabrizetto as his heir, but Fabrizio likes him no better than he had Paolo. His son Giovanni has become a successful diamond merchant, and his wife has died years ago. Unable to quite make it back to his own palace, the prince dies of a stroke in a hotel in Palermo, realizing that a whole older world is passing away with him. A mysterious female apparition, perhaps the embodiment of his earlier vision of the planet Venus, conducts him to the next world.

Relics (May 1910)

Twenty-two years later, the Salina palace at Palermo is now occupied by Concetta and two of her sisters, none of whom ever married. They have devoted themselves to religion and amassed a large collection of relics, which are undergoing an examination for authenticity by Church officials, who eventually reject most of them. Tancredi has died, but the sisters are still close to Angelica, who uses her wealth and influence to control politics on the island. She visits them and promises to keep the potentially scandalous exposure of their relics quiet. She brings with her Senator Tassoni, an old friend of Tancredi's from their days with Garibaldi, who wishes to meet the remaining members of his comrade's family. Tancredi had often told him of Concetta. He reveals that Tancredi had indeed intended to marry her, and the story of violating the

monastery had been a fiction, meant as a joking allusion to Tancredi's desire to conquer his cousin's chastity, but her rejection had made the situation impossible, so he had transferred his attention to another for political advantage. The immense weight of the misery of Angelica's life, which she had unintentionally and unknowingly inflicted upon herself, crushes down on her, but she also realizes that it is useless to indulge in this pain that will consume her. She orders the taxidermied body of the prince's dog Benedico destroyed; it is the last relic of her father.

CHARACTERS

Angelina

Angelina is the niece of Father Pirrone. His two brothers had long been feuding over a disputed land inheritance, and Angelina's uncle had arranged for his son to seduce her so as to force a marriage and bring the land back into his line of the family as a dowry. This is meant as a distorted reflection of the marriage arrangements first between Tancredi and Concetta and then of Tancredi and Angelica. (Angelina is a diminutive form of Angelica.) The affair causes Father Pirrone to reflect that peasants and nobles have the same ambitions and purposes, only on different scales.

Concetta Corbera

Concetta is the daughter of Don Fabrizio. The family expected that she would marry her cousin Tancredi, but she makes this impossible when she misunderstands a joke of Tancredi's that was actually intended to compliment her. She had been in love with him, and the rest of her life is spent in misery because of this romantic failure. The waste of her life competes with the general fall of the nobility that so concerns Fabrizio as the tragedy of the novel. She had imagined her whole life that Tancredi had purposefully outraged her by uttering what she considered blasphemy and hence had never loved her. The truth is revealed to her only at the end of the novel by one of Tancredi's friends who happens to visit her, plunging her into deeper despair than she had already known.

Fabrizietto Corbera

The prince's grandson has the same name and eventually the same titles as his grandfather, but he is called by the diminutive Fabrizietto. Don Fabrizio holds him in the same contempt he did his father, in particular because he adopts middle-class ways.

Don Fabrizio Corbera, Prince of Salina

From the beginning of the novel, Fabrizio is described in terms more godlike than human: "his huge frame made the floor tremble, and a glint of pride flashed in his light blue eyes at this fleeting confirmation of his lordship over both human beings and their works." He is "very large and strong; in houses inhabited by lesser mortals his head would touch the lowest rosette on the chandeliers; his fingers could twist a ducat coin as if it were mere paper. . . . But those fingers could also stoke and handle with the most exquisite delicacy." His mother, Princess Carolina, had come from Germany, and the prince is fair-skinned and blonde. He also has other Germanic characteristics that are seen as out of place in Sicily: "an authoritarian temperament, a certain rigidity in morals, and a propensity for abstract ideas; these, in the relaxing atmosphere of Palermo society, had changed respectively into capricious arrogance, recurring moral scruples, and contempt for his own relatives and friends, all of whom seemed to him mere driftwood in the languid meandering stream of Sicilian pragmatism." The narrative of the novel grows out of Fabrizio's habit of introspection, or thoughtfulness. The depth of his character and of his consciousness of class and place is the true subject of *The Leopard*. Don Fabrizio is the last link in the chain of noble tradition, a fact that makes him tower over his modern contemporaries. But at the same time, his isolation from political and economic affairs makes him powerless to control his own fate or halt the decline he sees everywhere around him. He eventually becomes dependent on bourgeois (middle-class, as opposed to aristocratic) culture in the form of Sedàra, the rich peasant mayor of Donnafugata, and even of his nephew Tancredi, who must become a politician in order to carry on the family's prestige, albeit in a form that is altered and diminished.

Francesco Paolo Corbera

His father considers him a "booby" compared with his favored nephew, Tancredi, and he is of minor importance as a character. He eventually dies in a riding accident.

Giovanni Corbera

Giovanni is Don Fabrizio's second son. Before the action of the novel, he had run away to England and taken up work as a lowly clerk, preferring his independence to being kept, as he saw it, almost as a pet in Sicily. Although he is the only child to physically resemble his father, he never returns to the family. He eventually finds success as a diamond merchant.

Maria Stella Corbera, Princess of Salina

Maria Stella is Don Fabrizio's wife. Maria, "restless and domineering," is a mystery to her husband. He complains that despite having several children with her, he has never seen her navel, but clearly has little interest in her as a companion or even as a human being. The narrative of the book presents her in a somewhat hysterical manner, as when "her fine crazy eyes glanced around at her slaves of children and her tyrant of a husband." She superstitiously believes, her husband notes, that comets are an ill omen. To Fabrizio the astronomer this is, of course, ridiculous. But it is also an indication of the gulf that separates them. They live in different worlds and he cannot even imagine trying to communicate with her. She eventually dies of diabetes, which could not be treated in the nineteenth century.

Angelica Falconeri (née Sedàra)

Though of a lower class, Angelica is able to marry into the prince's family because she brings much-needed wealth for the advancement of her husband Tancredi's political career. She is possessed of remarkable natural beauty and considerable intelligence, and Tancredi is able to train her in aristocratic manners so that she can be accepted in the highest circles without reserve. However, her character, hidden under a beautiful surface, remains essentially identical to that of her scheming, bourgeois father. She is shown as incapable of refined, genuine emotion: "Anyone deducing . . . that [Angelica] loved Tancredi would have been mistaken; she had too much pride and too much ambition to be capable of that annihilation, however temporary, of one's own personality without which there is no love." Ultimately she echoes her father's drives for power and control: "years later, she became one of the most venomous string pullers for Parliament and Senate."

Tancredi Falconeri

Tancredi is Don Fabrizio's beloved nephew, the son of his favorite sister, whom he looks on as his spiritual, if not his legal, heir: "Though the Prince never admitted it to himself, he would have preferred the lad as his heir to that booby Paolo." Nevertheless, Tancredi is deeply involved with liberal causes and eventually joins Garibaldi's army. Since *The Leopard* is told from the prince's perspective, much of Tancredi's importance in the novel comes from his relationship to his uncle. Tancredi "had become very dear to the irascible Prince, who perceived in him a riotous zest for life and a frivolous temperament contradicted by sudden serious moods." In other words, the prince saw his own character in his nephew. Tancredi is not betraying his class or family, however, as he realizes the only way to protect his interests is by controlling the course of the revolution from within. He therefore forges an alliance with the rising bourgeois class through his marriage to the heiress Angelica. Fabrizio at first excuses his nephew's immersion in the modern world of liberal politics—"Tancredi could never do wrong in his uncle's eyes"—but eventually comes to see that Tancredi acted in the best interests of his social class, even though his victories against the tide of revolution and modernization are limited.

Don Ciccio Ferrara

Ciccio is the prince's accountant. As indicated by the honorific *Don*, Ciccio is of a little higher social status than most of Fabrizio's servants. Nevertheless, to the prince, "he was a scraggy little man who hid the deluded and rapacious mind of a 'liberal' behind reassuring spectacles and immaculate cravats." To the prince, Ciccio seems to miss the essential qualities of the world around him and replace them with a sort of fictitious drama that describes only its surface. When he is through working with Ciccio and the concerns of the modern world he represents, Fabrizio feels he is "soaring back through the clouds."

Aimone Chevalley di Monterzuolo

Monterzuolo is a representative of the Piedmontese government. He journeys to Donnafugata to offer Don Fabrizio a place in the new government as a senator. His attitude favoring technology and modernization is in contrast with the prince's acceptance of tradition.

Father Pirrone

Pirrone is a Jesuit priest. As was normal for an aristocratic family in the old tradition, Don Fabrizio employs a priest to act as the family confessor and to lead them in their spiritual lives. But Pirrone is also a trained mathematician; he is Fabrizio's calculator (a term originally applied to human beings who carried out difficult computations) and assists him in his astronomical work. The narrator sometimes takes Pirrone's point of view to offer a more objective picture of events.

Pietro Russo

Russo is Don Fabrizio's chief manager of his extensive estates. With his traditional feelings about class, Fabrizio thinks of him as "some red-skinned peasant, which is what that name of [his] means." Yet Fabrizio is forced by circumstance to also form a very different opinion of Russo: "Clever, dressed rather smartly in a striped velvet jacket, with greedy eyes below a remorseless forehead, the Prince found him a perfect specimen of a class on its way up." Though he does not openly admit it, Russo is deeply involved in the revolutionary movement sweeping through Sicily and will presently gain political influence once it succeeds. Fabrizio is distressed by people like Russo because all they want is wealth, and in the future that wealth will give them a status approaching his own. To them, aristocratic lineage and airs are things they can acquire, not an essential part of themselves.

Calogero Sedàra

Sedàra is a bourgeois businessman who has accumulated vast wealth and the outward appearance of respectability by becoming the mayor of Donnafugata (hence his title of *Don*) but whose manners still mark him as a peasant who appears clownish to the prince: "Don Fabrizio found an odd admiration growing in him for Sedàra's qualities. He became used to the ill-shaven cheeks, the plebeian accent, the odd clothes, and the persistent odor of stale sweat, and he began to realize the man's rare intelligence." Once the marriage is set between Angelica and Tancredi, Sedàra uses his business experience to make himself useful to the prince, though only in ways that are contrary to Fabrizio's whole philosophy of life: "Problems that had seemed insoluble to the Prince were resolved in a trice by Don Calogero; free as he was from the shackles imposed on many other men by honesty, decency, and plain good manners, he moved through the jungle of life with the confidence of an elephant which advances in a straight line." Although contact with this representative of the modern world seems immediately helpful to the prince, it will ultimately destroy the Salina family: "Don Calogero's advice . . . was both opportune and immediately effective; but the eventual result of such advice, cruelly efficient . . . was that in years to come the Salina family were to acquire a reputation for treating dependents harshly, . . . without in any way halting the collapse of the family fortunes." Even while Sedàra remains the prince's dependent, the prince also becomes paradoxically dependent on Sedàra to maintain his own position in the new order of society, leaving him feeling lost and defeated.

Senator Tassoni

Tassoni is an old friend of Tancredi from his days in the Redshirts. He was also briefly Angelica's lover. In her old age his passing mention of Tancredi reveals to her that she had missed her chance of marrying her cousin.

Ciccio Tumeo

Tumeo is the organist in the church at Donnafugata and the prince's companion in hunting. Despite their class difference, a genuine friendship exists between the two men. Tumeo feels betrayed by Sedàra's fixing of the new election, considering that the new, more nearly republican form of government is falsified by the mere pretense that power is, just as before, really held in a few hands at the top.

THEMES

Politics

The Leopard was rejected by several publishers during Lampedusa's lifetime because it seemed unpublishable from a political viewpoint. And, indeed, when it was published after the author's death, at the beginning of the turbulent 1960s, *The Leopard* was attacked from both sides. It was attacked from the left for its seeming celebration of the aristocracy and its attacks on peasants, workers, and even the middle class, and from the right for its portrayal of the same aristocratic class as decadent, corrupt, and

impotent. But the fact is, Lampedusa (like his main character Don Fabrizio) is not very interested in politics but rather in the position of his own family. As he is dying, Don Fabrizio reflects:

> For the significance of a noble family lies entirely in its traditions, that is in its vital memories; and he was the last to have any unusual memories, anything different from those of other families. . . . The last Salina was himself. That fellow Garibaldi, that bearded Vulcan, had won after all.

The tragedy is not the end of old Italy but the end of the Salinas. Those around Fabrizio who hold conservative views express a conventional support for the monarchy: "For the King, who stands for order, continuity, decency, honor, right; for the King, who is sole defender of the Church; sole bulwark against the dispersal of property, 'The Sect's' ultimate aim." ("The Sect" means the Freemasons, which in nineteenth-century Italy was a caricature of any force opposed by conservatives, just as the labels *Socialist* and *Communist* have become in modern American politics.) But Fabrizio does not share these views. From before the time of the novel's opening, Don Fabrizio has realized that the Kingdom of the Two Sicilies is doomed because of the crown's incompetence. The only question is whether it would be replaced with a new, more vigorous monarchy (from Piedmont) or whether the monarchic system would collapse entirely into a republic, which would do away with the crown, the aristocracy, and probably his personal fortune.

Certainly Lampedusa's views cannot be confused with the reactionary politics of his own lifetime in Fascist Italy. Lampedusa hated the Fascists, since under Fascism real power lies with the industrial class, which rules with the consent of a public beguiled by a right-wing vision of an ideal past very different from any historical reality and very different from the one held dear by Don Fabrizio. Don Fabrizio's witness to a government of the newly rich who manipulate the peasants is Lampedusa's criticism of Fascism, not of liberalism. Lampedusa breaks out of his historical framework to speak quite openly of his own times: "No one mentions red shirts anymore; but they'll be back. When they've vanished, others of different colors will come; and then the red ones again. And how will it end?" While he begins with Garibaldi's Redshirts, he clearly moves on to the Fascist

TOPICS FOR FURTHER STUDY

- In the late nineteenth century, traditional Japanese culture was faced with the modern world and chose to modernize, in an era known as the Meiji restoration. There was a terrible social cost in terms of civil war and the eradication of a traditional, aristocratic way of life. The Japanese experience was similar to that of Italy at roughly the same time, although the disruption and transformation of culture was even more profound in the East. Alan Gratz's 2008 book *Samurai Shortstop* is a young-adult novel set in Meiji Japan. It tells the story of a teenage boy from an aristocratic family who witnessed his grandfather commit ritual suicide rather than change with the times. He finds, though, that the modern game of baseball is seemingly the only way he has to fit into the culture of his aristocratic boarding school, as well as the only field in which he can apply the training in the samurai ways he receives from his father. Comparing this novel with *The Leopard*, write your own story from the viewpoint of one of Don Fabrizio's teenage sons. How might his feelings about the relationship of the past and the present be different from his father's?

- *The Leopard* takes place in the early 1860s against the historical backdrop of the Risorgimento, the political and military crisis that

resulted in the unification of Italy. At the same time, the United States experienced the Civil War, a conflict between the economically disadvantaged, agricultural South and the industrialized, bourgeois North over the issue of national unity. Write a paper comparing the two conflicts, if possible with reference to the history of your own family during the Civil War.

- Tour companies in Sicily frequently use the popularity of *The Leopard* to promote their business and offer tour packages based on the places described in the novel. Consequently, *The Leopard* is frequently mentioned in blogs kept by tourists. Make a survey of these sites using Internet searches and especially searches of blogs. How does Lampedusa's nostalgia interact with the tourist experience? Write a paper explaining your conclusions.

- Many secondary works devoted to *The Leopard* are illustrated with photographs either from the Lampedusa family archives or of the buildings and places described in the book. Using these and any other sources that are available to you, make a presentation to your class showing images of the world described in *The Leopard*.

Blackshirts, while the return of the Redshirts expresses his concerns over the growth of the Italian Communist Party during the 1950s.

Past

The Leopard is an undoubted masterpiece, not so much in its evocation of the past as in its evocation of longing for the past. Don Fabrizio is sure on his deathbed that despite all his efforts, the modern world has swept away the old world that he knew. This means in turn that as the author, Lampedusa feels separated from the past by

modernity, which he considers a catastrophe. Fabrizio's nephew Tancredi famously reassures his uncle, "Unless we ourselves take a hand now, they'll foist a republic on us. If we want things to stay as they are, things will have to change." But things change and do not stay as they are, and as the crisis of modernity becomes more acute throughout Lampedusa's lifetime in the two world wars, the republic and the end of the princes of Lampedusa/Salina finally comes. The situation is shown allegorically when, early in the novel, the prince's family is served a dessert

The novel opens with Garibaldi's Redshirts landing on the Sicilian coast. (© mradlgruber | Shutterstock.com)

pudding that had been sculpted into the shape of a city. By the time it is served to Paolo, the prince's heir, "it consisted only of shattered walls and hunks of wobbly rubble." Like modernity, in T. S. Eliot's phrase in *The Wasteland*, it has become a heap of broken ruins. This foreshadows the state of Don Fabrizio's world when it is left to his descendants.

The Leopard is such a personal exploration that it is difficult to associate it with any particular philosophy (just as it is difficult to associate it with any political movement). In one sense it is an intensely political novel. But in another way, it is clear that the author has a marked distaste for politics. Strictly speaking, the politics of *The Leopard* are reactionary—that is, a conservative reaction against change. This is why Lampedusa could not find a publisher in his lifetime. But the novel was also a favorite of the surrealists, who, politically, were allied with the Communists. Yet there is one political philosophy with which *The Leopard* seems to have some affinities: traditionalism. Although this term has a vast range of meanings, it is in a narrow sense a political movement (as described in Mark Sedgwick's

Against the Modern World: Traditionalism and the Secret Intellectual History of the Twentieth Century). Traditionalism divides the past into two successive ages. During some golden age in the past, human life existed as an integrated whole full of wisdom and purpose. At some point human life was struck by a disaster that traditionalists refer to as modernity (and depending on the particular version of traditionalism, this can be as late as the Enlightenment or as early as the birth of Christianity or even the Iron Age), and life became a sordid affair stripped of all meaning and significance. Unlike other ideologies with a similar view of history, such as Marxism, traditionalism pointedly offers no solution to the problem it poses, except to patiently wait for the cycles of history to restore the significance that had been lost.

This philosophical view of history does have some correspondence to *The Leopard*: its hero, the introspective but creative and vigorous Don Fabrizio, who represents the humanity of the traditionalist golden age, is nevertheless helpless before the onslaught of modernity as it destroys the traditional world of which he feels himself a part. Traditionalism began in the 1920s in France, with the work of René Guénon, who saw a greater continuity with the traditional world in Islam than in Christian Europe; he eventually moved to Egypt and converted to Sufi Islam. In Italy, traditionalism was represented by Julius Evola, whose private spirituality centered on the practice of ceremonial magic. Lampedusa is not known to have had any contact with Evola, and traditionalists do not claim Lampedusa as one of their own, despite the at least superficial similarity of their ideas. The Nazi Party was founded by the traditionalist Rudolf von Sebottendorf, but Adolf Hitler's seizure of control in the party completely transformed its nature, and von Sebottendorf ended up in a concentration camp. Evola tried to exert influence over Italian Fascism, but his opposition to Christianity caused his writings to be censored by the government of Benito Mussolini. Traditionalism is a fringe movement, but traditionalist groups were responsible for a number of terrorist attacks in Italy throughout the 1960s. The prominent Romanian historian of religion Mircea Eliade was perhaps the best-known traditionalist because of his prominence in the scholarly community. Today, traditionalist parties are able to elect members of parliament in Greece and Russia.

STYLE

Symbolism

One reason for the initial cool reception of *The Leopard* by publishers was its defiance of modern literary trends, and even of accepted genre categories. The novel is unrelated to the neorealism that dominated Italian literature during the 1950s (comparable to the journalistic style familiar from well-known films like *Open City* and *The Bicycle Thieves*), and it is related still less to the avant-garde literature of the time. Its outward form is an old-fashioned nineteenth-century historical novel, so its surface narrative is sometimes compared to Margaret Mitchell's *Gone with the Wind*. However, one feature of *The Leopard* is that it is assembled from or uses elements from many styles that were current in the late nineteenth century, around the time of Lampedusa's birth. One of these is symbolism, a French school of literature whose best-known exponent was Paul Verlaine. Symbolism refers

to the rejection of the prevailing realism of nineteenth-century French literature and the production of literature with fantastic elements incorporated into the text as if they were real in a manner calculated to reveal an important psychological truth. Symbolist elements in *The Leopard* include the repeated description of figures in paintings, particularly of the pagan gods, as if they were actual characters, as well as the description of Don Fabrizio in superhuman terms. Both techniques are meant to stress that Fabrizio is a relic from an older, greater age. Similarly, when Fabrizio nears death, he sees a young woman on the train platform when he is traveling back home to Palermo from Naples where he had gone to see a specialist. The next day, as he is actually dying in a hotel, the same woman appears in his room among the crowd of his family and doctors. He recognizes her also as a vision he had seen in the stars, and then he dies. This is the intrusion into the narrative of the ancient myth of the valkyrie taking the dead hero to the afterlife. It signifies that the death of the prince is the end of a heroic age.

Decadence

Another style of late-nineteenth-century French literature that Lampedusa intrudes here and there into *The Leopard* is decadence, a movement represented in English in the works of Oscar Wilde. One element of decadence is the close association of the grotesque and the beautiful, and particularly the reconceptualization of the grotesque as the beautiful. Many passages of *The Leopard* are decadent in this sense, for instance, the description of the transformation of the brutality of medieval feudalism into a rare cultivated beauty:

> The wealth of many centuries had been transmitted into ornament, luxury, pleasure; no more; the abolition of feudal rights had swept away duties as well as privileges; wealth, like an old wine, had let the dregs of greed, even of care and prudence, fall to the bottom of the barrel, leaving only verve and color. And thus eventually it cancelled itself out; this wealth which had achieved its object was composed now only of essential oils—and like essential oils, it soon evaporated.

Most typical of decadence is the connection drawn between sex and death. While driving though an orange grove on his way to visit his mistress, Don Fabrizio inhales "that Islamic perfume evoking houris and fleshly joys beyond the

COMPARE & CONTRAST

- **1860s:** Italy is a patchwork of independent states, ruled either by hereditary monarchies or by the papacy (government headed by the pope).

  Today: Italy is a unified republic with no monarchic head of state. While the papacy remains politically independent, it is limited to a few acres (Vatican City), inside the city of Rome.

- **1860s:** Marriages at all levels of society are commonly arranged by parents or prominent relatives on the basis of family interest.

  Today: Marriage is essentially a private concern of the couple involved, and its impact on their families is a secondary consideration.

- **1860s:** Wealth was generally produced by agriculture, so there was no practical way to increase it. Thus, one class could rise economically only at the expense of another.

  Today: Wealth is generated by an industrial and postindustrial economy (although southern Italy remains economically disadvantaged compared with the north), and can be generally increased without a fixed limit.

grave." A repeated symbol in *The Leopard*, expressing the depth of the tragedy involved in the loss of the prince's world to modernity, is the image of a mutilated corpse. This occurs first in the dead Neapolitan soldier found in the prince's garden in Palermo with "a pile of purplish intestines [that] had formed a puddle under his bandoleer." The image constantly reasserts itself to the prince's mind:

> But the image of that gutted corpse often recurred, as if asking to be given peace in the only possible way the Prince could give it: by justifying that last agony on grounds of general necessity.

And it recurs finally after the ball in Palermo that is effectively the death of the prince's world and the beginning of Tancredi's, as the prince walks back to his palace and sees a vehicle on the road:

> A long open wagon came by stacked with bulls killed shortly before at the slaughter house, already quartered and exhibiting their intimate mechanism with the shamelessness of death. At intervals a big thick red drop fell onto the pavement.

In both cases the sign of death is, unexpectedly, its bright coloration.

HISTORICAL CONTEXT

The Risorgimento

During the French Revolution, France occupied northern Italy and reorganized its many medieval city-states into the Cisalpine Republic and then, under Napoleon, the Kingdom of Italy. This unification was reversed with the restoration in 1815, and Austria became the overlord of the many small Italian states. However, the Kingdom of Piedmont (or Sardinia) kept the idea of Italian unification alive and by 1860 had unified under its control most of Italy except for the Papal States, the Veneto (directly controlled by Austria), and the Kingdom of Naples (or the Two Sicilies) in the south. Giuseppe Garibaldi had acted as a military leader in many of the wars fought against France and Austria to achieve the goal of Italian unity, sometimes as a commander for Piedmont and sometimes on behalf of schemes to create an Italian republic in cooperation with the political revolutionary Giuseppe Mazzini. Garibaldi, however, was more important as an inspiring leader of the Risorgimento (or "Resurgence") than as an effective military commander.

In 1860, however, Garibaldi was starting to agitate against Piedmont, which had ceded his

The Leopard *can be viewed as an examination of the idea of the decline of Europe.* (© jele / Shutterstock.com)

home town of Nice to France. So the Piedmontese king Victor Emmanuel II and Prime Minister Camillo Cavour redirected Garibaldi by sending him to Sicily to join a revolt there against the Bourbon monarchy. He landed in Marsala with his volunteer corps, known as the thousand because of their small number and as the Redshirts because of their uniform. They soon succeeded in raising a general rebellion in Sicily, driving out the Bourbon troops, and invading the mainland of Naples. The young King Francis retreated to the fortress of Gaeta, which Garibaldi's irregular army lacked the artillery and equipment to assault. However, the Piedmontese finally sent a regular army through the Papal States and forced Gaeta to surrender in March of 1861. Shortly thereafter Victor Immanuel was declared king of Italy, which was unified except for the city of Rome and Austrian-occupied Venetia. These territories would be added by 1870.

The military and political revolutions that unified Italy also transformed Italian society, increasing the power of the bourgeoisie, or middle class, at the expense of the nobility and spreading ideals of equality and republican government. In *The Leopard*, the prince's nephew Tancredi joins Garibaldi's Redshirts shortly after their landing because he realizes the only way to preserve the prestige of the Salina family is to make it an important factor in the new bourgeois Italy that is coming into existence. The novel explores the tendency of the new political arrangements to inevitably weaken the nobility at the expense of wealthy merchants and industrialists, whatever lip service was at first paid to the aristocracy. The social structure was changed by Italy's entrance into the modern world in economic and political terms, so that the way of life idealized by the aristocracy quickly vanished, leaving only a memory for the prince of Lampedusa to cherish.

CRITICAL OVERVIEW

The first few chapters of David Gilmour's *The Last Leopard: A Life of Giuseppe di Lampedusa* sketch the history of the Tomasi family back to the sixteenth century, as far as it can reliably be traced, and draw comparisons between the historical reality and its fictional shadow in *The Leopard*. Gilmour finds the main point of *The Leopard* is the care of Lampedusa for his spiritual inheritance, the only thing he receives after the financial and political decline of his family. Correspondingly, this is the only inheritance that the fictionalized Don Fabrizio is concerned about leaving, but for which he finds no heir. Gilmour's researches in the Lampedusa family archives found that the real Prince Giulio, the model for Don Fabrizio, was a far more insignificant person than Fabrizio is in Lampedusa's idealization of his idea of family.

Initial reaction to *The Leopard* was generally negative (despite the book's rapid rise as an international best seller), with Socialist reviewers attacking Lampedusa's classism and conservatives attacking his anticlericalism and his portrayal of the aristocracy as decadent and impotent. Louis Aragon, however, a surrealist and a Communist, unexpectedly hailed it as one of the greatest novels ever written. American reviews, far removed from European politics, were more positive, even if more innocent, on the book's purely literary merits. Vivian Mercier gave a very favorable notice in the *Hudson Review*: "The old order is revealed, even while it is collapsing, as a beautiful thing, a genuine *order*. One almost wishes that the Prince of Salina had fought to preserve it."

An early study of *The Leopard*, Arthur and Catherine Evans's 1963 article in *Wisconsin Studies in Contemporary Literature*, establishes that the novel is not actually historical but is devoted to a particular response to history: "Lampedusa's novel is an analysis of the moral response to change on the part of a man, his class, and his country." The author is in love with a world that is dead, the authors find, so that, "fear, inertia, and pride paralyse land and people in a common death-urge." In their view, Don Fabrizio is desperately trying to maintain his position: "The Prince's response is a wasting fretfulness, a yearning for permanence guaranteed, so he hopes, at the price of compromise and a leonine disdain for others' happiness." The Evanses realize that much of the meaning of the novel is repeated over and over in different symbolic forms. Concentrating on the animal theme of *The Leopard*, they compare the decline from lion to hyena as a metaphor for the rulers whom Don Fabrizio expects will succeed him, with the dog Benedico (who instinctively rejects Angelica) as a symbol of loyalty to the traditions of the past, moth-eaten and discarded by the end of the novel. Stanley G. Eskin, in his 1962 article in *Italica*, also investigates *The Leopard*'s extensive use of animal symbolism and relates it to Lampedusa's interest in the symbolist movement. Richard O'Mara, writing in the *Sewanee Review* in 2008, interprets the hyenas and jackals that the prince fears will succeed him as the Sicilian mafia, rather than the more usual reading as a reference to the Fascists, relating it to a more generalized or contemporary experience than to Lampedusa's own.

CRITICISM

Rita M. Brown

Brown is an English professor. In the following essay, she examines The Leopard *from the viewpoint of Freudian psychoanalysis's conception of society.*

Although Freudian psychoanalysis is not mentioned in *The Leopard* (it hardly could be, since it takes place for the most part before Sigmund Freud was born), the novel is deeply influenced by that school of psychology. Lampedusa's wife was the leading Italian psychoanalyst of her generation and, if she did not psychoanalyze her husband, encouraged him to carry out a systematic introspection close to self-analysis, which was the spur to his journal keeping, which in turn led eventually to his writing *The Leopard*, a meditation upon his own past. The main psychoanalytic feature of the novel is Dan Fabrizio's constant reverie and self-examination, a habit that reflects the author more than his historical grandfather. But its outlook on society, which is often analyzed in political terms, is fundamentally psychoanalytic. In works like *Civilization and Its Discontents* and especially *The Future of an Illusion* (by which he meant "religion") Freud extended his science of mind far beyond the medical treatment of mental illness to produce a critique of civilization.

WHAT DO I READ NEXT?

- *Letters from Londonand Europe* (2010, translated by J. G. Nichols) publishes recently discovered correspondence from Lampedusa to his relatives in Italy during the 1920s. The letters are similar to the introspective style and concerns of *The Leopard* and have much in common with nineteenth-century travel literature.

- G. A. Henty began his career as an officer in the British army during the Crimean War of the 1850s. His letters home about the awful conditions the British army suffered during the campaign because of the incompetence of senior officers (the publicizing of which also made Florence Nightingale famous) were published in newspapers and Henty soon found himself working as a war correspondent. One of the campaigns he covered was Garibaldi's invasion of Sicily and Naples, the historical backdrop of *The Leopard*. In his later career, Henty devoted himself to writing young-adult literature, producing nearly a hundred novels all set during various historical military campaigns ranging in time from ancient Egypt to the Franco-Prussian War of the early 1870s. In fact, Henty was one of the creators of the young-adult genre. In 1901 he published *Out with Garibaldi: A Story of the Liberation of Italy*, about the adventures of a half-English, half-Italian teenager who becomes one of Garibaldi's thousand, the volunteer corps with which he made his initial landing in Sicily. Readers should note that, like many Victorian authors, Henty was xenophobic (disliking foreigners) and imperialistic by modern standards.

- The four novels that make up Yukio Mishima's *Sea of Tranquility* tetralogy (*Spring Snow*, 1969; *Runaway Horses*, 1969; *The Temple of Dawn*, 1970; and *The Decay of the Angel*, 1971) are among the few works of world literature whose themes and attitude compare to those of *The Leopard*. The novels, set between 1912 and 1975, chronicle the decay of Japanese society over the course of the twentieth century through the eyes of a narrator who begins as a high school student and ends as a retired judge. In particular he narrates the lives of four young people he encounters over time who become more vicious and debased, without, nevertheless, losing an essential beauty, but whose lives all end in suicide. The first is his best friend from high school, and the narrator believes the other three are reincarnations of his friend.

- Gerard Gefen's *Sicily: Land of the Leopard Princes* (2001), with photographs by Jean-Bernard Naudin, offers an illustrated tour through the places described in *The Leopard*, supplemented by family photos of the Lampedusas.

- The collection of material by Lampedusa translated by Archibald Colquhoun in *Two Stories and a Memory* (1962) includes "Places of My Infancy," the memoir with which Lampedusa began the process of composing *The Leopard*, as well as two short stories that are his only other fiction.

- George Macaulay Trevelyan's 1911 *Garibaldi and the Making of Italy* is a classic account of the *Risorgimento*, especially in its military aspect, which is treated in minute detail.

Freud's basic realization was that the human mind is compartmentalized. It contains the desires to kill (that is, to eat) and to procreate but also mechanisms that repress and control these desires, which make it possible for human beings to live in society. These mechanisms are first seen in small children, who come to realize that they must subordinate and identify themselves and their desires to those of their parents in order to survive. The state has the power to

> HOWEVER, FABRIZIO ALSO POSSESSES MERCY
> AND LOVE, AND IT IS THROUGH THESE THAT HE
> RESTRAINS HIMSELF, NOT FEAR."

command the individual, in Freud's view, because it is a larger version of the family, with the ruler and the ruling class modeled on the father. The rules of the family are obeyed because it is necessary to channel the energy of instinctual desires for survival to the group rather than the individual, and the state derives its power over its members from the same subordination of a person's desires to the state's authority.

The mind, Freud believed, reacts also to the external world of nature in human terms so that processes and phenomena that are mysterious, such as a storm or death, are conceived of in human terms, as if they were individuals: gods, in other words. The authority of the ruler and of a god are both modeled on the child's surrender to the authority of the father that is necessary for survival, and the progress of civilization fostered through the growth of society into larger structures is similarly based on the individual's surrender to the authority of the state and church. Freud believed that the progress of Western civilization since the Enlightenment had made this kind of identification and submission to authority unnecessary, as the most educated and advanced individuals replace submission with the understanding of their own interest. But for the greater mass of society, the working poor, Freud feared that enlightened self-interest and investment in society was not yet possible. At the same time, however, unquestioned obedience to state and church was breaking down, and with that would come the realization that society was not organized in the economic and other interests of the masses.

In *The Leopard*, Lampedusa explores these large social themes of Freud's work at the historical moment of transition from traditional to modern society (at least in Sicily). Drawing on the image of the tyrant in Plato's *Republic*, Freud supposes that there might be an individual free from the mechanism of repression, who acts to satisfy his desires without any responsibility.

This person, who lacked "the restrictions of civilization . . . would be a tyrant, a dictator, who had seized all means to power." It is tempting to identify Don Fabrizio as such an individual. But he is clearly not such a superhuman (or perhaps inhuman) character. Fabrizio is subject to the buffeting winds of history as much as anyone else. At the end of his life, he reckons all the time of happiness he has lived, which is to say the times when he fulfilled his desires rather than repressing them, and thinks it amounts at most to three of his seventy-three years. Though these moments include the most visceral satisfactions of his romantic conquests and the slaughter of animals in hunting, they are mostly the joy he took in the prospect of preserving his family and class traditions for his heirs, and in the recognition he had for his scientific work, which are very much pleasures of the subordination of the self to society.

Yet the *image* of the tyrant whose life is the unrestrained satisfaction of desire exists in Don Fabrizio. His very reckoning of his life's failure to achieve happiness except in fleeting moments shows that Fabrizio is aware of his drives and thinks that true happiness would lie in the satisfaction of those drives, beyond what is commonly allowed by civilization. This is symbolized at the very beginning of *The Leopard*, whose first scene shows the prince and his family saying the rosary together in the chapel of their palace. The text of their prayers (the Our Father and the Hail Mary) is too pervasive in Italian culture for Lampedusa to have to quote them, but they are profound statements of the willing subjection of the individual to the will of his parents, and thus to the state and to religion. But the point of the scene is to show the very limited meaning this self-subjection has in the prince's inner life. The narration concentrates instead on the mural decorating the ceiling, which shows the pagan gods of ancient Rome:

> The divinities frescoed on the ceiling awoke. . . . The major Gods and Goddess, the Princes among the Gods, thunderous Jove and frowning Mars and languid Venus . . . were amiably supporting the blue armorial shield of the Leopard. They knew that for the next twenty-three and a half hours they would be lords of the villa once again.

By being called princes and supporting his symbol, the leopard, they are clearly identified with Don Fabrizio and his inner drives. These primitive desires are the true rulers of the house, who pay no more than a half-hour daily lip service to the normalizing function of religion and its social control expressed in the rosary. The same point is driven home in the same scene by the dissatisfactions of the prince's heir, Paolo: his face

> was veiled in brooding melancholy. It had been a bad day: Guiscard, his Irish sorrel, had seemed off form, and Fanny had apparently been unable (or unwilling) to send him her usual lilac-tinted billet-doux [love letter]. Of what avail then, to him, was the Incarnation of his Saviour?

This is a realization that religion thwarts and tamps down rather than fulfills desires.

And yet neither the prince nor, indeed, his ineffectual heir takes on the mantle of Freud's tyrant, inflicting his will on the world about him for the sake of his own pleasure. Don Fabrizio knows, at least, that it is possible; he holds it as an idea in his mind that he considers ennobling as an ideal of absolute freedom. However, Fabrizio also possesses mercy and love, and it is through these that he restrains himself, not fear. It is just in this difference that he feels superior to others around him: his peasants and the rising middle class that he sees as terrified of noble antiquities like himself. He feels kinship with his nephew Tancredi and his daughter Concetta when he sees the same bravery of mind displayed in them, though to a lesser degree.

Fabrizio also sees his psychological freedom as having a political dimension. He is willing to act as a father to his dependents (for example, the peasants on his estates), and while he perhaps does not look after their real needs and interests but rather those it comforts him to imagine they have, he considers his paternalism benevolent. Calogero Sedàra, the mayor of Donnafugata, in contrast, makes a pretense of giving the same peasants their so-called freedom, and makes a show of treating them as free men able to determine their destinies for themselves. But he conceives of this as flattery and in fact treats them as lower creatures than Fabrizio imagines them to be. When they are given the chance to vote to determine their own futures (a task for which their prince's care has failed to prepare them), Sedàra, their elected leader, deceives them and crookedly fixes their vote in what he considered to be their interest. He is no less paternalistic than Fabrizio, but he fears to take on the responsibility of fatherhood over his people.

Freud also clearly saw the political dimension of his analysis of human behavior. Intellectuals like himself were freed by the Enlightenment from the constraints of tradition and so could confront their fellow men on the basis of shared liberty. But the greater mass of people were still ruled by their dependence on the paternalistic state and the patriarchal Church. Freud saw the civilization of the nineteenth century as failing its dependents, leaving them in a benighted condition of servitude and oppression, claiming that "the great mass of the uneducated and oppressed . . . have every reason for being enemies of civilization." When the oppressed realize that their so-called fathers have manipulated them and worn them down rather than enlightening them and using the fruits of their own labors to build them up— have failed to make them equal partners in civilization—their support for civilization might quickly vanish, and with it the mechanisms that civilization had used to control the masses. Freud is thinking of the revolutions that rocked Europe in the aftermath of World War I, bringing a Communist dictatorship to Russia and destroying the monarchies in Austria and Germany. Since the oppressed masses had been denied the chance to truly become free through education and the use of the wealth they produced, violence would naturally result when they realized that the paternalistic social controls that had been imposed on them had been mere illusions:

> If the sole reason why you must not kill your neighbor is because God has forbidden it and will severely punish you for it in this or the next life—then when you learn there is no God and you need not fear His punishment, you will certainly kill your neighbor without hesitation, and you can only be prevented from doing so by mundane force. Thus either these dangerous masses must be held down most severely and kept most carefully from any chance of intellectual awakening, or else the relationship between civilization and religion must undergo a fundamental revision.

The fear that the peasant masses would rise up in bloody revolt against their masters was part of Lampedusa's received tradition from his family. He recalls it in *The Leopard* when Father Pirrone is told by his Jesuit brothers in Palermo that "the authorities had noticed a silent ferment among the people; at the first sign of weakening control, the city rabble would take to looting and rape." Freud's analysis of the psychology of such a revolt lets Lampedusa understand what must have seemed irrational to his grandfather as he lived through those times. Or rather, Freud allows Lampedusa to come to what is after all a thoroughly modern understanding of those events that his grandfather could not have accepted in his own intellectual context.

Lampedusa has come to an understanding of his own past through a lifelong introspection informed by psychoanalysis. It is no wonder that he saw the tragedy of his own family, the tragedy of Europe, in Freudian terms. Like Freud, he saw that if the paternalism of the state and the church were suddenly ripped away from those it had oppressed rather than educated, it would end in them becoming tyrants, stealing whatever gave them pleasure and destroying whatever gave them displeasure. With the rule of the aristocrats, who had at least the freedom to take on the role of father, gone, it would mean the rule of the middle class, which would not mean freedom but only an ugly pretense of freedom: "We were the Leopards, the Lions; those who'll take our place will be little jackals, hyenas." The jackals and hyenas are of course the Fascists, but the indictment is also against the modern state itself, which continues to keep the masses in a state of dependency, denying them the freedom that it pretends to offer and that at least Don Fabrizio possessed. It is the loss of this freedom that Lampedusa chiefly mourns.

Source: Rita M. Brown, Critical Essay on *The Leopard*, in *Novels for Students*, Gale, Cengage Learning, 2014.

Alberto Manguel

In the following review, Manguel discusses how Tomasi's letters reveal the author's style of "tenderness, wisdom, and irony that is so captured in The Leopard*" and which helped make it the best-selling Italian novel of all time.*

'Every poet describes himself, as well as his own life, in his writings,' observed Giuseppe Tomasi di Lampedusa in one of his lectures on English literature, which he delivered twice a week to an audience of young people in his palazzo in Palermo. He was speaking of Shakespeare, whom he adored (he said his mistress, whom everyone considered plain, was *Measure for Measure*) but he could have been speaking of himself. Lampedusa published nothing during his lifetime except three articles in a confidential Genoese journal, but in his posthumous books— *The Leopard, Two Stories and a Memory*, and a

few others—the protagonist is always Lampedusa and the narrative that of Lampedusa's life.

Giuseppe di Lampedusa, Duke of Palma and Prince of Lampedusa, was born in 1896 to an old aristocratic Sicilian family. He was a lance-corporal during the first world war. Captured in Austria, he escaped and returned home on foot. During the second world war he travelled extensively in Europe. He met his Italian-Latvian wife, Alessandra Wolf Stomersee, in London and married her in Riga. After the war, he returned to Palermo, where he died of cancer in 1957. His masterpiece, *The Leopard*, was turned down by a number of publishers until it was accepted by Giorgio Bassani for Feltrinelli: to the annoyance of conceited publishers, haunted by the good books they have rejected, it has since become the best-selling Italian novel of all time.

During his travels, Lampedusa wrote extensively to friends and family. His correspondence (Gioacchino Lanza Tomasi tells us in an informative introduction to this edition), consists of two collections: the large one, comprising almost 400 letters between Lampedusa and his wife, is still being edited for publication in Italy; the smaller one covering the years 1925 to 1930, made up of 70 letters addressed to various friends and acquaintances, especially the Piccolo brothers, Casimiro and Lucio, his childhood friends.

In a short memoir, *Places of My Infancy*, Lampedusa writes: 'I can promise to say nothing that is untrue, but I don't think I shall want to say all; and I reserve the right to lie by omission. Unless I change my mind.' The correspondence is a fine example of this deliberately deceptive style. It appears factual, veers towards the confidential, seems to turn to derision and sarcasm, then adopts a serious, even melancholy tone. Reading the letters today, over the dead shoulders of their recipients, we wonder what to believe. It all sounds so true and so madeup at the same time. For instance, what are we to make of this missive addressed from the Hotel Excelsior in Bressanone to 'Lucio, crowned with laurel'?

> The Monster is doing really well in this little town of abbeys, cloisters, powerful bishops and clear flowing water and decorous hills. And he is reading and making shrewd annotations on the profound lyrics of the respectable dean of St Paul's. I have learnt of the numerous tragic deaths which have gladdened the summer over there. O my cradle, O city of

my childhood, why within the iron-coloured circle of your hills are you so filthy, sad and desperate? And why do you elect as your perpetual inhabitants, Tragedy without a soul and Grief without any light?

Here the editor's notes are invaluable. Literary readers may recognise the Dean of St Paul's as John Donne and the elegiac lines about 'the city of my childhood' as an adaptation of Dante's, but it also helps to know that it was Lucio Piccolo himself who nicknamed Lampedusa 'the Monster' for his voracious reading habits.

But in this letter, as in most of the rest of his correspondence, the pleasure for the unintended reader comes not from the slightly prurient feeling of putting one's nose in someone else's private business, but from the discovery, in the raw as it were, of the brilliant literary intelligence, the flare for language (exquisitely rendered into English by J. G. Nichols), the passionate interest Lampedusa had in the affairs and quirks and dramas of his fellow humans.

Early readers of *The Leopard* in its unfinished manuscript form (mainly dogmatic Italian Marxists for whom no aristocratic character could possibly be a worthy artistic subject) derided a style so far removed from the modernist experimentation and a theme so rooted in remembrance of things past. Today, when the status of *The Leopard* as a modern classic is no longer in dispute, the reading of Lampedusa's travel correspondence brings to light a draft, an essay of a certain voice, a first glimpse of that certain identifiable mixture of tenderness, wisdom and irony that became Lampedudsa's incomparable style.

Source: Alberto Manguel, "Tenderness, Wisdom and Irony," in *Spectator*, Vol. 315, No. 9515, January 8, 2011, p. 35.

Jeffrey Meyers

In the following excerpt, Meyers provides an insightful study of Lampedusa's use of recurrent and static symbols in The Leopard.

The Leopard is a richly symbolic novel from the first scene during the Rosary to the final moment when the carcass of Bendicò is flung out the window. The symbols form two categories: there are those which emerge and disappear only to be found later in a somewhat varied form, like a pattern of dolphins leaping through

> THE WARNINGS OF BENDICò AND FATHER PIRRONE ARE IGNORED, AND AT THE END OF THE NOVEL THE LAST OF THE SALINA'S ILLUSIONS ARE DESTROYED, FOR ONLY IN THE CHURCH HAD THEY MAINTAINED THEIR PREEMINENCE."

the sea. These may be called *recurrent* symbols, which only grow to their fullest meaning toward the end of the book, and through their very expansion advance the theme of the novel. Through repetition and variation they function also as leitmotifs and thereby effect a structural unity. The eviscerated soldier, the stars, Sicily itself, and Bendicò are recurrent symbols, woven like threads into the fabric and texture of Lampedusa's art.

The second mode of symbols are used more conventionally; they occur and evoke a higher meaning only once. But these *static* symbols often appear in an expanded moment which allows their meanings to reverberate through the novel and foreshadow the future. Prophecy is used structurally to link the present with the future and to give an air of predestined inevitability to important actions. The most successful symbols in this group are the series of *objects d'art* which illustrate and prophesy the love of Tancredi and Angelica.

The most famous art object in the novel is the glorious and sensual fountain of Amphitrite at Donnafugata that emanated the Keatsian "promise of pleasure that would never turn to pain" ("Forever wilt thou love and she be fair"). "Perched on an islet in the middle of the round basin, modelled by a crude but sensual hand, a vigorous smiling Neptune was embracing a willing Amphitrite."

According to the myth, Poseidon desired the sea goddess Amphitrite and sent a dolphin to look for her. When the dolphin brought her to Poseidon he married her, and as a reward, placed the dolphin among the constellations. This symbolic fountain, where Sedàra later spies Tancredi kissing Angelica, not only reflects the sensual nature of their love in the goddess whose wet navel gleams in the sun, but more importantly reveals the role of the Prince in the marriage. He is the dolphin, associated with the constellations, who is degraded to the role of Pandaro. Acting on the instructions in Tancredi's letter, he "swallows the toad" and completes the loathesome negotiations with Sedàra, in whose symbolical white tie and tails Fabrizio "saw Revolution." When the Prince is on his deathbed and the illusions about Tancredi's marriage have long since been shattered, he thinks once more of the delicious fountain and fears the grotesque metamorphosis it might suffer if sold to satisfy the debased pleasure of the bourgeoisie.

A series of art objects continue to reflect the love of Tancredi and Angelica and "the instincts lying dormant in the house" as these uncertain sensualists pursue each other through Donnafugata, that "mysterious and intricate labyrinth" which suggests Daedalus, King Minos, and the legend of how Ariadne saved Theseus from the Cretan minotaur (Sedàra). Donnafugata itself symbolizes the legacy of the decayed aristocracy to the young lovers who wander through its vastness "like the explorers of the New World," seeking to salvage something for the future. Behind the elegance and grandeur of its facade, a false front with no substance supporting it, were the ruined, empty, crumbling, and forgotten rooms. Donnafugata is foreshadowed in the first section by the huge desk in the Prince's office "with dozens of drawers, recesses, hollows, and folding shelves . . . decorated like a stage set, full of unexpected, uneven surfaces, and secret drawers."

In one of the secret rooms of Donnafugata Angelica "had hidden behind an enormous picture propped on the floor, and for a short time *Arturo Corbera at the Siege of Antioch* formed a protection for the girl's hopeful anxiety."

Tancredi is named after the Crusader and Prince of Antioch who played an important role in the capture of the city, which was overrun by the Turks in 1094. After an ineffectual siege of seven months, a force of 300,000 Crusaders stormed the city with the help of a traitor in 1098. Once in possession they were soon overtaken by disease and famine. This painting symbolizes the courtship of Tancredi who lays siege to the alien fortress of Angelica, and only wins her after the timely intervention of the Leopard, who betrays his daughter and his class.

Tancredi, Prince of Antioch, is also one of the principal heroes of Tasso's *Gerusalemme Liberata*, whose subject is the First Crusade; just as Angelica is one of the main heroines of Ariosto's *Orlando Furioso*. Tasso's Tancredi has many qualities of Castiglione's *Il Cortegiano*, with his noble heart and graceful manners, his courtesy and generosity. . . . But he is best known in the poem for his agonizing passions and romantic adventures. Ariosto's Angelica, a beautiful but selfish pagan, is a strong contrast to the passionate paladin Tancredi. All men fall in love with her, but she loves no one, not even the great hero Orlando. Finally she marries a simple soldier, Medoro, whom she finds wounded on the battlefield and nurses to health.

Tasso presents a triangle of lovers: Erminia loves Tancredi who loves Clorinda. The tender and helpless Erminia falls in love with Tancredi when he besieges Antioch, takes her prisoner, and treats her chivalrously. Completely overcome by her passion, she is unable to hide it. All this, of course, is reflected in *The Leopard*, for Concetta loves Tancredi who loves Angelica. And Concetta, unable to contain her feelings, confides them to Father Pirrone, who then tells the Prince.

The two lovers are surrounded at Donnafugata by other works of art that seem to encourage their "game full of charm and risk," their licentious desires in the decrepit rooms. Like Angelica "a shepherdess [is seen] glancing down consenting from some obliterated fresco"; and they find on the fireplaces "delicate intricate little marble intaglios, with naked figures in paroxysms." (This too evokes the "mad pursuit," the "struggle to escape," and the "wild ecstasy" of Keats' Grecian Urn). Even the accidental music of the *Carnival of Venice* to which "they kissed in rhythm" evokes at once the festivity and sensual outbursts of the present, and the hint of Lenten austerities (their marriage which "even erotically was no success") that must inevitably follow. Exotic Venice of fabled splendor, the most profligate of cities, the very seat of all dissoluteness, is the perfect setting for passionate abandon.

This mixture of passion and denial within a religious context leads the lovers to the climax of these scenes, the most intense and lyrical in the novel. In a secret apartment they find whips of bull's muscle, which of course are male symbols, but are afraid of themselves, leave the room immediately, and kiss as if in expiation. The following day they enter the apartment of the Saint-Duke who with the Blessed Corberà, foundress of the Convent that Fabrizio and Tancredi visit, represents the severe religious traditions of the Salina family. This time they find another whip, used by the Saint-Duke to scourge himself and redeem the earth with his blood, for "in his holy exaltation it must have seemed that only through this expiatory baptism could the earth really become his."

But his descendant Tancredi is a different sort of man, and finds his redemption through Angelica's beauty and her father's money. The religious traditions are embodied in Concetta whose indifference to Caviaghi, her ice-cold hands, and her denial of the flesh contrast strongly with Angelica's passion; and symbolize that Lombardy and Sicily can never be truly united. Ironically, Concetta becomes like the nuns in Tancredi's fictive convent—virginal, isolated, and afraid.

After Angelica prostrates herself and kisses the feet of the enormous and ghastly crucified Christ in the room of the Saint-Duke, Tancredi bites her lip in a rough kiss and draws blood. Angelica assumes the traditional posture of Mary Magdalene, and her fascinating mixture of sinfulness, holiness, and beauty, as if to pay for her sins before she commits them. He scourges himself by a degrading marriage to the woman he calls his whip, and offers her blood, not his own, for atonement. The family has changed considerably in the last two hundred years.

A few days later the lovers enter the most dangerous room with its "neat rolled-up mattress which would spread out again at a mere touch of the hand," like a Sicilian stiletto. That morning Angelica had said, "I'm your novice," offering herself for sexual rather than religious initiation. In the afternoon "already the woman had surrendered, already the male was about to overrun the man, when the Church bell clanged almost straight down on their prone bodies, adding its own throb to the others," and preventing the long-desired consummation. The religious traditions have sounded their final echoes. Tancredi is neither the scourging Saint, nor the predatory Prince who at least takes women when he wants them.

Symbolic paintings also illuminate the character of Fabrizio and prophesy his future, as do

references to literature. When Garibaldi's General visits the Prince after the successful landing at Marsala, he substitutes a neutral *Pool of Bethesda* for the portrait of Ferdinand II which hangs in the drawing room.

John v. 2-9 says "there is in Jerusalem a pool called Bethesda around which lay a multitude of invalids blind, lame, and paralyzed." Jesus found a sick man there and said "Rise, take up your pallet and walk;" and the man was healed. The invaders picture themselves as Jesus, coming like Chevalley to cure and heal the Sicilians; and Sedarà is their grotesque John the Baptist, for "whenever he passed secret groups were formed, to prepare the way for those that were to come." The Prince, "with his sensibility to presages and symbols," knows too well that the aristocracy is "blind, lame, and paralyzed."

Literature is the last art that is used symbolically, and three important references appear in *The Leopard*.

[Of these, the most] significant instance of the symbolic use of literature in the novel, occurs when Don Fabrizio quotes [from Baudelaire's "Un Voyage a Cythère"] as he leaves his mistress Marianina. . . . "Un Voyage a Cythère" describes the poet's futile quest for an Eldorado on the island where Aphrodite was supposed to have emerged from the sea, and where a famous temple was erected in her honor. His illusions are quickly destroyed when he finds a hanged man whose sexual organs have been torn out by birds of prey as punishment for his sexual excesses. The poet then identifies himself with the man on the gibbet, and realizes that the allegory is directed towards himself. He prays, in the last lines, for the strength and courage to accept his debased self.

The poem symbolizes the conflict in the Leopard between his intellectual and sensual, his heavenly and earthly, his spiritual and fleshly quests. His inability to dispel illusion and face reality, and to reconcile the strivings of his soul and body, are the core of the Prince's weakness. Thus, the lamentations and self-denunciations.

Here again Lampedusa uses symbols to explain the present as well as to reveal the future, thus forming a structural and a thematic effect. In Donnafugata, when Tancredi and Angelica are described as "two lovers embarked for Cythera on a ship made of dark and sunny rooms," the Baudelaire poem is immediately invoked, and we understand at the height of their lyrical love that their hopes for happiness will be disappointed. The sunny rooms are the present, the dark ones the future.

Another static symbol associated with the fountain of Amphitrite and the two lovers is that of the foreign peaches . . . which Fabrizio observes with Tancredi. "The graft with German cuttings, made two years ago, had succeeded perfectly; [the fruit] was big, velvety, luscious-looking; yellowish, with a faint flush of rosy pink on the cheeks." The Prince remarks, "They seem quite ripe . . . [and are] products of love, of coupling."

Unlike the Paul Neyron roses which had been "enfeebled by the strong if languid pull of the Sicilian earth," the grafted peaches thrive and prosper. The difference is that the French roses were planted directly in the Sicilian earth that has always been (passively) hostile to alien elements; while the German peach cuttings were grafted to Sicilian stems. Like his uncle, Tancredi also has German strains in his blood, and the material fruits of his marriage to Angelica are symbolized in the grafted peaches, just as their sensual desire is reflected in the "shameless naked flesh" of the fountain.

When Tancredi steals the peaches, with their "aphrodisiac and seductive properties," from his uncle and carries them to Angelica, whom they seem to resemble, he performs a symbolical marriage ceremony. "He sidestepped a sword-waving urchin [The Revolution], carefully avoided a urinating mule [Don Calogero], and reached the Sedàra's door." The Revolution and Angelica's father are the two dangerous elements which Tancredi must accept and adjust to if the "graft" to Angelica is to take place. Tancredi recognizes this when he says paradoxically, "if we want things to stay as they are, things will master. Fabrizio thinks of Marianina, who can refuse him nothing, as "a kind of Bendicò in a silk petticoat." Bendicò means the same to the spinster Concetta, even when he is dead and embalmed, a heap of moth-eaten fur and nest of spiderwebs, like her unused trousseau. She refused "to detach herself from the only memory of her past which aroused no distressing sensations."

The literary model for the dead Bendicò is Loulou, the parrot of the old maidservant Félicité in Flaubert's "A Simple Heart." "Though he was not a corpse, the worms had begun to devour the dead bird; one of his wings was broken, and the stuffing was coming out of his body. But Félicité kissed Loulou's forehead, and pressed him against her cheek . . . when Félicité woke up, she could see him in the dawn's light, and [like Concetta] she would recall painlessly and peacefully the old days." Both Bendicò and Loulou are adored household pets whose mistresses continue to be strongly attached to them for many years after their death, even though they are hideously decomposed. And both works conclude with the metamorphosis of the animal into another image which reveals something important about the illusions of their owners.

Bendicò's realistic approach to things and instinctive good sense is symbolized when he warns the Leopard at three crucial stages of the family's decline. These warnings are merely noted by the perceptive Prince, but not heeded. In the second scene of the novel Fabrizio sits "merely watching the desolation wrought by Bendicò in the flower beds," and remarks, "How human!" Here the dog is symbolically warning the fatalistic Fabrizio of the destruction and disasters of war, and the rapacity of Sedàra's class who will rape the Prince's lands. Bendicò's second warning comes when the enthusiastic Salina family greets the newly engaged Angelica. "Only Bendicò, in contrast to his usual sociability, growled away in the back of his throat." Finally, when the Leopard is speaking to Chevalley, Bendicò crawls into the room and falls asleep, failing to hear the wise Northern words just as his master does. (This device is later repeated when the herbalist falls asleep while Father Pirrone is explaining the political situation to him. But Pirrone, like Chevalley, keeps on talking.)

Father Pirrone, who is compared to a sheep dog, symbolically warns the Salinas in much the same way on two occasions. When Tancredi is courting Angelica and kissing her hand, the priest meditates over the Biblical stories of Delilah, Judith, and Esther, three women who betrayed famous and powerful men. When Fabrizio is contracting with Sedàra, Pirrone notices the falling barometer and predicts "bad weather ahead."

The warnings of Bendicò and Father Pirrone are ignored, and at the end of the novel the last of the Salina's illusions are destroyed, for only in the Church had they maintained their preeminence. The relics are cleared out of the family chapel by the priest-technician, who symbolizes the secularization of the Church just as the increasing gullibility of the spinster sisters represents the increasing piety of the aristocracy. Then Concetta's "inner emptiness was total. . . even poor Bendicò was hinting at bitter memories." As the faithful dog, the last relic, is flung through the window "his form recomposed itself for an instant; in the air could have seen dancing a quadruped with long whiskers, and its right foreleg seemed to be raised in imprecation. Then all found peace in a little heap of livid dust."

Bendicò forms the image of the Leopard over the solid but sagging door near the deep well of Donnafugata which "pranced in spite of legs broken off by flung stones," just as Loulou becomes an image of the Holy Ghost to the dying Félicité who "thought she saw in the opening heavens a gigantic parrot, hovering above her head." In the dust heap Bendicò symbolizes the end of all tradition, beliefs, position, and power of the once-great family. The Prince himself says that "the significance of a noble family lies entirely in its traditions, that is in its vital memories." The embodiment of these vital memories, Bendicò and at the same time Prince Fabrizio, is now cast out, and only the "inner emptiness" remains.

Source: Jeffrey Meyers, "Symbol and Structure in *The Leopard*," in *Italian Quarterly*, Vol. 9, No. 34–35, Summer–Fall 1965, pp. 50–70.

SOURCES

Eskin, Stanley G., "Animal Imagery in *Il Gattopardo*," in *Italica*, Vol. 39, No. 3, 1962, pp. 189–94.

Evans, Arthur, and Catherine Evans, "'Salina e Svelto': The Symbolism of Change in *Il Gattopardo*," in *Wisconsin Studies in Contemporary Literature*, Vol. 4, No. 3, 1963, pp. 298–304.

Freud, Sigmund, *The Future of an Illusion*, translated and edited by James Strachey, W. W. Norton, 1961, pp. 5–71.

Gilmour, David, *The Last Leopard: A Life of Giuseppe di Lampedusa*, Pantheon Books, 1988, pp. 1–14, 188–89.

Lampedusa, Giuseppe Tomasi di, *The Leopard*, translated by Archibald Colquhoun, Pantheon Books, 1960.

Mercier, Vivian, "Sex, Success and Salvation," in *Hudson Review*, Vol. 13, No. 3, 1960, pp. 449–56.

O'Mara, Richard, "The Leopard Reconsidered," in *Sewanee Review*, Vol. 116, No. 4, 2008, pp. 637–44.

Sedgwick, Mark, *Against the Modern World: Traditionalism and the Secret Intellectual History of the Twentieth Century*, Oxford University Press, 2004, pp. 95–117.

FURTHER READING

Beales, Derek, and Eugenio Biagiani, *The Risorgimento and the Unification of Italy*, Longman, 2003.
    This is a standard textbook that deals with the historical and cultural aspects of the reunification of Italy.

Finley, Moses I., *A History of Sicily: Ancient Sicily to the Arab Conquest*, Viking, 1968.
    Although technically outdated, Finley's classic is elevated in style and literary significance far above an ordinary textbook. His evocation of the tragic history of the island brought comparisons to Lampedusa's *The Leopard* from reviewers.

Gefen, Gerard, *Sicilian Twilight: The Last Leopards*, Vendome, 2001.
    Gefen attempts to recreate the world of *The Leopard* with a combination of period documents and photographs as well as modern photos of the places described in the novel.

Moe, Nelson, *The View from Vesuvius: Italian Culture and the Southern Question*, University of California Press, 2002.
    Moe discusses the current status of the integration of the former Kingdom of the Two Sicilies into the modern, unified Italian state.

SUGGESTED SEARCH TERMS

Giuseppe Tomasi di Lampedusa

The Leopard

traditionalism

psychoanalysis

Julius Evola

Palermo

ancien régime

Freemasons

One Flew over the Cuckoo's Nest

1975

Loyally adapted from the beloved 1962 best seller by 1960s countercultural icon Ken Kesey, *One Flew over the Cuckoo's Nest* (1975), directed by Miloš Forman, caused audiences to erupt in joy as they cheered on rebel convict Randle P. McMurphy (Jack Nicholson) in his fight for the souls of his fellow patients in a mental institution. Cowering under the influence of the head nurse, Nurse Ratched (Louise Fletcher), the men under her care have lost their ability to stand up for themselves. McMurphy rockets into this antiseptic world to start a fight to the death against Nurse Ratched and the chilling institutional power she wields against her patients. *One Flew over the Cuckoo's Nest* won five Academy Awards, the first time a film had swept all major categories since 1934: Best Actor in a Leading Role (Jack Nicholson), Best Actress in a Leading Role (Louise Fletcher), Best Director (Miloš Forman), Best Writing: Screenplay Adapted from Other Material (Lawrence Hauben and Bo Goldman), and Best Picture (Saul Zaentz and Michael Douglas). Kesey's novel may have depths that the film cannot reach, due to the directorial decision to eliminate the schizophrenic Chief Bromden's nuanced narration, but the film offers a horror story embedded in a rowdy comedy—a fusion that has fascinated and terrified audiences to this day. Looking back on the film in 2003, Roger Ebert noted, "I was present at its world premiere . . . and have never heard a more tumultuous reception for a film. . . .

© *Archive Photos | Moviepix | Getty Images*

After the screening, the young first-time co-producer, Michael Douglas, wandered the lobby in a daze." Such is the power generated by the clash of the mighty R. P. McMurphy and the dreadful Nurse Ratched.

PLOT SUMMARY

One Flew over the Cuckoo's Nest begins with Nurse Ratched's arrival on her ward. She greets her three orderlies and assistant nurse. The patients line up for medication time. Chief Bromden is briefly introduced, an enormous Native American who sweeps the ward floor continuously. The scene cuts to R. P. McMurphy's arrival on the ward. As he is checked in, he lets out a loud howl and kisses one of his guards. The nurses check in his belongings as McMurphy introduces himself to the other patients. He

approaches the Chief first, remarking on his remarkable size and teasing him with an Indian war cry. Billy Bibbit, a stuttering young man, explains that the Chief is a deaf mute. Next, McMurphy introduces himself to the patients playing cards: Billy, Cheswick, Martini, and Harding.

McMurphy is led to Dr. Spivey's office, where he has an initial interview. The doctor reads his file aloud: McMurphy was incarcerated in a work farm after being charged with five counts of assault and statutory rape. Dr. Spivey reveals that those in charge at the work farm think McMurphy is faking insanity to get out of prison. He will be evaluated at the hospital as to whether or not he is lying to the authorities. "I think we out to get to the bottom of R. P. McMurphy," McMurphy tells the doctor with a sly grin.

Back on the ward, Nurse Ratched leads the men in a group therapy session. She opens the

FILM TECHNIQUE

- Miloš Forman chose to shoot *One Flew over the Cuckoo's Nest* as realistically as possible, with a chronological plot using no flashbacks, no special effects, and simple cuts between scenes. The film is not in black and white, but what color there is hardly dazzles the eye. Shot during the winter in Oregon, even the trees, grass, and sky outside reflect the white-walled, featureless hallways of the ward. As she takes in the ward the night of the party, Rose can be heard saying, "This looks just like my high school!"

- The camera lingers over faces—not only those of Nurse Ratched, McMurphy, and Chief Bromden but over Washington, Billy, Scanlon, and the minor but ever-present wanderers of the same halls where McMurphy wages his war. The film's realism includes a strictly third-person observation of electroshock therapy—the audience witnesses as if they were another doctor in the already claustrophobic room, not as if they were experiencing McMurphy's extreme state themselves. The lack of subjective camera work turns the lens into a Ratched-esque observer: patient, clear-eyed, and uncompromising toward the real human suffering that steadily unfolds on the ward.

- After acclimation to the blandness of the halls, sudden colorful details such as Candy's and Rose's dresses the night of the party and the slippery fish the men use for bait on their commandeered boat seem to jump off the screen. Likewise, Nurse Ratched's face against her white uniform is rendered more harsh and alien than seems logically possible for a pretty movie actress. By adjusting his audience's eye to the void within the ward, Forman can then overwhelm the audience with just a suggestion of color. This is why the all-night party seems all the wilder for the thick brown liquor pouring out an IV tube, and why when Nurse Ratched retrieves her cap from Martini the next morning, the light dusting of dirt on the usually spotless ironed cloth is reason enough for McMurphy's destruction.

---

meeting with a brutally direct summary of Mr. Harding's feelings about his wife, whom he suspects is cheating on him. Then, one by one, she asks the men to comment on Mr. Harding's relationship with his wife. One by one, the men refuse. "You mean there's not a man here who has an opinion on the matter?" she asks. The viewer meets other patients such as Mr. Scanlon, Mr. Bancini (who, like many other patients, cannot participate in the meeting as he is too advanced in psychosis), and Taber. The camera slowly zooms in on Nurse Ratched and her assistant, Nurse Pilbow, the only females on the ward, as she continues to ask uncomfortably direct questions about Harding's relationship.

Mr. Harding blows up after a confrontation with Taber, triggering the other patients, who begin to yell and argue over one another. The camera returns many times to record McMurphy's reactions as at first he is entertained by the fight but becomes increasingly disturbed by the chaos he is witnessing. The scene ends as McMurphy watches Nurse Ratched's utterly expressionless face as she sits surrounded by screaming men.

A bus transports the men to recreation time, where McMurphy tries to teach Chief to play basketball. An orderly, Washington, tells McMurphy it is pointless, but Chief does follow some of McMurphy's basic directions to hold the ball and raise his arms.

At medication time that night, McMurphy asks Nurse Ratched if she can turn the record player down. She explains calmly that she will not turn it down. Back at the card table, McMurphy bets the other men he can break Nurse Ratched's calm in one week.

In a group therapy session, McMurphy requests to change the schedule so the men can watch the World Series. Nurse Ratched counters that the schedule is important to the men on the ward and cannot be changed. She suggests a vote, but the men do not raise their hands in support. That night, McMurphy sits silently in the tub room with his feet on a huge ceramic water fountain, with which he sprays the men to break up another banal fight between them over a board game. On a bet he tries to pick up the water fountain to throw it through the window, but after a mighty attempt he fails.

The next morning in group therapy, Nurse Ratched bullies Billy much as she did Mr. Harding, mentioning a secret proposal to a girl that Billy kept from his mother and a suicide attempt as a result of the girl's rejection. Objecting to Nurse Ratched's treatment of Billy, Cheswick calls for a new vote in part to change the topic of conversation. This time a majority of the men in the group vote to see the World Series. However, Nurse Ratched says the nine members of the group are only half of the ward, counting the other nine men who cannot participate (called the Chronics in the novel). Nurse Ratched adjourns the meeting just as McMurphy asks the Chief to vote. He raises his hand, to the delight of McMurphy. But Nurse Ratched tells him the vote does not count because the meeting was over. Frustrated, McMurphy begins narrating a baseball game in front of the blank television as the men gather around him, laughing and cheering along. From her nurse's station, Nurse Ratched, enraged, calls for the men to stop immediately.

The scene cuts to Dr. Spivey interviewing McMurphy in front of two other doctors. McMurphy complains about Nurse Ratched, while Dr. Spivey counters with an accusation that McMurphy shows no signs of insanity and is intentionally faking his mental problems.

At recreation, McMurphy stands on the Chief's shoulders and climbs over the barbed wire fence, to then hide inside the group's bus. When the men board the bus, he takes off without out the bus driver. McMurphy makes a stop to pick up a woman named Candy. They commandeer a boat from a harbor by posing as doctors from the state mental institution. Setting sail,

the men fish successfully while Billy flirts with Candy. They return to shore celebrating their catch, where the police and Dr. Spivey are waiting to take them back to the institution.

A meeting of doctors and nurses convenes to decide McMurphy's fate. They agree that he is dangerous but not necessarily crazy. Dr. Spivey suggests sending him back to the work farm. Nurse Ratched intervenes. She wants to keep him on her ward instead of passing her problem along to the next authority.

McMurphy organizes a basketball game between the patients and the orderlies. Chief becomes the star player when he makes a basket, following McMurphy's earlier lessons. In the pool, Washington reveals to McMurphy that he has been confined indefinitely to the ward and will not be out in sixty-eight days when his prison sentence would have been up. Shaken, McMurphy confronts the men at group therapy, asking why they let him antagonize Nurse Ratched when he was only damaging his chances of leaving the ward. Harding explains that he did not know McMurphy was committed—that most of the guys are voluntary. Only Chief, Taber, and McMurphy are committed. McMurphy cannot believe it: "What do you think you guys are, crazy or something?"

Instead of responding to McMurphy's challenge, the men bring up petty arguments about ward policy. Cheswick erupts over the policy on rationing cigarettes while the men toss around a cigarette stolen from Harding. The cigarette burns Taber's leg and the orderlies carry him away screaming. Cheswick throws a fit until finally McMurphy shatters the glass of the nurse's station to grab a carton of cigarettes. The orderlies begin to carry Cheswick away when suddenly McMurphy attacks Washington. They fight, but as McMurphy is wrestled to the ground, Chief drops his broom and comes to the rescue. The orderlies must pile on to restrain the enormous man.

On the disturbed ward, Cheswick, McMurphy. and Chief await electroshock therapy. Cheswick cannot stop crying in fear. The staff must carry Cheswick into the room as he screams for Mack. Alone, McMurphy and Chief sit together in silence. McMurphy offers Chief some gum. The Chief says, "Thank you." Stunned, McMurphy offers him another piece. The Chief smiles at the gum and says, "Juicy Fruit." McMurphy is beside himself with pleasure at finding a new friend in the Chief, who has been faking being deaf and mute. He makes plans to escape to Canada with the Chief. Cheswick rolls by unconscious on a gurney.

McMurphy is brought into the room next and given the electroshock treatment. His whole body convulses, and his face turns a terrible red.

On his return to the ward, McMurphy tricks the men into thinking he has been damaged by the electroshock, shuffling his feet slowly with a blank expression on his face. Nurse Ratched, aware of his trick, can hardly contain her impatience. She interrupts the boisterous celebration that ensues at his return by reminding him he is not the only one on the ward. McMurphy respectfully backs down. But after the nurses leave for the night, Randall sneaks into the nurse's station and calls Candy to tell her to come break him out and to bring liquor with her. McMurphy wakes Chief up to ask him to escape with him. Chief says he is not ready for the challenge of the outside world, that it is easier for McMurphy because he is not so big. But McMurphy laughs and says the Chief is as big as a tree trunk.

After bribing Turkle, the night guard, with liquor, money, and the company of Candy's friend Rose, a wild all-night party ensues on the ward as the men get drunk. Candy and Billy dance together at the end of the night. McMurphy decides it is time to leave but realizes Billy looks upset. After teasing him about his feelings for Candy, McMurphy decides to stay a little longer so that Billy and Candy can be alone together. He asks Candy if she will sleep with Billy and she agrees. The two go to a room alone while the rest of the patients wait.

Dawn comes, finding McMurphy asleep beside the open window. The ward is in total disarray. The door slams as Nurse Ratched arrives on the ward and begins giving orders to regain control. As the orderlies gather the patients, she takes in the destruction. Washington reports that Billy is missing. They search the rooms individually until they find Billy and Candy together. Billy runs after Nurse Ratched to explain himself, suddenly more confident and cured of his stutter. But when Nurse Ratched mentions Billy's mother, with whom she is friends, and her certain disappointment in him when she tells his mother what he has done, Billy breaks down completely, stuttering worse than

ever as he names McMurphy responsible for what happened.

He begs Nurse Ratched on his knees not to tell his mother, but she has him dragged away by the orderlies to await the doctor's arrival. Nurse Ratched turns her glare on McMurphy. He tries desperately to unlock the window but is caught and punches an orderly. He and the Chief prepare to escape. Washington approaches, but suddenly there is a scream from the nurse's station. Rose and Candy call from outside the window for McMurphy to escape, but he turns to follow the sound of the scream. The patients and staff pile into the nurse's station to find that Billy has killed himself. Nurse Ratched urges everyone to be calm and go on with their schedule. Instead, McMurphy attacks her, strangling her with all his strength. By the time the orderlies knock him unconscious and pull him away, she is purple and coughing for air.

The scene cuts to a card game, as Chief sweeps in the background. Nurse Ratched is back in the nurse's station with a brace around her neck. Rumors about the disappearance of McMurphy are rampant between the remaining patients. That night, as the Chief lays in bed awake, McMurphy is walked into the ward by two orderlies. Much like his earlier joke on the men when he pretended to be in a zombielike state, his eyes are unfocused and he shuffles his feet across the floor. The staff lay him in bed and leave. Chief inspects McMurphy to find he has two scars on his skull. He has been given a lobotomy. Chief shakes McMurphy, but he is unresponsive. Hugging him close, the Chief says he will not leave without McMurphy. He smothers him to death with a pillow.

Chief lifts the enormous water fountain off its base and throws it through the ward window. The camera cuts to the patients waking up at the crash of glass as Taber laughs and howls. The Chief runs toward the hills, free.

CHARACTERS

Bancini

Bancini is a Chronic member of the ward, too far advanced in mental illness to participate in the group therapy sessions. He can be heard repeating the phrase "I'm tired" and is seen in one of the first scenes of the movie strapped to his bed in the morning.

Billy Bibbit

Billy, an anxious young man with a stutter, has an irrepressible romantic side. However, Nurse Ratched, friends with Billy's mother (who in the novel works in the same hospital), uses this friendship to make Billy feel weak and powerless. After Billy meets and falls for Candy, McMurphy arranges for the two to sleep together. But when they are discovered and Nurse Ratched guarantees that Billy's mother will hear about his rebellion, Billy kills himself in the nurse's station.

Chief Bromden

Chief is a massive supposedly deaf-mute half Native American, who serves as the schizophrenic narrator of the novel. After watching his father's life destroyed by liquor and their native land lost, Chief is committed to the mental hospital without hope of release. He believes in the Combine, a metaphor for the power of authoritarian conformity that sweeps the weak beneath its blades. In the film, Chief (played by Will Sampson) does not narrate but plays a key role in the plot as McMurphy's friend. McMurphy always seems to include the Chief in his antics and teaches him to play basketball. Revealing he can actually hear and speak just before they go into shock therapy (the reason for the revelation in both film and novel is Chief's love of chewing gum), Chief and McMurphy become secret compatriots in the mission to escape. When McMurphy cannot physically escape with Chief after his lobotomy, Chief kills him out of mercy before escaping the ward.

Candy

Candy is a prostitute friend of McMurphy's who joins the patients on their fishing trip as well as the night of the party. Although she and McMurphy are something of a couple, she sleeps with Billy Bibbit at McMurphy's request after a night of dancing with him.

Cheswick

Cheswick is a patient on the ward who complains frequently and loudly when he feels uncomfortable. After one of his outbursts leads to McMurphy breaking the glass of the nurse's station, Cheswick is subjected to electroshock therapy along with Chief and McMurphy. In the novel, Cheswick drowns during recreation time in the pool, after an argument with McMurphy, whom he adores.

Harding

Harding, played by William Redfield, is an intellectual who has trust issues, especially concerning his attractive wife. He and McMurphy get along, though somewhat competitively, as the sanest of the insane on the ward.

Martini

Martini (Danny DeVito) is a childish patient on the ward who frequently tries and fails to cheat at card games and interrupts others while they are speaking.

Randle P. McMurphy

McMurphy, sometimes called Mack, is a thirty-eight-year-old convict with a history of violence. In an attempt to cheat his sentence at the work farm, he gets himself checked into the mental institution for an examination to determine if he is insane. Once on the ward, he cannot tolerate the oppressive rule of Nurse Ratched, betting the other patients he can upset her to the point that she will lose control of her expressionless facade. However, Mack does not know at first that once committed he will not be released until Ratched determines he has been cured. He is closest to the Chief, especially after finding out the Chief has been lying to the staff about his condition, but treats all the men on the ward as equals— encouraging them, entertaining them, and fascinating them much to the chagrin of Ratched, who feels the only cure for the patients is her cure, the bureaucratic methods of the institution. McMurphy represents the spirit of creativity and freedom that is trampled on by those who fear losing their power. Played by Jack Nicholson, who won the 1975 Academy Award for Best Actor for his performance, McMurphy is a sly gambling man with a compassionate heart for the other patients. He is the inspiration for each of the men to try a little harder rather than wallow in their misery. Elaine B. Safer notes in her essay "'It's the Truth Even if It Didn't Happen': Ken Kesey's *One Flew over the Cuckoo's Nest*," "Jack Nicholson plays McMurphy as an imaginative, attractive, sympathetic hustler, . . . a man who easily gains control of incapacitated men in a cuckoo's nest." He leads the lost men back to themselves, and is sacrificed for this defiance of Nurse Ratched's iron rule.

Nurse Pilbow

Nurse Pilbow is Nurse Ratched's assistant who rarely speaks. Like Nurse Ratched, she wears a fixed expression during group therapy, and she seems to emulate Ratched's behaviors.

Nurse Ratched

Nurse Ratched, known in the novel as Big Nurse, runs her ward strictly and without humor. Seeing herself as a dedicated professional, Ratched firmly believes that her actions are just and her methods helpful. Nothing makes her more furious than McMurphy's influence on her patients, yet when Dr. Spivey suggests sending him back to the work farm, she alone recommends that he stay on her ward for treatment. Louise Fletcher's performance is as cold as Jack Nicholson's is passionate, and for her chilling portrayal of the monster nurse she was awarded the 1975 Academy Award for Best Actress in a Leading Role. Pauline Kael states in her *New Yorker* review of the film, "Louise Fletcher gives a masterly performance. Changes in her flesh tone tell us what Nurse Ratched feels." Indeed, Nurse Ratched is so tightly wound, her jaw set so firmly, that she seems at all times about to explode. Though she believes she is healing them, her effect on her patients is devastating to their confidence. Emasculating and cruel in group therapy sessions, she preys on their weaknesses; for example, she uses her relationship with Billy's mother as a weapon against him whenever he shows signs of strength, most notably after his night with Candy. McMurphy challenges all that she stands for: the rules of the establishment, cleanliness, moral superiority, and the importance of structure. The two engage in a destructive war that claims both Billy and McMurphy's lives. In the novel, Nurse Ratched is a shape-shifting monster with little trace of humanity.

Rose

Rose is Candy's friend who arrives on the ward the night of the party to help Candy break McMurphy out of the mental hospital.

Scanlon

Scanlon is a very quiet patient on the ward and a member of the group therapy sessions.

Dr. Spivey

Dr. Spivey was played by Dean R. Brooks, the real head doctor of Oregon State Hospital at Salem, where the movie was filmed. The doctor doubts McMurphy's claim to insanity, believing he is simply hoping to escape the work farm.

After the fishing trip, Dr. Spivey wishes to send McMurphy back to the work farm, as he is a danger to the other patients.

Taber

Taber (Christopher Lloyd), who has issues controlling his anger, is always willing to take McMurphy up on his outrageous bets. In the novel, Taber is a former member of the ward who was moved to the disturbed ward (where the men receive electroshock therapy) after clashing with Nurse Ratched.

Turkle

Turkle is the night guard on the ward played by Scatman Crothers, who loses his job after allowing the all-night party on his watch. McMurphy bribes him with money and liquor, after which he falls asleep.

Washington

One of three orderlies who work for Nurse Ratched in both the film and novel, Washington dislikes McMurphy, frequently arguing and fighting with him. He is the one to tell McMurphy that it is up to Nurse Ratched's discretion when, or if, he will ever be released from the mental hospital.

THEMES

Mental Disorders

As in Kesey's novel, Miloš Forman's film emphasizes the question of who is truly out of their mind: those who break from the system or those who work to make it stronger. Despite Nurse Ratched's insistence that the men must adhere to a careful schedule or they will become confused, McMurphy's chaos and distractions fascinate them. Under his care, they make small steps forward: the Chief speaks, Billy finds a girl, Cheswick steers a boat singing sailor songs. Their progress only angers Nurse Ratched, who must see things done her way or not at all—as stubborn a psychosis as Martini's childish cheating at cards. McMurphy may or may not be insane. But as the doctors and Nurse Ratched evaluate his sanity, the audience evaluates the sanity of the mental institution, and the results are not positive. In fact, the results are horrific. Nurse Ratched personally drives Billy to suicide by shaming him after a happy if morally dubious night with Candy. McMurphy is her next victim,

READ, WATCH, WRITE

- What do you feel is the role of gender in *One Flew over the Cuckoo's Nest*, both novel and film? Watch the movie, focusing on how men and women are represented differently, and write an essay about the role of Dr. Spivey versus that of Nurse Ratched. How would the story change if the ward's head nurse were male? Use quotes in your essay from a relevant review of the film.

- What does this film teach its audience about mental illness, if anything? Do you agree with its portrayal of the patients? Watch the movie, focusing on the patients of the ward other than McMurphy. Take notes on the film's presentation of the mentally ill. After watching the film use the Internet to research mental illness, and draw similarities between mental illness and the film's portrayal. Lead a class discussion in which you detail your findings.

- Read the novel *One Flew over the Cuckoo's Nest*. Make a list of five specific instances of difference between the novel and film. Include in the list why you think these changes were made. If you were directing a film adaptation, how would you shoot it?

- Choose a scene from the novel and describe how you would present this scene visually and what instructions you would give your actors.

- Write a scene from Nurse Pilbow's point of view. What is life like working on Nurse Ratched's ward?

- After watching the film and reading the novel, focus on the fishing trip in both the film and novel. Many critics find the trip unrealistic in an otherwise extremely realistic film. How is this scene situated in the novel? What elements are added or eliminated in the film and to what effect? After organizing your thoughts on a piece of paper, discuss what you have found in a blog post. Allow your classmates to comment and share ideas.

- Read Ken Kesey's only children's book, *Little Trickster the Squirrel Meets Big Double the Bear* (1990). What is the moral or lesson of the story? What would you say is the moral or lesson of *One Flew over the Cuckoo's Next*, if any? Write a persuasive essay in which you make a case that the two stories are fundamentally similar to each other.

---

as she has him lobotomized after he attempts to strangle her. Her belief in the system is so strong that she has given herself over to it, and wishes the same for the others. Subsuming whatever personality she may have in order to present a flat, expressionless face and steady, calm and uncompromising voice, she considers those who do the same (like her silent assistant, Nurse Pilbow), to be good, those who do not, to be problems worth fixing. A lobotomized McMurphy will follow the rules because there is nothing left of him to fight, while a McMurphy sent back to the work farm would be free to continue his wild-child ways. This is her motivation for keeping him on the ward.

In the novel, the Chief's mental illness makes him an unreliable narrator. A hallucinogenic fog is always sneaking over the novel's scenes, obscuring reality and fantasy. The reader is told the story from within the insane mind, not without as in the film. The film's realism lessens the effect of the patients' real mental problems, as the hero McMurphy sees the group as regular guys. With the viewer knowing no better, the Chief of the film certainly seems strange but not like a man hanging on to reality by a thread. This extends to all the patients, who are lovable for their eccentricities and powerlessness against their common enemy, Nurse Ratched. But the men in the ward are there for a reason, and

© *Republic Pictures | Archive Photos | Getty Images*

perhaps McMurphy is at his most insane in treating each of them as regular folks. Where Nurse Ratched sees their debilitating weakness, McMurphy sees only strength.

Conformity

The enemy of both film and novel are the machines of institutional control meant to suck out the soul of any one individual who wages war against it. McMurphy does just that—going head to head in battle against Nurse Ratched, the representative of all that keeps individuality and creativity crushed beneath the pressure of conformity. In the novel, the Chief calls this evil machine the Combine, and he considers Nurse Ratched a worker for and part of the Combine's relentless efforts to mow down those who would define themselves in life, rather than be defined. Sane versus insane, right versus wrong, criminal versus innocent, moral versus immoral: the film asks where the line is truly drawn, and McMurphy asks if there is a line at all. To Nurse Ratched, these are black-and-white matters already set in stone. She has no doubts that her

actions are just, her plan is helpful, and her words are true. When she does lose control, when chaos erupts during meetings, when the staff wants to send McMurphy back to the work farm, and most notably on the night of the party, Nurse Ratched reacts with chilling calm to gradually regain her power. McMurphy passionately throws himself against this monolith of cold institutional superiority and loses his life in the fray that follows. Creativity, beauty, and life's natural messiness fall to the antiseptic powers of control and conformity. Only the Chief escapes.

STYLE

Narration versus Spectation

The greatest difference between the novel *One Flew over the Cuckoo's Nest* and its film adaptation is the style in which the story is written and that in which the film was shot. Chief Bromden's narration of the novel is unreliable because, as a schizophrenic, he is the frequent victim of paranoid visions and wild, rapid thoughts. To the Chief (and so to the reader of the novel), Nurse Ratched is a hideous monster with a doll's unmoving face, while McMurphy is a beacon of light in the dark. Safer, in her essay "'It's the Truth Even if It Didn't Happen': Ken Kesey's *One Flew over the Cuckoo's Nest*," quotes a 1970 *Rolling Stone* interview with Kesey, in which he discussed wanting to film the movie himself: "I could do it weird. I could do it so that people, when they left there, they couldn't find the exit."

Instead, Miloš Forman directed the film, choosing to eliminate Chief's role as narrator in favor of using the third-person point of view. What is lost in the transition is the deeply personal effect of experiencing this antiestablishment story from within the mind of a mental patient. But much is gained, despite the film adaptation's natural, necessary simplification of the novel's complex issues. Forman did away with the Chief's surrealist narration in favor of realism in all aspects of the film's visual design. A starkly white and static ward replaces the creeping fog that Chief battles in the novel. The evil Big Nurse is replaced by an actual human: Louise Fletcher in the difficult role of Nurse Ratched. Kael comments on the peculiar effect of a realistic Nurse Ratched: "Those who know the book will probably feel that Nurse Ratched is now more human, but those who haven't read it may be appalled at her inhumanity."

Both novel and film tell a humanistic story of individuals struggling under the repressive power of an unfeeling institution, and both are wildly funny thanks to McMurphy's personal magnetism whether on the page or screen. But because the novel is fed by surrealism, by a give-and-take relationship with reality, while the film is unquestionably realistic, the two cannot be reconciled in scope and meaning. It is the difference between witnessing and being, though Safer thinks it is for the best:

> Had Milos Forman used Bromden as narrator instead of employing objective narration, and had he used surreal details instead of realistic ones . . . he might have caused the cinema audience to be so shocked and distraught "when they left there, they couldn't find the exit."

Forman spares his audience, delivering instead a straightforward, unflinching high-stakes battle of good and evil, and one of the most beloved stories in American cinema.

Selective Adaptation

One aspect of the novel not adapted to the film was Kesey's description of the patients on the ward as either Acutes or Chronics. The Acutes are patients who can participate in group therapy sessions, while the Chronics are more serious cases who are not expected to recover. For example, Chief is a Chronic, while Harding is an Acute. In the film during group therapy sessions with the Acutes, the Chronics can be seen wandering in the background of the scene.

Cheswick's and Taber's roles were altered for the film, with both playing larger parts than in the novel. Cheswick's suicide was cut for the film, while Taber was added as a present member of the ward. Again, Chief's role as narrator was eliminated, dramatically altering the style with which the film was shot. Chief's backstory, admiration of McMurphy, and growth from emotionally weak to strong-willed are hinted at rather than occupying prominent positions in the plot.

Though changes were made in the transition between novel and film, the cast members were selected for their close resemblance to the characters described in Kesey's book, and no major absences can be found. Marsha McCreadie declares in her essay "*One Flew over the Cuckoo's Nest*: Some Reasons for One Happy Adaptation," "The momentum and the spirit of the original have been retained."

CULTURAL CONTEXT

Published in 1962, Kesey's *One Flew over the Cuckoo's Nest* came at a time when America was on the brink of a cultural upheaval (of which Kesey himself was a conspicuous leader). Robert Faggen states in his 2002 introduction to Kesey's novel, "By the end of the 1950s, psychiatry had reached the height of its prestige in the American imagination." Respected, trusted, and put into practice throughout the country—the separation of the insane from the sane was considered beneficial to both groups of people. What Kesey illuminates in his novel, which was ahead of its time in its criticism of the psychiatric establishment, is that rarely in life are boundaries so clear and definite as the establishment would have those under its power believe. Is McMurphy crazy? Certainly he is a dangerous man with too much charm. But his treatment on

One Flew Over the Cuckoo's Nest *was the first film since 1934 to sweep all five main categories at the* Academy Awards. *(© Keystone-France | Gamma-Keystone | Getty Images)*

the ward, and even the treatment he observes of the more believably institutionalized patients, is the stuff of horror stories. Ebert sums up the daily routine in his 1975 review of the film: "Their passive existence is reinforced by the unsmiling, domineering Nurse Ratched, who lines them up for compulsory tranquilizers and then leads them through group therapy in a stupor." The novel captures the young spirit of the 1960s, an era of rebellion against such essence-draining powers of control.

The film, premiering over a decade after the novel's publication in 1975, captured the new spirit of the land. By the 1970s, the impenetrable tower of psychiatry had begun to crumble as people—their minds expanded by the many human rights movements of the 1960s—recognized that the concept of a "normal" person is more a cultural construct than a reality. The '60s hippies and flower children had given

way to a culture burnt out on war and destruction, protests and death. Kael then noted, "The movie comes at a time when we're all prepared to accept a loony bin as the right metaphor for the human condition." The hallucinogenic aspects of the plot, especially Chief's narration, were eliminated completely for the movie in favor of a stark realism. No swirling psychedelic colors or mystical fog interrupt the action, no experimentation with sound or light; there is simply a white ward with staff in pressed white uniforms shot with clear-eyed camera work and edited with simple cuts between scenes. Ebert, in his 2003 review of the film, summarizes the effect:

> Toned down for the 1970s into a parable about society's enforcement of conformism, it almost willfully overlooked the realities of mental illness in order to turn the patients into a group of cuddly characters ripe for McMurphy's cheerleading.

Perhaps this willful overlooking of the patients' very real problems is a consequence primarily of the absence of Chief's narration as a man with schizophrenia, or perhaps Forman chose to lighten the burden of mental illness because his film is a comedy filmed at a time when people needed cheerleading. If Chief's narration of the novel represents the daring and fearless experimentation of the 1960s, then the film, with its unflinching realism, represents the coming-to-terms and reflection of Americans in the 1970s.

CRITICAL OVERVIEW

Critical reception of the film was overwhelmingly positive, as evidenced by the film's 1975 sweep of the five major categories of the Academy Awards. Especially noteworthy are accounts of the original audiences' reactions in theaters. Safer notes, "The film audience stamped and cheered McMurphy as he battled the terrors of the mental hospital."

While opinions vary as to the success of the film's wider metaphorical meanings (such as among those who view the mental ward as a stand-in for America), reviewers almost unanimously heap praise on the brilliance of the actors. Ebert, in his 2003 reflection on the film, feels that "Louise Fletcher's [performance], despite the Oscar, is not enough appreciated. This may be because her Nurse Ratched is so thoroughly contemptible." And in his 1975 review he states, "McMurphy is the life force, the will to prevail, set down in the midst of a community of the defeated. And he's personified and made totally credible by Jack Nicholson."

Kael is most impressed by the Chief: "Will Sampson, the towering full-blooded Creek who plays Chief Broom, brings so much charm, irony, and physical dignity to the role of the resurrected catatonic that this movie achieves Kesey's mythic goal." Vincent Canby writes in "Jack Nicholson, the Free Spirit of *One Flew over the Cuckoo's Nest*" that "the other patients in the ward . . . are never patronized as freaks but are immediately identifiable as variations on ourselves, should we ever go over the edge of what's called sanity."

For reviewers, the fishing trip is most problematic. While in the novel the fishing trip is an approved patient outing, in the film the scene is a stolen moment shared only by the patients. Ebert sums up the problem succinctly in his original 1975 review: "The scene causes an almost embarrassing break in the movie—it's Forman's first serious misstep—because it's an idealized fantasy in the midst of realism." But, and Ebert acknowledges this truth with some regret, the audience's delight is not diminished by this fantastical adventure on the high seas.

John Zubizarreta, in "The Disparity of Point of View in *One Flew over the Cuckoo's Nest*," puts the matter directly: "What audience . . . wouldn't cheer the rambunctious likes of Randle McMurphy, cavorting rebelliously through a celluloid landscape of sterile, white walls; inhuman, dictatorial nurses; insensitive, violent orderlies; and absurd, debilitating rules of order?"

CRITICISM

Amy Lynn Miller

Miller is a graduate of the University of Cincinnati and currently resides in New Orleans, Louisiana. In the following essay, she discusses what makes Forman's film adaptation of Kesey's One Flew over the Cuckoo's Nest *a successful and satisfying transition from literature to film.*

Film adaptations of novels are never a guaranteed success. Fans of a book await the release of a film version with a mix of both excitement and apprehension. Who will play the main character? Will a favorite scene be included? As the credits roll, the audience members make their decision, and in the case of *One Flew over the Cuckoo's Nest*, the general audience seemed thrilled. Ebert, in his 1975 review of the film, writes, "I can't get out of my mind the tumultuous response that *Cuckoo's Nest* received from its original audiences." Almost twenty years later, in 2003, he was still reeling from the reaction of the crowd at the film's world premiere. He had never seen, in two decades of reviewing new films, a more excited audience—"no, not even during *E.T.*"

What makes Forman's adaptation so thoroughly successful? The answers are myriad, but some important decisions can be isolated and observed. Screenwriters Lawrence Hauben and Bo Goldman preserved as much of the novel's original dialogue as possible. The cast was chosen to closely match the physical descriptions

WHAT DO I SEE NEXT?

- In director Terry Gilliam's mind-bending mystery *12 Monkeys* (Universal Pictures, 1995), futuristic prisoner James Cole (Bruce Willis) travels back in time to discover the source of a deadly virus that wiped out human life on the earth's surface. When the scientists who give Cole his mission accidentally send him to the wrong time, Cole is taken to an insane asylum, where he meets the eccentric Jeffrey Goines (Brad Pitt), involuntarily setting off a disastrous chain of events. This film is rated R for violence and language.

- Based on Susanna Kaysen's memoir, *Girl, Interrupted* (Columbia Pictures, 1999) tells the story of a group of women in a mental institution in the 1960s. When new patient Susanna (Winona Rider) forms a friendship with sociopath Lisa (Angelina Jolie), the two begin making trouble, eventually leading to their escape. Lisa's dangerous influence brings Susanna to a tipping point, at which she must accept the consequences of her mental illness and relent to doctors' orders or follow Lisa toward their mutual destruction. This film is rated R for sexuality, language, and violence.

- Jack Nicholson's shocking descent into madness in *The Shining* (Warner Bros., 1980) is brought on by the strange power of the secluded resort hotel where he serves as winter caretaker with his wife and sensitive young son. Director Stanley Kubrick's long tracking shots and cold symmetry provide an unsettling visual contrast to Nicholson's terrifying performance. Far from the dangerous but lighthearted McMurphy, Nicholson's Jack Torrance is a man consumed by both inner and outer evil. This film adaptation of Stephen King's novel is rated R.

- *Amadeus* (Orion Pictures, 1984), directed by Miloŝ Forman, is an expansive rendering of the life of composer Wolfgang Amadeus Mozart, told through the eyes of his jealous contemporary Antonio Salieri. Confined to an insane asylum, Salieri looks back with regret on his career as a composer in the shadow of Mozart's magnetism and talent. Set amid the decadent European aristocracy of the 1800s, ornate costuming and stunning sets dominate Forman's vision in *Amadeus* (rated R for brief nudity).

- Based on Kesey's second novel, *Sometimes a Great Notion* (Universal, 1970) follows the Stamper family during a logger's strike in Oregon. Torn between pressures to join the strike and the need to survive in troubling economic times, the Stampers battle demons both inside their home and within their community. Mental illness plays a role in Lee Stamper, who has returned from college deeply depressed after his mother's death.

- *Easy Rider* (Columbia Pictures, 1969) tells of the quest of two bikers in the 1960s riding cross-country to New Orleans, Louisiana, for Mardi Gras. Set in a time when men with long hair were considered dangerous nonconformists, Captain America (Peter Fonda) and Billy the Kid (Dennis Hopper) are captured and jailed in a small southern town, where they meet George (Jack Nicholson), who agrees to travel with them. Sharing many themes with *One Flew over the Cuckoo's Nest*, *Easy Rider* asks the cost of freedom in a restrictive society and challenges perceptions of good and evil. *Easy Rider* is rated R.

- Forman's *Man on the Moon* (Universal Studios, 1999) stars Jim Carrey as Andy Kaufman, an eccentric comedian who tested the limits of his audience's patience. Like McMurphy, Kaufman is an indefinable spirit of rebellion and change, intentionally resisting expectations of who and what he is. This biopic follows Kaufman's rise to fame and mysterious disappearance, with an emphasis on his strange and alienating performances. This film is rated R for language and nudity.

of the characters in the novel, and once they arrived on location at Oregon State Hospital at Salem, head doctor (and Dr. Spivey in the film) Dean R. Brooks placed the men with actual patients whose symptoms seemed similar to those of each actor's character.

All adaptations must be simplified: novels are complex, privately experienced media, while a movie is enormously loud and bright and must be taken in during a single sitting. But how the original material is simplified makes all the difference. In the case of *One Flew over the Cuckoo's Nest*, the simple version of Kesey's story is the battle between Nurse Ratched and McMurphy. Compelling details in the novel (the Chief's extensive backstory, for example, and Cheswick's death in the pool by possible suicide) fell on the axe in favor of focusing the camera's eye on the battle at hand. This proved successful, due in large part to the dynamic of Louise Fletcher's Nurse Ratched and Jack Nicholson's McMurphy.

Another significant simplification of the source material is the Chief's demotion from narrator to character. For Dale Wasserman's play version of the novel, much of the Chief's narration was retained, and certainly the film could have done the same, had Forman chosen. But by removing the Chief's hallucinations and interior struggle to stay silent and expressionless despite being able to hear and speak, Forman cut away the most thought-provoking depths of the novel, ensuring a commercially successful film. Kael writes, "Forman replaces the novel's trippy subjectivity with a more realistic view of the patients. . . . They seem not much more insane than the nurses, the doctors, the attendants."

Seen from the outside, instead of from within Chief's thoughts, the story is a simple hero's tale, as McMurphy comes to save the day and is sacrificed so that the Chief can finally be free. This basic movement is present in the novel as well, but as Zubizarreta points out, "The film gives the cinema audience the kind of story that Chief creates for himself out of need, the kind of blown-up, irreverent, comic hero adventure in which we participate vicariously." This is to say not that the novel is not a delight—there are as many laugh-out-loud moments to be found in both film and novel—but that the stakes, as high as they are in the movie, are even higher in the book. After all, when the Chief begins his story in the novel, he is careful

to explain, "It's still hard for me to have a clear mind thinking on it. But it's the truth even if it didn't happen." There is no room in Forman's realistic, crowd-pleasing interpretation for this mystifying ambiguity.

The major complaints of critics—the adventure on the fishing boat and the laughs drawn from the patients' eccentric behaviors—stem from Forman's simplification of the novel. With enough time, he could have shown McMurphy's process of getting Dr. Spivey to approve the fishing trip, and with a narrator, he could have shown the patients from inside a fellow patient's mind. But would a film as experimental as Kesey's novel have been as successful, not only commercially and critically, but in its legacy? Ebert acknowledges in his 2003 review that *One Flew over the Cuckoo's Nest* "is on every list of favorite films." This is due to the performances handed in by Nicholson and Fletcher, along with Forman's decision, as a director of comedies, to broaden the base of the story as widely as possible. McCreadie writes, "An innovative treatment of this metaphorical tale might have proven too much."

The overarching metaphor that America is one big asylum is not particularly strong in the movie, though we can easily relate to McMurphy's frustrations: each of us has been forced to subsume our creativity by a cold institution at one time or another. Watching McMurphy lose to Nurse Ratched is heart-wrenching, in part because, as Kael writes, "We all fear being locked up among the insane, helpless to prove our sanity, perhaps being driven mad; this fear is almost as basic as that of being buried alive." Punished disproportionately for his violent actions (electroshock for breaking the nurse's station window, a lobotomy for an attempt on Nurse Ratched's life), McMurphy puts up a good fight, but the powers that be, armed to the teeth with rules and regulations, win out in the end. Had he strangled Nurse Ratched and gone back to prison for life, McMurphy would have been happier than to have had his spirit sucked out of him through the lobotomy. After all, he has never missed a World Series game in prison. Chief knows McMurphy would never want to live as a catatonic. Under the cover of darkness, he, as Zubizarreta describes it,

> assumes Mack's role, lovingly suffocates the hero, and bursts through the windows of the institution by using the very same washtub basin that McMurphy had tried earlier to lift

unsuccessfully: the gesture signifies Mack's transferral of power to Chief.

With this new power, Chief runs for freedom, while Taber, identified as the only other man committed to the ward indefinitely, hoots and hollers in proud celebration.

Forman's film, based off Kesey's beloved tour de force, tells the same story of good and evil through a different filter—that of realism. The camera, patient and steady, is fixed firmly outside the characters' minds. But because the film ultimately respects the spirit of its source material, the actions of Ratched and McMurphy ring true. Sweeping the major Academy Awards and written into history as a best film, a favorite film, *One Flew over the Cuckoo's Nest* reminds us to be ourselves without apology, to help those who are weaker to become strong, and to show loyalty to those we love. Ebert writes in his 2003 reflection on the film, "McMurphy succeeds and prevails as a character, despite the imperfections of the film, because he represents that cleansing spirit that comes along now and again to renew us."

Source: Amy Lynn Miller, Critical Essay on *One Flew over the Cuckoo's Nest*, in *Novels for Students*, Gale, Cengage Learning, 2014.

Roger Ebert

In the following review, Ebert discusses how the film has remained "enduringly popular as an anti-establishment parable."

There is a curiously extended closeup of Jack Nicholson about four-fifths of the way through *One Flew Over the Cuckoo's Nest*. We notice it because it lingers noticeably. It shows his character, R.P. McMurphy, lost in thought. It comes at the balancing point between the pranks and laughter of the earlier parts of the film, and the final descent into tragedy. What is he thinking? Is he planning new defiance, or realizing that all is lost?

The mystery of what McMurphy is thinking is the mystery of the movie. It all leads up to a late scene where he is found asleep on the floor next to an open window. By deciding not to escape, he has more or less chosen his own fate. Has his life force run out at last? After his uprising against the mental institution, after the inmates' rebellion that he led, after his life-affirming transformations of Billy and the Chief, after his comeback from an initial dose

> THE MOVIE'S SIMPLISTIC APPROACH TO MENTAL ILLNESS IS NOT REALLY A FAULT OF THE MOVIE, BECAUSE IT HAS NO INTEREST IN BEING ABOUT INSANITY. IT IS ABOUT A FREE SPIRIT IN A CLOSED SYSTEM."

of shock therapy, has he come at last to the end of his hope?

One Flew Over the Cuckoo's Nest (1975) is on every list of favorite films. It was the first film since *It Happened One Night* (1934) to win all five of the top Academy Awards, for best picture, actor (Nicholson), actress (Louise Fletcher), director (Milos Forman) and screenplay (Lawrence Hauben and Bo Goldman). It could for that matter have won, too, for cinematography (Haskell Wexler) and editing (Richard Chew). I was present at its world premiere, at the 1975 Chicago Film Festival, in the 3,000-seat Uptown Theatre, and have never heard a more tumultuous reception for a film (no, not even during *E.T.* at Cannes). After the screening, the young first-time co-producer, Michael Douglas, wandered the lobby in a daze.

But what did the audience, which loved the film so intensely, think it was about? The film is remembered as a comedy about the inmate revolt led by McMurphy, and the fishing trip, the all-night orgy, and his defiance of Nurse Ratched (Fletcher)—but in fact it is about McMurphy's defeat. One can call it a moral victory, and rejoice in the Chief's escape, but that is small consolation for McMurphy.

The film is based on Ken Kesey's 1962 best-selling novel, which Pauline Kael observed "contained the prophetic essence of the whole Vietnam period of revolutionary politics going psychedelic." Toned down for the 1970s into a parable about society's enforcement of conformism, it almost willfully overlooked the realities of mental illness in order to turn the patients into a group of cuddly characters ripe for McMurphy's cheerleading. We discover that the Chief is not really mute, Billy need not stutter, and others need not be paralyzed by shyness or fear. They will be cured not by Nurse Ratched's pills, Muzak and discussion groups, but by McMurphy liberating them to be guys—to watch the World Series on TV, go fishing, play pick-up basketball, get drunk, get laid. The message for these wretched inmates is: Be like Jack.

The movie's simplistic approach to mental illness is not really a fault of the movie, because it has no interest in being about insanity. It is about a free spirit in a closed system. Nurse Ratched, who is so inflexible, so unseeing, so blandly sure she is right, represents Momism at its radical extreme, and McMurphy is the Huck Finn who wants to break loose from her version of civilization. The movie is among other things profoundly fearful of women; the only two portrayed positively are McMurphy's hooker friends Candy and Rose. I mean this as an observation, not a criticism.

McMurphy's past is hinted at early in the film; he was sentenced to a prison farm for criminal assault against an underage girl ("she told me she was 18"), and has been sent to the mental institution for "evaluation." He is 38 years old, obviously a hell-raiser, and yet deeply democratic: He takes the patients at face value, treats their illnesses as choices that can be reversed, and tries by sheer force of will to bust them loose into a taste of freedom. The movie sees the patients in the same way. The photography and editing supply reaction shots that almost always have the same message: A given patient's fixed expression is misinterpreted because of the new context supplied by McMurphy. Consider the scene where McMurphy has stolen the boat and has his friends on board. When he is questioned, he introduces them all as doctors, and there are quick cuts to closeups of each one looking doctorly on cue. This has nothing to do with mental illness but everything to do with comedy.

Nicholson's performance is one of the high points in a long career of enviable rebels. Jack is a beloved American presence, a superb actor who even more crucially is a superb male sprite. The joke lurking beneath the surface of most of his performances is that he gets away with things because he knows how to, wants to, and has the nerve to. His characters stand for freedom, anarchy, self-gratification and bucking the system, and often they also stand for generous friendship and a kind of careworn nobility. The key to the success of his work in *About Schmidt* is that he conceals these qualities—he becomes one of the patients, instead of the liberating McMurphy.

If his performance is justly celebrated, Louise Fletcher's, despite the Oscar, is not enough appreciated. This may be because her Nurse Ratched is so thoroughly contemptible, and because she embodies so completely the qualities we all (men and women) have been taught to fear in a certain kind of female authority figure—a woman who has subsumed sexuality and humanity into duty and righteousness. Dressed in her quasi-military nurse's costume, with its little hat and its Civil War-style cape, she is dominatrix and warden, followed everywhere by the small, unspeaking nurse who is her acolyte.

Because we respond so strongly to her we hardly see Fletcher's performance. But watch her preternatural calm, her impassive "fairness," her inflexible adherence to the rules, as in the scene where she demands McMurphy get a majority vote in order to turn on the World Series on TV—this despite the fact that a majority of the patients don't understand what they are voting on. At the end, when McMurphy's final fate is decided upon, note how the male administrator tentatively suggests he be sent back to the prison farm, but Ratched firmly contradicts him: "We must not pass our responsibilities on to someone else."

Is *One Flew Over the Cuckoo's Nest* not a great film because it is manipulative, or is it great because it is so superbly manipulative? I can see it through either filter. It remains enduringly popular as an anti-establishment parable, but achieves its success by deliberately choosing to use the mental patients as comic caricatures. This decision leads to the fishing trip, which is at once the most popular, and the most false, scene in the movie. It is McMurphy's great joyous thumb in the eye to Ratched and her kind, but the energy of the sequence cannot disguise the unease and confusion of men who, in many cases, have no idea where they are, or why.

Consider by comparison the quiet, late-night speech by the Chief (Will Sampson), who speaks of his father. This is a window into a real character with real problems, who has chosen to be considered deaf and mute rather than talk about them. McMurphy's treatment works for him, and leads up to the sad perfection of the very final scenes—during which, if he could see them, McMurphy would be proud of his star pupil.

Milos Forman, born in Czechoslovakia in 1932, has become one of the great interpreters of American manners and mores. A leader of the Czech New Wave, his early films like *Loves of a Blonde* (1965) and *The Fireman's Ball* (1968) won worldwide audiences their use of paradoxical humor. (In what was seen as a parable of life under communism, the firemen arrive too late to save a barn, but when the farmer complains of the cold, they helpfully move him closer to the flames).

After the "Prague spring" came the Soviet crackdown, and Forman fled to America, where he has had extraordinary success (his *Amadeus* in 1984, produced by *Cuckoo* co-producer Saul Zaentz, won seven Oscars, including best picture and director). Look at the quintessentially American topics of his films: The runaway young people and conventional parents of *Taking Off* (1971), the anti-war musical *Hair* (1979), the New York historical romance *Ragtime* (1981), the defense of a rabble-rouser in *The People vs. Larry Flynt* (1996), the portrait of the McMurphy-like prankster Andy Kaufman in *Man on the Moon* (1999). He sees his adopted land in terms of its best nonconformist and outsider traditions, at a time when conformity is the new creed. His McMurphy succeeds and prevails as a character, despite the imperfections of the film, because he represents that cleansing spirit that comes along now and again to renew us.

Source: Roger Ebert, Review of *One Flew over the Cuckoo's Nest*, in *Chicago Sun Times*, February 2, 2003.

A. D. Murphy

In the following review, Murphy argues that the ideas presented in the film are earth-shattering, revolutionary, and relevant, and "their transfer to the screen is potent, contemporary, compelling."

Despite its seeming more like a fabulous remake of a dated story rather than the first film version of a noted book and play, *One Flew Over the Cuckoo's Nest* is brilliant cinema theatre. Jack Nicholson stars in an outstanding characterization of Ken Kesey's asylum anti-hero, McMurphy, and Milos Forman's direction of a superbly-cast film is equally meritorious. Louise Fletcher is excellent as the arch-nemesis ward nurse of the piece, handsomely produced by Saul Zaentz (of Fantasy Records) and Michael Douglas. The R-rated comedy-melodrama is one of United Artists' more impressive releases this year.

The past 15 years have covered what seems to be a century of enlightenment. Kesey, a major intellectual catalyst of the Beatnik era, is virtually an elder statesman of the avant-garde; he and others were stirring up the mind when less aware kids were doing their *American Graffiti* numbers. What used to be theatre-of-the-absurd has become, via and after JFK, the Beatles, Vietnam, youthful rebellion, Watergate, etc., almost conventional, cliche storytelling.

Thus, this long-delayed film emerges with a dual impact. To those under the age of, say 25, it will be a theatrically powerful but not especially challenging ensemble showpiece, which poses the now-familiar question, who is insane—the keepers or the kept? To those over that age barrier, it is intellectual nostalgia (a revisitation of the days when causes didn't choke from mace attacks), Lawrence Welk consciousness-raising, or a first-class Maugham, Galsworthy, Maxwell Anderson or Arthur Miller revival.

Sadly, the ideas herein are today as earth-shattering as The Pill, as revolutionary as pot, as relevant as the Cold War. Gladly, however, their transfer to the screen is potent, contemporary, compelling. And so, the young in head like the young in age can be drawn equally to this film as they are to Bette Midler and Manhattan Transfer.

It was Nov. 13, 1963 that Kirk Douglas returned to Broadway in a David Merrick-Edward Lewis Seven Arts-Eric Productions presentation of Dale Wasserman's legit adaptation of Kesey's book, directed by Alex Segal. *Hello, Dolly!* was in its Detroit tryout that week, and John F. Kennedy had two weeks or so left to live. Eleven weeks later, *Cuckoo's* had closed, a financial flop. But Douglas for years tried to get a film version off the ground, finally yielding to son Michael who pulled it off with Zaentz; meanwhile, both from its ideas and its versatility as a performers' showcase, local legit productions abounded. (However, play had a very long run, starting March 24, '71, off-Broadway with William Devane in McMurphy role—Ed.)

The film, made independently for over $3,000,000 before UA bought into it, traces the havoc wrecked in Nurse Fletcher's zombie-run mental ward when Nicholson (either an illness faker or a free spirit) displays a kind of leadership which neither Fletcher nor the system can handle. The story is a dramatic staple: *Stalag 17, Mr.*

Roberts, etc. "Us" against "Them-in-authority." The latter win, but not without a fight.

Lawrence Hauben and Bo Goldman are credited with the adaptation of the book (Wasserman's legit version is given separate passing credit). Despite the pointed directions of empathy and revulsion in the original material, the screenplay draws no sharp lines: Fletcher is all the more chilling in her bland autocracy for being apparently sincere in her vocation; Nicholson's real motives (for the offbeat behavior in a work camp that has sent him to the asylum for observations) are never clarified. All hands appear equally propelled by a perverse destiny.

The lengthy (133-minute) film first stresses broad vulgarity, as if to get all that out of the way, before moving into an ambivalence where one knows not whether to laugh or cry, or both. The cumulative impact is compellingly downbeat (nobody wins, everyone loses) and at the same time confusingly ambiguous (as befits the shallow liberalism of the time it so well depicts).

One must therefore forget the whole and concentrate solely on the excellent theatrics of the parts. Nicholson, Fletcher, Forman, cinematographers Haskell Wexler, Bill Butler and William Fraker; production designer Paul Sylbert; composer Jack Nitzsche (providing some haunting musical excerpts both in complementary and counterpoint effect); supervising editor Richard Chew, among others.

In addition, the major supporting players (with their 1963 Broadway production counterparts noted parenthetically) emerge with authority: Brad Dourif (Gene Wilder), the acne-marked stutterer whose immature sexual fantasies are clarified on the night of Nicholson's aborted escape; Sidney Lassick (Gerald S. O'Loughlin), a petulant auntie; Will Sampson (Ed Ames), the not-so-dumb Indian with whom Nicholson effects a strong rapport; William Redfield (William Daniels), the over-intelligent inmate.

Also, Sherman (Scatman) Crothers (Milton J. Williams), the night ward attendant whose hankering for liquor and girls precipitates Nicholson's wild party; Dean R. Brooks (Rex Robbins), in real life a hospital superintendent who makes a superb acting debut as a skeptical chief doctor, plus being the film's technical advisor; Delos V. Smith (Malcolm Atterbury), William Duell (Charles Tyner), Danny De Vito (Al Nesor), Vincent Schiavelli (Wesley Gale), among other

ward-mates; Nathan George (Lincoln Kilpatrick), a male nurse. Joan Tetzel did the head nurse part Fletcher handles so well here. Christopher Lloyd rounds out the crew, while Marya Small and Louisa Moritz are very chipper chippies.

The film's pacing is relieved by a group escape and fishing boat heist, right out of Mack Sennett, and some stabs at basketball in which Nicholson stations the tall Indian for telling effect. This in turn makes the shock therapy sequences and Dourif's suicide scene awesomely potent. The film picks one up in a theatrical centrifuge for over two hours; the trip is more than enough to make one forget the mossbound Sixties' thrust.—until it's all over.

Murf.

Source: A. D. Murphy, Review of *One Flew over the Cuckoo's Nest*, in *Variety*, November 18, 1975.

SOURCES

Canby, Vincent, "Jack Nicholson, the Free Spirit of *One Flew over the Cuckoo's Nest*," in *New York Times*, November 28, 1975, http://www.nytimes.com/packages/html/movies/bestpictures/cuckoo-re.html (accessed November 30, 2012).

Ebert, Roger, "Great Movies: *One Flew over the Cuckoo's Nest* (1975)," rogerebert.com, February 2, 2003, http://rogerebert.suntimes.com/apps/pbcs.dll/article?AID=/20030202/REVIEWS08/302020301/1023 (accessed November 30, 2012).

———, Review of *One Flew over the Cuckoo's Nest*, rogerebert.com, January 1, 1975, http://rogerebert.suntimes.com/apps/pbcs.dll/article?AID=/19750101/REVIEWS/501010348 (accessed November 30, 2012).

Faggen, Robert, Introduction to *One Flew over the Cuckoo's Nest*, Penguin Books, 2003, pp. xv–xxii.

Kael, Pauline, "The Bull Goose Loony," in *New Yorker*, December 1, 1975, pp. 131–36.

Kesey, Ken, *One Flew over the Cuckoo's Nest*, Penguin Books, 2003, p. 8.

McCreadie, Marsha, "*One Flew over the Cuckoo's Nest*: Some Reasons for One Happy Adaptation," in *Literature/Film Quarterly*, Vol. 5, No. 2, Spring 1977, pp. 125–31.

One Flew over the Cuckoo's Nest, directed by Miloš Forman, Warner Home Video, 2002, DVD.

Safer, Elaine B., "'It's the Truth Even if It Didn't Happen': Ken Kesey's *One Flew over the Cuckoo's Nest*," in *Literature/Film Quarterly*, Vol. 5., No. 2, Spring 1977, pp. 132–41.

Zubizarreta, John, "The Disparity of Point of View in *One Flew over the Cuckoo's Nest*," in *Literature/Film Quarterly*, Vol. 22, No. 1, January 1994, pp. 62–69.

FURTHER READING

Kesey, Ken, *Kesey*, edited by Michael Strelow, Oregon State University Press, 2005.

This collection of Kesey's notes and sketches compiled by Michael Strelow illuminates the creative process of the novelist as he wrote *One Flew over the Cuckoo's Nest*. Sketches of patients at the hospital where Kesey worked are particularly interesting in comparison to the film's imagery.

McGilligan, Patrick, *Jack's Life: A Biography of Jack Nicholson*, W. W. Norton, 1994.

McGilligan's study of Jack Nicholson includes behind-the-scenes glimpses into the filming of Nicholson's major roles and his methods as one of the most successful actors of his time.

Wasserman, Dale, *One Flew over the Cuckoo's Nest: A Play in Three Acts*, Samuel French, 1963.

The play version of *One Flew over the Cuckoo's Nest* notably starred Kirk Douglas as the raucous McMurphy in its 1964 Broadway debut. The Douglas family purchased the movie rights, and Kirk's son Michael Douglas produced the 1970 film version.

Wolfe, Tom, *The Electric Kool-Aid Acid Test*, Picador, 1968.

Wolfe's exposé on Kesey's adventures in the 1960s is as infamous as it is entertaining. Written in the then-emerging style of New Journalism, Wolfe's playful retelling of the life of Kesey includes details of his inspiration and his writing process for *One Flew over the Cuckoo's Nest*.

SUGGESTED SEARCH TERMS

One Flew over the Cuckoo's Nest

1975 AND film

mental institution AND film

Lawrence Hauben AND Bo Goldman

Milos Forman

1975 AND Academy Awards

Jack Nicholson AND Louise Fletcher

Jack Nicholson AND R. P. McMurphy

Milos Forman AND Ken Kesey

Ragtime

1981 E. L. Doctorow's novel *Ragtime* was a critical and literary success when it was published in 1975. The task of translating the novel's multiple plot lines and dozens of characters into a coherent film was a daunting one. To accomplish this, director Miloš Forman and screenwriter Michael Weller cut some characters, abbreviated others, and changed the focus of the story, from a panoramic view of America at the turn of the twentieth century to the story of one man's fight for justice and the people who are affected by his plight.

The film of *Ragtime* that reached theaters in 1981 weaves in and out of the lives of historical and fictional characters from the book. It tells the story of Evelyn Nesbit Thaw, a former show-girl, and her husband Harry, from the prominent Cleveland Thaw family, who gunned down famous architect Stanford White in full view of hundreds of witnesses, one of the great true crimes of the twentieth century. It tells the story of a poor Jewish immigrant who begins the story as a street vendor and ends up as one of the most successful and powerful movie directors of his time. It tells the story of a middle-class family in suburban New York who represent the repressive yet hopeful standards of their day, living lives of calm prosperity until circumstances make each of them reconsider who they are. Most of all, however, it focuses on the story of Coalhouse Walker Jr., a black man, a successful piano player on the verge of starting a family

© *AF archive | Alamy*

before he is subjected to ridicule and humiliation while driving down the street one sunny afternoon. His struggle for justice after his car is defaced and vandalized eventually drives Walker to lead vigilante raids and then to take over the wealth-laden museum that is the J. Pierpont Morgan Library, creating a racial standoff at a time when racial divides were enforced, not discussed.

Ragtime was nominated for eight Academy Awards and features standout performances by Howard E. Rollins Jr., Elizabeth McGovern, and film legend James Cagney, to name just a few in a rich cast. It was originally rated R for brief nudity and for the use of racial slurs that were common at the story's time, though recent DVD versions have been edited for a PG rating.

PLOT SUMMARY

As the opening credits for *Ragtime* roll, viewers see a couple in formal attire on a darkened stage, dancing in a stilted, mannered way to a song that may have been popular in the nineteenth century. The scene soon changes to the hands of a black, cigar-smoking piano player, Coalhouse Walker Jr., playing music to accompany a silent news reel that announces breaking stories at the start of the twentieth century: a heat wave in New York; black social leader Booker T. Washington's famous dinner with President Roosevelt; a rare Gutenberg bible acquired by wealthy industrialist J. Pierpont Morgan; a tour by escape artist Harry Houdini; and the unveiling of a nude statue in the tower of Madison Square Garden, designed by famed architect Stanford White. Evelyn Nesbit Thaw, billed in the newsreel's title card as a "former model," denies having posed for the statue. This sequence mixes historical details. The heat wave was actually in 1911. Washington's dinner at the White House was in 1901. Nesbit married Harry Thaw in 1905, and she had nothing to do with the creation of Augustus Saint-Gaudens' statue *Diana* (which is shown in the film spinning in the wind, though the real bronze statue, sculpted in 1893, was too heavy to be moved that way). It is historically accurate that

FILM TECHNIQUE

- When Booker T. Washington enters the Morgan Library, Forman uses a wide shot: Washington is in the middle of the frame, but he is small, shot from a distance. The effect is to combine the grandeur of the building with the historic significance of the man. Later, when Coalhouse Walker exits the library, he is first viewed with a subjective camera, shot from over the shoulders of an armed policeman and Police Commissioner Waldo. After Waldo gives the command and the policeman shoots him, the camera shows him from a wide shot that is almost identical to the one that framed Washington. This repetition serves to give the renegade Walker status equal to the famous human rights activist Washington for a few seconds, before he falls over and dies.

- As Walker approaches the Emerald Isle Fire Station in his Model T, the camera angle is from over his shoulder, shot from the car's back seat. This subjective camera gives viewers a perspective that is similar to Walker's: the audience sees the fire engine as it is being moved into the road and, like Walker, does not recognize the danger at first, piecing together the implied hostility in the situation as the car slowly rolls to a stop.

- When the scene first moves to Spring Lake, Forman introduces the festive beachside setting with a low camera, shooting up at actors from below the waist, until it picks up the little boy running up the sidewalk from the Essex and Sussex Hotel. When he reaches the end of the sidewalk and runs along the boardwalk, away from the camera, the camera rises up in a crane shot and tracks his progress.

- The most commonly used camera angle in this film is the eye-level shot. The camera is positioned in a medium location using a medium lens, showing what a human observer would see from that location. It is a neutral angle that generally positions actors alone or in pairs, keeping viewers involved in the scene by making them look at the proceedings in the same way that they view the real world.

- Eye line matching is an editing technique that ensures continuity. It involves matching shots that follow one another, with the level of the character's eyes in the first shot matching that in the second shot, implying a conversation when each shot only shows one person. This technique is especially significant in the scenes with Police Commissioner Rhinelander Waldo. James Cagney, playing Waldo, was 82 years old when he made *Ragtime* and in fragile health, coming out of a twenty-year retirement. Many of the scenes of Waldo conversing with another character show only Cagney or the other actor, not both. With eye line matching, the film's editors were able to create the effect of a continuous conversation, whether Cagney was actually responding to the other actor or filming his lines at some later time.

- A voice-over is used at the end of the film. As Walker is trying to decide whether to give himself up or blow himself up, he prays aloud for guidance. As he speaks, the camera shifts to the outside of the library, showing a quick sequence of scenes of policemen moving into position, ready for action. While Walker's voice on the soundtrack conveys the emotional trouble in his heart, the visuals of armed men preparing to kill him convey the physical danger he is in. Each element works with the other to increase suspense as the film moves toward its climax.

Stanford White designed Madison Square Garden and that he commissioned the *Diana* statue for it, and that he had an affair with Evelyn Nesbit when she was young.

The story begins with a bacchanal dinner among socially prominent New Yorkers, dressed in tuxedos and wearing laurel wreaths. They are served by scantily clad dancing girls. Harry Thaw appears at the front door and tricks the doorman into admitting him, along with several armed men. He confronts White, shouting through the door, and then he and the other men break the door down. Seeing the men with their arms around the women, Thaw threatens to report the party to the police: in return, White points to the commissioner of police, Rhinelander Waldo, seated at one of the tables. Thaw leaves.

At an estate in New Rochelle, New York, a family sits down to dinner. The father announces that his factory has had a good month, giving credit to his wife's younger brother, who works at his factory designing fireworks displays. Before they can start their meal, they are interrupted by a scream, and through the open window they see a maid running across the lawn. She leads them to a newborn baby lying in their garden. The mother takes the child in her arms and orders that they call the family doctor.

The doctor is finishing his examination when some policemen arrive with Sarah, a young African American woman found hiding nearby. When she refuses to talk, the police inspector orders the doctor to examine her to see whether she has given birth recently. After hearing that Sarah will go to jail and the baby to an orphanage, the family's mother asks whether the police will let the young woman stay in their home. Her husband objects, but she takes him aside to talk to him.

In New York, Harry Thaw and Evelyn Nesbit Thaw talk to lawyers. Thaw bullies Evelyn into saying that she wants the statue, presumably modeled by her, taken down from public display. Thaw insists that White had put the statue there to humiliate him; Evelyn looks bored.

While Thaw and Evelyn attend a show at Madison Square Garden, the younger brother from the New Rochelle family notices her across the room, then looks up at the statue of Diana, making the connection in his mind. White enters to applause from the diners. Thaw goes to White's table, draws a gun, and shoots the

architect in the head. As people scream around him, Thaw calmly smiles and gives his pistol to a policeman.

The film shows another newsreel, with Coalhouse Walker again playing the piano accompaniment. In addition to stories about the vice president, Harry Houdini, and immigration, the newsreel announces that Mrs. Thaw, mother of the accused murderer, has returned from Europe.

In a meeting with Mrs. Thaw and her lawyers, Evelyn describes sadistic abuse she suffered from Harry. The lawyers want to use her testimony to prove that Harry was insane. After Mrs. Thaw leaves, her lawyers offers Evelyn a million dollars if she will help them with Harry's insanity defense and then divorce him. In the next scene, at Harry Thaw's trial, Evelyn testifies to the same sadistic acts, but this time she says it is Stanford White who beat her, and she testifies that she told Harry about this abuse shortly before he shot White.

Evelyn leaves the courthouse and is driven through the busy Jewish neighborhood of the Lower East Side of Manhattan, with the younger brother of the New Rochelle family, infatuated with her, following in another car. They are stopped by a delivery-wagon horse that has died in the street. Evelyn steps out to look and is called over by a man selling his artwork silhouettes, the character given the name Tateh in the film's credits. Tateh convinces her to pose for him. His young daughter sits nearby, and Evelyn is clearly enchanted by the child. Another man comes and talks to Tateh in Yiddish. Tateh excuses himself, leaving his daughter in Evelyn's care. He hurries to a clothes store and, finding the store locked, breaks through the window. He chases an undressed man from the store, followed by his wife. Tateh returns to take his child, takes her upstairs to his apartment, and throws his wife's belongings out the window on her. He symbolically severs his relationship with her by dramatically tearing his shirt.

The scene changes to Coalhouse Walker auditioning for the band at the Clef Club, showing his interest in working regularly. The Clef Club was a real nightclub in Harlem in the early 1900s.

Tateh and his daughter arrive in Philadelphia on an electric train. Wandering the street, he sees a toy store and asks his daughter to give him the book he made for her, a collection of pictures that show the figure of a girl ice skating as their pages are flipped. The owner of the shop offers to buy any flip books Tateh can produce.

At the Clef Club, Walker is a featured performer, introduced by name to the audience.

Evelyn returns to the Lower East Side with a present for Tateh's daughter. She is followed into his abandoned apartment by the younger brother. Winning over her skepticism and fear, he haltingly asks her for a date, and Evelyn accepts.

Back in New Rochelle, the family tires of waiting for the younger brother, so they begin dinner without him. They are interrupted, however, by Walker, who comes to the door looking for Sarah. The father checks with Sarah, but she refuses to see Walker. When he goes back to the kitchen, the father finds Walker with the baby in his arms, proud and delighted at first meeting his child.

A jury finds Thaw not guilty by reason of insanity: he has escaped the death penalty, but the judge sentences him to the mental institute at Mattawan. Thaw rejects the verdict, insisting on his sanity. Outside, Evelyn is shuttled away in a car, with great media attention. Her new publicity team—agent, dance instructor, manager, and lawyer—starts the process of exploiting her by having her pose with the now-scandalous *Diana* statue.

Arriving home drunk, she is met in her hall by the younger brother, who has not had a chance to talk to her. He is skeptical about her new team and offers to take more control of her career. Evelyn takes off her clothes, and, as they are kissing, she is served with a divorce decree from lawyers from Harry Thaw's mother, acting as Harry's legal guardian: instead of the million dollars promised, Evelyn will only receive twenty-five thousand because she has been having an affair. Evelyn is outraged, having just saved Harry's life. The young man offers to help her fight the charge, but Evelyn, resigned, signs the divorce document. She is paid the money in cash, and she counts it as they leave.

Because his brother-in-law handles the company's legal matters, the younger brother asks Evelyn to come to New Rochelle and meet his family. He is delighted when she accepts the invitation. In the next scene, however, she fails to show up for the dinner she agreed to attend. Once again, the doorbell rings as they sit down to eat—it is Coalhouse Walker, with flowers for Sarah. The note on the flowers moves Sarah to

tears. When she agrees to meet him, they fall into each other's arms. She agrees to marry him, and he leaves the house jubilant, dancing and skipping all the way to his car.

The younger brother goes to see Evelyn in the studio where she is learning her dance routine. As he becomes increasingly angry, acting as obsessive as Thaw had been, Evelyn's manager intervenes and pulls her away.

Walker is driving through New Rochelle when his car is stopped by a fire engine that has pulled out of the Emerald Isle firehouse into the street in front of him. Another engine blocks the back of his car. When Walker asks when the trucks will be moved, the firemen say that he must pay a toll of twenty-five dollars to drive on this road. Walker leaves to get a policeman: when he returns, has car has been moved into a horse stable, and horse dung has been thrown into the seat. Willie Conklin, the fire chief, tells the policeman that Walker parked illegally in front of the firehouse, and to keep peace, the officer tells Walker to just clean out his car and leave. Walker insists that the man who vandalized his car should clean it, and when he will not leave, he is arrested.

From jail, Walker phones the father, the only person he knows in New Rochelle, and the man posts his bail. When they return to the car, it has been vandalized with broken windows, broken mirrors, and tree branches thrown on it.

Walker sees a lawyer, an older black man, who tells him to just forget and accept what happened to him. The lawyer explains that he has more pressing issues to fight for. Walker then goes through several city departments for justice, but the staff of each department says that the matter is another department's responsibility.

While the father is talking to Sarah, trying to get her to have Walker drop the case, the younger brother comes in, incredulous. His father offers to pay for the car's repairs himself if Walker will just marry Sarah and forget his vengeance, but she says she cannot reason with him.

Sarah runs off during the night so that she can be at the train station in White Plains, New York, when Vice President Charles Fairbanks arrives on a whistle-stop tour. She races toward the vice president as he speaks, shouting that she wants justice for Coalhouse Walker, but a policeman stops her and beats her with a club.

They take her back to New Rochelle, but she only has time to speak to Walker once before she dies.

A call comes in to the Emerald Isle firehouse. As the firemen leave, they are shot down by masked men. One man asks a survivor where Conklin is and is told that he is off that night. At the police station the next day, the police chief reads a note from Walker, who insists that Conklin be turned over to him and that his car be repaired to its original condition. He threatens to keep burning fire departments and killing firemen. Conklin denies any responsibility for Walker.

After the police go to the family's house to suggest that the baby might be used to lure Walker out of hiding, the younger brother goes to the Clef Club to warn him. The people there deny knowing where Walker is, but they accept the younger brother's business card. The card ends up in the hands of the police. The younger brother promises to have nothing to do with Walker's problems, but he soon joins Walker's outlaw band, offering his expertise in fireworks and explosives.

Protesters, reporters, and newsreel cameramen surround the New Rochelle house. The father arranges to move the family away.

A delivery truck pulls up in front of the J. P. Morgan Library in Manhattan and leaves a box on the sidewalk. When the guard comes out to retrieve the box, armed men enter and send him running. The delivery truck returns with supplies for a siege. To draw attention, the insurgents set off a box of explosives in the middle of the street.

At Spring Lake, New Jersey, the family, including Sarah's baby, watches a movie being filmed on the beach. The star is Evelyn Nesbit; the director is Tateh, who has risen from a street peddler to a powerful film director. The young son of the New Rochelle family forms a silent, unspoken attachment to Tateh's daughter. The mother comes to take her son away, but Tateh tells her to stay. He gives the boy one of his flip books as a present. The attraction between Tateh and the mother is obvious—they both act a little guilty when the father arrives.

Policemen and crowds of onlookers surround the Morgan Library when Commissioner of Police Waldo arrives to run the situation. The library's curator explains that the building is filled with invaluable treasures. Waldo approaches the library with a megaphone, and a seventeenth-century goblet is thrown out into the street with the library's phone number. The police take over a nearby house in order to phone the library. Walker gives Waldo the same demands he gave the New Rochelle police: his car restored and custody of Willie Conklin.

Booker T. Washington is brought in to talk to Walker. He approaches the library and is admitted "in the name of our people." Washington explains to Walker how his violence is detrimental to the cause of racial justice in America. His life's work has been to convince white people to not fear black people, and Walker's actions feed the stereotypes and fears that Washington has been trying to erase. Walker, in tears, explains how Sarah died begging for justice. Washington assures him that his trial will be swift and that he will have a painless execution, but Walker continues to insist on the same demands he asked for before.

A nighttime attempt to raid the building is anticipated by the rebels, who set off explosives on the library's roof.

The father is called away from an elaborate dinner thrown by Tateh. Tateh speaks loftily about film aesthetics; Evelyn is bored, but Mother listens, enraptured. In the hall, the father and some policemen explain to the mother that they want to take Walker's baby away, but she refuses to permit that. She and her husband argue, and he leaves for New York.

Armed policemen break into a house looking for Conklin. They start pulling an elderly man out of bed before he points them toward Conklin, hiding on the floor next to the bed. Conklin is taken in his underwear to Commissioner Waldo, who puts Conklin on the phone with Walker. He is not able to talk Walker out of his demands, and a crowd of policemen carry him away.

Father arrives, and Waldo puts him on the phone with Walker, who agrees to see him. In the library, he asks whether Walker has talked to his brother-in-law, not knowing that the young man is sitting a few feet from him, hidden by a hood and blackface makeup.

Walker offers to let Conklin live if Waldo will deliver his restored car and allow his men to escape. When the father leaves, the men object, but Walker convinces them that he has a complex plot.

Waldo is suspicions of the offer. He believes that if Walker has a choice to either face execution (if he gives himself up) or blow himself and the library up, he will choose the latter. The father, trusting Walker's honesty, offers to wait in the library when the men leave, confident that Walker will not kill him. Walker, he explains, wants to have his case brought to court.

Before going to the library, the father tries to phone his family, only to find that they have checked out of the hotel and left no message for him.

The police plan to follow the car, assuming that it will be easy to trace a brand new Model T carrying a handful of black men. Walker has to convince his men that it makes sense for him to stay; they can spread the word about what happened to him, but if he went with them he would only be hunted, night and day. They leave reluctantly. They escape by having the black men hide down in the car while the younger brother, a white man whom the authorities do not know about, takes the wheel.

Walker receives a phone call from the younger brother, telling him that the men have escaped. Walker chases the father out and then anguishes over the decision of whether or not to blow up the library, praying for guidance before surrendering with his hands up. Waldo orders a police marksman to shoot the unarmed man dead on the library steps.

The same formal dancers shown during the opening credits are intercut with scenes of what happened to the characters later. Mother and Tateh drive off together from the New Rochelle house, taking the children with them, as the father watches from a window. Harry Thaw is released from the asylum at Mattawan, driving off with a carload of his wealthy friends, drinking champagne. Harry Houdini continues to perform amazing escapes as newspapers circulated in the crowd below him announce in full-page headlines "War Declared," a probable reference, given the film's time frame, to the outbreak of the First World War in 1914.

CHARACTERS

Baron Ashkenazy
See Tateh

Willie Conklin
Conklin is the chief of the fire station in New Rochelle. When Walker's car is stopped by the firemen, Conklin steps forward as the lead instigator in race-baiting. Although there is no proof that Conklin himself defaced the car, there is no doubt that he was involved.

When Walker's men attack Conklin's Emerald Isle Fire Station and threaten to attack others, Conklin refuses to accept any responsibility for what they are doing. When the Walker gang poses a serious threat to millionaire J. P. Morgan's library, the authorities turn on Conklin, having him dragged away in his underwear from the house where he is hiding. Police Commissioner Waldo shows open disgust with the lower-class Conklin and is clearly willing to turn him over to Walker if it will protect the library. Kenneth McMillan plays Conklin as a crude, ignorant bigot, his fumbling often played for comic effect.

Father
James Olson plays the soft-spoken, mild-mannered father of the New Rochelle family. The character is never named, and the role is listed simply as "father." He is cautious and conservative, hesitant to give aid to Sarah when she is found to have abandoned her newborn baby on his property and skeptical about allowing Coalhouse Walker into his house, asking him to enter through the back door, as was common for black Americans at the time. As the events of this story begin, the father seems pleased with his position in society and with his family's situation in the world.

Throughout the film, this man's sense of compassion grows. When Walker is put in jail for fighting against the people who damaged his car, the father posts bail for him and offers to restore the car himself if it will give Walker peace. He later leaves his family at the vacation hotel in Spring Lake to talk to Walker at the Morgan Library, eventually putting his life on the line by volunteering to become a hostage because he feels that Walker is an honest man. Still, he loses his wife and child when his wife runs off with the exciting film director, Baron Ashkenazy, taking their child with her.

Grandfather
The credits list the character of "grandfather," identifying the old man who is usually seen standing around the family from New Rochelle. This character has no lines, and he is never referred to on-screen.

Little Boy

The character identified in the credits as "little boy" is the son of the mother and father of the New Rochelle family. His diminished role marks one of the main differences between the film and Doctorow's novel. In the book, Doctorow gives readers his impressions from his point of view, leading many readers to assume that he is the narrator of the book. In the film, though, the character does not even have any speaking lines, and he is rarely seen.

Little Girl

The character identified as "little girl" in the credits is the daughter of Tateh and his unfaithful wife. When Tateh meets and falls in love with the mother of the New Rochelle family, he uses the close, immediate friendship between his daughter and her son to invite their family to his party.

Mother

Mother is the woman of the New Rochelle home; like the rest of that family, she is not named in the film. Mary Steenburgen plays her as a woman in transition. She is capable of making strong, iron-clad decisions, as when she insists that Sarah, who has had a baby but has been abandoned by her lover, should move into their house. She is also easily flustered, however, flying into a rage when the Coalhouse Walker story becomes a national event and police guards are placed in her house to watch Walker's baby. Throughout much of the story she is shown to be a woman who lives in the shadow of her husband but who is not afraid to express her opinions within her own household.

Forman makes it clear to audiences from the moment that she meets Baron Ashkenazy (Tateh) that she is attracted to him. He represents a kind of wild existence, from his ethnic background to his artistic livelihood in filmmaking, that is very different from her life with her husband. In Doctorow's novel, she marries Ashkenazy after the death of her husband, but in this film her husband watches as she drives away from his house with her family in Ashkenazy's car.

Evelyn Nesbit

Evelyn Nesbit was the first feature role for Elizabeth McGovern, who was nominated for an Academy Award for her work. She plays Evelyn as a naïve, sexually curious girl from a poor background who is overwhelmed when she marries into the prestigious Thaw family of Pittsburgh. Although she thinks nothing of her former affair with Stanford White, the thought of it drives her husband, Harry, to murder White. While describing Harry's sexual proclivities for his lawyers, she is easily persuaded to perjure herself by claiming on the witness stand that the things he did were in fact things that he found out White had done to her. When Harry's lawyers burst in on her in the middle of an affair with the younger brother, Evelyn does not cover her body while they talk money, and she accepts with worldly resignation the fact that they will not pay what they offered for her testimony. She goes on to anger the younger brother by drifting away from his life without explanation, showing her lack of concern for others.

A ten-minute segment covering Evelyn's seduction by Emma Goldman, a real-life activist for women's rights, was filmed, repeating a story line laid out in Doctorow's novel. It was cut from the final picture but is available as an extra on the DVD.

After losing the Thaw family money, Evelyn eventually moves into films. She has a successful relationship with the director Baron Ashkenazy, the character known in the film credits and throughout the novel as Tateh. When the family from New Rochelle watches them filming a pirate movie at Spring Lake, it is Evelyn's third collaboration with Ashkenazy.

Sarah

Sarah enters the story as a wild woman who has been captured by the police for abandoning her newborn child. The white family that owns the property where her infant was found takes her in as a household servant. When the baby's father, Coalhouse Walker Jr., comes to find her, Sarah refuses to see him; she has been abandoned by him once before and is not willing to trust him again. He eventually wins her confidence, however, and she agrees to marry him.

Sarah's death is caused by a combination of her loyalty and her ignorance. She goes to see the vice president while he is stopping in a nearby town, naïvely thinking that she can get close enough to him to tell him about Walker's struggle for restitution. When she approaches in the crowd, shouting toward the podium, the vice president's security forces beat her to the ground. She dies soon after from the injuries she sustains. She is happy when she is dying, though, telling Walker with pride that she has made his name known.

Tateh

Mandy Patinkin plays this character, who is called Tateh (the Yiddish word for "father") in the novel and the film credits. In just one place in the film he calls himself Baron Ashkenazy, which Doctorow's novel clarifies as the name he is known by in films.

Tateh starts life as a street vendor in the bustling squalor of Manhattan's Lower East Side. He is doing a silhouette portrait of Evelyn Nesbit when neighbors gives him disturbing news in Yiddish. He leaves his daughter with Evelyn and races to a nearby storefront, where he finds his wife (played by comedian Fran Drescher) having an affair with another man. He goes to their apartment and throws her belongings into the street.

He and the little girl move to Philadelphia, skipping a long segment in which the novel recounts his involvement in the famous textile mill strike in Lawrence, Massachusetts. In Philadelphia he finds a toy store that is willing to pay him for the moving-picture books that he makes with his silhouettes. The story catches up with Tateh years later, when he is a celebrated movie director, working with Evelyn as his leading lady.

In his rise from street artist in a crowded tenement to film director, dressed in fine clothes and hosting expensive dinners, Tateh represents the promise of American democracy.

Evelyn Nesbit Thaw

See Evelyn Nesbit

Harry K. Thaw

Thaw, an actual historical person, shot architect Stanford White to death on June 25, 1906. The film prepares viewers for this event by showing him in several early scenes to be a blustering, angry, insecure man who blames White for publicly humiliating his wife by using her as the model of a nude statue. When he shouts accusations at White, most of the people in the film look at Thaw with pity or disgust, recognizing him as a crazed zealot. After he shoots White, Thaw seems pleased with himself, and he cheerfully turns his gun over to the authorities. During his trial, his one objection is that his lawyers

are trying to make him sound insane: they are going for an insanity plea to save his life, but Thaw believes that his reputation should be upheld.

In a coda after the main story of the film is over, Thaw is shown leaving Mattawan, the asylum he was confined to after his trial. He shows no remorse as he climbs into a car with other wealthy friends as news cameras roll. They drink champagne and laugh, implying that Thaw has taken advantage of the legal system to avoid the death penalty.

Mrs. Thaw

Mrs. Thaw, the mother of Harry K. Thaw, is a society matron from Pittsburgh. She is devious and manipulative: once she takes over Harry's defense she arranges to bribe Evelyn for perjured testimony, and when Harry is found to be insane she takes over as his legal guardian to refuse Evelyn the bribe settlement she was promised.

Rhinelander Waldo

New York Police Commissioner Waldo was a minor character in Doctorow's novel, but he became a central focus of Forman's film when film legend James Cagney was offered any role in the movie that he wanted and he chose the part of the police commissioner. Although Cagney was 81 years old when the film was made (whereas the real Waldo was 32), the role was written for him, giving him many of the lines that in the book belong to the Manhattan district attorney, Charles Whitman, who does not appear as a character in the film.

Cagney plays Waldo as a canny, sympathetic character. He is corrupt enough to attend Stanford White's bacchanal party early in the film, and he is brash enough to threaten, late in the film, to turn Conklin over to the revolutionaries who will probably kill him, but he seems sympathetic to Walker's dispute. At the end of the story, when he orders Walker to be shot dead on the steps of the Morgan Library, it shows a cold, vicious side to his character that was not previously revealed.

Coalhouse Walker Jr.

The story of Coalhouse Walker Jr. was just one of the intertwining plots in Doctorow's novel. In choosing to focus the film on the Walker story, Forman and his screenwriter, Michel Weller, made an international name for Howard E.

Rollins Jr., who was nominated for an Academy Award for Best Supporting Actor.

Walker's character goes through a few changes in the course of this film. He starts off as an unidentified pianist, shown playing background music at a silent movie house. The first thing viewers know about him is that he abandoned Sarah after she became pregnant. When Walker finds secure employment at the Clef Club, he goes to find Sarah and is delighted to see his son, but when he is humiliated at the fire station he is not willing to let the insult go, as so many victims of racial abuse did at that time. He becomes a vigilante, unwilling to listen to the eminent black leader Booker T. Washington or the father of the New Rochelle family, who treats him respectfully as a friend.

The film's climax comes when Walker is left alone in the Morgan Library, which is wired with explosives. He does not have to worry about saving the lives of his men or of the father, who was sent in as a hostage. He can destroy the building, obliterating millions of dollar of historic treasures and artworks in return for the destruction of his car, and he prays for guidance. In the end he decides that he will not be destructive, even though he has no reason to let the library stand.

Booker T. Washington

Booker T. Washington was a real-life political and social figure, one of the most famous voices on the rights of African Americans at the turn of the twentieth century. Forman foreshadows his part of the story early in the film, when the silent newsreel announces that Washington was the first Negro to be invited to the White House to eat dinner with the president. This early mention reminds readers of the historical significance of the man. Later, when Walker and his men are a threat to the Morgan Library, Washington, as a leading Negro voice, is called upon to speak to him. Washington's authority is established when he stands outside of the library and calls out, in a deep voice, "In the name of our people, open this door!" Played by Moses Gunn, he sits down with Walker and, like the real-life Booker T. Washington, advocates nonviolent change to improve the position of black Americans. Walker is moved by the great man but eventually decides that his quest for vengeance is different from Washington's larger concern for his race.

Stanford White

The 1906 murder of Stanford White was one of the most famous news stories of the first decade of the twentieth century, and it stands as a centerpiece for this film. White was a world-famous architect who designed the new Madison Square Garden building after the old one burned down. Famed novelist Norman Mailer plays White in the film as a lively, promiscuous man who enjoys his wealth and the company of young ladies. The film does not verify whether he did or did not have an affair with Evelyn Nesbit, as history says he did: when Nesbit's husband, Harry K. Thaw, accuses White of "ruining" her, White just turns away, annoyed with the young man. The only thing that riles White out of his general sense of bemusement is when Thaw and his friends break down a door that White declares is "priceless."

Younger Brother

Brad Dourif plays the character who is named only as "younger brother" in both the film credits and the novel. He is a young man who lives in New Rochelle with the family of his sister, her husband, and their son.

Throughout the course of the film, the younger brother's motivation changes several times. At first, he is pleased to hear that his brother-in-law values his work and is considering him as a possible partner in the future at the plant manufacturing patriotic displays, where the younger brother is in charge of the fireworks. When he sees Evelyn, though, he is smitten. He follows her, asks her out, and eventually enters into an affair with her. When she stands him up, however, he turns his attention to helping Walker, who has become a fugitive. He finds Walker and asks to be allowed to use his knowledge of munitions, making him the only white person in Walker's band of renegades and giving the younger brother a sense of fulfillment in his life.

In Doctorow's novel, the younger brother ends up in Mexico, where he continues his experience of fighting for justice against the law by joining the famous Mexican revolutionary Emiliano Zapata in the Mexican Revolution. In the film, his white face is instrumental in helping the members of Walker's gang escape while police are looking for a car full of black men.

THEMES

Family

The film of *Ragtime* narrows the focus on the role of family, which was one of the less prominent themes in Doctorow's novel. The central story of Coalhouse Walker is tied together by his desire to marry Sarah and to raise his son with her, showing him to be a flawed man who once was willing to let her leave his life, a flaw that becomes relevant when his pride drives him to violence. Walker and Sarah are contrasted with a "typical" middle-class American family living in the New York suburb of New Rochelle, so typical that the family members are known only by their family identities: father, mother, younger brother. These characters, who seem at first to fit the stereotypes of their familial functions, surprise viewers throughout the film by growing beyond their designated roles. Father, for instance, starts the film as the sort of autocratic ruler of his household that one might expect of a father in the early 1900s, but actor James Olson plays him with a sensitivity that makes it entirely believable that this man would offer to become Walker's hostage. The younger brother, a rising young businessman working for his brother-in-law, finds himself pulled by passion, first for Evelyn and then for justice, abandoning his business career. The mother runs her household, but she also leaves her house to live with the film director who has filled her mind with a view of how exciting the creative life can be.

Doctorow's novel mirrors the New Rochelle family with another family whose members are only identified by their family position. By calling the film director Tateh and his wife Mameh, he introduces another aspect to the idea of family, drawing attention to the ways in which immigrant families and established American families are the same.

Racism

The way the firemen of the Emerald Island Fire Station mistreat Walker is indicative of a racist society. They pick a fight with him, stopping him from driving down the street, because they are offended to see that a black man has a better car than they can afford. They are bold enough to block his path and later, when Walker returns accompanied by a policeman, to vandalize his car, confident that the law will side with the majority race, regardless of who is right.

In his quest for justice, Walker runs into several people who speak to him about the sad, practical realities of the racist society he lives in. The black lawyer he consults, played by Ted Ross, refuses to take his case because there are many worse injustices against black people that he feels need addressing: the fact that Walker even owns a car to be vandalized tells this lawyer that he is better off than most black people of the time. Later, Police Commissioner Waldo sends Booker T. Washington in to talk to Walker. The character in the film explains a position that the real Washington took toward race relations: that black Americans must be patient and nonthreatening if they are to advance socially. Over the course of decades, many thinkers have disagreed with Washington's passive approach, feeling that social gains would come more quickly if whites were made to feel uncomfortable about society's inequality.

Social Class

This film highlights the strong divisions between social classes in America, a country that has always prided itself on being a classless society. The opening scenes establish what life was like for the wealthy in Stanford White's social circle. They attend parties where liquor flows and hired women dance provocatively. Significantly, Reinhardt Waldo, who is not a true member of the upper class, is allowed to associate with them, taking advantage of his position as the commissioner of police. After White is murdered in full view of witnesses at an extravagant dinner floor show, his murderer, Harry Thaw, escapes the death penalty only because Thaw's mother has the means to hire the best lawyers for him.

The family from New Rochelle represents the middle class. Unlike the members of White's or Thaw's social circle, the father has to work for a living, building his business up. They live in a large house and they have hired servants, but they also have extended family living with them. When the younger brother offers to have his lawyers look into Evelyn's situation, he does so almost bragging that his business gives him access to lawyers, but then he backtracks and admits that the lawyers do not actually work for him but for his brother-in-law.

At the bottom of the social spectrum in the world of this movie are people of notable ethnic and racial backgrounds. African Americans, of course, are relegated to the lowest social

READ, WATCH, WRITE

- Before Miloš Forman, Robert Altman was the producer's first choice to direct the film adaptation of *Ragtime*. Altman's customary style of interweaving many different stories into one film was considered to be natural fit for Doctorow's novel. Watch *Nashville*, one of Altman's most acclaimed films, released at the same time as Doctorow's novel in 1975. Choose three or four characters from the over two dozen that *Nashville* presents and write a treatment—a short summary in paragraph form—for a Forman-esque script that would make one movie focusing on these few characters.

- Read "Michael Kohlhaas," the 1811 novella by German writer Heinrich von Kleist. This story, about an actual historical figure who went from legal to illegal means when his horses were stolen from him as an illegal transit toll, is an acknowledged influence on the Coalhouse Walker story. Write your own adaptation of the Kohlhaas/Coalhouse story set in your own world, including a subsequent discussion of which elements you think carry over to the twenty-first century.

- Listen to the music of one of the great ragtime composers such as Scott Joplin, Eubie Blake, Jelly Roll Morton, or Fats Waller. Present the music to your class with an explanation of what elements of the compositions were truly revolutionary in their day.

- The momentous 1901 dinner between Booker T. Washington and President Theodore Roosevelt, mentioned in the newsreel footage at the beginning of the film, is covered at length in Deborah Davis's 2012 book *Guest of Honor: Booker T. Washington, Theodore Roosevelt, and the White House Dinner That Shocked a Nation*. After reading that book, compose a letter to the president making a compelling argument for a controversial figure you think the president probably would not *want* to host for dinner, but should.

- Anzia Yezierska's novel *Bread Givers* has been considered a classic of young-adult fiction since its first publication in 1925. It tells the story of Sarah, a Jewish girl who emigrates from Poland with her parents to live in the chaotic Lower East Side depicted in this film as the home of Tateh, his wife, and their daughter. Read Yezierska's novel and then lead a discussion for your class, with examples from the book, about the ways the film is true to the life of Jewish immigrants of the early twentieth century, and which elements of the film ring false.

- Doctorow won the National Book Award for his 1985 novel *World's Fair*. The book tells a much more direct, focused story about a family living in New York during the Great Depression in the 1930s. Read *World's Fair* and research the time period in which it is set. Write "parts" for two or three historical figures that you think could be included in the story, similar to the way that historical figures are used in *Ragtime*, and explain how adding these characters would help bring out the novel's themes.

- The true story of Stanford White's murder is covered in great length in historian Paula Uruburu's 2008 book *American Eve: Evelyn Nesbit, Stanford White, the Birth of the "It" Girl, and the Crime of the Century*. After reading the book, make a case for whether or not Nesbit should be included on a list of the most important people of the twentieth century, defining the standards that you used to reach your determination. Post your argument on a blog and allow your classmates to comment.

positions, which is what makes the lower-class white firemen so resentful that a man like Walker can afford a Ford Model T. Evelyn Nesbit, clothed in furs, runs into Tateh in the Jewish ghetto of New York City, where the streets are packed with immigrants who live in cramped housing conditions and who struggle to make a living.

The film retains Tateh's social rise from the novel, showing that the boundaries of social class are not frozen. Tateh begins as a poor man who is skilled in cutting out amusing silhouettes, but by the end of *Ragtime* his artistic sensibilities have enabled him to rise in rank, giving him the means to throw a dinner party that resembles the one that White threw at the film's beginning. With his social rise comes an ascent in rank, as he now goes by the name of Baron Ashkenazy. It is ironic that he acquired his "baron" title in America, a country that does not acknowledge aristocracy, showing that social advancement often includes lying to hide one's humble roots.

Marriage

Ragtime presents readers with several variations on the theme of marriage. The first is the marriage between Harry Thaw and Evelyn Nesbit Thaw. Thaw seems to oblivious to his wife, but he is obsessed with the social image that his wife projects. Readers can see that she is a sexually active but unintelligent young woman, but Thaw sees her only as an image of what the wife of a man like him should be. The names Mother and Father represent what the family in New Rochelle is all about: the man and the woman there seem to be partners in a joint venture, marriage, but they do not relate to each other as individual people. Similarly, the couple that starts out in the Jewish ghetto has the same names, but in Yiddish. Their relationship is one of passion, though: Mameh has an affair in the middle of the afternoon, and Tateh, finding out, throws her out into the street and tosses everything she owns from the apartment window. As a final gesture that their marriage is over, he stands in the street and tears the shirt from his chest.

All of these couples end up separating. Though the film does imply that Tateh's new, upper-class life with Mother might be just as sterile and impersonal as her former life was, there is still a chance that his artistic flair can give their marriage the spark of interest that the other lacked.

© *AF archive | Alamy*

STYLE

Framing

Forman uses two different techniques to frame the intertwined stories that are told in this movie. The first is the image of a couple dancing a formal dance onstage. Their costumes imply wealth, and the formality of their dance adds to that impression, establishing the concept that the wealthy are trapped in a formal if elegant dance that requires them to follow moves that they were trained to do. The fact that the woman is Elizabeth McGovern, whose Evelyn Nesbit character is trained to dance formally within the story, adds to the impression that Forman is commenting on class: in the story, Evelyn is awkward and uncouth, so to start the film by showing her as graceful but aloof shows that class can be attained, but only at the expense of personality.

The film also starts and ends with images of news that was current at the time. In the beginning of the film, news stories are presented onscreen at a silent movie theater, which serves to familiarize readers with what was happening at the time. Several of the stories mentioned come to be significant in the story, such as a headline about Booker T. Washington (who shows up in the film, played by Moses Gunn), and the mention of a rare antique Bible acquired by J. Pierpont Morgan, so that readers can understand the financial scope of the treasures held in his library. At the end of the film, Forman mirrors those opening scenes with shots showing characters from earlier in the film: Harry Thaw, mentioned in one newsreel clip, is released from the asylum at Mattawan, and Harry Houdini, who played a significant role in Doctorow's novel but was only mentioned in the opening newsreel footage of the film, performs an escape act in the film's last scene.

Open Sets

Some films are cluttered, claustrophobic, reflecting an uncomfortable world in which the characters feel confined. By contrast, *Ragtime* has an open and expansive look. Almost every scene shows wide open space and ample light. This is true of outdoor spaces, of course, such as the beach at Spring Lake, where Baron Ashkenazy is filming, and even the blocked road in front of the fire station. It is also true of indoor scenes that viewers might expect to be visually busy, such as the courtroom of Harry Thaw's trial or the inside of the Morgan Library. Even Evelyn Nesbit Thaw's sitting room is so expansive and open that she has to run to fall into the younger brother's arms.

Many of the indoor scenes are bright with sunlight. The upstairs room where Sarah sits avoiding Walker when he comes to court her, for instance, is as bright as the parlor where he plays the piano. Scenes that take place indoors at night are usually in opulent settings where ample lighting would be expected, adding to the film's open feeling. This visual scheme helps support the idea that this story takes place at a time when hope was abundant, when America was a young country that was just starting to realize its promising future.

CULTURAL CONTEXT

The End of the Gilded Age

One of the aspects most frequently mentioned about Doctorow's novel is the way that it uses actual historical persons to make the story come alive. While the film of *Ragtime* includes Evelyn and Harry Thaw, Stanford White, Booker T. Washington, Rhinelander Waldo, and wordless footage of escape artist Harry Houdini, the novel also includes full speaking roles for Houdini, automobile magnate Henry Ford, financier John Pierpont Morgan, founders of psychoanalysis Sigmund Freud and Carl Jung, women's rights leader Emma Goldman, Mexican revolutionary Emiliano Zapata, and more. What made all of these characters significant to the story is that they are all emblems of the cultural change that occurred in America and around the globe in the first decade of the twentieth century.

The last third of the nineteenth century is often called the Gilded Age, a term attributed to author Mark Twain. It was a time of great financial growth, when vast fortunes were amassed by individuals like Morgan, John D. Rockefeller (founder of Standard Oil), William Thaw (father of *Ragtime*'s Harry K. Thaw; he made fortunes in shipping and rail lines) and Andrew Carnegie (founder of Carnegie Steel). During a relatively short period between 1878 and 1889, the boom in the American economy and the need that boom created for transportation, building materials, and energy gave these individuals opportunities to amass wealth that was practically unimaginable. As Twain's name for the era suggests, it was a time when gold covered everything, but lightly, obscuring the fact that the shiny surface of wealth could hide dark and sinister roots.

By the start of the twentieth century, individual wealth was no longer looked on with fascination, but with contempt. The captains of industry were derided as "robber barons," while President Theodore Roosevelt gained the nation's admiration as a "trust buster" for breaking up railroads and other monopolies during his term in office, 1901 to 1909.

Historically, the time from the 1890s to the 1920s is looked upon as the Progressive Era, when social change rose up from the bottom, advancing the quality of life for laborers, women, and minorities. National unions were formed. Women fought for the right to vote (which was finally conferred with the Nineteenth Amendment, in 1920). Black Americans developed a voice and a social identity, mostly through the arts, such as ragtime music and the literature of the Harlem Renaissance. By the time that World War I started in 1914, an event identified at the very end of *Ragtime*, the millionaires were already looked at as relics of a distant age, while progressives like the film's Tateh or women's rights leader Emma Goldman, from the novel, were considered the people who embodied the country's promise.

Civil Rights in the 1970s

People often look at the 1960s as a time of progressive social upheaval, listing the civil rights movement, women's liberation, the youth movement, the American Indian movement, and other cases where there was a realignment of America's priorities. By the late 1970s—the period between the publication of the novel *Ragtime* in 1975 and the film's final production in 1981—the country had had a chance to slow down and absorb the changes that were going to be lasting.

By the late 1970s, for example, it was clear that the civil rights movement was no passing fad and that race relations in America were not going to return to what they had been in the century between the end of the Civil War in 1865 and the passage of the Civil Rights Act of 1964. The mid-1950s to the mid-1960s saw one victory after another for racial equality, with laws that gave the federal government the power to overcome segregation laws that oppressed black Americans, particularly in the South. Schools won desegregation with the Supreme Court's decision in *Brown versus the Board of Education of Topeka, Kansas*, in 1954; federal laws against segregation in transportation were enacted in 1955 after Rosa Parks was arrested for not moving to the back of a bus in Montgomery, Alabama; white students joined in the Freedom Rides of 1961 to draw attention to the violence being perpetrated upon black protesters. By the late 1960s, however, the civil rights movement had turned violent, with riots causing deaths and millions of dollars of destruction in cities across the country after the murders of Malcolm X in 1965 and Martin Luther King Jr. in 1968.

The two responses to the country's ongoing problem with racial inequality, represented by the sit-in demonstrations of the late 1960s and the violent riots of the late 1960s, can be seen in the film *Ragtime*, with Booker T. Washington speaking for the calm, measured approach that would create lasting change and Coalhouse Walker representing violent action against the unjust system. By the end of the 1970s, it was

Director Milos Forman gives instruction to actor James Cagney. (© NY Daily News Archive / New York Daily News / Getty Images)

clear to movie audiences that the violence of the race riots may have been instrumental in making people see how slow the country was to enact the Civil Rights Act, but that it would not be a continuing part of the country's evolution toward equality. White people who had been complacent about segregation before the 1960s had lived through a decade when it was a subject that they could not ignore, just as the white family in the film becomes involved in Walker's humiliation and vengeance. It was a discussion that was timely in late 1970s, a decade after the assassination of Dr. King, which may be why the filmmakers decided that the Coalhouse Walker story deserved to be at the film's center.

CRITICAL OVERVIEW

With a prestigious director, Miloš Forman, and a best-selling book for its source, *Ragtime* was released in 1981 to much critical attention and general, though not universal, acclaim. One sign that it was treated as a major artistic project is that it was nominated for an impressive eight Academy Awards and seven Golden Globe Awards, but critical skepticism of the film is shown in the fact that it did not win any of these nominations. Industry insiders seemed to want to like this film more than they could actually commit to declaring its excellence.

Almost all critics noted the cuts that Forman made to the novel's sprawling, freewheeling style. Many felt that the film's focus on a few of the book's stories was too limited. Richard Corliss, for example, writing in *Time* magazine, noted, "By taking 155 minutes to tell less than half of Doctorow's 270-page pageant, Forman and [scriptwriter] Weller have created an impressive but strangely lopsided movie." Corliss later returns to his main idea when pronouncing his final assessment, that Forman has "reduced a pageant to an anecdote, and sacrificed sweep for nuance." It was a sentiment made even more potently in the *National Review* by John Simon, who started his review by stating, "For once I am in complete agreement with the majority of my colleagues: *Ragtime*, the movie, does not work, largely because one misses the kaleidoscopic construction of the Doctorow novel." The choices that Forman and Weller made in compressing the material made it "a predominantly earnest social document," Simon felt, and its good intentions, "deprived of Doctorow's jazzy texture and mischievous mythmaking, emerge as conventional, indeed stolid, fare, with now and then a jaunty fillip."

Roger Ebert, the film critic for the *Chicago Sun-Times*, gave his approval for the choice to focus on the Coalhouse Walker story and focused his review on the performances that Forman was able to get from his actors. "Ragtime is a loving, beautifully mounted, graceful film that creates its characters with great clarity," he noted, concluding that "Forman's decision to stick with the story of Coalhouse is vindicated, because he tells it so well." Ebert's sentiment was echoed by Desmond Ryan, the film critic for the *Philadelphia Inquirer*, who acknowledged that there would be many different ways to film Doctorow's novel before declaring this film to be "clear-eyed, intelligent, and beautifully rendered. While this is certainly not the only possible approach to an extremely difficult book, the film is, in the end, a work of art that stands on its own." As was the case with other critics, Desmond and Ebert acknowledged the differences between the novel and the film, but they did not feel that those difference made the film any less significant.

CRITICISM

David J. Kelly

Kelly is an instructor in literature and creative writing. In the following essay, he examines how history has proven Forman's decision to focus on Coalhouse Walker in Ragtime *to be a prudent choice.*

It is a question that always arises in writing classes: why is a particular element included in a creative work? Writers are usually fine with leaving the question unanswered, writing it off as a vague mystery of psychology when they respond, "Because I felt like putting it there." For readers, however, the answer has to be more relevant. *How* something made its way into an artistic piece is not really that important, but *whether* it should be there is a question that every reader and every film viewer has to come to terms with.

A good example of why this question is always relevant would be Forman's 1981 film adaptation of E. L. Doctorow's 1975 novel *Ragtime*. Much of the criticism of the time found it difficult to separate the novel from the film, which led, unsurprisingly, to the film being found slight, superficial, and less emotionally engaging.

Putting a novel on-screen requires its reduction, for the same reason that a diagram might only hope to convey, at best, a reduced form of the information that can be packed into a paragraph. Adapting a novel for film also requires streamlining its story, so that viewers who are involved with it for just a few hours of their lives can make sense of what they see. Very few readers encounter a novel all in one sitting, which gives them days or weeks of down time to absorb and make sense of what they have read.

A film is a very different thing from a novel, and the two should not be held to the same expectations. Even with that in mind, though, it is fair for critics to question whether the choices that Forman made in editing and streamlining Doctorow's story were good choices.

WHAT DO I SEE NEXT?

- For years, F. Scott Fitzgerald's novel *The Great Gatsby*, often thought of as the great American novel, was considered impossible to film. Critics' responses to the 1974 version of it were mixed, but many consider it worth looking at, if only for the performances of Robert Redford and Mia Farrow, who embody the roles of Jay Gatsby and Daisy Buchanan. Directed by Jack Clayton, it is available on DVD from Paramount and rated PG.

- The story of Evelyn Nesbit was told in an historically inaccurate version in the 1955 film *The Girl in the Red Velvet Swing*, for which Nesbit herself served as a technical consultant. Starring Joan Collins, Ray Milland, and Farley Granger, it is a beautifully shot film, an example of the kind of artificiality that often comes with Hollywood biographies. The restored 2007 version is available from Twentieth Century Fox. This film is not rated.

- Having worked as a director in both his native Czechoslovakia and in the United States, Miloš Forman is probably best known for his 1975 film adaptation of Ken Kesey's classic novel *One Flew over the Cuckoo's Nest*, which won Academy Awards for Best Picture, Best Director, and Best Actor for star Jack Nicholson. It tracks the story of a convict who goes to a mental institution to avoid jail and finds that the tightly regimented life there might be causing him to lose his mind. Brad Dourif, who plays the younger brother in *Ragtime*, was nominated for a Best Supporting Actor award for that picture. The special edition DVD from 2002 is available from Warner Home Video and is rated R.

- Doctorow's novel had a more expansive role for escape artist Harry Houdini, who appears here only in news footage. Around or after the time that *Ragtime* takes place, Houdini was such an international sensation that he was recruited to star in several films. Released by Kino International in 2008, the three-disk unrated *Houdini: The Movie Star* collects films featuring Houdini in a variety of heroic roles, from detective to submarine pilot. The films offer insight into what captured the imaginations of the people in *Ragtime*.

- In 1982, the year that *Ragtime* was nominated for eight Academy Awards, Warren Beatty was nominated as a director for his film *Reds*. Like Forman's film, it is a historical epic about political upheaval, but taking place predominantly during the Russian Revolution of 1917. The all-star cast includes Beatty, Diane Keaton, Jack Nicholson, Gene Hackman, and Polish novelist Jerzy Kosinski. The special twenty-fifth anniversary edition of the film, rated PG, was released on DVD by Paramount in 2006.

- The 1975 movie *Dog Day Afternoon* (rated R) plays the armed standoff as a modern tragicomedy: Al Pacino plays an ordinary man who tries to rob a bank to pay for his lover's sex-change operation and ends up the center of a media circus when the bank is surrounded by police, news reporters, and jeering mobs. John Cazale and Charles Durning co-star. The two-disk special edition is available from Warner Home Video.

- Booker T. Washington became a world-famous civil rights leader and the founder of the Tuskegee Institute (now Tuskegee University), one of the most influential of the historically black colleges that came into being in the late nineteenth century. Young viewers who are unfamiliar with Washington can learn by watching the story of his youth, *Booker*, an esteemed film made for PBS in 1984 (unrated), starring LeVar Burton, Shelley Duvall, and Shavar Ross as Washington. This unrated short film is available on DVD.

❝
KNOWING WHY FORMAN WENT ABOUT FOCUSING THE STORY IN THE WAY THAT HE DID DOES NOT NECESSARILY MAKE IT RIGHT. CRITICS WERE RIGHT TO QUESTION WHETHER THE CHANGES THAT FORMAN MADE WERE WELL CHOSEN.❞

The first thing to do would be to eliminate those choices that clearly, admittedly have nothing to do with artistic intent. One can blame a film for taking a work of art and making a piece of fluff out of it, but it is not clear that that is what *Ragtime* is doing. The film probably suffered in the eyes of some critics the minute the rights to Doctorow's novel were bought by producer Dino De Laurentiis, who was better known in the 1970s for producing pop-culture kitsch like *Death Wish*, *Orca, the Killer Whale*, and a forgettable remake of *King Kong* than he was for bankrolling quality works like Sidney Lumet's *Serpico* or Robert Altman's *Buffalo Bill and the Indians*. A De Laurentiis movie might have been done well, but it might not have, too. It was going to be a film for mass release, not an art-house movie, so any expectations about the way that the book *Ragtime*, an expensive best-selling property, was going to be put on the silver screen would have to take that into consideration. Altman, who was De Laurentiis's first choice for director, was a master at weaving intertwining stories together in his films, and he would have been the ideal choice for adapting Doctorow's sprawling narrative: as storytellers, the two men seemed to think alike. When Altman dropped out of the production, however, it was inevitable that whoever the project fell to would trim and focus the story.

Forman made his reputation in his native Czechoslovakia, as one of the directors who brought the Czech New Wave to international prominence in the 1960s. By 1975, though, he was known worldwide for his adaptation of Ken Kesey's novel *One Flew over the Cuckoo's Nest*, for which he won the Best Director Oscar. Though an "art" director, he was not a director of epics, while *Ragtime* the novel was a strange hybrid of both.

Interviewed about the film, Forman explained why it was the narrative of Coalhouse Walker, among all of the novel's story threads, that interested him most. Reading the book, he was particularly moved by the scene of Walker standing beside his car, looking at a pile of horse dung that has been left on its seat, and knowing that somebody should have to pay for what had been done to him but that nobody was likely to. Having been raised in a totalitarian political system behind the Iron Curtain, Forman was well familiar with having to swallow his pride and accept whatever was thrown at him. In that sense, it was natural that he would gravitate to the plight of black Americans, as filtered through history and through Doctorow, more than to other narratives in the novel such as the comings and goings of millionaires, social upstarts, factory owners, or the politically naïve.

What interests one man, though, is not necessarily going to capture the imaginations of the movie-going masses. Knowing why Forman went about focusing the story in the way that he did does not necessarily make it right. Critics were right to question whether the changes that Forman made were well chosen.

A good representative of the critics' disappointment with Ragtime's transition from the page to the screen—one that captures with eloquence the major charges levied against Forman—can be found in a review in *Literature Film Quarterly* titled "Ragtime without a Melody," by Leonard and Barbara Quart. This review, published the year after the film's release, shows appreciation for many of the film's attributes, but the writers' most strident point is made about Forman's decision to make Coalhouse Walker's story more significant than the rest. The Quarts felt that the Walker saga "does not justify its centrality," in their words, because "the struggle with the racist firemen—all filled with working class resentment—is too gross and caricatured to be of genuine interest or relevance."

The Quarts' explanation for the film's shortcomings, like those of even the most engaging and probing critics, can be reduced to the same basic argument that novels are better than films because they are able to be more nuanced. A movie critic emphasizing this point is no more helpful to moviegoers than a food critic telling a diner that the food at the corner bistro is fresher and more nuanced than the food they will be served at a chain restaurant. Though the objection stated by the Quarts falls on that same spectrum, it is not exactly the same. They do not fault Forman's film for narrowing the book's focus to one storyline; instead they object to this particular storyline and the film's handling of it.

One reason their objection falls flat to modern viewers is that time has proven Forman's instinct to be more insightful than they gave him credit for. In the 1980s, the working-class resentment that the Quarts found irrelevant might have seemed on its way out, but it never really went away. In fact, since then, it has ballooned. There has always been grumbling against the idle rich and the politically connected, represented by Forman as chubby, tuxedoed men (including the commissioner of police) swilling champagne, their heads adorned with wreaths of garland and their laps adorned with giggling girls. But the poor blaming other poor for their troubles, which used to be the basis of lower-class whites' racism, has become more entrenched than ever in the twenty-first century. It is a society where a substantial number of people at or below the poverty line vote against taxing the wealthy, choosing to cut benefits for the poor instead.

Racism, too, is a piece of ugliness that may have seemed on its way out back when the film was made, but it just will not go away. The fact that an African American was elected to the presidency in 2008 raised expectations that America was ready to move on into a "post-racial" world, but the backlash, though political and not often violent, has served as a reminder that racism still exists. A direct line can be drawn from the doubts raised about President Obama's American citizenship and the foremen in *Ragtime* who ask Coalhouse Walker whose car he is driving: both, whether stated sincerely or not, are incredulous about a black man's achievement.

Working with the novel, Forman might have made the movie version of *Ragtime* about Harry Houdini, and he would have served up a satisfying and thought-provoking entertainment. He might have focused on the younger brother's descent into militantism and tapped into some strain of percolating resentment that exists across class and time. He could have devoted most of the story to Tateh, a socialist back when socialism was in vogue, who sells out

when he starts making money, or the mother, who bails on her traditional family to seek her liberation in the hands of an artist. There is no good reason to believe that any of these approaches would have resonated with audiences, either when the film was made or now, any more than the framing that Forman chose does. One thing is for sure—there is no way that the film of *Ragtime* could have offered viewers an audio-visual presentation of the world that Doctorow brought alive in his novel. The choices the film makers made here reflect commercial considerations and personal considerations. The result is an appropriately enlightening and entertaining experience.

Source: David J. Kelly, Critical Essay on *Ragtime*, in *Novels for Students*, Gale, Cengage Learning, 2014.

Paul Skenazy

In the following excerpt, Skenazy points out the problems with the cameo motif, and suggests that the director failed to translate tone, time, and style to the film.

Ragtime, the film, is an uncertain and confused movie, often marvelous and as often boring, innovative yet derivative, iconoclastic while reassuring. It doles out a bit of this and a bit of that, unsure where it is going or what it is saying. The lack of decision is apparent in the pacing, in the contradictions built into several characterizations, and in the dangling, often only half-finished stories. It is both solidly professional and a bungled, technical mess of unexplained and unconnected ideas and devices most of which, separately, are clever, and some of which are quite original.

Like Forman's last two films—*One Flew Over The Cuckoo's Nest* and *Hair*—*Ragtime* takes its title from a financially and critically successful, politely blasphemous work voicing the restless underside of American life in the 1960s and 1970s. In its advertisements, *Ragtime* even borrows the type design from the 1975 novel by E. L. Doctorow: the curved, outlined letters, rolled at their ends, underscored by the extended tail of the capital "R." The ads assume the draw of the name, repeating it down the page. The name represents a novel, an era and (if confusedly) a style. It serves as a kind of shorthand for Forman, indicating his subject and implying his point of view. It is a style and title that read double, a curving turn of protective, lilting pleasure rhythmically disciplined into patterns of regret.

Forman is not a translator; his conceptions are his own. But his titles circumscribe his imagination. He is bound to some echoes of the original that holds copyright to the public imagination: names, scenes, beginning and end, tone, relationships. In this he is like Doctorow, who as a novelist writes within the parameters of historical event. Coalhouse Walker Jr. cannot blow up the Morgan Library; in *The Book of Daniel*, Daniel Isaacson's parents (modeled on the Rosenbergs) must die whatever he might, as narrator, discover about their guilt or innocence. The aesthetic limits both artists impose on themselves imply their concern with how much perception can claim and control event. Whether it was fiction that taught film to be self-conscious about how form makes meaning, or vice-versa, both have become rather adept—even tedious—by now at reminding us how much fantasy and faith there are in those stories of the past we agree to call history, and how much effort we expend to conclude that we can, safely, believe in them.

One of the reasons the reviews of *Ragtime* compare the film to the novel is because the novel is easier to explain. For all its multiplicity of character and its intricate webbing of fiction and fact, famous and homey, historical and imaginary, the novel is about the interconnections of social and personal acts. Doctorow asks seriously if irony and play can control the pandemonium of our national history. The anachronistic point of view represents the problem of inheritance: how to live in the house of the past, knowing its foundations are myth and fiction resting precariously on a ground of fact; knowing the interior needs to be gutted and rebuilt, insulated and reformed, materialized to accommodate contemporary convenience and necessity.

Forman doesn't know what he wants to do with this tone, this time, these problems—except borrow them. He seems most of all to be after style, or really two kinds of style: the grand manner of the turn-of-the-century, and the self-examining one of modernist art. The first he brings off skillfully, if deceptively, in the sets, in the bright colors, in the elaborate recreation of Atlantic City and bustled dresses and cars and trains and cobblestones and gas lamps. As long as the camera remains in the territory of wealth,

or portrays the comforts of middle-class family life, the sharply detailed features of lattice and cabinet and dress are marvelous to watch.

But while Forman defines the interior of the home with delicate attention, his presentation of lower-class worlds is distinctly inappropriate. The street market is antiseptic, with clean curbs and more light than a photographer's studio. Tateh's stumbling, immigrant English is peppered by the most extraordinary Latinate words. The basement hideout of Coalhouse and his cohorts is also spotless, not so much a rebel hideaway in Harlem as an artist's study in browns. Such obvious artificiality suggests that style has overcome story, destroying the necessary class contrasts.

Similar imbalances disrupt the tone. Why is Tateh's wife's adultery a farce, the fireman's wife's bed history Keystone Cops slapstick, and Tateh's affair with Mother a discreet, off-camera event? What are we to make of the presentation of the police invasion of the house across from the Library? Are these just cheap laughs to hold our interest, or are they meant to serve other purposes (for instance, to be echoes of early film motifs, or to comment by counterpoint on the tragedy of principle occupying center stage)?

Confusion is also my response to a more interesting device in the film, the cameo casting. It is of two sorts. First is the traditional use of familiar Hollywood faces in small roles: the guest appearances of Donald O'Connor, Pat O'Brien and, especially, the much-publicized return to films of James Cagney as Police Commissioner Waldo. More interesting is the selection of Norman Mailer to play Stanford White.

The presence of these notables provides the simple pleasure of recognitions: of the actors, of Mailer. Forman presumes a range of viewing and reading, of "keeping up," from his audience. He "develops" his characters through memory and recognition glossed by the immediate film image, working our literacy against the actual roles. The casting highlights questions of real and unreal, event and the mediating life of imagination. Because of their identification with aspects of film history, the actors function as part of Forman's emphasis on film as an emergent form, played against the equally new, fearful sounds of ragtime, against stage reviews and other forms of entertainment (Houdini, for example), against "real" events (like melodramatic shootings and bombings and love affairs and rich men who whip their wives).

Conceptually, then, the cameo motif fits. It echoes the "newsreel" device as well as Tateh's resurrection as Ashkenazy the film director. Technically, however, the cameos fail. O'Brien is given no lines of interest, and he speaks with the intonation of a zombie. O'Connor, portly but still a graceful entertainer, seems planned for more footage than he finally gets. Some of his scenes must have been cut, or else his presence too is only some vagabond, flighty imaginative whim. . . .

Source: Paul Skenazy, "Doing Time," in *Threepenny Review*, No. 10, Summer 1982, pp. 21–23.

John Simon

In the following excerpt, Simon claims that the film version of Ragtime *does not stay true to the kaleidoscope effects of the book.*

For once I am in complete agreement with the majority of my colleagues: *Ragtime*, the movie, does not work largely because one misses the kaleidoscopic construction of the Doctorow novel. Milos Forman, the director, and Michael Weller, the scenarist, chose what they felt to be the principal strands of this multifarious web: Evelyn Nesbit and the celebrated murder case; Coalhouse Walker Jr., the black musician with his fanatical and fatal quest for justice; Tateh, the impoverished Jewish immigrant who works himself up into a movie director; and the typical turn-of-the-century American family that gets itself embroiled with all of them.

Some of the many subplots and characters beyond these make all but subliminal appearances (e.g., Houdini), some ended up on the cutting-room floor (e.g., Emma Goldman), and quite a few (e.g., Henry Ford, J. P. Morgan, Dreiser, Freud, Zapata) never even passed their screenplay test. So, instead of free-wheeling ragtime, we get a fugue, and a rather unbalanced one at that, with Coalhouse and his vendetta given top priority. A good deal of Doctorow's irreverent, ahistoric, but politically satiric jocularity bites the dust in the process. But could the filmmakers have stayed faithful to the novel? The printed page can work as a kaleidoscope because the reader takes the shuffling and reshuffling images at his own pace, making his quietus whenever he may choose; but a screen-sized kaleidoscope shimmying around relentlessly for several hours would leave audiences dizzy and confused—if it did not just make them leave, period.

So *Ragtime* was doomed from the beginning, and with what may well have been additional pressure from the crass producer. Dino De Laurentiis, Forman ended up making a predominantly earnest social document, a film whose piously liberal intentions, deprived of Doctorow's jazzy texture and mischievous mythmaking, emerge as conventional, indeed stolid, fare, with now and then a jaunty fillip. When history is monkeyed with as recklessly as it is in the novel, it turns out, paradoxically, more acceptable than when it undergoes fewer, lesser distortions, which now sound like false notes in a solemn music. And since the Coalhouse story becomes so important, it cannot help revealing how inferior it is in moral fervor, psychological complexity, and sublime irony to Heinrich von Kleist's masterly novella *Michael Kohlhaas*, from which Doctorow derived the tale as a respectful but reductive *hommage*.

We are left with some very handsome production values—John Graysmark's set designs, Anna Hill Johnstone's costumes, and Miroslav Ondricek's cinematography; individual scenes that work, but are surrounded by others that don't; and a mixed bag of performances. Howard E. Rollins is a superbly restrained yet emotionally resonant Coalhouse, and there is excellent support from Kenneth McMillan, Elizabeth McGovern, Debbie Allen, Robert Joy, and a couple of others; acceptable performing from Brad Dourif, Mandy Patinkin, and quite a few more; but plodding contributions from James Olson and Mary Steenburgen as father and mother. Norman Mailer is rather stiff as Stanford White even before, mercifully soon, he becomes a stiff; and poor old Jimmy Cagney, as the police commissioner, even though one gets the feeling that he is moved about on casters, still manages to exude cocky authority. In this lean period of the cinema, I cannot reprove whoever admits to having caught the movie, but I doff my hat to him who can say: "No, but I've read the book." . . . .

Source: John Simon, "Wrong-Note Rag," in *National Review*, February 5, 1982, pp. 122–23.

Robert James Hatch

In the following excerpt, Hatch considers the film with its strong cast to be a "well-constructed, coherent, eventful period drama."

E.L. Doctorow's fat and flamboyant novel *Ragtime* is a set of overlapping and entwined scenarios, a series of *tableaux vivants* which highlight a rich segment of American history. One could carve from it any number of movies, from a psychological biography of Harry Houdini, to the domestic amours of Harry K. Thaw, to a winter with Admiral Peary at the North Pole.

Milos Forman, with his screen writer, Michael Weller, has operated on the book to expose what is no doubt its central cord—the short, stirring and tragic life of Coalhouse Walker Jr., a black man who demanded justice half a century too soon. Doctorow's readers will recognize other strands of his chronicle, but they have all been subordinated to the main theme in varying degrees; some have been dropped entirely. Walker's effect on the lives of Father, Mother and Younger Brother is portrayed at length, though more superficially than in the novel, but Houdini is a mere newsreel curiosity; Emma Goldman is banished, along with J.P. Morgan and Henry Ford; Tateh's lyric trolley-car journey from Mulberry Street to New England with his little daughter is dispensed with, though the ghetto silhouette-artist does reappear as the resplendent Baron Ashkenazy, filming an early serial on the beach at Atlantic City.

What remains is a well-constructed, coherent, eventful period drama that embraces a social theme more serious than such entertainments usually attempt. The film is much more sober than the novel; the wild, ingenious coincidence that was the latter's wit has been disciplined to plausibility. The matter-of-fact intercourse between actual and invented persons that gave the book its seductively dreamlike quality is less felt on the screen, where all the characters are bathed in the same amber light of high theatricality. But though much is lost, some visual pleasures are gained. Doctorow tells us how Thaw stalked across the crowded floor of Madison Square Garden's rooftop theater to empty his gun into the head of Stanford White; it is a vivid passage. But Forman, tossing money about like Croesus himself, builds a facsimile of the place, stages a big Floradora spectacle from *Mamzelle Champagne* and shows us the frightened Evelyn Nesbit, watching as her whey-faced lunatic of a husband forges his way through the babble of New York City's dining and drinking high society toward the table of the unsuspecting White (played, by the way, with lusty arrogance

by Norman Mailer). The opulence of the scene and its evocative power are stunning. Similarly, when the racist hoodlums of the White Plains volunteer fire department desecrate Walker's car, thus starting the clock of his rage, the episode carries an extra shock because we have been feasting our eyes on the brass-trimmed elegance of the proud black's antique Ford. So, though the film has less depth than the book, and though Forman avoids some of the bolder leaps in Doctorow's choreography of history, it drives through a nostalgic panorama of the ragtime era to its bitter, foregone conclusion.

The cast, which fairly gleams with larger-than-life vitality under Forman's direction, is far too large for individual mention. Here are a few of the players whose performances struck me most forcefully. Robert Joy, the Canadian actor who made his screen debut as the dope pusher in *Atlantic City* and who is the most implacable of the zealots in *Ticket to Heaven*, plays the insanely jealous, perhaps totally insane, Harry K. Thaw. Elizabeth McGovern's portrayal of Evelyn Nesbit is more Anita Loos than E.L. Doctorow, but she carries off her big scene, in which she springs stark naked from the arms of Younger Brother (Brad Dourif) to bargain with the lawyers employed by Thaw's mother, with a hilarious poise remarkable in a 19-year-old actress. Mandy Patinkin is a Tateh straight out of Chagall and a Baron Ashkenazy just in from Ruritania. Kenneth McMillan is by turns loathsome, pathetic and clownish as Willie Conklin, fire chief, neighborhood bully and nigger hater. . . .

Then there is Howard E. Rollins, an actor with considerable TV experience here appearing in his first movie as Coalhouse Walker Jr., the ragtime pianist, wayward father and Harlem dude who proves himself ready to kill and be killed in an attempt to prove that a black man is an American citizen and entitled to the rights of that estate. Rollins revels in *Ragtime*'s theatricality. He is patiently tender with Sarah (Debbie Allen), his ill-used sweetheart; forbearingly polite in the presence of Father's well-intentioned racism; icily dignified when goaded by the beer-bellied firemen; sadly deferential toward Booker T. Washington (Moses Gunn); quietly lethal as the leader of the outlaw band. He strikes sparks whenever he appears and is the unmistakable star of *Ragtime*.

And here arises an unintended bit of irony, for Rollins is not billed as the star. That honor falls on James Cagney, who has emerged from twenty years of retirement to play Rheinlander Waldo, Police Commissioner of New York City. It is fine to have Cagney back on the screen, and great to discover that he has lost none of his Irish bravado. But his part, though rich, is brief, and the center of tension remains with Rollins even while Cagney is cutting capers in the police stakeout across the street from the gang's last stand in the Pierpont Morgan Library.

I recognize that billing Cagney above Rollins, and shining the publicity on the old white man instead of the young black man, is not bigotry but show business. Cagney is a folk hero of the movies whom the public will flock to see in what may well be his last appearance Rollins is relatively unknown; the role of Walker is a big step up for him, and there will be plenty of time to give him his due. However, the central point of *Ragtime*, made more strongly on the screen than in the book, is that in those bully Teddy Roosevelt days, a black man had to die to have his rights acknowledged, and even then was cheated of them. The implication is that in this respect, at least, we are better than our grandfathers, and no doubt that is so. But some latter-day brothers and sisters of Coalhouse Walker's may be wryly amused by the box office calculations of Paramount Pictures.

Source: Robert James Hatch, Review of *Ragtime*, in *Nation*, December 12, 1981, pp. 650–51.

Roger Ebert

In the following review, Ebert calls Ragtime *a "loving, beautifully mounted, graceful film that creates its characters with great clarity."*

Milos Forman apparently made a basic decision very early in his production of E.L. Doctorow's best-selling novel, *Ragtime*. He decided to set aside the book's kaleidoscopic jumble of people, places, and things, and concentrate on just one of the several narrative threads. Instead of telling dozens of stories, his film is mostly concerned with the story of Coalhouse Walker, Jr., a black piano player who insists that justice be done after he is insulted by some yahoo volunteer firemen.

Doctorow's novel was an inspired juggling act involving both actual and fictional characters, who sometimes met in imaginary scenes of good wit and imagery. The Coalhouse story was more or less equal with several others. A film faithful to the book would have had people walking in and out of each other's lives in an astonishing series of coincidences. That might have been a good film, too. It might have looked a little like Robert Altman's *Nashville* or *Buffalo Bill*, and indeed Altman was the first filmmaker signed to direct *Ragtime*. But we will never see what Altman might have done, and Forman decided to do something different. He traces the ways in which Coalhouse Walker enters and affects the lives of an upstate New York family in the first decade of the century. The family lives in White Plains, New York, in a vast and airy old frame manor, and it consists of Father, Mother, and Younger Brother, with walk-ons by a grandfather and a young son.

For Younger Brother, the sirens of the big city call, in the form of an infatuation with the chorus girl Evelyn Nesbit (Elizabeth McGovern). That's before the saga of Coalhouse Walker alters his life. Coalhouse (in a superb performance by Howard E. Rollins, Jr.) meets the family by accident, or maybe by fate. A young black woman gives birth to Coalhouse's son, and then the family takes in both the woman and her son, hiring her as their maid. Coalhouse comes calling. He wants to marry the mother of his child. He has earned enough money. Everything's all set for the ceremony, when an event takes place that changes everything. The local volunteer firemen, enraged that a black man would own his own Model T, block the car's way in front of their station. They pile horse manure on the front seat. And Coalhouse, quite simply, cannot rest until he sees his car restored to him in its original condition. The story develops quickly into a confrontation. Coalhouse barricades himself into New York's J. Pierpont Morgan Library, and issues a set of demands. The library is surrounded by police and guardsmen, led by Police Commissioner Rhinelander Waldo (the great James Cagney, out of retirement). Father (James Olson) gets drawn into negotiations, and Younger Brother (Brad Dourif) is actually one of Coalhouse's lieutenants, in blackface disguise. Meanwhile, Mother is running off with a bearded immigrant who started out making cutout silhouettes on the streets and is now one of the first film directors.

The story of *Ragtime*, then, is essentially the story of Coalhouse Walker, Jr. Forman, a Czechoslovakian with an unusually keen eye for American society—his credits include *One Flew over the Cuckoo's Nest* and *Hair!*—has made a film about black pride and rage and not only white racism, which we sort of expect, but also white liberalism.

The great achievement of *Ragtime* is in its performances, especially Howard E. Rollins, Jr. and the changes he goes through in this story, from youthful romantic love to an impassioned cry "Lord, why did you fill me with such rage?" Olson, quiet and self-effacing, is subtly powerful as Father. Mary Steenburgen is clear-voiced, primly ethical Mother who springs a big surprise on everyone. Pat O'Brien has two great scenes as a corrupt, world-weary lawyer. Kenneth McMillan blusters and threatens as the racist fire chief. And when Cagney tells him "people tell me you're slime," there is the resonance of movie legend in his voice.

Ragtime is a loving, beautifully mounted, graceful film that creates its characters with great clarity. We understand where everyone stands, and most of the time we even know why. Forman surrounds them with some of the other characters from the Doctorow novel (including Harry Houdini, Teddy Roosevelt, and Norman Mailer as the architect Stanford White), but in the film they're just atmosphere window dressing. Forman's decision to stick with the story of Coalhouse is vindicated, because he tells it so well.

Source: Roger Ebert, Review of *Ragtime*, in *Chicago Sun Times*, January 1, 1981.

Variety

In the following review, a contributor states that the chaotic plot of the novel was realized almost completely in Miloš Forman's "superbly crafted screen adaptation."

The page-turning joys of E.L. Doctorow's bestselling *Ragtime*, which dizzily and entertainingly charted a kaleidoscopic vision of a turn-of-century America in the midst of intense social change, have been realized almost completely in Milos Forman's superbly crafted screen adaptation.

Within a myriad of characters who include the likes of Evelyn Nesbit, Stanford White, Booker T. Washington and J. Pierpont Morgan, the film charts the syncopated social forces that truly ushered in 20th-century America by pivoting them around a nameless upper-crust family unexpectedly caught up in the maelstrom.

Overriding focus of the film is on the travails of a fictional black ragtime pianist (Howard E. Rollins), whose common-law wife (Debbie Allen) is taken in by The Family after she abandons her newborn child in their garden.

Juggling the scores of characters that Doctorow intertwined in his quirky blend of historical and fictional people and events, Forman and scripter Michael Weller were forced into some occasional truncation and shortcutting, but ultimately win the chess game hands down. . . .

Source: Review of *Ragtime*, in *Variety*, December 31, 1980.

SOURCES

"Awards for *Ragtime*," IMDb, http://www.imdb.com/title/tt0082970/awards (accessed December 27, 2012).

Barbour, John, and Gary Khammar, executive producers, "Remembering *Ragtime*," *Ragtime* (DVD extra), Light Source & Imagery, 1984.

Corliss, Richard, "One More Sad Song," in *Time*, November 23, 1981, p. 101.

Ebert, Roger, Review of *Ragtime*, in *Chicago Sun-Times*, January 1, 1982.

Quart, Leonard, and Barbara Quart, "Ragtime without a Melody," in *Literature Film Quarterly*, Vol. 10, No. 2, 1982, p. 73.

Ragtime, directed by Miloš Forman, Paramount, 1981, DVD.

Ryan, Desmond, "A Clear Vision of *Ragtime*," in *Philadelphia Inquirer*, December 21, 1982, p. B04.

Simon, John, "Wrong-Note Rag," in *National Review*, February 5, 1982, pp. 122–24.

"Theodore Roosevelt: Presidential Accomplishments," National Park Service website, http://www.nps.gov/history/logcabin/html/tr3.html (accessed December 27, 2012).

"Timeline: Civil Rights Era," PBS.org, http://www.pbs.org/wnet/aaworld/timeline/civil_01.html (accessed December 27, 2012).

FURTHER READING

Forman, Miloš, *Turnaround: A Memoir*, Villard Press, 1994.

> Forman explains his immigration to the United States and his associations with great European and American artists. The book includes extensive information about the filming of *Ragtime*.

Moore, Jacqueline, *Booker T. Washington, W.E.B. Du Bois, and the Struggle for Racial Uplift*, Rowman & Littlefield, 2003.

> Around the time this film takes place, two leading black American intellectuals represented different ways of approaching racial repression: Washington stood for gradual improvements while DuBois led the movement for immediate recognition of equal rights. Moore's book outlines the two views, which are important for fully understanding Walker's actions.

Morris, Christopher D., ed., *Conversations with E. L. Doctorow*, University Press of Mississippi, 1999.

> Viewers hoping to understand this film would do well to look at the thoughts of the man who invented the characters. Doctorow discusses *Ragtime*, his most commercially successful book, several times in the interviews collected here.

Rapf, Joanna E., "Volatile Forms: The Transgressive Energy of *Ragtime* as Novel and Film," in *Literature Film Quarterly*, Vol. 26, No. 1, 1998, p. 16.

> This scholarly comparison of the novel and the film draws parallels between the two works, with an emphasis on the author's literary analysis of the book. Younger readers might find this work a little complex.

Sobchack, Tom, "*Ragtime*: An Improvisation on Hollywood Style," in *Literature Film Quarterly*, Vol. 13, No. 3, 1985, pp. 148–54.

> Sobchack takes a rare look at the film by giving insight into how Forman's style matches the style of music that gives the book and movie their title.

Sterritt, David, "Milos Forman and the Tricky Business of Filming *Ragtime*," in *Christian Science Monitor*, December 10, 1981.

> This article, available online at the *Christian Science Monitor* website, was published at the time that the film was released. It goes into Forman's thoughts about the novel and his process for adapting it, along with his views of race relations and the events the film depicts.

SUGGESTED SEARCH TERMS

Ragtime AND Doctorow

Ragtime AND Forman

Ragtime AND Cagney

Ragtime AND Evelyn Nesbit

Evelyn Nesbit AND twentieth century

Ragtime AND Howard E. Rollins Jr.

Ragtime AND racism

Coalhouse Walker Jr.

Stanford White AND Harry K. Thaw

Ragtime AND privileged class

Ragtime AND social ladder

The Salt Eaters

Toni Cade Bambara's debut novel *The Salt Eaters* was published in 1980. Among students and critics it has garnered a reputation for being somewhat inaccessible because it is written in a fragmented style that jumps abruptly back and forth between an array of characters with little explanation or exposition. At the same time it is known for being a beautifully written, highly lyrical, and emotionally powerful book. Bambara has stated that her intention in writing it was to produce a work that demonstrated how the spiritual, psychic, and political forces in a community could all exist in harmony with one another. To this end, the work involves themes of community, connectedness, and healing. The title of the work itself is a reference to healing, as salt is a natural antiseptic and is often used to help heal wounds. Bambara uses the story of the healing of Velma Henry, a troubled woman who has attempted suicide, to demonstrate how these three forces can work together to create healthy and whole individuals and, in turn, a healthy and whole community.

TONI CADE BAMBARA

1980

AUTHOR BIOGRAPHY

Bambara was born Miltona Mirkin Cade on March 25, 1939, to Helen Brent Henderson Cade in New York City. For the first ten years of her life the family lived in Harlem, New York.

Afterwards, the family lived in different locations around New York and New Jersey. She has stated that the environment she grew up in had a great influence on her writing style, and also that her mother, with whom she was very close, was her greatest influence and inspiration. She changed her name from Miltona to Toni when she was around the age of five, and in 1970 she added Bambara, the name of a West African ethnic group.

In 1959, Toni Cade graduated from Queens College with a BA in theater arts and English. In the same year, her first published story, "Sweet Town," was released and was awarded the John Golden Award for Fiction. After her graduation from Queen's College, Bambara spent some time traveling and studying in Italy and France before returning to further her studies in the United States. Bambara completed her master's degree in American Studies at City College, New York, in 1965, and taught in the Search for Education, Elevation, and Knowledge (SEEK) program at City College until 1969. It was during this phase in her life that Bambara began to embrace activism and became involved in many social and political causes such as the civil rights and women's movements. She was a major figure in the black arts movement. Her 1970 anthology *The Black Woman* featured work by Nikki Giovanni, Audre Lorde, Alice Walker, Paule Marshall, and others, and became known as an important artistic product of the movement. Bambara edited a second anthology, *Tales and Stories for Black Folks*, which was published in 1971. The next year she published a collection of her own original short stories, *Gorilla, My Love*. In this collection she introduced what would become a recurring theme in her work: the importance of community, especially among black women. Bambara stated that the short story was her favorite mode of creative writing.

Between 1972 and 1975 Bambara traveled extensively. In 1973 she visited Cuba, where she worked with several women's organizations. The next year she moved to Atlanta with her daughter, Karma, and took a teaching position at Spelman College. In 1975 she went to Vietnam as a guest of the Women's Union and was deeply affected by her work there. Some of the stories in her 1977 collection *The Sea Birds Are Still Alive* were inspired by her travels in Vietnam. Bambara began working on her first novel, *The Salt Eaters*, in 1978. It was written in an experimental style involving a nonlinear narrative and a multitude of characters that many critics enjoyed, though some criticized it for being overly complicated. The work received the American Book Award and the Langston Hughes Society Award in 1981.

In the 1980s, Bambara continued to write and edit, but also returned to one of her previous passions: the performing arts. She worked as writer and narrator for Louis Massiah's 1986 documentary *The Bombing of Osage Avenue*. Bambara continued to work in film and continued to write books, including her last novel, *Those Bones Are Not My Child*, even after she was diagnosed with colon cancer in 1993. She succumbed to the cancer on December 9, 1995, at the age of fifty-six. Her works continue to be widely read and anthologized and have received countless awards.

PLOT SUMMARY

Chapter 1
At the beginning of *The Salt Eaters*, Velma Henry, the protagonist of the novel, is clad in a hospital gown and sitting on a stool in front of Minnie Ransom, a well-known local healer. Velma feels stiff and uncomfortable. She is unable to move or speak and is disoriented. Minnie, on the other hand, is wearing bright, colorful clothing, and moves around Velma, asking her if she is ready to be well. Because the novel is written in a somewhat cryptic style with little exposition, it is not immediately clear that the two women are in a room at the Southwest Community Infirmary in the fictional town of Claybourne, Georgia, in 1978. Velma is in the hospital recovering from a suicide attempt that presumably took place earlier that day and involved her slitting her wrists and putting her head in a gas oven. Minnie has been summoned to heal her. Both of the women are black, which is important to note as race is a major factor in the novel. Most of the chapter takes place inside Velma's mind as she slips in and out of lucidity, trying to understand exactly what Minnie means when she tells her stories and asks her questions.

Surrounding the two women are a multitude of people. The twelve who are physically closest to Minnie and Velma, forming a protective chain around them, are a group of spiritual leaders known as The Master's Mind. Also in the room are a number of visiting medical practitioners, as well as various members of the clinic staff and patients who have come to watch. This is not unusual as the infirmary is not structured like a traditional hospital, but rather includes all types of medicine. To everyone's surprise, Velma's loving godmother, Sophie "M'Dear" Heywood, who has been present for every major event in Velma's life, abruptly leaves the room.

While Minnie continues to struggle with Velma, the scope of the novel broadens to the rooms surrounding Velma's. Buster and Nadeen, a teenage couple who take parenting classes at the clinic, are there so that Buster can interview a doctor. Sophie sits in Doc Serge's office reflecting on her own tragic past. She thinks about her son, Smitty, who was beaten to death in a war protest, and about her own beating at the hands of her neighbor Portland Edgers, who was forced to do it by a white police officer.

The remainder of the chapter consists of Velma's personal reflections on her suicide attempt, on the history of her relationship with her husband, Obie, on a meeting she attended with members of a women's action committee, and on an uncomfortable protest march in which she participated.

Chapter 2
The second chapter of the novel is a conversation between Minnie and Old Wife, her spirit guide. Old Wife is a "haint," or a ghost who helps Minnie in her work as a healer. Minnie asks Old Wife what is going on with Velma, why she chose to commit suicide and why she is presently unreachable. Minnie is finding Velma to be one of her most difficult patients. While Old Wife engages Minnie in conversation, she does not provide her with any concrete answers. Minnie laments the current state of the youth population, which to her seems to be having an increasing incidence of self-harm. She also chastises Old Wife for not remembering some of the details of one of their previous healing sessions. Minnie and Old Wife make fun of each other in a good-natured way. After much urging, Minnie agrees to meet Old Wife in the "Chapel," a place where they both go to commune. Minnie agrees to join her, but her journey there is not normal. It is more like it used to be early in her healing career, following what many members of her family feared was a mental collapse. The Chapel

is actually a place in Minnie's mind where she can go to receive messages from the Source.

This chapter also introduces Dr. Julius Meadows, the physician at the clinic, who is observing the healing. Buster and Nadeen also witness parts of the healing though Buster reluctantly has to leave to conduct an interview with Doc Serge, the man who runs the clinic.

Chapter 3
Chapter 3 takes place on a bus driven by Fred Holt, a lonely, embittered man who silently mocks many of his passengers. Among the passengers on the bus are a multiracial performing arts group called the Seven Sisters, which includes Cecile, Inez, Mai, Chezia, Nilda, Iris, and Palma, who is Velma's sister. They all know Velma, who used to tour with the group, playing piano. The women are on their way to participate in the Claybourne Spring Festival, a celebration that is organized by members of the Academy and meant to help unify many different leftist activist groups with similar interests. They make small talk among themselves while Fred Holt thinks about how crazy they are and what his late friend Porter would say if he were there to hear them. Porter was one of the only other black bus drivers who worked with Fred, and the two lobbied together against workplace discrimination. In addition to thinking about Porter, Fred also spends a good amount of time regretting that he ate chili for lunch, worrying that it might make him ill and that he will be late getting into Claybourne to pick up his second load of passengers for the day. The passengers begin to ask him why they are running late, but rather than answering, Fred continues to think about his past and continues to lament Porter's death. Porter had been his best friend and confidant until he died after being stabbed in the neck by a passenger with a pair of knitting needles. Now Fred is left alone with his wife, Margie, though the two do not get along very well. Before the passengers arrive in Claybourne, a sense of mental clarity comes over everyone on the bus at the same time, though none of them know exactly how to pinpoint it.

Chapter 4
Chapter 4 follows Velma's husband, Obie, as he goes about his business at the Academy. He reflects on the ideological splits that are happening within all of the activist factions he used to be familiar with. He thinks about the upcoming

Spring Festival and how it is merely a temporary measure that he and the other leaders hope will foster a sense of unity until they can come up with a more drastic plan to bring all the factions back together. He thinks about how he misses Velma's working at the Academy and how things are more difficult without her. He laments the fact that their marriage is failing and that he is falling down on the job both at home and at work. He thinks about his brother, who is in jail for rape, and generally feels lost and confused.

Chapter 5

In Chapter 5 Nadeen candidly observes Velma's healing with rapt interest. Even though she does not know Velma, she feels connected to her. She is fascinated by seeing something unexplainable fall away from Velma's face. She believes that what she is witnessing is real and true healing, and somehow, through her sense of kinship with Velma, she begins to feel like a grown woman. Meanwhile, other infirmary patients and staff continue to move in and out of Velma's room. Nadine watches closely as the cuts around Velma's wrists heal and once again thinks about how this is the most authentic kind of healing she has ever seen. Velma, who is still not fully conscious, is not able to comprehend the meaning of the questions Minnie is asking her.

Suddenly the perspective of the narrative shifts, and readers are let into Velma's hallucinations, which involve spinning and skating and playing the piano when her mother was still alive. In a sudden moment of lucidity, she claims that health is her right.

Later in the chapter Buster finally gets the interview he wanted with Doc Serge, who runs the infirmary, but Buster realizes in the middle of the conversation that Serge will not tell him what he came to find out: what the big reenactment would be at the Spring Festival this year. Instead, Serge just lectures him about economics, not missing a beat even when Buster brings up Serge's history as a pimp.

Chapter 6

Chapter 6 revolves around the inner reflections of three individuals. Palma is worried about Velma, Sophie is worried about Velma, and Fred continues to reflect on his late friend Porter. Palma, who had been worrying about Velma on the trip, becomes even more overwhelmed with the sense that something bad has

happened after she gets off the bus in Claybourne. She thinks about Velma's slip into madness and instability, including an incident one morning when she bit through a juice glass. The other women on the bus decide to go for food at a nearby café.

Sophie sits in Doc Serge's office trying to figure out what went wrong with Velma, lamenting the fact that she has become so lost. After a while her mind drifts to the traumatic events in her own life, including the time she was beaten in prison by her neighbor Portland Edgers.

Fred makes his way to the infirmary where he is planning to have a check-up. He tries to make small talk with a young boy and some drunk men, but he does not find either interaction satisfying. As he travels through the town, he thinks of how hurt he was when both his ex-wife, Wanda, and his friend Porter accepted their respective religions and shut him out of their lives.

Chapter 7

Chapter 7 begins with Obie getting a massage from his Korean masseuse, Ahiro. Though he tries to relax, he cannot get his mind off Velma. Ahiro recommends that Obie have a good, long cry, but he shrugs off her suggestion.

A dance class occurs somewhere nearby, and the music can be heard in the infirmary. Velma, still rocking back and forth on her stool, reflects upon the one time she visited the salt marshes of Georgia, which are known for their healing powers. As she listens to the music and feels Minnie's hands on her, she thinks about how in the end her trip to the marshes had not done her any good.

At the end of the chapter Campbell avoids paying his rent and watches Velma and Obie's son, Lil James, bike up a hill.

Chapter 8

Chapter 8 follows Dr. Meadows as he roams around Claybourne, a town in which he still does not feel comfortable. He carries with him a notebook in which he has been recording ways that the locals pronounce words. Out of nowhere, three black men dressed in drag amble toward him wishing him a happy Mardi Gras. They try to convince him to don a dress and join them on their adventures. He declines their offer, and after they leave, the street he is on is empty and quiet once again. He accidentally meanders into the poor part of town, where he feels uncomfortable. After accidentally stepping on a man's feet he is worried that the man and his friend want to start a fight with him, but actually they just want to talk to him about their problems with the nearby nuclear plant. One of the men turns out to be Nadeen's uncle, and the other is a friend of his. Dr. Meadows spends some time talking to the two men, and then continues walking.

Chapter 9
Chapter 9 takes place at the Avocado Pit Café where Jan and Ruby are enjoying a meal together and conversing about the latest news. Their waiter, Campbell, is particularly eager to talk to Jan and serves their table with special attentiveness. A mysterious and seemingly drunk man moseys up to Jan, asks her if she teaches at the Academy and then leaves. The two wonder if Velma will show up, but they are doubtful since she failed to keep her appointment with a lawyer that morning. Jan tells Ruby that Velma has been working at the Transchemical plant and has wiped out all of their computer records and was in the process of being interrogated about it.

Meanwhile Campbell signals to his writer friends at the café that it will be a few more minutes before he can meet them. He can't wait to tell them about a board game that he has invented. He serves a group of regulars from the plant who frequently play games at the café. He then returns to Jan and Ruby's table to flirt with Jan some more. After he leaves, Ruby confides to Jan that Velma had been asking her questions about suicide. This makes Jan extremely worried, though Ruby shrugs it off.

Chapter 10
Chapter 10 is the shortest chapter in the novel. Nearly all of it consists of a hallucination or daydream that Sophie has while sitting in Doc Serge's office. In the dream, Velma tells Sophie about a bad dream she has had, and Sophie comforts her. Toward the end of the chapter the action pans over to Velma's hospital room, where Minnie is still trying to connect with her.

Chapter 11
In Chapter 11 six of the Seven Sisters, minus Palma, from Fred's bus earlier are eating at a round table in the Avocado Pit Café, where Jan and Ruby are eating. Mai attempts to record one of her grandmother's stories while a man across

the bar checks her out. A distant rumbling sound makes everyone in the café feel uneasy.

In the hospital Velma has a flashback to the time in her life when she felt most cared for. She had a cold and her mother, Sophie, Palma, and Smitty all tended to her. Other dreams come to her, including a time she collected oysters with Sophie. Then she reflects on the time she confronted Obie about his affair, and he did not deny it.

Back in the café, the diners realize that an approaching train is causing the mysterious rumbling. Some people still feel uneasy. The two groups of women—Jan and Ruby and the Seven Sisters—continue to eat and talk. Velma comes up continually in both conversations. Jan and Ruby discuss whether or not Velma is self-centered and try to decide on the best thing to do about the nearby power plant. Out of nowhere a tremendous thunderstorm bursts from the sky, causing everyone at the café to crowd in for cover.

Chapter 12
The final chapter of the novel is also the most cryptic. As the healing session comes to a climax, Velma's hallucinations become fast-paced and disorienting as she hurls through space and time. In her head she runs through the entire town passing familiar places and faces and visiting her memories. This portion of the book, like many of the other dream and hallucination scenes, is imaginative and fantastical. Many parts of her dream include her godmother, Sophie. After an encounter with a rude woman from Velma's past, the narrative shifts back to Old Wife and Minnie observing her on the stool. They put on some music from the 1920s, which reaches through to Velma. Slowly Velma begins to come closer to reality as she dances to the music both in her dream and in real life. Old Wife instructs Minnie to let her dance. As Velma dances, she begins to realize that she is about to surrender to the healing. As Velma understands that she could really have died as a result of her suicide attempt, she recalls all of the other times in her life when she might have died.

While this is happening, Minnie receives a strong message in her left bicuspid and begins to panic, but Old Wife comforts her. Just a moment later, the storm hits and shakes the room. Later, Velma would remember it as the moment she began to rejoin the land of the living.

The next several pages depict how all of the other characters in the story reacted to the first crack of thunder. At that same time, through the infirmary window Fred thinks he sees Porter across the street. He frantically goes to chase him but finds no one there when he gets to the spot. Campbell suspects that a rumble of such a magnitude has to signal more than a storm. Palma ducks into the arms of Marcus Hampden, her lover. Obie was in the whirlpool at the gym. He then receives a phone call from the infirmary and instantly knows something must have happened with Velma. As he rushes toward the infirmary, she finally comes out of her stupor, standing up and casting off her shawl.

CHARACTERS

Ahiro
Ahiro is Obie's Korean masseuse.

Buster
Buster is a headstrong young journalism student who is Ruby's cousin. He has accepted paternity of Nadeen's soon-to-be-born child under duress from her Uncle Thurston, though he is not entirely convinced that the child is his. Buster and Nadeen take parenting classes together at the Academy, though on the day that the action of the novel occurs, they are at the hospital so that Buster can witness Velma's hearing and interview Doc Serge for a paper he is writing.

Campbell
Campbell is an investigative reporter and a waiter at the Avocado Pit Café. Though a gifted reporter, he has not yet earned any clout in the journalism community because he writes for a small local paper in Claybourne. He is eager to break a big story that will earn him a reputation. He eavesdrops on customers at the café, hoping to get a lead on a story. He also eavesdrops on Jan and Ruby because he is infatuated with Jan. They will later marry. Over the course of the novel Campbell develops a theory that all systems of knowledge in the universe, whether scientific or religious or something completely different, are actually the same system.

Cecile
Cecile is one of the Seven Sisters, a performing arts group that travels around performing for leftist political causes. While Velma is in the hospital, the Sisters are riding the bus back to Claybourne to participate in the Spring Festival. Cecile is known as the Sister of the Plantain.

Chezia
Chezia is one of the Seven Sisters, a performing arts group that travels around performing for leftist political causes. While Velma is in the hospital, the Sisters are riding the bus back to participate in the Spring Festival.

Cleotus (The Hermit)
Cleotus is a mysterious figure in the novel. He is referred to by other characters repeatedly, but he only appears once, to Jan, and will not tell her his name. The Hermit teaches classes on spirituality to a select few.

Portland Edgers
Portland Edgers is Sophie's neighbor. He was forced by a white policeman to beat Sophie when they were in jail together after being arrested at a political event.

Marcus Hampden
Marcus Hampden is a member of the Coalition of Black Trade Unionists and Palma's lover.

Lil James "Jabari" Henry
Lil James Henry is Velma and Obie's son.

Obie Henry (James Lee Henry)
Obie is Velma's husband and the leader of the Academy of Seven Arts, also known as the Academy, a collective at which the educated and motivated black people take classes and develop political strategies. Though Obie and Velma's marriage has been disintegrating for a long time, he does not want it to fall apart. He feels that he has no way to communicate with Velma, and that she has shut him out completely. He has been having an affair behind Velma's back, though she has been able to figure it out and eventually confronts him about it. Obie has always been a strong orator and leader, but lately his troubles at home have been detracting from his leadership skills.

Palma Henry
Palma is Velma's older sister, a painter, and an active member of Women for Action as well as one of the Seven Sisters (known as the Sister of the Yam.) Palma is interested and active in

politics but not to the extent that Velma is. She is very flirtatious and is having an affair with Marcus Hampden. Palma spends a lot of her time caring for and worrying about her sister, Velma, whom she was watched slip deeper into mental illness for a long time. Because Velma does not share her schedule with anyone or tell her family when she is leaving town, Palma is constantly trying to track her down and ensure that she is safe.

Velma Henry

Velma Henry, also sometimes called Vee, is the protagonist of the novel. Increasing mental instability compounded by a myriad of daily stresses make Velma attempt suicide prior to the beginning of the novel by slitting her wrists and placing her head in a gas oven. Her marriage to Obie has been slowly collapsing, exacerbated by her discovery that he is having an affair. She also became frustrated and exhausted by the fracturing of the network of political activist groups in Claybourne, which were becoming increasingly ineffective. To further add to her stress, she is being investigated for committing fraud by manipulating the computer files at the local nuclear power plant where she works. The pressure of all of these things along with her own inner instability has caused her to unravel and act strange. Once she bit clear through a glass in front of her sister Palma, who had to extract the shards from her lips. At the beginning of the novel Velma finds herself in a lot of pain, propped up on a stool in the local infirmary in front of Minnie Ransom, a faith healer. Though Minnie's healing sessions usually take only fifteen minutes, Velma's situation is so dire that she takes much longer. Throughout the novel Velma drifts in and out of lucidity, trying to resist Minnie's attempts to heal her, though in the end she eventually succumbs. While in the hospital she reflects on events from her past—experiences with her husband and political marches she has taken part in—and she also sometimes slips into waking dreams.

Sophie "M'Dear" Heywood

Sophie Heywood is Velma's godmother and the owner of a local boardinghouse. Sophie has supported Velma her entire life, even when Velma's own mother, Mama Mae, did not. She is a spiritual woman who believes that people could understand a great deal more about life if they would just open themselves up to it. Sophie is so upset and outraged by Velma's suicide attempt that she becomes temporarily mute and cannot even stay in the room with her. She hides out in Doc Serge's office to reflect and compose herself.

Fred Holt

Fred Holt is a charter bus driver who is carrying a group of people into Claybourne for the Spring Festival. He feels exhausted and sick from being overworked and having had chili for lunch that has upset his stomach. Fred is deeply unhappy with his lot in life and resents almost everyone in it, especially since the death of his best friend, Porter, the only other black bus driver who worked in this region at his company. He spends a lot of his time thinking about how Porter would react to situations and wondering how he would be spending his time if he were still alive. Shortly before Porter's death Fred felt betrayed by his interest in taking spiritual classes with The Hermit, whom they used to make fun of together. Fred also felt betrayed and abandoned when his first wife, Wanda, decided to convert to Islam and later left him. He is now married to a woman named Margie, whom he resents for not being intimate with him. He is sometimes cruel to Margie.

Inez

Inez is one of the Seven Sisters, a performing arts group that travels around performing for leftist political causes. While Velma is in the hospital, the Sisters are riding the bus back to participate in the Spring Festival. Inez is a Chicana and is known as the Sister of the Corn.

Iris

Iris is one of the Seven Sisters, a performing arts group that travels around performing for leftist political causes. While Velma is in the hospital, the Sisters are riding the bus back to participate in the Spring Festival.

Jan

Jan is a friend of Ruby and Velma's. She used to work at the Academy but was fired recently. She is an astrologer who always carries tarot cards and star charts with her. There are clues in the work that suggest that she ends up marrying Campbell, a waiter at the Avocado Pit Café, after the end of the novel.

Mama Mae

Mama Mae is Velma and Palma's deceased mother.

Mai

Mai is one of the Seven Sisters a performing arts group that travels around performing for leftist political causes. While Velma is in the hospital, the Sisters are riding the bus back to Claybourne to participate in the Spring Festival. Mai, who is of Asian decent and has moved from San Francisco, is known as the Sister of the Rice.

Margie

Margie is a white woman with stringy blonde hair who is married to Fred Holt.

Dr. Julius Meadows

Dr. Meadows is light-skinned doctor who is new to Claybourne and who has not yet figured out how to fit in with the locals.

Nadeen

Nadeen is a fifteen- or sixteen-year-old girl who is pregnant with Buster's child. She is not the most intelligent young girl, though she has an acute sense of intuition. She is at the hospital with Buster on the day that Velma's healing is taking place and finds herself captivated and drawn in by the process.

Nilda

Nilda is one of the Seven Sisters, a performing arts group that travels around performing for leftist political causes. While Velma is in the hospital, the Sisters are riding the bus back to participate in the Spring Festival. She is from India.

Old Wife

Old Wife is Minnie Ransom's wise-cracking spirit guide. She is a "haint," or a ghost, who has been dead for many years. She helps Minnie figure out how to best heal patients.

Jay Patterson

Jay Patterson is a local official who meets with the Women for Action.

Porter

Porter is the only other black bus driver who worked with Fred Holt. The two were good friends. Shortly before he was stabbed to death with a pair of knitting needles, he became interested in studying with the Hermit.

Minnie Ransom

Minnie Ransom is the faith healer who tries to calm and heal Velma throughout the course of the novel. She grew up in a well-to-do family that was shocked when she ended up having an apparent mental collapse while away at a Bible college when she rolled in the mud and ate dirt. Following that event she became a spiritual healer who has access to forces that are beyond this world. Usually all she has to do is spend a few minutes with people and place her hands on them, but Velma turns out to be a more challenging case.

Ruby

Ruby is a friend of Velma's and a member of Women for Action. She has been marching with Velma since the 1960s. She is pragmatic and highly political and known for being rather tactless and abrasive. She is also a jewelry maker.

Doc Serge

Doc Serge is a smooth-talking former pimp who runs the infirmary.

Smitty

Smitty is Sophie's son, who was murdered at a Vietnam War protest.

Wanda

Wanda was Fred's first wife. She left him shortly after her conversion to Islam, and he still feels her absence.

THEMES

Community

One of the major themes in *The Salt Eaters* and in Bambara's work in general is the importance of community. Bambara's stories often show that people are at their happiest and healthiest when they make choices based on what is best for the greater community around them rather than what is best for themselves as individuals. *The Salt Eaters* is no exception. Bambara demonstrates that if Velma had been successful in committing suicide, her loss would have radiated outward to her immediate family and friends, her partners in activism, and her colleagues. Bambara shows that our bodies are not our own, that they belong to our community and to the people who care about us, with whom it is

TOPICS FOR FURTHER STUDY

- *The Salt Eaters* incorporates heavy use of an African American dialect. The use of dialect in literature is an excellent way to add a feeling of authenticity to the work and make it seem more realistic. With several classmates, write a play that is set in a time or place where people speak differently than you do; incorporate that dialect into your writing. Then act out the play with your group members in front of your class.

- In *The Salt Eaters* Velma suffers from a psychological disorder that causes her to attempt suicide. Even though she was exhibiting many warning signs weeks before her attempt, her friends and family were still surprised by it. Using the Internet, research a psychological disorder of your choosing, and then create a PowerPoint presentation educating your classmates about that disorder. Be sure to include the common causes, symptoms, warning signs, and ways that individuals who may be suffering from that disorder can seek help.

- Read the young-adult novel *The Nature of Jade* by Deb Caletti. Jade is a young girl who suffers from panic attacks that send her into terrifying and dizzying states of being disconnected from reality. Compare and contrast the figurative language that Caletti uses to portray Jade's panic attacks with the language that Bambara uses to describes Velma's waking dreams and hallucinations. Do the authors use similar or dissimilar techniques to convey the fact that their characters are caught up in an irrational state? Write a paper compiling your findings.

- Music plays a large role in *The Salt Eaters*. Velma is a talented musician who used to go on tour, playing the piano with her women's group. Minnie Ransom uses different types of music to ground Velma and bring her back to reality. The drums from the Spring Festival are pervasive throughout the novel. With a classmate choose a passage in which music is explicitly mentioned. Using context clues about what is going on at that point in the novel, create your own interpretation of what the music might sound like. Record it and play it for your classmates.

---

our moral responsibility to engage. Active participation in one's community provides stability, support, and comfort, while choosing the path of isolation as Velma does leads to suffering and death.

Connectedness

A theme that is closely related to community is that of connectedness. This theme is manifest in the extensive web of characters who are all connected to each other in some way through their interpersonal relationships and are also connected on a higher, spiritual level. There are several instances throughout the work when characters feel connected to one another in an intangible but deeply profound way. Just as Minnie Ransom is connected to her spirit guide, Old Wife, she is also connected to and heals Velma simply by touching her. Palma is so connected to her sister that she is able to sense that there is trouble with her sister before anyone tells her. Even Nadeen, who has never before met Velma, feels drawn to and connected to Velma as she observes Velma's healing in the hospital. Merely watching Velma be healed causes Nadeen to realize things about herself, such as the fact that she is a woman and not a child.

Activism

The majority of characters in the novel are involved in some sort of activism. Ruby and Jan used to march at protests together in the

The Salt Eaters *takes place in the fictional town of Claybourne, Georgia.* *(© chloe7992 | Shutterstock.com)*

1960s and are now in the Women for Action group with Palma and Velma and many others. Velma's husband, Obie, was also an activist in the 1960s and now runs the Academy of Seven Arts, a place where those who want to bring about change can gather and learn and think. Even most of the novel's minor characters are involved in some sort of activist group or cause. However, activism is also an important part of the novel in the general sense of the word. Bambara seems to argue that it is absolutely essential for individuals to take an active interest in their community, to be activists, rather than pacifists, on a day-to-day basis. In the novel pacifism equates with stagnation and defeat, as exemplified by Velma's giving up her causes and surrendering to death.

Struggle

The struggle to heal and the struggle to become whole are experienced by many characters in the novel, with Velma, of course, being the character who struggles most obviously. Even though she is eventually healed by a sort of divine intervention through Minnie, Bambara makes it clear that her healing was not miraculous; it was a lot of work and will continue to be a lot of work until she dies. While Velma struggles to resist Minnie, Minnie struggles to bring her back in what is one of the most difficult cases of her career. Buster and Campbell both struggle to find a story worth writing about. Fred struggles to make it to his destination without becoming sick or accidentally killing his passengers. Obie struggles to "take care of business," to salvage his relationship with his wife. Sophie struggles to make sense of her goddaughter's actions. All of the characters struggle with their own battles, making it clear that life is almost never without struggle regardless of one's situation.

STYLE

Postmodern Literature

Stylistically, Bambara drew on several aspects of postmodern literature in the creation of *The Salt Eaters*. Works described as postmodern do not follow traditional realistic narrative structures, and usually involve experimental techniques or ideas. The format of a postmodern work can flexibly be altered so that the author can more clearly convey their message. The splitting of the narrative into fragments that transition suddenly from one to the next without warning or explanation is indicative of postmodern influence. Bambara's rejection (through Campbell) of the idea that any one religion or scientific theory can provide an adequate explanation for the meaning of human experience is also in line with postmodern values. The novel seems to support Campbell's claim that all systems of knowledge are not only equal, but the same. The fact that the meaning or moral of the novel is extremely complicated, difficult to summarize, and perhaps even contradictory, is another indicator that Bambara was influenced by postmodernism. *The Salt Eaters* presents a picture of life that is messy, difficult, dangerous, and constantly changing. There are many different conclusions that readers might draw from it depending on their previous life experiences.

Black Dialect

A stylistic element that many of Bambara's critics have praised in her work is her keenly intuitive ear for writing dialogue in an authentic black dialect. This means that throughout the

COMPARE
&
CONTRAST

- **1970s:** As witnessed in *The Salt Eaters*, nuclear power is a source of major contention and frequent protest in the United States. One of the largest protests takes place in Washington, DC, in May 1979. That same year Musicians United for Safe Energy (MUSE), which includes Crosby, Stills, and Nash, Bonnie Raitt, Jackson Browne, and Bruce Springsteen, holds a series of "No Nukes" concerts in New York City in support of the movement.

  Today: On February 9, 2012, the Nuclear Regulatory Commission approves the nation's first new nuclear power plant since 1978. The plant will be located near Augusta, Georgia.

- **1970s:** The black feminist movement marks its official inception with the 1973 founding of the National Black Feminist Organization (NBFO) in New York.

  Today: The NBFO disbands in 1977 never to regroup, though some branches continue to meet until 1980. Presently no black feminist group of equal membership and influence exists.

- **1970s:** According to the National Center for Biotechnology Information, as of 1978, the year of the novel's publication, suicide rates per one hundred thousand people are 12.4 among 15- to 24-year olds, 16.3 among 25- to 44-year olds, 17.6 among 45- to 64-year olds, and 19.9 for those over the age of 65.

  Today: As of 2002 those rates drop significantly in all categories to 9.9 among 15- to 24-year olds, 14.0 among 25- to 44-year olds, 14.9 among 45- to 64-year olds, and 15.6 for those over the age of 65.

novel she spells words to mimic the way they would actually sound when spoken out loud by a community of black people in Georgia in the 1970s. She also incorporates common slang terms. By using black dialect Bambara not only makes the novel seem realistic, but she also affirms the relevance and legitimacy of a way of speaking that is not Standard English. Though writing in black dialect may not seem very shocking to contemporary readers who have encountered it many times before, in the 1970s, when Bambara was writing the novel, use of black dialect was less widespread.

HISTORICAL CONTEXT

Black Arts Movement

In the 1960s and 1970s, Bambara was a significant contributor to the black arts movement, also known as the artistic branch of the black power movement. Though the movement ended in the mid-1970s, Bambara's experiences with it continued to influence her work throughout the years. The movement was closely related to the civil rights movement in that the art created by its participants championed racial equality in all facets of life. The movement began in 1965 when LeRoi Jones (also known as Amiri Baraka) moved to the largely African American neighborhood of Harlem and, with other African American activists, founded the Black Arts Repertory Theatre/School (BARTS). This was significant because it gave black artists a place in which to congregate and work where they could also support and encourage one another. The Academy of the Seven Arts in *The Salt Eaters* is somewhat reminiscent of BARTS. BARTS provided a place for a community of black artists to grow, which it did rapidly. Such an outpouring of art by African American artists had not been seen since the Harlem Renaissance of the 1920s and 1930s. The Western literary canon, which had always been and is still today dominated by white males, experienced an influx of African American contributors thanks to the movement. Bambara was the editor of an anthology published in 1970 called *The Black Woman*. The volume was one of the first explicitly feminist anthologies, especially unusual in that it featured writings by black women. Contributors included Nikki Giovanni, Audre Lorde, Alice Walker, Paule Marshall, Bambara herself, and others. The powerful and influential work became a cornerstone piece of the black arts movement.

Bambara has stated that it took her a long time to realize that art, and her writing in particular, was an effective form of activism. She worked with many women's activist groups before she discovered that writing something with a powerful message could be just as influential as—or in some cases more influential than—working with people on a personal basis. The works of the black arts movement were political at the core, as the movement was in many ways born out of the black power movement. Larry Neal described it as the "aesthetic and spiritual sister of the Black Power concept" in his 1968 essay "The Black Arts Movement," published in the *Drama Review*. Black power activists generally endorsed radical tactics to achieve their goals. Bambara herself was not directly associated with the black power movement, though she did work with many different activist groups to bring about change.

Black Feminism

Bambara was deeply entrenched not only in African American rights movements, but also in feminist movements. She belonged to many different women's organizations and her works, including *The Salt Eaters*, frequently feature black feminists. These types of organizations began becoming popular in the mid-1970s, just a few years before *The Salt Eaters* was published. Proponents of black feminism argued that because African American women were socially situated in a very different position from that of white women, especially in terms of political rights and social influence, they needed separate organizations to advocate for their particular needs and interests. African American women were somewhat marginalized by both the black power movement, which tended to be largely organized and run by men, and the feminist movement, which was run by white women. Elements of these struggles are depicted in Bambara's works.

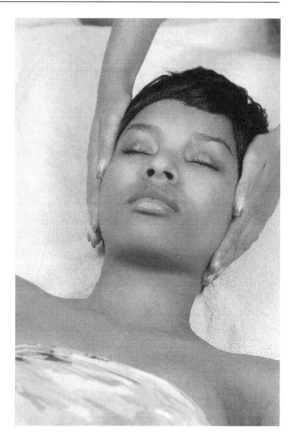

The Salt Eaters centers around "healers" Minnie Ransom and Old Wife as they try to heal Velma Henry after her attempted suicide. *(© Sanjay Deva / Shutterstock.com)*

CRITICAL OVERVIEW

Though *The Salt Eaters* has generally been a positively received work, many critics pointed out that it could potentially be a difficult novel for average readers to penetrate. For example, Margot Anne Kelley in her essay "'Damballah is the First Law of Thermodynamics': Modes of Access to Toni Cade Bambara's *The Salt Eaters*," published in 1993 in the *African American Review*, commented: "Of the ten novels we read [in a senior seminar on African American women's novels], *The Salt Eaters* was the only one that all of the students found inaccessible." However, Kelley goes on to explain that she found drawing analogies between the novel and certain scientific theories was a particularly effective way to open up students' minds to the book.

Yet other critics such as Carole Walley, who wrote about the novel in the *Feminist Review* in 1986, find the *The Salt Eaters* to be most instructive when, as a reader, one surrenders to the text and stops trying to make sense of it. Walley writes: "The book requires the reader to let go—and to give thought to the step-by-step struggles, dilemmas and relationships which are being narrated. Nothing is taken for granted. We are put in touch with the writer's work of slowing down." Walley adds, "Bambara forces us to pay attention to the detail of our lives."

In fact, many other critics, including Derek Alwes, who discussed the work in the *African American Review* in 1996, claim that the novel has an instructional effect on readers and forces them to closely consider their lives: "Ultimately, [Toni Morrison's] *Jazz* and *The Salt Eaters* have identical agendas—to direct their readers (especially, if not exclusively, their African American readers) to discover the most rewarding path to self-realization, liberty, power, and happiness."

Another critic who makes a similar argument is Janelle Collins, writing in *MELUS* in 1996. She states:

> The demand for the reader's participation is intentional and necessary. . . . With *The Salt Eaters*, the poetics and politics of postmodernism fuse; the question left to us—as readers, teachers, scholars, activists—is whether we will let ourselves remain fragments fissioned into the dominant power system or fuse our energy into a chain reaction of change.

Many critics agree that while *The Salt Eaters* may not be the easiest book to read, the effort invested will pay off with significant rewards in the end. If it was Bambara's goal to force readers into contemplating their own lives after reading this work, many critics agree that she has achieved it.

CRITICISM

Rachel Porter

Porter is a freelance writer who holds a bachelor of arts in English literature. In the following essay, she argues that in The Salt Eaters, *interactions between characters who subscribe to opposite belief systems help the reader decode Bambara's moral message and derive meaning from the work.*

As many critics have argued, one of Bambara's predominant themes in *The Salt Eaters* is the

WHAT DO I READ NEXT?

- *The Dark-Thirty: Southern Tales of the Supernatural*, published in 1992, is a collection of eerie tales featuring supernatural elements for young adults. The book, which was written by Patricia C. McKissack and illustrated by Brian Pinkney, won a Coretta Scott King Award.

- *Dragon Ladies: Asian American Feminists Breathe Fire*, edited by Sonia Shah with a preface by Yuri Kochiyama and a foreword by Karin Aguilar-San Juan, was published in 1999. The work contains writings from some of the most significant contributors to Asian American feminism.

- The 2006 book *New Thoughts on the Black Arts Movement*, edited by Lisa Gail Collins and Margo Natalie Crawford, includes essays by scholars analyzing the black arts movement from a contemporary perspective. This book will help to contextualize the movement, particularly for younger readers.

- Bambara's 1972 collection of fifteen short stories, *Gorilla, My Love*, is written in a more realistic style than *The Salt Eaters* but addresses similar themes, including community and responsibility.

- Toni Morrison's 1970 novel *The Bluest Eye* is about a young black girl named Pecola who feels deeply inferior because of her dark skin and eyes. Throughout the novel she suffers so much emotional, physical, and sexual abuse that she is driven insane.

- Kate Chopin's 1899 novel *The Awakening*, though also set in the American South, depicts an entirely different time and culture than *The Salt Eaters*. However, both books feature female protagonists who feel so smothered by their lives that they attempt suicide, and both books document their emotional collapse.

overriding importance of unity and community rather than divisiveness and isolation in all aspects of life. This philosophy renders the significance of personal beliefs and convictions if not entirely null, at least much less essential to a person's sense of identity than most Westerners believe it to be. In her essay "What It Is I Think She's Doing Anyhow: A Reading of Toni Cade Bambara's *The Salt Eaters*," Ashaka Gloria Hull claims that the character Campbell is a mouthpiece for Bambara's personal beliefs on this topic. For example, while working on a news article about nuclear energy Campbell has an epiphany: "All the systems were the same at base—voodoo, thermodynamics, I Ching, astrology, numerology, alchemy, metaphysics, everybody's ancient myths—they were interchangeable, not all separate much less conflicting. . . . How simple universal knowledge is." Later in the work Campbell muses:

> Of course everything was everything. . . . Damballah is the first law of thermodynamics and is the Biblical wisdom and is the law of time and . . . everything that is now has been before and will be again in a new way, in a changed form, in a timeless time.

To Bambara it is important to believe something, though exactly what that something is does not really matter so long as one accepts the universality and interconnectedness of all belief systems from science to religion. One of Bambara's most effective ways of demonstrating this throughout the novel is by using her characters symbolically. Nearly all of the interpersonal activity in the novel takes place between two individuals or two groups of individuals who are in some way diametrically opposed. Where balance is found, peace is maintained. Where it is lost, isolation and suffering abound. This phenomenon is particularly evident in the interactions between Velma and Minnie Ransom, Jan and Ruby, Fred Holt and his late friend Porter, and the conflict that Sophie Heywood experiences in her own mind as she struggles to understand Velma's actions.

Aside from Velma and Minnie, Jan and Ruby are the characters in the novel who are most clearly having a one-on-one debate. As they sit at the café enjoying a meal together and discussing their lives and the lives of the women who are close to them, they frequently come across topics they disagree about. Ruby is a no-nonsense, pragmatic political activist. She and Velma have a long history: they marched together in the 1960s. Ruby does not suffer fools gladly and has no problem putting people in their place when she thinks they are being impractical. She is a woman of action who takes practical steps to

> NEARLY ALL OF THE INTERPERSONAL ACTIVITY IN THE NOVEL TAKES PLACE BETWEEN TWO INDIVIDUALS OR TWO GROUPS OF INDIVIDUALS WHO ARE IN SOME WAY DIAMETRICALLY OPPOSED. WHERE BALANCE IS FOUND, PEACE IS MAINTAINED. WHERE IT IS LOST, ISOLATION AND SUFFERING ABOUND."

solve a problem as soon as she identifies it. Jan, on the other hand, is far more mild mannered, a teacher turned astrologer who used to teach academic classes for troubled students at the Academy. She keeps tarot cards in her purse and chimes in with astrological advice from time to time, much to the annoyance of Ruby, who thinks astrology is ridiculous. Jan also has no regard for politics. While they are eating, Jan is approached by Cleotus, the mysterious hermit and spiritual leader, which emphasizes Jan's strong connection to the mystical world. Unlike many other characters in the novel, Jan and Ruby are able to work together effectively in spite of their drastically different personalities. They function harmoniously as two halves of the same symbolic whole; despite their dissimilar belief systems, both work toward the same end. Though they have different viewpoints concerning the future of the Women for Action and Velma's health, they are always able to resolve their differences quickly to their mutual benefit. They serve as a model of balance in the novel.

At the opposite end of the spectrum, the bus driver Fred Holt serves a model of complete imbalance, which is at the root of his suffering. He is a grumpy and bitter old man who spends the majority of his time physically, mentally, and emotionally disconnected from other human beings in the driver's seat of his bus. He fantasizes about shooting his passengers when he becomes annoyed with them for asking him simple questions, and he is cruel to his wife, Margie, whom he deeply resents, deliberately telling her things that he knows will upset her. He feels betrayed and abandoned by his best friend, Porter, and his ex-wife, Wanda, the only people he ever seemed to have any respect for, though in reality he pushed them both away. Fred felt disconnected and betrayed by Wanda when she became interested in Islam, and disconnected from Porter when he decided that he wanted to study with the hermit Cleotus. In both instances Fred allowed the fact that someone in his life adopted a new belief system, or merely expressed an interest in a different belief system, to drive a wedge between himself and his loved one. As Fred explains: "The hurtingest part was the voice, something in Porter's voice like Wanda's when she found 'the way,' joined up with them Muslim people, talked off the wall in a voice that shut him out." It is this voice that prevented Fred from ever taking Wanda up on her many invitations to the temple, and the same voice that makes him feel he has lost Porter as a friend. In both situations his loved ones vanished from his life shortly after he came to this conclusion. Wanda left, and Porter died, leaving him alone with Margie, whom he resents. Fred is hateful, judgmental, and cruel; he does not accept others' need for exploration and is oblivious to the unity of all humanity and human knowledge. By the logic of the story he is therefore destined to be alone and unhappy. Yet Fred cannot understand that he is the source of his own unhappiness and isolation. If his dogma were not so exclusive, he would not be trapped in a cycle of pushing people away from him every time they become curious about a new belief system.

With Sophie "M'Dear" Heywood Bambara provides a sharp contrast to Fred. Sophie has had her closest loved ones, both her son Smitty and her husband Daddy Dolphy, ripped away from her in cruel ways. Yet unlike Fred, Sophie looks for meaning in these events and focuses on healing herself from them rather than despairing. As a deeply spiritual person and a sign reader, she believes that everyone can be clairvoyant if they allow themselves to tap into it. Sophie, a respected community leader, appears as a symbol of unity throughout the novel. Even when, shocked and hurt by her godchild's suicide attempt, she needs to retreat inside herself for a moment to heal, she thinks about the importance of acceptance and unity. In her dreamlike state she says to Velma: "Not all wars have casualties, Vee. Some struggles between old and new ideas, some battles between ways of seeing have only victors."

Of course Velma and Minnie are the most obvious and prevalent example of two people at

Bambara's novel explores the relationships between African Americans, particularly between genders. (© REDAV / Shutterstock.com)

odds with one another in the story. They engage in a battle of wills throughout the novel: Minnie struggles to bring Velma back to life and wholeness while Velma struggles to resist. Their belief systems could not be more opposite: Minnie is a faith healer who miraculously heals people's ailments and communes with witches while Velma is a computer programmer and a hyperorganized, overworked community activist. In the course of the novel, the reader learns that Velma has undergone several fearful, traumatic experiences that have caused her to retreat into herself, while the community around her failed to keep her connected. As Velma suffers alone, she retreats from all of the important relationships in her life including her failing marriage and her relationship with her son. The more Velma isolates herself from her family and her town, the further she slips away from sanity. But ultimately it is Minnie Ransom's hands, the literal touch of another human, that bring Velma back to the land of the living. When she finally allows Minnie to get through to her, she earns a second chance at life, a "burst cocoon," in a hospital in which faith healers, spirit guides, and practitioners of Western medicine coexist peacefully.

These character interactions and many more in the story serve to illustrate Bambara's moral, that independence and radicalism lead to isolation, psychological breakdown, and death, while cooperation and community interaction lead to emotional stability and life. As Sophie Haywood is contemplating Velma's horrific actions, she muses to herself: "Did you think that your life was yours alone to do with what you please? That I, your folks, your family, and all who care for you have no say-so in the matter? Whop!" Bambara's work rejects the notion that individuals are the sole owners of their own lives just as adamantly as Sophie does. Indeed, through moral lessons Bambara's *The Salt Eaters* does not simply encourage, it demands that readers let their communities and their loved ones into their lives for the greater benefit of all.

Source: Rachel Porter, Critical Essay on *The Salt Eaters*, in *Novels for Students*, Gale, Cengage Learning, 2014.

David Ikard

In the following excerpt, Ikard explores how Bambara "casts light on how black men and women impose unrealistic gender standards on each other that foster intraracial conflicts and violence."

. . . In *The Salt Eaters* (1980), Toni Cade Bambara's first and most highly regarded novel, she provides critical insights into the cultural variables that frustrate gender relations in the black community. In particular, she casts light on how black men and women impose unrealistic gender standards on each other that foster intraracial conflicts and violence on both sides of the gender line. Unable and, at times, unwilling to address these intraracial gender conflicts, her characters (women and men) become co-conspirators in their own racial and/or gender oppression.

Though Bambara certainly emphasizes the problematics of black male victimhood and privilege, her aim is not to place the onus of intraracial gender discord on black men. Rather she wants to illuminate how internalized "white supremacist" notions of gender roles have fostered—and foster—intraracial gender and cultural unrest. To this end, she does not simply

replace the victimized black male motif (that absolves black men of moral and social responsibility because of racial oppression) with a version emphasizing black female victimhood. Rather she establishes modes of cultural analysis to empower blacks across gender differences. Most critically, she shows that black feminist discussions that address black men as if they enjoyed the racial privileges of white men are as problematic as the black nationalist discourse that labels any woman who takes initiative an emasculator.

In *The Salt Eaters* Bambara provides a strategy for gender-cultural empowerment and conciliation by introducing a vision of black cultural restoration premised on the existence of a real and accessible ancestral power latent within black Americans. Remarking on the cultural vision in the novel, Bambara explains that "What compelled me to tackle [the issue of cultural wholeness] . . . in *Salt* was the amount of psychic and spiritual damage that is being done to us, and the fact that we're encouraged to ignore or laugh at the damage" (Chandler 348). Bambara argues that achieving this cultural wholeness comes at a high social cost. In effect, those who acquire it must accept responsibility for self and cultural determination, rejecting as they do the idea that oppression (of any sort) robs them of social agency. For these reasons, Bambara observes, most blacks do not desire wholeness. She writes, "To be whole—politically, psychically, spiritually, culturally, intellectually, aesthetically, physically, and economically whole—is of profound significance. It is significant because there is a correlative to this. There is a responsibility to self and to history that is developed once you are 'whole,' once you are well, once you acknowledge your powers" (348). Acknowledging the existence and viability of these cultural powers is for Bambara the first and most crucial step towards achieving cultural healing and wholeness. . . .

Source: David Ikard, "'So much of what we know ain't so': The Other Gender in Toni Cade Bambara's *The Salt Eaters*," in *Obsidian III*, Vol. 4, No. 1, Spring–Summer 2002, p. 76.

Margaret Mazurkiewicz

In the following essay, Mazurkiewicz provides an overview of Bambara's career, and considers the style of The Salt Eaters *to be "almost dreamlike."*

Toni Cade Bambara is a well-known and respected civil rights activist, professor of English and African American studies, editor of two anthologies of black literature, and author of short stories and novels. According to Alice A. Deck in the *Dictionary of Literary Biography*, "In many ways Toni Cade Bambara is one of the best representatives of the group of Afro-American writers who, during the 1960s, became directly involved in the cultural and socio-political activities in urban communities across the country." Deck points out that "Bambara is one of the few who continued to work within the black urban communities (filming, lecturing, organizing, and reading from her works at rallies and conferences), producing imaginative reenactments of these experiences in her fiction. In addition, Bambara established herself over the years as an educator, teaching in colleges and independent community schools in various cities on the East Coast."

Bambara's first two books of fiction, *Gorilla, My Love* and *The Sea Birds Are Still Alive*, are collections of her short stories. Susan Lardner remarks in the *New Yorker* that the stories in these two works, "describing the lives of black people in the North and the South, could be more exactly typed as vignettes and significant anecdotes, although a few of them are fairly long. . . . All are notable for their purposefulness, a more or less explicit inspirational angle, and a distinctive motion of the prose, which swings from colloquial narrative to precarious metaphorical heights and over to street talk, at which Bambara is unbeatable."

In a review of *Gorilla, My Love*, for example, a writer assesses in the *Saturday Review* that the stories "are among the best portraits of black life to have appeared in some time. [They are] written in a breezy, engaging style that owes a good deal to street dialect." A critic writing in *Newsweek* makes a similar observation of the author's second collection of short stories, *The Sea Birds Are Still Alive*, commenting, "Bambara directs her vigorous sense and sensibility to black neighborhoods in big cities, with occasional trips to small Southern towns. . . . The stories start and stop like rapid-fire conversations conducted in a rhythmic, black-inflected, sweet-and-sour language." In fact, according to Anne Tyler in the *Washington Post Book World*, Bambara's particular style of narration is one of the most distinctive qualities of her writing. "What pulls us along

is the language of [her] characters, which is startlingly beautiful without once striking a false note," notes Tyler. "Everything these people say, you feel, ordinary, real-life people are saying right now on any street corner. It's only that the rest of us didn't realize it was sheer poetry they were speaking."

In terms of plot, Bambara tends to avoid linear development in favor of presenting "situations that build like improvisations of a melody," as a *Newsweek* reviewer explains. Bell Gale Chevigny in the *Village Voice* observes that despite the "often sketchy" plots in *Gorilla, My Love*, the stories are always "lavish in their strokes—here are elaborate illustrations, soaring asides, aggressive sub-plots. They are never didactic, but they abound in far-out common sense, exotic home truths."

Numerous reviewers have also remarked on Bambara's sensitive portrayals of her characters and the handling of their situations, portrayals that are marked by an affectionate warmth and pride. Laura Marcus writes in the *Times Literary Supplement* that Bambara "presents black culture as embattled but unbowed. . . . Bambara depicts black communities in which ties of blood and friendship are fiercely defended." In addition, Deck remarks that "the basic implication of all of Toni Cade Bambara's stories is that there is an undercurrent of caring for one's neighbors that sustains black Americans. In her view the presence of those individuals who intend to do harm to people is counterbalanced by as many if not more persons who have a genuine concern for other people."

C. D. B. Bryan admires this expression of the author's concern for other people, declaring in the *New York Times Book Review* that "Bambara tells me more about being black through her quiet, proud, silly, tender, hip, acute, loving stories than any amount of literary polemicizing could hope to do. She writes about love: a love for one's family, one's friends, one's race, one's neighborhood and it is the sort of love that comes with maturity and inner peace." According to Bryan, "All of [Bambara's] stories share the affection that their narrator feels for the subject, an affection that is sometimes terribly painful, at other times fiercely proud. But at all times it is an affection that is so genuinely that her stories are *genus homo sapiens* not only black stories."

In 1980, Bambara published her first novel, a generally well-received work entitled *The Salt*

Eaters. Written in an almost dream-like style, *The Salt Eaters* explores the relationship between two women with totally different backgrounds and lifestyles brought together by a suicide attempt by one of the women. John Leonard, who describes the book as "extraordinary," writes in the *New York Times* that *The Salt Eaters* "is almost an incantation, poem-drunk, myth-happy, mudcaked, jazz-ridden, prodigal in meanings, a kite and a mask. It astonishes because Toni Cade Bambara is so adept at switching from politics to legend, from particularities of character to prehistorical song, from LaSalle Street to voodoo. It is as if she jived the very stones to groan."

In a *Times Literary Supplement* review, Carol Rumens states that *The Salt Eaters* "is a hymn to individual courage, a sombre message of hope that has confronted the late twentieth-century pathology of racist violence and is still able to articulate its faith in 'the dream'." John Wideman notes in the *New York Times Book Review*: "In her highly acclaimed fiction and in lectures, [Bambara] emphasizes the necessity for black people to maintain their best traditions, to remain healthy and whole as they struggle for political power. *The Salt Eaters*, her first novel, eloquently summarizes and extends the abiding concerns of her previous work."

Source: Margaret Mazurkiewicz, "Toni Cade Bambara: Overview," in *Reference Guide to American Literature*, 3rd ed., edited by Jim Kamp, St. James Press, 1994.

Beverly Guy-Sheftall and Toni Cade Bambara

In the following interview, Bambara comments on her literary influences and her approach to fiction writing.

[Guy-Sheftall]: Have women writers influenced you as much as male writers?

[*Bambara*]: I have no clear ideas about literary influence. I would say that my mother was a great influence, since mother is usually the first map maker in life. She encouraged me to explore and express. And, too, the fact that people of my household were big on privacy helped. And I would say that people that I ran into helped, and I ran into a great many people because we moved a lot and I was always a nosey kid running up and down the street, getting into everything. Particular kinds of women influenced the work. For example, in every neighborhood I

> **THERE ARE TIMES WHEN YOU HAVE TO PUT ASIDE WHAT YOU INTENDED TO WRITE, WHAT GOT YOU TO THE DESK IN THE FIRST PLACE, AND JUST GO WITH THE STORY THAT IS COMING OUT OF YOU, WHICH MAY OR MAY NOT HAVE ANYTHING TO DO WITH WHAT YOU PLANNED."**

lived in there were always two types of women that somehow pulled me and sort of got their wagons in a circle around me. I call them Miss Naomi and Miss Gladys, although I'm sure they came under various names. The Miss Naomi types were usually barmaids or life-women, nighttime people with lots of clothes in the closet and a very particular philosophy of life, who would give me advice like, "When you meet a man, have a birthday, demand a present that's hockable, and be careful." Stuff like that. Had no idea what they were talking about. Just as well. The Miss Naomis usually gave me a great deal of advice about beautification, how to take care of your health and not get too fat. The Miss Gladyses were usually the type that hung out the window in Apartment 1-A leaning on the pillow giving single-action advice on numbers or giving you advice about how to get your homework done or telling you to stay away from those cruising cars that moved through the neighborhood patrolling little girls. I would say that those two types of women, as well as the women who hung out in the beauty parlors (and the beauty parlors in those days were perhaps the only womanhood institutes we had—it was there in the beauty parlors that young girls came of age and developed some sense of sexual standards and some sense of what it means to be a woman growing up)—it was those women who had the most influence on the writing.

I think that most of my work tends to come off the street rather than from other books. Which is not to say I haven't learned a lot as an avid reader. I devour pulp and print. And of course I'm part of the tradition. That is to say, it is quite apparent to the reader that I appreciated Langston Hughes, Zora Hurston, and am a product of the sixties spirit. But I'd be hard pressed to discuss literary influences in any kind of intelligent way. . . .

[Have] your travels revealed to you how American black and other Third World women can link up in their struggles to liberate themselves from the various kinds of oppression they face as a result of their sexual identity?

Yes, I would say that two particular places I visited yielded up a lot of lessons along those lines. I was in Cuba in 1973 and had the occasion not only to meet with the Federation of Cuban Women but sisters in the factories, on the land, in the street, in the parks, in lines, or whatever, and the fact that they were able to resolve a great many class conflicts as well as color conflicts and organize a mass organization says a great deal about the possibilities here. I was in Vietnam in the summer of 1975 as a guest of the Women's Union and again was very much struck by the women's ability to break through traditional roles, traditional expectations, reactionary agenda for women, and come together again in a mass organization that is programmatic and takes on a great deal of responsibility for the running of the nation.

We missed a moment in the early sixties. We missed two things. One, at a time when we were beginning to lay the foundations for a national black women's union and for a national strategy for organizing, we did not have enough heart nor a solid enough analysis that would equip us to respond in a positive and constructive way to the fear in the community from black men as well as others who said that women organizing as women is divisive. We did not respond to that in a courageous and principled way. We fell back. The other moment that we missed was that we had an opportunity to hook up with Puerto Rican women and Chicano women who shared not only a common condition but also I think a common vision about the future and we missed that moment because of the language trap. When people talked about multicultural or multiethnic organizing, a lot of us translated that to mean white folks and backed off. I think that was an error. We should have known what was meant by multicultural. Namely, people of color. Afro-American, Afro-Hispanic, Indo-Hispanic, Asian-Hispanic, and so forth. Not that those errors necessarily doom us. Errors may result in lessons learned. I think we have the opportunity again in this last quarter of the twentieth century to begin forging those critical ties with other communities. It will be done. That is a certainty. . . .

You are one of the few black literary artists who could be considered a short story writer primarily. Is this a deliberate choice on your part or coincidental?

It's deliberate, coincidental, accidental, and regretful! Regretful, commercially. That is to say, it is financially stupid to be a short story writer and to spend two years putting together eight or ten stories and receiving maybe half the amount of money you would had you taken one of those short stories and produced a novel. The publishing companies, reviewers, critics, are all geared to promoting and pushing the novel rather than any other form.

I prefer the short story genre because it's quick, it makes a modest appeal for attention, it can creep up on you on your blind side. The reader comes to the short story with a mind-set different than that with which he approaches the big book, and a different set of controls operating, which is why I think the short story is far more effective in term of teaching us lessons.

Temperamentally, I move toward the short story because I'm a sprinter rather than a long-distance runner. I cannot sustain characters over a long period of time. Walking around, frying eggs, being a mother, shopping—I cannot have those characters living in my house with me for more than a couple of weeks. In terms of craft, I don't have the kinds of skills *yet* that it takes to stay with a large panorama of folks and issues and landscapes and moods. That requires a set of skills that I don't know anything about yet, but I'm learning.

I prefer the short story as a reader, as well, because it does what it does in a hurry. For the writer and the reader make instructive demands in terms of language precision. It deals with economy, gets it said, and gets out of the way. As a teacher, I also prefer the short story for all the reasons given. And yes, I consider myself primarily a short story writer. . . .

That leads me into the next question which is about the process involved in your writing a story. Do you have the whole idea of it before sitting down to write, or does it unfold as you're writing?

It depends on how much time you have. There are periods in my life when I know that I will not be able to get to the desk until summer, until months later, in which case I walk around composing while washing dishes and may jot down little definitive notes on pieces of paper which I stick under the phone, in the mirror, and all over the house. At other times, a story mobilizes itself around a single line you've heard that resonates. There's a truth there, something usable. Sometimes a story revolves around a character that I'm interested in. For example, "The Organizer's Wife" in the new collection. I've always been very curious about silent people because most people I know are like myself—very big-mouthed, verbally energetic, and generally clear as to what they're about because their *mouth* is always announcing what they're doing. That story came out of a curiosity. What do I know about people like that? Could I delve into her? The story took shape around that effort.

There are other times when a story is absolutely clear in the head. All of it may not be clear—who's going to say what and where it's taking place or what year it is—but the story frequently comes together at one moment in the head. At other times, stories, like any other kind of writing, and certainly anybody who's writing anything—freshman compositions, press releases, or whatever—has experienced this, that frequently writing is an act of discovery. Writing is very much like dreaming, in that sense. When you dream, you dialogue with aspects of yourself that normally are not with you in the daytime and you discover that you know a great deal more than you thought you did. So there are various kinds of ways that writing comes.

Then, too, there is a kind of—some people call it automatic writing—I call it inspiration. There are times when you have to put aside what you intended to write, what got you to the desk in the first place, and just go with the story that is coming out of you, which may or may not have anything to do with what you planned at all. In fact, a lot of stories (I haven't published any of these because I'm not sure they are mine) and poems have come out on the page that I know do not belong to me. They do not have my sense of vision, my sense of language, my sense of reality, but they're complete. Each of us has experienced this in various ways, in church, or fasting, or in some other kind of state, times when we are available to intelligences that we are not particularly prone to acknowledge, given our Western scientific training, which have filled us with so much fear that we

cannot make ourselves available to other channels of information. I think most of us have experienced, though we don't talk about it very much, an inspiration, that is to say, an inbreathing that then becomes "enthusiasm," a possession, a living-with, an informing spirit. So some stories come off like that.

Do you make many revisions before the story is finished and ready for publication?

Oh yes. I edit mercilessly. Generally, my editing takes the form of cutting. Very frequently, a story will try to get away from me and become a novel. I don't have the staying power for a novel, so when I find it getting to be about thirty or forty pages I immediately start cutting back to six. To my mind, the six-page short story is the gem. If it takes more than six pages to say it, something is the matter. So I'm not too pleased in that respect with the new collection, *The Sea Birds Are Still Alive*. Most of those stories are too sprawling and hairy for my taste, although I'm very pleased, feel perfectly fine about them as pieces. But as stories, they're too damn long and dense. . . .

One of the characteristics of your fiction which is apparent in Gorilla, My Love, *an older collection of short stories, as well as in* The Sea Birds *is the extent to which—though one knows you're there—you can remove yourself from the narrative voice. You don't intrude. Is that deliberate?*

Well, I'm frequently there. You see, one of the reasons that it seems that the author is not there has to do with language. It has to do with the whole tradition of dialect. In the old days, writers might have their characters talking dialect or slang but the narrator, that is to say, the author, maintained a distance and a "superiority" by speaking a more premiumed language. I tend to speak on the same level as my characters, so it seems as though I am not there, because, possibly, you're looking for another voice.

I rarely get the impression that your fiction comes directly out of your personal experience, even though it's obvious that what you have written about has been filtered through your consciousness. I don't have the impression that these particular characters or that particular incident are very close to what you may have actually experienced. Is that correct?

Yes, that's correct. I think it's very rude to write autobiographically, unless you label it autobiography. And I think it's very rude to use friends and relatives as though they were occasions for getting your whole thing off. It's not making your mama a still life. And it's very abusive to your developing craft, to your own growth, not to convert and transform what has come to you in one way into another way. The more you convert the more you grow, it seems to me. Through conversion we recognize again the basic oneness, the connections, or as some blood coined it: "Everything is Everything." So, it's kind of *lazy* (I think that's the better word) to simply record. Also, it's terribly boring to the reader frequently, and, too, it's dodgy. You can't tell to what extent things are fascinating to you because they're yours and to what extent they're useful, unless you do some conversion.

What can we expect from you in the future?

I'm working on several things—some children's books, a new collection of short stories, a novel, some film scripts.

"Children of Struggle" is a series I've been working on that dramatizes the role children and youth have played in the struggle for liberation—children of the Underground Railroad, children of Frelimo, children of the Long March, of Granma, of El Grito de Lares, The Trail of Tears, and so forth. . . .

Source: Beverly Guy-Sheftall and Toni Cade Bambara, "Commitment: Toni Cade Bambara Speaks," in *Sturdy Black Bridges*, edited by Roseann P. Bell, Bettye J. Parker, and Beverly Guy-Sheftall, Anchor Press/Doubleday, 1978, pp. 230–49.

SOURCES

Alwes, Derek, "The Burden of Liberty: Choice in Toni Morrison's *Jazz* and Toni Cade Bambara's *The Salt Eaters*," in *African American Review*, Vol. 30, No. 3, Fall 1996, pp. 353–65.

Bambara, Toni Cade, *The Salt Eaters*, Vintage Books, 1992.

"But Some of Us Are Brave: A History of Black Feminism in the United States," MIT website, http://www.mit.edu/activities/thistle/v9/9.01/6blackf.html (accessed December 10, 2012).

Collins, Janelle, "Generating Power: Fission, Fusion, and Postmodern Politics in Bambara's *The Salt Eaters*," in *MELUS*, Vol. 21, No. 2, Summer 1996, pp. 35–47.

Copeland, Larry, "Nuclear Agency Approves First Nuclear Reactors since 1978," in *USA Today*, February 10, 2012, http://usatoday30.usatoday.com/news/washington/story/2012-02-09/us-nuclear-reactors-approve/53027204/1 (accessed December 10, 2012).

Horsley, Sarah K., "Toni Cade Bambara," FemBio website, http://www.fembio.org/english/biography.php/woman/biography/toni-cade-bambara/ (accessed December 10, 2012).

Hull, Akasha (Gloria), "What It Is I Think She's Doing Anyhow: A Reading of Toni Cade Bambara's *The Salt Eaters*," in *Home Girls: A Black Feminist Anthology*, edited by Barbara Smith, Rutgers University Press, 2000, pp. 124–42.

Kelley, Margot Anne, "'Damballah Is the First Law of Thermodynamics': Modes of Access to Toni Cade Bambara's *The Salt Eaters*," in *African American Review*, Vol. 27, No. 3, Fall 1993, pp. 479–93.

Mathes, Carter A., "Scratching the Threshold: Textual Sound and Political Form in Toni Cade Bambara's *The Salt Eaters*," in *Contemporary Literature*, Vol. 50, No. 2, Summer 2009, pp. 363–96.

McKeown, Robert E., Steven P. Cuffe, and Richard M. Schulz, "U.S. Suicide Rates by Age Group, 1970–2002: An Examination of Recent Trends," in *National Center for Biotechnology Information*, October 2006, http://www.ncbi.nlm.nih.gov/pmc/articles/PMC1586156/ (accessed December 10, 2012).

Neal, Larry, "The Black Arts Movement," in *Drama Review*, Vol. 12, No. 4, Summer 1968, pp. 29–39.

Reed, Daphne S., "LeRoi Jones: High Priest of the Black Arts Movement," in *Educational Theatre Journal*, Vol. 22, No. 1, March 1970, pp. 53–59.

Schirack, Maureen, and Lauren Curtright, eds., "Toni Cade Bambara," University of Minnesota website, August 11, 2004, http://voices.cla.umn.edu/artistpages/bambaraToni.php (accessed December 10, 2012).

Walley, Carole, Review of *The Salt Eaters*, in *Feminist Review*, No. 24, Fall 1986, pp. 116–18.

Ya Salaam, Kalamu, "The Black Arts Movement," aalbc.com, http://aalbc.com/authors/blackartsmovement.htm (accessed December 10, 2012).

FURTHER READING

Bambara, Toni Cade, ed., *The Black Woman: An Anthology*, New American Library, 1970.

Bambara's first edited anthology, *The Black Woman*, was a significant work of the black arts movement. The collection includes fiction and poetry by black women authors who were already somewhat established at the time of its publication as well as works by newcomers.

Brown, Diane R., and Verna M. Keith, eds., *In and Out of Our Right Minds: The Mental Health of African American Women*, Columbia University Press, 2003.

In *In and Out of Our Right Minds* the authors assert that while African American women are often portrayed as being calm, stable, and strong in the face of trauma or adversity, in reality they are statistically at higher risk of psychological disorders because they have a greater number of stresses in their lives.

Hurston, Zora Neale, *Their Eyes Were Watching God*, Harper Perennial, 2006.

Originally published in 1937, *Their Eyes Were Watching God* is the most famous work of Zora Neale Hurston, whom Bambara has cited as one of her major influences. The novel follows a young African American woman as she grows to adulthood and faces racial discrimination in the midst of the Harlem Renaissance.

Rojas, Maythee, *Women of Color and Feminism*, Seal Press, 2009.

In this work Maythee Rojas, an associate professor of women's, gender, and sexuality studies at California State University, Long Beach, explores how race and socioeconomics can affect the feminist experience.

SUGGESTED SEARCH TERMS

Toni Cade Bambara

The Salt Eaters

Toni Cade Bambara AND the Salt Eaters

Toni Cade Bambara AND novels

Toni Cade Bambara AND writing

Toni Cade Bambara AND activism

Toni Cade Bambara AND feminism

Toni Cade Bambara AND black arts movement

Toni Cade Bambara AND postmodern novel

black arts movement AND feminist literature

The Third Life of Grange Copeland

ALICE WALKER

1970

The Third Life of Grange Copeland is the first novel of one of America's most prominent contemporary authors. Published in 1970, when Alice Walker was twenty-six years old, the novel follows the lives of three generations of one African American family in the South, from 1920 to the mid-1960s. The title refers to the three stages in the life of Grange Copeland, who begins as a sharecropper in Georgia, moves to New York to improve his lot, and then returns to the South for his "third life," in which he forms a close and loving relationship with his granddaughter Ruth. This redeems him in some measure from the failures of his "first life," in which he abused and neglected his wife and son. In its exploration of concepts such as black masculinity, African American gender relations, the nature of racist oppression, and the hopes created by the civil rights movement, *The Third Life of Grange Copeland* is a thoughtful and engaging novel that remains as relevant in the 2010s as it was at its first publication.

Readers should be cautioned that the novel does contain some violent scenes of domestic abuse.

AUTHOR BIOGRAPHY

Alice Walker was born on February 9, 1944, in Eatonton, Georgia, the last of eight children born to Willie Lee Walker and Millie Lou

Alice Walker (© Araya Diaz | WireImage | Getty Images)

writer, poet, and essayist. Her short-story collections include *In Love and in Trouble* (1972) and *The Way Forward Is with a Broken Heart* (2000). Her most notable novel is *The Color Purple* (1982), which was awarded the Pulitzer Prize in Fiction in 1983; this was the first time the award was given to an African American woman. The novel also won the National Book Award. Walker's other novels include *The Temple of My Familiar* (1989), *Possessing the Secret of Joy* (1992), and *Now Is the Time to Open Your Heart* (2004). Walker's essay collections, in which she discusses issues of race and gender, include *In Search of Our Mothers' Gardens* (1983) and *We Are the Ones We Have Been Waiting For* (2006).

PLOT SUMMARY

Part 1

The novel begins in 1920 in Greenfield County, Georgia. Brownfield Copeland is a young boy who works with his father, Grange, in the cotton fields. Brownfield is neglected by both his parents. His father becomes violent when he drinks and refuses to send his son to school. Brownfield develops a dream to escape to the North where his cousins live. His parents also talk of moving north, but Grange lacks the initiative to do so.

Five years later, Brownfield finds himself expected to care for a new baby boy named Star, who is neglected by his mother and father. By this time Brownfield is working at a factory with his mother, Margaret. He still dreams of moving north. Tragedy strikes when Grange leaves the family and Margaret kills herself and the baby. Brownfield goes to work for Mr. Shipley, who owns the cotton plantation.

Part 2

Fed up with working for Shipley, Brownfield leaves and tries to head north but does not know where he is going. He wanders into a town, enters a bar and grill, and meets the owner, Josie, and her daughter, Lorene. It happens that Josie is a former lover of Grange, Brownfield's father. She invites Brownfield to work for her and live with her and Lorene. Josie and Brownfield become lovers, although he does not yet know of her former relationship

Grant Walker. Her father was a sharecropper, and her mother worked as a maid. In 1961, Walker attended Spelman College in Atlanta, Georgia, on a scholarship. She transferred to Sarah Lawrence College in New York in 1963 and graduated from there in 1966. In the same year, she met Melvyn Leventhal, a Jewish civil rights lawyer. They married in 1967 and moved to Jackson, Mississippi, at a time when interracial marriages were rare. Two years later their child, Rebecca, was born. The marriage ended in divorce in 1976.

Walker's first published short story appeared in 1967, as did her first published essay. In 1968, her first book of poems, *Once*, was published. That year she became writer-in-residence at Jackson State College in Mississippi. In 1970, her first novel, *The Third Life of Grange Copeland*, was published and won her national acclaim. The following year she accepted a fellowship at Radcliffe College of Harvard University. Since then Walker has had a distinguished career as novelist, short-story

MEDIA ADAPTATIONS

- An audiobook of *The Third Life of Grange Copeland* was produced in 2008 by Recording for the Blind & Dyslexic.

with his father. When he does learn of this, he transfers his affections to Lorene.

Brownfield meets Josie's niece, Mem, a quiet, educated girl. He and Mem become involved with each other, and she tries to teach him to read and write. They marry, leaving Josie's house and going to live as sharecroppers in the country. They hope to move north in a couple of years. However, three years later, with one child, Daphne, and Mem pregnant with their second, they are too poor to contemplate moving.

Part 3

Unhappy with being in debt with no prospects of escaping their situation, Brownfield becomes depressed. He also becomes abusive toward Mem and irresponsible with money. Their two children, Daphne and Ornette, are afraid of their father. He becomes an alcoholic and beats Mem, who wants to leave him but has nowhere to go.

Brownfield renews his friendship with Josie, who tells him she knew his father before he married Margaret. She claims that Grange loved her and only married Margaret because of pressure from his family. Josie and Grange continued to see each other even after the marriage. When Grange returns to Georgia, Josie rejects Brownfield in favor of Grange, and they marry.

Part 4

Mem gives birth to another child, Ruth. Brownfield is drunk at the time and offers no assistance. Grange has become a regular visitor to their home and brings gifts for the children. He and Josie are comfortably off, in contrast to the poverty in which Brownfield and his family live. Grange lights a fire to provide some warmth

for the new baby and makes a stew. He sees that Brownfield has not helped Mem at all.

As the three daughters grow older, Brownfield continues on his downward spiral. He is frequently drunk and offers them no affection.

Part 5

Captain Davis, who owns the dairy farm on which Brownfield works, reassigns Brownfield to the dairy farm owned by his son, J.L. Brownfield hates the white men he works for because he can never get out of debt. He is ready to move the family to J.L.'s farm, but Mem refuses to go. The next day, Mem tells Brownfield she has taken out a lease on a house in town. She insists that they move to town and that he take a job in a factory. He is furious. She tells him she has already obtained a job and will be able to afford the rent. On Saturday night, Brownfield returns home drunk and beats Mem up. When he wakes, Mem turns the tables on him, threatening him with a shotgun and hitting him in the head with it. She tells him he must reform and treat her and the children well. He must not drink in the house or come home drunk. Humiliated, Brownfield reluctantly agrees to her demands.

Part 6

The family moves to the new house, and Brownfield works in a factory. He goes along with Mem's house rules while secretly plotting his revenge against her. For a while they live fairly normally, but after two pregnancies that result in still births Mem becomes ill. Eventually she is unable to continue working. The heating bill is not paid for two months, and the family receives an eviction order. The family is forced to move to a house on J.L.'s farm that is in terrible condition. Brownfield returns to his old ways, insulting Mem. He tells her she cannot compare to Josie.

Several years pass. The family continues to live in squalor. Ruth begins to attend school. Mem gives birth to a son who dies in infancy, possibly because he froze to death. Mem recovers her health and accepts a job as a maid for a white family.

Part 7

One day when Mem returns from work, Brownfield shoots and kills her. Ruth goes to live with her grandfather, Grange, while Daphne and Ornette are sent north to live with their maternal grandfather. Grange develops a warm relationship with

Ruth, but Josie resents the presence of the child. Grange and Ruth do day-to-day activities together, and he builds her a cabin to play in. They dance together, and Grange sings. Josie becomes more jealous. She begins to visit Brownfield, who is serving a prison term for murder.

Grange tries to explain to Ruth how black people are discriminated against. He tells her about slavery and segregation and his hatred of white people. He wants her to learn about the ways of the world. However, when he tells her that the suicide of his wife can be blamed on the old white man he worked for, Ruth does not believe him.

Grange thinks back to the time he spent in New York, before he returned to the South to be with Josie. He did not find success in the North. He was destitute and forced to beg for money. He committed many robberies, and his hatred for white people grew worse. He would get involved in fights with white people in order to take out his frustrations on them. As he raises his granddaughter, he decides not to tell her of this aspect of his life.

Part 8

Brownfield is serving ten years in prison for the murder of Mem. He blames her for her own death. Josie tells him about Grange's warm relationship with Ruth, and Brownfield becomes angry at the thought of his child being raised by Grange. Josie still resents the presence of Ruth, and Brownfield tells her of his plan to regain custody of his daughter after his release from prison. He tries to reassure Josie that once Ruth is gone from their house, Grange will love her again.

Part 9

Grange thinks back to the time when he was married to Margaret, which he now thinks of as his first life. He realizes he is partly responsible for her death. He continued to see Josie, which undermined Margaret's self-esteem, causing her to go with other men, including Shipley, the white employer, who was the father of Margaret's baby, Star. Margaret killed herself because she was in despair and believed herself to be a sinner.

Ruth hates going to school and listening to the lectures given by the teacher, Mrs. Grayson. The textbook they use is handed down from the white school and contains unflattering images of black people. Ruth daydreams during class, and one day Mrs. Grayson beats her with a strap. Ruth stands up to her, they trade insults, and Ruth walks out of the class. Ruth has no friends at school and has low social standing there because of her family history. She eventually makes one friend, a girl named Rossel, who also has a troubled family background.

As Ruth enters her teens she considers what she is going to do with her life. She does not want to leave her grandfather, but she knows there are limited options for her. She does not want to be a teacher, but she also finds out that all the best jobs are reserved for white people. Grange says he hopes things will change. He then explains to Ruth how in what he calls his second life he came to hate white people but also learned to love himself. In his third life, however, after he returned to the South, he abandoned hatred and learned to love someone else and make that person, Ruth, the focus of his life. He continues to teach her everything he knows.

Part 10

Josie has gone to live with Brownfield. One day, as Grange accompanies Ruth home from school, they encounter Brownfield and Josie. Brownfield says he wants Ruth back, which shocks Grange. Brownfield insists the courts will side with him. Ruth is scared she will be forced to return to live with a father she despises. Fearful of what may happen, Grange opens a bank account for Ruth and puts his own savings in it. Ruth is now sixteen years old. She learns how to drive, and Grange puts the car in her name.

One day Ruth encounters Brownfield on her way to school. He brings her a gift, but she rejects it. He says he loves her and that she is his possession and must leave her grandfather. She rejects all his arguments. That night Brownfield tells Josie he has a plan to gain custody of Ruth. While he was in prison he did some work for a judge, and he plans to ask the judge to help him in his court battle.

Part 11

Ruth learns from television about the civil rights movement and enthusiastically embraces it, although Grange is skeptical about what it might accomplish. He believes white racism has been around too long for there to be meaningful change. During the summer there are civil rights demonstrations in the town, and Ruth accepts a flyer from a young man named Quincy and then places it in the mailbox of her white neighbors. Quincy later looks for Ruth and drives to her house with several other civil rights workers. They tell Grange and Ruth about the work they do. Grange feels they are wasting their time, although he likes them personally.

In the courtroom, Judge Harry (Brownfield's friend) awards custody of Ruth to Brownfield, but Grange does not accept the decision. He shoots Brownfield, killing him, and leaves the courtroom with Ruth. He returns home with Ruth as the police pursue them. Leaving Ruth in the house, he heads for the cabin with his guns but is shot and killed by the police.

CHARACTERS

Angeline

Angeline is Brownfield's cousin and Lincoln's sister. She lives in Philadelphia and on her visits to Georgia passes on to the young Brownfield family gossip that is unfavorable to his family.

Uncle Buster

Uncle Buster is Grange's uncle. When Grange was a boy, Uncle Buster made Grange accompany him to church, saying he would beat the boy if he refused to join the church. Uncle Buster goes to sleep during the service.

Brownfield Copeland

Brownfield Copeland is the son of Grange and Margaret Copeland. He had a hard childhood, being sent to work in the cotton fields when he was six years old. His father gives him no affection, and Brownfield comes to hate him. After his mother's death, Brownfield tries to find his way to the North but ends up not too far away from his childhood home. He stays with Josie, and they become lovers. Soon he meets Josie's niece Mem and they marry. However, the marriage is not a happy one. Brownfield, frustrated with his life of poverty and debt, becomes abusive, beats his wife, and neglects his children. Although Mem temporarily gets the upper hand while they live in the city and Brownfield works in a factory, he plots to get his revenge. Eventually he kills Mem and serves seven years in prison for his crime. When he is released, he is determined to gain custody of his youngest daughter, Ruth. Ruth does not want to go back

with her father, but Brownfield manages to win custody of her in court. Brownfield is then killed by Grange.

Daphne Copeland

Daphne Copeland is the eldest daughter of Brownfield and Mem Copeland. At the age of five, she is put to work in the cotton fields. After the death of her mother, she is sent to the North to live with her maternal grandfather.

Grange Copeland

Grange Copeland goes through three distinct stages in his life. In what he later calls his first life as a sharecropper who works in the cotton fields, he is morose and uncommunicative. He drinks a lot and fights with his wife, Margaret. He continues to see his lover, Josie. He is also afraid of the white men who have control over his life. In 1926, fed up with his existence, he leaves his wife and heads north, ending up in New York City. This is the second stage of his life. He finds that the North is not a hospitable place. He does whatever he has to do in order to survive, including selling bootleg whiskey (this is during Prohibition, when the sale of alcohol was illegal) and drugs, as well as robbing people. Often he goes hungry. He also learns to hate white people even more.

Eventually Grange returns to the South and is the wiser for his experience. He shows that he has the ability to change his life in a positive way. He marries Josie, forms a loving relationship with Ruth, his granddaughter, and sees his own life in a different perspective. He realizes that he was partly responsible for his first wife's suicide. He starts to live more selflessly than before, inspired by his love of Ruth. He becomes so attached to his granddaughter that he cannot bear to part with her when the court awards custody of her to Brownfield. He shoots his son in the courtroom and then drives home, where he is killed by police.

Josie Copeland

Josie Copeland is Grange's lover before he marries Margaret. He continues to see her while he is married to Margaret. Josie owns the Dew Drop Inn, and later, when Brownfield finds his way there, Josie takes up with him for a while. When Grange returns from the North, she marries him, selling the inn to help pay for Grange's farm. When Ruth comes to live with them, Josie is jealous of Grange's relationship with the girl and feels she has been replaced in his affections. Josie's early life was troubled. She was raped when she was sixteen, as a result of which she gave birth to a daughter, Lorene. She is haunted by this experience and the fact that her father refused to help her when she was being raped by his friends.

Margaret Copeland

Margaret Copeland is Grange's first wife and Brownfield's mother. She works at a bait factory canning worms. As a young woman she was beautiful (Grange later recalls), but she is ground down by the hardness of her life with her abusive husband. Angry with him, she takes other lovers, including Shipley, who fathers her son, Star. She gave in to Shipley because she thought that by doing so she could help Grange get out of debt. Eventually, tormented by guilt, she kills herself and her baby son.

Mem Copeland

Mem Copeland is Josie's niece who marries Brownfield. Mem is a quiet girl who attended school in Atlanta. When Brownfield meets her at Josie's inn, he is fascinated by her because she is more refined and educated than he is. She teaches young children at the school, and at Brownfield's request she tries to teach him to read and write. They soon marry and move onto a cotton farm. Their aim is to save money to enable them to move to the North, but this never happens. Instead, they find themselves in poverty and debt, and Mem's life goes downhill when Brownfield starts to abuse her. She loses her former good looks, worn down by the hardness of her life and the beatings she suffers from her husband.

However, Mem is a strong woman, and she has more initiative than her husband. She leases a house in town and gets a job there, virtually forcing her husband to go with her and their three children. For a while their life is more tranquil, but Mem gets sick from overwork, and Brownfield forces the family to move to J.L.'s farm. Back in the country, Mem is once more subject to her husband's abuse and desire for vengeance. He kills her one evening as she returns home from work.

Ornette Copeland

Ornette Copeland is the second daughter of Brownfield and Mem. She is a rebellious child, unloved by her father. When her mother is murdered, she is sent north with her sister Daphne to live with their maternal grandfather. Later she becomes a prostitute.

Ruth Copeland

Ruth Copeland is the youngest daughter of Brownfield and Mem Copeland. At the age of six, after her mother is murdered, she goes to live with Grange, her grandfather, with whom she forms a tight bond. It is through Ruth that Grange discovers the better side of his own nature. She seems wise beyond her years, and she does not accept her grandfather's negative view of all white people. She is drawn to the civil rights movement when she first hears about it on television, and she seems set for a more fulfilling life than any other member of her family has achieved, although she is undecided about what she plans to do. When Ruth is sixteen, her father tried to reclaim her, but she has no relationship with him and no desire to live with him. She prefers to stay with Grange.

Captain Davis

Captain Davis is the old white man who owns the dairy farm on which Brownfield works. Brownfield hates him because Davis has power over him, but to the captain's face he is always respectful and polite.

J.L. Davis

J.L. is the son of Captain Davis. He owns the dairy farm where Brownfield works after he leaves Captain Davis's farm.

Mrs. Grayson

Mrs. Grayson is Ruth's teacher when she is in sixth grade. Ruth does not think she is a good teacher, and when Mrs. Grayson beats her with a strap, Ruth insults her and walks out of the class.

Judge Harry

Judge Harry is the judge who is acquainted with Brownfield from Brownfield's time in prison. Judge Harry takes Brownfield's side in the legal fight over custody of Ruth.

Helen

Helen is a civil rights worker and Quincy's wife. She and Quincy visit Grange and Ruth, and Helen expresses the hope that the political situation can be changed by black people exercising their right to vote. Grange is impressed by her.

Lincoln

Lincoln is Brownfield's cousin and Angeline's brother. He lives in Philadelphia. When he visits the young Brownfield, he tells him about life in the North.

Lorene

Lorene is Josie's daughter. She is a tough woman with a masculine appearance. She lives with her mother at the Dew Drop Inn, and Brownfield, before he meets Mem, takes her as a lover, even though he is also involved with Josie. Lorene later moves to the North.

Sister Madeleine

Sister Madeleine is a fortune teller. Josie consults her about her violent dreams. Madeleine is Quincy's mother.

Aunt Marilyn

Aunt Marilyn is Margaret Copeland's sister, Uncle Silas's wife, and Angeline and Lincoln's mother.

Rossel Pascal

Rossel Pascal is a girl at the school Ruth attends. Like Ruth, she has had a bad home life. Her father is an alcoholic, and her mother is dead. Also like Ruth, she is not popular at school. Because of the similarities in their situations, the two girls become friends.

Quincy

Quincy is a young, college-educated civil rights activist in Georgia. Ruth notices him and finds him attractive. With his wife, Helen, he visits Grange and Ruth. He is ambitious and hopes one day to become mayor of Greene County.

Mr. Shipley

Mr. Shipley is the white man who owns the cotton field where Grange and Brownfield work. He also owns the house in which the family lives. Grange is afraid of him. Shipley is the father of Margaret's child, Star. Margaret gave in to Shipley's desire because she thought it would help to pay off the family's debts.

Uncle Silas

Uncle Silas is Margaret's brother-in-law. He lives with his wife, Marilyn, and their two children, Lincoln and Angeline, in Philadelphia. Although he appears to have prospered in the North, he is in reality a drug addict. He is killed robbing a liquor store.

Star

Star is Margaret's son by Shipley. He is given little care, and Brownfield resents him. He is poisoned by his mother at the age of two, just before she commits suicide.

Walt Terrel

Walt Terrel is the richest black man in the local area. He is a World War II hero, and Rossel decides in twelfth grade that she wants to marry him. Her wish comes true.

THEMES

Domestic Violence

The novel shines a light on African American gender relations and domestic abuse in the South over two generations, beginning in 1920. Of the three marriages depicted (Grange and Margaret, Brownfield and Mem, and Grange and Josie), the first two start well but soon degenerate into abuse and violence. Both Grange and Brownfield feel powerless in their lives because they are dominated by whites who keep them in poverty and debt. The only way they can assert their masculinity is to bully someone weaker than themselves, which in both cases means they beat their wives.

As a black woman married to a man who is frequently drunk and abusive toward her, Margaret is completely powerless. She is deeply angry about Grange's behavior and the fact that he has a mistress, Josie, in town. In spite of all the abuse she suffers, she still loves Grange, but the marriage is dysfunctional in the extreme.

It is not surprising that Brownfield, who grows up observing the fractious relationship between his parents, behaves the same way toward his wife, Mem, as his father did toward Margaret. Brownfield and Mem are happy at first, but Brownfield has no more education, skills, or prospects than his father did, and he feels the same frustration about it. He is poor and in debt, controlled by white men who keep him in a dependent situation. He beats his wife because for a few moments it eases his own pain.

When Mem shows the courage and initiative to alter their situation for a while, there is a glimpse of how an empowered woman can alter

TOPICS FOR FURTHER STUDY

- Domestic abuse plays a large role in *The Third Life of Grange Copeland*. How serious a problem is domestic abuse today? Using the Internet, research the facts and give a class presentation about domestic abuse and what more can be done to prevent it. Display your findings with a PowerPoint presentation.

- Read *Alice Walker*, by Tony Gentry (Chelsea House Publishers, 1992), a biography of Walker for young people. Write an essay in which you explain how her life up to the late 1960s might have influenced the themes of *The Third Life of Grange Copeland*.

- Create a blog with two other classmates in which you discuss how you react to the character Grange Copeland. Do you like him? Is he a sympathetic character or not? Invite your classmates to contribute their comments.

- Create a brief civil rights time line that covers the period of the novel, from the 1920s to the 1960s, concluding with the Voting Rights Act of 1965.

a marriage for the better, but the odds against Mem's success are too great. When she succumbs to ill health, Brownfield, who has been humiliated by her taking the lead in finding a house and a job in town, relishes the prospect of retaking control and dragging her down again. The theme that emerges is that black men are so badly damaged by the racism inherent in Southern society that they find it impossible to create stable, loving families. They quickly resort to their cruder instincts in order to preserve some twisted semblance of self-worth, no matter how damaging this might be for others.

Redemption

Redemption is shown in the novel by the surprising ability of Grange Copeland to rise above his past, in at least some respects, and put someone other than himself at the center of his life: Ruth, his granddaughter. Grange undergoes quite a change from the sullen sharecropper of his youth and the hustler he became in New York. The change he goes through upon his return to the South could not have been predicted, based on his life up to that point.

It is not that his marriage to Josie is especially successful—there are unresolved tensions in it from the beginning—but in caring for Ruth he shows a love and concern that was not present at all when he was married to Margaret and raising Brownfield. Toward Brownfield, he felt nothing but indifference, but to Brownfield's daughter, Grange offers his devotion and life experience in an attempt to raise her well and ensure her future success in life. Grange also shows an unexpected ability for thoughtful and even compassionate reflection on his life with Margaret, realizing that he must take some responsibility for what happened to her.

Grange's redemption shows that a man is not entirely determined by his past. He can rise above it if he has an incentive to do so. In this case, it is the presence of the little girl, Ruth, who quite unconsciously acts as a kind of savior for Grange. At the end of the novel, Grange acts as a savior for her. He sacrifices his own life so that Ruth does not have to return to the abusive Brownfield, thus freeing her from the cycle of domestic abuse that had dogged the family for two generations.

STYLE

Realism

The novel is a realistic portrayal of the way life was for African Americans in the South from the 1920s to the 1960s. In other words, the story is presented in a way that is meant to be true to life, in all its details. Walker intended the novel to be what she called in an interview with Claudia Tate in 1983 "rigorous realism." She explained:

> I wanted the reader to be able to sit down, pick up that book, and see a little of Georgia from the early twenties through the sixties—the trees, the hills, the dirt, the sky—to feel it, to feel the pain and the struggle of the family, and the growth of the little girl Ruth.

The Third Life of Grange Copeland is set in rural cotton-era Georgia. (© Keystone-France | Gamma-Keystone | Getty Images)

Third-Person Point of View

Point of view refers to how the story is told. This novel is told by an omniscient, third-person narrator. This means that the narrator stands outside the action of the story but has insight into the minds of all the major characters and knows all that is necessary about the events in order to tell the story. Because the novel covers a long stretch of time and several different locations, this was the obvious choice for the author when deciding how to tell her story.

Symbolism

Throughout *The Third Life of Grange Copeland*, the poor rural South is contrasted with the more prosperous urban North. The African Americans in the South have an almost mythical view of the North as a place where they can flourish in ways impossible in the South. The contrast between North and South is shown symbolically in the first pages of the novel, in which Brownfield's Uncle Silas and Aunt Marilyn and their children drive off in their brand new Buick. The car is described in great detail: it is

> long and high and shiny green with great popping headlights like the eyes of a frog. Inside the car it was all blue, with seats that were fuzzy and soft. Slender silver handles opened the doors and rolled the astonishingly clear windows up and down.

The car symbolizes modernity, the prosperity that was coming to America in the 1920s, but that was only a distant dream for the African Americans in the South, unless they were willing to make the trek north. The contrast between North and South is further brought out in the fact that the road upon which Brownfield's relatives drive away is in terrible condition and damages the car. The top is scratched by tree branches, and there are numerous potholes in the road, which "was for mules, wagons, and bare feet only."

HISTORICAL CONTEXT

Sharecropping in the South

During the 1920s, when the novel begins, share-cropping was widespread in Georgia and throughout the South. A sharecropper was a laborer who owned no land but worked on farms owned by others. Sharecroppers were paid at the end of the season with a share of the crop. This system was in place in Georgia from the end of Reconstruction in 1877 and lasted well into the twentieth century. In 1910, 37 percent of the farms in Georgia were operated by share-croppers. More than half of the sharecroppers at this time were African American. The labor system favored the landlords, and sharecroppers might be paid only one-third of the value of the crop. Sharecroppers in many cases were also compelled to buy essential supplies from the landowner or local merchants, such as fertilizer, seed, clothing, and sometimes food. They were given credit to make these purchases and often ended up in debt that they could never hope to repay, thus binding them further to an unfair system. Illiterate sharecroppers (like Brownfield in the novel) could easily be cheated by unscrupulous landowners and others.

The Great Migration

In the novel, Brownfield's Uncle Silas and Aunt Marilyn moved from Georgia to the North sometime during the early 1900s, and in the mid- or late 1920s Grange also goes North, to New York City. Brownfield thinks of doing so as well, although he never manages to get out of Georgia. This movement of African Americans from the South to the North, as well as to the Midwest and the West, during the period from about 1910 to 1970, is known as the Great Migration. At the end of the nineteenth century, nine out of ten African Americans lived in the South, but racist laws made it difficult for them to succeed, so they looked to the North, where their prospects were better. As many as six million African Americans took part in the Great Migration during this sixty-year period. The migration resulted in a shift from rural to urban locations, as African Americans swelled the populations of cities such as Chicago, Detroit, St. Louis, and New York. Many did find the greater prosperity they sought. However, just as in the novel, in which Margaret, Grange's wife, believes that life in the North is not all it is made out to be, African Americans also faced discrimination in the North.

Civil Rights Movement

The civil rights movement began in 1955 with a bus boycott by African Americans in Montgomery, Alabama. In the novel, Grange and Ruth come into direct contact with the movement in the 1960s, when protests take place in Baker County, in southwest Georgia, where they live. Four young civil rights activists, campaigning for voter registration, visit their home. In Georgia, there had been a surge of black activism after World War II aimed at ending discrimination, but by the mid-1950s, this had faded, and segregation was strictly and often violently enforced. During the early 1960s, however, the civil rights movement energized African Americans in Georgia once again, especially in the larger cities such as Atlanta, Albany, and Savannah. In rural areas, civil rights protests were less common, and Baker County was one of the so-called Black Belt rural counties, in which white supremacy was upheld ruthlessly by local police and reinforced by continuing black poverty.

CRITICAL OVERVIEW

Reviews of *The Third Life of Grange Copeland* were mixed. In *Library Journal*, as quoted by Evelyn C. White in *Alice Walker: A Life*, Victor A. Kramer writes that the novel "presents hatred . . . within a plot that seems near fantasy." Kramer also notes, "Walker's characters are not pretty ones. Yet this is the point: dignity cannot be maintained amidst intense degradation."

Over the years since its publication, the novel has continued to receive attention from critics. In a 1984 *New York Times* essay on Walker's work, David Bradley has high praise for the characterization of Grange Copeland, who emerges "as one of the richest, wisest and most moving old men in fiction. His speeches, never preachy, always set perfectly in context, ring with complex truth." In the *Dictionary of Literary Biography*, Thadious M. Davis identifies "the vision of survival" as the main theme of the novel. However, in spite of this, "Walker delivers a bleak message. The traditional family disintegrates primarily from the attitudes and actions of its members. The family offers neither

COMPARE
&
CONTRAST

- **1920s:** During the Great Migration, large numbers of African Americans leave the rural South in search of better opportunities in the North, Midwest, and West.

  1960s: When the Great Migration ends in 1970, the African American demographic has changed considerably. Less than 50 percent of African Americans live in the South, and only one-quarter live in rural areas. Overall, about 80 percent of African Americans live in cities.

  Today: Because of new economic opportunities in the South and better race relations, many African Americans are returning to the South in what has been called the New Great Migration.

- **1920s:** The Back to Africa movement led by Marcus Garvey gains some support among African Americans in Georgia. The movement believes that white racism will not end and that African Americans would be better off returning to Africa.

  1960s: Albany, Georgia, is in the national spotlight in 1961–62 during the civil rights movement. Mass protests against racial discrimination lead to mass arrests, with over one thousand African Americans jailed. The movement, however, fails to force the city to desegregate.

  Today: There is a trend toward resegregation in American public schools, including those in the South. In six Southern states, including Georgia, at least 30 percent of black students attending public schools go to schools that are 95 percent black.

- **1920s:** The Harlem Renaissance nurtures the career of Zora Neale Hurston, whose novel published in the following decade, *Their Eyes Were Watching God* (1937), is regarded as a seminal work in African American and women's literature.

  1960s: The civil rights movement and the women's movement nurture many new black women writers. *I Know Why the Caged Bird Sings*, an autobiography by Maya Angelou, is published in 1969. Other African American women writers who came of age in the 1950s and 1960s are ready to make their publishing debuts in the early 1970s. In addition to Alice Walker, these authors include Toni Cade Bambara and Toni Morrison.

  Today: Popular young African American women writers include ZZ Packer, who is perhaps best known for her short-story collection *Drinking Coffee Elsewhere* (2004); Kalisha Buckhanon with her debut novel, *Upstate* (2006); and Tayari Jones, whose third novel, *Silver Sparrow* (2011), is a coming-of-age story.

---

solace nor strength; it assures nothing." Maria Lauret in *Alice Walker*, reads the history of the Copeland family

> not only as a microcosmic representation of the history of African Americans but of America as a whole . . . a history of violence and oppression that is passed down a chain of racial, class, and gender supremacies from which education and the entry into modernity can provide only a partial release.

CRITICISM

Bryan Aubrey

Aubrey holds a PhD in English. In the following essay, he analyzes The Third Life of Grange Copeland *as a story of personal transformation, as seen in the life of Grange Copeland.*

The Third Life of Grange Copeland is a remarkable novel because it manages at once to

WHAT DO I READ NEXT?

- *In Love and Trouble: Stories of Black Women* (1973) is Walker's first collection of short stories. The thirteen stories are about black women of varying backgrounds and the challenging situations they face in the American South. The collection is available in an edition published by Mariner Books in 2003.

- *In Search of Our Mothers' Gardens* (1983) is a collection of thirty-six nonfiction pieces by Walker, written between 1966 and 1982. The works include essays, reviews, and speeches on topics such as feminism, black writers, the civil rights movement, anti-Semitism, and the antinuclear movement

- *Miles to Go for Freedom: Segregation and Civil Rights in the Jim Crow Years* by Linda Barrett Osborne (2012) is a well-reviewed book for young-adult readers. It presents an account of racial segregation and the drive toward civil rights during the period from the 1890s to 1954 in the United States. The book has many photographs and first-person accounts as well as a time line and bibliography.

- *The Third Life of Grange Copeland* gives a vivid picture of one African American family over three generations in Georgia. *Bone* (1993), a novel by Chinese American author Fae Myenne Ng, accomplishes the same for the Chinese American community in San Francisco. The novel tells the story of one Chinese American family over two generations as it tries to understand why a young family member took her own life.

- *Breath, Eyes, Memory* (1998) is the first novel of Edwidge Danticat, a writer who was born in Haiti and moved to the United States when she was twelve. The book tells the coming-of-age story of Sophie, a girl from Haiti whose early years are spent with her aunt and grandmother until she moves to New York City to be with her mother, whom she has never seen.

- *The Civil Rights Reader: American Literature from Jim Crow to Reconciliation* (2009), edited by Julie Buckner Armstrong and Amy Schmidt, is an anthology of drama, essays, fiction, and poetry from the 1890s to the present that focuses on the civil rights movement. Writers represented include Claude McKay, Langston Hughes, James Baldwin, Flannery O'Connor, Eudora Welty, Robert Hayden, Malcolm X, Amiri Baraka, Rita Dove, and Nikki Giovanni. The book also includes a chronology of important events.

be realistic yet visionary. It takes as its subject the grim, despairing lives of a black family in the American South over two generations. The Copeland family appears to be locked into an unending cycle of poverty, abuse, and violence, yet Walker is at pains to show that another way is possible. The novel moves from darkness to some measure of light. Harsh though it frequently is, it offers, against all the odds, hope and redemption. Although racism and the virtual economic slavery it imposes upon black people is the basic poison that sends the Copeland family into its downward spiral, the engine of redemption in this novel is a radical change not in the social order but in the individual's attitude toward himself. *The Third Life of Grange Copeland* is a novel of personal, rather than societal, transformation.

The transformation presented is in the life of Grange Copeland. Given the way Grange is described in the early chapters, his transformation into the responsible, loving grandfather who raises Ruth could not have been predicted. Grange has been beaten down by his life as a poor sharecropper, exploited by the white landowners. He is so intimidated by white people that he cannot look them in the eye. His son,

> HE REVEALS HIMSELF, IN SPITE OF ALL HIS HARDSHIPS AND FAILURES, TO BE A THOUGHTFUL, REFLECTIVE MAN WHO HAS THE INTELLIGENCE TO UNDERSTAND WHY HIS OWN LIFE UNFOLDED AS IT DID AND WHAT HE HAS TO DO TO CHANGE IT AND THE DETERMINATION TO CARRY THOSE CHANGES OUT."

Brownfield, notices that around white people, his father is even more silent than he usually is. It is as if he freezes up in their presence. So despairing is Grange about his life that he can offer no love to his son. Once, when he is drunk, Grange says to Brownfield, "I ought to throw you down the goddam well." Grange is moody, frequently gets drunk, quarrels violently with his wife, and will not give up his lover, Josie, even though he is married.

An incident early in the novel reveals his sense of hopelessness. He goes outside and surveys the run-down, two-room cabin in which they live and points out all the things that need repair. Brownfield observes his father's bewilderment at his own powerlessness. Grange just shrugs, and Brownfield knows what that means: "his father saw nothing about the house that he could change and would therefore give up gesturing about it and he would never again think about repairing it." The incident serves as a metaphor for Grange's life with his family at this point. There is nothing to be done about it. It cannot be altered. The only thing Grange can do is leave it all behind, which he does, without warning, but with terrible consequences—the suicide of his wife, her murder of her baby son, and Brownfield's growing alienation and despair.

Grange's "second" life in the North seems to offer no more prospects than his first one. He is lured to the North because to African Americans in the South, the North appears to offer so much. This is shown symbolically at the very beginning of the novel. The gleaming, brand-new automobile in which Brownfield's Uncle Silas and Aunt Marilyn drive down to visit Grange and his family represents mobility, freedom, success, modernity—everything the South is not but that

can be obtained in the North, or so the belief goes. It is not surprising that Grange makes his way north, and not surprising either that he finds life in New York City not what it is reputed to be. He lives on the margins of society, resorting to criminality just to survive.

Grange Copeland's saving grace is that he reveals himself, in spite of all his hardships and failures, to be a thoughtful, reflective man who has the intelligence to understand why his own life unfolded as it did and what he has to do to change it and the determination to carry those changes out. Nothing in his past could have predicted this change, but it happens nonetheless, and as a result he experiences a "total triumph over his life's failures." He succinctly explains to Ruth the pattern of his life. First he was hated by the whites, and he hated himself. Then, when he was in New York City, he tells her, "I started hating them in return and loving myself. Then I tried just loving me, and then you." Grange's second life in New York is not presented directly in the novel but only recalled by him later, so when Grange says that in New York he learned to love himself, to overcome the self-hatred that had been his legacy from the racism of society, the reader must take his word for it. Walker is certainly at pains to show him at peace with himself and his understanding of life, dedicated to raising his granddaughter and preparing her to face life's realities.

The main plank of Grange's newfound philosophy is taking responsibility for oneself and not blaming others. This is what becoming a man means to him, as he explains to Brownfield. A confrontation between father and son takes place when Grange and Ruth encounter Brownfield as Grange escorts his granddaughter home from school. Brownfield is presented as a stark contrast to his father: Grange learns from his experiences and grows as an individual. Brownfield, on the other hand, seems incapable of growth; he blames the whites and his father for all his troubles, which means he will never overcome them. Grange tries to explains to his son that such an attitude leads only to weakness and the feeling that a person is not responsible for anything that happens to him, which allows him always to put the blame on someone else, with terrible consequences:

> Then you begins to think up evil and begins to destroy everybody around you, and you

After killing Meme, Brownfield is jailed for seven years. (© albund / Shutterstock.com)

blames it on the crackers. . . . Nobody's as powerful as we make them out to be. We got our own *souls*, don't we?

It is Grange's responsibility to himself, his own soul, that allows him to transcend selfishness and extend himself in love for Ruth. He has a vision for how her life should be. It is not enough just to survive, he tells himself; what he wants for Ruth is that she will "survive *whole*," which means living in the present and experiencing fully what each day has to offer: "Each day must be past, present and future, with dancing and wine-making and drinking and as few regrets as possible."

In saving his own life from failure and despair, Grange also saves Ruth from the terrible legacy she inherited. If the male line of the Copeland family experienced suffering, the female line endured it in double measure. Grange's wife, Margaret, and Brownfield's wife, Mem, were oppressed not only by white racism but also by the disaffected, depressed black male that racism produced, whose only source of power lay in his ability to abuse his own wife. As the child of a murdered mother and the granddaughter of a suicide, Ruth does not appear to have much of a chance in life, a situation that is reinforced by the isolation and hostility she experiences at school. By some

miracle, however, not all of which is attributable to the tender care offered by Grange, she seems to emerge unscathed by these experiences.

Ruth is like a pure spirit emerging from the most unpromising of backgrounds. Often she seems wiser even than Grange, certainly wiser than her few years would suggest. She refuses to accept, for example, Grange's hatred of white people, which seems to be the one flaw in Grange's later makeup. Although he has learned to ignore white people and create a life for himself in which he does not have to deal with them, his hatred seems to live on. Ruth argues with him about it. Indeed, she, though a young girl, seems able to teach him something. When Grange tells Ruth that the whites "can be hated to the very bottom of your guts," she rebukes him, saying he is just as bad as her father. Later, when Grange talks about their white neighbors, saying that all they do is plot how to take his land, Ruth gently ridicules his comments and says "I mean, what I want to know, is did anybody ever try to find out if they's real *people*." She knows already that for black people to stereotype whites is the same error that whites have long made in their view of blacks.

Thus does Alice Walker, writing in the late 1960s, reveal through her portrayals of Grange's "third life" and of Ruth her positive vision for black families in the South. The way is always going to be hard, but in spite of racism and generations of violence, there is light at the end of the tunnel. The older generation, personified in Grange, can learn a better way, and the young, personified in Ruth, can be free.

Source: Bryan Aubrey, Critical Essay on *The Third Life of Grange Copeland*, in *Novels for Students*, Gale, Cengage Learning, 2014.

J. Samuel Kirubahar and Mary Rosalene Beulah

In the following excerpt, Kirubahar and Beulah examine the novel through the lenses of violence, oppression, and gender.

COPELAND—A MAN

. . . Alice Walker's *The Third Life of Grange Copeland* is her debut novel and considered by many as an autobiographical one. The Copeland family can be considered as a microcosm of their community and the American society. They belong to a community that has been for long time marginalized, devalued and demeaned. In her novel, Walker tells the story of Grange Copeland, a man who lives a life full of degradation and oppression, and accepts it as a natural state. However, because of some extraordinary changes he made in his life, he is able to break out of the rut of socially and personally accepted oppression, and changes his life for the better.

GRANGE—THE OTHER

The existential problem is reflected in the story from the beginning. Communities are divided by some aspects of identity and cannot create a sense of collective purpose or meaning. In the family circle, Grange Copeland permits the overwhelming pressure of oppression to divide them. The story begins in rural Georgia during the 1920's. Grange is a Black share cropper, living in destitution with his wife, and son, Brownfield. From the outset, it is plain that they live miserable lives. Grange works all day in an atmosphere of oppression. He is expected to act as though he is the social inferior of his employer, the man drives the truck, Mr. Shipley. Grange feels totally dehumanized. He sees himself as a "stone," a "robot" and a "cipher." These symbolic images are incapable of autonomous decision making or self determination. His own concept of his "otherness" is revealed here. This "otherness" also comes as a result of the social

THE WOMEN IN *THIRD LIFE OF GRANGE COPELAND* ARE BRUTALLY VICTIMIZED AND THEY GO ABOUT SILENTLY EXPOSING THEIR HUMILIATION AND INDIGNITY TO THEMSELVES AND THEIR WORLD."

construction of oppression and subjugation due to racism prevailing in the society.

'When the truck came [Grange's] face froze into an unnaturally bland mask . . . A grim stillness settled over his eyes and he became an object . . . Some of the workers laughed and joked with the man who drove the truck, but they looked at his shoes . . . never into his eyes.'

This passage shows just what kind of racial tension Grange and the others have to live under. To his boss, he truly is an object, and he knows this, 'he worked for a cracker and . . . the cracker owned him.' His reaction, to freeze, is one of fear and rage. The fear was Shipley's superior air, which Brownfield described, made him seem like something alien, 'the man was a man, but entirely different from [Grange].' The rage is over that fear, and the feelings of inadequacy that come with it.

GRANGE'S FEELINGS AND ACTS

Margaret and Brownfield are forced to play the submissive role to make up for Grange's feelings of lack of manhood around Shipley, and the whites in general. Brownfield states, 'his mother was like their dog in some ways. She didn't have a thing to say that did not . . . show her submission to his father.' Grange, at regular intervals, 'would come home lurching drunk, threatening to kill his wife and Brownfield, stumbling and shooting off his shotgun.' It is a way to gain some feeling of power through his feelings of subjugation. He needs to seem powerful to someone. Grange is physically, verbally and psychologically abusive towards his wife, and his son, Brownfield, as the mechanisms of oppression have dehumanized him. The family is unable to connect in a shared optimism for a better future and in their search for an assertion of identity. The Copelands and their community are entities in an existential crisis.

ESCAPE

At the end of each drunken tirade Grange would roll out of the door and into the yard, crying like a child in big wrenching sobs. His weeping is his only release. In the end it is too much for him, and he flees north, to New York. In the North, Grange is overcome by his first change. To the Southern Blacks, the North represents some kind of Promised Land. "He had come North expecting those streets paved with gold," but soon receives a rude awakening. Where the South looked contemptuously down on him, in the North "to the people that he met and passed daily he was not even in existence." From this hostile setting came the catalyst for moral change.

THE REVELATION

While begging in Central Park in the dead of winter, during his third year in New York, he comes upon a pregnant woman, a White. He watches her, and is soon joined by her lover, a soldier. They speak, and exchange "chaste kisses . . . as befitted soon-to-be parents." This is a kind of human intimacy that he had not experienced while in the city, and naturally it touches him. After such a long period of isolation in the North, this closeness between the woman and the soldier opens his mind to new ideas.

The woman, at this point in the story, comes to symbolize to Grange a kind of unselfish, pure high emotion. She represents exactly how Grange believes, through his oppressive experiences, that Whites behave, in a way higher than blacks. "Grange had watched the scene deteriorate from the peak of happiness to the bottom of despair. It was honestly the first human episode he had witnessed between white folks."

Because it is the first time, the woman becomes symbolic, and her actions influence his views on Whites as a whole. Her transition from a symbol of pure love into something horrible and human destroys Grange's early misconception that Whites were somehow more than human, and forces him to reevaluate his life. It mirrors the aggressive patterns that have characterized his entire life. Grange Copeland is no longer afraid of oppression and he has now turned the tools of the oppressors against them in order to wrest meaning from their hands. The death of the woman liberated him. He wants to live again. This drives him back to his home again in the South to reclaim his life and take all efforts to create possibilities for his grand-daughter, Ruth, to make it possible for her to dream of defining the meaning of her own life, free from the influence of institutionalized oppression.

According to existential philosophy, all people want to make meaning out of their own lives. This is often thwarted by social conditions, where one's free will is robbed; thereby creating an environment that is conducive to create a vicious cycle of violence. At this point, the life changing epiphany takes place. The pregnant woman had symbolized to Grange all that was good in the Whites. Her contemptuous actions towards him destroyed all of that, making her, and all Whites symbols of corruption. Her symbolic transformation and death represents his loss of fear, and of love, "her contempt for him had been the last straw; never again would he care what happened to any of them."

HOMEWARD JOURNEY

Grange is now in his second life, his fear of the Whites has disappeared, his rage, intensified but different. After the Central Park incident, he spends weeks fighting with any white he sees. He now blames them for the evils he did to his family, 'every white face he cracked, he cracked in his sweet wife's name.' He is a different man from the poor sharecropper. With his newfound philosophy, he returns home to Georgia. Brownfield has married, and has fallen into the same trap of oppression and domination that Grange did; setting into a more violent, but otherwise identical, pattern to his father's a few years before. Grange marries a woman Josie, with money, and buys an isolated farm, self-sufficient and free of Whites, free in his hatred and isolation.

RUTH

Ruth finds a place in Grange's heart. Ruth's story is existential in outlook. Her story is a flight from twentieth century forms of Southern bondage. She does not grow up in the kind of spiritual and emotional vacuum which blighted Brownfield's life. Ruth is raised by a mother. She considers her as a "saint" who makes heroic efforts to meet her human needs. Mem literally gives up her life opposing Brownfield's acceptance of his "place" in Southern society. After Mem is murdered literally by Brownfield and symbolically by the Southern society, Grange Copeland comes to love Ruth, his grand-daughter. He takes care of her and becomes her surrogate father. Grange sees Ruth as a unique and beautiful person in the midst of a harsh and ugly environment which did not nourish him. Grange nourishes her mind and soul. Like the pregnant woman in the past, Ruth is the catalyst of Grange's transition into his third life, a transition that leads him to an opposite conclusion to his previous one. Ruth is young and new to the world; she has no set ways or bigotries, unlike the white pregnant woman. Where the woman inspires hate, Ruth inspires love. He treats her the way he wished he had Brownfield. She is his second chance, and he attempts to make up for his mistakes, and begins to change again.

TRANSFORMATION

Grange's meaning of life begins to change, 'the older Grange got the more serene and flatly sure of his mission he became. His one duty in life was to prepare Ruth for some great and herculean task . . . some harsh and foreboding reality.' He begins to doubt his hate philosophy. Words and intelligence and not raw violence have power to transform the world experience by creating understanding and control over life. Grange connects Ruth to the life giving tradition of the Black folk art of the South. Folk art and the Holy Ghost give her vital access to an imaginatively rich, emotional potent world, which the psychologically under developed Brownfield never becomes aware of. Grange helps her achieve independence from her father and the Southern life in general. Towards the end of the novel, he says to Ruth, 'I know the danger of putting [all] the blame on somebody else for the mess you make out of your life. I fell into the trap myself!' His admission of this shows a metamorphosis of thought and leads him close to a third life of selflessness. He continues, 'he gits . . . the feeling of doing nothing yourself . . . and begins to destroy everybody around you, and you blame it on the crackers.'

OPPRESSION = VIOLENCE

The varied fates of the Grange family members and other characters in the novel demonstrate how the very dynamics of oppression turns into a vicious cycle of violence. The oppressed characters go through their lives desperately and mechanically. Margaret chooses a violent end and chooses to kill herself—not as an act of free will and thoughtful choice but simply to escape the unbearable conditions, abandoning the fifteen year old Brownfield, who imitates

the behavior of his parents. The wheel goes turning round and round. Mem marries Brownfield though she knows that he is ignorant, no-good and illiterate. She teaches him how to write his name. Hope falls to the ground in the rural South. Twenty years later, the pernicious system that claimed Grange Copeland claims his son also:

> He thought of suicide and never forgot it, even in Mem's arms. He prayed for help, for a caring President, for a listening Jesus. He prayed for a decent job in Mem's arms. But like all prayers sent up from there, it turned into another mouth to feed, another body to enslave to pay his debts. He felt himself destined to become no more than an overseer, on the white man's plantation, of his own children.

BROWNFIELD—A VICTIM

In time, like his father, Brownfield also becomes a victim of the system and he vents his rage against a black woman who comprehends and endeavors to calm his pain. The worse he treated her, the more she was compelled to save him. He blamed Mem for his failures and his inability to produce a crop at the end of the farming season. He beat her. He did not fear her as he did the white men whose power choked him and refused him his manhood and who gave him dried potatoes and sickly hogs at the end of the year. Brownfield had to hit back at something, and his mission was to pull his wife down 'beneath him so his foot could rest easy on her neck.'

Brownfield complained about her refined speech: 'Why don't you talk like the rest of us poor niggers!' . . . Why do you have to always be so damn proper? Whether I says 'is' or 'ain't' ain't, no damn humping off your butt.' His trampled ego and pride makes him pull down Mem also from being a school teacher to his level. His rage could and did blame everything, everything, on her.' He advises his friends that the only way to keep a black woman down is to beat her. He tells his friends, 'Give this old black snake to her . . . and then I beats her ass. Only way to treat a nigger woman.' Mem took his ill treatment and fell down on her knees, grew ugly, gave birth to her babies in cold damp rooms all alone because, more often Brownfield would be too evil and drunk to get a midwife for her.

Mem's weakness is representative of a steady stream of suffering throughout Walker's fiction. She carries the burden of guilt and it is a heavy and cumbersome load on her back. Mem wants Brownfield to 'quit wailing like a seedy jackass.' Mem understands that it is the white racists who are responsible for Brownfield's degradation, but she rejects it as an excuse for his transgressions against his family. Walker writes that Brownfield did not have the courage to imagine life without the existence of white people as a prop.' Brownfield is beyond reach. Bitter and self consumed by self-hatred, he chooses to punish his father than assume responsibility for his life and family. He chooses sorrow over joy, and revenge over responsibility (Wades-Gayles, 307). Once she took advantage of his drunken state, and tried to overturn her weakness, placed the shotgun to his head, and reminded him:

> I put myself to the trouble of having all these babies for you . . . To think I let you drag me around from one corncrib to another just cause I didn't want to hurt your feelings . . . And just think of how many times I done got my head beat by you so you could feel a little bit like a man . . . And just think how much like an old no-count dog you done treated me for nine years . . . .

MEM—LIBERATION

Mem's liberation is short-lived. She does not understand what is evil and all the sunshine, comfort and cleanliness that she brought into the house is destroyed. Brownfield plans for her destruction. He takes her back to his shack, where she has to abide by [his] rules. Her role is clearly defined. She is a woman. He is lord. She must please him. He is free to please only himself. His cruelty seems too harsh to believe. But Walker knows men like him. They exist and there is no way to avoid them.

Grange's woman, Josie is also a victim of sexist culture that causes Margaret's suicide. Disowned and humiliated by her father, she vows never again to be dependent on any man for anything, 'like a phoenix who rises from the ashes with unfurled wings, she soars above male control to become the richest and most powerful black person, male, female, in the community. Her liberation from male control does not put her in touch with her personhood. As a prosperous prostitute, she is still confined to a role that requires woman's service to man' (Wade-Gayles, 304).

Bettye asks a few interesting questions. Mem had an identity as a school teacher and why did she accept such violent treatment

against her body and the 'violent expressions that chiseled away at her soul? What kind of lethargy was it that allowed her to take beatings, even the threat of them, time after time? How many bitches could she be?' The women in *Third Life of Grange Copeland* are brutally victimized and they go about silently exposing their humiliation and indignity to themselves and their world. Mem and Margaret seem to love the others but not themselves. The impact of unemployment on the African American family, and particularly on the black male, is the least understood of all. There is little analysis because there has been almost no inquiry.

WOMEN AND THE WHITE EMPLOYER

The women seem to understand their husband's predicament in the hands of the White employers and silently bear the humiliation. They fail to stand up against the violence and allow their men to have their space in their own home, which is revealed only through violence. They don't want to victimize the men. Frustration and violent pent up anger could be directed only towards the people who knew them and on whom they could exert some power. It is not only the women who suffer, but also the children. Walker and many African American women writers depict how slavery and subsequent racist social structures have stripped black men of paternal authority and ensured that they have not a proud cultural heritage but an unresolved and often inarticulable history of trauma and suffering to pass on (Read, 527).

END—THE MESSAGE

Walker's message shown through the progression of Grange's thoughts is that it is possible to lift themselves out of their constraints, to make a change so drastic that they become seemingly different people. The possibility of reclaiming one's agency, autonomy, and decision making power is possible though not an easy one. The simple binaries that made up imperial and post-colonial studies have in some way become redundant with regard to literature. Copeland embraces his hybridized position "not as a badge of failure or denigration, but as a part of the contestational weave of culture."

Robert Young comments on the negativity that is associated to the term "hybridity." On the other hand Ashcroft focuses on the hybrid nature of post-colonial culture as strength rather than a weakness and the same is true in Grange Copeland's life. It is proof that even when a person is caught in the vicious cycle of violence that is a product of racism, he can come out of it and survive and become an integral part of the new formations which arise. This what Bhabha refers to as "liminal" space. Ashcroft also mentions that hybridity is a means of evading the replications of the binary categories of the past and develop a new hybrid identity as Copeland's transformation shows in his third life.

Source: J. Samuel Kirubahar and Mary Rosalene Beulah, "The Vicious Cycle of Violence in Alice Walker's: *The Third Life of Grange Copeland*," in *Language in India*, Vol. 12, No. 9, September 2012, pp. 163–85.

Robert James Butler

In the following excerpt, Butler claims that Alice Walker uses the character of Grange to portray one's regenerating return to the South.

. . . The third major narrative in the novel incorporates the visions of the South implicit in the other two narratives and offers one more critically important perspective on the South. Whereas Grange Copeland's "first" life powerfully reinforces the bleakly pessimistic view of the South implicit in Brownfield's narrative, and his "second" life is very similar in certain ways to Ruth's story, because it is a flight from the slavery of the segregated South, Grange's "third" life contains an important element missing in the other two narratives—his remarkable return to the South, which regenerates him as a human being. It is this return, like Celie's return to Georgia at the end of *The Color Purple*, which underscores Walker's most affirmative vision of the South. In returning to Baker County, Grange achieves "his total triumph over life's failures," creating a new place for himself by transforming the racist society which has withered Brownfield into a genuine "home" which nurtures Ruth and also causes him to be "a reborn man." Like the hero described in Joseph Campbell's *Hero with a Thousand Faces*, Grange attains truly heroic status by a three-part journey involving the leaving of a settled, known world; the experiencing of tests in an unknown world; and the returning home with a new mode of consciousness which transforms his life and the lives of others.

Walker, who knew the most brutal features of the rural South firsthand, is careful not to

> IT IS GRANGE'S ACHIEVEMENT OF A 'HOME' IN GEORGIA WHICH PROVIDES HIM WITH A GENUINE HUMAN CONVERSION."

romanticize the South to which Grange returns. She emphasizes that Grange goes back to Georgia not because of a sudden nostalgia for magnolias and wisteria but simply because the circumstances of his life have made him a Southerner, for better or for worse: ". . . though he hated it as much as any place else, where he was born would always be home for him. Georgia would be home for him, and every other place foreign." Crucial to Grange's creation of a new home for himself in the South is his securing of land. Using the money he obtained in various devious ways in the North and the money he gets from Josie's sale of the Dew Drop Inn, he builds a farm which constitutes "a sanctuary" from the white world which has victimized him economically and poisoned him with hatred. As his name suggests, he is able to "cope" with his "land" so that he can build a "grange" or farm which will nourish himself and others. This "refuge" not only provides him with food from his garden and a livelihood from his sale of crops but, more importantly, gives him the independence and freedom he needs to assume meaningful roles which his earlier life lacked: ". . . he had come back to Baker County, because it was home, and to Josie, because she was the only person in the world who loved him. . . ."

Accepting the love from Josie which he had earlier rejected because he found it "possessive," he marries her shortly after returning from the North, thus embracing the role of husband. In this way he transforms her Dew Drop Inn from the whorehouse which was a grotesque parody of a human community into a real place of love between a man and a woman. Not long after this he begins to assume the role of father when he assists Mem in the delivery of Ruth on Christmas Day, a time when Brownfield is too drunk to be of much use to his family. After Brownfield murders Mem, Grange fully undertakes the role of father, providing Ruth with the love and care which he was unable to extend to Brownfield in his "first" life. In all these ways Grange is able to create a small but vital black community separated from the larger white world intent on destroying the black family.

Grange's journey north failed him because it poisoned him with the same kind of hatred which damaged his previous life in the South. His Northern experiences are revealed in the terrifying epiphany when he gloats over stealing a white woman's money while watching her drown in Central Park Lake. The whole experience becomes a grotesque inversion of a religious conversion, very much like Bigger Thomas's killing of Mary Dalton in *Native Son*. Like Bigger, who feels a grisly sort of "new life" when he savors the death of Mary Dalton, Grange feels "alive and liberated for the first time in his life" as he contemplates the image of withdrawing his hand from the drowning woman. He thus commits in a different form the same sin which brought his "first" life in the South to such a disturbing close. Just as Grange is partly responsible for the deaths of his wife and stepchild, whom he abandons when he is no longer able to cope with the societally induced hatred which poisons all of his human relationships, so too does he abandon the pregnant white woman when societally induced hatred causes her to call him a "...." Withdrawing his hand from her also echoes an earlier gesture of withdrawing his hand from his son shortly before he abandons him. Just as his hand "nearly touche[s]" the woman's in Central Park, his hand has earlier "stopped just before it reached [Brownfield's] cheek." In both cases his withdrawal of human sympathy from people is a clear index of how Grange has been emotionally damaged by the racist society in which he lives.

The South and North, therefore, are portrayed in Grange's first two lives as dehumanized and dehumanizing environments. But whereas the South has turned him into a "stone" and a "robot," the North converts him into the kind of invisible man classically described in African American literature by Du Bois and Ellison:

> He was, perhaps, no longer regarded merely as a "thing"; what was even more cruel to him was that to the people he met and passed daily he was not even in existence! The South had made him miserable, with nerve endings raw from continual surveillance from contemptuous eyes, but they *knew he was there*. Their very disdain proved it. The North put him into solitary confinement where he had to manufacture his own hostile stares in order to see himself. . . . Each day he had to say his name to himself over and over again to shut out the silence.

Although both environments pose severe threats to his humanity, Grange finally chooses the South over the North because he is humanly visible to Southerners, whereas Northern society is completely blind to him. Although Southern whites regard blacks with "contemptuous eyes" which distort their vision, they at least focus upon blacks as human beings; the white Northerners Grange meets would reduce blacks to complete anonymity. Thus, Grange experiences a condition of "solitary confinement" in the North but in the South is given the opportunity to feel the "sense of *community*" which Walker has extolled in her essays as a particularly important feature of Southern black life.

It is Grange's achievement of a "home" in Georgia which provides him with a genuine human conversion. He returns to Baker County with disturbing vestiges of his first two lives, fits of depression which lead him to contemplate suicide and express an "impersonal cruelty" which frightens Ruth. But his recovery of the meaningful roles of husband, father, and farmer lead to his regeneration, providing him with a "third" life.

Josie's love, though flawed, is deeply experienced for a while, and Ruth is able, with "the magic of her hugs and kisses," to bring him out of his bouts of suicidal depression. As the novel develops, he admits to Ruth that she has "'thaw[ed]'" the "'numbness'" in him. Whereas early in the book Grange seems "devoid of any emotion . . . except that of bewilderment" and whereas in the middle of the book he is blinded by a nearly demonic hatred of whites, he finally becomes a fully developed, even heroic, person because of his recovery of a "home" in the black South.

Walker, however, consciously avoids idealizing Grange's Southern home. As the novel's ending makes clear, it is a small oasis of human love surrounded by the same kind of Southern racism which has blighted the lives of scores of black people in the novel. Southern courts continue to mete out injustice, and Southern violence continues to take the lives of innocent people, most notably Fred Hill, who is murdered when his son attempts to integrate a previously all white school. And as Ruth's narrative demonstrates, even Grange's home has its restrictive features. Although such a pastoral "refuge" satisfies Grange with a sense of place and continuity with the past, Walker clearly endorses Ruth's desire to leave it for the open space which her young spirit desires. Grange's story may contradict Thomas Wolfe's notion that you can't go home again, but Ruth's story emphasizes the fact that staying home or returning home for good can stifle certain kinds of people. Although Grange's Southern home provides Ruth with an essential foundation for human growth, ultimately she must leave that home if she is to continue to grow.

As Alice Walker has observed in *In Search of Our Mother's Gardens*, her sense of reality is inherently dialectical:

> "I believe that the truth of any subject comes out when all sides of the story are put together, and all their different meanings make one new one. Each writer writes the missing parts of the other writer's story. And the whole story is what I'm after."

The Third Life of Grange Copeland succeeds as a novel because it consciously avoids an oversimplified vision which expresses only one "side" of Southern life. Artfully mixing its three main narratives in order to include the "missing parts" absent from any single narrative, the novel suggests a "whole truth" about the South which is complex and many-sided. The book thus remains true to its author's deepest prompting and her most profound sense of her Southern black heritage.

Source: Robert James Butler, "Alice Walker's Vision of the South in *The Third Life of Grange Copeland*," in *African American Review*, Vol. 27, No. 2, Summer 1993, pp. 192–204.

SOURCES

Bradley, David, "Novelist Alice Walker Telling the Black Woman's Story," in *New York Times*, January 8, 1984, http://www.nytimes.com/books/98/10/04/specials/walker-story.html (accessed December 8, 2012).

Davis, Thadious M., "Alice Walker," in *Dictionary of Literary Biography*, Volume 6: *American Novelists since World War II, Second Series*, edited by James E. Kibler Jr., Gale Research, 1980, pp. 350–58.

DiSalvio, Daniel, "The New Great Migration," in *New York Times*, January 4, 2012, http://www.nytimes.com/roomfordebate/2011/07/25/how-budget-cuts-will-change-the-black-middle-class/the-black-middle-class-is-leaving-the-north (accessed November 23, 2012).

Giesen, James C., "Sharecropping," in *The New Georgia Encyclopedia*, 2009, http://www.georgiaencyclopedia.org/nge/Article.jsp?id = h-3590 (accessed November 23, 2012).

"Great Migration," History.com website, http://www.history.com/topics/great-migration (accessed November 23, 2012).

Lauret, Maria, *Alice Walker*, 2nd ed., Palgrave MacMillan, 2011, pp. 58–59.

Person, David, "The Next Fight: Resegregation," in *USA Today*, May 18, 2010, http://usatoday30.usatoday.com/news/opinion/forum/2010-05-19-column19_ST_N.htm (accessed November 23, 2012).

Tate, Claudia, and Alice Walker, "Interview with Claudia Tate from *Black Women Writers at Work* (1973)," in *The World Has Changed: Conversations with Alice Walker*, edited by Rudolph P. Byrd, New Press, 2010, pp. 58–59.

Tuck, Stephen, "Civil Rights Movement," in *The New Georgia Encyclopedia*, 2009, http://www.georgiaencyclopedia.org/nge/Article.jsp?id = h-2716 (accessed November 23, 2012).

Walker, Alice, *The Third Life of Grange Copeland*, Harcourt, 2003.

White, Evelyn C., *Alice Walker: A Life*, W. W. Norton, 2004, p. 188.

FURTHER READING

Butler, Robert James, "Alice Walker's Vision of the South in *The Third Life of Grange Copeland*," in *African American Review*, Vol. 27, No. 2, Summer 1993, pp. 192–204.

Butler examines how Walker presents both the bad and good sides of the African American experience in the South.

Grant, Donald L., *The Way It Was in the South: The Black Experience in Georgia*, University of Georgia Press, 2001.

This book covers the history of African Americans in Georgia from slavery to the present.

Lemann, Nicolas, *The Promised Land: The Great Migration and How It Changed America*, Knopf, 1991.

Lemann tells the story of the migration of African Americans from the rural South to the urban North from 1940 to 1970.

Washington, J. Charles, "Positive Black Male Images in Alice Walker's Fiction," in *Obsidian II*, Vol. 3, No. 1, Spring 1988, pp. 23–48.

Washington counters the view sometimes expressed that Walker presents only negative images of black men.

SUGGESTED SEARCH TERMS

Alice Walker

The Third Life of Grange Copeland

Great Migration

sharecropping

civil rights movement

voting rights

Georgia AND history

domestic violence

African American literature AND South

The Way of All Flesh

SAMUEL BUTLER

1903

The Way of All Flesh is a novel written by Samuel Butler, a nineteenth-century British author known as an eccentric freethinker and iconoclast. His story about multiple generations of the Pontifex family is a caustic satire targeting what he saw as the suffocating values, pieties, enthusiasms, and hypocrisies of the Victorian age. In large part, the novel is a thinly veiled autobiography: Much of the Pontifex family's frustration, repression, and unhappiness reflect Butler's attitude toward his own family. Despite numerous setbacks, however, Butler's protagonist, Ernest Pontifex, is able to break away from his repressive upbringing and find fulfillment as a writer, much as Butler himself did.

Butler began writing the novel in 1873 and worked on it for more than a decade. He put the novel aside, however, out of reluctance to publish it as long as members of his family were still alive, for he did not want to alienate his family any more than he already had. As it happened, two of his sisters were still alive in 1903, the year after Butler's death, when his literary executor published the novel.

Butler is not generally regarded as among the top rank of Victorian novelists. The sole work on which his reputation rested during the late Victorian period was the satirical novel *Erewhon*. *The Way of All Flesh*, however, is now regarded as a masterpiece. The novel is available in numerous editions, including one

Samuel Butler (© *Pictorial Press Ltd | Alamy*)

published by Random House in 1998, and can also be found online at Project Gutenberg.

AUTHOR BIOGRAPHY

Butler was born on December 4, 1835, at Langar Rectory, near Bingham, Nottinghamshire, England. His father, Thomas Butler, was an Anglican clergyman. He attended the Shrewsbury School, where his grandfather, also named Samuel Butler, had been headmaster for decades. Later, in 1858, Butler earned a degree in classics from St. John's College at Cambridge University. He intended to pursue a career in the ministry, but when he began to doubt his faith, he refused to take orders in the church. After quarreling about the matter with his disappointed father, he emigrated to New Zealand, where he became a sheep farmer. (Ironically, he was originally headed for western Canada, but his plans changed at the last moment; the ship on which he was first booked was lost at sea.) During this period he read *On the Origin of Species* (1859), the groundbreaking book on evolution written by Charles Darwin (who also attended Shrewsbury School), and for the next quarter century he was preoccupied with the clash between traditional religion and the new theories about evolution, which called into question the biblical account of Creation.

In 1864, Butler returned to England and, having long aspired to become a painter, took art courses. In time, several of Butler's paintings were exhibited at the Royal Academy, but by the 1870s it was becoming clear even to him that his artistic talents were limited. A friend suggested that he turn to writing, so in 1872 he published what was at the time considered his major work, *Erewhon* (an anagram of the word *nowhere*), a satirical novel in the tradition of Jonathan Swift's *Gulliver's Travels*. The novel further alienated his parents, who banned him from their house. This novel was followed by *The Fair Haven* (1873), a "defense" of the gospels that in fact satirically denounces Christian doctrine. At about this time he began writing *The Way of All Flesh*. In the years that followed, he wrote a considerable amount of nonfiction, much of it examining the implications of Darwinism—which Butler began to suspect was faulty and perhaps even a sham, a view that led to a minor public spat with Darwin and his followers. Among these texts were *Life and Habit* (1877), *Evolution, Old and New* (1879), *Unconscious Memory* (1880), and *Luck, or Cunning, as the Main Means of Organic Modification* (1886).

In the final years of his life, Butler pursued a number of interests, including art history, music, and literature. He published a travel narrative that celebrated the Italian countryside, a biography of his grandfather Samuel Butler, a book arguing that Homer's epic poem the *Odyssey* was in fact written by a Sicilian woman, a translation of the Homeric epics, and a book contending that Shakespeare wrote his sonnet sequence for a homosexual lover. In 1901, he returned to the theme of his first novel to publish *Erewhon Revisited*.

Butler never married, although in New Zealand a woman named Mary Brittan declined his offer of marriage, and in England he had a relationship with Eliza Savage, whom he met in one of his art courses. She was a close confidante, and she reviewed chapters of *The Way of All Flesh* as Butler finished them. There were also rumors of a liaison with one Lucie Dumas, a much younger woman, but little is known about their relationship. Some biographers have speculated that Butler may have been gay. Butler died at a nursing home in London on June 18, 1902, of unspecified causes. *The Way of All Flesh* was published the following year.

Butler is not to be confused with the seventeenth-century poet of the same name who wrote the satirical poem *Hudibras* (1663–1678). Nor is he to be confused with his grandfather of the same name, who achieved a measure of fame as a schoolmaster and Anglican bishop in the late eighteenth and early nineteenth centuries.

PLOT SUMMARY

Chapters I–XVI

Although the main character of *The Way of All Flesh* is Ernest Pontifex, the novel opens with an extensive examination of Ernest's paternal ancestors. The story is narrated by Edward Overton, a family friend and Ernest's fictional biographer. Ernest's great-grandfather was John Pontifex, a carpenter as well as a gifted musician and artist. His only child, George, grew up to take over an uncle's London business as a publisher of conventionally pious books. A cruel man, George beat and broke the will of his children, including his son Theobald who would become Ernest's father. Theobald longs for a career at sea, but he is too weak to resist his father's plans for him to become a minister. After his ordination, he takes a post at a parish where he becomes engaged to one of the pastor's daughters, Christina. He puts off the marriage but finally acquiesces when he is given a parish of his own. He and Christina settle into the parsonage at Battersby-on-the-Hill.

Chapters XVII–XXI

Five years later, Ernest is born. To mark the occasion, George retrieves a bottle containing water from the river Jordan to be used for Ernest's baptism. He drops the bottle, but his servant sponges up enough for use during the baptism. Dinner is attended by Theobald's sister and Ernest's godmother, Alethea, and by Overton, Ernest's godfather; the reader learns that Overton has asked Alethea to marry him, but she has inexplicably refused. George Pontifex dies of liver failure brought on by excessive drinking and eating. Ernest is a toddler when

MEDIA ADAPTATIONS

- A 2004 unabridged audio version of *The Way of All Flesh*, read by Frederick David-son and with a running time of fifteen hours and eighteen minutes, is available from Blackstone Audio.

- Another unabridged audio version of *The Way of All Flesh* is available in a 2010 edition by Tantor Audio. The novel is read by Antony Ferguson and has a running time of fifteen hours and twenty-one minutes.

- *The Way of All Flesh* is available as an MP3 download. The novel, in severely abridged form, is read by Tom Conway and is available from Saland Publishing. It was produced in 2010; the running time just under fifty-three minutes.

his parents begin to subject him to harsh disciplinary treatment. Theobald is a tyrant who beats Ernest and his siblings to ensure that they do not exhibit any self-will.

Chapters XXII–XXVI

Overton describes Ernest's intolerable Victorian Sundays as a child; the only spark of joy for the children is that they can choose their own hymns to sing during evening services. Christina wants to be more affectionate, but she, too, is under the thumb of Theobald. Ernest continues to endure beatings for being self-willed and naughty—as, for example, when he is unable to pronounce the word *come* correctly. Overton reports that much later, when he questioned Ernest about his upbringing, Ernest refused to express a wish that he had been treated differently. Ernest came to believe that the concept of "family" should be restricted to lower species. Overton reproduces a letter Christina wrote to her children when she was pregnant and fearful that she would not survive childbirth. Her concern is entirely for how her children will be judged at death and not for their earthly happiness.

Chapters XXVII–XXXI

Ernest, now twelve years old, is enrolled at the Roughborough grammar school some fifty miles from home. The school is run by Dr. Skinner, who has a reputation for being a sound theologian and an effective headmaster. Ernest soon learns, however, that Skinner is little different from Theobald in his treatment of children and that he is, in fact, a pretentious and petty bully. Ernest is unhappy at school, but he takes solace in being free from his father's bullying. Ernest manages to get along with the other boys, largely by avoiding his studies and by taking up drinking and smoking.

Chapters XXXII–XXXVIII

Ernest enjoys a happy period in his life after Alethea visits him at Roughborough. She is drawn to him because he has an agreeable personality and loves music, so she decides to take an interest in him. She takes a small house in Roughborough, where she forms acquaintances among the students and teachers and where she can give Ernest refuge from his oppressive life at school. Ernest learns carpentry and is given tools and materials to use in the construction of an organ. Alethea, however, is stricken with typhoid fever and dies. Before she dies, she dictates a will leaving the bulk of her money in trust with Overton for Ernest's benefit; Ernest is to receive the money when he reaches the age of twenty-eight. At home at Battersby, a young servant, Ellen, becomes pregnant, prompting Theobald to dismiss her.

Chapters XXXIX–XLIV

Ernest learns of Ellen's dismissal and runs after the carriage taking her away. After he intercepts the carriage, he offers Ellen money, along with such valuable objects as his silver watch. Ellen promises to repay him in the future. Ernest makes up a story to explain the loss of these objects to his parents, but Theobald later discovers the watch at a pawnbroker's shop. He uses this discovery to compel his son to confess to his charity to Ellen and to his and other boys' transgressions at school: drinking, smoking, using profanity, and incurring debt. Theobald makes a chart outlining these transgressions and gives it to Dr. Skinner. Ernest confesses to his school chums that he betrayed them, but they forgive him because of his honesty to them. By the time Ernest leaves the school, he has actually earned a bit of respect from Dr. Skinner, although the headmaster wishes that Ernest had spent more time studying and less time practicing the organ.

Chapters XLV–L

Ernest enrolls at Emmanuel College at Cambridge University, where his newfound freedom, comfortable surroundings, and friends provide him with the first real happiness he has known. He is not much of a student, but he acquires a reputation as an intellectual by arguing in an undergraduate magazine that the ancient Greek dramatists are overrated. In time, he will complete an honors degree in mathematics and classics. He plans to enter the ministry, and during his last year in college, he becomes more interested in religious matters. He is attracted to the evangelical Simeonites and their voluntary poverty. He reports his religious enthusiasm to his parents, who are disturbed, feeling that even religious ardor should be exercised in moderation. These events occur just at the time when religious skepticism is beginning to run through Victorian Britain.

Chapters LI–LV

Ernest takes his degree and is ordained. He accepts a position as a curate in a London parish under the supervision of Pryer, a conservative, high church Anglican and the parish's senior curate. Ernest finds that Pryer's views are as appealing as those of the evangelical Simeonites had been. Pryer espouses the view that clerics should be granted a great deal of latitude in their views, whereas laypersons should adhere strictly to church tenets. Ernest finds himself agreeing, and the two make plans to form a College of Spiritual Pathology in which they would treat people's souls in the same way that doctors treat their bodies. In this way, religious practice would keep up with developments in science. He pledges his money to the enterprise and writes long, stuffy letters to his old college friends describing his plans for England's spiritual regeneration. Overton pays a visit and is distressed by Ernest's intentions—as is Mrs. Jupp, Ernest's Cockney landlady at Ashpit Place. Ill-advisedly, Ernest gives Pryer responsibility for investing his money in the stock market, intending to use the profits to implement their plan.

Chapters LVI–LX

While waiting for the stock market to rise and provide him with profits, Ernest tries to implement his plans in his own neighborhood. He comes across an old college friend who devastates Ernest by confessing that he does not like poor people. Ernest then decides to turn his attention to Mrs. Jupp's other tenants, but one puts Ernest in fear for his physical safety; one couple almost manage to convert him to Methodism; one causes him to doubt his belief in the Resurrection of Christ; and one, an attractive young woman, nearly seduces him. Back in his room, Ernest kicks his Bible, then forces himself into the room of another tenant—this one, too, an attractive, young woman whom he supposes to be a prostitute but who is in fact respectable. The terrified woman runs into the street and finds a policeman, who arrests Ernest on a charge of attempted assault.

Chapters LXI–LXV

Overton and a friend try to help Ernest, but their efforts fail, and Ernest is sentenced to six months in jail. He contracts a case of brain fever and spends two months in bed in the prison infirmary. As he recovers, he realizes that becoming a clergyman was a mistake, and he convinces himself that the cornerstone of Christianity, the Resurrection of Christ, is false doctrine. In this way he converts to a rationalist philosophy and is determined to try to undo all the wrong that he and others have suffered from Christian doctrine. He even resolves to try to get the archbishop of Canterbury to repudiate Christianity. Overton is pleased to learn that Theobald, in shame, has renounced his son, believing that Ernest will be able to prosper without interference from his family.

Chapters LXVI–LXXII

Ernest continues to convalesce in prison. He discovers that Pryer has run off with all his money. He learns to become a tailor, and he finds relief from the restrictions of prison life as the chapel organist. He thinks about life after his release from prison, and he resolves to be independent and self-sufficient. Accordingly, even though his father relents toward him after he finally leaves prison, he rejects his father's offer of help in obtaining a position as an office clerk. His break with his parents is complete. He moves in briefly with his godfather, Overton, and then finds rooms of his own. He tries to find work as a tailor, but he meets with little success; other tailors reject him because they see him as too genteel. At the depth of his despondency, he

runs into Ellen, the dismissed servant from Battersby, who now has become a streetwalker, although Ernest does not realize this. Ernest becomes infatuated with her, to the dismay of Overton, who nonetheless offers the couple financial help in a scheme to open a used clothing shop.

Chapters LXXIII–LXXVIII

Ernest and Ellen are married, and their shop has become successful. The two attend concerts and plays and take hikes, and Ernest enjoys reading, playing the piano, and writing about scientific and philosophical subjects. Ellen, however, begins to act strangely. He comes home to find her crying hysterically, and he assumes that she is in a bleak mood because she is pregnant. In fact, Ellen is drinking, particularly when Ernest is away. To pay for the liquor, she is sneaking money out of the shop cash drawer. Money worries begin to dog him, and he falls into a state of despair. Ellen suddenly is stricken by a case of delirium. She pledges abstinence, and her relationship with her husband improves after she gives birth to a second child. But she gradually loses Ernest's respect, and when she again begins to drink, Ernest comes to hate her. His fortunes change after a chance encounter with a coachman from Battersby, who tells Ernest that he and Ellen married shortly after her dismissal and are still married. Thus, Ellen's marriage to Ernest is invalid. Overton arranges a separation, turns Ernest's children over to the care of his laundress, and employs Ernest as a secretary.

Chapters LXXIX–LXXXIII

Ernest's ordeal leads to an attack of nerves. He rests, visits the Zoological Gardens, and travels to France and Italy with Overton. Back in England, he seeks work as a writer, but misfortune strikes again (for instance, when one of his publishers goes out of business), and he has little real success. When he reaches the age of twenty-eight, he inherits the money left to him by Alethea and becomes more of a gentleman. His father summons him to Battersby because Christina is dying. On her deathbed, she imagines that Ernest will become prime minister of England.

Chapters LXXXIV–LXXXVII

Ernest travels abroad in an effort to find societies composed of the best people. After three years, he returns to England and takes up a career as a writer. He publishes anonymously a collection of essays that are well received by the public and by critics. When his identity is made public, he becomes famous, but his later writings are less successful, principally because their subject matter is too controversial. Theobald dies at an advanced age. Ernest's two children are placed with foster parents who treat them well, and they grow up to become responsible, healthy, and attractive. Overton lives into his eighties and continues to urge Ernest to write with the public in mind. Ernest, however, remains indifferent to the opinions of others, believing that later generations will read and appreciate his work.

CHARACTERS

Ellen

Ellen is a pretty servant at the Pontifex home at Battersby, but she is dismissed after she becomes pregnant. Much later, Ernest encounters her in London. He fails to recognize that she has become a streetwalker, and he finds her very attractive. Ultimately the two marry and make their living running a used clothing shop. Ellen drinks to excess, however, and in time the marriage collapses. Ernest later learns that Ellen was already married to the Battersby coachman, rendering her marriage to Ernest invalid.

John

John is the name of the coachman from Battersby who later brings about a reversal of fortune in Ernest's life by informing him that he married Ellen not long after the two of them left the service of Ernest's parents. The result is that Ernest is not legally married to Ellen.

Mrs. Jupp

Mrs. Jupp, Ernest's lower-class landlady in the East End of London, is a comic figure.

Edward Overton

Edward functions as Ernest's biographer and as the narrator of the novel. He takes an intense interest in his godson and adopts the role of an older and wiser adviser and confidant. In some ways Overton is the parent that Ernest wishes he had had (he was born in the same year as Theobald); in other respects he represents an older Ernest, perhaps even an older Samuel Butler, who recognizes the many ways in which Ernest's

family upbringing, religion, and education stifled him. Throughout, it is Overton's perceptions that Ernest comes to share.

Alethea Pontifex

Alethea is Ernest Pontifex's godmother and Theobald's younger sister. She is charming and independent, a woman who enjoys life and loves the arts. Overton describes her as a "freethinker" in matters of religion. She dies suddenly of typhoid fever during Ernest's school days. She leaves the bulk of her estate to Ernest, who will inherit the money when he turns twenty-eight. Alethea is depicted as a role model for a person who lives a fulfilled, independent life.

Christina Pontifex

Christina, Ernest's mother, is depicted as hysterical, melodramatic, and mentally weak. She wants to treat Ernest and his siblings with affection, but she is unable to resist the tyranny of her husband. She dies thinking that Ernest will become England's prime minister and that another son will become archbishop of Canterbury.

Ernest Pontifex

Ernest, the novel's protagonist, does not appear in the novel until chapter XVII, making clear that his development would be influenced by three generations of his ancestors. Ernest is a trusting, gentle, open, intelligent child and man, but because of his upbringing, his appealing qualities often get him into trouble. During his years at school, at university, and as a young man, he repeatedly succumbs to views that have appeal for him, only to reject them later when new, also appealing views present themselves to him. He also makes disastrous decisions, such as the decision to turn his money over to Pryer and to marry Ellen. Through his many failures and setbacks, Ernest, with the help of his prudent and wise godparents (Overton and Alethea), eventually breaks with his past, triumphs over his many adversities (for example, his imprisonment), and achieves a measure of success and fulfillment on his own terms.

George Pontifex

George is Ernest's grandfather. He became the sole owner of a publishing business that appeals to the conventional pieties of the public. He treated his sons, including Theobald, with cruelty, beating them for their own good.

John Pontifex

John is Ernest's great-grandfather. He made his living as a carpenter, and he was naturally gifted as an artist and musician. John lived simply and unpretentiously, and he is cast as something of an idealized founder of the Pontifex family.

Theobald Pontifex

Theobald is Ernest Pontifex's father and an Anglican clergyman. He is portrayed as cruel, unfeeling, parsimonious, and even sadistic. He intends for Ernest to follow him into the ministry, but when Ernest refuses to take orders, he rejects his son. Later in the novel, he makes conciliatory gestures to Ernest, but Ernest concludes that he has to make a complete break from his oppressive father.

Pryer

Pryer is depicted as a closeted homosexual and as the emblem of high church hypocrisy. As a senior curate, he is Ernest's supervisor at their London parish. He wins Ernest over to his conservative views, and he and Ernest plan to form a College of Spiritual Pathology at which souls would be treated in the same way that doctors treat bodies. He is given responsibility for investing Ernest's money to fund the plan, but he runs off with the money.

Dr. Skinner

Dr. Skinner is the headmaster of the public school Ernest attends at Roughborough. He is satirically portrayed as the emblem of the savage and repressive headmaster.

THEMES

Parent-Child Relationships

One of Butler's chief purposes in *The Way of All Flesh* was to demonstrate the need for individuals to evolve away from elements of their upbringing—family, religion, education, class, culture, belief systems, manners—that can repress them or inhibit their development into fully self-reliant adults. To this end, the novel depicts dysfunctional parent-child relationships. In the early chapters, the reader learns about Ernest's grandfather, George Pontifex, who publishes pious religious texts but who also beats his weak-willed son Theobald, to ensure that his son exhibits no self-will. George emerges as an agent of tyranny, passing that tyranny along to the next generation, where Theobald and his wife, Christina, become themselves victims of a tyranny that they try to exercise over their son Ernest. Theobald is interested entirely in maintaining his position in the world; along with other characters, he represents what Butler saw as a toxic mix of avarice and religion. Christina remains locked in her daydreams. Their marriage is loveless and essentially sterile; it came about entirely through the pressures of money, family, and possessions, and Christina in effect "wins" Theobald in a card game. As a couple, the two work to preserve domestic order, not to provide their children with happiness, fulfillment, or growth. Old John Pontifex, Ernest's great-grandfather, is held up as one figure in the family tree who lived an instinctual, artistic, natural life; it becomes Ernest's goal to cast off his parents to reclaim the type of life his distant ancestor enjoyed.

Loss of Faith

Much of *The Way of All Flesh* is taken up with religious belief. George Pontifex, Ernest's grandfather, publishes religious texts that appeal to his market's pious tastes. Theobald Pontifex is an Anglican minister, and it is assumed that his son Ernest will attend university and himself take orders as a minister. Ernest enrolls at the University of Cambridge and, particularly during his last year at Cambridge, becomes absorbed by religious matters. He finds himself attracted to the ascetic low church Simeonites, but after he completes his education and takes a position as a curate in London, he finds himself equally attracted to the high church views of Pryer. After he is arrested and jailed, he has an epiphany when he concludes that the Resurrection of Christ, the foundational doctrine of Christianity, is false. He comes, then, to reject much of the religious faith of his father and grandfather to become a freethinker. In chapter LXXXIII, Overton comments on Ernest's views:

> The spirit behind the Church is true, though her letter—true once—is now true no longer.... The Theobalds, who do what they do because it seems to be the correct thing, but who in their hearts neither like it nor believe in it, are in reality the least dangerous of all classes to the peace and liberties of mankind.

TOPICS FOR FURTHER STUDY

- One object of Butler's satire is the English public school system. Conduct research into British education in the nineteenth century. How do the British and American uses of the word *public* to describe schools differ? What were some of the most prominent English public schools? Write an oral report, perhaps a satirical one in the voice of Butler's Dr. Skinner, and present the results of your findings to your classmates.

- Using the Internet or print sources, examine the educational system at the University of Cambridge in the 1850s. Why were there separate colleges, such as St. John's and Emmanuel? Did students attend classes, or did they meet more frequently with tutors? What types of degrees were awarded, and what subjects did students study? What is a "poll degree," and what is the "Classical Tripos"? What was the social life like? Who were the Simeonites at Cambridge? Prepare a written report answering some of these questions or any others you believe are relevant to your understanding of Ernest Pontifex.

- Prepare a chart in which you outline the structure of the Church of England during the Victorian era. Be prepared to explain the roles of various members of the church hierarchy, including bishops, deacons, deans, chaplains, vicars, archdeacons, and curates. Share your chart with your classmates.

- The British scientist Charles Darwin was the author of *On the Origin of Species by Means of Natural Selection* (1859). Darwin is thought of as the originator of the theory that higher forms of life evolved from lower forms through the process of natural selection and survival of the fittest (though earlier scientists had proposed similar views). Conduct research to determine the impact Darwin and his followers had on the Victorian age, in particular, on Victorian religious beliefs. Try to imagine a dialogue between Darwin and Butler about these issues (about which they ultimately disagreed), and with a classmate present your dialogue to your class.

- Select a scene from *The Way of All Flesh* that you believe could be turned into a dramatic presentation. Write the script (or screenplay) for the scene and post it on a blog. Invite your classmates to comment. With one (or more) of those classmates, perform the scene for your class.

- Alex Haley is perhaps best known for his Pulitzer Prize–winning saga *Roots*. He is also the coauthor (with David Steven) of the 1993 novel *Queen*, a multigenerational saga that examines the ancestry of the author's African American father; Queen is the name of the woman who would become Haley's grandmother. Read *Queen* and prepare an oral report in which you comment on how its tone and purpose differ from those of Butler's multigenerational saga of family life.

- *The Chosen* (1967), by Chaim Potok, is a novel originally written for a wide audience but that has since come to be regarded as a young-adult novel. The story, set in Brooklyn in the 1940s, is about fathers, sons, and the questioning of religious faith. Read the novel, then imagine a conversation about religious faith between Ernest Pontifex and one of the major characters of Potok's novel—Daniel, a Hasidic Jew, or Reuven, a secular Jew (or perhaps among all three). Publish your dialogue on a blog and invite your classmates to comment.

Overton goes on: "The man to fear is he who goes at things with the cocksureness of pushing vulgarity and self-conceit." Ernest, then, has struggled to learn that strict dogma is not the way to fulfillment; his struggle is finally successful, but only after he latches on to, then rejects, various dogmas and beliefs.

The Way of All Flesh *looks into the social discord of the Victorian era.* *(© Hulton Archive / Getty Images)*

Education

One of the targets of Butler's satire is the British educational system. At his school at Roughborough, Ernest is profoundly unhappy most of the time, for he is subjected to bullying and ill treatment from students and teachers alike, although some of the teachers are kindlier than others. Many of the details of Ernest's life at the school are presented ironically; the emphasis on Greek and Latin and on the recording of transgressions such as smoking or drinking beer provide good examples. Near the end of chapter XXVIII, Butler, in the voice of Overton, draws the reader's attention to the tyranny of the British school system at the time:

> O schoolmasters . . . bear in mind when any particularly timid, drivelling urchin is brought by his papa into your study, and you treat him with the contempt which he deserves, and afterwards make his life a burden to him for years— bear in mind that it is exactly in the disguise of such a boy as this that your future chronicler will appear.

Overton goes on:

> Never see a wretched little heavy-eyed mite sitting on the edge of a chair against your study wall without saying to yourselves, "Perhaps this boy is he who, if I am not careful, will one day tell the world what manner of man I was."

Thus, the narrative takes the position that the British school system of the nineteenth century failed to meet the emotional and psychological needs of its students and that a person had to cast off its damaging effects in order to become a self-actualized, happy person.

STYLE

Caricature

Butler satirizes various types of characters in *The Way of All Flesh*. One way in which he does so is through caricature, that is, through a portrait that exaggerates or distorts a person's characteristics for comic or satiric effect. One way he creates caricatures is through documents written in their own hands. The novel, purportedly written by Ernest Pontifex's "biographer," Edward Overton, includes such documents as report cards, sermons, musical notations, epitaphs, and in particular letters. A good example of a document that caricatures its writer is the 1841 letter Christina Pontifex writes to her children when she is pregnant and convinced that she will not survive childbirth. The letter, reproduced in chapter XXV, is absurd, for at this point, Ernest, the oldest child, is only about five years old. Christina writes:

> When I think about leaving you all, two things press heavily upon me: one, your father's sorrow . . . the other, the everlasting welfare of my children. I know how long and deep the former will be, and I know that he will look to his children to be almost his only earthly comfort.

Nonsensical statements such as this—nonsensical because her husband, Theobald, has no interest in or affection for his children—add to the caricature of Christina as weak-minded and afflicted with a melodramatic religiosity. Yet another example of this kind of caricaturing through documents occurs at the end of chapter XLII, when Theobald, based on information provided by Ernest, prepares a chart listing the boys at the Roughborough school ("Smith," "Brown," "Jones," "Robinson") and the number of their transgressions for smoking, drinking beer, and swearing and using obscene language.

Third-Person Point of View

The Way of All Flesh is narrated by Edward Overton, an old family friend (he is the same age as Theobald Pontifex) and Ernest Pontifex's godfather and fictional biographer. Butler, though, is not entirely consistent in his use of a fictional narrator; conventionally, such a narrator would be able to report only on events and conversations at which he was present or that were reported to him by other characters. Overton, however, sometimes quietly becomes more like an all-seeing "omniscient" narrator, providing the reader with insights into Ernest's state of mind.

Overton is not hesitant about commenting on his godson and the circumstances of his life, interpreting them for the reader and placing them in context. Examples occur on virtually every page. In chapter XLII, when Ernest's parents

are trying to wrest from him information about the other boys at school, Overton remarks:

> Nothing should have cajoled or frightened [Ernest] into telling tales out of school. Ernest thought of his ideal boys: they, he well knew, would have let their tongues be cut out of them before information could have been wrung from any word of theirs. But Ernest was not an ideal boy, and he was not strong enough for his surroundings.

These kinds of comments suggest that Overton is more than just a narrator; he is, in effect, a mouthpiece for the author, for it is unlikely that Overton could have known in any detail what Ernest's thoughts were when Ernest was just a boy.

Bildungsroman

The essential plot structure of *The Way of All Flesh* is that of the bildungsroman, a German term used to refer to a novel (*Roman*) of "formation" or "education" (*Bildung*, which can be literally translated in various ways, including "formation," "growth," "education," or "development"). A bildungsroman, then, is a novel that traces the development and education of a character, usually a young man. Two of the most important such novels in literary history are *The Sorrows of Young Werther* (1774), by the German writer Johann Wolfgang von Goethe, and *A Portrait of the Artist as a Young Man* (1916), by the Irish novelist James Joyce. Quite often, the bildungsroman deals with the education of a young man with an artistic temperament, as the title of Joyce's novel suggests. Although Ernest Pontifex is not particularly artistic, he shows an interest in music and is finally able to take up a career as a writer, living according to his own emotional needs. The thrust of the novel's episodic plot is to demonstrate how his family, education, and religion stifled him and then how he was able to liberate himself from these influences and from false beliefs (for example, those of the Simeonites and of Pryer) to achieve the kind of independence enjoyed by his godparents, Edward Overton and Alethea Pontifex.

HISTORICAL CONTEXT

The principal historical events surrounding *The Way of All Flesh* have to do with religion. The Victorians took religious issues seriously, and religion—its theology, forms, rituals, scriptures,

COMPARE
&
CONTRAST

- **1870s:** Charles Darwin's evolutionary theory provokes controversy. Many prominent scientists attack Darwin's ideas, but many others, including Joseph Hooker, Thomas Huxley, Henry Bates, and Alfred Russel Wallace, publicly defend him and his theories.

  Today: Evolution and the theory of natural selection continue to be controversial, with the theory of intelligent design offered by some as an alternative view of how Creation unfolded.

- **1870s:** Women begin to attend one of two women's colleges, Girton and Newnham, at Cambridge University; by 1879, twelve women are enrolled at Cambridge's Girton College, though women would not be full members of the university until 1947. The abolition of religious tests opens places and fellowships to applicants of all religions.

  Today: The University of Cambridge is a comprehensive international university that enrolls approximately twelve thousand undergraduates and more than six thousand graduate students in thirty-one colleges. As of 2005, women made up almost 48 percent of Cambridge's enrollment.

- **1870s:** The 1870 Education Act establishes a system of school boards to construct and manage schools in areas where they are needed; the act is passed in the face of resistance from religious institutions that want to retain control over education.

  Today: Under the provisions of the Education Reform Act of 1988, "all pupils in attendance at a maintained school shall in each school day take part in an act of collective worship" of a broadly Christian character (although parents retain the right to withdraw students from worship or provide for worship reflecting another faith tradition).

---

and practices—were matters for frequent and ongoing reflection, debate, and writing. Indeed, it would be little exaggeration to say that in some way religion permeated virtually every aspect of Victorian life. For centuries, England had been a Protestant nation. Largely for political purposes, King Henry VIII broke with the Church of Rome (the Catholic Church) in the 1530s to form what would become the Anglican Church, or the Church of England, called the Episcopal Church in the United States. In the centuries that followed, English Catholics and Protestants remained sharply at odds, to the point even of engaging in armed conflict.

But Protestantism in England itself contended with internal divisions. One faction within the church consisted of "high church" Anglicans, who practiced a version of Protestantism that was closer to pre-Reformation Catholicism. It shared many doctrines with the Catholic Church, and it was not opposed to ritual and ornamentation (priestly vestments, incense, statues, music, stained-glass windows, and the like). The other faction, often referred to as "low church," consisted of evangelical Christians. The distinction between the two had less to do with bedrock theology and more to do with such matters as the organization of the church, forms of worship, religious observance and rituals, and one's general outlook on religious life and the role of religion in the public arena. In general, evangelicals tended to distrust hierarchy and formal theology, which they associated with Catholicism. Their interpretation of the Bible was literal. They believed in a personal relationship with Christ, achieved through strict adherence to precepts contained in the Bible, an impulse reflected in chapter XXIII, when Overton reports having half listened to Theobald Pontifex reading verses from the fifteenth chapter of the Old Testament book of Numbers. Evangelicals were opposed to ritual and the ornamentation usually found in Catholic churches (and in many Anglican churches), which they believed erected a barrier between the believer and God. They were proponents of thrift, sobriety, and industry, virtues that appealed primarily to the upwardly mobile middle class.

High church Anglicans, in contrast, tended to be somewhat more aristocratic, more associated with the well-to-do or with educated people, and more liberal in their theological outlook. Many were thought to have a "broad church" or "Latitudinarian" outlook, meaning that they accepted diverse views and forms of worship within the Anglican Church. High church views were inculcated at Oxford University, in contrast to Cambridge University, where the religious atmosphere tended to be more evangelical and low church. Evangelicals—active, vigorous, and enthusiastic—saw high church Anglicans as complacent, too content with their earthly benefits, and lacking in deep spirituality. But among high church Anglicans, evangelicalism was associated with a lack of sophistication and refinement. High church clergy regarded themselves as gentlemen; in their view, evangelical clergymen were common. These at least were the perceptions the two factions had of each other.

Butler would have assumed that most of his readers were familiar with this split, so in *The Way of All Flesh* he was able to make reference to various ecclesiastical events without explaining them in detail. Take, for instance, a brief passage near the beginning of chapter XLVII. Ernest has returned to Cambridge in 1858. The narrator notes that "the year 1858 was the last of a term during which the peace of the Church of England was singularly unbroken." Reference is made to the 1844 "Vestiges of Creation"; the full title is *Vestiges of the Natural History of Creation*. This anonymous book, which in many ways anticipated Charles Darwin's evolutionary theories, created enormous controversy. Reference is also made to "Essays and Reviews," a volume of seven essays, each written separately by six English clergymen and one layman in 1859 (and scheduled for publication that year, although publication was delayed until 1860). These essays provoked controversy because they took the liberal position that God's revelation was ongoing, that the presumed "miracles" of the Bible defied God's laws, and that Darwin's *On the Origin of Species*, published just months earlier, offered a legitimate view of how the natural world unfolded—a shocking view to many people at the time. Interestingly, this volume of *Essays and Reviews* sold more copies in two years than *Origin of Species* did in the first seventeen years after its publication.

Further, mention is made of Tractarianism, a movement founded by, among other important theologians, John Henry Newman, an Anglican minister and a professor at Oxford University; the movement is therefore often called the Oxford Movement. "Tractarianism" refers to the publication of ninety *Tracts for the Times*, a series of disquisitions on matters of faith and religion written primarily by Newman from a high church position. As Newman's religious beliefs evolved, he concluded that the differences between Anglicanism and Catholicism were insignificant, and in 1845 he underwent a public and very controversial conversion to Catholicism. For nearly two decades, he endured harsh criticism for this decision, along with attacks on the priesthood and on Catholic doctrine. He responded in one of the most widely read nonfiction books of the Victorian era, *Apologia pro vita sua*, or *Defense of One's Life*, first published in 1864.

Another work that provoked controversy and referred to in chapter XLVII of the novel was Bishop John Colenso's *The Pentateuch and Book of Joshua Critically Examined*, in which he argues that the Bible was literally true and that the English clergyman was required to believe, for example, "in the historical truth of Noah's Flood, as recorded in the Bible, which the Church believed in some centuries ago, before God had given us the light of modern science." Yet further subjects of religious contention were the Gorham and Hampden controversies. George Gorham was a clergyman who was denied a parish because he was suspected of harboring Calvinist (low church) religious views; Renn Hampden was nominated to a bishopric by Prime Minister Lord John Russell in 1847, raising the question of the relationship and respective powers of the state and the Church of England, particularly given that Hampden's liberal religious views were suspect in some quarters. These and other issues and controversies formed a significant part of the intellectual backdrop of Ernest Pontifex's life, particularly during his formative college years.

Butler's experience with faith while growing up influenced his writings, as is reflected in The Way of All Flesh. *(© Radek Sturgolewski / Shutterstock.com)*

CRITICAL OVERVIEW

Early critics of *The Way of All Flesh* recognized that Butler's novel was an important document in the early-twentieth-century reaction against the Victorian age. For example, a reviewer for the *Times Literary Supplement* in London in 1903 writes:

> The book is concerned chiefly with the years 1835 to 1867—a period which for average readers is obsolete without being strange—and having in it a strong militant purpose, seems to be fighting a battle already lost and won.

The reviewer goes on to comment favorably on the work:

> From those, however, for whom the humanity of the last or preceding generation can be as interesting, in its material customs and spiritual conflicts, as that of other generations, and who have intellect enough themselves to enjoy the working of an intellect both powerful and nimble, the work is sure of a ready and attentive acceptance.

In an introduction to a 1916 edition of *The Way of All Flesh*, William Lyon Phelps remarks on, and defends, Butler's attack on Christianity:

> I think that the terrific attack on "professing Christians" made in this novel will be of real service to Christianity. . . . The Church needs clever, active antagonists to keep her up to the mark; the principle of Good is toughened by constant contact with the principle of Evil.

Phelps concludes: "Thus, although I firmly believe this is a diabolical novel, I think it will prove to be of service to Christianity."

The British novelist Virginia Woolf comments favorably on the novel in a *Times Literary Supplement* review in 1919. While praising Butler's "vigorous powers of delineation," she writes that "his gifts were such as to produce a novel which differs from most professional novels by being more original, more interesting, and more alive." Woolf continues:

> Endowed with these formidable qualities and a profound originality which wrought them to the sharpest point, Butler sauntered on unconcernedly until he found a position where he could take up his pitch and deliver his verdict upon life at his ease.

Later critics continued to admire the novel. For example, Morton Dauwen Zabel, in "Samuel Butler: The Victorian Insolvency," an essay first published in 1956, calls the novel "one of the milestones in the history of the English novel." For Zabel, it was a milestone because it is "a book that marks as distinctly as any the point of division between the Victorian age and the Twentieth Century." F. W. Dupee, however, in an essay dated 1967, also calls attention to what he regarded as the novel's faults: "The story bumbles along agreeably while defying many of the novelistic refinements that were in force as far back as 1873." Dupee refers to Butler's "defiance of sophisticated novelistic procedures" and calls the narrative "shaky, tending to lapse into single episodes or sequences of episodes or into impromptu performances of virtuosity on the author's part."

CRITICISM

Michael J. O'Neal

O'Neal holds a PhD in English. In the following essay, he examines The Way of All Flesh *as an important document in the reaction against Victorianism in the late nineteenth and early twentieth centuries.*

WHAT DO I READ NEXT?

- Butler's other major work is *Erewhon*, published anonymously in 1872. The title of the novel is an anagram for the word *nowhere*. The book is thus about a fictional nation, in the tradition of Jonathan Swift's *Gulliver's Travels*. While it has some utopian elements, it is largely a satire on Victorian society and institutions; for example, Butler attacks religious hypocrisy in a chapter titled "The Musical Banks," where cathedrals are compared to banks, with each issuing its own "currency" (religious beliefs) that other "banks" will not accept.

- Readers interested in the role of religion in mid- to late Victorian English literature might start with J. Russell Perkin's *Theology and the Victorian Novel* (2010).

- An alternative to the Perkin book is Julie Melnyk's *Victorian Religion: Faith and Life in Britain* (2008), a relatively brief introduction to the complicated matter of religion and its impact on nearly every aspect of life in Victorian England.

- Philip Pullman's controversial trilogy of young-adult fantasy novels, *His Dark Materials*, comprises *The Golden Compass* (1995), *The Subtle Knife* (1997), and *The Amber Spyglass* (2000). The trilogy is a coming-of-age story about two children who wander through parallel universes. The novels comment on a range of issues, including religion; they are in part a recasting and inversion of the epic poem *Paradise Lost* by John Milton and present a negative portrayal of religion in general and Christianity in particular.

- *Coming of Age in America* (1994) is a collection of short stories and novel excerpts edited by Mary Frosch. Included are works by authors from a range of ethnic and racial groups, all writing about the common process of growing up and coming of age. Among the authors included are Julia Alvarez, Frank Chin, Dorothy Allison, Adam Schwartz, Reginald McKnight, and Tobias Wolff.

- A parallel book is *Coming of Age around the World* (2007), edited by Faith Adiélé and Mary Frosch. This collection presents twenty-four stories by major international authors about the experience of young people struggling for an individual identity.

The word *Victorian*—a reference to Queen Victoria, who warmed the throne of Great Britain from 1837 until her death in 1901 and who left an indelible stamp upon the age—bears numerous connotations. Used to describe a grandmother's living room, it implies ornate, old-fashioned dustiness and fussiness. Many people associate Victorianism with extreme prudery with regard to sexual matters—a half-truth, for this prudery was restricted to the "respectable" middle class (and women) but was in less evidence among the lower and upper classes (and among men).

Victorianism carries other connotations as well. The age, for example, was one of sweeping political reform. In 1832, a reform act extended the franchise (the right to vote) from a small percentage of property owners to about one in seven men. In 1867, a second reform bill extended voting eligibility to about two of five men, and a third reform bill, passed in 1884, extended the franchise to all male householders, adding about six million men to the voting roles. (Women, like the dowager countess's granddaughter, would have to wait until 1928 to achieve the right to vote in Great Britain.) Britons were enormously proud of their liberties and political institutions, regarding them as models for the rest of the world.

The age, too, was one of empire. By the early 1890s, Great Britain, perhaps the greatest

> AFTER THE NOVEL WAS PUBLISHED IN 1903, IT ENJOYED A PERIOD OF WIDESPREAD AND GROWING POPULARITY, FOR WRITERS, PHILOSOPHERS, PSYCHOLOGISTS, SOCIAL SCIENTISTS, AND OTHER INTELLECTUALS WERE ELATED BY ITS BARBED REJECTION OF STUFFY, PIETISTIC VICTORIAN VIEWS IN FAVOR OF NEW, MORE MODERN, PROGRESSIVE ATTITUDES ABOUT A RANGE OF ISSUES."

imperial power in world history, controlled millions of square miles and hundreds of millions of people. The "jewel in the crown" of the British Empire was India. During Victoria's reign numerous lands came into British possession, among them Brunei, Cyprus, Sarawak, the Gold Coast, Natal, Zululand, New Guinea, New Zealand, and Queensland (in Australia). Truly, "the sun never set on the British Empire." During the *Pax Britannica*, Britain's might, buttressed by the world's most powerful navy, maintained relative peace at sea for a century.

The age was one of science and commerce. By the mid- to late nineteenth century, Britain had become the world's dominant industrial power. The nation's railway system expanded exponentially. Steam power, mechanized power looms, and numerous other technological developments boosted the standard of living. Britain was regarded as the "workshop of the world," a nation in which the production of crude iron and steel and the mining of coal doubled and redoubled during the Victorian era. The 1851 Great Exhibition was a monument to Britain's triumphs in science, industry, and architecture. London was the most important city in Europe, growing from just under two million to six million in population during Victoria's reign.

One consequence of all these developments was that Britain grew smug and self-satisfied about its government, culture, and institutions. But not everything ran smoothly. Despite Britain's growing prosperity, slums and poverty were facts of life. Many people, particularly those in the weaving industries and agriculture,

were displaced by technology, and many moved into crowded slums in industrial cities, where they enjoyed few rights and virtually no security. Although the "political economy" of Adam Smith and his book *An Inquiry into the Nature and Causes of the Wealth of Nations* (1776) and the utilitarianism of Jeremy Bentham were products of the eighteenth century, they were views that continued to be influential during the Victorian age. Together with these notions, the radical revision of views concerning historical processes by Karl Marx in *Das Kapital* (1867–1894) and the *Communist Manifesto* (1848) and the evolutionary theories of Charles Darwin were, in the opinion of many, failing to take into account people's spiritual needs. In particular, the age was one of religious doubt, as science, especially the relatively new science of geology, was calling into question many of the tenets of the Judeo-Christian tradition and as German biblical criticism was convincing a growing number of people that the Bible is simply a historical text, not the revealed word of God. This atmosphere of skepticism and doubt prompted evangelical Christians in particular to push back in their defense of a literal interpretation of the Bible.

Which brings us finally to *The Way of All Flesh* and its reaction against Victorianism, for Butler took as his target the smugness and restrictiveness often thought of as characteristic of the Victorian age. At the time of the novel's composition, many people were beginning to reject the traditional Victorian values of piety, earnestness, domestic propriety, and sense of high moral purpose. This revaluation of Victorianism pervades Butler's novel. After the novel was published in 1903, it enjoyed a period of widespread and growing popularity, for writers, philosophers, psychologists, social scientists, and other intellectuals were elated by its barbed rejection of stuffy, pietistic Victorian views in favor of new, more modern, progressive attitudes about a range of issues.

One was the patriarchal system, represented to great effect by George Pontifex and his son Theobald, with support from the vapid and ineffectual Christina Pontifex. Another was what could be called romantic religiosity, embodied by Christina and her dreams about her sons. Marriage and family are obvious targets of Butler's satire. Old John Pontifex and his wife are exemplars of people who led simple, instinctual lives, unhampered by the repressions of an antiquated and unresponsive educational system. George and his family, followed by Theobald and his, are examples of the type of dysfunctional family from which, Butler argues, one had to seek liberation. Notice, by the way, that Overton, like Butler himself, remains a bachelor, and although Ernest marries Ellen, the marriage is invalid, so Ernest in the end is in essence a bachelor. Alethea Pontifex is the only member of the family who engages the reader's sympathy, largely because of her intellect, her independence, and her love of the arts. She, too, remained unmarried.

Yet another target of Butler's satire is the educational system, which he saw as stunting students' natural development. Twentieth-century educators, who were beginning to see children as children and not as miniature adults, could gleefully sneer at a character like Dr. Skinner. Butler writes in chapter XXXI:

> Latin and Greek had nothing in them which commended them to [Ernest's] instinct as likely to bring him peace. . . . The deadness inherent in these defunct languages themselves had never been artificially counteracted by a system of *bona fide* rewards for application.

Butler continues: "There had been any amount of punishments for want of application, but no good comfortable bribes had baited the hook which was to allure him to his good." Butler ends by expressing the traditional, hidebound Victorian view: "We were put into this world not for pleasure but duty, and pleasure had in it something more or less sinful in its very essence." At the university level, Butler satirizes the fads and intellectual fashions that students were susceptible to, including, for example, the Simeonites.

The use of the word *instinct* in the passage from chapter XXXI is telling. In the early decades of the twentieth century, social scientists were questioning the presumed superiority of developed Western cultures. They were adopting a posture of cultural relativism and finding substantial value in technologically primitive, instinctive cultures and their ability to fulfill human needs—cultures that in some cases were dominated by British imperialism. In many of these cultures, boys had close relationships with their fathers. Social scientists were learning that in so-called primitive cultures, children absorbed from their families skills and values that were too often denied to Victorian children. In Victorian

culture, at least among upwardly mobile classes, sons—and daughters, too—often remained alienated from their parents. They could be almost strangers in their families. If they misbehaved, a good beating, followed by the reading of a religious sermon or tract, would bring them to heel. A good "modern" of, say, 1920 would have smirked at these views, seen as belonging to a thankfully distant past.

In the twenty-first century, *The Way of All Flesh* has perhaps lost some of its power, for the battle between Victorianism and the modern age has long been won by the forces of modernity. The makeup of the social structure, of the family, and of educational institutions has profoundly altered. So, too, have cultural values, attitudes toward religion, and beliefs about the place of science and technology. The straitjacketing moral and social sanctions of Victorianism have largely been loosened. But Butler's novel survives because of its wit, its sharp satire, and in particular its continuing ability to undermine the very concept of adherence to and belief in whatever manners and morals happen to predominate at a given point in history.

Source: Michael J. O'Neal, Critical Essay on *The Way of All Flesh*, in *Novels for Students*, Gale, Cengage Learning, 2014.

Peter Faulkner

In the following essay, Faulkner provides an overview of Butler's career, noting that The Way of All Flesh *had an impact on the Victorian family ideal of the time.*

Samuel Butler was one of the most independent minds of the later 19th century: his interest in social ideas links him with such Victorian sages as Carlyle, Ruskin, and Arnold, but his preference for irony and paradox brings him close to Bernard Shaw and Oscar Wilde. The fact that he is so hard to classify would undoubtedly have pleased him, but it may account for the varied and fluctuating assessments of his importance.

Erewhon is his most stimulating book. A story in the tradition of *Gulliver's Travels*, it uses its conventional Evangelical protagonist Higgs and his adventures to raise many significant lines of thought—a possible analogy between crime and disease, the inauthenticity of much contemporary religious observance, the abstractness of upper-class classical education, the dangers of mechanisation, the extravagances

Ernest experiences theological doubt as a young man. *(© Kuzma / Shutterstock.com)*

of moral dogma, and, above all, the hold of conventions on the mind. And Butler does all this in a highly entertaining way. He clearly saw himself as a free-thinker, and his mission [was] to challenge, by argument and irony, the conventional wisdom of his day. Above all, his insight into the extent to which human beliefs are the products of social environment is impressive, especially at a time when thinkers were apt to believe in absolutes. He writes of an Erewhonian judge: "He could not emancipate himself from, nay, it did not even occur to him to feel, the bondage of the ideas in which he had been born and bred." Butler's distinction was his awareness of the awaiting bondage.

In some cases Butler's determination not to be dragooned into orthodoxy led him to extravagances of his own. Many would feel that this is true of his protracted campaign against Darwin's idea of evolution. In a series of books including *Life and Habit*, *Unconscious Memory*, and *Luck or Cunning*, Butler argued that the evolutionary process was directed by some kind of life-force. He thus introduced a new and complicating note into the controversy between Science and Religion.

Sometimes his love of heterodoxy led him to attack accepted assumptions irresponsibly, but there was usually enough behind his arguments to make attention to them an enlivening experience. In *The Authoress of the Odyssey* he argued from internal evidence that the poet must have been a woman, and in *Shakespeare's Sonnets* that they were addressed to a plebeian lover.

His *Notebooks* perhaps best reveal the wide range of his interests, but his best-known book is *The Way of All Flesh* which, published posthumously in 1903, dealt a massive blow to the Victorian family ideal. In it Butler mixes autobiography with experiences of his own ideas, thoroughly debunking the attitudes represented by the father, Theobald Pontifex. The book had a liberating effect on many young writers of the time, and its attitude to Victorianism underlies the criticisms of the 1920's. The early scenes have great vividness, but there are elements of complacency in the later part which mark Butler's limitations. He lived very much to himself and this comes out in the somewhat inhuman ideal which is propounded at the end. The comment made on Ernest Pontifex shows, however, a just awareness on Butler's part of how he was regarded: "With the general public he is not a favourite. He is admitted to have talent, but it is considered generally to be of a queer, unpractical kind, and no matter how serious he is, he is always accused of being in jest." Butler's jests often retain for the modern reader an interest which can no longer be accorded to the conventional wisdom of the age which he strove to educate by his paradoxes.

Source: Peter Faulkner, "Samuel Butler: Overview," in *Reference Guide to English Literature*, 2nd ed., edited by D. L. Kirkpatrick, St. James Press, 1991.

Carl Woodring

In the following review, Woodring describes the plot of the novel and dubs it "a genealogical narrative that knocked the stuffing out of Victorian morality."

When Samuel "Erewhon" Butler died in 1902, he left behind a novel he had begun in 1873 and fretted over until 1884. The disheveled manuscript bore the title *Ernest Pontifex; or, The Way of All Flesh. A Story of English Domestic Life.* Butler's literary executor tidied up the work and published it in 1903 as *The Way of All Flesh*. Sardonically autobiographical concerning the protagonist's relation to his parents, the novel meant to its first readers all that Butler could have hoped for—a genealogical narrative that knocked the stuffing out of Victorian morality. The satire pretends, through irony, to a disinterested realism from an ingenuous narrator, who gives in full letters from successive parents that are transparently hypocritical or obtuse. Except for the several levels of irony and the sayings of a leering Dickensian landlady, Mrs. Jupp, the style is as flat as a millstone.

Butler had published several books that rejected Darwinian "luck" in favour of evolutionary "cunning." Every creature, he argued, by unconscious memory does best what it learned to do within the bodies of its ancestors. Although Christianity is repeatedly thrashed in the novel, Butler's evolutionary theories are only passively present.

Old Mr. Pontifex improved the family's genes; successive generations alternately strengthened and impaired the line. Old Pontifex, a carpenter, was a self-taught artist and musician. He lived up to the meaning in Latin of his surname, bridge-builder. Later Pontifexes justified instead the connotation of pomposity. George, son of old Pontifex and his obstinate wife, was educated too rapidly by London relatives into an empty sophistication as a self-assured publisher of religious books. When his son Theobald expressed scruples against ordination as a clergyman, George threatened to cut him off until Theobald acquiesced. Theobald would have conceded when George again "shook his will" against marriage to Christina Allaby, but the Allabys had trapped the dull-witted Theobald.

Their son Ernest was baptized in water from the Jordan sponged up, after an accident, from the cellar floor. From birth to college, Ernest suffers parental oppression without reserve. Whenever Theobald's temper clouded, a rain of blows, verbal and physical, fell on little Ernest. The headmaster of Roughborough School, Dr. Skinner, a combination of Arnold of Rugby and Dickens's Pecksniff, continues the skinning of Ernest. When the servant Ellen is dismissed for pregnancy, Ernest gives her a watch bestowed by his aunt Alethaea; he is caught in a lie when Ellen pawns the watch locally, but he cannot even guess what his mother means by a suspected loss of purity.

Ernest, who was born as Butler was in 1835, went to Cambridge when Butler did. There, learning the dogmas needed to make a clergyman of him and reading "literary garbage" by Kingsley, Dickens, and others who taught respect for poverty, he encountered distasteful Evangelicals, post-Tractarian thieves who invest his money (from Alethaea) in a college of Spiritual Pathology, and, a true revelation to Ernest, the handsome, smoothly accomplished, irreligious, and amoral Townley. Ordained and eager to regenerate the Church, Ernest takes lodgings in Ashpit Place near Drury Lane. There he quickly discovers that Cambridge did not teach him how to counter the scepticism of a tinker who had read Robert Chambers's *Vestiges of the Natural History of Creation* and has not taught him how to tell a respectable young lady from a prostitute. His consequent error, when he determines to free himself from purity, results in his being sentenced, by a magistrate shocked that blameless parents and every effort to shield the boy from impurity have failed, to six months at hard labour.

Realism, subverted mostly by satiric irony in the early chapters, turns to parable in the encounters with the doubting tinker, the demure prostitute Miss Snow, and, when Miss Snow was busy with Townley, Miss Maitland, who flees flushed and trembling from Ernest into, by chance, a policeman. The later chapters, retaining realism of tone, pursue didactic fantasy. In a reversal of Victorian autobiography and fiction, Ernest undergoes a conversion from Christianity and determines never to see his parents again and to take no money from them. Butler himself had suffered the Prufrockian paralysis of detesting his father but not daring to abandon his inheritance. Ernest has the better fortune of being assured by his godfather, Edward Overton (our narrator), that Alethaea has left an allowance for him. By coincidence Ernest encounters Ellen; against the bachelor Overton's advice, he marries her. They open a shop and prosper until her drunkenness undoes them. By a coincidental discovery that she has been married before, Ernest at 26 is again free. There are two children, whom Ernest pays a bargeman at Gravesend one pound a week to raise lest they be miseducated as he was. When Ernest receives from Overton the full inheritance from Alethaea, he first experiences anew the insincerities of his family, then travels for a few years, and finally, with several Victorian illusions still to be deflated, he begins to write "semi-theological, semi-social" books and essays of the kind Butler had written.

Source: Carl Woodring, "*The Way of All Flesh*: Overview," in *Reference Guide to English Literature*, 2nd ed., edited by D. L. Kirkpatrick, St. James Press, 1991.

Francis Hackett

In the following review, Hackett commends the iconoclastic spirit manifested in The Way of All Flesh.

[In] Samuel Butler there is little of the conventional rococo which endears Winston Churchill, poor man, to his enormous and quite uncritical audience. But the astonishing and delightful thing about Samuel Butler is that he does not write *The Way of All Flesh* to satisfy the lovers of pure and plain principle and clap them on the back. He does not seek to justify the select few to their estimable selves, at the expense of the purveyors of conventional fodder. No, indeed. Samuel Butler's sword is not only Castilian but double-edged. With one edge he undoubtedly attacks the uncritical, but with the other, and the keener, he cuts into the supercilious prig. It would be a mistake to say that his novel shows indifference to idealism. It is limited in its appeal precisely because it can interest only those who

have endured introspection and the tortures of conscience and the agonies of self-criticism. But the small company that has an intellectual sense (usually a proud intellectual sense) of affinity with Hamlet need not suppose that Samuel Butler is going to do for them what the Russian novelists have done. On the contrary, the whole burden of his novel is the follies of Hamletry. If his book is merciless to the ordinary religious father and mother in England, it is equally relentless toward their mollycoddle son. But there is this difference: Samuel Butler understands the mollycoddle to the core and loves him: and he exhibits his evolution because he knows that the follies which he detects could not exist except in a soul that is to be valued.

Ernest Pontifex, Samuel Butler's hero, suffers horribly from idealism. When at last he begins to see the idiocy of trying to be absolutely perfect, it is only to discover that the huge majority of the men have never been troubled by any such idiocy, but have quite naturally adopted the Eleventh Commandment, "Thou Shalt Not Be Found Out." It stands to reason that those who have never worried morbidly about their imperfection will take a thoroughly Rooseveltian attitude toward Ernest, call him a mollycoddle, and have done with it. The curious thing is that Butler himself seems to agree with Roosevelt. He singles out one Towneley as the graceful, lovable, well bred, "red-blooded" type—an empiric man who would generally echo John Mitchel's dictum that a certain nation of mollycoddles "would have been saved long ago if it wasn't for their damned souls." Ernest Pontifex adores Towneley and he sums up the difference between that eupeptic gentleman and his confused self in these words: "I see it all now. The people like Towneley are the only ones who know anything that is worth knowing, and like that of course I can never be. But to make Towneleys possible there must be hewers of wood and drawers of water—men, in fact, through whom conscious knowledge must pass before it can reach those who can apply it gracefully and instinctively as the Towneleys can. I am a hewer of wood, but if I accept the position frankly and do not set up to be a Towneley, it does not matter."

This attitude of Butler's is summed up in the phrase, "The result depends upon the thing done and the motive goes for nothing." But there is a difference, after all, between this scorn for fine-spun and high-flown theories that don't work out in practice and the ordinary scorn of the rationalist. Ultimately Butler is not a red-blood. Ultimately he has "confidence that it is righter and better to believe what is true than what is untrue, even though belief in the untruth may seem at first most expedient." But he is sick of the writers who do nothing except prate about idealism. He is sick of the idealistic pimple that is priggishness. He is sick of the people, unconventional or conventional, whose ideals are heard but not seen.

The hatred of rules is no small part of Samuel Butler's nature, especially the rules of parents and schoolmasters. The only rules he regards as worth knowing are not the fixed rules of institutions, but the rules of thumb by which human beings are living. Over and over again he parallels that philosophy which says that an actress who remains chaste is a prig. "Extremes are alone logical, and they are always absurd, the mean is alone practicable and it is always illogical. . . . Sensible people will get through life by rule of thumb as they may interpret it most conveniently without asking too many questions for conscience's sake." This lesson, of course, would be wasted on the Average Man, who is seldom even aware of his illogicality. It would be wasted on the ordinary American, who would be bored even at hearing it discussed. But it will not be wasted on those who, like Samuel Butler himself, want primarily to live a life as honest as is compatible with happiness, and who are feeling like Judge Grosscup, the deplorable "need for honesty" in others. *The Way of All Flesh* is, in the clever phrase of H. G. Wells, a Dreadnaught. It is of about the same length as *Tono-Bungay* and little shorter than *The Old Wives' Tale*, or *It Never Can Happen Again*. To my mind it is a wiser book than any of these, which is saying a good deal. It has less brilliance than *Tono-Bungay* and less suggestiveness. It has less background and less social idiom than Bennett's great book. It is less whimsical and less ingratiating than De Morgan's. But it knows more about the old Adam than any of the three, and can give them fifty yards in a hundred for critical intelligence. Occasionally in novels you read of a Great Writer whose work is so stupendous that the novelist doesn't dare to quote from it (unless he be as foolhardy as May Sinclair). Well, Samuel Butler would be an ideal figure for that Great Writer. In *The Way of All Flesh* there is not (me judice) one meretricious line. The same might be said of *The Old Wives'*

Tale, but the difference between a successful novel of ideas and successful novel of manners is like the difference between exploding dynamite and discharging a rifle.

Butler admits you into an easy and humorous free masonry, if you happen to be his sort. Not with a wink, but quietly and serenely. He tells you what you've always privately known, but never admitted, and he also clears up many things you thought you knew, but didn't. He is not above a certain perversity about the idealist, but he makes no easy jokes and works off nobody else's wisdom or sentiment. What he has is his own, and it is very astonishing and shrewd of its kind.

Source: Francis Hackett, Review of *The Way of All Flesh*, in *Horizons: A Book of Criticism*, B. W. Huebsch, 1918, pp. 83–91.

Times Literary Supplement

In the following review, a contributor to the Times Literary Supplement *describes the book's final impression on the reader as one of despair, bitterness, and hopelessness.*

It is very unlikely that [*The Way of All Flesh*] by the late Mr. Samuel Butler will command the immediate reputation achieved by his *Erewhon* thirty years ago; but we think it likely enough that this, more than the former, work will preserve his memory. Fresh and novel speculation, brightly and forcibly delivered, will, with luck, delight an author's contemporaries; but by the time that "posterity" has arrived the speculation is apt to have become a little stale. But posterity will not tire of vivid and informed accounts of life in previous ages. It is more interesting now to read Fielding than Locke—not that Mr. Butler, with all his various and considerable gifts, is to be compared to the one or the other. *The Way of All Flesh* is, of course, full of theory and argument, for theory and argument were the breath of Mr. Butler's nostrils. The main theme of the book, however, inspired though it is by a theory, is the life of a man, written in detail, and plainly with a strong personal emotion. That fact, we think, will say something to posterity. Unfortunately for its present popularity, however, the human interest of the book falls between two stools; it has for average readers neither the piquancy and importance of the present nor the curiosity of the fairly remote past. The book is concerned chiefly with the years 1835 to 1867—a period which for average readers is obsolete without being strange—and, having in it a strong militant purpose, seems to be fighting a battle already lost and won. From those, however, for whom the humanity of the last or preceding generation can be as interesting, in its material customs and spiritual conflicts, as that of other generations, and who have intellect enough themselves to enjoy the working of an intellect both powerful and nimble, the work is sure of a ready and attentive acceptance.

To come to details. Internally the writing, as well as the subject, is plainly "dated," as they say of plays; but we are furthermore furnished with a note by the editor, Mr. R. A. Streatfeild, which tells us that Mr. Butler began to write *The Way of All Flesh* in 1872 and finished it in 1884. But there is more significance in the chronology than that indicates. The hero, whom Mr. Butler takes in detail from his birth to his thirty-third year, was born in 1835. Now that is the year of Mr. Butler's own birth; and, when the reader observes the bitterness with which the hero's early years are described, he cannot help the suspicion (though the writer is supposed to be the hero's godfather and not the hero himself) that there may be something of personal recollection—so far as concerns boyhood and childhood, for later on there can be no correspondence. Knowing nothing of the matter, we are content sincerely to hope that this is not the case, and even that some one who does know may set the suspicion at rest; for anything more lamentable than this childhood and boyhood can hardly be imagined. Mr. Butler sets out with the theory that the bringing up of children was thoroughly bad, that they were constantly sacrificed to the ignorance, selfishness, and vanity of their parents, and that this was especially the case with the children of clergymen. Clearly he meant his hero's case to be typical. We cannot believe it; we are convinced he exaggerates. The Rev. Theobald Pontifex (the father) is represented as a vindictive, malevolent, cruel bully, but also as a man who persuaded himself that he meant well and was doing his duty. Now could such a one beat a child of seven for saying "tum" instead of "come"? All this part of the book is painful to the last degree, and fills an ordinarily kind-hearted reader with maddening wrath. Exaggerated or not, it has little or no application to the present day. We treat children very differently; and the Rev. Theobald and his wife would hear of the S.P.C.C.

When the boy escapes to school the cloud lifts a little, and the portraits, still sketched with the bitter irony of which Mr. Butler was a master, are relieved with more humour. Our author is still, of course, in opposition. Witness his treatment of Dr. Skinner, who is given as the popular ideal of the earnest schoolmaster—one's imagination fears to suggest which incarnation of that ideal may be intended. "Whatever else a Roughborough man might be, he was sure to make any one feel that he was a God-fearing, earnest Christian, and a Liberal, if not a Radical, in politics. Some boys, of course, were incapable of appreciating the beauty and loftiness of Dr. Skinner's nature. . . . They not only disliked him, but they hated all that he more especially embodied, and throughout their lives disliked all that reminded them of him." Then follows a delightfully wicked account of a supper at Dr. Skinner's. We have no space to pursue the story; it is enough to say that the hero's evil up-bringing has its evil results, and that his nature ultimately triumphs over them, and that these matters are presented with a wealth of observed detail. The book is at times perhaps too full—as when an essay and a sermon are given at length; but the careful student of developments will welcome them also. We do not attach great importance to Mr. Streatfeild's statement that the work is a practical illustration of the theory of heredity embodied in *Life and Habit*. The hero seems to throw back to his great-grandfather, and we are reminded that we are largely the creatures of our ancestry, and that is about all. The author is really concerned to denounce evil systems of training, false ideas of respectability, and what he believed to be bad conventions generally, and to illustrate the benefits which may be got by defying them. Many readers, perhaps most, will disagree with a great deal of what he says. But none who have humour or appreciation of effective writing can fail to admire the ironical presentment of character and the pithy, caustic phrases in which the book abounds. "The successful man will see just so much more than his neighbours as they will be able to see too when it is shown them, but not enough to puzzle them." "They would have been equally horrified at hearing the Christian religion doubted and at seeing it practised." "Those virtues which make the poor respectable and the rich respected." Such flashes are on every page.

As for the philosophy, it appears to us to be wholly negative. The dogmas of religion are put aside, but so are the dogmas of science. "The spirit behind the Church is true, though her letter—true once—is now true no longer. The spirit behind the high priests of science is as lying as its letter." Professedly the teaching is that the only criterion of virtue is worldly success and comfort. That, we perceive, is ironical; but the author recurs to this irony again and again; and when once the irony is removed the philosophy is one of despair. And we cannot help thinking that he is often very near this despair. That, or something very like it, is the impression the book finally leaves on us. It is the work of a man who saw the contrasts, the futilities, and the hypocrisies of life very clearly, and who could exhibit them very wittily—but who felt them bitterly and almost hopelessly. We admire Mr. Butler almost more in this book than in anything else he did; but we liked him better when he was using his intellect and knowledge to prove that the *Odyssey* was written by a woman.

Source: "A Bitter Legacy," in *Times Literary Supplement*, No. 71, May 22, 1903, p. 158.

SOURCES

Atterbury, Paul, "Steam and Speed: Industry, Power and Social Change in 19th-Century Britain," Victoria and Albert Museum website, http://www.vam.ac.uk/content/articles/s/industry-power-and-social-change (accessed November 30, 2012).

Beckwith, Roger, "*Essays and Reviews* (1860): The Advance of Liberalism," in *Churchman*, Vol. 108, No. 1, 1994, http://www.churchsociety.org/churchman/documents/Cman_108_1_Beckwith.pdf (accessed November 26, 2012).

"A Bitter Legacy," in *Times Literary Supplement*, May 22, 1903, p. 158.

"A Brief History of the University: The Revived University of the Nineteenth and Twentieth Centuries," University of Cambridge website, http://www.cam.ac.uk/univ/history/19c.html (accessed February 14, 2013).

"Butler, Samuel," in *Merriam-Webster's Encyclopedia of Literature*, Merriam-Webster, 1995, p. 191.

Butler, Samuel, *The Way of All Flesh*, Random House, 1998.

"The City in European History: London in the Nineteenth Century," University of North Carolina at Pembroke website, http://www.uncp.edu/home/rwb/london_19c.html (accessed December 3, 2012).

Clifford, David, "Samuel Butler (1835–1902)," Victorian Web, 2007, http://www.victorianweb.org/science/butler.html (accessed November 12, 2012).

Cockshut, A. O. J., *Religious Controversies of the Nineteenth Century*, University of Nebraska Press, 1966, pp. 8–9.

Dupee, F. W., "Butler's Way," in *New York Review of Books*, August 24, 1967, pp. 26–31.

"The 1870 Education Act," British Parliament website, http://www.parliament.uk/about/living-heritage/transformingsociety/livinglearning/school/overview/1870educationact/ (accessed November 30, 2012).

Ellison, Robert H., "John Henry Newman: A Brief Biography," Victorian Web, 1996, http://www.victorianweb.org/authors/newman/jhnbio2.html (accessed December 2, 2012).

"Fact and Figures: January 2012," University of Cambridge website, http://www.admin.cam.ac.uk/offices/communications/services/cambridgeand/cambridgefactsfigures.pdf (accessed February 13, 2013).

IntelligentDesign.org Home Page, http://www.intelligentdesign.org/ (accessed February 13, 2013).

Kaplan, Lillian, "Vestiges of Creation: A Centenary," in *Journal of Heredity*, Vol. 36, No. 1, 1945, p. 8.

Landow, George P., "Bishop Colenso and the Literal Truth of the Bible," Victorian Web, 2012, http://www.victorianweb.org/religion/colenso.html (accessed November 26, 2012).

Leavis, Q. D., "That Great Controversy," in *Collected Essays*, Vol. 3, *The Novels of Religious Controversy*, Cambridge University Press, 1989, p. 44.

Montgomery, Stephen, "Charles Darwin and Evolution: How Did the Victorian World Respond to Darwin?" Christ's College Cambridge website, http://www.christs.cam.ac.uk/darwin200/pages/index.php?page_id=d7 (accessed February 13, 2013).

Phelps, William Lyon, Introduction to *The Way of All Flesh*, E. P. Dutton, 1916, pp. v–ix.

"Religious Education and Acts of Worship," Campaign for Real Education website, http://www.cre.org.uk/docs/re.html (accessed November 30, 2012).

Robinson, Roger, "Butler, Samuel," in *Dictionary of New Zealand Biography*, 2012, http://www.TeAra.govt.nz/en/biographies/1b55/1 (accessed November 12, 2012).

Shea, Victor, and William Whitla, eds., *Essays and Reviews: The 1860 Text and Its Reading*, University Press of Virginia, 2000, pp. 25–26.

"Student Numbers," in *Cambridge Student Reporter*, Vol. 135, Special No. 19, August 26, 2005, http://www.admin.cam.ac.uk/reporter/2004-05/special/19/studentnumbers2005.pdf (accessed February 13, 2013).

"Universities Tests Act 1871," legislation.co.uk website, http://www.legislation.gov.uk/ukpga/Vict/34-35/26 (accessed February 14, 2013).

Woolf, Virginia, Review of *The Way of All Flesh*, in *Times Literary Supplement*, June 26, 1919, p. 347.

Zabel, Morton Dauwen, "Samuel Butler: The Victorian Insolvency," in *Craft and Character: Texts, Method, and Vocation in Modern Fiction*, Viking Press, 1957, pp. 97–113.

FURTHER READING

Hackett, Francis, ed., *The Note-Books of Samuel Butler*, Nabu Press, 2010.

This edition of Butler's notebooks—Butler carried notebooks with him and wrote in them constantly—is a reproduction of an edition first published in 1923. The book consists of numerous short entries, some just a sentence or two and others a paragraph or two. The entries all have a witty, epigrammatic quality and provide insight into Butler's unique take on his culture and society.

Moran, Maureen, *Victorian Literature and Culture*, Continuum, 2007.

This volume is a handbook on the relationship between literature and culture in the Victorian era. It includes information not only about literature but also about the era's cultural, historical, economic, philosophical, and intellectual background.

Paradis, James G., ed., *Samuel Butler: Victorian against the Grain: A Critical Overview*, University of Toronto Press, 2007.

This collection of essays takes an interdisciplinary approach to Butler and his works, placing that work within the Victorian age's cultural framework. The essays examine Butler's many roles: satirist, art historian, painter, theologian, novelist, student of evolution, and others.

Raby, Peter, *Samuel Butler: A Biography*, University of Iowa Press, 1991.

Few biographies of Butler are available. Raby's is one of the more recent ones that remains available. In the first half it focuses on Butler's life and upbringing and in the second half on the relationship of his major works to his life.

Sutherland, John, *The Longman Companion to Victorian Fiction*, 2nd ed., Longman, 2009.

First published in 1988, this volume is a massive compendium of information about Victorian fiction. It includes plot summaries of hundreds of novels as well as biographical information on the principal authors.

Warwick, Alexandra, and Martin Willis, *Victorian Literature Handbook*, Continuum, 2008.

This volume is an alternative to Moran's *Victorian Literature and Culture*. It places greater emphasis on authors, literary texts, and critical approaches to Victorian literature, and it includes a time line of key literary and cultural events.

SUGGESTED SEARCH TERMS

Anglican Church

Cambridge University

Church of England

Samuel Butler AND Erewhon

Samuel Butler AND novelist

Samuel Butler AND Way of All Flesh

Simeonites

Tractarianism

Victorian fiction

Victorian religion

Zorro

ISABEL ALLENDE

2005

The Chilean American novelist Isabel Allende almost refused to write her 2005 novel *Zorro*. She was indeed interested in the legendary character. She enjoyed watching modern film versions of his story with her grandchildren and, in the interview "Loving Zorro, Writing *Zorro*," admitted, "As a young woman I was in love with Zorro." However, when the owners of the character's copyright approached her with the idea of writing a novel about him, she was almost insulted: she remembered thinking, "I am a serious writer, I don't write on commission." But the idea of inventing Zorro's youth—telling the tale of what turned him into a masked hero—captured Allende's imagination. She threw herself into the project, researching the period, traveling to all of the novel's locations, and even taking fencing lessons. The result is a book rich with historical detail. The novel is both a fun adventure story and an in-depth exploration of timeless themes like friendship, justice, and the role of religion in society. There are some mature topics in the novel, such as sexual situations and violence, making it more appropriate for older students.

AUTHOR BIOGRAPHY

Isabel Allende Llona was born on August 2, 1942, in Lima, Peru. Her family lived there because her father was the Chilean ambassador

Isabel Allende (© *AFP | Getty Images*)

to Peru. Allende did not see Chile, her native country, until she was four years old, when her father abandoned the family. Allende's mother took her three children and moved back home to Santiago with her parents. Some years later, Allende's mother was married again, to a man who was also a diplomat, and Allende spent much of her adolescence in Bolivia and Lebanon. The family was in Beirut when civil war broke out in Lebanon, and Allende was sent home. She was sixteen years old and lived with her grandparents again. She traveled extensively with her grandfather and learned to truly love Chile.

Allende married Miguel Frías in 1962. They had two children together, Paula in 1963 and Nicolás in 1966, but it was not a happy marriage. They were divorced in 1987, and Allende married an American, Willie Gordon, a year later. As of 2012, they were living in San Rafael, California.

Allende began her writing career working as a journalist in Chile. In 1973, a military coup led by General Augusto Pinochet overthrew the Chilean government, including the president, who was a cousin of Allende's. For a while Allende worked with a group trying to help victims of Pinochet's oppressive and violent regime, but two years later, her family fled the country,

fearing for their safety. They lived in Venezuela for thirteen years.

In 1981, Allende learned that her grandfather was dying. She wrote him a long letter, full of memories of her childhood, and that letter became the inspiration for her first novel, *The House of the Spirits*, which was originally published in Spanish in 1982. Since then, Allende has written more than a dozen novels, among them *Eva Luna* (1985), *The Infinite Plan* (1991), *Daughter of Fortune* (1999), and *Zorro* (2005). Allende has also published nonfiction, including her memoir *Paula* (1994), which describes her daughter's illness and death from porphyria, a hormonal disorder.

Allende has earned many international awards, and her work has been translated into more than thirty languages from her native Spanish. Allende frequently visits her home country of Chile, but she became an American citizen in 1993.

PLOT SUMMARY

Prologue
The brief prologue establishes that the first-person narrator is a character who knows Diego de la Vega, who will later become Zorro, but does not indicate who the narrator is.

Part One: California, 1790–1810
The narrator introduces Padre Mendoza, the leader of the San Gabriel mission. Mendoza learns that the nearby Shoshone tribe is planning an attack on the mission and asks for help from Captain Alejandro de la Vega. In the battle, the leader of the Native Americans is wounded, and the men are shocked to learn that she is a woman. Alejandro falls in love with the young woman, whose name is Toypurina. He marries her in spite of his prejudice against her mixed blood.

Alejandro and his wife, now baptized and called Regina, have a son, Diego. Regina falls ill after the birth and is saved only by the healing skills of her mother, White Owl. The housemaid Ana nurses Diego along with her own recently born son, Bernardo, which starts the boys' life-long friendship. Alejandro does not approve of this friendship because of the boys' different social status.

MEDIA ADAPTATIONS

- In 2006, HarperAudio released an unabridged audiobook of *Zorro: A Novel* on CD, read by Blair Brown.
- A few episodes of early radio plays of Zorro stories are available for free at http://archive.org/details/TheAdventuresOfZorro.

Diego attends school in the village, although Bernardo is not allowed to go, being the son of a servant. Diego is driven to pay more attention in class so that he can later repeat the lessons to Bernardo. Both boys are also taught traditional Native American wisdom by White Owl.

Diego and Bernardo save a boy named García from the bullying of Carlos Alcázar and his friends, earning García's undying loyalty. The three friends carry out a dangerous prank, drugging a bear and bringing it into the town.

Pirates attack the de la Vega house one night while Alejandro is away on business. Regina once again becomes a warrior to defend her son and her home, but she is gravely injured. Diego is able to hide with her, saving her, and Ana hides Bernardo, but Ana herself is killed by the pirates. After his mother's death, Bernardo does not speak for weeks, eventually years. He is sent to White Owl, and she understands that his muteness is a form of mourning. Bernardo meets Light-in-the-Night. His friendship with her quickly turns to love. Diego is surprised to find that Bernardo has become a man while in the Indian village.

White Owl sends Diego and Bernardo separately into the wilderness to seek their spirit guides. Bernardo sees a foal, and he speaks to it—the first time he has talked in years. Diego sees a *zorro*, a fox, and then is bitten by a snake. Bernardo finds him and carries him back to White Owl.

The village of the Native American tribe is destroyed by Don Juan Alcázar and the soldiers.

Diego objects, but his father tells him there is nothing they can do.

Alejandro throws a lavish party for Diego's fifteenth birthday. After the celebration, Diego is to leave for Spain to receive a proper education. Bernardo is to accompany him.

Part Two: Barcelona, 1810–1812

Diego and Bernardo sail away from California on the ship of Captain José Díaz. Diego passes the time on board climbing the ropes and playing cards with the sailors. The boys leave the ship and cross over the Panama isthmus to Portobelo to board another boat, which will carry them to Spain. The captain is Santiago de León. He teaches Diego through conversation and by letting him read from his library. Diego also learns magic tricks from Galileo Tempesta, one of the sailors.

In Spain, the boys are to live with Tomás de Romeu, an old friend of Diego's father. De Romeu has two daughters. Juliana is the oldest and is very beautiful, and Diego quickly falls in love with her. Isabel, the younger daughter, is eleven years old and awkward. De Romeu enjoys Diego's company and talks about religion and politics. Diego takes fencing lessons from Maestro Manuel Escalante. Juliana is courted by Rafael Moncada, but Diego quickly learns that Moncada is dishonest, paying another man to serenade Juliana on his behalf.

Napoleon is in power in France, and his soldiers are fighting Spanish guerrillas in the countryside. Diego does not take sides in the battle but helps whoever seems to need it most. He warns those in danger when he learns the French soldiers are due to attack, and he alerts the French to poisoned bread that might have killed thirty men.

At a party, Diego sees Moncada cheating at cards and makes his suspicions clear. Because he is angry at Diego, Moncada strikes Bernardo with his cane, prompting Diego to challenge him to a duel. In the duel, Moncada shoots Diego, but when Diego has his chance to return fire, he shoots into the ground rather than killing or injuring Moncada. Moncada is humiliated.

Diego befriends a beautiful gypsy girl named Amalia. He and Bernardo join the gypsy circus, using the rope-climbing skills they learned aboard ship.

Escalante tells Diego about La Justicia, a secret society that works to defend the weak and helpless without spilling innocent blood. Diego is initiated into the society in an elaborate ceremony. He takes the code name Zorro, thinking of the spirit guide he saw in the California wilderness. Diego performs his first mission for La Justicia: sneaking into the bedroom of Roland Duchamp, the French commander, to demand that he release people unfairly imprisoned in La Ciudadela, a military prison in Barcelona. Once Diego is able to secure the paper ordering their release, he escapes from Duchamp's room, tracing a large letter *Z* on the wall.

Part Three: Barcelona, 1812–1814

Moncada pressures de Romeu to allow him to marry Juliana, but de Romeu will not force his daughter to marry against her will. Moncada comes up with a plan to impress Juliana. He hires a few thugs to attack Juliana, Isabel, and their chaperone, Nuria, when they leave the house to do charity work. Moncada then pretends to rescue them. Juliana seems to be fooled, but Isabel sees through the trick.

Diego also suspects the truth, and he brings Amalia to Juliana so that she can hear the whole story. Amalia admits that her brother Pelayo was among the men that Moncada paid to "attack" Juliana and her sister. It is also revealed that Pelayo was the one who serenaded Juliana. Juliana is upset by these revelations.

Moncada fears that Pelayo may blackmail him and plans to get rid of him by causing the gypsy camp to be destroyed. Bernardo learns of the plan through a network of servants, and he and Diego are able to spread a warning. The gypsies flee, and Diego, dressed as Zorro, stays behind to confront the soldiers.

Padre Mendoza sends a letter explaining that Light-in-the-Night has given birth to a son. Bernardo knows he is the father. He returns to California, leaving Diego on his own in Spain.

Spain's war with France progresses. Duchamp senses that Napoleon will not be in power much longer and decides to return to Paris. He warns de Romeu, who does not hide his liberal beliefs, that he might want to take his family abroad as well, but de Romeu does not listen. Once the Spanish king returns to power, "a heartless persecution was unleashed against dissidents, opponents, liberals, [and] Francophiles."

De Romeu decides to flee, but his accountants tell him he cannot afford to do so.

Diego continues his work for La Justicia, including rescuing Escalante from unjust imprisonment. De Romeu is arrested. Juliana agrees to marry Moncada if he will help free her father, but Moncada is not able to help. Juliana goes to Doña Eulalia, who is Moncada's aunt. She offers to buy all of de Romeu's remaining property so that the girls have money to build a new life.

The girls visit their father in prison. He tells them that Moncada will not help because he was the one to denounce de Romeu. Diego promises de Romeu that he will always watch over his daughters, and de Romeu is executed. Juliana confronts Moncada about betraying her father, and Diego steps in to protect her when Moncada becomes aggressive. Isabel, who has secretly been studying fencing, also picks up a sword. They lock Moncada in a secret room and must flee.

Part Four: Barcelona, Late 1814–Early 1815

Diego, Juliana, Isabel, and Nuria leave Barcelona disguised as religious pilgrims. Diego struggles with the heavy responsibility of looking after the young women. They meet up with Amalia's tribe of gypsies and travel with them for a while. Pelayo makes Diego a sword.

When they reach La Coruña, Diego sees his old sailor friend Galileo, who leads him to Captain de León. De León agrees to take the fugitives to America.

The ship is attacked by pirates led by the historical figure Jean Lafitte. He is a fair leader: the rules of his pirate band are "reasonable," and "everything was decided by vote." Lafitte is handsome and dashing, and Juliana falls in love with him. He is attracted to her in return, but he is already married, with an infant son. Lafitte's mother-in-law, Madame Odilia, decides that Juliana is a worthy replacement for her daughter, Catherine, who has essentially died. Madame Odilia has kept Catherine half-alive with the help of a voodoo priestess. Juliana stays with Lafitte in New Orleans.

Part Five: Alta California, 1815

Diego is frustrated and in tears that Juliana, the girl he still loves, is staying with Lafitte, but he returns home with Isabel and Nuria. When the ship arrives on the California coast, Bernardo is there waiting for them. Bernardo takes the travelers to the mission.

Padre Mendoza tells Diego all that he has missed while he was away. Alejandro and Regina have lived apart for five years. When Diego left for Spain, Regina returned to live with her mother's tribe. Alejandro "never got used to her absence and had aged in his sorrow." Moncada arrived with power granted by the Spanish king that put him above the California governor. Moncada took over the de la Vega hacienda and put Alejandro in jail on an "unfounded charge of treason." Mendoza did what he could to protect the Indians, but Moncada now hates him for it, and the mission is "in ruins." Carlos Alcázar, the childhood bully, is in charge of the prison where Alejandro is imprisoned.

Moncada arrives with a group of soldiers and is furious to learn of Juliana's marriage to Lafitte. Diego recognizes his old friend García among Moncada's men. García tries to defend Alejandro, but it only makes Moncada more angry.

Diego tells his friends that he is going to Monterey to ask the governor to help his father but instead disguises himself as a priest and goes to the prison. The lovely Lolita Pulido offers him a ride in her carriage, believing him to be a priest. She is kind to the prisoners when they arrive at the prison.

Diego manages to find his father. Alejandro is ecstatic to see his son but seems to be an old man now. Diego promises to release Alejandro and his fellow prisoners. As Zorro, with the help of Bernardo and the Shoshone tribe, Diego frees the prisoners. He learns that the prisoners have been forced to dive for pearls. Alcázar has been stealing more than his share of the treasure, without Moncada's knowledge. Diego take the pearls from Alcázar and steals a kiss from Lolita before fleeing.

Diego brings the pearls to Padre Mendoza but does not remove his Zorro costume. He swallows his pride, allowing Mendoza to believe he is a foppish, weak man.

Moncada arrives and has Diego arrested. Diego is held prisoner in his own house, which Moncada is using as a headquarters. García is there, but he refuses to neglect his duty as a soldier and release Diego outright. However, when he ties Diego up, he leaves the ropes loose. Moncada suspects that Diego is Zorro, but while he is questioning him, Zorro appears outside the house. (It is later revealed that both Bernardo and Isabel dress as Zorro to fool Moncada's soldiers.) In the confusion that follows, Diego is able to escape through a secret passage that he and Bernardo discovered when they were boys.

Diego returns and forces Moncada to sign a paper confessing to planning a colonial rebellion against the king of Spain. Diego tells Moncada to leave and vows if he ever returns, the confession will be sent to the courts so that Moncada will be arrested for treason. Diego, Bernardo, and Isabel vow to work together to fight for justice.

Part Six, Brief Epilogue and Final Period: *Alta California, 1840*

The narrator reveals herself to be Isabel de Romeu. She explains a bit more about what happened to several of the major characters.

CHARACTERS

Carlos Alcázar
Carlos is a bully at Diego's school when they are boys. As an adult, Carlos is still a bully, having become one of the powerful but dishonest men that Diego, as Zorro, fights against.

Don Juan Alcázar
Don Juan Alcázar is Carlos's father and Lolita's uncle. When Diego is a boy, Alcázar is in charge of the town's soldiers and allows them to mistreat the Native Americans.

Amalia
Amalia is the beautiful gypsy girl that Diego meets in Barcelona. Although Diego is in love with Juliana, he enjoys Amalia's company and finds comfort in her arms.

Ana
Ana is a Native American woman who becomes a servant in the de la Vega household. She gives birth to Bernardo just before Regina has Diego, and because Regina is unwell, Ana nurses Diego along with her own son. This starts a bond between the two boys as "milk brothers" that lasts their whole lives.

Bernardo
Bernardo is Ana's son and Diego's "milk brother" and constant boyhood companion.

Although the boys are very different, they always seem to understand each other, and Bernardo helps Diego with everything from childhood pranks to dangerous adventures as Zorro. After Ana is killed in a pirate attack on the de la Vega house, Bernardo does not speak for three years.

Doña Eulalia de Callís

Doña Eulalia is the elegant Spanish lady who helps transform the Native American leader Toypurina into Regina, who can be a socially accepted wife for Alejandro de la Vega. Diego meets Doña Eulalia again when he travels to Spain.

Alejandro de la Vega

Alejandro is Diego's father. He loves Diego and tries to be a good father. Most of his life, he feels strongly that his pure Spanish blood makes him important and better than his mestiza wife, Regina. However, by the end of the novel, when he is unfairly imprisoned, the kindness of his fellow prisoners, three Indian men, "succeeded in dissolving the sense of superiority the Spanish hidalgo had displayed all his life long."

Diego de la Vega

Diego is the central character in the novel. Allende tells Diego's story from the time his parents meet until he becomes an adult. Diego changes from a playful but intelligent boy into a brave and honorable man. In the course of his education, Diego discovers Native American wisdom with White Owl, discusses political philosophy with Captain de León, and learns about swordplay, justice, and honor from Maestro Escalante until he is ready to become Zorro and fight to protect those who are treated unfairly.

Regina María de la Inmaculada Concepción de la Vega

Regina begins her life as Toypurina, the leader of the Shoshone warriors who attack Padre Mendoza's mission to free the neophytes. She fights so fiercely that Mendoza and de la Vega are shocked to discover that she is not a man. De la Vega falls in love with her, and they marry, though de la Vega can never forget that she is not of pure Spanish blood. Their marriage is not a completely happy one. Regina sends Diego and Bernardo to her mother, White Owl, to learn the valuable lessons that their Native American tradition has to offer.

Captain Santiago de León

De León is the captain whose boat takes Diego and Bernardo from Central America to Spain. He is an educated man and allows Diego to read from his library. His books and his conversation teach Diego about rebellion, democracy, and justice. Diego later learns that de León is a member of the secret organization La Justicia.

Isabel de Romeu

Isabel is Tomás de Romeu's younger daughter. She is less beautiful and cultured, perhaps, than her sister, Juliana, but she is brave. By the close of the story, she becomes as much a helper to Diego in his fight for justice as Bernardo. Her given name, the same as Allende's, hints at the fact that she is the narrator of the story, though this fact is not confirmed until the end of the book.

Juliana de Romeu

Juliana is de Romeu's older daughter. Diego falls in love with her because she is beautiful and kind, but she treats him like a brother. Moncada wants to marry Juliana. She accepts only to help her father escape from being unjustly arrested, but Moncada betrays the family. When Jean Lafitte captures the boat traveling to America, Juliana immediately falls in love with him, and she stays with him when her sister, Diego, and Nuria continue on to California.

Tomás de Romeu

Tomás de Romeu is an old friend of Alejandro de la Vega and offers to look after Diego while he is receiving his gentleman's education in Spain. De Romeu's two daughters, Juliana and Isabel, become good friends with Diego. De Romeu is executed because of Moncada's treachery.

Captain José Díaz

Díaz is the captain of the ship that takes Bernardo and Diego from California to Panama on their way to Spain.

Roland "Le Chevalier" Duchamp

Duchamp is the leader of the French troops in Barcelona. He is known as "Le Chevalier."

Maestro Manuel Escalante

Escalante is Diego's fencing instructor. He teaches Diego about more than just swordsmanship, however, also discussing topics like justice and honor and introducing Diego to the secret society La Justicia.

Pedro Fages

Fages is the governor of California at the beginning of the story. Doña Eulalia is his wife, and after his death, she returns to Spain.

García

García is a boy in Diego's class at school. He is bullied by Carlos Alcázar. Diego stands up for him—his first fight against injustice. When Diego returns from Spain, García is a soldier, but he is loyal to his old friend Diego.

Jean Lafitte

Jean Lafitte is a pirate who captures the boat carrying Diego, Juliana, Isabel, and Nuria from Spain to America. Lafitte is the leader of the pirates, but he is very fair to his followers. He is handsome and charming, and both sisters are smitten with him, but it is Juliana that Lafitte falls in love with. The character of Jean Lafitte is based on a true historical figure.

Marie Laveau

Marie Laveau is the voodoo priestess who helps Madame Odilia keep her daughter Catherine half-alive until a new mother is found for Catherine's baby. The character of Marie Laveau is based on a true historical figure.

Le Chevalier

See Roland "Le Chevalier" Duchamp

Light-in-the-Night

Light-in-the-Night is a beautiful young woman whom Bernardo meets when he is taken to White Owl after his mother's death so that she can try to cure his muteness. They become good friends, and eventually they fall in love and have a son together.

Padre Mendoza

Padre Mendoza is the Catholic priest who leads the mission in San Gabriel, Alta California. Although he is a religious man and takes very seriously his work of converting Native Americans to Christianity, he is also a practical man. He believes that "it is easier to save the soul if the body is healthy" and is therefore kind to the people under his care, making sure they have food, clothing, and medical care. He is also willing to fight to defend his church and his mission, whether from attacks by tribes who resent Spanish interference or by unfair Spanish leaders who threaten his flock.

Rafael Moncada

Moncada is the villain of the novel. He is a young man who wants to marry Juliana de Romeu, though she despises him. This sets up a rivalry between him and Diego. Moncada is dishonest and becomes Zorro's nemesis.

Nuria

Nuria is the chaperone of de Romeu's daughters, Juliana and Isabel. Originally Nuria disapproves of Diego, but she comes to like and respect him. She leaves Spain with the three young people after de Romeu is executed.

Madame Odilia

Madame Odilia is Catherine Villars's mother. Using voodoo, she keeps her daughter alive as a sort of zombie in order to protect her grandson, Pierre. She seems to dislike Juliana but finds her worthy of taking Catherine's place as Jean Lafitte's wife and baby Pierre's mother.

Count Orloff

Orloff is one of the guests at Diego's fifteenth birthday party. He is the Russian leader in charge of the Alaska territory. His presence hints at foreign interest in valuable Spanish colonial territory.

Pelayo

Pelayo is the gypsy whom Moncada hires to sing to Juliana on his behalf. Pelayo also does other jobs for Moncada but eventually befriends Diego and helps him.

Lolita Pulido

Lolita is Don Juan Alcázar's niece and Carlos Alcázar's cousin. She is nothing like either of them, however, and Diego falls in love with her.

Galileo Tempesta

Galileo is one of the sailors on the ship that carries Diego and Bernardo to Spain. Galileo teaches Diego magic tricks that help him when he becomes Zorro.

Toypurina

See Regina María de la Inmaculada Concepción de la Vega

Catherine Villars

Catherine is Jean Lafitte's wife. She has died but is kept in a kind of zombie state by her mother, Madame Odilia, and the voodoo priestess, Marie Laveau, until Madame Odilia can find a suitable replacement mother for Pierre, Catherine's son with Lafitte.

White Owl

White Owl is Regina's mother and a Native American healer. When Regina is unwell after giving birth to Diego, White Owl is able to save her. When Diego and Bernardo are boys, White Owl teaches them about the five virtues of *okahué*: "honor, justice, respect, dignity, and courage."

Zorro

See Diego de la Vega

THEMES

Justice

It should be no surprise that in a book about Zorro, who fights for those who cannot help themselves, justice is an important theme. From his boyhood, Diego fights against injustice almost as a reflex. When he and Bernardo come upon Carlos and his bully friends harassing García, a situation where most schoolboys would avoid confrontation, Diego steps in to help. He is driven by the same impulse to try to help the Native Americans he sees being attacked by a group of colonial soldiers. He can do little himself to help and goes to his father, who knows "the class system too well to harbor any hope of righting the wrong." Diego, however, cannot accept the unfairness. He "never forgot that lesson; the bad taste of justice denied would remain forever in the deepest part of his memory, and would emerge again and again, determining the course of his life."

Diego's natural inclination to fight injustice is encouraged by his fencing instructor, Maestro Escalante, who, when he meets Diego, "felt that finally his life had a high purpose: to guide this young man to follow in his footsteps, to convert him into a paladin of just causes." When Diego is about to fight a duel with Moncada for hitting Bernardo, who was unarmed, Escalante challenges him, "Do you truly believe that life is fair, Señor de la Vega?" Diego answers, "No,

TOPICS FOR FURTHER STUDY

- Research the history of Spanish colonization in America, including the missions in California. Create a map, either on poster board or using a computer, showing the territory that was New Spain. Indicate where missions and towns were established. Show on your map where different Native American tribes lived, and mark the dates and places where these tribes rebelled against Spanish control.

- Read Sherman Alexie's 2007 young-adult novel *The Absolutely True Diary of a Part-Time Indian.* Just as Diego is caught between the heritage of his mestizo mother and that of his hidalgo father, the hero of Alexie's book, Arnold, struggles to find his ethnic identity. Write an essay comparing Diego and Arnold and how they find their places in the world.

- Critics have praised Allende for her detailed portrayal of the setting in *Zorro.* Find images that represent the California setting of the story, including such things as mission buildings, the haciendas of wealthy landowners, pictures of the surrounding countryside and plant life, and traditional Native American art of the area. Create a PowerPoint presentation of these images, and share it with your class while providing informed commentary.

- Allende wrote *Zorro* to detail the backstory of a character who has been beloved since the publication of the first Zorro story, Johnston McCulley's 1919 novella *The Curse of Capistrano.* Since then, the character has been featured countless times in print, on film, and on television. Think of some of your favorite characters from books or movies, and create a backstory for one of them, imagining in detail what kind of life events would have influenced and shaped that character. Write a scene, either as a short story or as dialogue from a play, that portrays one of these formative experiences.

maestro, but I plan to do everything in my power to make it so."

Because Diego is passionate about fighting for justice, Escalante introduces him to a secret society, La Justicia. The members of this society take an oath "To seek justice, nourish the hungry, clothe the naked, protect widows and orphans, give shelter to the stranger, and never spill innocent blood." Diego joins the group, and there is a secret rite to induct him. When he later tells Bernardo about the ceremony, Bernardo "pointed out how similar the principles of La Justicia were to those of the *okahué* of his tribe," the principles of "honor, justice, respect, dignity, and courage." Diego names his sword "Justine, because it will always serve just causes," and vows to make fighting for justice as Zorro "the foundation of my life."

Religion

Throughout *Zorro*, Allende provides comments about religion that might seem, at first glance, to be condemning religion. The idea is introduced in the first few pages, which describe the confusion of the Native Americans regarding what the missionaries tell them about Christianity. The narrator explains that the Native people "could not understand the advantage of living contrary to their inclinations in this world in order to enjoy a hypothetical well-being in another," meaning that they did not want to change their established way of life for the vague possibility of heaven in the future. This lack of understanding might not necessarily be seen as a criticism of Christianity itself, but Allende also describes the punishment the missionaries enacted on those who did not wish to convert: "the friars went out to hunt down and lasso the deserters and then whipped their doctrine of love and forgiveness into them." Such treatment certainly does not seem to fit into the teachings of "love and forgiveness."

Padre Mendoza is not the kind of man who would resort to whipping people, preferring "to win followers among the Indians through persuasion." However, Allende lists his missionary work as one of "many chores—farming, herding cattle, and Christianizing Indians." This description portrays Mendoza's efforts to convert the Native Americans not as a holy calling but instead only as a mundane and vaguely unpleasant job that needs to be done.

Allende also makes Captain de León critical about religion. He tells Diego, "There is nothing

Zorro is a cultural icon, but before Allende's novel, no one had written an origin story about him. *(© Nulman Vladyslav / Shutterstock.com)*

holy about Holy Scriptures. They were written by men, not God." De Romeu is also negative, describing convents as places where "poor young girls were fodder for evil nuns who filled their heads with demons, and for clergy who pawed them under the pretext of confessing them." It is in these two quotes that the reader might find a clue about Allende's true thoughts about religion. In both cases, it is not religion or God who is criticized, but people who use religion for their own purposes.

This view is supported when one considers Allende's descriptions of Native American religious traditions: both Bernardo and Diego come to greater understanding of themselves and what kind of men they want to be through White Owl's teachings. Also significant is the fact that when Diego, Juliana, Isabel, and Nuria are fleeing from Spain after de Romeu's death, they pretend to be going on a religious pilgrimage. At first, it is only a way to keep themselves safe, but as they travel,

> an unexpected transformation took place
> among the four false pilgrims. The peace and

silence forced them to listen, . . . to open their hearts to the unique experience of following in the footsteps of the thousands of pilgrims who had walked that road for nine centuries.

Allende clearly values this kind of religious experience, an introspective pilgrimage undertaken freely out of true devotion.

STYLE

Magical Realism

As the term implies, *magical realism* combines elements of magic with reality. Magical realism is not the same as pure fantasy, where any and all aspects of the story might be unrealistic. Instead, magical realism uses very realistic settings, situations, and characters and then introduces certain supernatural aspects, which are accepted by the characters as authentically real rather than as something unusual or fantastic.

Magical realism became especially popular in Latin America beginning in the 1940s. The political turmoil that was widespread in Latin American countries in the second half of the twentieth century seemed suited to magical realism: the fantastic elements of magical realism capture the revolutionary spirit. The Chilean Allende is considered a magical realist, as are Colombian author Gabriel García Márquez and American novelist Toni Morrison.

Several elements of magical realism appear in *Zorro*. For example, the supernatural world enters into the story when Diego and Bernardo are sent out into the wilderness to find their totem animals. Each young man sees his spirit guide, and the experience is profound and moving. However, the descriptions in these scenes are completely grounded in reality: Allende describes how Bernardo feels ill, how Diego gets lost because he does not share his friend's sense of direction, and how both boys are cold and exhausted. The fantastic visions of the animals are blended with the authenticity of the boys' trek through the very real rocks, hills, and trees while suffering realistic physical discomfort.

Another aspect of magical realism that Allende puts to good use in *Zorro* is that of authorial reticence. This literary term refers to a technique whereby the author, or the narrator, is unable or unwilling to clearly confirm or deny that the events described are absolutely true or that the beliefs of the characters in the story are valid. This distance from the action in the story allows the magic and the realism to exist side by side. If the author or narrator were to embrace the supernatural aspects too closely, the story might turn into complete fantasy, and the story would lose its realism. However, if the author does write respectfully about the magical elements, they become more meaningful.

Allende tells the story through a narrator who is also a character in the story and not always present during the events described. The narrator writes near the end of the novel that Bernardo described to her many of the events she was not present to witness. "In the episodes in which he was present, I have been obliged to write with a certain rigor," Isabel explains; "he does not allow me to interpret events in my own manner. I have more freedom in other places." Allende also uses Isabel to question the truth of the story. She admits that she has "embellished the memorable episodes," "made generous use of adjectives" and "added suspense to Zorro's feats." Isabel feels this is an acceptable practice; as she explains it: "This is called literary license and, as I understand it, it is more legitimate than all-out lies." The device of using Isabel as the narrator, making it clear that she is telling a story rather than writing a true history, allows Allende to describe both the magical and the realistic parts of the story but keep just enough distance to maintain authorial reticence.

Coming-of-Age Story

The novel *Zorro* tells the story of Diego's coming of age. A coming-of-age story—often referred to as a *bildungsroman*—describes a character's journey from childhood to adulthood. It is more than simply a chronological description of events in a person's life; it attempts to portray how a character grows into the kind of person he is as an adult. In *Zorro*, the reader sees Diego experiencing many different kinds of education, starting with the town schoolhouse and leading into White Owl's teaching him and Bernardo about the virtues of *okahué*. Then Diego leaves home and travels halfway across the world, which can be an education in itself. Also, in talking with Captain de León, Diego learns about philosophy and democracy and is "amazed to discover that there were many ways to think." This awareness that the world contains more than the ideas that one might learn from one's parents and schoolteachers is an important step

COMPARE
&
CONTRAST

- **1810s:** A person's role in Spanish society is fixed. The reputation and wealth of a person's family determine everything, from how much education he or she receives to what type of work he or she might do, to the marriage that would be arranged.

  Today: There is much more social mobility in Spain, as in most modern societies. The importance and wealth of one's family is still important, but a person can improve his or her social standing through education or through achievement in business.

- **1810s:** In every class of Spanish society, men and women lead very different and separate lives in almost every aspect. Marriages are arranged for social alliance and financial gain. Women can inherit property, but upon marriage they give up control of that property to their husbands. Divorce is socially unacceptable and forbidden by the Catholic Church.

  Today: Men and women in Spain still often follow the tradition of spending their leisure time separately. However, women have financial independence and legal rights

fully equal to those of men. Marriages are no longer arranged, and divorce is permitted, if frowned upon by the Church.

- **1810s:** The Spanish Inquisition, which worked to put an end to heresy (beliefs that contradicted the Catholic Church), declines throughout the seventeenth and eighteenth centuries, but its courts still hold trials until the French invasion of Spain in 1808. Many conservatives believe the courts are important to uphold Spain's national identity and morals. The Inquisition is finally ended in 1834, but throughout the nineteenth century, Spain continues to be a strictly Catholic country, with the Church's beliefs influencing both social and legal matters.

  Today: Church and state in Spain are not completely separate until Spain's 1978 constitution takes effect, and Spain is still very much a Catholic country. Non-Catholics amount to less then 2 percent of Spain's population, and Catholic beliefs still heavily influence what people think is socially appropriate.

in growing up. Diego's fencing teacher and membership in La Justicia also help him discover what is important to him, so that by the time he returns home, he has truly become a man, determined to fight injustice.

HISTORICAL CONTEXT

Spanish Colonization of California

The colony of New Spain covered a huge area, including much of what is now the United States west of the Mississippi River, as well as modern-day Mexico, Guatemala, Belize, El Salvador, Honduras, Nicaragua, and Costa Rica. The colony was highly profitable for Spain because of the

vast amounts of natural resources and the opportunities for trade the area presented. Because the colony was so valuable, it attracted the attention of other world powers, and Spanish leaders were concerned that the sparsely populated northern borders were vulnerable. Therefore, there was a push in the last third of the eighteenth century to encourage people to settle in Alta California (what became the US state of California).

Planned communities were settled, and there were two prominent features in each town. The first was the mission, which was run by the church, which hoped to spread Christianity in the New World by converting Native Americans. The other was the presidio, home of the military leaders and soldiers whose job was to defend both the town and Spain's claim on the

The character of Zorro is renowned for his black mask, sword, and the Z shape he makes with his sword. *(© Featureflash | Shutterstock.com)*

territory. As Allende portrays in *Zorro*, in these isolated border towns, there were clearly defined social classes. *Hidalgos*, those of purely Spanish descent, were at the top of the social ladder. They held the important military and government posts and had the most wealth. People of mixed Spanish and Native American blood, called *mestizos*, were looked down upon by most upper-class hidalgos, as seen in the treatment of Regina in the novel. The Native American people formed the lowest class and were tolerated only as servants or possible converts to Christianity.

Although Padre Mendoza is a kindly, sympathetic character in *Zorro*, the general effect of the California missions on Native Americans was disastrous. Children were taken from their parents at the age of five or six so that they might be brought up without the influence of Native American traditions. By law, adults were baptized, but it is unlikely that many were true converts, understanding and embracing Christianity. Once they

were baptized and became neophytes, they were put to work, without pay, and could be whipped, jailed, or otherwise punished if they did not obey. Unmarried women were locked into barracks, nominally to protect their virtue, and were released only to work until they were married and could live with their husbands.

There was resistance. Some Native Americans refused to learn Spanish or pretended that they did not understand the language so that they could ignore orders. Some did their work poorly, only faking the appearance of obeying. Some ran away, but the punishment for escape attempts was often brutal. The bravest fought against the Spanish, as do Toypurina and her followers in *Zorro*. There was one devastating consequence of Spanish colonization that none could resist, however: disease. Germs to which the Native Americans had no resistance claimed the lives of hundreds of thousands of people.

CRITICAL OVERVIEW

Critical reaction to *Zorro* has been overwhelmingly positive. Misha Stone in *Library Journal* calls the novel "enthralling reading" and dubs Allende "a beguiling storyteller." The review in *Publishers Weekly* describes Zorro as a "lively retelling," a "page-turner" that "explodes with vivid characterization and high-speed storytelling." Brad Hooper's review in *Booklist* praises "Allende's mesmerizing narrative voice," which "never loses timbre or flags in either tension or entertainment value."

Several reviewers noted the gamble Allende took in writing such a sensational story: it would have been very easy to allow the exaggerated drama of the adventures to take center stage. However, as a contributor to *Kirkus Reviews* states, "Allende's tale risks but resists descending into melodrama at every turn." In the *Globe and Mail*, Paul Quarrington agrees, explaining how "the penny-dreadful tone is actually a lovely device that Allende employs." Quarrington admits that *Zorro* is

> a book rife with coincidence, love at first sight, pirates, secret societies—hey, it's a book where a guy can put on a mask, draw a little moustache on his face and fool people who have known him all of their lives.

Regardless of this, according to Quarrington, *Zorro* is "hugely enjoyable" and a "wonderful novel." Perhaps Allende managed to escape melodrama by grounding her story in a thoroughly researched historical context. In his *Booklist* review, Hooper praises Allende's "complete familiarity with setting," both in terms of the time period and in terms of the locations in California and Spain.

CRITICISM

Kristen Sarlin Greenberg

Greenberg is a freelance writer and editor with a background in literature and philosophy. In the following essay, she examines the social class distinctions in Allende's Zorro.

In her novel *Zorro*, Isabel Allende imagines the childhood and young adulthood of a famous and beloved character. Zorro is best known as a defender of the weak against danger and injustice, and in order to show how Diego de la Vega evolved into this kind of hero, Allende portrays him witnessing and experiencing various kinds of injustice. Perhaps one of the most prominent forms of injustice in the book is prejudice based on social class.

Diego's fifteenth birthday party is a snapshot of California colonial society in the late eighteenth century. It is a large, dramatic affair, with acrobats, fireworks, and a bullfight, and food is "served to five hundred guests for three days in accordance to social class." First, of course, are the hidalgos, "pure-blooded Spanish," who are seated for their meals "comfortably shaded beneath a grape-laden arbor, at the main tables set with tablecloths" that are imported from Spain. Next come the "*gente de razón*, respectable people," who are mestizos of mixed Spanish and Native American blood. They are considered by the hidalgos to be somewhat worthy of notice, because they are not "Indians and servants." They are "dressed in their Sunday best at tables to the side but still in the shade." Last of all are the "Indians in full sun on the patios." Each person knows his position in society, which is represented by his seat at the tables at Diego's party.

Allende's portrayal of this strict social hierarchy starts early in the story, when Alejandro falls in love with Toypurina. He tries to forget her, because she is a mestiza: her father was Spanish and her mother Native American. Alejandro has been taught that "a de la Vega, an hidalgo, a man of honor and lineage, could never dream of living his life with a mestiza woman."

WHAT DO I READ NEXT?

- At the urging of her grandchildren, Allende wrote a trilogy of novels for young adults: *City of the Beasts* (2002), *Kingdom of the Golden Dragon* (2004), and *Forest of the Pygmies* (2005). Like *Zorro*, the novels are filled with exciting adventures and show some characteristics of magical realism.

- The theme of justice echoes through Ying Chang Compestine's 2007 book *Revolution Is Not a Dinner Party: A Novel*. The story takes place during China's Cultural Revolution, which brought huge social change and political turmoil to the lives of so many, including the novel's young heroine, Ling. Compestine based the novel in part on the experiences of her own family, giving the characters powerful realism.

- The University of Oregon maintains a site called Web de Anza, "An Interactive Study Environment on Spanish Exploration and Colonization of 'Alta California' 1774–1776" (http://anza.uoregon.edu). The site includes primary source documents—actual letters and journal entries—from colonists in California in the eighteenth century.

- In 2012, celebrated Native American author Louise Erdrich published *The Round House*. This novel centers on an Ojibwe boy coming of age in the aftermath of a racist attack in which his mother is almost killed.

- *One Hundred Years of Solitude* (1967) by Nobel Prize–winning author Gabriel García Márquez is a classic work of magical realism. The novel follows the Buendía family through seven generations.

- Toni Morrison is an American writer who uses some of the elements of magical realism. Her novel *Tar Baby* (1981) examines some of the issues central to *Zorro*: the search for identity and the clash of different cultures and social classes. The book tells the story of Jadine, a young woman torn between her aunt and uncle, who are servants, and their employer, who has funded Jadine's education.

Although Alejandro is "tormented," he is finally able to overcome his doubts and decides to marry the woman he loves. She is "baptized under the name of Regina María de la Inmaculada Concepción, but she immediately forgot most of it and went only by Regina." This indicates that she is largely unchanged, but Alejandro seems content to have her made socially acceptable, if only superficially.

Not everyone is so willing to forget Regina's background. The people in town talk about her "behind her back, . . . commented on her unsociable and arrogant nature, her more than doubtful origins, her escapades on horseback, her naked bathing in the sea." They are willing to accept her socially only because Doña Eulalia and her husband, the governor of California, take her under their wing. Alejandro, meanwhile, tolerates Regina's behavior, trying to dismiss her escapades as "bad habits" that he hopes motherhood will "cure."

Although it seems romantic that Alejandro overcomes his prejudice against Regina's mixed blood, the issue ultimately prevents them from being happy together. In that society,

> No rancher would admit to having an Indian ancestor. To a man they claimed Spanish heritage: white skin and pure blood. That Regina did not even try to hide her origins was not something they could forgive.

Alejandro "never questioned the ideas he had inherited from his ancestors." He is always "ashamed that she was a mestiza. Because he was proud, he pretended not to notice that a narrow-minded colonial society ostracized her, but with time he began to blame her."

The strict distinctions between social classes are also highlighted in Alejandro's reaction to Diego calling Bernardo his "brother." Allende stresses that Alejandro does not approve of Diego's friendship with Bernardo. Alejandro worries that this friendship shows "a weakness in his son's character," firmly believing that "Diego and Bernardo were different by birth; they would never be equals." Alejandro's ideas are so fixed that a reader might be led to question how Allende herself feels about the social hierarchy—could she possibly support such divisions?

However, Allende is able to describe Alejandro's ideas while making clear that "they were not appropriate to the reality of America." Indeed, one only has to look at the behavior of Diego, who, after all, is set up in the novel as the ultimate defender of justice, to see that Allende could not possibly support prejudice based on race, social status, or wealth.

Diego's friendship with Bernardo begins almost as soon as they are born. Because Regina is ill after giving birth, Bernardo's mother, Ana, nurses both boys. Thus they become "milk brothers," and they continue to refer to each other as "brothers" even when they are grown. They see the world very differently and have very different temperaments, as is illustrated by their very different styles of swimming: "While Diego wore himself our thrashing through the waves, Bernardo maintained an unhurried rhythm for hours, breathing slowly and letting himself be carried by the mysterious currents of the sea." Diego throws himself into life, always pushing, whereas Bernardo is more willing to quietly follow. Perhaps because of their different natures, Bernardo "assumed the role of protecting Diego, who he believed was destined for great things, like the heroic warriors in White Owl's storehouse of myths."

The boys become so close, they seem to read each other's minds, and "Bernardo taught Diego the Indians' sign language, which they then enriched with their own additions and used for communicating when telepathy . . . failed." When the two boys are reunited after some time apart, "Diego felt as if he had gained back half his soul." They are so attuned to one another that at times, Diego thinks he feels "his brother's pounding heart in his own chest." Surely this level of understanding and affection is not presented critically; Allende knows that what binds Diego and Bernardo together as friends is far more important than arbitrary considerations of social class.

Diego's friendship with Bernardo crosses all boundaries. Bernardo is Native American, and Diego is hidalgo, or at least his father wants him to appear to be a member of the highest class. Diego's family is wealthy, while Bernardo's mother is a servant and leaves him with nothing when she dies. However, the boys' friendship is the most stable relationship in the novel. Diego and Bernardo never doubt one another and are always there to help one another. Even their romances do not put an end to their intimacy and their confidence in one another. Their devotion endures over time, hardship, and separation, showing that Allende thinks little of the class distinctions that Alejandro, as well as colonial society, assumes are vital and unquestionable.

The novel begins in San Gabriel mission in California. *(© Lowe R. Llaguno / Shutterstock.com)*

Source: Kristen Sarlin Greenberg, Critical Essay on *Zorro*, in *Novels for Students*, Gale, Cengage Learning, 2014.

Publishers Weekly

In the following review, a contributor claims that Zorro is "a page-turner that explodes with vivid characterization and high-speed storytelling."

Allende's lively retelling of the Zorro legend reads as effortlessly as the hero himself might slice his trademark "Z" on the wall with a flash of his sword. Born Diego de la Vega in 1795 to the valiant hidalgo, Alejandro, and the beautiful Regina, the daughter of a Spanish deserter and an Indian shaman, our hero grows up in California before traveling to Spain. Raised alongside his wet nurse's son, Bernardo, Diego becomes friends for life with his "milk brother," despite the boys' class differences. Though born into privilege, Diego has deep ties to California's exploited natives—both through blood and friendship—that account for his abiding sense of justice and identification with the underdog. In Catalonia, these instincts as well as Diego's swordsmanship intrigue Manuel Escalante, a member of the secret society La Justicia. Escalante recruits Diego into the society, which is dedicated to fighting all forms of oppression, and thus begins Diego's construction of his dashing, secret alter ego, Zorro. With loyal Bernardo at his side, Zorro hones his fantastic skills, evolves into a noble hero and returns to California to reclaim his family's estate in a breathtaking duel. All the while, he encounters numerous historical figures, who anchor this incredible tale in a reality that enriches and contextualizes the Zorro myth. Allende's latest page-turner explodes with vivid characterization and high-speed storytelling.

Source: Review of *Zorro*, in *Publishers Weekly*, Vol. 252, No. 9, February 28, 2005, p. 39.

Brad Hooper

In the following review, Hooper remarks that Allende is an intelligent and inventive novelist.

Allende, born in Peru and raised in Chile, now resides in California, and out of her abiding interest in Spanish American and California history and culture, she has fashioned her historical fiction (including the companion novels *Daughter of Fortune*, 1999, and *Portrait in Sepia*, 2001). In her latest historical novel, she imaginatively creates, in the words of the narrator, "the origins of the legend"—the legend being none other than Zorro, the famous Robin Hood of eighteenth-century colonial California. The novel's conceit is that the testimony offered here is a bird's-eye view of the provenance of Zorro as recorded by someone who knew him well, but the identity of that person is not revealed until the novel's end. Allende's complete familiarity with setting includes not only the "custom of the country" in Southern California when still in Spanish hands but also the complicated political atmosphere of Spain itself during the Napoleonic era, to which Diego de la Vega is dispatched as a teenager for his formal education. It is in Spain where the physical disguise of Zorro and the social-reform mentality that motivates him first bear adult fruit. (Diego is one-quarter Native American and thus understands the downtrodden.) Allende's mesmerizing narrative voice never loses timbre or flags in either tension or entertainment value. To describe her as a clever novelist is to signify that she is both inventive and intelligent.

Source: Brad Hooper, Review of *Zorro*, in *Booklist*, Vol. 101, No. 12, February 15, 2005, p. 1035.

Misha Stone

In the following review, Stone recommends Allende's retelling of Zorro, *which displays her storytelling capabilities.*

Allende's retelling of *Zorro* displays her essential belief that the fabric of the story—the making of the man—is as important as the actions. Born to an aristocratic Spanish father and a tamed Shoshone warrior in 18th-century California, Diego de la Vega learns the lessons of injustice early. His mother's Indian blood and the violence perpetrated against the Native Americans by European settlers ignite a slow-burning fire in Diego. When Diego is sent to Barcelona with his "milk" brother Bernardo to be educated in the ways of his forebears, he studies with a fencing master and joins an underground resistance group, where Zorro the romantic revolutionary is truly forged. Allende's Zorro is not quite the violent, swashbuckling rogue that Johnston McCulley created in his serial potboilers, but this Zorro doesn't have to be for his character to be compelling. One does long for a little more swordplay, but Diego's crisis of identity, his relationship with Bernardo, and his love for a woman he cannot have make for enthralling reading. Allende (*Daughter of Fortune*) is a beguiling storyteller, and *Zorro* provides a rich palate for her customary embellishments. Recommended for all public libraries.

Source: Misha Stone, Review of *Zorro*, in *Library Journal*, Vol. 130, No. 4, March 1, 2005, p. 74.

Barbara Mujica

In the following excerpt, Mujica claims that though Zorro *is not Allende's best novel, it is "an entertaining, humorous adventure story full of dashing swashbucklers, dastardly villains, wise women, damsels, and clever younger sisters."*

. . . If you're planning a fall vacation and want to take along some light reading, by all means pack a copy of *Zorro*. This new novel by Isabel Allende is fun and, for the most part, lively, although the plot occasionally becomes mired in wordiness.

Allende's book is an account of the youth and formation of the fictional character Zorro, created in 1919 by Johnston McCulley. The original author introduced Zorro in a novel called *The Curse of Capistrano*, which appeared in installments in a pulp magazine. McCulley's book became enormously Successful, and his hero inspired films and a television series, as well as new characters, such as Batman, created by Bob Kane. Allende now enriches the legend by filling in the blanks regarding Zorro's upbringing, education, and early exploits. Set in the late eighteenth and early nineteenth centuries, the book reflects Allende's interest in California history, evident in earlier novels such as the first-rate *Portrait in Sepia* and *Daughter of Fortune*.

Allende's Zorro is the son of Alejandro de la Vega, a landed aristocrat, and Toypumia [Toypurina], a mestiza Shoshone warrior. When Indians attack San Gabriel Mission, Alejandro, the Spanish captain charged with defending it, wounds Toypumia, who is disguised with a [wolf's] head. (Her name means Daughter-of-Wolf). Upon discovering she is a woman, he nurses her back to health and takes her to Eulalia de Callis, the governor's wife, who teaches her European ways. In spite of the taboo against marrying non-whites, the smitten Alejandro takes Toypumia as his bride and settles her on his splendid hacienda. However, he cannot destroy her strong attachment to her people, and when their son Diego is [born], the boy learns Indian lore from his mother as well as Spanish culture from his father. His ties to the Shoshones are strengthened by his intimate friendship with Bernardo, an Indian servant born the same day as he, who is as close to him as a brother. In an elaborate Indian rite of passage in which the boys participate, they learn the significance of the zorro (fox). Diego's antagonist is Carlos Alcazar, the spoiled, cruel son of an overbearing Spanish rancher. Over the years Diego observes terrible abuses of Indians by Spaniards, in particular, by the elder Alcazar, and appeals to his father to deal with the Injustices. However, the system is stacked irremediably against the Indians.

When Diego is old enough, he leaves for Barcelona to continue his education, accompanied by Bernardo, his inseparable companion. On the long voyage across the Atlantic, he amuses himself performing daring acrobatic feats on the ship's rigging, a skill that will be essential to his transformation into Zorro. The two young men take up residence in the home of

Tomas de Romeu, a liberal intellectual. The French have just occupied Spain, and it's not long before Romeu's pro-French politics get him into trouble. Romeu has two daughters, the beautiful but aloof Juliana and the plain but adventurous Isabel. Diego falls head-over-heads in love with Juliana, who pays no attention either to him or to her other suitor, the perfidious Rafael Moncada. Later, when the Spaniards expel the French and the ultra-conservative regime of Fernando VII comes to power, Moncada betrays Romeu and hands him over to the government with hopes of forcing Juliana to marry him.

While he is in Barcelona, Diego studies swordsmanship with the famous master Manuel Escalante and soon becomes a first-rate fencer. Always a champion of the outcast, he befriends a community of gypsies, a group as marginalized as the California Indians. The idea of Zorro is born when Diego decides to perform acrobatic stunts in the gypsy circus, wearing a mask and a black outfit and identifying himself only as Zorro. Later, Diego saves the gypsies by forewarning them of an impending assault on their encampment. From then on, he performs daring rescues and acts of bravery wearing his Zorro costume, always slashing a Z on a nearby wall to identify himself. Thus is the legend of Zorro born.

Diego manages to snatch Juliana and Isabel from Moncada's clutches and embark on the trip back home. He plans to return to California and assume his proper role of landowner with Juliana at his side. However, on the way his ship is attacked by pirates, who take Diego, the two girls, and their governess to New Orleans, where the dashing buccaneer Jean Lafitte controls a vast empire, complete with slaves. Lafitte could sell Juliana into prostitution, but fate has another plan—one that separates her from Diego. Allende's descriptions of New Orleans, a vibrant, exhilarating, multi-racial city are especially poignant now, in the aftermath of Hurricane Katrina. African sensuality, French elegance, Spanish vigor, and American business acumen combine to make this a truly unique city.

Once again back in California, Diego faces impending disaster. His old enemy Moncada has made his way to the New World, and has joined forces with Alcazar. The partners have imprisoned Diego's father and exploit the Indians with impunity. With the help of Bernardo and Isabel, Diego assumes the role of Zorro and stages a breathtaking rescue that sets things aright. Then he goes on to make a career of righting wrongs and defending the oppressed.

Allende's novel is rich in its celebration of diverse cultures, although her depictions of Indian and African customs are colorful rather than profound. Her characters are not particularly memorable. Zorro's personality was established by McCulley, and the female characters are conventional—even the clever Isabel. Predictably, Allende's villains are all Spaniards (although not all her Spaniards are villains), while the gypsies, Africans, and Indians are all righteous. In *Zorro* the author uses narrative tricks she has used before. For example, she keeps the narrator's identity a secret until the end, a technique she used effectively in *The House of the Spirits*, but in *Zorro* the mystery is easy to solve and doesn't matter much anyhow. *Zorro* is not Allende's best novel, but it is an entertaining, humorous adventure story full of dashing swashbucklers, dastardly villains, wise women, damsels, and clever younger sisters—certainly an enjoyable read. . . .

Source: Barbara Mujica, "Zorro and the Zahir," in *Americas* (English Edition), Vol. 57, No. 6, November–December 2005, p. 62.

SOURCES

Allende, Isabel, *Zorro: A Novel*, translated by Margaret Sayers Peden, Harper Perennial, 2005.

———, "Loving Zorro, Writing *Zorro*: A Conversation with Isabel Allende," in *Zorro: A Novel*, Harper Perennial, 2005, p. PS8.

"California Indians: Spanish Colonization," in *U-X-L Multicultural CD: A Comprehensive Resource on African Americans, Hispanic Americans and Native North Americans*, U-X-L, 2003.

Freeman, Susan Tax, "Spain," in *Countries and Their Cultures*, edited by Carol R. Ember and Melvin Ember, Vol. 4, Macmillan Reference USA, 2001, pp. 2064–85.

Hooper, Brad, Review of *Zorro*, in *Booklist*, Vol. 101, No. 12, February 15, 2005, p. 1035.

Jackson, Robert H., "New Spain, Colonization of the Northern Frontier," in *Encyclopedia of Latin American History and Culture*, 2nd ed., edited by Jay Kinsbruner and Erick D. Langer, Vol. 4, Charles Scribner's Sons, 2008, pp. 817–19.

Moore, Lindsay, "Magical Realism," Postcolonial Studies, Emory University website, 1998, http://www.english.

emory.edu/Bahri/MagicalRealism.html (accessed December 15, 2012).

Nalle, Sara Tilghman, "Inquisition, Spanish," in *Europe, 1450 to 1789: Encyclopedia of the Early Modern World*, edited by Jonathan Dewald, Vol. 3, Charles Scribner's Sons, 2004, pp. 272–75.

Quarrington, Paul, "Z," in *Globe and Mail*, May 21, 2005, p. D8.

Review of *Zorro*, in *Kirkus Reviews*, Vol. 73, No. 4, February 15, 2005, p. 187.

Review of *Zorro*, in *Publishers Weekly*, Vol. 252, No. 9, February 28, 2005, p. 39.

"Spanish Settlement in California," in *DISCovering Multicultural America: African Americans, Hispanic Americans, Asian Americans, Native Americans*, Thomson Gale, 2003.

Stone, Misha, Review of *Zorro*, in *Library Journal*, Vol. 130, No. 4, March 1, 2005, p. 74.

Ward, Jason L., "New Spain," in *History of World Trade since 1450*, edited by John J. McCusker, Vol. 2, Macmillan Reference USA, 2006, pp. 530–32.

happened hundreds of years ago, but this nonfiction work makes clear that injustice still occurs in the twentieth and twenty-first centuries. Bausum's book depicts immigrant experiences that are worlds away from the American dream.

Leffingwell, Randy, *California Missions and Presidios: The History and Beauty of the Spanish Missions*, Voyageur Press, 2005.
    The photography in Leffingwell's book captures the unique beauty of colonial architecture, including presidios, missions, and adobes. The accompanying text illuminates the history of Spanish colonization of California.

Silko, Leslie Marmon, *Ceremony*, Penguin Books, 2006.
    Silko's critically acclaimed novel, originally published in 1977, describes the struggle of a half-Laguna, half-white veteran to recover after World War II. Traditional Native American ceremonies and spirituality finally help him find a way to heal.

FURTHER READING

Allende, Isabel, *The House of the Spirits*, translated by Magda Bogin, Everyman's Library, 2005.
    In this, her debut novel, Allende presents the story of three generations of the Trueba family as their country experiences political upheaval.

Bausum, Ann, *Denied, Detained, Deported: Stories from the Dark Side of American Immigration*, National Geographic, 2009.
    The mistreatment of Native Americans by Spanish colonists might be something that

SUGGESTED SEARCH TERMS

Isabel Allende AND Zorro

Isabel Allende AND historical novel

Isabel Allende AND Latino identity

Isabel Allende AND magical realism

Zorro AND history

New Spain

California missions

Native American AND Shoshone

Glossary of Literary Terms

A

Abstract: As an adjective applied to writing or literary works, abstract refers to words or phrases that name things not knowable through the five senses.

Aestheticism: A literary and artistic movement of the nineteenth century. Followers of the movement believed that art should not be mixed with social, political, or moral teaching. The statement "art for art's sake" is a good summary of aestheticism. The movement had its roots in France, but it gained widespread importance in England in the last half of the nineteenth century, where it helped change the Victorian practice of including moral lessons in literature.

Allegory: A narrative technique in which characters representing things or abstract ideas are used to convey a message or teach a lesson. Allegory is typically used to teach moral, ethical, or religious lessons but is sometimes used for satiric or political purposes.

Allusion: A reference to a familiar literary or historical person or event, used to make an idea more easily understood.

Analogy: A comparison of two things made to explain something unfamiliar through its similarities to something familiar, or to prove one point based on the acceptedness of another. Similes and metaphors are types of analogies.

Antagonist: The major character in a narrative or drama who works against the hero or protagonist.

Anthropomorphism: The presentation of animals or objects in human shape or with human characteristics. The term is derived from the Greek word for "human form."

Anti-hero: A central character in a work of literature who lacks traditional heroic qualities such as courage, physical prowess, and fortitude. Anti-heroes typically distrust conventional values and are unable to commit themselves to any ideals. They generally feel helpless in a world over which they have no control. Anti-heroes usually accept, and often celebrate, their positions as social outcasts.

Apprenticeship Novel: See *Bildungsroman*

Archetype: The word archetype is commonly used to describe an original pattern or model from which all other things of the same kind are made. This term was introduced to literary criticism from the psychology of Carl Jung. It expresses Jung's theory that behind every person's "unconscious," or repressed memories of the past, lies the "collective unconscious" of the human race: memories of the countless typical experiences of our ancestors. These memories are said to prompt illogical associations that trigger powerful emotions in the reader. Often, the emotional process is primitive, even primordial. Archetypes are the literary images that grow out of the "collective unconscious." They appear in literature as incidents and plots that repeat basic patterns of life. They may also appear as stereotyped characters.

Avant-garde: French term meaning "vanguard." It is used in literary criticism to describe new writing that rejects traditional approaches to literature in favor of innovations in style or content.

B

Beat Movement: A period featuring a group of American poets and novelists of the 1950s and 1960s—including Jack Kerouac, Allen Ginsberg, Gregory Corso, William S. Burroughs, and Lawrence Ferlinghetti—who rejected established social and literary values. Using such techniques as stream of consciousness writing and jazz-influenced free verse and focusing on unusual or abnormal states of mind—generated by religious ecstasy or the use of drugs—the Beat writers aimed to create works that were unconventional in both form and subject matter.

Bildungsroman: A German word meaning "novel of development." The *bildungsroman* is a study of the maturation of a youthful character, typically brought about through a series of social or sexual encounters that lead to self-awareness. *Bildungsroman* is used interchangeably with *erziehungsroman,* a novel of initiation and education. When a *bildungsroman* is concerned with the development of an artist (as in James Joyce's *A Portrait of the Artist as a Young Man*), it is often termed a *kunstlerroman.*

Black Aesthetic Movement: A period of artistic and literary development among African Americans in the 1960s and early 1970s. This was the first major African-American artistic movement since the Harlem Renaissance and was closely paralleled by the civil rights and black power movements. The black aesthetic writers attempted to produce works of art that would be meaningful to the black masses. Key figures in black aesthetics included one of its founders, poet and playwright Amiri Baraka, formerly known as LeRoi Jones; poet and essayist Haki R. Madhubuti, formerly Don L. Lee; poet and

playwright Sonia Sanchez; and dramatist Ed Bullins.

Black Humor: Writing that places grotesque elements side by side with humorous ones in an attempt to shock the reader, forcing him or her to laugh at the horrifying reality of a disordered world.

Burlesque: Any literary work that uses exaggeration to make its subject appear ridiculous, either by treating a trivial subject with profound seriousness or by treating a dignified subject frivolously. The word "burlesque" may also be used as an adjective, as in "burlesque show," to mean "striptease act."

C

Character: Broadly speaking, a person in a literary work. The actions of characters are what constitute the plot of a story, novel, or poem. There are numerous types of characters, ranging from simple, stereotypical figures to intricate, multifaceted ones. In the techniques of anthropomorphism and personification, animals—and even places or things—can assume aspects of character. "Characterization" is the process by which an author creates vivid, believable characters in a work of art. This may be done in a variety of ways, including (1) direct description of the character by the narrator; (2) the direct presentation of the speech, thoughts, or actions of the character; and (3) the responses of other characters to the character. The term "character" also refers to a form originated by the ancient Greek writer Theophrastus that later became popular in the seventeenth and eighteenth centuries. It is a short essay or sketch of a person who prominently displays a specific attribute or quality, such as miserliness or ambition.

Climax: The turning point in a narrative, the moment when the conflict is at its most intense. Typically, the structure of stories, novels, and plays is one of rising action, in which tension builds to the climax, followed by falling action, in which tension lessens as the story moves to its conclusion.

Colloquialism: A word, phrase, or form of pronunciation that is acceptable in casual conversation but not in formal, written communication. It is considered more acceptable than slang.

Coming of Age Novel: See *Bildungsroman*

Concrete: Concrete is the opposite of abstract, and refers to a thing that actually exists or a description that allows the reader to experience an object or concept with the senses.

Connotation: The impression that a word gives beyond its defined meaning. Connotations may be universally understood or may be significant only to a certain group.

Convention: Any widely accepted literary device, style, or form.

D

Denotation: The definition of a word, apart from the impressions or feelings it creates (connotations) in the reader.

Denouement: A French word meaning "the unknotting." In literary criticism, it denotes the resolution of conflict in fiction or drama. The *denouement* follows the climax and provides an outcome to the primary plot situation as well as an explanation of secondary plot complications. The *denouement* often involves a character's recognition of his or her state of mind or moral condition.

Description: Descriptive writing is intended to allow a reader to picture the scene or setting in which the action of a story takes place. The form this description takes often evokes an intended emotional response—a dark, spooky graveyard will evoke fear, and a peaceful, sunny meadow will evoke calmness.

Dialogue: In its widest sense, dialogue is simply conversation between people in a literary work; in its most restricted sense, it refers specifically to the speech of characters in a drama. As a specific literary genre, a "dialogue" is a composition in which characters debate an issue or idea.

Diction: The selection and arrangement of words in a literary work. Either or both may vary depending on the desired effect. There are four general types of diction: "formal," used in scholarly or lofty writing; "informal," used in relaxed but educated conversation; "colloquial," used in everyday speech; and "slang," containing newly coined words and other terms not accepted in formal usage.

Didactic: A term used to describe works of literature that aim to teach some moral, religious, political, or practical lesson. Although didactic elements are often found in artistically pleasing works, the term "didactic" usually refers to literature in which the message is more important than the form. The term may also be used to criticize a work that the critic finds "overly didactic," that is, heavy-handed in its delivery of a lesson.

Doppelganger: A literary technique by which a character is duplicated (usually in the form of an alter ego, though sometimes as a ghostly counterpart) or divided into two distinct, usually opposite personalities. The use of this character device is widespread in nineteenth- and twentieth-century literature, and indicates a growing awareness among authors that the "self" is really a composite of many "selves."

Double Entendre: A corruption of a French phrase meaning "double meaning." The term is used to indicate a word or phrase that is deliberately ambiguous, especially when one of the meanings is risqué or improper.

Dramatic Irony: Occurs when the audience of a play or the reader of a work of literature knows something that a character in the work itself does not know. The irony is in the contrast between the intended meaning of the statements or actions of a character and the additional information understood by the audience.

Dystopia: An imaginary place in a work of fiction where the characters lead dehumanized, fearful lives.

E

Edwardian: Describes cultural conventions identified with the period of the reign of Edward VII of England (1901-1910). Writers of the Edwardian Age typically displayed a strong reaction against the propriety and conservatism of the Victorian Age. Their work often exhibits distrust of authority in religion, politics, and art and expresses strong doubts about the soundness of conventional values.

Empathy: A sense of shared experience, including emotional and physical feelings, with someone or something other than oneself. Empathy is often used to describe the response of a reader to a literary character.

Enlightenment, The: An eighteenth-century philosophical movement. It began in France but had a wide impact throughout Europe and America. Thinkers of the Enlightenment valued reason and believed that both the individual and society could achieve a state of perfection. Corresponding to this essentially humanist vision was a resistance to religious authority.

Epigram: A saying that makes the speaker's point quickly and concisely. Often used to preface a novel.

Epilogue: A concluding statement or section of a literary work. In dramas, particularly those of the seventeenth and eighteenth centuries, the epilogue is a closing speech, often in verse, delivered by an actor at the end of a play and spoken directly to the audience.

Epiphany: A sudden revelation of truth inspired by a seemingly trivial incident.

Episode: An incident that forms part of a story and is significantly related to it. Episodes may be either self-contained narratives or events that depend on a larger context for their sense and importance.

Epistolary Novel: A novel in the form of letters. The form was particularly popular in the eighteenth century.

Epithet: A word or phrase, often disparaging or abusive, that expresses a character trait of someone or something.

Existentialism: A predominantly twentieth-century philosophy concerned with the nature and perception of human existence. There are two major strains of existentialist thought: atheistic and Christian. Followers of atheistic existentialism believe that the individual is alone in a godless universe and that the basic human condition is one of suffering and loneliness. Nevertheless, because there are no fixed values, individuals can create their own characters—indeed, they can shape themselves—through the exercise of free will. The atheistic strain culminates in and is popularly associated with the works of Jean-Paul Sartre. The Christian existentialists, on the other hand, believe that only in God may people find freedom from life's anguish. The two strains hold certain beliefs in common: that existence cannot be fully understood or described through empirical effort; that anguish is a universal element of life; that individuals must bear responsibility for their actions; and that there is no common standard of behavior or perception for religious and ethical matters.

Expatriates: See *Expatriatism*

Expatriatism: The practice of leaving one's country to live for an extended period in another country.

Exposition: Writing intended to explain the nature of an idea, thing, or theme. Expository writing is often combined with description, narration, or argument. In dramatic writing, the exposition is the introductory material which presents the characters, setting, and tone of the play.

Expressionism: An indistinct literary term, originally used to describe an early twentieth-century school of German painting. The term applies to almost any mode of unconventional, highly subjective writing that distorts reality in some way.

F

Fable: A prose or verse narrative intended to convey a moral. Animals or inanimate objects with human characteristics often serve as characters in fables.

Falling Action: See *Denouement*

Fantasy: A literary form related to mythology and folklore. Fantasy literature is typically set in non-existent realms and features supernatural beings.

Farce: A type of comedy characterized by broad humor, outlandish incidents, and often vulgar subject matter.

Femme fatale: A French phrase with the literal translation "fatal woman." A *femme fatale* is a sensuous, alluring woman who often leads men into danger or trouble.

Fiction: Any story that is the product of imagination rather than a documentation of fact. Characters and events in such narratives may be based in real life but their ultimate form and configuration is a creation of the author.

Figurative Language: A technique in writing in which the author temporarily interrupts the order, construction, or meaning of the writing for a particular effect. This interruption takes the form of one or more figures of speech such as hyperbole, irony, or simile. Figurative language is the opposite of literal language, in which every word is truthful, accurate, and free of exaggeration or embellishment.

Figures of Speech: Writing that differs from customary conventions for construction, meaning, order, or significance for the purpose of a special meaning or effect. There are two major types of figures of speech: rhetorical figures, which do not make changes in the meaning of the words, and tropes, which do.

Fin de siecle: A French term meaning "end of the century." The term is used to denote the last decade of the nineteenth century, a transition period when writers and other artists abandoned old conventions and looked for new techniques and objectives.

First Person: See *Point of View*

Flashback: A device used in literature to present action that occurred before the beginning of the story. Flashbacks are often introduced as the dreams or recollections of one or more characters.

Foil: A character in a work of literature whose physical or psychological qualities contrast strongly with, and therefore highlight, the corresponding qualities of another character.

Folklore: Traditions and myths preserved in a culture or group of people. Typically, these are passed on by word of mouth in various forms—such as legends, songs, and proverbs—or preserved in customs and ceremonies. This term was first used by W. J. Thoms in 1846.

Folktale: A story originating in oral tradition. Folktales fall into a variety of categories, including legends, ghost stories, fairy tales, fables, and anecdotes based on historical figures and events.

Foreshadowing: A device used in literature to create expectation or to set up an explanation of later developments.

Form: The pattern or construction of a work which identifies its genre and distinguishes it from other genres.

G

Genre: A category of literary work. In critical theory, genre may refer to both the content of a given work—tragedy, comedy, pastoral—and to its form, such as poetry, novel, or drama.

Gilded Age: A period in American history during the 1870s characterized by political corruption and materialism. A number of important novels of social and political criticism were written during this time.

Gothicism: In literary criticism, works characterized by a taste for the medieval or morbidly attractive. A gothic novel prominently features elements of horror, the supernatural, gloom, and violence: clanking chains, terror, charnel houses, ghosts, medieval castles, and mysteriously slamming doors. The term "gothic novel" is also applied to novels that lack elements of the traditional Gothic setting but that create a similar atmosphere of terror or dread.

Grotesque: In literary criticism, the subject matter of a work or a style of expression characterized by exaggeration, deformity, freakishness, and disorder. The grotesque often includes an element of comic absurdity.

H

Harlem Renaissance: The Harlem Renaissance of the 1920s is generally considered the first significant movement of black writers and artists in the United States. During this period, new and established black writers published more fiction and poetry than ever before, the first influential black literary journals were established, and black authors and artists received their first widespread recognition and serious critical appraisal. Among the major writers associated with this period are Claude McKay, Jean Toomer, Countee Cullen, Langston Hughes, Arna Bontemps, Nella Larsen, and Zora Neale Hurston.

Hero/Heroine: The principal sympathetic character (male or female) in a literary work. Heroes and heroines typically exhibit admirable traits: idealism, courage, and integrity, for example.

Holocaust Literature: Literature influenced by or written about the Holocaust of World War II. Such literature includes true stories of survival in concentration camps, escape, and life after the war, as well as fictional works and poetry.

Humanism: A philosophy that places faith in the dignity of humankind and rejects the medieval perception of the individual as a weak, fallen creature. "Humanists" typically believe in the perfectibility of human nature and view reason and education as the means to that end.

Hyperbole: In literary criticism, deliberate exaggeration used to achieve an effect.

I

Idiom: A word construction or verbal expression closely associated with a given language.

Image: A concrete representation of an object or sensory experience. Typically, such a representation helps evoke the feelings associated with the object or experience itself. Images are either "literal" or "figurative." Literal images are especially concrete and involve little or no extension of the obvious meaning of the words used to express them. Figurative images do not follow the literal meaning of the words exactly. Images in literature are usually visual, but the term "image" can also refer to the representation of any sensory experience.

Imagery: The array of images in a literary work. Also, figurative language.

In medias res: A Latin term meaning "in the middle of things." It refers to the technique of beginning a story at its midpoint and then using various flashback devices to reveal previous action.

Interior Monologue: A narrative technique in which characters' thoughts are revealed in a way that appears to be uncontrolled by the author. The interior monologue typically aims to reveal the inner self of a character. It portrays emotional experiences as they occur at both a conscious and unconscious level. images are often used to represent sensations or emotions.

Irony: In literary criticism, the effect of language in which the intended meaning is the opposite of what is stated.

J

Jargon: Language that is used or understood only by a select group of people. Jargon may refer to terminology used in a certain profession, such as computer jargon, or it may refer to any nonsensical language that is not understood by most people.

L

Leitmotiv: See *Motif*

Literal Language: An author uses literal language when he or she writes without exaggerating or embellishing the subject matter and without any tools of figurative language.

Lost Generation: A term first used by Gertrude Stein to describe the post-World War I generation of American writers: men and women haunted by a sense of betrayal and emptiness brought about by the destructiveness of the war.

M

Mannerism: Exaggerated, artificial adherence to a literary manner or style. Also, a popular style of the visual arts of late sixteenth-century Europe that was marked by elongation of the human form and by intentional spatial distortion. Literary works that are self-consciously high-toned and artistic are often said to be "mannered."

Metaphor: A figure of speech that expresses an idea through the image of another object. Metaphors suggest the essence of the first object by identifying it with certain qualities of the second object.

Modernism: Modern literary practices. Also, the principles of a literary school that lasted from roughly the beginning of the twentieth century until the end of World War II. Modernism is defined by its rejection of the literary conventions of the nineteenth century and by its opposition to conventional morality, taste, traditions, and economic values.

Mood: The prevailing emotions of a work or of the author in his or her creation of the work. The mood of a work is not always what might be expected based on its subject matter.

Motif: A theme, character type, image, metaphor, or other verbal element that recurs throughout a single work of literature or occurs in a number of different works over a period of time.

Myth: An anonymous tale emerging from the traditional beliefs of a culture or social unit. Myths use supernatural explanations for natural phenomena. They may also explain cosmic issues like creation and death. Collections of myths, known as mythologies, are common to all cultures and nations, but the best-known myths belong to the Norse, Roman, and Greek mythologies.

N

Narration: The telling of a series of events, real or invented. A narration may be either a simple narrative, in which the events are recounted chronologically, or a narrative with a plot, in which the account is given in a style reflecting the author's artistic concept of the story. Narration is sometimes used as a synonym for "storyline."

Narrative: A verse or prose accounting of an event or sequence of events, real or invented. The term is also used as an adjective in the sense "method of narration." For example, in literary criticism, the expression "narrative technique" usually refers to the way the author structures and presents his or her story.

Narrator: The teller of a story. The narrator may be the author or a character in the story through whom the author speaks.

Naturalism: A literary movement of the late nineteenth and early twentieth centuries. The movement's major theorist, French novelist Emile Zola, envisioned a type of fiction that would examine human life with the objectivity of scientific inquiry. The Naturalists typically viewed human beings as either the products of "biological determinism," ruled by hereditary instincts and engaged in an endless struggle for survival, or as the products of "socioeconomic determinism," ruled by social and economic forces beyond their control. In their works, the Naturalists generally ignored the highest levels of society and focused on degradation: poverty, alcoholism, prostitution, insanity, and disease.

Noble Savage: The idea that primitive man is noble and good but becomes evil and corrupted as he becomes civilized. The concept of the noble savage originated in the Renaissance period but is more closely identified with such later writers as Jean-Jacques Rousseau and Aphra Behn.

Novel: A long fictional narrative written in prose, which developed from the novella and other early forms of narrative. A novel is usually organized under a plot or theme with a focus on character development and action.

Novel of Ideas: A novel in which the examination of intellectual issues and concepts takes precedence over characterization or a traditional storyline.

Novel of Manners: A novel that examines the customs and mores of a cultural group.

Novella: An Italian term meaning "story." This term has been especially used to describe fourteenth-century Italian tales, but it also refers to modern short novels.

O

Objective Correlative: An outward set of objects, a situation, or a chain of events corresponding to an inward experience and evoking this experience in the reader. The term frequently appears in modern criticism in discussions of authors' intended effects on the emotional responses of readers.

Objectivity: A quality in writing characterized by the absence of the author's opinion or feeling about the subject matter. Objectivity is an important factor in criticism.

Oedipus Complex: A son's amorous obsession with his mother. The phrase is derived from the story of the ancient Theban hero Oedipus, who unknowingly killed his father and married his mother.

Omniscience: See *Point of View*

Onomatopoeia: The use of words whose sounds express or suggest their meaning. In its simplest sense, onomatopoeia may be represented by words that mimic the sounds they denote such as "hiss" or "meow." At a more subtle level, the pattern and rhythm of sounds and rhymes of a line or poem may be onomatopoeic.

Oxymoron: A phrase combining two contradictory terms. Oxymorons may be intentional or unintentional.

P

Parable: A story intended to teach a moral lesson or answer an ethical question.

Paradox: A statement that appears illogical or contradictory at first, but may actually point to an underlying truth.

Parallelism: A method of comparison of two ideas in which each is developed in the same grammatical structure.

Parody: In literary criticism, this term refers to an imitation of a serious literary work or the signature style of a particular author in a ridiculous manner. A typical parody adopts the style of the original and applies it to an inappropriate subject for humorous effect. Parody is a form of satire and could be considered the literary equivalent of a caricature or cartoon.

Pastoral: A term derived from the Latin word "pastor," meaning shepherd. A pastoral is a literary composition on a rural theme. The conventions of the pastoral were originated by the third-century Greek poet Theocritus, who wrote about the experiences, love affairs, and pastimes of Sicilian shepherds. In a pastoral, characters and language of a courtly nature are often placed in a simple setting. The term pastoral is also used to classify dramas, elegies, and lyrics that exhibit the use of country settings and shepherd characters.

Pen Name: See *Pseudonym*

Persona: A Latin term meaning "mask." *Personae* are the characters in a fictional work of literature. The *persona* generally functions as a mask through which the author tells a story in a voice other than his or her own. A *persona* is usually either a character in a story who acts as a narrator or an "implied author," a voice created by the author to act as the narrator for himself or herself.

Personification: A figure of speech that gives human qualities to abstract ideas, animals, and inanimate objects.

Picaresque Novel: Episodic fiction depicting the adventures of a roguish central character ("picaro" is Spanish for "rogue"). The picaresque hero is commonly a low-born but clever individual who wanders into and out of various affairs of love, danger, and farcical intrigue. These involvement may take place at all social levels and typically present a humorous and wide-ranging satire of a given society.

Plagiarism: Claiming another person's written material as one's own. Plagiarism can take the form of direct, word-for-word copying or the theft of the substance or idea of the work.

Plot: In literary criticism, this term refers to the pattern of events in a narrative or drama. In its simplest sense, the plot guides the author in composing the work and helps the reader follow the work. Typically, plots exhibit causality and unity and have a beginning, a middle, and an end. Sometimes, however, a plot may consist of a series of disconnected events, in which case it is known as an "episodic plot."

Poetic Justice: An outcome in a literary work, not necessarily a poem, in which the good are rewarded and the evil are punished, especially in ways that particularly fit their virtues or crimes.

Poetic License: Distortions of fact and literary convention made by a writer—not always a poet—for the sake of the effect gained. Poetic license is closely related to the concept of "artistic freedom."

Poetics: This term has two closely related meanings. It denotes (1) an aesthetic theory in literary criticism about the essence of poetry or (2) rules prescribing the proper methods, content, style, or diction of poetry. The term poetics may also refer to theories about literature in general, not just poetry.

Point of View: The narrative perspective from which a literary work is presented to the reader. There are four traditional points of view. The "third person omniscient" gives the reader a "godlike" perspective, unrestricted by time or place, from which to see actions and look into the minds of characters. This allows the author to comment openly on characters and events in the work. The "third person" point of view presents the events of the story from outside of any single character's perception, much like the omniscient point of view, but the reader must understand the action as it takes place and without any special insight into characters' minds or motivations. The "first person" or "personal" point of view relates events as they are perceived by a single character. The main character "tells" the story and may offer opinions about the action and characters which differ from those of the author. Much less common than omniscient, third person, and first person is the "second person" point of view, wherein the author tells the story as if it is happening to the reader.

Polemic: A work in which the author takes a stand on a controversial subject, such as abortion or religion. Such works are often extremely argumentative or provocative.

Pornography: Writing intended to provoke feelings of lust in the reader. Such works are often condemned by critics and teachers, but those which can be shown to have literary value are viewed less harshly.

Post-Aesthetic Movement: An artistic response made by African Americans to the black aesthetic movement of the 1960s and early '70s. Writers since that time have adopted a somewhat different tone in their work, with less emphasis placed on the disparity between black and white in the United States. In the words of post-aesthetic authors such as Toni Morrison, John Edgar Wideman, and Kristin Hunter, African Americans are portrayed as looking inward for answers to their own questions, rather than always looking to the outside world.

Postmodernism: Writing from the 1960s forward characterized by experimentation and continuing to apply some of the fundamentals of modernism, which included existentialism and alienation. Postmodernists have gone a step further in the rejection of tradition begun with the modernists by also rejecting traditional forms, preferring the anti-novel over the novel and the anti-hero over the hero.

Primitivism: The belief that primitive peoples were nobler and less flawed than civilized peoples because they had not been subjected to the tainting influence of society.

Prologue: An introductory section of a literary work. It often contains information establishing the situation of the characters or presents information about the setting, time period, or action. In drama, the prologue is spoken by a chorus or by one of the principal characters.

Prose: A literary medium that attempts to mirror the language of everyday speech. It is distinguished from poetry by its use of unmetered, unrhymed language consisting of logically related sentences. Prose is usually grouped into paragraphs that form a cohesive whole such as an essay or a novel.

Prosopopoeia: See *Personification*

Protagonist: The central character of a story who serves as a focus for its themes and incidents and as the principal rationale for its development. The protagonist is sometimes referred to in discussions of modern literature as the hero or anti-hero.

Protest Fiction: Protest fiction has as its primary purpose the protesting of some social injustice, such as racism or discrimination.

Proverb: A brief, sage saying that expresses a truth about life in a striking manner.

Pseudonym: A name assumed by a writer, most often intended to prevent his or her identification as the author of a work. Two or more authors may work together under one pseudonym, or an author may use a different name for each genre he or she publishes in. Some publishing companies maintain "house pseudonyms," under which any number of authors may write installations in a series. Some authors also choose a pseudonym over their real names the way an actor may use a stage name.

Pun: A play on words that have similar sounds but different meanings.

R

Realism: A nineteenth-century European literary movement that sought to portray familiar characters, situations, and settings in a realistic manner. This was done primarily by using an objective narrative point of view and through the buildup of accurate detail. The standard for success of any realistic work depends on how faithfully it transfers common experience into fictional forms. The realistic method may be altered or extended, as in stream of consciousness writing, to record highly subjective experience.

Repartee: Conversation featuring snappy retorts and witticisms.

Resolution: The portion of a story following the climax, in which the conflict is resolved.

Rhetoric: In literary criticism, this term denotes the art of ethical persuasion. In its strictest sense, rhetoric adheres to various principles developed since classical times for arranging facts and ideas in a clear, persuasive, appealing manner. The term is also used to refer to effective prose in general and theories of or methods for composing effective prose.

Rhetorical Question: A question intended to provoke thought, but not an expressed answer, in the reader. It is most commonly used in oratory and other persuasive genres.

Rising Action: The part of a drama where the plot becomes increasingly complicated. Rising action leads up to the climax, or turning point, of a drama.

Roman à clef: A French phrase meaning "novel with a key." It refers to a narrative in which real persons are portrayed under fictitious names.

Romance: A broad term, usually denoting a narrative with exotic, exaggerated, often idealized characters, scenes, and themes.

Romanticism: This term has two widely accepted meanings. In historical criticism, it refers to a European intellectual and artistic movement of the late eighteenth and early nineteenth centuries that sought greater freedom of personal expression than that allowed by the strict rules of literary form and logic of the eighteenth-century neoclassicists. The Romantics preferred emotional and imaginative expression to rational analysis. They considered the individual to be at the center of all experience and so placed him or her at the center of their art. The Romantics believed that the creative imagination reveals nobler truths—unique feelings and attitudes—than those that could be discovered by logic or by scientific examination. Both the natural world and the state of childhood were important sources for revelations of "eternal truths." "Romanticism" is also used as a general term to refer to a type of sensibility found in all periods of literary history and usually considered to be in opposition to the principles of classicism. In this sense, Romanticism signifies any work or philosophy in which the exotic or dreamlike figure strongly, or that is devoted to individualistic expression, self-analysis, or a pursuit of a higher realm of knowledge than can be discovered by human reason.

Romantics: See *Romanticism*

S

Satire: A work that uses ridicule, humor, and wit to criticize and provoke change in human nature and institutions. There are two major types of satire: "formal" or "direct" satire speaks directly to the reader or to a character in the work; "indirect" satire relies upon the ridiculous behavior of its characters to make its point. Formal satire is further divided into two manners: the "Horatian," which ridicules gently, and the "Juvenalian," which derides its subjects harshly and bitterly.

Science Fiction: A type of narrative about or based upon real or imagined scientific theories and technology. Science fiction is often peopled with alien creatures and set on other planets or in different dimensions.

Second Person: See *Point of View*

Setting: The time, place, and culture in which the action of a narrative takes place. The elements of setting may include geographic location, characters' physical and mental environments, prevailing cultural attitudes, or the historical time in which the action takes place.

Simile: A comparison, usually using "like" or "as," of two essentially dissimilar things, as in "coffee as cold as ice" or "He sounded like a broken record."

Slang: A type of informal verbal communication that is generally unacceptable for formal writing. Slang words and phrases are often colorful exaggerations used to emphasize the speaker's point; they may also be shortened versions of an often-used word or phrase.

Slave Narrative: Autobiographical accounts of American slave life as told by escaped slaves. These works first appeared during the abolition movement of the 1830s through the 1850s.

Socialist Realism: The Socialist Realism school of literary theory was proposed by Maxim Gorky and established as a dogma by the first Soviet Congress of Writers. It demanded adherence to a communist worldview in works of literature. Its doctrines required an objective viewpoint comprehensible to the working classes and themes of social struggle featuring strong proletarian heroes.

Stereotype: A stereotype was originally the name for a duplication made during the printing process; this led to its modern definition as a person or thing that is (or is assumed to be) the same as all others of its type.

Stream of Consciousness: A narrative technique for rendering the inward experience of a character. This technique is designed to give the impression of an ever-changing series of thoughts, emotions, images, and memories in the spontaneous and seemingly illogical order that they occur in life.

Structure: The form taken by a piece of literature. The structure may be made obvious for ease of understanding, as in nonfiction works, or may obscured for artistic purposes, as in some poetry or seemingly "unstructured" prose.

Sturm und Drang: A German term meaning "storm and stress." It refers to a German literary movement of the 1770s and 1780s that reacted against the order and rationalism of the enlightenment, focusing instead on the intense experience of extraordinary individuals.

Style: A writer's distinctive manner of arranging words to suit his or her ideas and purpose in writing. The unique imprint of the author's personality upon his or her writing, style is the product of an author's way of arranging ideas and his or her use of diction, different sentence structures, rhythm, figures of speech, rhetorical principles, and other elements of composition.

Subjectivity: Writing that expresses the author's personal feelings about his subject, and which may or may not include factual information about the subject.

Subplot: A secondary story in a narrative. A subplot may serve as a motivating or complicating force for the main plot of the work, or it may provide emphasis for, or relief from, the main plot.

Surrealism: A term introduced to criticism by Guillaume Apollinaire and later adopted by Andre Breton. It refers to a French literary and artistic movement founded in the 1920s. The Surrealists sought to express unconscious thoughts and feelings in their works. The best-known technique used for achieving this aim was automatic writing—transcriptions of spontaneous outpourings from the unconscious. The Surrealists proposed to unify the contrary levels of conscious and unconscious, dream and reality, objectivity and subjectivity into a new level of "super-realism."

Suspense: A literary device in which the author maintains the audience's attention through the buildup of events, the outcome of which will soon be revealed.

Symbol: Something that suggests or stands for something else without losing its original identity. In literature, symbols combine their literal meaning with the suggestion of an abstract concept. Literary symbols are of two types: those that carry complex associations of meaning no matter what their contexts, and those that derive their suggestive meaning from their functions in specific literary works.

Symbolism: This term has two widely accepted meanings. In historical criticism, it denotes an early modernist literary movement initiated in France during the nineteenth century that reacted against the prevailing standards of realism. Writers in this movement aimed to evoke, indirectly and symbolically, an order of being beyond the material world of the five senses. Poetic expression of personal emotion figured strongly in the movement, typically by means of a private set of symbols uniquely identifiable with the individual poet. The principal aim of the Symbolists was to express in words the highly complex feelings that grew out of everyday contact with the world. In a broader sense, the term "symbolism" refers to the use of one object to represent another.

T

Tall Tale: A humorous tale told in a straightforward, credible tone but relating absolutely impossible events or feats of the characters. Such tales were commonly told of frontier adventures during the settlement of the west in the United States.

Theme: The main point of a work of literature. The term is used interchangeably with thesis.

Thesis: A thesis is both an essay and the point argued in the essay. Thesis novels and thesis plays share the quality of containing a thesis which is supported through the action of the story.

Third Person: See *Point of View*

Tone: The author's attitude toward his or her audience may be deduced from the tone of the work. A formal tone may create distance or convey politeness, while an informal tone may encourage a friendly, intimate, or intrusive feeling in the reader. The author's attitude toward his or her subject matter may also be deduced from the tone of the words he or she uses in discussing it.

Transcendentalism: An American philosophical and religious movement, based in New England from around 1835 until the Civil War. Transcendentalism was a form of American romanticism that had its roots abroad in the works of Thomas Carlyle, Samuel Coleridge, and Johann Wolfgang von Goethe. The Transcendentalists stressed the importance of intuition and subjective experience in communication with God. They rejected religious dogma and texts in favor of mysticism and scientific naturalism. They pursued truths that lie beyond the "colorless" realms perceived by reason and the senses and were active social reformers in public education, women's rights, and the abolition of slavery.

U

Urban Realism: A branch of realist writing that attempts to accurately reflect the often harsh facts of modern urban existence.

Utopia: A fictional perfect place, such as "paradise" or "heaven."

V

Verisimilitude: Literally, the appearance of truth. In literary criticism, the term refers to aspects of a work of literature that seem true to the reader.

Victorian: Refers broadly to the reign of Queen Victoria of England (1837-1901) and to anything with qualities typical of that era. For example, the qualities of smug narrowmindedness, bourgeois materialism, faith in social progress, and priggish morality are often considered Victorian. This stereotype is contradicted by such dramatic intellectual developments as the theories of Charles Darwin, Karl Marx, and Sigmund Freud (which stirred strong debates in England) and the critical attitudes of serious Victorian writers like Charles Dickens and George Eliot. In literature, the Victorian Period was the great age of the English novel, and the latter part of the era saw the rise of movements such as decadence and symbolism.

W

Weltanschauung: A German term referring to a person's worldview or philosophy.

Weltschmerz: A German term meaning "world pain." It describes a sense of anguish about the nature of existence, usually associated with a melancholy, pessimistic attitude.

Z

Zeitgeist: A German term meaning "spirit of the time." It refers to the moral and intellectual trends of a given era.

Cumulative Author/Title Index

Cumulative
Nationality/Ethnicity Index

Cumulative Nationality/Ethnicity Index

Subject/Theme Index

Black culture
    The Salt Eaters: 241–242
    The Third Life of Grange
       Copeland: 269, 273
Black nationalism
    The Salt Eaters: 246
Black-white relations
    Ragtime: 207, 215, 216, 220,
       223–224
    The Salt Eaters: 232, 246
    The Third Life of Grange
       Copeland: 265, 266
Black womanhood
    The Salt Eaters: 242, 246, 249
Blame
    The Third Life of Grange
       Copeland: 265, 269
Bravery
    Zorro: 314
British colonialism
    Clear Light of Day: 101–104
British history
    The Way of All Flesh: 284–286,
       288–289
Bureaucracy
    One Flew over the Cuckoo's
       Nest: 192

C

Care
    The Salt Eaters: 247
Change (Philosophy)
    The Third Life of Grange
       Copeland: 257, 264–267, 270
Characterization
    The American: 15–18, 24
    The Antelope Wife: 41, 45
    The Book Thief: 58–60
    Clear Light of Day: 91, 106,
       113–114
    The Hundred Secret Senses:
       128–129, 136
    The Leopard: 169
    One Flew over the Cuckoo's Nest:
       201, 202
    Ragtime: 225–226, 229
    The Salt Eaters: 244, 247
    The Third Life of Grange
       Copeland: 262
    The Way of All Flesh: 283–284,
       295
    Zorro: 309, 312–314
Children
    The Third Life of Grange
       Copeland: 270
Chinese culture
    The Hundred Secret Senses:
       132–135
Chinese history
    The Hundred Secret Senses:
       127–128

Christianity
    The Way of All Flesh: 279, 287,
       293, 295
    Zorro: 306
Circularity
    A Canticle for Leibowitz: 87
    The Hundred Secret Senses: 132,
       134
Civil rights
    The Leopard: 258
    Ragtime: 220
    The Third Life of Grange
       Copeland: 253, 256–257,
       262
Civil war
    The Leopard: 166
Cold War
    A Canticle for Leibowitz: 72,
       82–84
Colonialism
    Zorro: 308–309
Comedy
    The American: 9, 11, 14
    A Canticle for Leibowitz: 73
    One Flew over the Cuckoo's Nest:
       187, 202
Coming of age
    Clear Light of Day: 112
    Zorro: 307–308
Communications
    The Book Thief: 66
    Johnny Got His Gun: 143, 145,
       156, 161
Community
    Clear Light of Day: 107
    The Salt Eaters: 231, 238–239,
       243, 246, 247
    The Third Life of Grange
       Copeland: 272
Compassion
    The American: 7
    One Flew over the Cuckoo's Nest:
       192
    Ragtime: 212
Conflict
    The American: 11
    The Leopard: 184
    The Salt Eaters: 246
Conformity
    One Flew over the Cuckoo's Nest:
       192, 195, 197, 201, 203
    The Way of All Flesh: 289
Connectedness
    The Antelope Wife: 39–40, 44
    The Hundred Secret Senses: 134
    The Salt Eaters: 231, 234, 239, 244
Consciousness
    Clear Light of Day: 107
Contrast
    The Third Life of Grange
       Copeland: 261
    The Way of All Flesh: 296

Control (Psychology)
    One Flew over the Cuckoo's Nest:
       195, 197
Cooperation
    The Salt Eaters: 246
Courage
    The Salt Eaters: 248
Creativity
    One Flew over the Cuckoo's Nest:
       192, 195, 200
Cruelty
    The Antelope Wife: 40–41
    One Flew over the Cuckoo's Nest:
       193
    The Salt Eaters: 245
Cultural conflict
    The American: 1, 2
    The Antelope Wife: 43, 44
    Clear Light of Day: 98, 107
Cultural identity
    The American: 11
    Clear Light of Day: 109, 112–113
    The Hundred Secret Senses: 117,
       130–132
    The Salt Eaters: 246
Culture
    Clear Light of Day: 108

D

Daily living
    The Antelope Wife: 44
Death
    The Book Thief: 50, 69, 70
    The Hundred Secret Senses: 130
    Johnny Got His Gun: 146, 153,
       155, 157
    The Leopard: 168, 175
    One Flew over the Cuckoo's Nest:
       191
    The Salt Eaters: 246
    The Third Life of Grange
       Copeland: 272
Decadence
    The Leopard: 174–175
Decay
    The Leopard: 183
Deception
    The Antelope Wife: 40
    Zorro: 301
Defeat
    One Flew over the Cuckoo's Nest:
       201
Defiance
    The American: 17
    One Flew over the Cuckoo's Nest:
       192
    The Way of All Flesh: 295
Deformity
    A Canticle for Leibowitz: 75
Democracy
    Johnny Got His Gun: 154